CW01507724

In the Cause of Humanity

In the Cause of Humanity is a major new history of the emergence of the theory and practice of humanitarian intervention during the nineteenth century when the question of whether, when and how the international community should react to violations of humanitarian norms and humanitarian crises first emerged as a key topic of controversy and debate. Fabian Klose investigates the emergence of legal debates on the protection of humanitarian norms by violent means, revealing how military intervention under the banner of humanitarianism became closely intertwined with imperial and colonial projects. Through case studies including the international fight against the slave trade, the military interventions under the banner of humanitarian aid for Christian minorities in the Ottoman Empire, and the intervention of the United States in the Cuban War of Independence, he shows how the idea of humanitarian intervention established itself as a recognized instrument in international politics and international law.

Fabian Klose is Professor of International History and Peace and Conflict Studies at the University of Cologne. He is the author of *Human Rights in the Shadow of Colonial Violence* (2013), and Editor of *The Emergence of Humanitarian Intervention* (2016) and *Humanity. A History of European Concepts in Practice* (2016). The German edition of *In the Cause of Humanity* received the Carl Erdmann Prize of the German Historical Association 2018 and Geisteswissenschaften International 2020.

Human Rights in History

Edited by

Stefan-Ludwig Hoffmann, University of California, Berkeley

Samuel Moyn, Yale University, Connecticut

This series showcases new scholarship exploring the backgrounds of human rights today. With an open-ended chronology and international perspective, the series seeks works attentive to the surprises and contingencies in the historical origins and legacies of human rights ideals and interventions. Books in the series will focus not only on the intellectual antecedents and foundations of human rights, but also on the incorporation of the concept by movements, nation-states, international governance, and transnational law.

A full list of titles in the series can be found at:
www.cambridge.org/human-rights-history

In the Cause of Humanity

A History of Humanitarian Intervention in the Long Nineteenth Century

Fabian Klose

University of Cologne

CAMBRIDGE
UNIVERSITY PRESS

CAMBRIDGE
UNIVERSITY PRESS

University Printing House, Cambridge CB2 8BS, United Kingdom

One Liberty Plaza, 20th Floor, New York, NY 10006, USA

477 Williamstown Road, Port Melbourne, VIC 3207, Australia

314–321, 3rd Floor, Plot 3, Splendor Forum, Jasola District Centre,
New Delhi – 110025, India

103 Penang Road, #05–06/07, Visioncrest Commercial, Singapore 238467

Cambridge University Press is part of the University of Cambridge.

It furthers the University's mission by disseminating knowledge in the pursuit of
education, learning, and research at the highest international levels of excellence.

www.cambridge.org
Information on this title: www.cambridge.org/9781316516201
DOI: 10.1017/9781009029186

© Fabian Klose 2022

This publication is in copyright. Subject to statutory exception
and to the provisions of relevant collective licensing agreements,
no reproduction of any part may take place without the written
permission of Cambridge University Press.

The translation of this work was funded by Geisteswissenschaften International -
Translation Funding for Humanities and Social Sciences from Germany, a joint
initiative of the Fritz Thyssen Foundation, the German Federal Foreign Office,
the collecting society VG WORT and the Börsenverein des Deutschen Buchhandels
(German Publishers & Booksellers Association).

First published 2022

Printed in the United Kingdom by TJ Books Limited, Padstow Cornwall

A catalogue record for this publication is available from the British Library.

Library of Congress Cataloging-in-Publication Data
Names: Klose, Fabian, author.
Title: In the cause of humanity : a history of humanitarian intervention in the long
    nineteenth century / Fabian Klose, University of Cologne.
Other titles: Habilitation. English
Description: Cambridge, United Kingdom ; New York, NY : Cambridge
    University Press, [2022] | Series: Human rights in history | "Originally presented as the
    author's second dissertation, Habilitation" – Acknowledgements. | Includes
    bibliographical references and index.
Identifiers: LCCN 2021029847 (print) | LCCN 2021029848 (ebook) |
    ISBN 9781316516201 (hardback) | ISBN 9781009012881 (paperback) |
    ISBN 9781009029186 (epub)
Subjects: LCSH: Humanitarian intervention–History–19th century. | Antislavery
    movements–History–19th century. | Religious minorities–History–19th century. |
    Turkey–History–Ottoman Empire, 1288-1918. | Humanitarian assistance,
    American–History–19th century. | Cuba–History–Revolution, 1895-1898.
Classification: LCC JZ6369 .K5615 2022 (print) | LCC JZ6369 (ebook) |
    DDC 341.5/84–dc23
LC record available at https://lccn.loc.gov/2021029847
LC ebook record available at https://lccn.loc.gov/2021029848

ISBN 978-1-316-51620-1 Hardback

Cambridge University Press has no responsibility for the persistence or accuracy
of URLs for external or third-party internet websites referred to in this publication
and does not guarantee that any content on such websites is, or will remain,
accurate or appropriate.

Contents

Acknowledgements

The present monograph began life as a second dissertation (*Habilitation*), which I submitted to the Faculty of History and the Arts of the Ludwig Maximilian University of Munich in September 2016. I was thrilled to see it receive, in October 2018, the Carl Erdmann Prize of the German Association of Historians (VHD). The English translation of my book was made possible by a prize awarded in March 2020 as part of the Geisteswissenschafen International programme, sponsored by the Fritz Thyssen Foundation, VG Wort, the German Publishers' and Booksellers' Association (Börsenverein des Deutschen Buchhandels) and the German Federal Foreign Office, for which I am sincerely grateful. Researching this book and putting together the manuscript were stages in an exhilarating journey that took me to a wide variety of places and allowed me to meet many wonderful people to whom I owe a great deal. I would not, therefore, want to miss this opportunity to thank them all for their tremendous support in helping bring this book into being.

I would first of all like to extend my heartfelt thanks to the staff of the libraries and archives I used. Without their knowledge and expert assistance, my work as a historian would have been impossible to accomplish. My gratitude is due to the staff of the Bavarian State Library and the University Library in Munich, the Library of the Leibniz Institute of European History (IEG) and the University Library in Mainz, the British Library in London, the Firestone Library in Princeton, the Library of Congress in Washington, DC. and the New York Public Library. My thanks also go to the archivists at the National Archives, Kew, the National Maritime Museum, Greenwich, the National Museum of the Royal Navy, Portsmouth, the Archives des Affaires Étrangères in Paris, the Service historique de la défense, Vincennes, the Archivo General de Indias, Seville, the Archivo General de Simancas, Valladolid, the Archivo Histórico Nacional, Madrid, the Austrian Haus-, Hof- und Staatsarchiv, Vienna, the National Archives, Washington, DC. and the Archive of the International Committee of the Red Cross, Geneva (with special thanks to Jean-Luc Blondel and Daniel Palmieri).

These research trips and archival visits – and ultimately the writing itself – would not have been possible without generous financial support from several organizations. The German Academic Exchange Service (DAAD) generously funded a year's postdoctoral research, which took me to the University of Minnesota and Princeton University. I hugely benefited from conversations with scholars at both these universities, and am particularly indebted to Eric Weitz, Elena Schneider and Samuel Moyn. The German Research Foundation (DFG) allowed me to continue my project at Munich University's history department. In the process of preparing my *Habilitation*, the constructive suggestions of my mentors – namely Martin Baumeister, Martin Geyer, Johannes Paulmann and Bernhard Zangl – proved invaluable, and I wish to underscore my gratitude to them all.

Finally, I enjoyed, for nearly six years, the privilege of working at the Leibniz Institute of European History (IEG) in Mainz, where I was able to take advantage both of the excellent working conditions and the stimulating environment offered by the institute in order to complete this book's original version. My sincere gratitude therefore goes to the institute's visiting scholars and fellows, and above all to my colleagues in all parts of the institute, who did so much to enrich my time there through innumerable discussions and conversations.

It was, therefore, particularly gratifying to me that this book's original publication should have taken place under the institute's auspices and imprint, published by Vandenhoeck & Ruprecht. It is wonderful to see its English version taken on by Cambridge University Press and to work with Michael Watson and his team. I also want to express my appreciation to Joe Kroll, whose translation brings my book to English-language readers. My sincere gratitude is due to everyone involved in the translation and publication of my book. For valuable advice, constructive criticism and inspiring discussions I am, moreover, indebted to Michael Geyer, Till van Rahden, Jorge Luengo, Tobias Grill, Sarah Panter, Arvid Schors, Claus Kreß, Andrew Thompson, Kerstin von Lingen and Barbara Müller.

In my academic growth and development as a historian, one person has played a key role in giving me advice and support at critical moments. Martin Geyer was the first to suggest I consider embarking on the *Habiliation* project, and was unwavering in his support and advice during all the years leading up to its completion. My heartfelt thanks are due to him for his companionship on a long academic journey.

My manuscript received its final polish from a team of reliable and indefatigable proofreaders, who cast a critical eye on individual chapters or even the whole book and were forthcoming with helpful comments.

For this, I would like to thank Barbara, Joe, Marianne, Martin, Sepp, Tobias and Ulrike, to whose suggestions and constructive criticism this book owes a great deal. Any remaining errors are, of course, entirely my own responsibility.

My concluding words of thanks go to my family, which has always been an indispensable support to me along life's path. My special thanks are therefore due to Hans Brandl, Sepp Brandl, Gerhard Grochowski and my mother, Marianne Klose, for their fantastic support. A good deal of all this could not have been done without them. This book is dedicated to another person who is very special to me, and she knows why.

Abbreviations

ACICR	Archives du Comité International de la Croix-Rouge
ADM	Records of the Admiralty
AF	Ancien Fonds
AGI	Archivo General de Indias
AGS	Archivo General de Simancas
AHN	Archivo Histórico Nacional
BFSP	British and Foreign State Papers
BPP	British Parliamentary Papers
CO	Colonial Office
DD	Documents Diplomatiques
DO	Dominions Office
DPKO	Department of Peacekeeping Operations
EGO	Europäische Geschichte Online
FO	Foreign Office
HHStA	Österreichisches Haus-, Hof- und Staatsarchiv
HMS	His/Her Majesty's Ship
HMSO	His/Her Majesty's Stationery Office
ICISS	International Commission on Intervention and State Sovereignty
ICRC	International Committee of the Red Cross
ILA	International Law Association
LoC	Manuscript Division Library of Congress
MAE	Ministère des Affaires Étrangères
NATO	North Atlantic Treaty Organization
NGO	non-governmental organization
NMM	National Maritime Museum
NMRN	National Museum of the Royal Navy
R2P	Responsibility to Protect
SHD	Service historique de la défense

TNA	The National Archives
UN	United Nations
UNGA	United Nations General Assembly
UNHCR	United Nations High Commissioner for Refugees
UNSC	United Nations Security Council
USS	United States Ship

Introduction

The emerging global convention of a 'Responsibility to Protect' was conceived as a universal principle of protecting fundamental human rights – not as a license to make war in the name of peace.[1]   Kofi Annan, 2012

The Continuing Problem

In the year 2000, to coincide with the turn of the millennium, Kofi Annan, the then secretary-general of the United Nations, released a report in which he discussed at length the role of the UN and the challenges faced by the organisation in the twenty-first century.[2] Annan's detailed reflections extended from questions of globalisation, peacekeeping, the global struggle to overcome poverty, and long-term environmental and climate protection to the structural reform of the UN and its various agencies and sub-organisations. They were intended as proposals to the member states of the UN ahead of its millennium summit, at which joint solutions to pressing problems both present and future were to be discussed. A central concern of Annan's was the propagation of universal human rights, and he accordingly pushed to bolster the international protection mechanisms already in place. His proposed strategies not only included the establishment of the International Criminal Court and the general strengthening of international humanitarian law, but also implied the concept of humanitarian intervention – the direct intervention, ultimately backed up by force, in the internal affairs of a sovereign state for the purpose of protecting humanitarian norms.[3]

Annan, who before being elected the seventh secretary-general of the UN had for three years headed the organisation's Department of Peacekeeping Operations (DPKO), was fully aware of the contradiction to the principle of state sovereignty this entailed:

I also accept that the principles of sovereignty and non-interference offer vital protection to small and weak states. But to the critics I would pose this

1

question: if humanitarian intervention is, indeed, an unacceptable assault on sovereignty, how should we respond to a Rwanda, to a Srebrenica – to gross and systematic violations of human rights that offend every precept of our common humanity? We confront a real dilemma. Few would disagree that both the defence of humanity and the defence of sovereignty are principles that must be supported. Alas, that does not tell us which principle should prevail when they are in conflict.[4]

Although Annan here was clearly aware of the dilemma of intervention, he concluded with a plea in favour of armed military intervention as a last resort in order to retain an effective instrument against mass murder and crimes against humanity. Annan's position was clearly influenced by his own dramatic experiences as head of the DPKO from 1993 to 1996 and reflects the lessons learned from the international community's abject failure during that period.[5] The UN and its locally stationed peacekeeping troops were completely out of their depth and proved unable to prevent either the genocide of an estimated 800,000 Tutsi by their Hutu compatriots in Rwanda or that of over 8,000 Bosnian Muslims by Serb forces in the so-called safe area declared by the UN around the town of Srebrenica.[6]

The secretary-general's words did not go unheeded. It was in reaction to his proposals and against the backdrop of fierce political controversy over the UN Security Council's incapacity for concerted action – this time brought on by the 1999 Kosovo crisis and the subsequent military intervention carried out by the North Atlantic Treaty Organization (NATO) without a UN mandate – that the International Commission on Intervention and State Sovereignty (ICISS), which had been founded specifically for that purpose, addressed the subject of humanitarian intervention in September 2000.[7] After a year of deliberation the expert panel, which had been founded at the suggestion of the Canadian government, delivered its final report in December 2001. Entitled *The Responsibility to Protect*, it redefined the principle of sovereignty.[8] Sovereignty, it argued, was to be understood not only as a state's power and right under international law to control its internal affairs as it saw fit, but also entailed an overriding obligation to ensure the protection of individuals in its territory. In cases where a state was found no longer to be fulfilling this duty, the ICISS argued that: 'Where a population is suffering serious harm, as a result of internal war, insurgency, repression or state failure, and the state in question is unwilling or unable to halt or avert it, the principle of non-intervention yields to the international responsibility to protect.'[9] In other words, if and when a state should prove unable to guarantee its populations basic rights, the principle of non-intervention is rendered void and the responsibility to protect passes to the international community, which may exercise it – as a last resort – by force.[10] The concept of the responsibility to protect (R2P) was heralded as a decisive normative breakthrough in international relations and given international recognition at the 2005 UN summit. On the occasion of the sixtieth anniversary of the UN's founding, all its member states joined officially to affirm that '[e]ach individual State has the responsibility to protect its populations from genocide, war crimes, ethnic cleansing and crimes against humanity'.[11]

The robustness and practicability of this new R2P formula was first put to the test by two conflicts which, at the time of writing, remain unresolved. Following severe assaults on the civilian population by the Libyan regime of Muammar Gaddafi, on 17 March 2011 the UN Security Council adopted Resolution 1973, in which the council referred explicitly to the concept of the responsibility to protect in authorising UN member states to take such measures as might be necessary to protect the civilian population of Libya.[12] As a consequence of this decision, NATO launched air strikes against Gaddafi's forces, thereby intervening in the civil war on the opposition side and contributing decisively to the regime's collapse. In a later interview, Jan Eliasson, deputy secretary-general of the UN, justified the international military intervention by arguing that Gaddafi's public announcement of atrocities against Libyan civilians constituted a 'Srebrenica moment' in which the international community was bound to intervene.[13] This application of R2P notwithstanding, the international community remains divided on the question of whether and when severe human rights violations might authorise intervention in the internal affairs of a sovereign state. The continuing civil war in Syria in particular underscores how this question is still one of the most controversial in international politics today.[14]

The dilemma between unqualified respect for state sovereignty and the protection of universal humanity as it presents itself today is not, however, one that made its first appearance at the turn of the twenty-first century. Already during the long nineteenth century[15] – in the period, that is, from the French Revolution to the First World War – the question was not only the subject of much fervent controversy in international politics, it also surprisingly often concerned the same trouble spots that dominate contemporary debates. Over 150 years ago a civil war in what was then the Ottoman province of Syria mobilised international public opinion and subsequently led to a multilateral military intervention. Yet humanitarian crises throughout the Balkans and in Africa also repeatedly gave rise to similar debates within the Concert of Europe. A key part here was played by the problem of the transatlantic slave trade, which – involving as it did the abduction and transport by force of more than

12 million Africans – must surely rank among the greatest humanitarian disasters of all time. The slave trade and its suppression posed fundamental questions in politics and international law that contributed crucially to the development of a humanitarian concept of intervention, including the use of armed force. The United Kingdom, which had first deployed naval squadrons off the coast of West Africa to suppress the slave trade in 1808 and kept them there for over sixty years, took on a central role in this international endeavour.

The nineteenth century, as this book will argue, was the true 'century of humanitarian intervention', in which the idea of protecting and enforcing humanitarian norms by military force emerged across a variety of theatres in Africa, Asia, Europe and America, took on a definite shape in colonial and imperial contexts, and ultimately was enshrined in core texts in international law. Starting with the abolitionist efforts made under British leadership, this book will consider further historical examples, such as the repeated interventions by the great powers for the protection of Christian minorities within the Ottoman Empire or that of the United States in the Cuban war of independence, and reveal the ways in which they were connected. Its aim is above all to demonstrate the reciprocal relations between theoretical discourses and the practical enforcement of norms of international law, thereby tracing the historical process of development by which a concept of humanitarian intervention took shape. How was it possible for the idea of humanitarian intervention to become a firm part of international politics? The task at hand is to show which actors left their respective marks on the concept of humanitarian intervention and how it is intertwined with established narratives of humanitarianism and internationalism as well as colonialism and imperialism.

At the analytical level, this study takes its cue from a definition of humanitarian intervention as it has been convincingly proposed by such political scientists as Jeff L. Holzgrefe. According to Holzgrefe, the term denotes 'the threat or use of force across state borders by a state (or group of states) aimed at preventing or ending widespread and grave violations of the fundamental human rights of individuals other than its own citizens'.[16] Although the definition varies slightly across the extant literature, most scholars agree on the three core elements, namely outside intervention in the internal affairs of a sovereign state, the predominance of humanitarian intentions and the forceful nature of the intervention.[17] Many studies thus use the term to refer straightforwardly to the use of military means of coercion as distinct from other forms of humanitarian action. Accordingly, the manifold activities of international organisations in the twentieth century – such as the United Nations High Commission for Refugees (UNHCR), the International Red Cross Committee (ICRC) and Médecins Sans Frontières – are not usually considered humanitarian interventions, but instead described as 'humanitarian aid', 'humanitarian protection' or 'humanitarian assistance'.[18] Several authors have, in this context, pointed out the importance of maintaining a clear, methodical distinction between military and civilian measures in order to maintain conceptual precision.[19]

From a historical perspective in particular, it seems highly desirable to limit the analytical scope of the concept of intervention to the aspect of coercion. In its conceptual history the term, which became established in political usage only in the course of the nineteenth century, did in fact refer primarily to the outside intervention by force in the internal affairs of another state – though below the threshold of all-out war.[20] The present study therefore focuses on foreign policy and military intervention as practised by states – government policy, in other words, aimed at the resolution of humanitarian crises. Yet this should not be taken to imply that, conversely, non-state actors and developments in civil society were of no consequence for this analysis. The opposite is the case: Social reform movements, which often acted in international concert, frequently played a decisive part in initiating key debates and pushing governments to take action in the first place. Even before the twentieth century, non-state actors were often the driving force behind policies of intervention in the name of humanity, thereby exerting a significant influence on international politics in the nineteenth century.

A closer look reveals a multifaceted history of interconnection between actors, both state and non-state, encompassing a broad range of groups and individuals including African slaves, abolitionists, slave traders, naval captains, diplomats, cabinet ministers, public lawyers and journalists. The methodical linkage established here between developments in civil society, transnational campaigns, foreign policy initiatives and military intervention means that this book is situated at the intersection of international political, legal, cultural, intellectual and diplomatic histories. The aim of this multi-perspectival and integrative approach is to offer a foundational contribution to the new historiography of international relations, international law and international humanitarianism in the long nineteenth century.

In the present context, humanitarianism cannot be understood apart from the history of violence. Recent scholarship has ever more forcefully connected the phenomenon's historical origins with the subject of imperialism, thereby establishing the notion of an 'imperial humanitarianism' or a 'humanitarian imperialism'.[21] This book owes much to these studies, although they tend largely not to discuss instances of outright military intervention. By contrast, here I shall argue that the concept of humanitarian intervention by force materially influenced a variety of practices applied in the colonial and imperial context. In fact, it was an element central to colonial and imperial infiltration, for it allowed states to take concrete measures to intervene in the internal affairs of other sovereign states across the world under the banner of humanity and civilisation. Understood thus, humanitarian imperialism did not consist only of religious missionary activity, civilian reform projects for the benefit of indigenous peoples or humanitarian relief in cases of famine or natural disaster, but explicitly also of concrete military operations and the means and measure of coercion they entail. It is this violent aspect of humanitarianism in the long nineteenth century which is often over-looked and which deserves closer consideration in its broader historical context.

The State of the Question

Over the past twenty years, humanitarian intervention and related topics have been discussed mostly by scholars of international law and political scientists who, between them, have produced a vast and thriving body of literature. At the methodical level, both disciplines clearly favour a nor-mative approach. Among scholars of international law, the dominant question naturally concerns the lawfulness of this form of outside inter-vention and specifically, assuming such lawfulness to be conceivable, what legal criteria might be applied to interventions by force in the name of humanity. The principal focus lies on the dilemma in international law, already outlined, between safeguarding the principle of state sover-eignty and the growing importance accorded to the idea of protecting universal human rights. Some scholars of international law take a long view of legal history, considering the medieval doctrine of international law and sixteenth- and seventeenth-century natural law approaches in the work of Hugo Grotius and Emer de Vattel as well as the development of positive law in the nineteenth century.[22] Scholars of international law draw on these historical precedents to establish whether a doctrine of humanitarian intervention might already be said to have existed prior to 1945 in international customary law. Aside from such exercises in legal history, however, much recent scholarship considers current debates over a right to intervention within the framework of the Charter of the United Nations and whether the concept might be developed to include a responsibility to protect on the part of the international community.[23] The 1999 intervention in Kosovo, carried out by NATO without a UN mandate, is often invoked as the cause célèbre against which to weigh questions of the legality and legitimacy of humanitarian interventions and their far-reaching consequences for international law.[24]

Political scientists, meanwhile, largely restrict their analyses to the twentieth and twenty-first centuries, situating the question of humanitarian intervention in the context of contemporary international politics and analysing it through the lens of various theoretical approaches to international relations. In examining the political dilemma of intervention, more recent studies favour a multidimensional analysis in which a variety of ethical, legal and political aspects are interwoven.[25] The role of the international community and the mechanisms by which it responds to human rights violations continue to be the central questions. Across the disciplinary boundary, political scientists and scholars of international law broadly agree that the emergence of a new world order after the end of the Cold War marks the decisive watershed. While East and West were locked in a stand-off, military interventions on humanitarian grounds did not look like a viable option for several decades. Among the rare exceptions are India's intervention to protect the civilian population of East Pakistan (Bangladesh) in 1971, that of Vietnam in Cambodia in 1978, which put an end to the atrocities of the Khmer Rouge regime, and Tanzania's intervention in Uganda, which unseated the murderous dictator Idi Amin in 1979. In the conventional view, then, the 1990s witnessed a veritable 'explosion of intervention with largely humanitarian justifications'.[26] The end of the bipolar global order brought on by the collapse of the Soviet Union allowed the United Nations to assume a more active role in promoting international security and peace. Something of a series of new conflicts – from Iraq and Somalia to the former Yugoslavia – combined with this new scope for action to increase the UN's involvement in humanitarian crises in both qualitative and quantitative terms.[27]

Taken together, these interpretations form a genealogy in which humanitarian intervention appears as a phenomenon of the present day and recent past, and at any rate one lacking a long and complex history. The dominant normative approach leaves little scope for a historical interpretation and marginalises relevant cases from previous centuries. Most studies make at best cursory mention of such historical precedents as the intervention of the great powers of Europe in the Greek war of independence (1827) or the Syrian civil war (1860–61).[28] While some authors leave it at such isolated references, others – such as Gareth Evans, former deputy head of the ICISS – go so far as to call the 400 years between the Peace of Westphalia and the Holocaust an age of institutionalised indifference to humanitarian concerns. Evans argues that the principle of unlimited sovereignty enshrined in the Westphalian system had meant that virtually no intervention during that period could be ascribed to purely humanitarian motivations rather than to interests of national security.[29]

Such a view invites contradiction. If purely humanitarian motives were to be adduced as the sole valid criterion for a humanitarian intervention, then no such thing would ever have existed. It would be a fundamental misapprehension to suggest that a state would ever lay its military resources and the lives of its troops on the line from pure altruism and in answer to the call of humanity. In the past no less than in the present, humanitarian interventions were virtually always driven by a mixture of motives on the part of those involved. Humanitarian motives, as this book will argue, are only one of a whole range of motivations that might at any given time include economic, colonial, imperial, geostrategic and security concerns.[30] What is more, a sweeping dismissal of the period from the mid-seventeenth to the first half of the twentieth century as an era of 'humanitarian indifference' completely disregards the thriving historical research into the early history of humanitarianism and human rights. Recent historical scholarship has been explicit in locating a genuine 'humanitarian revolution'[31] in that very period. People began to empathise with their fellow human beings, and not only close to home, in familiar contexts, but across borders and even continents. Far from being indifferent, individuals were mobilised by a sentimental and moral 'humanitarian narrative' to take an interest in the plight of strangers and to campaign for the relief of their suffering.[32] This burgeoning new sensibility precipitated a wave of humanitarian reform projects in western European and North American societies, leading ultimately to the founding of a number of humanitarian movements.

Yet historical scholarship long neglected the connection between this emergent humanitarianism and policies of state intervention – a connection that forms the focus of this book. Only a few studies of the early history of minority protection and human rights as well as on nineteenth-century international politics so much as hint at this connection. For instance, although Carole Fink's important *Defending the Rights of Others: The Great Powers, the Jews, and International Minority Protection 1878–1938* examines the European great powers' diplomatic interventions on behalf of persecuted religious minorities, she focuses largely on Jewish populations while overlooking earlier international interventions in support of Christians in the Ottoman Empire. Her assertion that 'when several thousand Maronite Christians were massacred in Lebanon in 1860 and hundreds of rebels slaughtered in Crete in 1866, the western powers were silent' is inaccurate.[33] Even Paul Gordon's *The Evolution of International Human Rights: Visions Seen* gives only the very briefest sketch of these interventions by the great powers.[34] Although the accounts of the history of nineteenth-century international relations by such historians as Jürgen Osterhammel and Matthias Schulz place a stronger emphasis on the overall question, they mention humanitarian intervention only in passing.[35] Mark Mazower not only omits case studies of humanitarian intervention in the nineteenth century from *Governing the World: The History of an Idea*, his history of internationalism, but even devotes a chapter to repeating the political science view that links the emergence of both the concept and the practice solely with the end of the Cold War.[36]

Only some of the more recent English-language studies display a shift towards an understanding of humanitarian intervention in its own right and draw up a genealogy in which the concept's long history is rendered visible. The seminal work here is *Freedom's Battle: The Origins of Humanitarian Intervention*, in which Gary Bass examines the various interventions by the great powers in the Ottoman Empire over the course of the nineteenth century.[37] While Bass does discuss some aspects of intervention as a historical phenomenon, his overall concern is less historiographical than political: to vindicate and to propound the concept of humanitarian intervention as such. Historical precedent is accordingly invoked as a set of guidelines to be deduced directly from the past – lessons, he states explicitly, to be heeded in the political decision-making processes of today: 'The nineteenth century shows how the practice of humanitarian intervention can be *managed*.'[38] But this political agenda comes at the cost of a thorough historical analysis of the phenomenon of humanitarian intervention as it relates to the emergent concept of humanitarianism and the development of international law, but also and not least its manifold intertwining with colonialism and imperialism.[39]

Like Bass, Davide Rodogno, in his book *Against Massacre: Humanitarian Interventions in the Ottoman Empire 1815–1914*,[40] concentrates exclusively on the various instances of great power intervention in the Ottoman Empire. Instead of pursuing a political agenda, however, Rodogno's perspective is thoroughly historical, and his is the first genuinely historical monograph on the topic. The story it tells is one in political history, and its aim is to show how humanitarian intervention emerged from the peculiar relationship between the European great powers and the Ottoman Empire. Rodogno situates the practice of intervention in the international context of the simmering 'Eastern Question' and its various geostrategic implications. In his account, nineteenth-century humanitarian intervention appears as a practice that served only to protect Christian minorities and was restricted to a clearly defined geographical area – that of the Ottoman Empire – where it was repeatedly enacted.[41]

As valuable as Rodogno's analysis of these historical precedents and their significance is, he has nothing to say about interventions on behalf of non-white, non-Christian populations in other parts of the world. This question is addressed in *Humanitarian Intervention: A History*, a collection of essays edited by Brendan Simms and David Trim, which marks the first attempt to present a history of humanitarian intervention covering multiple areas of the world in a *longue durée* perspective ranging from the sixteenth to the twentieth century.[42] Their narrative is structured chiefly along geopolitical coordinates and their shift over the course of four centuries. Against the 'Westphalian paradigm', the notion of the absolute validity of the territorial principle of sovereignty, they maintain 'that the concept of Westphalia as originating a system of states whose sovereignty was absolute simply is not true'.[43] It was therefore possible, under certain circumstances, for humanitarian and geopolitical concerns to fuse and create a space for humanitarian interventions. In answering the question of how far back the history of humanitarian intervention might be traced, the editors make a conscious choice in favour of including examples from the early modern period, which, they argue, represents something of an incubation period. Early modern notions of interests common to Christendom formed the point of departure for subsequent evolutionary steps, taking a linear course via the history of Enlightenment thought to modern-day concepts of humanitarian intervention and universal human rights.[44]

Another publication, by the political scientist Alexis Heraclides and the historian Ada Dialla, also concentrates almost exclusively on the well-examined case studies from the Ottoman Empire.[45] Yet the book's division into one section on the theory and another on the practice of humanitarian intervention means that each subject is treated in isolation rather than both being considered in their interrelatedness. Moreover, Heraclides and Dialla, whose book is based entirely on secondary literature without drawing on archival research, do not situate their book in the thriving field of research on the history of humanitarianism, and nor do they refer to its key debates. In their book, as well as in the other studies briefly discussed here, the abolition of the slave trade is barely considered at all, meriting at most a passing mention.[46]

Structure and Sources

Against this backdrop of debates in contemporary scholarship, this book follows a new approach, departing from the geographical and thematic focus on interventions in the Ottoman Empire. Instead, it considers cases of intervention across four continents – Africa, Asia, the Americas and Europe – and a range of thematic contexts. This significantly broadened perspective is intended to reveal the interconnectedness of various cases of intervention and moreover to embed the developmental process of the concept of humanitarian intervention in the wider imperial context of nineteenth-century international politics. At the same time, the present study aims for a decisive re-evaluation of the early history of humanitarian intervention. It locates the crucial juncture not in efforts for the relief of Christian minorities, but rather in the international measures directed at the suppression of the greatest crime of its time, the Atlantic slave trade, in the early nineteenth century, and places them at the centre of its analysis.[47] The argument developed in the following is that the struggle against the slave trade, in which Great Britain took the lead, provided a framework enabling a humanitarian understanding of intervention to emerge. It was in this context that military intervention in defence of humanitarian norms and for the purpose of their enforcement became an option in international politics. A space opened up in the public realm as well as in politics and international law which proved decisive for subsequent cases. Yet as the founding instance of humanitarian intervention, the struggle to put an end to the slave trade was not limited to a clearly defined and narrowly bounded imperial space, but played out on a global stage which spanned a variety of locations both at sea – in the Mediterranean and Caribbean seas and in the Atlantic and Indian oceans – and on the African and American mainland.

In selecting a temporal perspective, I purposely chose not to take a *longue durée* view tracing a linear development back to the early modern era. My focus is instead squarely on the long nineteenth century as the formative period for the concept of humanitarian intervention as enforcing an international norm, a concept distinct from the particularistic early modern idea of coming to the relief of neighbouring co-religionists. The guiding assumption here is that there developed, between the end of the eighteenth and the beginning of the twentieth century, a significant fusion of nascent humanitarianism and state interventionism, which took place against the backdrop of growing internationalism.

Accordingly, Chapter 1 begins by discussing the nineteenth century as the age of internationalism, forms of which developed in various realms. International relations underwent a significant degree of legalisation and a law-based international order emerged along the lines of supposed European 'civilisational standards', enshrining clear hierarchies of 'civilised' and 'uncivilised' states and thereby preparing the further course of European colonialism and imperialism. In the realm of civil society, social and political reform movements began to form cross-border networks and explore new means of exerting influence in the transnational sphere, making deliberate use of the 'public sphere' as a resource to rally support for their causes. Yet at the state level, too, the period following the Congress of Vienna of 1814–15 saw a tremendous increase in international cooperation between the European great powers. In intense diplomatic consultation at regular conferences and meetings of ambassadors and in special committees, the 'Concert of Europe'[48] tried to find joint solutions to international conflicts, civil wars and humanitarian crises. Accordingly, this form of cooperation and collective crisis management is often regarded as one of the first forms of international governance.

The function of intervention, in this context, was to act as a corrective in international politics. Fundamental questions posed by this practice of intervention by force in the internal affairs of a sovereign state will be addressed in Chapter 2, which locates them in the context of the Vienna order. What can be observed here is, first, the emergence of an anti-revolutionary paradigm of intervention, by means of which the 'Holy Alliance', made up of the continental powers Russia, Austria and Prussia, made a collective attempt to prevent and suppress internal unrest and revolutionary movements. Second, and in parallel to these efforts, the British struggle to suppress the Atlantic slave trade gave birth to a more far-reaching conception of intervention centred on the military enforcement of an internationally agreed humanitarian norm.

Addressing the question of the movements in the history of ideas that gave rise to such a novel conception of intervention, Chapter 3 considers the intellectual origins of humanitarianism. Beginning in the mid-eighteenth century, various religious, philosophical and literary currents combined to mould a humanitarian sensibility, under the influence of which people developed empathy for their fellow human beings and took active measures to relieve the suffering of others across national and even continental divides. Rather than building their campaigns on a discourse of rights, civil society groups appealed instead to the idea of 'humanity', thereby making it a key normative reference in both national and international politics. This book, then, is intended as a contribution to the history of humanitarianism as distinct from the early history of human rights.

Part II focuses on the struggle against the Atlantic slave trade and the emergence of a humanitarian understanding of intervention. It begins (Chapter 4) by briefly outlining the system of transatlantic traffic in slaves, which, by reducing human beings to a mere commodity in a circular trading system, constituted one of history's worst humanitarian disasters. One of the central concerns of the abolitionists, who towards the end of the eighteenth century grew from a small cohort of well-connected activists to a mass movement, was to reverse this process of dehumanisation and render slaves visible in public discourse as fellow human beings who were suffering and in need of help. The focus is thus placed on the successful humanitarian mobilisation of the public by means of a targeted 'humanitarian narrative' and an unprecedented combination of multifarious instruments of appeal. For strategic reasons, the abolitionists concentrated their efforts on the slave trade, which was to be terminated by means of state intervention. A close interlinkage of mobilisation in parliament and civil society can be observed here, for the activists used petitions and legislative initiatives in their attempts to make their cause the official policy of the British government. In doing so, the abolitionists were the first to link humanitarianism with the policy and practice of state intervention.

All this resulted in the British Slave Trade Act of 1807, which also marked the beginning of the Royal Navy's operations off the coast of West Africa. Chapter 5 concentrates on the developments that led from a national ban on the slave trade and its unilateral military enforcement by the United Kingdom to its international and multilateral implementation. A crucial turning point is marked by the Congress of Vienna, at which the political pressure built up by the abolitionists was so great that, for the first time, the proscription of the slave trade was jointly proclaimed and enshrined as a humanitarian norm in international law. This interdict then formed the point of reference for a series of highly controversial negotiations between the European states to decide on collective measures to be taken against this border-crossing problem. A bilateral approach between Britain and the continental powers finally resulted in a mechanism for implementation to be set up, which consisted of a previously unheard-of combination of military and legal measures and which, in the shape of the Mixed Commissions for the Abolition of the Slave Trade, produced one of the first forms of international jurisdiction.

This form of international cooperation offered completely new possibilities for the suppression of a system of human trafficking that operated across oceans and continents, but at the same time it conflicted with the interests of particular states and their own mutual rivalries and on several occasions threatened to founder on the limitations imposed by national sovereignty rights. Alongside the viability of the agreed measure, then, Chapter 6 looks at the diplomatic wrangling by which the British government tried to secure treaty obligations from as many states as possible and to overcome massive political resistance, notably from Spain,

Portugal, Brazil, France and the United States. Yet this decades-long process of negotiation produced a mounting international consensus, particularly from the mid-1840s onwards, condemning slavery as a 'crime against humanity'. One telling sign of this new moral climate was the emergence of one of the first international treaty regimes, which extended from Europe across North and South America and the Arab World to eastern and western Africa. Its foundational idea was to enforce agreed humanitarian norms by military means if necessary. The fight against the slave trade, it is argued, gave rise to a new conception of intervention, and abolitionism became established as a key international guiding norm for 'civilisational' action in the long nineteenth century.

Part III discusses the striking triangular relationship between colonialism and imperialism, humanitarianism and interventionism in various parts of the world. It asks to what extent the idea of humanitarian intervention solidified in international politics as a colonial and imperial practice. Indeed, Chapter 7 will show how closely the struggle against the slave trade was intertwined with the colonial and imperial penetration of Africa. In western Africa British anti-slavery measures, which for strategic reasons increasingly shifted from seaborne military operations to dry land, led to direct interference in the internal affairs of African principalities. A particularly prominent case was Lagos, which ended up being formally annexed by the United Kingdom. From the middle on the century onwards, the by now tried and tested intervention measures came to serve as an example for the suppression of the slave trade in eastern Africa, increasingly turning the idea of abolition into a decisive catalyst and trailblazer for European expansionism across the African continent. At two international conferences – first in Berlin (1884–85) and then in Brussels (1889–90) – the 'civilised' states signed treaties by which they gave themselves a mandate in international law and an effective carte blanche for direct intervention, in the name of civilisation, in the internal affairs of African realms.

This telling fusion of humanitarianism, interventionism and imperialism can, however, also be found in altogether different parts of the world and in other international constellations. Chapter 8 accordingly considers three key case studies of collective European great power intervention for the protection of Ottoman Christians, doing so in the imperial context of the so-called Eastern Question. The first of these cases is the intervention in the Greek war of independence of 1821–30. Unlike in much of the existing literature, however, this is not understood here as heralding the birth of the modern concept of humanitarian intervention. Instead, this study argues that the reaction of the Concert of Europe was decisively conditioned by abolitionist ideas and was based on the very conception of humanitarian intervention that had crystallised in the fight against the slave trade. The intervention in Greece did, however, mark a precedent in its novel linkage between abolitionist themes and those of the protection of minorities, with a distinct narrowing of the idea of international protection to the Christian population. This selective conception of intervention was then ready to be reactivated by the European powers, as testified to by the crises in Lebanon (1860–61) and the Balkans (1876–78), against the Ottoman Empire, which was repeatedly branded as 'uncivilised', 'barbaric' and 'despotic'. What is remarkable about these instances of intervention is the increasing degree to which practices of international governance emerged in the form of international commissions alongside rudimentary forms of international criminal prosecution and minority protection. Above all, though, this period witnessed the consolidation in international law of the doctrine of humanitarian intervention, with the decisive impetus coming from the fight against the slave trade on the one hand and the relief of Christian minorities on the other.

The final chapter in Part III (Chapter 9) looks at the United States, which serves as something of an extra-European mirror in which European practices of intervention are reflected. The first conclusion to draw is that the US government regarded interventions by the Concert of Europe in the internal affairs of sovereign states as a colonial threat to its own national security interests, which led to the formulation in 1823 of the Monroe Doctrine and its paradigm of non-intervention. A fundamental change came when the United States embarked on its own course of colonial expansion and increasingly came to adapt the practice of intervention to its own purposes. The key role here was played by the Caribbean island of Cuba, where a war of independence precipitated a humanitarian crisis. In the context of that crisis, the US government began to invoke European interventions as precedents and examples by which its own military action against Spain might be justified both legally and morally.

The United States can thus be seen to have claimed the same right to humanitarian intervention in international politics in order to assert its own role as arbiter of power in the western hemisphere and as such to uphold by force the principles of civilisation and humanity – even against a Christian European state. Set alongside European interventions, the American case vividly shows how closely the idea of humanitarianism was interwoven with colonialism and imperialism. An attempt to understand the historical subject of humanitarianism should not, therefore, allow itself to be reduced to a choice between 'Humanitarianism or Imperialism',[49] as in the question posed by Gary Bass in his opening chapter, but rather be guided by the interconnection between humanitarianism and colonialism or imperialism. Rather than standing in opposition to one another, these concepts must be understood as forming a highly potent symbiotic unit.

Finally, the book's Epilogue turns its attention to the further developments undergone by the concept of humanitarian intervention in the twentieth and twenty-first centuries. What is striking is the degree to which the examples of the nineteenth century remained in people's minds and took on the function of a discursive frame of reference in subsequent debates in international law. Their function was that of a surface onto which further developments of the idea towards current concepts and debates were projected and in which they could be reflected. All the while, however, there was a tendency to ignore their colonial and imperial aspects.

The present study draws on a wide range of sources. My research took me to a number of archives and research libraries in the United Kingdom, France, Germany, the United States, Switzerland and Austria. The unpublished sources I consulted consist largely of diplomatic and military documents giving detailed accounts of both the military and political aspects of individual cases of intervention. Of crucial importance are the voluminous records preserved by the British Foreign Office (FO) and Colonial Office (CO) as well as the Records of the Admiralty (ADM) kept at the National Archive (TNA) in Kew. They not only offer insights into interventions in the Ottoman Empire, but also give a detailed account of British measures taken against the slave trade. Among these documents are diplomatic correspondence, Royal Navy dispatches, court records of the Mixed Commissions, consular reports and the proceedings of the various commissions and diplomatic conferences. With regard to the Royal Navy's missions against slavers, I drew upon smaller holdings at both the National Maritime Museum (NMM) in Greenwich and the National Museum of the Royal Navy (NMRN) in Portsmouth.

In France, my research focused on the copious records of the French foreign ministry held at the Archives des Affaires Étrangères (MAE) in Paris and the Service historique de la défense (SHD) in Vincennes. Both holdings allow a detailed insight into the French position regarding the respective interventions – a position which, particularly with regard to the suppression of the slave trade, was highly ambiguous and controversial. This critical perspective on British abolition measures and the international treaty regime was supplemented by examining smaller Spanish holdings at the Archivo General de Indias (AGI) in Seville, the Archivo General de Simancas (AGS) in Valladolid and the Archivo Histórico

Nacional (AHN) in Madrid, together with files from the Österreichisches Haus-, Hof- und Staatsarchiv (HHStA) in Vienna. In the United States, I consulted the National Archives and the Library of Congress, both in Washington, DC. Of particular relevance were the voluminous congressional records of debates over an international ban on the slave trade and intervention in the Cuban war of independence, with the *Annals of Congress of the United States* and *United States Congressional Serial Set 1817–1980* proving particularly valuable. The Manuscript Division of the Library of Congress (LoC), with the *Papers of President William McKinley* and the *Clara Barton Papers*, was also illuminating with regard to the humanitarian crisis in Cuba, as was the correspondence of Clara Barton, the founder of the American Red Cross, with the International Committee of the Red Cross. This correspondence is preserved at the Ancien Fonds (AF), Courrier reçu Etats-Unis 1893–1913 of the Archives du Comité International de la Croix-Rouge (ACICR) in Geneva.

Several important published editions of documents and sources proved a useful supplement to these archival holdings. Besides a plethora of published government documents, the *British and Foreign State Papers* (BFSP), the *Hansard Parliamentary Debates* and the *British Parliamentary Papers* (BPP) were particularly helpful, as were, in France, the *Documents Diplomatiques* (DD) series and, in the United States, the collections *Spanish Diplomatic Correspondence and Documents, 1896–1900* and *Speeches and Addresses of William McKinley*. Aside from these official government documents, however, this study also relies heavily on sources produced by a variety of civil society actors. These include the contemporary publications of the *African Institution* and reports from missionaries, explorers and journalists as well as legal treatises by eminent scholars of international law. Where the various campaigns of humanitarian mobilisation are concerned, public petitions, pamphlets and newsletters as well as newspaper articles are key sources that are central to the analysis presented here. Finally, this also includes visual sources in the form of paintings, prints, cartoons and photographs deployed by abolitionists, philhellenes and the champions of *Cuba libre*.

Part I

Interventionism and Humanitarianism under the Sign of Internationalism

People begin to feel that not only is every nation entitled to a free and independent life, but also that there are bonds of international duty binding all the nations of this earth together. Hence, the conviction is gaining ground that if on any spot of the world, even within the limits of an independent nation, some glaring wrong should be done ... then other nations are not absolved from all concern in the matter simply because of large distance between them and the scene of the wrong.[1]   Giuseppe Mazzini, 1851

1 The Nineteenth Century as the Age of Internationalism

In 1916 the British writer and political theorist Leonard Woolf published two reports on the subject of *International Government* for the Fabian Society. Woolf, who was married to the celebrated novelist Virginia, was an ardent supporter of liberal internationalism. His report argued for the creation of an international organisation which would be able to prevent wars and secure a lasting world peace. Far from being a figment of a utopian imagination, Woolf maintained that such a body could be conceived of as rooted in some of the principal achievements of the nineteenth century.[1] The Congress of Vienna (1814–15) had inaugurated an entirely new system of international relations based on one decisive insight:

> The recognition of international interests, and that national interests are international interests, and vice versa, was the great social discovery of the last 100 years. This discovery has operated in many different ways, all of which throw light upon the problem of International Government.[2]

This new internationalism expressed itself in various forms of international government, which Woolf understood in the broadest sense to refer to the regulation of relations between states, nations and peoples on the joint basis of international agreements.[3] Woolf provided a detailed analysis of the history and structure of international cooperation in the nineteenth century in such diverse realms as communication, public health and disease control, and technology and industry. Under the heading of 'Morals and Crime', he stressed not only the struggle against 'white slavery' – the traffic in women and girls for prostitution – but especially the international efforts to abolish slavery and the slave trade. Woolf traced these efforts from the proscription of the slave trade at the Congress of Vienna to their culmination in the Brussels Conference Act of 1890 and the founding of an international bureau in Zanzibar to supervise its implementation.[4]

With regard to the idea of securing international peace, Woolf emphasised the key part played in the nineteenth century by conferences and congresses, at which the European great powers had found solutions to simmering international crises before they erupted into full-scale European wars. As a particularly impressive example of successful crisis management, Woolf cited the case of the Greek war of independence, discussing in some detail the great powers' collective intervention which, after successive diplomatic meetings, culminated in the Battle of Navarino (1827), at which an allied naval squadron completely destroyed the Ottoman fleet.[5] According to Woolf, this joint military action was not a war but rather a new phenomenon in international law which he described in the following terms:

A blockade and a naval action between isolated sovereign Powers involves war, whether some of them call themselves mediators or anything else. But if the decisions of an international conference are binding upon the nations of Europe, then a blockade, or even a naval massacre, to enforce those decisions, undertaken in the name of Europe, can reasonably be called pacific.[6]

In a supplementary note, Woolf referred to debates on the question of collective intervention in international law and concluded by restating his position: 'There is a real difference between a nation enforcing its own will by violence and one enforcing the will of an international authority by violence. It is the difference between a hooligan and a policeman.'[7] Although the European powers had not been able to prevent all bloodshed in the Greco-Turkish conflict, they had nonetheless largely succeeded in settling matters of severe dissension which, but for their intervention, would have led to incessant massacres and fighting.[8]

At the time of the report's publication in 1916, Woolf's claims must indeed have struck the overwhelming majority of his readers as completely utopian. A plea for cooperative internationalism, and particularly the idea that joint military action by the European great powers might prevent bloodshed and secure international peace, must have seemed absurd while the conflagration set off by the same powers' nationalism was claiming lives in unprecedented numbers on the battlefields of the Somme and Verdun. Nonetheless, Woolf's arguments remained relevant and decisively influenced the British government's position with regard to setting up a post-war international body. The Foreign Office's proposals for an 'International Government under the League of Nations' in many respects reflected the ideas that Woolf had derived, during the First World War, from his careful study of nineteenth-century internationalism.[9]

By increasingly referring to the nineteenth century as the 'age of internationalism',[10] recent historians have to some extent adopted Leonard Woolf's perspective. Contrary to earlier traditions in historical scholarship, this new interpretation understands the era to have been distinguished less by a divisive and provocative nationalism on the part of individual states and more by the processes of acceleration and compression which brought not only nations, but entire global regions into closer contact with one another than ever before.[11] This resulted in a significant increase in cross-border activities and cooperation that was reflected in the founding of international organisations and institutions. Between 1815 and 1914 alone, more than 500 such associations were founded – a startling figure that vividly illustrates this new development.[12] The conceptual history of the term 'internationalism' can be traced to the late eighteenth century, specifically to 1780, when the British philosopher and social reformer Jeremy Bentham, in his book *An Introduction to the Principles of Morals and Legislation*, became the first writer to use the adjective 'international' – and to do so, moreover, with reference to international law, its definition and demarcation.[13] By the mid-nineteenth century, Bentham's neologism had established itself as a term in its own right. According to a broad definition and taking into account the nineteenth-century understanding of the term, internationalism comprises

on the one hand social and political movements campaigning for reforms within states and between peoples at an international level; on the other hand, it includes practical internationalisation in commerce, culture and society. Various forms ranging from non-governmental organisations via intra-governmental bodies to informal networks fall under this rubric.[14]

The 'mechanics of internationalism' began to exert a formative influence on the very character of nineteenth-century politics, with manifold forms of internationalism developing in nearly every sphere of public life.[15] A key role fell to the sectors of transport, trade and communications, where the rapid growth of cross-border transactions called for international regulation. Among frequently cited milestones are such creations as the Central Commission for the Navigation of the Rhine (1815), the International Telegraph Union (1865) and the General Postal Union (1874; renamed Universal Postal Union in 1878).[16] Science and technology, too, witnessed a rapid expansion of international cooperation. Experts from different states organised themselves in networks and made increasing use of congresses and conferences as new forums for the exchange of ideas and to set common standards for weights and measures as well as units of currency and time.[17] The outcomes of these efforts at standardisation were then codified in treaties under international law, leading to a marked expansion of international treaty law and heralding a historic shift 'from a law of coexistence to one of cooperation'.[18] In sum, the rapidly growing number of norm-setting treaties led to an unprecedented positivisation of international law, thereby laying the ground for the further juridification of international relations.[19]

These developments were accompanied by a parallel growth of the academic study of international law, one consequence of which was the founding in 1873 of the Institut de droit international. The institute was set up in Ghent; its founding members included the Belgian Gustave Rolin-Jaequemyns and Swiss Gustave Moynier and Johan Caspar Bluntschli. To advance their goals of the professionalisation of the field and the further codification of international law, they published the *Revue de droit international et de législation comparée*, which had originally been started by Rolin-Jaequemyns. Drawing its members from the international elite of legal scholars, the members of the Institute, whom the Finnish legal historian Martti Koskenniemi has called 'the men of 1873', considered themselves a liberal moral instance and nothing less than 'the legal conscience of the civilised world'.[20]

Yet 'the men of 1873' did not regard this increasing global reach of international law as creating an egalitarian international legal order which all states were equally and unconditionally entitled to join. Admission instead depended, as the title of Bluntschli's legal treatise *Das moderne Völkerrecht der civilisirten Staten als Rechtsbuch dargestellt* (The modern law of peoples of the civilised states presented in the form of a law-book)[21] implied, on their respective 'standard of civilisation', defined exclusively in European terms.[22] Like many of their contemporaries, these jurists too were in thrall to the idea of the superiority of European civilisation as it had emerged from the mid-eighteenth century onwards and become firmly established by the end of the nineteenth. From this conviction they derived a joint mission on the part of European states to carry civilisation abroad, an attitude Bluntschli described in the following terms:

It is the destiny of the Earth's surface to serve human culture, and it is the destiny of mankind in its progress to spread civilisation across the Earth. Yet this destiny cannot be fulfilled except by the civilised states taking in hand the education and guidance of the savage tribes. To this end, it is necessary to extend the reach of civilised state authority.[23]

In his influential treatise on *The Institutes of the Law of Nations* (1883), another of the Institute's co-founders, the legal scholar and philosopher James Lorimer of the University of Edinburgh, divided humankind into the three categories of 'civilised', 'barbarous' and 'savage' and argued in favour of establishing a corresponding hierarchy of law and of diplomatic recognition:

As a political phenomenon, humanity, in its present condition, divides itself onto three concentric zones or spheres – that of civilised humanity, that of barbarous humanity, and that of savage humanity. To these, whether arising from peculiarities of race or from various stages of development in the same race, belong, of right, at the hands of civilized nations, three stages of recognition – plenary political recognition, partial recognition, and natural or mere human recognition.[24]

According to Lorimer, full political recognition was due only to the European states and their colonial territories – and of the latter only those settled by people of European descent – as well as the countries of North and South America that had gained their independence from European imperial powers. Partial diplomatic recognition was due to the Ottoman Empire and the historic states of Asia that had not come under European control, notably Persia, China, Siam and Japan. The rest of humankind was consigned to the third category – understood only in the natural and human rather than in the political sense – which Lorimer suggested be further divided into 'progressive and non-progressive races'.[25]

In this view, international law referred above all to relations between the civilised states. It was for scholars of international law, Lorimer argued, to explore the extent to which it might also be applied to other categories of humankind. Yet he expressly warned against hasty concessions to 'savages' and 'barbarians', citing the Ottoman Empire, which had been accepted into the community under international law after having fought Russia alongside France and Britain in the Crimean War (1853–56), as a warning example: 'In the case of the Turks we have had bitter experience of the consequences of extending the rights of civilization to barbarians who have proved to be incapable of performing its duties, and who possibly do not even belong to the progressive races of mankind.'[26]

Scholars of international law hotly debated the nature of legal relations with such non-European states as Persia, Siam, China, Japan and the Ottoman Empire. Notwithstanding such objections as those raised by Lorimer, certain concessions were made over the course of the nineteenth century, with an enhanced standing in international law first for the Ottoman Empire and then, from the 1890s on, for Japan. Yet no such concessions were made with regard to the 'savage' peoples of Africa, a section of humanity that remained categorically excluded from the community of international law. Indeed, a large majority of the 'men of 1873' were active supporters of imperial and colonial policy, providing as they did the justification in international law for European expansion.[27] In so doing, certain scholars of international law – such as Sir Travers Twiss, an Englishman in the service of King Leopold II of Belgium – materially advanced the cause of European colonialism.[28]

This fatal commingling of legal internationalism and European colonialism was particularly in evidence at the Berlin Conference of 1884–85, at which the European great powers, under the pretext of a civilising and humanitarian mission, laid the foundations for their colonial endeavours in Africa and met with broad approval from the 'men of 1873'.[29] A particularly ardent proponent of European colonial undertakings in the Congo basin was the aforementioned Gustave Moynier, co-founder of the Ghent Institute and also of the International Committee of the Red Cross (ICRC), as the president of which he served till his death in 1910. To further the cause, Moynier published the monthly journal *L'Afrique explorée et civilise* from 1879 to 1894, as well as a range of other publications devoted to colonial propaganda.[30] These efforts were rewarded with the dubious honour of the consulship of the Congo Free State in Switzerland – the diplomatic representation, that is, of the private colony of King Leopold II that became the site of one of the greatest humanitarian catastrophes of the nineteenth century.

The internationalisation of law in the nineteenth century not only transcended borders and brought countries into closer cooperation, but also codified international hierarchies in a community of international law, membership of which was limited almost exclusively to European and American nations.[31] Global differences were thereby legally cemented along supposed civilisational boundaries, which in turn were clearly reflected in the provisions of nascent international humanitarian law. When the states assembled at the Hague Peace Conference of 1899 tried to regulate and 'humanise' military conflict by proscribing such devices as poison gas and expanding bullets, they had only conflicts between 'civilised' nations in mind,[32] explicitly leaving the 'uncivilised' portion of humanity excluded from the Hague Convention. One consequence was that the use of Dum Dum bullets,[33] which expand on impact, thereby causing severe injury and loss of blood, remained legal in overseas territories.[34] This form of codification of international humanitarian law effectively enshrined colonial conflict as a category outside the usual rules of engagement, thereby legitimising its pursuit as, in Kipling's phrase, 'savage wars of peace'.[35]

Defining internationalisms were emerging in other areas besides international law. A variety of movements for social and political reform began to form international networks and use the new opportunities for cooperation that were arising in the transnational sphere. Activists from all manner of countries cooperated across borders in the fight against slavery and the slave trade, against traffic in women and girls, for workers' rights and to secure world peace.[36] In so doing, these civil society groups were fully aware of the decisive role played by a mobilised public, which grew in importance with the revolution in communications, becoming nothing short of a defining 'feature of the nineteenth century'.[37] The telegraph created a global network of news which, together with the emergence of mass-market newspapers, led to information being transmitted at greater speed and intensity and opened up entirely new opportunities for communication and agitation.[38] Accordingly, the various social and political activist groups deliberately used 'publicity' as a resource to raise awareness of their causes and rally support, thereby becoming influential 'pressure groups' that as civil society actors came to exert an often decisive influence on political decisions made at the level of nation states. In his classic account of the history of nineteenth-century internationalism, Francis Lyons called this process the 'growth of an international social conscience', that social conscience being embodied by civil society groups:

By bringing together like-minded people from various countries to periodic conferences, by their reports and statistics, by their publications and propaganda, they not only moulded, or even created, public opinion, but often became influential pressure-groups, revealing the disparities between governments in their approach to social evils and badgering the more backward to close the gap between them and the more advanced. In a word, they made themselves in large measure the social conscience of Europe.[39]

On the whole, Lyons considers this era as being marked by a strong 'humanitarian impulse', which reached an early peak – both symbolically and institutionally – in the founding of the Red Cross in 1863.[40]

This cross-section of the various spheres in which defining internationalisms began to emerge illustrates the degree to which the nineteenth century was not only an age of internationalism but moreover one in which it was 'a structural component of international relations'.[41] Core features of this development were the lasting establishment of institutions, congresses and conferences as forums for communication and cooperation, defining efforts at setting norms and standards, the juridification of international relations by the successive codification of law and the emergence of transnational networks and civil society groups. Owing to the huge increase in these developments, the later nineteenth century in particular – it being a matter of emphasis whether it is taken to begin in the 1860s or the 1880s – is generally thought of as the peak of nineteenth-century internationalism.[42] This characterisation largely holds true for the spheres described here, not least because this period marks the foundation of many international institutions and organisations.[43] With regard to governmental internationalism, however, it sets in too late, for many preconditions for this overall development were put in place in the early years of the century. A decisive moment was the Congress of Vienna (1814–15),[44] which heralded not only the redrawing of the continent's political map, but also a fundamental trans-formation of relations between European states.[45] Such a contemporary observer as Friedrich von Gentz, closest adviser to the Austrian foreign minister Metternich and the 'secretary of the congress', were aware of this epochal break. In 1818, Gentz wrote:

> The political system that has established itself in Europe since 1814 and 1815 is a phenomenon unprecedented in the history of the world. The principle of balance or rather of counter-weights formed by separate alliances – a principle by which Europe had been governed, and all too often rocked and bloodied, for three centuries – has given way to a principle of general unity, connecting the totality of states by a federative bond under the guidance of the five main powers.[46]

Based on a notion of political equilibrium that was founded less on equality of material power than on equal status and the consensus of the great powers, the Allies that together had defeated Napoleon – the United Kingdom, Russia, Prussia and Austria – began to introduce new standards of behaviour and new mechanisms in the cooperation between states.[47] This 'Concert of Europe', which France joined in 1818 at the Congress of Aachen, forming the European 'pentarchy', now assumed the role of a collective authority in charge of the continent's destiny and acted as a supranational force for order. In close consultation at regular conferences, especially between 1815 and 1822, the great powers jointly sought solutions to international conflicts, civil wars and humanitarian crises, codifying their collective decisions in the form of treaties binding under international law.[48] The idea of a coordinated policy on the part of the great powers to resolve conflicts and secure peace thereby became established as a distinctive trait of the nineteenth century. This form of intra-state cooperation, which came into being from 1815 onwards, is hence considered one of the earliest instances of internationalism in the political sense[49] and indeed as 'the very first model of international government'.[50] According to another interpretation, the Concert of Europe was even something of a 'security council', a first successful model of international crisis management.[51]

And the Vienna settlement really did inaugurate a virtually unpreced-ented period of peace in Europe following more than twenty years of armed struggle. Jürgen Osterhammel is right to state that the near-century between 1815 and 1914 was, certainly compared to previous and subsequent eras, one of extraordinary peaceability, for which he credits above all the durable order established at the Congress of Vienna.[52] The mechanisms of cooperation put in place by the Concert of Europe – conferences of ambassadors and foreign ministers, processes of mediation and the creation of European commissions for special purposes – proved durable enough even to survive the crises of 1853–56 and 1870–71. Both the Crimean War, which marked the first armed confrontation between members of the Concert (Great Britain and France on one side, Russia on the other) since 1815, and the Franco-Prussian War were undoubted watersheds and wrought lasting changes to the international order, but they did not put an end to these new forms of international cooperation.[53] Instead, these practices and procedures remained central to the repertoire of international politics and helped ensure that such severe crises as the Crimean War remained localised and finite conflicts rather than engulfing the entire continent. The measure of stability in international relations that was thus guaranteed was one of the main conditions for the flowering of internationalism in the other spheres briefly alluded to.[54] Without the fundamental transformation of international relations inaugurated at the Congress of Vienna, it would be hard to imagine the subsequent age of internationalism. In short, 'If the Concert was a response to Napoleon, internationalism as the nineteenth century understood the term was nothing if not a response to the Concert'.[55]

Although the Concert of Europe performed admirably as a first model of international government, providing a lasting guarantee of peace and stability, this should not be taken to mean that the five members of this European directory always agreed over the scope and limits of their collective authority. In fact, even the early period of their cooperation was marked by fundamental differences over the authority of the Concert, particularly with regard to the key question of whether the European powers were entitled to intervene directly in the internal affairs of sovereign states.[56] Dissension arose on the occasion of the wave of revolutions that swept southern Europe between 1820 and 1823 and seriously endangered the survival of its absolutist monarchies. Whereas the 'Holy Alliance' consisting of the conservative continental powers Russia, Austria and Prussia vehemently pleaded for direct military intervention in support of the threatened monarchies in the Italian and Iberian peninsulas, the United Kingdom was no less adamant in rejecting this as a severe overstepping of authority and violation of the principle of sovereignty. Intervention as a corrective in international politics can thus be seen to have formed a core issue of contention between conservative and liberal powers in the early nineteenth century.[57]

2 Intervention as a Corrective in International Politics

The term 'intervention' to denote the temporally limited involvement from outside in the internal affairs of another state, by use of coercive measures, and the topical deployment of power this implies[1] became established in the language of politics only over the course of the nineteenth century.[2] As a form of the deployment of military force, it is frequently associated with the phenomenon of war. Writers on this topic, however, point to the indistinct boundary between these two forms of deploying force and explicitly situate intervention somewhere between the states of war and peace, being as it were 'a kind of war in peace'.[3] Moreover, what begins as a military operation of limited scope may often by a series of steps turn into a full-blown war, a problem of which nineteenth-century observers were well aware. The influential British Liberal politician Vernon Harcourt described this gradual slide:

> Intervention may be wise, may be right, – nay, sometimes may even be necessary. But let us not deceive ourselves; intervention never has been, never will be, never can be short, simple or peaceable. Conducted under the most favourable circumstances, we have seen that it almost inevitably before its solution results in war.[4]

Military intervention was, however, not a genuinely new phenomenon of the nineteenth century, but rather one whose roots in theory and practice are discernible already in the early modern age. Especially during the wars of religion in the sixteenth and seventeenth centuries, European powers repeatedly intervened in neighbouring countries on the pretext of protecting their (Protestant or Catholic) co-religionists from the 'tyranny' of their respective rulers. Queen Elizabeth I of England actively supported the struggle of the French Huguenots and even directly intervened on the side of the Dutch Calvinists in their rebellion against Catholic Spain. For its part, the Spanish crown dispatched an expeditionary force to support an Irish rebellion against English rule. In the Thirty Years War, the various European powers repeatedly intervened in the internal affairs of the Holy Roman Empire – both to provide military support to their co-religionists and to assert their own strategic interests. Following a massacre of Protestant Waldensians in Piedmont at Easter, Oliver Cromwell, Lord Protector of England, did not hesitate to make credible diplomatic threats – in 1655, seven years after the Peace of Westphalia had been concluded – that ultimately led Charles Emmanuel II, Duke of Savoy, to relent and make concessions to the persecuted minority.[5] The momentous invasion of William III of Orange to depose his father-in-law James II of England in the Glorious Revolution of 1688 can likewise be seen as conforming to this early modern pattern of intervention to protect foreign subjects from religious persecution.[6]

The first theoretical approaches to the question of intervention can accordingly be found in the writings of that era's eminent jurists and political thinkers, most of whom were still influenced by the medieval tradition of just war theory and hence discussed chiefly the legitimacy of military intervention.[7] In his seminal *De jure belli ac pacis* (1625), Hugo Grotius, who is widely considered one of the founders of the modern theory of international law, also considered the question of whether a war fought for the protection of foreign subjects from their own masters might be legitimate.[8] While Grotius firmly denied subjects any right of resistance to their authorities even under extreme duress, he was prepared to grant a third party the right to intervene, which he justified with reference to the right, developed earlier on, to wage war as a punitive measure:

The fact must also be recognised that kings, and those who possess rights equal to those kings, have the right of demanding punishments not only on account of injuries committed against themselves or their subjects, but also on account of injuries which do not directly affect them but excessively violate the law of nature or of nations in regard to any persons whatsoever.[9]

Although Grotius recognised the principle of sovereignty as a pillar of international law, he made an exception in the case of gross violations of natural law, which he considered just cause for the use of military force within the borders of another sovereign commonwealth.[10]

The writings of Grotius were key points of reference for later figures influential in the development of international law who critically reappraised the idea of intervention he postulated.[11] The legal philosopher Christian Wolff, a native of Breslau (Wroclaw), argued for the absolute validity of state sovereignty, from which he concluded that any form of intervention was illegitimate and a violation of the natural freedom of nations.[12] In their own influential writings, the German scholar Samuel von Pufendorf and the Swiss Emer de Vattel likewise defended the inviolability of sovereignty and strongly denied any general right to interference supposedly derived from natural law.[13] Unlike Wolff, however, they did allow for one, albeit strictly limited, exception: Only if the people had already risen up against the tyranny of their own ruler did they consider an intervention permissible – and then only if the people had expressly sought foreign aid and the intervening party was not pursuing interests of its own.[14] With reference to William of Orange's 1688 invasion of England, Emer de Vattel justified a limited right of intervention in the following terms: 'But if the prince, by violating the fundamental laws, gives his subjects a legal right to resist him, – if tyranny becoming insupportable obliges the nation to rise in their own defence, – every foreign power has a right to succour an oppressed people who implore their assistance.'[15] By either rejecting the right of intervention altogether or by admitting it only under exceptional circumstances, these legal scholars of the late seventeenth and eighteenth centuries bolstered the principle of state sovereignty in the theory of international law.[16]

That this concept, so central to international relations and international law, should have become firmly established was long associated, especially by political scientists and scholars of international law, with the Peace of Westphalia and portrayed as a key feature of the supposedly new order of the European system of states to which it had given rise.[17] Meanwhile, however, a number of authors have raised objections to this interpretation, accusing it of being one-dimensional and fixated on a specific moment in time. They point out that an absolute principle of sovereignty and a general principle of non-intervention by no means follow directly from the provisions of Münster and Osnabrück,[18] but on the contrary that these treaties explicitly granted France and Sweden, their foreign guarantors, the right to continue intervening in the affairs of the Holy Roman Empire. Brendan Simms has thus found the treaties to constitute 'nothing less than a charter for intervention'[19] and cites numerous instances of such direct interventions in the eighteenth century.[20] If we accept this point, the year 1648 does not stand for the establishment of the absolute validity of state sovereignty and the beginning of a political culture of non-intervention. In fact, intervention in the internal affairs of foreign states remained a firm part in the repertoire of international policy, was hotly debated in legal theory and repeatedly applied in practice.[21]

The debate flared up again towards the end of the eighteenth century as a result of the French Revolution. Instrumental in this was Edmund Burke, a Whig politician, philosopher and political thinker who became one of the revolution's most ardent and articulate opponents.[22] Burke saw events in the neighbouring country first of all as a threat to the national security of Great Britain, which on account of mere geographical proximity was exposed to the danger of Jacobin doctrines undermining the order of the state. Moreover, Burke saw in the spread of revolutionary ideas a serious threat to the whole 'Commonwealth of Europe'. To prevent it from being plunged into chaos, in his numerous pamphlets Burke forcefully urged for military intervention in France to put an end to revolutionary upheaval and to protect both national and international order.[23] Whereas the practice of intervention had previously been determined largely by religious and confessional considerations, the concept was now also interpreted to include the role of a defence mechanism against revolution.

Far from receding with the end of the Napoleonic Wars, this intervention paradigm found unprecedented acceptance in international politics and assumed the role of a key control mechanism in the nascent system of international governance.[24] The Congress of Vienna ushered in not only a reordering of the political map of Europe, but also the construction of a peacetime order based on the idea of political equilibrium.[25] In this context, the continental powers felt that there was a clear purpose to the practice of intervention: Internal unrest and revolutions, which were considered the principal cause of wars between states and the main threat to the international order, were under all circumstances to be prevented by collective intervention.[26] In the international politics of the early nineteenth century, this practice thus assumed the corrective function of protecting a threated order. As Jürgen Osterhammel put it, 'little wars were to stand in for the big wars they had prevented'.[27]

This right to interference, as it was incorporated in the Vienna settlement, was expressed chiefly through the policy of the Holy Alliance. The alliance formed by Russia, Prussia and Austria at the tsar's suggestion in Paris on 26 September 1815 had initially only set general guidelines for political cooperation to be guided by Christian principles. Moreover, the three monarchs involved – Tsar Alexander I, King Frederick William III and Emperor Francis I – had given each other only a rather vague promise of mutual support.[28] The measures agreed by the monarchs became more concrete with the first wave of nineteenth-century revolutions, which threatened the existence of the absolute monarchies of southern Europe from 1820 onwards.

The opening salvo, as it were, was the mutiny of parts of the liberally minded Spanish officer corps on 1 January 1820 at the port of Cadiz, where troops were to embark to suppress independence movements in the South American colonies. The revolt against the reactionary regime of Ferdinand VII quickly spread across the country, ultimately forcing the king to agree to the reintroduction of the liberal constitution of

1812 and to swear an oath to uphold it.[29] Besides the upheaval this spelled for the domestic affairs of Spain itself, the events of 1820 resonated in other countries and acted as a clarion call to further insurrections inspired by liberal ideas.[30] In July, a military coup in the Kingdom of the Two Sicilies, which like Spain was ruled by a Bourbon monarch, forced Ferdinand I likewise to accept a liberal constitution; a similar sequence of events unfolded in Portugal only one month later.

Within the conservative circle of the Holy Alliance, these developments in southern Europe caused extreme consternation. The fear was that revolutionary ferment might spread to other countries in a kind of chain reaction, extending into their own domains and ultimately jeopardising the entire international order established at the Congress of Vienna. It was at first above all the Austrian foreign minister Prince Clemens von Metternich who demanded that steps be taken against seditious activities and argued in favour of a policy of active intervention.[31] What worried Metternich was that the situation in Naples, the capital of the Kingdom of the Two Sicilies, might directly affect Austrian interests in the Italian peninsula and that liberal movements in general posed a threat to the absolutist model of rule in the multinational Habsburg Empire.[32] The aim of the congress that gathered in the town of Troppau (Opava) in Upper Silesia in October 1820 was therefore to agree on a joint policy to be adopted by the European great powers.

Whereas France and Great Britain, which both rejected a policy of active intervention against the revolutionary states, merely sent their ambassadors as observers to Troppau, the three monarchs of the Holy Alliance were present in person. In the 'Protocole pour déterminer le droit d'intervention des grandes Puissances', they committed themselves to refusing, on principle, to recognise any political change caused by revolution while reserving for themselves the right to intervene by force in the states concerned.[33] The purpose of these policies was to protect allied ruling houses and to reassure them by offering the prospect of military assistance in an emergency. With its anti-revolutionary paradigm of intervention, the Troppau Protocol signalled the specification of principles that previously had been only vaguely defined. Cloaked in the presumption of legitimacy, the monarchic form of rule was to be kept in power and protected from revolution by all means necessary, including military intervention in the internal affairs of sovereign states.[34] This was a clear attempt 'to hold all of Europe to a reactionary model of government and society'.[35]

The Troppau Protocol sealed the end of liberal constitutionalism in southern Europe and allowed the reactionary powers to prepare to retaliate. Having received, at the Congress of Laibach (Ljubljana) in early 1821, a mandate from Russia and Prussia for military intervention in southern Italy, Austria invaded the Kingdom of the Two Sicilies in March with 60,000 men, defeating the revolutionary forces and restoring the Bourbons to absolute rule. That same month, Vienna successfully pursued the same approach to political unrest in the Kingdom of Piedmont-Sardinia.[36] Spain, from which the wave of liberal revolutions had spread, suffered the same fate in the spring of 1823. At the Congress of Verona in 1822, the members of the Holy Alliance had agreed, albeit against massive resistance from the United Kingdom, to respond to Ferdinand VII's call for help with a military intervention, which France was charged with carrying out.[37] The French government's willingness to take this step was due less to any particular enthusiasm it might have felt for this new intervention paradigm than to its staunch refusal to allow foreign troops to march through its territory. Dispatched in April 1823, the French expeditionary corps soon put an end to the liberal project and fully restored the Spanish king to his previous position of power.[38] Within less than three years, all liberal constitutional designs and the models of government associated with them had been swept aside by the anti-revolutionary policy of intervention on the part of the conservative powers.

Not all the founding members of the Concert of Europe supported the right of intervention propounded by the Holy Alliance. The United Kingdom was strongly opposed to it and made its opposition clearly known several times over the course of the intervention debates. In May 1820 Castlereagh, the foreign secretary, rejected the Russian proposal for joint action against revolutionary Spain. In a memorandum, he outlined the principles on which the British position rested:

The principle of one State interfering by force in the internal affairs of another, in order to enforce obedience to the governing authority, is always a question of the greatest possible moral as well as political delicacy, and it is not meant here to examine it. – It is only important on the present occasion to observe that to generalize such a principle and to think of reducing it to a System, or to impose it as an obligation, is a Scheme utterly impracticable and objectionable.[39]

As an exception in which the United Kingdom too would be willing to intervene, Castlereagh admitted only an acute threat to Britain's national security and to European peace in general: 'We shall be found in our place when actual danger menaces the System of Europe, but this Country [i.e. the United Kingdom] cannot, and will not, act upon abstract and speculative Principles of Precaution.'[40]

London's reaction to the Troppau Protocol consisted of an unambiguous restatement of its familiar position. In a circular addressed to British diplomatic missions in 1821, Castlereagh condemned the intervention doctrine pursued by the Holy Alliance as wholly incompatible with the principles of both the British constitution and international law.[41] Moreover, the foreign secretary found the prospect of arbitrary intervention in the internal affairs of states to be a serious treat in itself:

But as they [i.e. the British government] regard the assumption of such right as only to be justified by the strongest necessity, and to be limited and regulated thereby, they cannot admit that this right should receive a general and indiscriminate application to all revolutionary movements without reference to their immediate bearing upon some particular state and states, or to be made prospectively the basis of an alliance. They regard its exercise as an exception to the general principle, of the greatest value and importance, and as one that only properly grows out of the circumstances of the special case.[42]

Castlereagh firmly rejected the anti-revolutionary automatism of intervention set in motion by Prussia, Russia and Austria. Intervention was to remain the exception, not be established as the norm. After all, it was hardly a desirable general principle, as Castlereagh reaffirmed before the House of Commons a few months later, that states should be permitted to interfere in each other's affairs simply because they disapproved of a change in the form of government.[43] That certain states should stand in judgement over others was nothing short of presumption and flew in the face both 'the law of nations and the principles of common sense'.[44]

Castlereagh's suicide in August 1822 did nothing to change the British stance. His successor George Canning continued Castlereagh's foreign policy.[45] If anything, the lingering conflict between the United Kingdom and the Holy Alliance over the right to intervene against revolutionary uprisings came to a head when, in April 1823, France invaded Spain at the behest of the Holy Alliance and put a violent end to that country's liberal project. The French invasion caused a public outcry in Britain, with some voices even calling on their own government to take military countermeasures. Having issued strongly worded protests and a warning to Paris not to seek territorial gains in the Iberian Peninsula or the Spanish colonies in South America – and to respect the territorial integrity of Portugal, a British ally – London decided to remain neutral while keeping a close eye on developments on the continent.[46]

It is hardly surprising then that the United Kingdom, which had emerged from the Napoleonic wars with undisputed mastery over the seas, should on account of this apparently clear stance be perceived above all as an advocate of non-intervention in the context of nineteenth-century international politics.[47] For the period from 1815 to 1827, John Bew has even found a broad 'anti-intervention consensus', supported by both main parties, to have applied in the United Kingdom.[48] While this is surely the case with regard to intervention as understood and practised by the Holy Alliance, it is not the whole picture. It entirely fails to account for another area of international politics that was only just emerging and where Britain was in the vanguard of defining an altogether new idea of intervention, that in which military power was deployed to enforce an internationally agreed humanitarian norm.[49]

Since 1808 units of the Royal Navy had been operating off the coast of West Africa in order to bring military pressure to bear against the Atlantic slave trade. This struggle was fast moving to the forefront of the United Kingdom's foreign policy. By cooperation with the other European great powers Britain tried to negotiate an international ban on the slave trade and to ensure that it was enforced. These early British efforts culminated in the 'Déclaration des 8 Cours, relative à l'Abolition Universelle de la Traite des Nègres', adopted by the European powers at the Congress of Vienna on 8 February 1815.[50] The declaration condemned the slave trade as a flagrant violation of the principles of humanity and universal morals. The states signatory to the declaration, which formed part of the final act of the Congress, recognised the need for urgent action against human trafficking. With the proscription of the slave trade now for the first time codified in international law, the British government stepped up its attempts to build a multilateral mechanism to implement the newly established humanitarian norm, thereby laying the foundation for humanitarian intervention as an instrument of international politics.[51] The struggle against the slave trade may thus be considered the template for the doctrine of humanitarian intervention in international law.[52]

Although attempts have occasionally been made to attach the label 'humanitarian' to early modern interventions – for instance Cromwell's efforts on behalf of the persecuted Waldensians of Piedmont in 1655 – and thereby to extend the concept's genealogy, they do not bear closer scrutiny.[53] These early modern instances were clearly motivated by confessional solidarity and their purpose was to provide relief to co-religionists in danger in nearby European countries.[54] There was, by contrast, an entirely new quality to the Royal Navy's interventions against the slave trade, first off the western African coast and ultimately throughout the Atlantic. The aim of these military operations was to put a stop to a humanitarian crisis in geographically remote areas for the benefit of people who were not of one's own denomination or even members of the wider Christian communion. But why was it the United Kingdom which, while taking a staunchly non-interventionist stance in European politics, should at the same time have put itself in the vanguard of an idea of intervention driven by humanitarian concerns, thereby coming to be regarded as 'the birthplace of humanitarian intervention'?[55] What currents in the history of ideas fed the intellectual soil on which such a novel idea of intervention could arise and be put into practice in the early nineteenth century?

3 The Rise of the Humanitarian Sensibility and the Emergence of Humanitarianism

The answer to these questions is to be found in the context of the emergence of humanitarianism,[1] which from the mid-eighteenth century matured into a highly influential factor in national and international politics, gathering force as a 'humanitarian revolution' and in the nineteenth century constituting something like that era's international 'social conscience'.[2] People began to develop empathy for their fellow human beings and work towards alleviating the suffering of others not just in their own countries, but across borders and even in other continents. A characteristic expression of this development was the veritable wave of humanitarian reform movements that began to spread across western European and North American societies. While the movement for the abolition of the Atlantic slave trade may have been the most prominent of these and wide-ranging in its outcomes, it was far from being the only one of its kind. Activists began publicly to decry existing abuses, demand fundamental reforms and sometimes even work simultaneously in other areas such as criminal justice and penal reform, the impressment of sailors, care for the poor and the sick, and related social causes.[3] The founding impetus came from both individuals strongly influenced by Enlightenment ideas and religious groups and evangelicals or Quakers and other nonconformists. In the groups that now formed, secular and religious motivations can accordingly be observed to merge.[4] Activists not only created national networks with like-minded individuals and groups, but also connected internationally.[5] A typical example is Granville Sharp, co-founder of the British abolitionist movement, who forged close transatlantic links with American abolitionists around the Quaker Anthony Benezet.[6] By means of their respective national and international networks, they tried to raise awareness of humanitarian issues to bring aid to people in need.

In the mid-eighteenth century the idea of an obligation to mutual humanitarian aid that underpinned these activities also began to take shape at the international level, specifically in the realm of international law. One example is the aforementioned Emer de Vattel, who in *The Law of Nations* (1758) had this to say about mutual obligations as the founding principle of relations between states:

The offices of humanity are those succours, those duties, which men owe to each other, as men, that is, as social beings formed to live in society, and standing in need of mutual assistance for their preservation and happiness, and to enable them to live in a manner conformable to their nature. Now the laws of nature being no less obligatory on nations than on individuals ... whatever duties each man owes to other men, the same does each nation, in its way, owe to other nations ... Such is the foundation of those common duties, – of those offices of humanity, – to which nations are reciprocally bound towards each other. They consist, generally, in doing everything in our power for the preservation and happiness of others, as far as such conduct is reconcilable with our duties towards ourselves.[7]

As a prime example of this humanitarian obligation to mutual 'succour', de Vattel referred to the material aid provided by Great Britain and Spain to Portugal following the earthquake of 1 November 1755, which almost completely destroyed Lisbon and claimed somewhere between 30,000 and 100,000 lives.[8] The Portuguese capital's close economic links with all major European trading centres meant that news of the disaster spread across the continent with relative rapidity, and foreign merchants from London and Hamburg were the first to dispatch ships laden with provisions for the relief of the afflicted people of Lisbon.[9]

But how did this revolutionary development and the emergence of a humanitarian consciousness in the mid-eighteenth century come about? The American historian Thomas Haskell argues for a close connection with the rise of a capitalist market order, of which certain motivations for the emergence of a 'humanitarian sensibility' were an accidental by-product.[10] In Haskell's account, the growth of both contractual law and economic ties between distant regions of the world contributed to an understanding of a causal link between the actions of people in one place and their consequences in another. Applied to the humanitarian problem of the slave trade, this might for instance mean that a link was perceived between the consumption of goods produced by slave labour – and hence one's own lifestyle – and the fate of African slaves working on the plantations. Haskell considers this awareness a key factor in the emergence of abolitionism and other humanitarian movements. The establishment of global market relations also spelled a significant expansion of the sphere of moral responsibility and the scope of humanitarian action it entailed.

Cultural historians meanwhile emphasise the importance of a radically new way of feeling that emerged in the age of Enlightenment, which found expression in a veritable 'culture of sensibility'.[11] Among its first intellectual precursors were the English 'Latitudinarians' of the late seventeenth century. These Protestant clergymen were opposed to Puritanism and the secular notion, associated chiefly with Thomas Hobbes, of people as selfish creatures striving mainly for their own comfort and happiness and concerned with maximising their advantage. In their writings and sermons, the Latitudinarian divines instead emphasised the social nature of human beings, who were born with a propensity for virtuous action and compassion for the suffering of others.[12]

Such moral philosophers as Anthony Ashley-Cooper, the third earl of Shaftesbury, and prominent figures of the Scottish Enlightenment such as Francis Hutcheson, David Hume and Adam Smith picked up these ideas and developed them further in their own works over the course of the eighteenth century.[13] Their innovative philosophical theory of 'moral sense' placed human feeling at the centre of their arguments, where it figured as the determining factor for moral action. In these accounts, the concept of 'sympathy' came to assume a central role.[14] To Hume, for instance, the ability to imagine the feelings of others was nothing less than elementary and universal principle of what it meant to be human, as he argued in one of his main works, *An Enquiry Concerning the Principles of Morals* (1751):

It is needless to push our researches so far as to ask, why we have humanity or a fellow-feeling with others. It is sufficient, that this is experienced to be a principle in human nature. ... No man is absolutely indifferent to the happiness and misery of others. The first has a natural tendency to give pleasure; the second, pain. This every one may find in himself. It is not probable, that these principles can be resolved into principles more simple and universal, whatever attempts may have been made to that purpose.[15]

These reflections on sympathy were largely shared by Hume's friend Adam Smith. In his principal philosophical work, *The Theory of Moral Sentiments* (1759), Smith likewise described a concern with the plight of others to be a principle rooted in human nature, while also defining 'pity or compassion' as 'the emotion which we feel for the misery of others, when we either see it, or are made to conceive it in a very lively manner'.[16]

In so doing, Smith broadened the theory of sympathy to include the key aspect of the human faculty of imagination,[17] which alone enabled one person to empathise and even to identify mentally with the suffering of another, as Smith explained:

By the imagination we place ourselves in his situation, we conceive ourselves enduring all the same torments, we enter as it were into his body, and become in some measure the same person with him, and thence form some idea of his sensations, and even feel something which, though weaker in degree, is not altogether unlike them. His agonies, when they are thus brought home to ourselves, when we have thus adopted and made them our own, begin at last to affect us, and we then tremble and shudder at the thought of what he feels.[18]

According to Smith, the imagination, the capacity for 'changing places in fancy with the sufferer', was 'the source of our fellow-feeling for the misery of others'.[19] From this idea it followed that to visualise human suffering and to narrate it in the most vivid terms possible had a key part to play in mobilising compassion.

An opportunity for doing so presented itself above all in literature, which alongside philosophy was the principal means for the expression of the new 'culture of sensibility'.[20] The literary genre of the sentimental novel, which thrived from the mid-eighteenth century onwards, made a significant contribution to this flowering of sensibility, conveying emotional messages to a broad readership and thereby popularising them. Such novels as *Pamela* (1740–41) and *Clarissa* (1747–48), both by Samuel Richardson,[21] were bestsellers in their day, triggering 'torrents of emotion' in their readers.[22] A decidedly sentimental narrative style confronted readers directly with the tragic fates of the novels' protagonists, allowing them to enter into and ultimately identify with them. This development was by no means restricted to the English-speaking world. French novels such as Jean-Jacques Rousseau's *Julie ou la Nouvelle Héloïse* (1761) were likewise widely feted and highly influential.

Against this backdrop some historians have considered the effects of this bourgeoning new world of sentiment on the social and political order of France in the run-up to the revolution.[23] Lynn Hunt, a noted authority on the revolutionary period, has stressed that reading sentimental novels gave rise to a new kind of identification with the plight of others and thereby contributed significantly to social disapproval of torture and other cruel punishments.[24] In her book's central argument, however, Hunt goes further still:

Readers learned to appreciate the emotional intensity of the ordinary and the capacity of people like themselves to create on their own a moral world. Human rights grew out of the seedbed sowed by these feelings. Human rights could only flourish when people learned to think of others as their equals, as like them in some fundamental fashion.[25]

The implication here is that an entirely new sense of equality took hold across the boundaries of class and estate imposed by the *ancien régime*, laying the ground for the Declaration of the Rights of Man of 1789 and thereby for the modern idea of human rights.

This genealogy, which draws a long line of continuity from 1789 via the Universal Declaration of Human Rights of 1948 to the present, is subject to much discussion and critical scrutiny in current debates on the history of human rights.[26] Yet Hunt's argument also poses elementary questions for the connection between the histories of humanitarianism and human rights: how did these developments relate to and influence one another? Or to put it another way, did the emergence of a new 'humanitarian sensibility' inevitably lead to the formulation and establishment of individual rights at the end of the eighteenth century? The two concepts share certain intellectual-historical roots and can often be observed to intersect. Especially with regard to the twentieth and twenty-first centuries, this makes the two fields hard to separate; somewhat inevitably, there is a 'blurred boundary between humanitarianism and human rights'.[27] Yet although the two concepts refer to related issues and both share human beings as their foremost concern, they are certainly not congruent. It is thus all the more important to make a clear methodical distinction between a discourse of granting equal human rights to all on the one hand and one concerned with putting an end to human suffering on the other.[28]

The effort to alleviate people's suffering and provide relief in humanitarian emergencies is by no means inextricably linked to the idea of defending human rights and the cause of legal equality. There is no necessary contradiction between humanitarian practices and their taking place within unequal legal frameworks – both nationally and internationally – and in a thoroughly paternalistic spirit. British abolitionism, the second key movement in the history of humanitarianism, offers a vivid case in point. Although the abolitionist movement, which had formed in the late eighteenth century from a number of religious groupings, was passionate in campaigning for an end to the Atlantic slave trade and the suffering of the African peoples concerned, this did not automatically mean that it was uniformly in favour of the full and immediate legal emancipation of slaves.[29] Under the given circumstances, abolitionists even denied enslaved Africans civil rights, judging them unable to exercise them responsibly. If slaves were to be granted civil rights, the precondition and task at hand was to raise their intellectual and moral capacities. William Wilberforce, who led the abolitionist cause in the House of Commons, argued accordingly in the great debate of April 1791 on the abolition of the slave trade:

The Negroes, he [Wilberforce] said, were creatures like ourselves: they had the same feelings, and even stronger affections than our own; but their minds were uninformed, and their moral characters were altogether debased. Men, in this state, were almost incapacitated for the reception of civil rights. In order to become fit for the enjoyment of these, they must, in some measures, be restored to that level from which they had been so unjustly and cruelly degraded. To give them power of appealing to the laws, would be to awaken in them a sense of the dignity of their nature. The first return of life after a swoon, was commonly a convulsion, dangerous, at once, to the party himself, and to all around him. Such, in the case of the Slaves, Mr. Wilberforce feared, might be the consequence of a sudden communication of civil rights.[30]

To abolitionists, then, recognition of African slaves as human 'creatures' possessed of 'the same feelings, and even stronger affections' as Europeans did not necessarily entail their eligibility for equal rights.[31]

In this context, the American literary historian Lynn Festa has shown how British abolitionists consciously adopted narrative techniques and established patterns familiar from the realms of successful sentimental literature in their campaign materials.[32] They placed an emphasis less on legal considerations than on the abstract notion of 'humanity'[33] and its various aspects. Understanding it as inclusion in the human community, the abolitionists began by describing the sufferings of Africans along the slave routes in as vivid and sentimental a manner as possible in order to emphasise their humanity. Slaves, who at the time were treated as one commodity among the many traded across the Atlantic, were to be rendered visible as human beings.[34] By this deliberate portrayal of Africans as part of the human community, the abolitionists appealed to the 'humanity' (in the philosophical sense of compassion) of their fellow Britons and called upon them to take action. The abolitionist message was that the slave trade was a flagrant violation of the elementary principles of humanity. One of the leading supporters of abolition, Lord Grenville, made this point in a speech to the House of Lords in June 1806:

My Lords; if we were to define humanity, what should we say it was? What are its attributes; what is its character? 'A sympathy of feeling for the distress of others – a desire to accomplish good ends by good means.' Let any man examine these qualities, and tell you, if he can, how the Slave Trade agrees with either of them; and if he cannot, I think we can have no difficulty in saying, that the Slave Trade is contrary to humanity.[35]

By the transition from the eighteenth to the nineteenth century, the rise of a humanitarian sensibility in such areas as international law, philosophy and literature had created the intellectual preconditions which civil society groups could now take advantage of for the purposes of their humanitarian campaigns. In the course of these developments, the idea of humanity emerged as the core normative reference in both national and international politics,[36] which helps account for the seeming absence or even 'disappearance of human rights' in the nineteenth century.[37] The abolitionists played a key role in this development by endowing the at first abstract notion of 'humanity' with a specific meaning, from which they were the first to derive the demand for a policy of direct humanitarian intervention. In so doing, they bridged the gap, for the first time, between the two concepts of nascent humanitarianism and state interventionism. The nineteenth century as the 'age of internationalism' characterised by the juridification of international relations, the operation of reform movements across national boundaries, the growing importance of 'publicity' as a resource, and its forms of intergovernmental cooperation and international governance offered an excellent framework for the development of a humanitarian notion of intervention and ultimately a doctrine of humanitarian intervention.

Part II

The Struggle against the Atlantic Slave Trade and the Emergence of a Humanitarian Understanding of Intervention

I was not aware till I had been some time here [in London] of the degree of frenzy existing here about the slave trade. People in general appear to think that it would suit the policy of the nation to go to war to put an end to that abominable traffic; and many wish that we should take the field on this new crusade.[1]   Lord Wellington, July 1814

4 Dehumanisation and Humanitarian Mobilisation

From Human Being to Commodity: The System of the Atlantic Slave Trade

It was the African American historian and civil rights pioneer W. E. B. Du Bois who wrote of the Atlantic slave trade as 'the most magnificent drama in the last thousand years of human history'.[1] Between the end of the fifteenth and the middle of the nineteenth century Europeans forcibly transported more than 12 million Africans to the Americas. Enslavement and traffic along the slave routes on the African continent having already claimed countless lives, an estimated further one and a half million human beings perished along the 'Middle Passage', the infamous crossing of the Atlantic.[2] For the 10 million or so survivors, arrival in the 'New World' generally meant lifelong servitude on the plantations and in the mines of the European colonies, with life expectancy reduced to just a few years by what were mostly extremely tough working conditions.[3] In view of this human tragedy suffered by millions upon millions, the Atlantic slave trade must, from a modern perspective, undoubtedly rank among the greatest crimes in the history of humankind.[4]

Yet to the minds of the overwhelming majority of contemporaries, the human traffic between the two continents was, for the nearly four centuries of its duration, seen not as a criminal act, but rather as a firm institution and an elementary part of an international economic system that contributed to shaping the entire Atlantic sphere.[5] In its early stages, the slave trade was dominated by Spain and Portugal, but by the seventeenth century other European states – the Netherlands, Denmark, Sweden and Brandenburg – began to carve out shares in this new and thriving sector. They remained, however, distinctly in the shadow of the new main players France and Great Britain.[6]

The decisive factor in the boom in the slave trade was the so-called sugar revolution, which brought profound changes to the entire Atlantic world.[7] A fall in the price of tobacco and a simultaneous rise in demand for sugar, which was on its way to becoming a mass commodity in

49

Europe, led to sugar cane becoming the major colonial cash crop from the mid-seventeenth century onwards. Enormous new plantations were cleared and sugar cane cultivated in monoculture in the Caribbean islands, with Barbados and Martinique as the principal centres.

'King Sugar' was now the uncontested ruler of the 'New World' and the decisive impetus in the emergence of an economic system often referred to as the 'Atlantic triangular slave trade'.[8] European slave traders exported firearms, gunpowder, iron goods and above all textiles on a large scale, exchanging them for human cargoes in West Africa. The western African coast and its hinterland – extending from Senegambia in the north via Guinea, the Gold Coast, the Bight of Benin, Biafra and the Loango Coast to Angola in the south – thus became the region on which the Atlantic slave trade was centred.[9] The slaves acquired here were transported to forced labour in the Americas, from where the products of the colonies were shipped back to the metropolises of Europe.[10] This highly simplified model fails, however, to account for the highly complex trade relations engendered by the slave trade.[11] For instance, rising demand for particularly desirable commodities also stimulated the manufacture and intra-European trade in textiles and firearms produced expressly for the African market. At the same time, the immense capital required to finance slave ships encouraged the growth of the entire banking and insurance sector. This meant that not only the maritime states, but also the countries of the European continent participated in and profited from this new economic activity.[12]

With West Africa also known as the 'white man's grave' on account of its fatal tropical diseases,[13] Europeans were moreover dependent on the cooperation of their local trading partners. While slavery and the slave trade had been widespread throughout much of the continent long before the first Europeans arrived there, it now reached a new level both qualitatively and quantitively.[14] Faced with huge European demand for slave labour, Africans took on the task of supplying it by waging targeted campaigns against other ethnic groups. The aim was to take as many prisoners as possible and to trade them profitably for European products. Entire kingdoms, such as Dahomey, profited from the abduction of slaves and were able to strengthen their own positions vis-à-vis their local competitors.[15] To this extent, certain African groups were autonomous actors in the Atlantic slave trade, making terms with European traders on an equal footing and pursuing their own specific objectives.[16] With its increasingly global implications, the Atlantic slave trade was undoubtedly 'one of the most complex economic enterprises known to the pre-industrial world'.[17]

The sites at which business was transacted between African and European slavers were the latter's fortified coastal bases and the established trading posts at the great estuaries, where slaves could be sold directly onto passing ships. For the prisoners, this spelled a violent transformation from a human being to a commodity in the Atlantic trading system, and indeed a forfeiting of any claim to humanity.[18] Having been selected for their physical fitness and traded for such goods as cloth and spirits, they were now a precious cargo and branded as such by hot irons. They were entered in the ship's bill of lading not by name but by number, and they were chained together and stowed in the hold to use the available space most efficiently.[19] In transporting this human cargo, captains of slave ships were guided by economic considerations alone. Their stated aim was to deliver alive as large a number of slaves as possible to American ports and thereby to make a good return on investment, which averaged an impressive 10 per cent.[20] Since a high mortality of slaves on the Middle Passage meant a proportionately high financial loss, attempts were constantly made to improve conditions on board, if only from entirely pecuniary considerations. Average mortality on the passage to the Americas was thus lowered from 20 per cent before 1700 to 5 per cent in the nineteenth century.[21]

Yet some captains also found it to be more 'economical' to throw slaves overboard alive, the reason being that insurance policies protected slave ships and their cargo from dangers at sea. This insurance compensated traders for slaves – the cargo in question – who drowned, but not for those who fell victim to disease while at sea.[22] With a view to securing the insurance premium, captains therefore decided to throw sick slaves overboard before they died, marking the ultimate degradation of human beings to mere commodities and the negation of any humanity.[23] The most notorious case took place in 1781 on board the British slave ship *Zong*, which owing to navigational error took nearly four months to reach its destination, Jamaica, from Africa. At twice the usual length, a large number of captives fell ill during the passage, whereupon Captain Luke Collingwood decided to throw 122 of them overboard.[24] The subsequent dispute between the ship's owner and the insurance company, which refused to pay compensation, was brought before an English court. It was not, however, a trial for mass murder.[25] As the presiding judge Lord Chief Justice Mansfield (William Murray) made clear, this was a civil case and was to be judged accordingly – by the same legal standards 'as if horses were killed'.[26]

Such captives as did arrive at their destination ports in relative health were, before disembarking, subjected to attempts to conceal the most obvious physical ravages of their gruelling journey.[27] A contemporary observer described how 'care is taken to polish them for sale'[28] in order that slaves might be presented to prospective buyers in as appealing a condition as possible. Whereas for the European slave traders the Atlantic crossing was above all a commercial risk, to the enslaved Africans it represented suffering that can barely be imagined and of which William Wilberforce, the abolitionist leader, trenchantly remarked 'that never can so much misery be found condensed into so small a place as in a slave ship during the middle passage'.[29]

There were indeed many elements that made up the suffering of the enslaved along their journey. Their violent abduction and the privations of the forced march to the coast were followed by the shock of being made to board the waiting ships of the white aliens. On arrival, captives were first stripped of their clothes and then, completely naked, subjected to a humiliating medical examination.[30] They were then shackled by their hands and feet, chained to one another and crammed below deck in cramped conditions.[31] Having had no previous contact with Europeans and no inkling of their fate, the enslaved Africans often feared that they had fallen into hands of cannibals and evil spirits.[32] The sailing of the ship marked the irreversible loss of all previous social and family ties and of any sense of cultural belonging centred on their village communities.[33]

After this traumatic beginning, the crossing to the West Indies, which took two months in good weather,[34] was marked by physical hardship and brute violence. On board, the captives were subject to the whims of the ship's crews, which reacted with draconian brutality to any form of rebellion, real or imagined. Women and girls, who were kept unchained in separate quarters from the male slaves, were frequently raped by members of the crew.[35]

The principal cause of the millions of deaths on board the slave ships were the disastrous conditions on the decks, one of the best-known and most harrowing accounts of which is provided by Olaudah Equiano in his autobiography *The Interesting Narrative of the Life of Olaudah Equiano*, first published in 1789. By his own account, Equiano was abducted as a boy of eleven from an Igbo village in the south-west of modern Nigeria and taken on the Middle Passage to Barbados. Given the chance to buy his freedom, he settled in England, where his book made him an icon of the abolitionist movement.[36] In it, he gave the first detailed account of the inhuman conditions on board from the perspective of the captives themselves:

The stench of the hold while we were on the coast was so intolerably loathsome that it was dangerous to remain there for any time ...; but now that the whole ship's cargo were confined together it became absolutely pestilential. The closeness of the place and the heat of the climate, added to the number in the ship, which was so crowded that each of us had scarcely room to turn himself, almost suffocated us. This produced copious perspirations, so that the air became unfit for respiration from a variety of loathsome smells, and brought on a sickness among the slaves, of which many died, thus falling victims to the improvident avarice, as I may call it, of their purchasers. This wretched situation was again aggravated by the galling go the chains, how become insupportable, and the filth of the necessary tubs, into which the children often fell and were almost suffocated. The shrieks of the women and the groans of the dying rendered the whole scene of horror almost inconceivable.[37]

Coupled with complete physical exhaustion, seasickness, poor diet and stale water, these atrocious hygienic conditions encouraged the outbreak of disease.[38] Besides such endemic tropical diseases as malaria and yellow fever, the highest death toll was exacted by gastrointestinal infections such as dysentery, which rapidly swept through the cramped quarters.[39] According to the contemporary account of Alexander Falconbridge, a former surgeon on a British slave ship, once disease had taken hold the lower decks of the slave ships came to resemble 'a slaughter-house',[40] with the emaciated sick lying in their own excrement. Like Olaudah Equiano, he depicts a 'scene of horror':

The place allotted for the sick negroes is under the half deck, where they lie on the bare plank. By this means, those who are emaciated, frequently have their skin, and even their flesh, entirely rubbed off, by the motion of the ship, from the prominent parts of the shoulders, elbows, and hips, so as to render the bones in those parts quite bare. And some of them, by constantly lying in the blood and mucus, that had flowed from those afflicted with the flux [dysentery], and which, as before observed, is generally so violent as to prevent their being kept clean, have their flesh much sooner rubbed off, than those who have only to contend with the mere friction of the ship. The excruciating pain which the poor sufferers feel from being obliged to continue in such a dreadful situation, frequently for several weeks, in case they happen to live so long, is not to be conceived or described.[41]

The captains of the slave ships had the dying and dead simply tossed overboard, where their bodies vanished in the expanses of the Atlantic Ocean or were consumed by waiting sharks, entire schools of which followed slave ships across the Atlantic in anticipation of prey.[42] For the slaves, the grisly sight of their fellow suffers being mauled by sharks meant a further step in their degradation to mere merchandise, which could be disposed of without ceremony or even the slightest acknowledgment of human dignity. To the enslaved Africans, death on the ships marked a twofold trauma: Physical death was compounded by being deprived of the ability to respond to it in a culturally appropriate way and to ease the transition of the dead to the world of their ancestors.[43]

Yet the enslaved Africans did not suffer the violence against them passively, but resisted it fiercely and in manifold ways.[44] It should therefore be remembered that active protest against the system of the Atlantic slave trade came first not from white abolitionists, but from African slaves themselves.[45] Soon after their abduction, captives would try to seize any opportunity for escape while being transported to the coast or held in makeshift prisons along the coast before embarkation. Even while being loaded onto the ships many were undeterred even by the dangers of drowning and the waiting sharks and made one last desperate attempt to reach the seemingly nearby coast by plunging themselves into the sea.[46] During the passage, too, the horrendous conditions on board and their apparently hopeless situation compelled many of the enslaved to seek escape by suicide. While some chose a quick death by leaping overboard, others refused food and water.[47] Fearing financial loss from the starvation of their 'human cargo', slavers would take to force-feeding their prisoners, brutally opening their jaws with a tong-like instrument called the *speculum oris* and forcing food into them.

Besides escape and self-harm, however, captives would also try to escape enslavement by violence directed against their abusers. Their inhuman treatment repeatedly caused African slaves to band together and attempt to bring slave ships under their control, thereby forcing their return to Africa.[48] Such shipboard revolts, which according to recent estimates affected about one in ten slave transports, were a constant danger of which the crews were well aware and which, in turn, redoubled their own readiness to visit violence on their captives.[49] Yet with only few exceptions, these mutinies were unsuccessful. Although dominant in numbers, the largely unarmed Africans were usually no match for sailors armed with guns and muskets. Revolts usually ended with a bloodbath among the mutineers and cruel vengeance against the survivors.[50] In the long term, however, the uprisings were not entirely without effect. They compelled slave traders to increase security measures on board, including larger crews. The slave revolts thereby not only added to the commercial risk of each sailing, but raised the costs of the doing business in general, contributing, in David Richardson's estimation, to weakening the Atlantic slave trade overall.[51]

Nor did resistance end when the enslaved Africans were landed in American ports and sold in local slave markets. Besides such everyday forms of resistance as disobedience, refusal to work and flight, the European regime of oppression was challenged above all by numerous violent uprisings, such as at Barbados, Jamaica and Bahia.[52] In nearly all cases, the white colonial masters succeeded in putting the rebellion down with great severity and restoring the previous order of things. An important exception was the slave revolt in Saint-Domingue, the French section of the island of Hispaniola, which had become one of the world's major producers of sugar cane and was thus considered a pearl among French possessions. The shockwaves emitted by the French Revolution led first to violent disputes between European settlers of different social classes and then to an uprising of the slave population. Led not exclusively, but critically, by the freed slave François-Dominique Toussaint Louverture, the black rebels ultimately succeeded in bringing the entire island under their control and fending off Spanish, British and French invasion attempts. The Haitian Revolution, as it became known, led to the complete abolition of slavery and finally, on 1 January 1804, to the proclamation of the first independent state in Latin America.[53]

Yet the successful Haitian Revolution and the destabilising effects of the various forms of African resistance were not enough to topple the firmly established system of slavery and the Atlantic slave trade. As long as this system was based on a broad elite consensus and was largely supported by the European populace, governments were prepared to commit their resources to protecting and upholding it. Any discussion of putting a stop to human trafficking and ultimately freeing the slaves had therefore to begin in the metropolitan centres of power and change minds there. This called for the founding of a well-organised protest movement, but above all for a shift of social awareness towards a recognition of the inhuman character of the Atlantic slave trade.[54]

The Rise of the Abolitionist Movement and Successful Humanitarian Mobilisation

It was at the very peak of the Atlantic slave trade in the 1780s, when more than 80,000 Africans a year were being transported to the Americas,[55] that a small group of activists in Great Britain – by far the dominant nation in the slave trade at the time – began to organise civilian resistance to this established economic system and thereby lay the foundations for a successful mass movement. The roots of the abolitionist movement reach back into the seventeenth century and are closely interwoven with the history of the Quakers.[56] This Christian community, which emerged in the 1650s and was known to its own members as the Society of Friends, was a genuinely 'Atlantic community'[57] in that many of its members had settled in the English colonies in America while remaining in touch with their co-religionists in the country of their founding. In keeping with their religious convictions, the Friends considered it sinful to enslave other human beings and began to campaign against slavery. The centre of early

Quaker abolitionism was Pennsylvania, where the first anti-slavery petition was issued in 1688 in Germantown, now part of Philadelphia.[58]

The Quakers were thus the first faith organization in the Atlantic world
to speak out collectively against the slave trade and increasingly were
identified by the title 'Friends of Humanity'.[59] One of the leaders of these
early anti-slavery efforts was Anthony Benezet, who tried to reach a wider
audience by publishing his arguments in pamphlet form.[60] Benezet's
publications went beyond the dominant religious line of argument by
consciously adapting concepts from natural law, thereby enhancing the
appeal of his plea beyond Quaker circles.[61]

The style of Benezet's arguments, too, broke new ground and was to
influence the argumentative strategy of abolitionist pamphleteering more
generally.[62] His first tract, 'Observations on the Inslaving, Importing,
and Purchasing of Negroes', published in 1759, began with a brief
description of the present sufferings of his white countrymen, caused
by enslavement and the forced separation from their families in the
turmoil of the Seven Years' War in the Americas.[63] Benezet used this
image, with which his contemporaries would have been all too familiar
(some of them at first hand), to highlight the horrors of the Atlantic slave
trade with explicit reference to the divine injunction 'To do unto all men,
as we would they should do unto us'. In his pamphlet, Benezet was also
the first to draw on eyewitness accounts by European observers of the
situation in West Africa.[64] A key motif was the abduction of Africans
from the bosom of their family, to which the following appeal to readers
was appended:

Let but any one reflect, that each individual of this number had some tender
attachment which was broken by this cruel separation; some parent or wife, who
had not even the opportunity of mingling tears in a parting embrace; or perhaps
some infant whom his labour was to feed and vigilance protect; or let any
consider what it is to lose a child, a husband or any dear relation, and then let
them say what they must think of those who are ingaged in, or encourage such a
trade.[65]

The slave trade was therefore, in conclusion, a grave offence to 'natural
justice and the common feelings of humanity'.[66] By making an intuitively
plausible connection between the suffering of the Seven Years' War,
familiar to Americans, and the horrors of the Atlantic slave trade
Benezet tried, on the one hand, to elicit sympathy among his countrymen
for the similar plight of enslaved Africans. On the other hand, he also
made clear that these Africans, who responded to the loss of their
children and loved ones with common human emotions of pain and
grief, were by nature fellow human beings and members of the human
community who were not to be degraded to the status of a material

commodity. Depicting as it did the slave trade as a fundamental violation of the common and unifying norm of 'humanity', this argument was a direct appeal to the growing humanitarian sensibility among his contemporaries. This aspect was to be central to subsequent abolitionist campaigning.[67]

The stylistic devices used by Benezet were to be as influential as his line of argument. Such works of his as *Some Historical Account of Guinea*,[68] in which he assembled writings on the subject by slavers, lawyers and philosophers, became something of a blueprint for other campaigners and their publications. The already existing close ties between Quaker communities on both sides of the Atlantic encouraged a brisk flow of ideas in both directions. Not only were plans and strategies for combating the evil of slavery discussed, but tracts were exchanged for publication in both Britain and the American colonies.[69] Benezet did not limit his efforts to his co-religionists in England, however, but was keen to work with anyone who shared his concerns.

Perhaps the most striking example of Benezet's quest for allies was his close collaboration with Granville Sharp, who at the time campaigned virtually single-handedly for the rights of black people in Great Britain. As a lawyer, he had had a spectacular success in the summer of 1772 defending the escaped slave James Somerset.[70] By invoking the principle of *habeas corpus*, Sharpe secured Somerset's release and prevented his forced transportation to Jamaica, where his owner had intended to sell him on. In strict legal terms, the ruling of Lord Chief Justice Mansfield – who was to preside over the *Zong* trial nearly ten years later – merely limited the rights of slaveholders to remove their slaves from English soil against their will. However, the ambiguous phrasing of the judgment led to many newspapers misinterpreting it as signalling a general freeing of slaves in England. Its legal significance aside, the case of *Somerset* v. *Stewart* had a considerable symbolic impact, the detailed press coverage bringing the matter of slavery to the awareness of a wider British public for the first time.[71]

The events surrounding *Somerset* v. *Stewart* brought Sharp and Benezet into ever closer collaboration[72] and laid the groundwork for a transatlantic abolitionist network which David Brion Davis accurately called the 'antislavery international'.[73] Although the turmoil of the American revolution made communication between activists on either side of the Atlantic more difficult, established links were never broken. If anything, the colonists' rebellion was a boon to the cause in that the revolutionary rhetoric of liberty was also applied in political debates on slavery in both Britain and America. This allowed ideas to take root which the abolitionists were able to use for their own purposes. The loss of the thirteen American colonies was even portrayed, in this context, as 'divine retribution' for Britain's involvement in the slave trade, which itself was framed as a 'national sin'.[74]

As soon as the American War of Independence had ended, American and British Quakers again joined forces in 1783, each addressing – for the first time ever – an anti-slavery petition to the Continental Congress of the nascent United States[75] and to the House of Commons, respectively.[76] Efforts were additionally made to win the support of politically influential individuals by the targeted sending of pamphlets. In Britain alone, the Quakers sent out over 10,000 copies of their parliamentary petition, reprinted under the title *The Case of Our Fellow-Creatures, The Oppressed Africans*,[77] to prominent members of the clergy as well as to all members of parliament and the entire royal family. Alongside a specific alternative economic proposal – to utilise the natural resources of the African continent instead – the pamphlet reiterated the abolitionist critique of slavery as an elementary violation of 'humanity'.[78]

Joseph Woods, who had launched the campaign in Britain with other Quaker abolitionists, returned to this line of argument in his *Thoughts on the Slavery of the Negroes*.[79] The essay explains his commitment to abolishing the slave trade in terms of the 'humanity of the present age',[80] thereby contextualising abolitionism as one aspect of an emerging concept of humanitarian action on behalf of suffering human beings. Woods stressed that Africans must be seen as members of the human community and treated accordingly whatever the circumstances: 'They cannot be denied to be men, and the inhumanity of treating them worse than brutes, can derive no justification from thence.'[81] Woods held the entire British nation to be implicated in the slave trade, since manufacturers, merchants and consumers benefited from the products made by slaves no less than the government that levied taxes on these goods. He appealed to parliament to intervene to end the system of slavery for good.[82]

In spite of their dedicated efforts, the Quaker abolitionist campaign was not a success with the general public in Great Britain. Its failure to mobilise wide support and make an impact was due in large part to the marginal position occupied by the Quakers as religious dissenters in a society dominated by the Anglican church.[83] As such, many doors remained closed to them and their appeals were doomed to go unheeded. Nor did they succeed in channelling their campaigning efforts into a single recognisable movement.[84] The goal had therefore to be to create a highly effective organisation by bringing together as many hitherto disparate abolitionist forces as possible and to make a concerted effort to win public favour.

A decisive step in this direction was made in spring 1787 and is associated with the name of Thomas Clarkson.[85] Clarkson's interest in the problem of slavery was first aroused when he was reading for holy orders at the University of Cambridge. In May 1785 he entered a Latin essay competition on the topic 'Is it lawful to make slaves of others against their will?' and in researching his answer first encountered abolitionist literature, including the work of Anthony Benezet, which made a lasting impression on him.[86] Having won the prestigious prize with his essay, Clarkson decided to devote his life to fighting slavery.[87] It was in looking for a publisher for his essay that he met the Quaker James Philipps in London, who printed it in an English translation under the title *An Essay on the Slavery and Commerce of the Human Species, Particularly the African*.[88] Through his publisher Clarkson went on to make the acquaintance of several more Quaker abolitionists, whose cause he had come passionately to share.

As an Anglican and a Cambridge man, Clarkson was in a position to forge links beyond the Quaker community and introduce wider sections of British society to the abolitionist cause.[89] This included one William Wilberforce, a close friend of Prime Minister William Pitt (the Younger) and member of parliament for Hull. As these links grew stronger, the abolitionists were encouraged in their idea of uniting their forces, with Wilberforce spearheading the abolitionist campaign in the House of Commons.[90]

The first tangible result of these plans was the founding on 22 May 1787, in John Philipps's London house and printing shop, of a joint committee.[91] Aside from raising the necessary funds, the new association saw its principal task as gathering and publishing information that would decisively advance the abolitionist cause in the public mind. Granville Sharp was chosen as its first chairman, already known as a pioneering anti-slavery campaigner and, as an Anglican, above suspicion of religious heterodoxy.[92] Although Sharp, followed by Clarkson and then increasingly Wilberforce, was the committee's public face, the role of the Quakers in the background was decisive, and not only because nine out of twelve founding members belonged to the Society of Friends.[93] It was also their pre-existing network that provided much of the financial support and informal infrastructure that would be needed for the campaigns ahead.[94]

The committee first had to address the key question of its strategic approach: Ought it direct its efforts simultaneously against the slave trade and the institution of slavery as such? While Sharp was in favour of an all-out attack, Clarkson and other members preferred a different strategy,[95] fearing that a two-pronged approach might overstretch their organization and ultimately deliver no progress at all. It was thus agreed to concentrate efforts on fighting the slave trade. The idea was that this would attack the roots of the overall problem as well as helping to improve the lot of the slaves already labouring in the colonies. A ban on transatlantic slave transports would cut off the supply of new slaves and force slaveholders to take better care of the slaves they already owned.[96] While the full emancipation of slaves was retained as a long-term goal, the name the committee gave itself was, in line with its guiding policy, the Society for Effecting the Abolition of the Slave Trade.

Another factor in deciding on this approach was an estimate of its likely political success and the viability of the society's demands. By focusing its campaigning exclusively on the slave trade, it made a conscious decision to avoid involving itself in legal wrangles over the property rights of the influential plantation owners in their slaves or in the powers of the government in London to involve itself in legislation in the colonies.[97] The right of the British government to regulate trade was undisputed, and hence a ban on the slave trade could be proclaimed by act of parliament and enforced with the instruments of the Crown:

By asking the government of the country to do this, and this only, they were asking for that, which it had an indisputable right to do; namely, to regulate or abolish any of its branches of commerce; whereas it was doubtful, whether it could interfere with the management of the internal affairs of the colonies, or whether this was not wholly the province of the legislatures established there. By asking the government, again, to do this and this only, they were asking what it could really enforce. It could station its ships of war, and command its custom-houses, so as to carry any act of this kind into effect.[98]

Already in their founding phase, the abolitionists had very specific ideas of how their humanitarian goals might be fulfilled through a policy of state intervention.

Having embarked upon the path of persuading the government to intervene directly against the slave trade, the abolitionists decided on a strategy that was pathbreaking and remains key to the work of humanitarian NGOs to this day. In a circular sent out in the summer of 1787, the committee expressed the purpose of its founding as follows: '[T]o excite still more the public attention to the Slave Trade, and to collect such evidence or information as may tend to its discouragement, and finally, to its abolition.'[99] Men of different Christian denominations had come together 'in the cause of humanity and justice' to mobilise the public throughout Great Britain against the slave trade by means of targeted campaigns and to exert direct pressure on political decision-makers:

[I]t is to be wished that the general sense of the nation (which we are persuaded is in favour of liberty, justice, and humanity) may be expressed by Petitions to

Parliament, and by applications to their Representatives, in order to procure their assistance. In the distribution of the Tracts, we therefore recommend this purpose may be kept in view.[100]

Religious motives were certainly key to the group, which sometimes was mockingly called the 'Saints' and sometimes the 'Clapham Sect', after its meeting place in south London.[101] Influenced by new evangelical tendencies, many members saw in Britain's huge role in slavery and the slave trade a form of national sin in need of redemption if the country was to restore its 'moral capital'.[102] To that end, it was important to acquaint as many British people with the horrors of the slave trade and to raise awareness of the humanitarian problem, thereby encouraging them to participate in the political process by addressing petitions to parliament.[103]

In organising and executing this project, the driving role fell once more to Clarkson, the 'moral steam-engine'[104] of the cause.[105] Directly the London Committee had decided on its course of action, Clarkson embarked on the first of many journeys to forge contacts across the country and to push for the founding of local committees.[106] Clarkson also visited the ports of Bristol, Liverpool and Lancaster, centres of the slave trade, where he hoped to gather reliable evidence and first-hand knowledge of the situation.[107] His meticulous inquiries took him on board slave ships, where he obtained a glimpse of the cramped decks and the testimonies of numerous sailors and captains. During his investigations Clarkson also met Alexander Falconbridge, whose account of the cruel regime on board the slave ships has already been cited. The report of the ship's surgeon, which the London Committee published in the following year, told not only of the sufferings of the enslaved captives, but also described the abuse perpetrated on sailors by their superiors and the high mortality among the crews of slave ships.[108] The plight of British sailors was another angle on which the abolitionists campaigned.[109]

Falconbridge served Clarkson not only as a valuable eyewitness, but also as an armed bodyguard of sorts. Unsurprisingly, Clarkson's inquiries were not welcome, leading first to threatening letters and finally to an attempt upon his life in the Liverpool docks.[110] When after several months of thorough and sometimes dangerous investigations Clarkson returned to London, he had gathered a great deal of material for his own publications and for the campaign now being launched by the abolitionist movement.[111] This material included not only a wealth of information, but also implements acquired in Liverpool, such as iron shackles, thumbscrews and the infamous *speculum oris* used in force-feeding – shocking evidence of the inhumanity of the slave trade, illustrations of which were included in subsequent abolitionist publications.[112]

Meanwhile the London Committee had begun to address circular letters to potential supporters in the British Isles and abroad, informing them of the new organisation's founding. In so doing it established itself as a key node in an international network of abolitionists of various stripes from the United States to France.[113] Indeed, it was in France in particular that the activities of the London Committee found a lively echo, leading to the founding of a French counterpart following the English example: the Société des Amis des Noirs, founded in Paris in February 1788 by Jacques-Pierre Brissot de Warville and Étienne Clavière.[114] The British abolitionists provided not only financial support, but also campaign literature in specially produced French translations. Clarkson kept in close touch with his French allies by letter and travelled several times to consult with them in person, ultimately becoming an eyewitness to the revolution.[115] These close ties notwithstanding, the French abolitionists pursued their own strategy, remaining an elite circle of some 140 upper-class members aiming not at mass mobilisation but rather at putting an end to French involvement in the slave trade by exerting direct influence on leading politicians.[116] This influence, however, remained circumscribed and in any case was soon overshadowed by the French Revolution, which claimed the lives of many leading members and caused the society to fold in 1793. The first French emancipation of slaves, proclaimed by the National Convention in February 1794, was therefore due less to the efforts of the Société des Amis than to the events of the revolution itself.[117]

By contrast, the strategy of the British abolitionists was clearly to mobilise as wide a section as possible of the general public.[118] To the London Committee as campaign headquarters fell the key task of promoting the distribution of abolitionist literature.[119] This material was printed by John Philipps, above whose workshop the committee had been founded, and then sent to known supporters and newspaper editors. With this clear strategy, the committee flooded Britain with information on the slave trade, making abolitionist tracts the linchpin of their publicity campaign.[120]

In their publications, authors often availed themselves of the sentimental narrative style, which has already been discussed as being especially popular in the eighteenth century and could therefore be expected to appeal to the zeitgeist and to readers' growing humanitarian sensibility.[121] The authors' stated aim was not so much to convey abstract knowledge about the problem of the slave trade than vividly to depict the suffering it caused and render visible the slaves' humanity. Eyewitness James Field Stanfield, who had himself been a sailor on a slave ship, left no gory detail of the Middle Passage out of his *Observations on a Guinea Voyage,*[122] the very purpose of which was to confront readers as directly as possible with his shocking experiences. But even the most detailed account was not enough, in Stanford's opinion, to convey the true horror he had witnessed:

> But no pen, no abilities, can give more than a very saint resemblance of the horrid traffic. One real view – one MINUTE, absolutely spent in the slave rooms on the middle passage, would do more for the cause of humanity, than the pen of a Robertson, or the whole collective eloquence of the British senate.[123]

In their efforts to portray the atrocities of the slave trade as vividly as possible to the public, the abolitionists did not limit themselves to the written word, but also made use of the suggestive power of images.[124] In selecting an official seal the committee chose a design from the workshop of Josiah Wedgwood, a successful manufacturer of porcelain and avowed abolitionist. The design chosen depicted an African kneeling while raising his manacled hands to the heavens in supplication, framed by the legend 'Am I not a man and a brother?'[125] This image rapidly became the most readily identifiable symbol of the abolitionist cause, not least because Wedgwood produced large quantities of it in the then-popular form of the cameo, an image set off in relief against the background.[126] Soon the motif of the imploring slave spread from the original medallion to such other objects as jewellery, hairpins, snuff boxes and even entire tea services: 'At length, the taste for wearing them became general; and thus fashion, which usually confines itself to worthless things, was seen for once in the honourable office of promoting the cause of justice, humanity, and freedom.'[127]

Under Wedgwood's leadership, the abolitionists pioneered marketing techniques of the nascent consumer society in the late eighteenth century and put fashion to the use of advertising their humanitarian cause.[128] The movement's official seal thereby became a key campaigning tool that was instantly recognisable and invited strong identification. Yet an arguably even greater visual impact was achieved by another abolitionist icon depicting a Liverpool slave ship, the *Brookes*. In November 1788 the committee's Plymouth chapter first published a bird's-eye view of the ship's slave deck, showing how the captives were crammed into any nook available like sardines in a can.[129] The slaves were shown not as individuals with distinct features, but only in outline, vividly illustrating how the Atlantic trading system negated Africans' humanity and turned them into mere merchandise. To Clarkson's mind, this image succeeded in conveying the boundless suffering of the Middle Passage[130] and the London Committee accordingly soon decided to print an expanded version of its own. The resulting pamphlet, entitled 'Plan and Sections of a Slave Ship', was published in 1789 and contained not only the bird's-eye view, but also several cross-sections through the various slave decks alongside a detailed description of the shockingly cramped conditions on board.[131] The accompanying text appealed directly to readers to take steps to fight the evils described.

This astute combination of visual and literary propaganda did not fail to have an effect on public perception. Of the pamphlet, Clarkson said: 'No one saw it but he was impressed. It spoke to him in a language, which was at once intelligible and irresistible. It brought forth the tear of sympathy in behalf of the sufferers, and fixed their sufferings in his heart.'[132] So great was the impact that the committee had the images of the *Brookes* reprinted in various forms – in over 8,000 copies in 1788 and 1789 alone – as well as in newspapers, handbills and publicly displayed posters.[133] Alongside the image of the 'kneeling African', the depiction of the hopelessly overcrowded slave ship became the most visible icon of abolitionist efforts at rallying the public to their cause.[134]

Yet the nascent campaign also used and generated other images, not least because it inspired artists such as the well-known painter George Morland to produce works tackling the horrors of the slave trade. Morland's 1788 painting *Execrable Human Traffic* depicts the brutal separation of an African family: while the mother and her toddler are dragged onto a waiting boat, the father is forcibly held on the shore by European slave traders and threatened with a savage dog. His *African Hospitality*, completed three years later, presents a striking contrast in the scene of a white family shipwrecked in a storm off Africa and their rescue by benevolent natives.[135] The pairing was designed to juxtapose the cruelty of the slave traders with the human kindness of the Africans and thereby to appeal to the audience's moral conscience. Engravings were made of both paintings, allowing them to circulate widely in Britain as well as abroad.[136]

All these devices, ranging from pamphlets and forceful images to specially produced artefacts, were part of a culture of mobilisation. The abolitionists used them all to make the human catastrophe of the slave trade visible to the public, to raise awareness and ultimately elicit compassion for its victims. They helped shift perception of the trafficking of human beings across the Atlantic from an abstract political question to relatable stories of human suffering – all the more so by emphasising the dimension of human pain, which allowed for identification with victims at a visceral level.[137] It was this aspect that the theologian and abolitionist William Priestly emphasised in a sermon preached in 1788:

What these poor wretches are made to suffer while they are conducted to such a distance, for such a purpose, before they reach the ships; what they suffer in the ships, and in their cruel bondage afterwards by us, may in some measure be imagined by us, when we consider that these men have the same feelings with ourselves, and conceive themselves to be as unjustly treated as we should do, if we were violently seized, conveyed away from all our friends, and confined to hard labour all our lives in Africa.[138]

There are two principal themes to the humanitarian narrative deployed here by the abolitionists. The horrors of the slave trade, particularly during the Middle Passage, form one key theme. By depicting chains and instruments of torture, showing conditions on board the *Brooks* and sharing eyewitness accounts of them, the movement confronted the public directly with the plight of the slaves, barely any awareness of which had previously existed. Second, the abolitionist campaign stressed the common humanity of Africans, of which the slogan 'Am I not a man and a brother?' was a particularly pithy expression.[139] This was an attempt to reverse the transformation of human beings into pure commodities that the Atlantic system had effected and to represent the slave as a fellow human being with the same human feelings.[140] The idea was to make the suffering of the captives relatable to the British public. This strategic choice, with its focus on inducing empathy, was an abolitionist innovation that proved definitive for all subsequent humanitarian campaigns.[141]

A special role fell to Olaudah Equiano and the autobiography he published in 1789. Himself a former slave, he was of incomparable value to the abolitionist cause as a star witness speaking with an authentic voice.[142] His life story soon became a bestseller of its day, selling several thousand copies as well as being distributed abroad and translated into Dutch, German and Russian. Equiano went on several lecture tours to promote his book and advance the abolitionist cause.[143] His narrative described both the horrors he had suffered on the Middle Passage and the human tragedy of the separation of families, both during enslavement in Africa and on being sold in slave markets in the Americas. Serving the movement as a victim, a witness and an activist, Equiano and his story personified the suffering of millions and was able to elicit a correspondingly direct reaction from his new compatriots in Great Britain.[144]

Intertwined Agitation in Civil Society and Parliament

These campaigns struck home, triggering nothing short of an 'abolitionist revolution of public opinion'.[145] The problem of the slave trade, of which a large majority of the public had hitherto barely been aware, was thrust into the centre of public attention. All that was needed now was to turn the great potential represented by a mobilised public into political capital. Strongly influenced by abolitionist propaganda, large sections of the public now put their names to petitions calling on parliament to suppress the slave trade, thereby putting pressure on their representatives.[146] Such petitions were far from being an abolitionist invention, having been used to initiate previous political reform projects and becoming established as an expression of the public will in late-eighteenth-century Great Britain, especially during the American War of Independence.[147] Yet the sheer quantity of petitions for abolition grew into something of a boom. Between 1788 and 1792 alone their number increased fivefold from 102 to 519, the largest number ever submitted to parliament in relation to a single cause.[148] This made petitions a key element in the abolitionist strategy, forming a link between public agitation outside and the exercise of political influence inside Westminster.[149] Their general effect was a distinct broadening of direct political participation on the part of emergent British civil society.

The key part in setting up and running the petitions fell to the local committees that were forming throughout the county. They composed a petition's text, which was then displayed at gatherings or in such publicly accessible spaces as town halls, inns, banks and taverns as well as being reprinted in newspapers.[150] A pioneer was the Manchester Committee, which by these means succeeded in gathering over 10,000 signatures in the first half of 1788.[151] Support was particularly large in such cities of the rapidly industrialising north of England as Manchester, Sheffield and Newcastle-upon-Tyne.[152] But committees in other parts of the country, such as those of Exeter and Plymouth, also ran campaigns coordinated by the London Committee that achieved remarkable feats of public mobilisation.[153] All this meant that the abolitionist movement could claim considerable public support. In 1792 alone, some 13 per cent of the adult male population of England, Scotland and Wales put their names to petitions to parliament to stop the slave trade.[154]

The signatories belonged above all to the rapidly expanding middle classes and covered a wide range of occupations and professions.[155] Besides religious motivations, the petitions' framers tended to invoke mainly secular and humanitarian arguments. A principal concern was the inhumanity of the Middle Passage while underscoring Africans' status as 'fellow creatures' within the human community. Referring to themselves as 'friends of humanity' and in the name of 'Justice, Liberty, and Humanity', the petitioners demanded that the state intervene immediately against human trafficking.[156] In further testimony to the campaign's impact, the core humanitarian themes of abolitionist propaganda were thus incorporated directly into the parliamentary petitions.

Abolitionist efforts to stir the British public to direct political participation proved a resounding success. The first wave of petitions submitted in 1788 was already strong enough to ensure that the Atlantic slave
trade became a firm item on the political agenda and one that parliamentary debates could no longer ignore.[157] Under the impression of the large
numbers of petitions reaching parliament from all parts of the country,
William Pitt could not but conclude that the slave trade was now an issue
'which, it was evident from the great number and variety of petitions
presented to that House respecting it, had engaged the public attention
to a very considerable extent, and consequently deserved the most serious notice of that House'.[158] From the various petitions Pitt also
deduced a general desire for change to the existing system and charged
the Privy Council with establishing how parliament might best be
enabled to make a decision based 'on principles of humanity, justice,
and sound policy'.[159]

It was during the same debate that Sir William Dolben, member for
the University of Oxford, vividly described the horrific conditions under
which slaves were transported on the Middle Passage. In view of this
humanitarian emergency, he pressed for parliament to take immediate
action, stating that another 10,000 lives were at risk of being lost by the
next parliamentary session.[160] His proposals included concrete improvements to the conditions under which slaves were transported, setting a
limit to the number of slaves permitted to be carried per ton of shipping,
minimum measurements for their quarters, and rules concerning venti-
lation and the provision of food. Dolben's motion set off further debates
and ultimately led to the passing of the Slave Trade Regulation Act,
which legislated rules for the transport of slaves and thereby marked
the first instance of the British government's direct intervention in the
slave trade.[161]

This attempt at regulation was not enough for the abolitionists, whose
goal remained the complete suppression of the slave trade. Some of them
even publicly rejected the law, suspicious that any legal regulation might
be interpreted as implicitly condoning the act and be politically abused to
that effect.[162] The committee's reactions accordingly came in the form a
new version of the *Brookes* illustrations, which were to demonstrate to the
public just how little was due to change on the slave decks for the African
captives.[163] Yet the debate over the Slave Trade Regulation Act did
mean an important milestone for the abolitionist movement, whose
cause had finally made the transition from civil society to parliament.

The time had now come for the abolitionists to bring their parliamentary spearhead into play. In May 1789 William Wilberforce took the
opportunity of the Privy Council presenting its final report to raise the

problem of the slave trade before the House of Commons.[164] In a speech lasting several hours, Wilberforce began by refusing to apportion blame and acknowledging his own complicity:

I mean not to accuse any one, but to take the shame upon myself, in common, with the whole parliament of Great Britain, for having suffered this horrid trade to be carried on under their authority. We are all guilty – we ought all to plead guilty, and not to exculpate ourselves by throwing the blame on others.[165]

A highly gifted orator, Wilberforce was able to incorporate into his speech the findings of the report that had only just been put before the House. He described both the destruction wrought by the slave trade in Africa and the cruelty suffered by the slaves during transportation and on arrival in the Caribbean. Yet he also sought to dispel economic fears and offer alternative scenarios. An end to the supply of new slaves would, Wilberforce argued, lead to the more humane treatment of labourers and in turn to reduced mortality and a higher birth rate, with broadly positive effects on the plantation economy of the West Indies. Trade in human beings could be replaced with trade in other commodities of equal value, by which Great Britain would moreover contribute to the economic development of Africa. Wilberforce concluded not by proposing legislation to abolish the slave trade altogether, but by presenting twelve resolutions aiming in that general direction as a basis for further parliamentary debates.[166] He had initially taken a purposely moderate stance in order to win other MPs over to his cause. In the subsequent debates, which the influential parliamentarian Charles James Fox accurately described as turning on 'a question between humanity on the one side and interest on the other',[167] it was indeed the West Indian interest that kept the upper hand and postponed a decision on the question indefinitely.[168] Yet Wilberforce was undeterred by such opposition and made sure that abolition remained on the parliamentary agenda. Following heated debates in the Commons and the setting up of a parliamentary select committee,[169] Wilberforce's efforts culminated in a bill for the abolition of the slave trade that was put before the House. It was, however, the opponents of abolition who emerged victorious from the two days of debate, roundly defeating the bill by 163 to 88 votes.[170]

From this severe blow the abolitionist movement concluded that if 'justice and humanity'[171] were to prevail, parliament would have to be made to feel the pressure of public opinion more strongly than ever. The campaign redoubled its efforts and a new wave of publications came off James Phillips' printing press, including 5,000 copies of a condensed version of the parliamentary select committee's findings.[172] A new element of mobilisation and protest was introduced in the call to boycott West

Indian products.[173] Such pamphlets as *An Address to the People of Great Britain on the Propriety of Abstaining from West India Sugar and Rum* by William Fox drew a clear link between the mass consumption of sugar in Great Britain and the human suffering caused by the captivity of slaves and their forced labour in the Caribbean plantations.[174] Pledging not to buy sugar and rum from the West Indies gave individuals a practical way of terminating their own participation in the iniquitous system of slavery and contributing to the abolitionist cause by exercising their personal power as consumers.

The London Committee itself was initially reluctant to endorse this form of protest, which had been initiated by individual activists. Wilberforce was worried that such an aggressive stance against the West Indian Lobby might alienate moderate political allies and weaken support for the abolitionist cause.[175] Clarkson meanwhile welcomed the new campaign as a further weapon in the arsenal of mobilisation.[176] Travelling around the country in the winter of 1791–92, he was delighted to find that more than 300,000 people from all walks of life were participating in the boycott. Entire families had pledged their support, with Clarkson noting that 'even children, who were capable of understanding the history of the sufferings of the Africans, excluded, with the most virtuous resolution, the sweets, to which they had been accustomed, from their lips'.[177] An important role here fell to women, whose place in the household put them in a position to make a conscious decision against the purchase of West Indian sugar and thereby play an active part in combating the slave trade.[178]

In terms of mobilisation, the first humanitarian consumer boycott in history was a resounding success – a success reflected in the fact that 519 petitions were submitted to parliament in 1792, bearing a total of some 400,000 signatures demanding an immediate end to the slave trade. The colonial interest, as represented by the Society of West India Planters and Merchants, tried to win support by publishing newspaper articles and pamphlets of their own as well as by political lobbying, but could claim only four petitions in its favour.[179] Owing to successful mobilisation, support for the abolitionist cause reached a new peak in spring 1792.

Wilberforce thus seized his chance to introduce a new bill for the abolition of the slave trade before the House of Commons on 2 April.[180] Into the heated debate that followed, Henry Dundas, the powerful home secretary, stepped with a proposal of his own for the gradual abolition of the slave trade, which succeeded in winning the necessary support with 230 to 85 votes.[181] A further vote fixed 1796 as the year by which the trade was to be ended for good.[182] This historic event – the first time a national legislature had passed a law opposed to the slave trade as such – was not, however, enough to dispel abolitionist misgivings. Wilberforce and Clarkson saw in these moves for 'gradual abolition' above all a delaying tactic on the part of their political opponents.[183] They found their suspicions confirmed by the rejection of the bill in the House of Lords, which decided instead to pursue further investigations of its own.[184] Nonetheless, public support was such that in 1792 the abolitionist cause could justifiably feel that success was within its reach.

Yet this hopeful prospect was soon overshadowed by events abroad. The news from across the channel, culminating in the execution of King Louis XVI in Paris on 21 January 1793, was worrying to Britain's political elites in particular, who feared revolutionary unrest in their own country. Only a few weeks later, the newly proclaimed French republic declared war on Great Britain. Almost simultaneously, news reached Britain of ever more atrocities and massacres perpetrated against the white population by slaves who had risen up in the successive revolutions that shook Saint-Domingue. These graphic accounts of the horrors of revolution on either side of the Atlantic confirmed the British establishment in its deep-seated fear of such radicalism rearing its head at home,[185] and the opponents of abolition were quick to take advantage of this new political climate for their own ends.[186] The House of Lords was once more debating the abolition of the slave trade in April 1793 when the Earl of Abingdon directly accused the abolitionists of conspiracy with the French enemy. By way of evidence he cited the correspondence between French and British abolitionists, accusing the latter of being nothing short of 'our Robespierres'. In Lord Abingdon's view, the idea of abolition was based on the same dangerous principles of 'liberty and equality' that had underpinned the French Revolution and whose true, murderous face had been exposed in the recent outrages in Paris and Saint-Domingue.[187] Lord Abingdon proceeded to reject the petitions seeking the abolition of the slave trade, denying the legitimacy of their motives: 'It is, say the petitioners, the ground of humanity; but humanity, as I have shown, is no ground for petitioning: humanity is a private feeling, and not a public principle to act upon: it is a case of conscience, and not a constitutional right.'[188] By calling into doubt the very concept of humanity, Lord Abingdon took aim at the key abolitionist motive and thereby sought to discredit their entire cause.

Confronted with the serious charge of being Jacobins in disguise and collaborators with the enemy, the abolitionist side was forced to make a change of strategy by which, however, they surrendered their most valuable weapon. To counter accusations of fomenting revolution, the movement abandoned its highly successful public campaigns[189] and instead concentrated on changing policy by parliamentary politics. Every year the indefatigable Wilberforce introduced a new bill on the slave trade, and every year his bill failed to win a majority in the House of Commons.[190] Without the weight of overwhelming public support behind it, abolitionist legislation lacked the punch able overcome resistance in parliament. It must surely rank among history's paradoxes that the French Revolution and the Haitian slave revolt – both historic events in which oppression of one form or another was shaken off – should have spelled such a setback for the abolitionist cause, all but bringing its efforts to a standstill. During subsequent wars with revolutionary France, which also made for a more repressive atmosphere domestically, the abolitionist movement began to fray.[191] Leading activist Clarkson retired, physically weakened by his tireless efforts,[192] regional committees folded and even the London Committee met only sporadically, and from 1797 to May 1894 not at all.[193]

Yet Wilberforce remained steadfast in his commitment to the cause, whose major achievement he kept alive by introducing his annual bill to the House of Commons. In the previous decades, the abolitionists had established a new 'humanitarian narrative' and shown great creativity in rallying the British public to their side.[194] This broad support had enabled them to bring the question of the slave trade from the public sphere into parliament. Although Wilberforce was long frustrated in his efforts, he was instrumental in keeping abolition on the political agenda. However, the next decisive step in bringing about a legal ban on the British slave trade backed up by government measures would require a new strategic approach, which was to succeed only in the spring of 1807.

5   From National Ban to International Implementation

The 1807 Slave Trade Act and the Beginning of Military Intervention

In spite of their considerable success in rallying the public to their cause, in twenty years of humanitarian campaigning the abolitionist movement had not succeeded in having its demands put into law by parliament and seeing the slave trade suppressed. Humanitarian motivation alone proved not nearly enough to win a decisive parliamentary majority. With Britain at war and Napoleonic France presenting a direct threat, the time seemed to have come to place less emphasis on humanitarian considerations and adopt a different strategy. The man able to seize this moment was James Stephen, an eminent maritime lawyer. He was also Wilberforce's brother-in-law, had already published pamphlets of his own against the slave trade and had repeatedly spoken up in debates.[1] His strategy aimed to fuse legal and political arguments to make a compelling argument for abolition.[2] Stephen's 1805 treatise *War in Disguise or the Frauds of the Neutral Flags* seemed at first to have no bearing on the struggle against the slave trade.[3] Its ostensible purpose was to condemn the deliberate use of ships sailing under the flag of a neutral state – particularly the United States – by means of which Britain's enemies France and Spain maintained vital trading links with their overseas possessions in wartime, thereby eluding the grasp of the Royal Navy. Stephen accordingly demanded an immediate end to this abuse and maintained that in the meantime Britain ought to use its dominance of the seas to make lawful 'prizes'[4] of these ships, thereby putting an end to enemy trade.

The treatise found a wide readership and sparked political debate in Britain over the extent to which British subjects and British capital were involved in giving crucial aid the enemy, for British slave traders continued to transport their 'human cargo' to St Thomas and St Croix unimpeded. These Caribbean islands were possessions of neutral Denmark and thus became entrepôts for the entire region, ensuring the supply of slaves to French and Spanish colonies.[5] The British prime minister was now Lord Grenville, an active supporter of the abolitionist cause. His argument was framed not in humanitarian terms, but as an astute combination of considerations of economic policy and military expediency. As Grenville told the House of Lords:

> If it was clear and obvious policy that we should not give advantages to our enemies, it was surely equally clear that we should not supply their colonies with slaves, thereby affording them additional means of cultivation, contributing to increase the produce of their islands, and thus enabling them to meet us in the market upon equal terms of competition, or perhaps to undersell us.[6]

In consequence of this debate, on 23 May 1806 parliament voted by a wide margin in favour of a bill drafted largely by James Stephen which, couched in terms of national interest, forbade under severe penalty any direct or indirect involvement by British subjects in the slave trade with other states.[7] The bill had been declared an important part of the war effort and a piece of legislation 'in which humanity and sound policy were united'.[8] As such, it easily passed both Houses and handed the abolitionists a long-awaited victory, as it were, by the back door. As an expert in maritime trade, James Stephen had rightly predicted that such a law was bound to have far-reaching consequences. The act dealt a decisive blow to the British slave trade, two-thirds of which involved foreign states and territories.[9]

The abolitionist cause hoped to capitalise on this success by pushing for the final, decisive step, in which the remainder of the British slave trade would be eliminated. Already in June 1806 a resolution was submitted to both Houses condemning the slave trade as 'contrary to the principles of justice, humanity, and sound policy'[10] and thereby restating the link between humanitarian considerations and those of realpolitik. Moreover, with a general election called later in the year, abolition came to be regarded as an important issue in a number of constituencies. The abolitionist members, who worked hard to win over their fellow parliamentarians, began to find the numbers shifting in their favour. A key part fell to the prime minister, Lord Grenville, who along with other members of his 'Ministry of All the Talents' brought his influence to bear on the House of Lords, which had hitherto frustrated many abolitionist projects, and changed many minds for good.[11] These efforts bore fruit when in the spring of 1807 first the House of Lords (by 100 votes to 34) and then House of Commons (by an overwhelming 286 votes to 16) voted in favour of a bill outlawing any British involvement in the slave trade. On 25 March 1807, King George III signed his assent to the Act of the British Parliament for the Abolition of the Slave Trade.[12] The abolitionist cause had triumphed. Following a humanitarian campaign that had been passionately fought for twenty years, a cause which had emerged in the realm of civil society had been adopted as government policy – as the policy of the United Kingdom, no less, which hitherto had been the leading nation in the slave trade. A humanitarian policy thereby became a key paradigm in the foreign policy of the nineteenth century's most powerful nation.

The preamble to the Slave Trade Act of 1807 referred to the resolution of the preceding year, thereby invoking its principal motives of 'justice, humanity, and sound policy', with the latter term covering considerations of economic policy, the ongoing war with France and global strategy. Coming into force on 1 May 1807, the act itself prohibited British subjects and any persons in British territories to engage in the slave trade in any form on penalty of a fine set at the considerable sum of £100 per slave traded.[13] Likewise prohibited was indirect participation in the slave trade in any form, which included equipping, manning and navigating slave ships as well as insuring both them and their cargo.[14] Moreover, the British government undertook to enforce this ban by all means at its disposal. The Slave Trade Act accordingly gave clear instructions to the Royal Navy and other officials:

And be it further enacted, that all Ships and Vessels, Slaves or Natives of Africa, carried, conveyed, or dealt with as Slaves, and all other goods and effects that shall or may become forfeited for any offence committed against this Act, shall and may be seized by any Officer of His Majesty's Customs or Excise, or by the Commanders or Officers of any of His Majesty's Ships or Vessels of War.[15]

If a slave ship was seized, the act promised the crews involved in the seizure a bounty per freed slave, which was set at £40 for a man, £30 for a woman and £10 for a child.[16] Adjudication of the associated legal claims and bounty payments was left to the Courts of Admiralty.[17]

Britain's Slave Trade Act marked a watershed in the battle against the Atlantic slave trade. Its effects were far-reaching: Not only did it ban what had previously been the leading nation in the slave trade from any further involvement, the act also legislated specific measures for its implementation. Unlike the national ban on the slave trade proclaimed only twenty-three days earlier in the United States,[18] which W. E. B. Du Bois had declared a 'dead letter'[19] for lacking any meaningful mechanisms for its implementation, the British law did more than just lip service to the principles underpinning it. By providing a legal basis for the Royal Navy to enforce the ban on the Atlantic slave trade, for the first time it put into practice the idea of upholding a humanitarian norm by military means.

To this end, the Admiralty dispatched two warships – the frigate HMS *Solebay* and the sloop HMS *Derwent* – to the coast of West Africa, where they were to operate from Freetown in Sierra Leone.[20] That port itself, situated on a fine natural harbour, owed its foundation to British abolitionists. Led by Granville Sharp, in 1787 they had begun to settle freed slaves in a 'Province of Freedom', many of whom had earned their freedom by fighting for the Crown in the American War of Independence. Originally settled in the British colony of Nova Scotia, the plan was to resettle them on African soil.[21] This project reflected the abolitionist conviction that the colonisation of West Africa as a rich agricultural region would lead to a thriving trade in African goods that would make the slave trade obsolete.[22]

However, this private settlement project suffered a number of setbacks from conflicts with indigenous Africans and from French attacks. The British government took over the territory's administration from the Sierra Leone Company in 1807, turned it into a crown colony and developed the port of Freetown into a permanent naval base. Both the ongoing struggle against Napoleonic France and the French presence in West Africa more generally provided a strong strategic incentive for doing so.[23] The private colonisation project that had been begun in the spirit of abolitionism thus became a full part of the British Empire and a pillar of Britain's interest in the region.[24]

It was from Freetown that the *Derwent* sailed on its first patrol against the seaborne slave trade on 15 January 1808, marking the beginning of the first – and, continuing for more than sixty years, the longest – humanitarian intervention in history. The earliest form of this doctrine in international law was being put into practice for the first time. And indeed the frigate succeeded in seizing two American schooners carrying a total of 167 slaves and returned them as prizes to Freetown, where the Africans disembarked and were freed.[25] With over 3,000 miles of coastline to police, from the Cap-Vert peninsula in modern Senegal to Cape Fria in what is now Namibia, the presence of two British warships could at first have little more than symbolic value. With its many estuaries and offshore islands, this enormous theatre of operations made the hunt for slavers more difficult still. Unsurprisingly perhaps, the Royal Navy had only modest successes to report during the early phase of its operations, liberating a mere 1,191 slaves between 1808 and 1811.[26] Britain's priority remained the overthrow of Napoleon, and war against France continued to tie up the larger part of the navy's resources. The Admiralty was thus unwilling or unable to redeploy more ships from blockading French ports and guarding home waters to operations against the slave trade off West Africa.

However, once parliament had strengthened the legal basis for abolition in 1811 – engagement in the slave trade was now a felony punishable by transportation with hard labour to the colonies rather than merely carrying a fine[27] – maritime operations began to be stepped up. Yet it was only after the end of the Napoleonic wars that the West Africa Squadron truly became a force to be reckoned with, its strength being steadily increased from 1815 onwards to a peak of more than thirty ships in the 1830s and 1840s.[28] Lasting for over sixty years, this military operation placed a considerable burden on the British treasury and perhaps was even the 'most expensive international moral effort in modern world history, with most of the cost paid by one country',[29] as the political scientists Chaim Kaufmann and Robert Pape have concluded. They estimate the death toll among the navy's personnel at over 5,000 and the economic cost of all abolition measures taken together at an average of 1.8 per cent of national income for every year from 1808 to 1867.[30]

In view of the costs imposed by this policy, the question inevitably arises why the United Kingdom should have pursued it over several decades. Historians long debated whether the Slave Trade Act of 1807 and the measures taken in consequence of it were motivated primarily by humanitarian concerns or rather by considerations of good business and realpolitik.[31] In his book *Capitalism and Slavery*, first published in 1944, Eric E. Williams argued that the British decision was driven not by the humanitarian campaigning of the abolitionist movement, but rather by economic factors. A native of Trinidad and Tobago, Williams stipulated a direct connection of the suppression of the slave trade with the (supposed) crisis of the plantation economy in the West Indies and the industrial revolution and rise of capitalism in Great Britain.[32]

In the subsequent debate, other historians criticised Williams' claims as one-dimensional, pointing out – most forcefully Seymour Drescher and David Eltis – that ceasing to engage in the slave trade came with costs to Britain that amounted to little less than an 'econocide' – that is, an act of economic suicide.[33] It would therefore be wrong to reduce Britain's decision against the slave trade and in favour of a policy of active intervention to a single, all-powerful motive. The 'principles of justice, humanity, and sound policy' so often invoked in the crucial debates surrounding the Slave Trade Act of 1807[34] stand for the shifting constellation of reasons that were mutually compatible under the circumstances.

It was in the name of these principles that the first humanitarian intervention in history was carried out by the Royal Navy off the western African coast. As in comparable situations in more recent times, this intervention was driven by a conspicuous amalgam of humanitarian, geostrategic and economic-political motives.[35] Moreover, as Seymour Drescher has astutely observed: 'Humanitarian and economic motives clearly overlapped once the British had abolished their own slave trade.'[36] This was because, once they had done so, it was clearly in the interest of the British government not to let other nations enjoy the economic benefits of the lucrative trade and put their own West Indian colonies at a marked disadvantage. This observation is confirmed by the fact that once abolition had been decided on, representatives of the West Indian planters and slaveholders quickly came round to supporting vigorous measures against the slave trade.[37] Yet even leaving these economic interests aside, no British government could afford to ignore the public pressure created by the abolitionist campaigns, instead finding it more expedient to adopt their humanitarian goals as part of its own foreign policy agenda.[38] The fight against the slave trade thus became a key paradigm for British foreign policy throughout the nineteenth century.[39] Yet the Royal Navy's patrols and policing of Atlantic shipping, although purportedly taking place for the disinterested purpose of enforcing abolition, also provided an excellent opportunity to consolidate Britain's maritime hegemony, which had become ever more apparent since the victory at the battle of Trafalgar in 1805 and for which *Pax Britannica* became the byword. It was a means of establishing spheres of influence not only in western African waters, but throughout the Atlantic.[40] 'Successful abolitionism', as Linda Colley has noted, 'became one of the vital underpinnings of British supremacy in the Victorian era, offering – as it seemed to do – irrefutable proof that British power was founded on religion, on freedom and on moral calibre, not just on a superior stock of armaments and capital'.[41]

The form of maritime intervention practised by the British navy affected the principle of the 'freedom of the seas', which was beginning to be established in international law and according to which the high seas – the seas beyond each nation's coastal waters – were beyond the jurisdiction of any particular nation and open to free and equal use by all.[42] Only in wartime might this freedom be circumscribed by maritime law, granting belligerent states the right to inspect foreign ships and search them for contraband – that is, for goods destined for the enemy. The operations of the West Africa Squadron in an area lacking well-defined sovereign borders on land and even less at sea were therefore bound to raise some fundamental questions in international law: What operations were the officers of the Royal Navy even legally authorised to carry out? What mandate did the Slave Trade Act equip them with? Were they entitled to stop, search, impound and hand over to a court not only suspected British slave ships on the high seas, but also those sailing under the flags of other nations? These questions touched upon jealously guarded sovereign rights and hence were likely to spark serious diplomatic disputes.[43]

To clarify the legal issues raised by the maritime intervention and above all to try the ships seized in its course, the British government set up a special Court of Vice Admiralty in Freetown. The scope of its authority, however, was largely a matter for the local officials to interpret.[44] Slave ships sailing under the flags of enemy nations such as France presented no legal difficulties, being legitimate prizes under maritime law.[45] But neutral ships, such as American ones, and those of allied nations, such as Portugal and later Spain, raised the fundamental question of whether Britain's national ban was applicable to these countries as well. In the absence of clear instructions from London, the decision was up to the chief judge, Justice Robert Thorpe. An avowed abolitionist, Thorpe saw the task of the court less in administering justice impartially than in unilaterally enforcing a universal ban on the slave trade and, to that end, to try ships of all nations.[46] In defence of his stance, Thorpe invoked both natural law and the Slave Trade Act itself, which he read as having established the fundamental injustice and inhumanity of the slave trade according to the 'law of nations' and thereby entitled Britain to act against other nations' slave trade.[47]

This broad interpretation of the national ban was supported by many of the leading abolitionists, who on 14 April 1807 founded the African Institution. Its ranks included eminent members of the clergy and the aristocracy, with the king's nephew, the Duke of Gloucester, acting as its first president and patron.[48] The institution's stated aim was to advance the spread of European civilisation on the African continent and thereby to effect the complete abolition of the slave trade. To this end, the institution made it its core mission to gather all relevant information and compile it in the form of annual reports, which could then be used in lobbying the relevant authorities.[49] Its statues moreover defined the institution's core mission as being

to watch over the execution of the laws, recently enacted in this and other countries, for abolishing the African Slave trade; to endeavour to prevent the infraction of those laws; and from time to time to suggest any means by which they may be rendered more effectual to their objects; and likewise to endeavour, by communicating information, and by other appropriate methods, to promote the Abolition of the African Slave Trade by Foreign powers.[50]

In taking on the dual role of both observers and promoters, the institute saw its efforts as directed not only at high circles of government in London, but also at the local officials tasked with enforcing the Slave Trade Act. The institution directly addressed officers of the Royal Navy to encourage them in their fight against the slave trade, not least by drawing their attention to the bounties to be earned for captured slave ships and freed slaves.[51] It also had digests of the key laws, ordinances and legal judgments produced, which, accompanied by legal explications, were to serve as guidelines for officers and judges working in or off Africa.[52] In its sixth annual report, issued in 1812, the institution could justly claim:

> The Directors have lost no opportunity of dispersing information, on the subject of the Slave Trade, throughout the Navy; ... They have also taken care to furnish the different Judges of the Vice-Admiralty Courts abroad with such information as was likely to be of use to them in the trial of cases connected with the Slave Trade.[53]

The abolitionist movement did not see the passing of the Slave Trade Act as ending its struggle, a struggle which now continued in its effort to ensure the enforcement of the ban for which it had campaigned so hard. By setting themselves up as advisers, activists repeatedly involved themselves in government measures to enforce its policy, underscoring once more how closely the public sphere and state policy were interwoven in this, the first humanitarian intervention in history.

Operating on a broad interpretation of the British ban, the Royal Navy seized slave ships sailing under other flags and took them to be tried in such British prize courts as that in Freetown. The somewhat ambiguous legal situation produced a series of controversial judgments in which foreign slavers had both their ships and their precious 'human cargo' confiscated.[54] As a result, the principal nations affected by these measures – notably Portugal[55] and above all Spain – increasingly complained about Britain's unilateral action through diplomatic channels and sought compensation for their mounting financial losses.[56] As this conflict simmered on, it threatened to turn into a serious diplomatic crisis between the allies who were still jointly fighting Napoleon. To prevent further escalation, the British side reconsidered its unilateralist policy of intervention. Even in the Admiralty there were serious misgivings about the legality of the navy's actions, and calls for a legally sound approach grew louder, especially when the end of the Napoleonic wars in 1814–15 resulted in an entirely new constellation in politics and international law.[57]

An end was put to this state of legal suspense by Sir William Scott, judge of the High Court of Admiralty, and his landmark decision in the case of *Le Louis*.[58] *Le Louis* was a French slave ship which on 11 March 1816 – after, that is, the conclusion of the war with France and hence in peacetime – was seized after a brief skirmish by HMS *Queen Charlotte* off Cape Mesurado (in modern Liberia) and condemned as a rightful prize by the Court of Vice Admiralty in Freetown. On appeal, however, Scott overturned the Freetown court's decision and ruled the seizure of *Le Lois* to have been unlawful.[59] As it stood, Scott argued, international law did not provide for the boarding of foreign ships in peacetime, even if they were engaged in the slave trade. Instead, all sovereign nations were equally entitled to the free and unrestricted use of the high seas:

In places where no local authority exists, where the subjects of all states meet upon a footing of entire equality and independence, no one state, or any of its subjects, has a right to assume or exercise authority over subjects of another. I can find no authority that gives the right of interruption to the navigation of states in amity upon the high seas, excepting that which the rights of war give to both belligerents against neutrals.[60]

The only exception mentioned by Scott was that of piracy, an enemy of all states with which no state of peace could ever obtain.[61] Yet Scott emphasised that the slave trade had hitherto neither been condemned as tantamount to piracy nor even been recognised as a crime by all states. He therefore concluded that even such a morally justified end as the suppression of the slave trade could not justify the use of illegal force and curtailing the sovereignty of other European states:

To press forward to a great principle by breaking through every other great principle that stands in the way of its establishment; to force the way to the liberation of Africa by trampling on the independence of other states of *Europe*; in short, to procure an eminent good by means that are unlawful; is as little consonant to private morality as to public justice. ... But a nation is not justified in assuming rights that do not belong to her, merely because she means to apply them to a laudable purpose; not in setting out upon a moral crusade of converting other nations by acts of unlawful force.[62]

With the full authority of the chief law officer of the High Court of Admiralty, Scott clearly ruled against the Royal Navy's practice of unilateral action against foreign slave ships, underscored the narrow limits of Britain's national ban and restated that Britain, while it may have enjoyed naval hegemony, was nonetheless bound to respect the principles of international law. The dilemma between enforcing a general humanitarian cause while respecting the sovereign rights enjoyed by other states under international law could therefore be resolved only internationally. The end of the Napoleonic wars and the attendant rise of political internationalism and the emergence of new mechanisms of cooperation between states offered a promising outlook for such a project.

The Congress of Vienna and the International Proscription of the Slave Trade

British abolitionists saw the end of the Napoleonic wars in April 1814 as an opportunity to fulfil their long-held dream of outlawing the slave trade by international treaty.[63] As William Wilberforce confessed to his friend William Hey on the allied victory and the abdication of Napoleon: 'I am just now extremely occupied, both mind and thoughts, with considering about, and taking measures for, effecting a convention among the great powers for the Abolition of the slave trade. It would be indeed a glorious termination of the hurricane.'[64]

To Wilberforce and his associates, it was clear that this was an opportunity not to be missed and they had to raise their cause at the imminent peace talks. They sought to enter into personal contact with such leading foreign statesmen as Charles-Maurice de Talleyrand, the French foreign minister, King Louis XVIII of France and Tsar Alexander I of Russia in order to win their support for an international ban on human trafficking.[65]

Wilberforce naturally also tried to get the British government to commit to this aim. Speaking in the House of Commons, he pointed to the exceptionally favourable circumstances for finally pushing for a general ban on the slave trade. The long war had reduced the European states' slave trade to a trickle while support for abolition had grown.[66] In the name of justice and humanity and for the protection of the African continent it was absolutely necessary to stop the trade from resuming.[67]

It was at Wilberforce's instigation that each of the Houses of Parliament addressed a petition to the prince regent. In the Address of the House of Commons of 3 May 1814, the signatories expressed their hope 'that His Majesty's Government would employ every proper means to obtain a Convention of the Powers of Europe for the immediate and universal abolition of the African Slave Trade'.[68] In view of the steps towards abolition taken by Britain and in the name of 'common humanity', they felt in a position to demand that other governments adopt comparable laws. By virtue of its position as the leading maritime and colonial power, Britain was under a special obligation to take the initiative and seek change from friendly states.[69] The address of the House of Lords reiterated these points, likewise calling for an immediate and general ban on the slave trade 'on the behalf of the interest of humanity'.[70] Both Houses of Parliament thereby expressed their strong support for abolitionist goals and gave a correspondingly clear mandate to the British delegation for the forthcoming negotiations in Paris. The idea was that a peace treaty with France was to be coupled with definite abolitionist policies. As a bargaining chip, Wilberforce suggested using the French colonies conquered in the preceding war, which were to be returned to France only on condition of a complete ban on the importation of slaves.[71]

Yet the negotiations in Paris soon dealt these high hopes a bitter blow.[72] Castlereagh, the foreign secretary and head of the British delegation, found that France, under the restored Bourbon monarchy of Louis

XVIII, refused to accede to British demands. His French counterpart, Talleyrand, explained that imposing such conditions for the return of its colonies was incompatible with his country's honour. What was more, the economic interest of major French trading cities was opposed to immediate abolition, and these cities might emerge as destabilising factors for the new French government if the policy were to be pushed through against their will.[73] All that was left in the end was a clause appended to the peace treaty in which France undertook to abolish, by its own initiative and with no pressure from Britain, its slave trade after a grace period of five years.[74] In spite of repeated efforts, this was the most that Castlereagh could get the French to concede.[75] Yet he also told the prime minister, Lord Liverpool, that it was counterproductive to put France under too much pressure in the circumstances. It would be wiser, he argued, to win the French government over to the British position in preparation for the Congress of Vienna, when joint pressure might be brought to bear on Spain and Portugal to agree a general ban on the slave trade.[76] To this end, Castlereagh informed the Austrian, Prussian and Russian governments of the agreement that had been reached while not missing the opportunity to solicit the allies' support for Britain's stance on the slave trade.[77]

Castlereagh returned to London with a sense of accomplishment, and a large majority in the House of Commons, elated at having emerged victorious from twenty years of war, greeted his presentation of the peace treaty with standing ovations.[78] Yet Wilberforce's voice was missing from the chorus of well-wishers. The compromise regarding the slave trade had been a shock to him, as he noted in his diary.[79] Wilberforce gave free rein to his disappointment in the parliamentary debate that followed, calling the celebrated treaty nothing less than 'the death-warrant of a multitude of innocent victims, men, women, and children'.[80] Instead of banning it, the treaty allowed the French slave trade to resume for another five years, with all the disastrous consequences for Africa this would entail.[81]

In response to this setback, the abolitionist movement fell back on its tested strategy for rallying public resistance. 'Let the nation', Wilberforce declared, 'loudly and generally express its deep disappointment and regret, and most earnestly conjure both Houses, but especially the House of Commons, to use its utmost efforts in behalf of the unhappy Africans.'[82] Abolitionist pamphlets attacked the treaty, accusing the British government of acting contrary to its own policy.[83] While the Royal Navy had been deployed to act against slave traders by force off the coast of West Africa and the Court of Vice Admiralty had been set up in Sierra Leone to condemn slave ships, free the slaves and settle them in the colony, Britain now stood by while France resumed its slave trade. Worse still, by signing the peace treaty, Britain risked squandering the progress hard won over the past twenty-five years.[84] The disheartening conclusion was that the 'golden opportunity of achieving this great work of humanity is, however, now lost, never perhaps to be recovered'.[85]

Yet the abolitionists took care not to question the peace treaty as such, and less still the great national victory over Napoleon. They instead called on the public to support petitions asking parliament for a specific amendment to the controversial supplementary clause.[86] This quickly turned out to be one of the most successful campaigns in the movement's history. Parliament was inundated by more than 800 petitions bearing around a million signatures and coming from all parts of the country.[87] The force of public sentiment surprised even the war's great hero, the Duke of Wellington, then on a brief visit home:

I was not aware till I had been some time here [in London] of the degree of frenzy existing here about the slave trade. People in general appear to think that it would suit the policy of the nation to go to war to put an end to that abominable traffic; and many wish that we should take the field on this new crusade.[88]

Riding high on this wave of support, Wilberforce once more pushed his case in parliament. He made astute use of the personal presentation in the House of Commons of a petition of 38,000 Londoners to launch two further parliamentary petitions.[89] They were addressed to the prince regent, whom both Houses asked to exercise his personal influence to obtain concessions from the French government on the one hand and push for a complete ban on the slave trade at the forthcoming Congress of Vienna on the other.[90] Once again the abolitionists had succeeded in obtaining a commitment from parliament, but this direct appeal to the prince regent, coupled with massive public support, further increased the pressure on the British government. Even the prince regent now felt compelled to inform the French king of parliament's resolutions and to request his closer cooperation in matters of the slave trade.[91]

Wellington, acting in his new capacity as British plenipotentiary, personally delivered the letter to Paris, where he resumed bilateral talks about the controversial supplementary clause.[92] It was in this context that the British delegation raised the possibility of enforcing a ban on the slave trade by prohibiting the import of colonial goods from countries that refused to bow to it.[93] This was indeed the first time ever that economic sanctions were proposed in support of a humanitarian norm. Wellington also presented Talleyrand with proposals for a joint intervention against the slave trade: In a precisely defined exclusion zone in the north Atlantic, the navies of each country were to be permitted to search each other's merchant ships in order to seize slave ships and hand them over for trial to the Admiralty courts.[94]

The flood of petitions also acted as a catalyst to British foreign policy, in which a more severe tone towards its wartime allies Spain and Portugal now became discernible.[95] Faced with pressure at home, the government demanded substantial concessions towards a ban on the slave trade. These demands were underpinned by threats to cut off much-needed financial support to the countries concerned.[96] In the case of Spain, this meant that London made a loan of 10 million Spanish dollars conditional on the Madrid government enacting an immediate ban on the slave trade.[97]

For their part, the abolitionists also sought to make their presence felt at the international level and intensified their contacts with leading statesmen.[98] Wilberforce maintained a lively correspondence with such influential figures as Talleyrand and even met, in London, Tsar Alexander I and Frederick William III of Prussia in person, on which occasion both monarchs assured him of their support.[99] The strategy now being pursued was to provide key decision-makers with detailed information on the horrors of the slave trade and thereby to influence the stance they would take in negotiations, particularly in the forthcoming Congress of Vienna. It was for this purpose that Thomas Clarkson produced a shortened version of his *Evidence on the Subject of the Slave Trade*, which had originally been compiled for the British parliament, for translation into Spanish, French and German. His preface was directed at the assembled European rulers, to whom Clarkson appealed to make the moment of their own liberation from Napoleonic oppression the occasion for ridding the peoples of Africa from the scourge of the slave trade.[100] In just a few pages Clarkson provided a vivid and concise account of the general problem before calling, in the name of humanity, on the heads of state to use the forthcoming congress to declare the slave trade a violation of international law.[101] This pamphlet was distributed to the various diplomats and delegates.

Not content, then, with mobilising support at home, the abolitionist movement tried firmly to establish the problem of the slave trade on the international agenda and to bring the weight of civil society to bear on international policymaking. The movement's aim was to create a favourable political climate ahead of the Congress of Vienna. This was felt most acutely by the British government, which faced pressure at home to deliver tangible results. Parliament had given the British delegation a clear mandate, and the prime minister, Lord Liverpool, accurately described what was expected of it:

I had a letter from Wilberforce yesterday, which proves to me that the Abolitionists in this country will press the question in every possible shape. We must do therefore all we can, and at least be able to show that no efforts have been omitted on our part to give effect to the Addresses of the two Houses of Parliament.[102]

These high expectations now had to be met in the Austrian capital. Rarely in the history of British diplomacy had a delegation travelled to an international conference with so clear a mandate.[103] Yet the congress was not merely a burden, but rather a great opportunity to conclude what hitherto had been arduous bilateral negotiations by agreeing on an international ban on the slave trade and thereby to provide sanction under international law for the operations of the West Africa Squadron.[104]

At the Congress of Vienna, which began in September 1814, were gathered nearly all European heads of state, with the great powers Austria, Prussia, Russia, Great Britain and France taking the leading roles. The aim of the summit was to place on secure grounding the political map of Europe, which had been significantly altered in the course of the Napoleonic wars. Questions of power and its balance naturally predominated, and with them conflicts of interest between the great powers that affected the territorial future of Poland and Saxony.[105] It seemed at first that no room would be left for such humanitarian concerns as abolitionism.[106] Castlereagh nonetheless missed no opportunity to raise the issue of an immediate ban on the slave trade with delegates from various nations, although French cooperation remained the crucial prize.[107] Talleyrand, however, remained firm in his rejection of British proposals, particularly for a mutual right to search shipping, invoking France's national interest.[108] Yet as a gesture of goodwill, he did offer his continued support for British efforts to push for an international ban at the Congress.

In keeping with this offer, and above all to ensure British support in such other important matters as that of Italy, it was indeed the French foreign minister who placed the problem of the slave trade on the congress' official agenda.[109] To address it, he proposed setting up a commission composed of delegates from Britain, France, Spain, Portugal, Prussia, Austria and Sweden.[110] This proposal at first met with resistance from the two Iberian nations, which feared that their own position would be weakened if any states other than the four directly concerned colonial powers were involved. The other delegations rebutted this objection, maintaining that human trafficking was a question of general morality, indeed of 'humanité', and as such of concern to all nations. The commission of eight accordingly took up its work in January 1815.[111]

In the first session, Castlereagh took the lead[112] and, invoking the principles both of the Christian faith and of humanity and morality more generally, tried to persuade the other states to issue declarations in favour of an immediate and sweeping ban on the slave trade.[113] Although all the commission's members expressed their support in principle, the Spanish and Portuguese envoys demanded a critical amendment, according to which the time for abolition should be left up to individual states.[114] France showed some sympathy for this position, itself insisting on the five-year transition period agreed in the Paris Peace Treaty. In light of such opposition, Castlereagh was forced to acknowledge that an immediate ban was not an option for the time being. He therefore changed tack, seeking to obtain concessions from France, Portugal and Spain with a view to creating an exclusion zone north of the equator and ensuring that any agreement would come into force as soon as possible.[115] The foreign secretary also proposed joint maritime intervention measures[116] as well as setting up a permanent commission that would address the problem of the slave trade once the Congress of Vienna had ended.[117] The British delegation explicitly restated the threat of an import ban on colonial products, as it had already made against France, in order to give weight to its demands.[118]

The continental powers Russia, Prussia and Austria, which were not involved in the slave trade, and Sweden, which had already agreed to complete abolition by treaty with Great Britain in 1813,[119] largely supported Castlereagh's proposals. While France tried to hold an intermediate position, the greatest resistance came from Spain and Portugal. In return for British compensation for seized slave ships amounting to £300,000[120] and the liquidation of £600,000 of war credit, the Portuguese government agreed to a ban on the slave trade north of the equator, but refused any further concessions.[121] Both Spain and Portugal considered an immediate ban, and the measures proposed to implement it imposed severe infringements on their national sovereignty and economic interests.[122] They declared that they would be prepared to ban human trafficking completely only after a grace period of eight years.[123]

The negotiations in Vienna thus produced a compromise, the substance of which was announced on 8 February 1815 in the 'Déclaration des 8 Cours, relative à l'Abolition Universelle de la Traite des Nègres'. In the spirit of the Enlightenment and the name of all 'civilised nations', the eight signatory states condemned the slave trade as contrary 'to the principles of humanity and universal morality'.[124] Recognition was given to the necessity of doing something about it and the desire expressed to do away with this scourge that had ruined Africa, demeaned Europe and harrowed humanity as a whole. The signatories affirmed their willingness to institute a universal ban as soon as possible and with all means at their disposal – with the proviso, however, that the particular interests of various nations and populations would be duly considered. The joint declaration was therefore unable to set a date for a global end to the slave trade, which was left up to negotiations between individual powers. It closed with a call to all 'civilised nations' to support this noble cause and contribute to its success.

The Vienna Declaration thus was not the legally binding ban that the British delegation had hoped to achieve, but was merely a statement of intent. Nonetheless, the government in London was not altogether displeased with what had been accomplished, particularly in view of the treaty that had been concluded with Portugal.[125] Even abolitionist criticism was largely muted and acknowledged Castlereagh's sincere efforts.[126] The declaration's importance should indeed not be underestimated. Its adoption as part of the final act[127] of the Congress of Vienna underscored its significance in international law, for it meant that the proscription of the slave trade was a goal supported not only by the eight member states of the commission, but by all nations represented at the congress. It was on this broad foundation that the declaration for the first time turned a humanitarian idea into a concrete norm, thereby placing it within the scope of international law.[128] Although it was not legally binding, the Vienna Declaration was able to exert humanitarian pressure in future negotiations and may therefore justly be called one of the first major humanitarian documents of international law in history.[129]

Yet doubt was soon to be cast on all that had been achieved in Vienna – on all, that is, bar the agreements relating to the slave trade, which would soon be unexpectedly surpassed. While the great powers were still negotiating, Napoleon escaped the island of Elba to which he had been exiled and landed with a band of loyal followers in southern France on 1 March 1815. He reached Paris on 20 March, inaugurating the 'Hundred Days' of his second reign. Well aware of British public opinion, Napoleon used the question of abolition with a view to winning support on the other side of the English Channel.[130] By decree, on 29 March he banned the French slave trade with immediate effect.[131] Although Napoleon was banished for good after his defeat at Waterloo on 18 June 1815, the decree was never rescinded. Indeed, the allies and foremost Great Britain had made Louis XVIII's re-assumption of his throne conditional on its confirmation.[132] This left the French king with no alternative but to outlaw the French slave trade in his turn. To be outdone by the Corsican 'despot' and his 'humanitarian' ruling was simply not an option.[133] It is surely one of history's ironies that the hard-won compromise between France and Britain was swept away by a decree of Napoleon's and that this was what finally placed France in opposition to the slave trade. In an additional article to the Second Treaty of Paris, the French government undertook to honour the agreement on the slave trade reached in Vienna and to participate constructively in the follow-up conference that the two governments were planning.[134]

The Struggle for International Implementation

The front against universal abolition was beginning to crack, with the Iberian states its principal holdouts. Spain in particular, which unlike Portugal objected to restrictions on slavery even north of the equator, thus moved into the focus of abolitionist attention.[135] In 1816, James Stephen, who had been the legal architect of the Foreign Slave Trade Act of 1806 and the Slave Trade Act of 1807, published a pamphlet entitled *An Inquiry into the Right and Duty of Compelling Spain to Relinquish Her Slave Trade in Northern Africa*. Stephen began this seminal treatise by stating that the declaration of Vienna had obliged the nations under international law to enact a universal ban on the slave trade.[136] Given the Spanish government's foot-dragging, Stephen asked what steps the other European states were entitled to take in order to meet this obligation. Key references for the British lawyer were Grotius and de Vattel, founding figures of international law, both of whom had conceded a right of intervention against severe violations of natural law.[137] Since the slave trade was now recognised as a gross contravention to the laws of nature and of peoples, it followed, according to Stephen, that force might rightfully be used:

To maintain the law of nature and of nations, to punish, or at least restrain, enormous violations of it, to succour an unhappy people oppressed by such offences, to promote by all the means in our power the social and moral improvement and happiness of other countries, are duties, and therefore rights, not peculiar to Great Britain, ... but belong to all the branches of the human family, and pre-eminently to every civilized nation.[138]

With this argument, based on both natural and international law, Stephen provided one of the first general legal justifications for intervening by force against human trafficking, to which he added considerations of realpolitik. The United Kingdom, he pointed out, certainly possessed the requisite military means – such as the naval squadron operating off the coast of West Africa – which it now ought to deploy against Spanish slave ships.[139] The risk of provoking war with Spain was, in Stephen's view, negligible: Its government lacked the resources, both military and financial, to pursue such a war and hence would put up no serious resistance to British measures.[140] Accordingly, Stephen recommended that the British government take advantage of the situation to make a show of strength and put an end to the Spanish slave trade – by force, if necessary.[141] He concluded with a rhetorical question:

Other countries perhaps have had their Nelsons, and their Wellingtons; but where will the historian find another people, by whom, in the very zenith of their glory, justice was preferred to power, and mercy to extended empire; and who, at the most triumphant conclusion of the most arduous wars, asked nothing so earnestly from the Government ... as reparation to the injured, succour to the wretched, and deliverance to the oppressed, in distant regions of the earth?[142]

What gave additional urgency to the question of military intervention for humanitarian reasons was not, however, the trade in African so much as that in European slaves. From the early sixteenth century on, the pirates of the 'Barbary Coast' of North Africa – with Algiers, Tunis and Tripoli as their principal bases – had included humans in the booty they sought in their raids on the Mediterranean coast and beyond. These captives were either held for ransom or sold into slavery.[143] According to recent estimates, well over a million human beings were enslaved in this way, making the Barbary pirates or 'corsairs' a threat not only to the maritime trading routes, but also to the inhabitants of the Mediterranean seaboard.[144] It was due above all to the efforts of one man that this problem reappeared on the agenda of international politics once the Napoleonic wars had ended. Sir William Sidney Smith, a retired admiral in the Royal Navy, had witnessed the activities of the North African pirates while on duty in the Mediterranean and had made it his personal project to combat them.[145] In the wake of the abolitionist campaign, he too approached a number of leading statesmen and asked for their support ahead of the Congress of Vienna. In a pamphlet published on 31 August 1814 he emphatically appealed to the European states to launch a joint naval operation to put an end to the Barbary states' piracy and slave trading.[146] With the help of influential friends, Smith was able to attend the congress as a private citizen. He made his cause known to the assembled princes by organising elaborate charity events as well as soliciting donations for the benefit of enslaved Christians. Smith's campaign continued beyond the congress, astutely interweaving the plight of Christians in Muslim hands with that of African slaves.[147]

Great Britain had previously not paid much notice to the Barbary pirates, whose activities had ceased to affect British shipping. From the late seventeenth century onwards, the strength of the Royal Navy had grown to the point where they avoided any direct confrontation with British ships and citizens,[148] instead attacking those of weaker nations – the small Italian and German states – as well as plundering the Mediterranean coast. Indeed the Barbary states, far from threatening British interests, were valuable suppliers of provisions to the British garrisons in Gibraltar and Minorca as well as providing the indirect benefit of weakening potential commercial rivals in the Mediterranean.[149] Such considerations meant that Britain also turned a blind eye to attacks on US merchant shipping and allowed the North African corsairs to pass through the Straits of Gibraltar in order to pursue American-flagged ships in the Atlantic.[150] These depredations did considerable damage to America's Mediterranean trade, leading Washington to embark on large-scale military operations in 1801 and 1815. In these 'Barbary Wars', which became the founding legend of the US Navy and brought American foreign policy into sharper relief, the United States pursued its commercial interests by military means while aiming to eliminate the danger to its own citizens of being captured and enslaved in the Mediterranean.[151]

The British policy of tolerating and even capitalising on the activities of the Barbary pirates underwent a fundamental transformation in the course of the debates over international abolition – debates that Britain had done so much to initiate. The more Britain put the fight against the Atlantic slave trade at the centre of its foreign policy, the more the problem of Christian slaves in North Africa put its moral credibility to the test.[152] Once a high-ranking naval officer such as Smith had made it his personal cause to draw a parallel between the enslavement of Africans and that of Europeans, the British government found itself in an increasingly awkward position with regard to Spain and Portugal. How could it be that the world's leading naval power was using force against Spanish and Portuguese slave ships while allowing the enslavement of Christians by Muslim pirates to continue unchecked?[153] For its part, the Spanish government refused to make any further concessions to the campaign against the Atlantic slave trade, reminding Britain of its obligation towards the white slaves: 'On the other hand nothing can appear to be more flattering to the philanthropy of the British Government, in whose consideration the liberty of the Whites of Europe cannot be of less importance than that of the Blacks of Africa.'[154]

This apparently unequal approach fed the suspicion that Britain's fight against the slave trade was motivated not so much by concern with humanity, but rather selectively, by considerations of strategic interest.[155] Castlereagh himself, writing to the British ambassador to St Petersburg, declared 'that it is only by making the Slave Trade and the question of the Barbary Powers go *pari passu*, that we can fully meet the wishes of the Emperor [tsar] and the other powers, who press the latter point as one of universal interest'.[156] In order to prove the sincerity of its commitment to abolitionism, the British government now found itself compelled to commit itself to the liberation of enslaved Christians. From March to May 1816, the Admiralty dispatched a squadron commanded by Lord Exmouth to the coast of North Africa with the aim of forcing a diplomatic solution.[157] Negotiations with the various Barbary rulers resulted in Exmouth purchasing the freedom of more than 1,000 Sardinians, Sicilians, Neapolitans, Genoese and Germans as well as signing new peace treaties, also on behalf of Sardinia and the Kingdom of the Two Sicilies.[158] Separate treaties were signed with the rulers of Tunis and Tripoli, according to which captives were henceforth not to be enslaved, but to be treated humanely as prisoners of war and exchanged with no demands for ransom.[159] Only Omar Agha, the dey of Algiers, refused to sign such a treaty, which would have put an end to what was an extremely lucrative trade in Christian slaves.

Lord Exmouth's mission was criticised in various quarters at home, however. Complaints were made in *The Times* that liberating enslaved foreign nationals, even if they were Christian, was a waste of taxpayers' money and military resources. A straitened budget, it was claimed, left no scope for such 'Quixotism'. If weaker states were to claim British protection from Barbary pirates, it was up to them to foot the bill.[160] The negotiations came in for criticism from the abolitionist side, too, albeit for different reasons. In parliament, abolitionists accused the government of having given tacit recognition to the North African pirates by paying them ransom money as well as having jeopardised Britain's international standing.[161] The time had come, they argued, to stop the suffering caused by the Barbary states for good – not by further diplomatic efforts, but by means of targeted strikes by the Royal Navy.[162]

This naked plea for the use of military force was not made in vain. In June 1816 the Admiralty again sent Lord Exmouth to Algiers, this time at the head of a task force of 15 warships and over 6,000 men. The provocation was the murder of some 200 Italian coral fishers under British protection at Bône in Algeria, which was found to be in breach of the newly signed peace treaty.[163] Lord Exmouth this time sailed with firm orders to obtain from the dey, by any means necessary, the immediate release of all Christian slaves and the final cessation of the slave trade. An ultimatum to that effect having passed unanswered, the British squadron, which had been joined by six Dutch warships, opened fire on Algiers on 27 August 1816. The bombardment lasted several hours and destroyed nearly the entire pirate fleet and large parts of the city's fortifications.[164] Omar Agha had little choice but to bow to all British demands unconditionally.[165] Besides releasing 1,624 European slaves and paying 382,500 Spanish dollars in reparations, the dey was now forced to accede unreservedly to the additional treaty promising to end the enslavement of Christians, which he had refused to sign in May.[166] The military strike had thus accomplished all its objectives. Whereas the

American operation of the previous year had pursued an entirely national goal, the British expedition had liberated mostly foreign subjects from slavery[167] as well as obtaining a treaty from which all Christian nations stood to benefit.

Victory in North Africa was enthusiastically celebrated in Great Britain. Lord Exmouth and his officers were honoured and decorated for their endeavours. The prince regent created him a viscount, and he received orders of chivalry from the kings of Spain, the Netherlands and the Two Sicilies.[168] As far as the British government was concerned, the value of this military success lay above all in its usefulness for foreign policy more generally. As Castlereagh put it in a personal letter of thanks to Lord Exmouth:

You have contributed to place the Character of the Country above all suspicion of mercenary policy, the great achievements of the War had not eradicated some lurking suspicion that we cherish'd Piracy as a commercial Ally; you have dispelled this cloud and I have no doubt the National Character in Europe will be Essentially Enobled by your Services.[169]

In the course of a later parliamentary debate on the official honours for the admiral and his Dutch ally, Castlereagh even labelled the strike against Algiers as a 'war of justice and humanity' against the Barbary pirates, selflessly undertaken by the British nation in defence of the rights of all European states.[170] This victory could now serve as a token of British foreign policy's sincere humanitarian commitment while also sending out the clear signal that Britain would not hesitate to use massive force in order to enforce a ban on the slave trade.[171]

Energised by its involvement in North Africa, the British government was now able to redouble its efforts to implement general abolition. With explicit reference to the agreements struck at Vienna and to the additional article to the second Paris Peace Treaty, it invited the great powers of France, Russia, Prussia and Austria to a conference in London.[172] Within the framework provided by the conference of ambassadors, a new mechanism of international cooperation that was emerging as part of the Vienna settlement, the envoys addressed the problem anew. Castlereagh began by presenting the other delegations with a plan for the foundation of a temporary naval league that was both to suppress North African pirates and to enforce the conclusive abolition of the slave trade.[173] The aims and purpose of this new alliance were clearly defined:

It is submitted that as any attempt at African colonization or conquest might give rise to political as well as military difficulties of considerable magnitude, that the proposed defensive concert should be purely maritime, and that it should be solely directed to afford, ... to each State a reasonable security for an unmolested enjoyment of the blessings of peace and a due observance of those civilized principles which the said regencies have lately been compelled by Lord Exmouth's operations to recognize.[174]

The idea behind restricting intervention to the maritime theatre from the outset was to prevent conflicts between the allies over possible territorial gains on the African continent. Meanwhile, the reference to Lord Exmouth underscored the character of the military operation he had led as a precedent for a policy of suppressing the slave trade by force of arms. For the purpose of implementing their common aims, the allies were each to contribute a set number of ships to an international naval squadron. There was to be a joint high command, based in Paris, which was to be controlled by a commission on which each of the powers was to have one seat. Besides a mutual right to stop and search suspicious ships sailing under allied flags, the proposal also made provisions for joint legal proceedings against intercepted vessels.

This proposal for a purely maritime intervention held clear advantages for and promised considerable influence to Great Britain as the leading naval power. Yet Britain's dominance on the high seas also meant that the other participants were wary of such designs, which entailed the surrender of certain sovereign rights. The French government in particular saw the plan above all as another British stratagem intended to bolster its rule over the seas and thereby to wound France's national honour.[175] With such fears in mind, the five powers were likewise unable to agree on concrete measures at their subsequent regular consultations, although the British foreign secretary tirelessly extolled the benefits of international cooper-ation to the other delegates, stressing that 'the endeavours of these Powers must be ineffectual, unless backed by a general Alliance, framed for this especial purpose. The rights of all nations must be brought to co-oper-ate'.[176] The conference of the great powers at Aachen in the autumn of 1818, among the outcomes of which was the withdrawal of the remaining allied forces of occupation from France and hence its re-joining the Concert of Europe, provided Castlereagh with a welcome opportunity once more to present his proposals for implementation.[177] The foreign secretary's main goal was to secure agreement to a 'right of mutual visit' of suspicious vessels. To reassure the other powers, he pointed to the bilateral treaties with Spain, Portugal and the Netherlands, with which such a right had been established along with 'Mixed Commissions for the Abolition of the Slave Trade' by which slave ships were legally condemned. With particular regard to France, which was still smarting from its recent defeat, Castlereagh was at pains to dispel any concerns over the curtailment of national sovereignty.[178] At the same time, he stressed the crucial practical and moral significance of so important a naval power as France participating in a system of joint naval measures for the effective suppression of the slave trade. Nonetheless, British proposals continued to find little favour with the other powers.[179]

While Austria made its agreement conditional on the attitude of the other states,[180] the Russian delegation made a proposal of its own, according to which all Christian nations were to set up a joint organisation based on the African coast. Equipped with a naval squadron and legal powers of its own, its task would be to enforce the ban on the Atlantic slave trade.[181] In the Russian view, there were no objections to granting a right to visit and impound ships to such a body, since it would in no way prejudice the commercial or maritime interests of any particular nation. Even the British delegation, however, had strong doubts about the practicability of this visionary idea of an international supervisory agency.[182] Prussia and France, meanwhile, flatly rejected any sweeping 'right to visit', fearing abuse and regarding it as a source of potential conflict.[183] The French delegation in particular predicted that, in view of its country's long-standing rivalry with Great Britain, exercising such a right would inevitably lead to violent confrontations between them.[184] The idea of a jointly run judiciary – the Mixed Commissions – was likewise rejected as a severe infringement of French sovereign rights. France made a more general argument against the need for joint implementation measures, pointing to the fact that it had already deployed a naval squadron of its own to the coast of Senegal, where it was fighting the French slave trade.[185] Yet ultimately it had been the prospect of surrendering sovereign rights by submitting to an abolition regime dominated by Great Britain that drove France to launch a military intervention of its own off the western African coast.

Aside from a joint address asking the king of Portugal to set a date for the termination of his country's slave trade,[186] the negotiations in Aachen ended without any tangible results. The great powers of Europe were unwilling to agree to a mutual right to visit: Too great was their concern that they were not only signing away their sovereign rights but, in doing so, further strengthening the hegemony of Great Britain, already the dominant maritime power. The failure to agree on collective measures of implementation was due in the last instance to the fact that joint public proclamations in favour of humanitarian action against the slave trade were not nearly enough to outweigh considerations of realpolitik.[187] Britain thus found itself compelled to abandon hope for a multilateral solution and follow a different path. Yet diplomatic talks at and after the Congress of Vienna had produced a scheme for a combined military and legal approach to abolition that could serve as the basis for further negotiations.[188]

The Bilateral Model: Intertwining Legal and Military Powers of Implementation

The United Kingdom was not deterred by the failure of a multilateral implementation mechanism and instead pursued a bilateral solution.[189] In one-on-one negotiations with a variety of states, the British government now tried to win support for the already mooted model in which military and legal measures were combined. Bilateral treaties – including with Portugal (1810), Sweden (1813),[190] the Netherlands[191] and Denmark (1814)[192] – had from the outset been at the heart of British efforts to push for restrictions or even a ban on the slave trade at the international level. The government in London stuck to this two-pronged strategy even during multilateral talks with the other great powers, as evidenced by the aforementioned Anglo-Portuguese treaty signed at the Congress of Vienna.[193] By means of this policy, the British government succeeded in concluding treaties binding under international law with Spain and Portugal (1817), the two staunchest opponents of general abolition, and with the Netherlands (1818). What made these treaties based on the principles of the Vienna Declaration remarkable was that they prescribed, for the first time, concrete measures for implementation and thereby became models for future agreements.

The first was the additional convention between Great Britain and Portugal of 28 June 1817, which was appended to the already existing treaty between the two nations.[194] The convention began by affirming the ban on the slave trade north of the equator,[195] while to the south subjects of the Portuguese crown holding a special royal dispensation[196] were permitted to continue their trade between the Portuguese colonies. Britain reiterated its promise to pay Portugal compensation of £300,000 (plus interest) for the illegal seizure of Portuguese vessels after 1 June 1814. In a treaty signed on 23 September 1817, Spain too decided to enter into legal cooperation with Great Britain, making explicit reference to 'the cause of humanity'.[197] This agreement likewise created an exclusion zone north of the equator, but also stipulated that the Spanish slave trade would become illegal on 30 May 1820. Compensation to Spain was set at £400,000.

It was indeed financial necessity rather than humanitarian conviction that led Spain and Portugal to conclude their respective treaties with the United Kingdom, causing *The Times* to ask: 'Why should England pay Spain for performing an act of humanity and justice?'[198] The long war against Napoleon and France's occupation of the Iberian Peninsula had drained the treasuries in Lisbon and Madrid and made both governments dependent on British aid. Spain was under additional strain from insurrection in its Latin American colonies and used the payment from Britain secretly to buy five Russian frigates and three ships of the line in an effort to regain control of the situation.[199] Britain deliberately exploited the economic and military weakness of both countries in order to force them into a treaty regime against the slave trade. Only with the Netherlands was a ban with no payoffs or geographical restrictions agreed on 4 May 1818.[200] By this time the Dutch government had already passed a ban on the slave trade, which had lost any importance it may once have had for the country's economy, and was hence in no need of a financial incentive to agree to a treaty.[201]

Aside from the various areas to which they applied and their other qualifications, these treaties had one notable feature in common.[202] With an unprecedented combination of military and legal means, which were able to develop their full force only by being intertwined, they backed up the newly passed humanitarian treaties for abolition with a well-defined implementation mechanism operating at an international level. First, the contracting parties granted each other a 'right to visit': that is, to stop and search each other's merchant ships sailing in international waters in peacetime. This meant that the right of mutual control, which both the abolitionists in parliament and British delegations at international conferences had demanded, was at last enshrined in international law.[203] This was, in Castlereagh's opinion, of nothing less than fundamental importance: 'It is the basis of the whole without which treaties to abolish it are mere waste paper.'[204] The navies of the countries concerned were now permitted to stop ships suspected of carrying slaves in the designated areas, to search them and confiscate any slaves found to be on board illegally, and to deliver the ships to the closest port for trial.[205] Only warships granted special written permission (in the language of both parties) and strictly bound to a shared set of rules were permitted to perform these operations.

These detailed instructions were an integral part of the treaties and provided binding operational guidelines to the navies of Britain, Portugal, Spain and the Netherlands.[206] The result was a remarkable standardisation of military executive power across the navies of four countries with the clear aim of avoiding diplomatic upsets from the start and to make international cooperation as frictionless as possible, as the following article indicated:

Whenever a ship of war shall meet a merchant vessel liable to be searched, it shall be done in the most mild manner, and with every attention which is due between allied and friendly nations; and in no case shall the search be made by an officer holding a rank inferior to that of lieutenant in the navy.[207]

The inspection of foreign vessels was to be performed only by senior officers, for only they were trusted to possess the diplomatic tact required for such a delicate task.

Since all three treaties also stipulated compensation for breach of contract, officers were held to scrupulous routines of evidence-gathering. They were to make a sworn report of when, under what circumstances and at what exact location at sea the ship was stopped and under what flag it was sailing.[208] This was to prevent the nationality and the probable course of the suspected slaver from being concealed. The number and sex of any slaves found on board were to be recorded minutely, as was their physical condition. Yet the instructions also expressly forbade removing the captives from the ship and landing them in port except in cases of extreme urgency. This provision was justified by arguing that, if a special tribunal found a ship to have been wrongfully impounded, this would make the return of seized property easier to accomplish.[209] A ship being intercepted by a naval vessel did not, then, automatically entail the liberation of the people crammed below deck – only the judgment of the tribunal determined whether they might leave their floating prison and when.

This is because there was also a crucial legal component to the three treaties of 1817 and 1818:

> In order to bring to adjudication, with the least delay and inconvenience, the vessels which may be detained for having been engaged in an illicit traffick of Slaves, there shall be established, within the space of a year at furthest from the exchange of the ratifications of the present convention, two mixed commissions, formed of an equal number of individuals of the two nations, named for this purpose by their respective sovereigns.[210]

This passage, which was enshrined in all three treaties, provided the basis on which the so-called Mixed Commissions for the Abolition of the Slave Trade were founded.[211] The idea of international arbitration bodies was already familiar to nineteenth-century diplomats, such bodies having been set up to resolve territorial and compensation claims between former belligerents after the American War of Independence and the Napoleonic wars.[212] The system of Mixed Commissions, however, went much further in its temporal and geographical scope. Mixed Commissions were set up on either side of the Atlantic – in Freetown, Luanda, Cape Town, Boa Vista in the Cape Verde Islands, Rio de Janeiro, Paramaribo in Suriname, Spanish Town in Jamaica, Havana and New York – and between 1819 and 1871 ruled on what to do with slave ships seized by the participating navies.[213] They were the main pillar of international law in combating the Atlantic slave trade and marked the beginning of an international judiciary.[214]

Their form and manner of functioning were clearly defined by regulations set down in the bilateral treaties. As with the military executive measures, the legal side of the treaty entailed an unprecedented degree of standardisation, with a fixed composition and set procedures for the Mixed Commissions spread around the Atlantic littoral. Each signatory nation appointed one commissary judge and one commissioner of arbitration each, who were supported by a registrar appointed by the nation in whose territory the Mixed Commission was situated.[215] Under the 'Regulations for the Mixed Commissions', members were strictly prohibited from receiving payments of any kind from parties involved in a case.[216] The costs of running the commissions, which came to several thousand pounds a year, were instead borne equally by the contracting parties.[217] Staff were recruited mainly from the diplomatic corps of the countries concerned and did not, as a rule, have specialist legal training.[218] Their salaries and pensions were graded according to their postings. A British commissary judge in Freetown earned an annual salary of £4,000, a commissioner of arbitration £2,000 and a registrar £1,000.[219] In spite of these financial incentives, the posts, particularly in Sierra Leone, often proved hard to fill. The prospect of working in Sierra Leone, known as the 'white man's grave' on account of its climate, was not an attractive one to most candidates. Tropical diseases were often caused the death or temporary incapacitation of members of the commissions,[220] in which case the regulations stipulated that, if the official concerned was a subject of the colonial power in whose territory the commission was situated, a high-ranking member of the colonial administration such as the governor or captain general should step in. In foreign territory, the task would fall either to the consul of the country concerned or else the commission's remaining members were charged, on an equal footing, to proceed with cases. The contracting parties were under express obligation to fill vacant posts as soon as possible.[221] Ensuring the functioning of the courts at all times was the guiding concern.

The procedures set down in the regulations stipulated close cooperation between the commissions' legal staff and the naval officers involved in operations. Directly on arrival in port with a seized ship, the officer responsible was required to submit an affidavit concerning the operation to the court.[222] He was also to provide additional evidence in form of the ship's log and any other papers which, assuming them not to have been manipulated, would contain information on the ship's nationality, cargo and planned route. The court registrar interviewed witnesses from among crews of both ships involved, using a standardised list of questions aimed at establishing the nationality of the ship's captain, crew and owner, its intended route, the freight it carried and the circumstances of its seizure.[223] The evidence thus established was submitted to the judges for assessment.

In view of the continuing presence of the captives on board ship, the entire process was to take no longer than twenty days, with an extension to a maximum four months only in exceptional circumstances, for instance to gather additional evidence.[224] Based on the evidence and having heard the arguments of the counsel for either side, the two judges made their ruling against which no appeal was possible. If the judges were unable to reach a unanimous decision, lots were drawn between the two commissioners of arbitration to choose which of them would cast the deciding vote.[225]

In the case of an acquittal – as would have to be given if, for instance, a ship was stopped outside the agreed zones – the ship and its cargo were to be returned to the slaver immediately and it was permitted to continue its voyage, putting an end to the desperate hopes of the slaves remaining crammed on board. Moreover, explicit provision was made for compensating the ship's owner for any damage suffered by the ship's wrongful impoundment, unless its captain had deliberately misled the authorities as to the facts of the matter. Personal responsibility for confiscations lay with the commanding naval officer, while his country vouched for the costs incurred, which in turn were decided by the appropriate Mixed Commission.[226] The list that had been drawn up to adjudicate claims for compensation accounted for any damage done to the ship and its cargo, demurrage to be paid for each day of internment and calculated by tonnage, and a per diem of one shilling per slave for their provision. Increases to insurance premiums were accounted for, as was an interest rate of 5 per cent per annum until compensation had been paid in full. The agreements also stipulated compensation 'for any diminution in the value of the cargo of slaves, proceeding from an increased mortality beyond the average amount of the voyage, or from sickness occasioned by detention'.[227] This compensation was to be calculated according to the price slaves might be expected to command at their port of destination. By providing for such compensation, which also factored in the increased mortality of slaves in transit and thereby put a price on human life, the Mixed Commissions somewhat paradoxically submitted to the cruel logic of the very trade they had been put in place to stop. What won the day here were not humanitarian principles, but rather the implacable laws of a market in which human beings were reduced to the status of merchandise in the Atlantic trading system.

This legalised way of dealing with the slaves on board the seized ships stands in clear contradiction to the legal scholar Jenny Martinez's claim that the Mixed Commissions were the 'first international human rights courts'.[228] In fact, these special tribunals ruled on the fate of the human beings crammed below deck not on the basis of universal human rights, but on prize and property law. Nor does the line of historical development and continuity Martinez draws from the Mixed Commissions via the international criminal jurisdiction of twentieth century with the military tribunals of Nuremberg and Tokyo to the International Criminal Court in the twenty-first century stand up to scrutiny.[229] The special tribunals of the nineteenth century had no authority to punish slave traders, proscribed though their activities might have been. Penalties remained up to the jurisdiction of their respective home countries, where slave traders usually went unpunished.

All that the regulations for the Mixed Commissions provided for was that, if a ship was condemned, it and its non-human cargo were declared a rightful prize and put up for public auction.[230] In some cases the buyer was the Admiralty itself, which added the former slave ships to Britain's own fleet. Renamed *Black Joke*, the former Brazilian slave brig *Henriquetta* thus became one of the most successful British slave chasers.[231] Yet it was not unheard of for slave traders to buy, either directly or through middlemen, confiscated ships and put them back to their original use.[232] So extensive was this practice that in the 1830s Britain moved to selling ships only once they had been broken down into parts.[233] Proceeds from the sale were shared equitably between the treaty partners and frequently used to pay for the operating costs of the commissions as well as for bounties.[234] With regard to the ships' human cargo – and this was the humanitarian aspect of the courts' work – the Mixed Commissions freed the slaves found on board and issued them each with a 'certificate of emancipation'. With this document in hand, they were to apply to the government of the country in whose territory the Mixed Commission resided for the right to settle as servants or free labourers. The treaty partners undertook to guarantee the freedom of the former slaves.[235]

The historical significance of the Mixed Commissions is to be found not in their supposed role as forerunners of the international protection of human rights or international criminal prosecution, but rather in the fact that they were the decisive legal component in the implementation of a norm that was – and this distinction is crucial – humanitarian, but not based on the idea of human rights. They certainly were the first form of international jurisdiction, and as such they provided a legal grounding and guarantee to the achievements of the military efforts against the Atlantic slave trade. The successful intertwining of military and legal elements was essential to the success of both. A well-functioning Mixed

Commission not backed up by a strong military executive force would have been as useless as the capture of a slave ship without subsequent legal process.[236]

This completely novel machinery of implementation, distinguished as it was by the standardisation of regulations and processes between nations throughout the Atlantic seaboard, is indeed a prime example of the mechanisms of international cooperation that emerged in the nineteenth century. It also gave impressive testimony to how firmly the first humanitarian intervention in history, against the Atlantic slave trade, was rooted in early-nineteenth-century internationalism while in turn shaping its further development. New possibilities for action opened up as the scope of international policymaking grew wider, although competing national interests continued to set limits to the most ambitious projects.

6 Possibilities and Limits of International Cooperation

International Implementation in the Shadow of National Interests

On paper, the machinery for implementation set up by the treaties between Britain, Portugal, Spain and the Netherlands of 1817 and 1818 seemed to allow for robust international enforcement of the ban on the slave trade. But how did the plans for international cooperation really work out in the reality of nineteenth-century politics? As far as the military executive was concerned, Britain bore virtually the sole responsibility for and burden of naval operations off the coast of West Africa. The British government put the Royal Navy's mission on a permanent footing and kept broadening its scope. In 1819 it dispatched a new squadron of seven ships under the experienced command of Commodore Sir George Ralph Collier to the western African theatre.[1] Yet even this detachment was nowhere near enough for the effective surveillance of 3,000 miles of coastline with countless estuaries, inlets and offshore islands that provided slavers with convenient hideouts. Accordingly, the British government steadily increased the number of ships in the West Africa Squadron, significantly adding to its capabilities and restating its firm political will to enforce its foreign policy paradigm of abolition by military means for as long as necessary.[2]

Although the treaties granted each signatory state the right to search the others' ships, the three other nations by and large declined to dispatch naval forces of their own to West Africa. One reason was that abolition was no great political priority or, as in the case of Spain and Portugal, even perceived as contrary to the national interest. Moreover, these countries had seen their navies decimated by the Napoleonic wars and preferred to use the forces remaining to them in line with their specific priorities.[3] Spain, for instance, needed every ship it still had to preserve and reconquer its colonial possessions in Latin America, which were clamouring for independence. The Spanish government, which had just spent the £400,000 it had received in compensation from Great

Britain on warships from Russia,[4] did not for a moment consider deploying naval forces of its own to enforce a policy to which at heart it objected. Both the Spanish and Portuguese governments were content to leave the Royal Navy to carry out these missions, which were not only costly but also, on account of tropical diseases, extremely dangerous to the ships' crews.[5]

This attitude did not, however, apply equally to the legal component, in which all signatories actively participated and the outcomes of which they were thus in a position to influence. In line with the treaties' provisions, the Anglo-Spanish Mixed Commission in Havana, the Anglo-Dutch Mixed Commission in Paramaribo and the Anglo-Portuguese Mixed Commission in Rio de Janeiro (which was to become the Anglo-Brazilian Mixed Commission after independence) took up work in 1819, as did their counterparts in Freetown.[6] The special tribunals were not, however, settings where untroubled international cooperation played out. The attitudes taken by their various members were largely determined by their respective government's position on the slave trade and the national interest involved.

For instance, the British judges on the Mixed Commissions were officially bound to administer justice impartially and 'to combine a fair and conscientious zeal for the prevention of the illegal traffick in slaves, with the maintenance of the strictest justice towards the parties concerned, and with the promotion of a spirit of conciliation and harmony between His Majesty's Subjects and those of the Kings of Spain and Portugal'.[7] In practice, however, they tended to take a hard line on slave traders and often acted as counsel for the prosecution rather than as judges.[8] In so doing they carried the policy of abolition adopted by their government into the courts and spearheaded its interpretation of international law.

Besides their contractually defined function in these international bodies, however, the British commission members had another important task to fulfil. From their various postings around the Atlantic seaboard, they sent countless dispatches to the Foreign Office in which they not only accounted for their regular activities and finances, but also gathered all manner of useful material on the slave trade. They compiled lists detailing the names of slave ships, their dates of arrival and departure, their ports of origin and destination, the numbers of crew and slaves and also the fatalities among those transported.[9] Slave traders were identified by name and descriptions given of the ships and their armaments as well of their tactics and their bases on the African coast.[10]

In addition, the British commissioners exercised a kind of supervisory function, ensuring adherence to the treaties and their provisions by exposing the collaboration of local authorities with slave traders. In March 1822, for instance, officials of the Mixed Commission in Sierra Leone reported that the Spanish colonial authorities were in the habit of renewing or forging the limited royal licences for slave trading that were supposed to have fixed expiry dates.[11] Having got wind of this practice, the Foreign Office made representations to the Spanish government, asking it to put an immediate stop to these activities by its agents and to abide by the treaty of 1817. Some years later, in March 1834, Palmerston, at the time a minister in the Foreign Office, received reports from the British commissioners in Sierra Leone and Havana concerning abuses on the part of the Spanish authorities and again reminded Spain of its obligations under international law.[12] Britain's commissioners formed a tight network whose news-gathering provided the government in London with up-to-date details of the slave trade, based on which it was able to coordinate diplomatic and military measures to enforce abolition.[13]

For their part, the Spanish, Portuguese and later Brazilian commissioners likewise played a dual role, albeit of a different kind. Their own attitude towards slave traders on trial tended to be lenient in the extreme; where the British tended to prosecute, they assumed the part of counsel for the defence. Their chief concern was often to protect the mercantile interests, including the slave trade, of their compatriots from British interference and to correct (as they saw it) the results of the Royal Navy's actions. Some of them, such as the Brazilian Commissioner Gomes, a member of the Sierra Leone Mixed Commission, maintained close contacts with known slave traders whose cases they tried.[14] In extreme cases, judges might even openly represent the slaveholding interest themselves. Such men as José Maria Herrera y Herrera and José Buenaventura Esteva not only served as the Spanish judges on the Cuban Mixed Commission in the 1840s and 1850s, but were also among the island's largest slaveowners.[15] Buenaventura Esteva even recruited labourers for his own plantations from among the slaves that had been freed by the commission. Having become aware of such activities, in August 1846 the foreign secretary had Palmerston enquire through Foreign Office channels 'whether the Marques de las Delicias [Buenaventura Esteva], being so great a slave-holder, is well fitted to be a member of the Mixed Commission'.[16] In Palmerston's view, the government in Madrid would do well to entrust the office of judge only to such persons as had as little involvement as possible in the criminal activities that they were sent to try.[17]

According to the commissioners' reports, the local Spanish, Portuguese and Brazilian authorities often lacked any political will to enforce the ban on the slave trade that had been declared under international law.[18] Public opinion in these countries generally perceived abolition to be an instrument whereby British power might be brought to bear on the internal affairs of sovereign states. In January 1825 Henry Kilbee, Britain's first commissary judge in Cuba, accordingly described the attitude of the Cuban public in the following terms: 'It is universally believed that the Abolition was a measure which Great Britain, under the cloak of philanthropy, but really influenced by jealousy of the prosperity of this Island, forced upon Spain.'[19] In Kilbee's view, the Spanish regarded the slave trade not as a crime, but as a means for the promotion of Cuban economic interest as well as having the side effect of thwarting a British policy that was considered largely self-serving. His sobering conclusion was: 'The Abolition by Spain, therefore, is merely nominal; and instead of promoting, only serves to injure the cause of justice and humanity.'[20]

Writing to the Foreign Office in January 1827, Kilbee and a fellow commissary judge, W. L. Macleay, restated these accusations, pointing out that the slave trade in Cuba continued unabated, in open defiance of the ban.[21] Slave ships sailed for Africa from Havana and returned without attracting the attention of the authorities, which were stirred to action only when the British commissioners asked the Spanish captain general to investigate the matter. As a rule, however, the authorities acquitted the ships without much ado and the case was closed. So far did this collaboration go, according to Kilbee and Macleay, that it was possible to land slaves at a public wharf and drive through Havana in broad daylight without there being a witness willing to testify to these events in court. The British commissioners thus felt 'justified by past experience in believing, that the legal authorities will exert all their ingenuity to evade the fulfillment of whatever orders may be received from Spain, the object of which is the suppression of the Slave-trade'.[22] To put Spain's inaction into figures, more than 43,000 African slaves were trafficked to Cuba between 1822 and 1829 in defiance of international law.[23]

The Mixed Commissions thus relied on the support of local authorities and their respective members for their effectiveness, as the statistics for their various locations suggest. In the clear lead were the special tribunals in Sierra Leone, which tried a total of 528 cases between 1819 and 1845. During the same period, their counterparts in Havana made a mere fifty judgments and those in Rio de Janeiro forty-four.[24] The principal reason was of course that the Royal Navy operated off the coast of West Africa and the ships intercepted there were the responsibility of the Freetown tribunals. Yet surely it is also the case that the British authorities were particularly ardent in fulfilling their treaty obligations – and given that their foreign counterparts were often absent from Sierra Leone, they had a free hand in using the Mixed Commissions as a targeted legal instrument against the slave trade.[25] This shows how the Mixed Commissions were not just sites of early international cooperation, but also arenas in which national interests might be pursued. This is underscored by the likelihood of a suspected slave ship being condemned or acquitted. Whereas only 1.8 per cent of trials in Freetown resulted in an acquittal, the figure was 10 per cent in Havana and an astonishing 32 per cent in Rio de Janeiro.[26] Over the period of their existence from 1819 to 1871 the Mixed Commissions examined over 600 cases and freed over 60,000 captives, preserving from being transported to the Americas as slaves.[27]

Yet the number of freed captives should not deceive us as to the weaknesses of the Mixed Commission system. Although the commissions had judicial power over the ships and their cargo, they had no legal mandate for sentencing slave traders. The owners and crews of seized ships continued to be subject to laws of their countries of origin, where a lack of appropriate legislation or the political will to enforce it meant that they usually went scot-free. Any deterrent effect the penalties might have had was thus limited to their material aspects, as shown by the report of a British commission of 15 May 1824. The case concerned one Brandão, the leading Portuguese slave trader operating around the Cape Verde Islands. When in February 1822 his ship, the *Conde de Villa Flor*, was stopped and seized by the Royal Navy before being legally condemned, Brandão openly announced 'that it was his intention to have retired from the trade, but that he is determined now, out of a spirit of defiance, to pursue the Slave Trade with all the means in his power'.[28] In spite of his public defiance of the law, the Freetown Mixed Commission could do nothing about Brandão, other than to hope that the Portuguese authorities would arrest and sentence him. This, however, they failed to do, and in the following year the commission reported that Brandão had redoubled his efforts, acquiring new ships and cementing his position as the leading slaver in the Cape Verde Islands.[29] Further weak points were the sentencing itself and the manner in which the courts dealt with the victims of the slave trade. If the judges failed to reach a unanimous verdict, lots were drawn for the commissioner of arbitration who would cast the deciding vote. Whether or not a ship was condemned then depended, as the British consul in Havana remarked, 'not nearly so much on fact, or law, or the merits of the case, as on the less fallible doctrine of chances'.[30] The fate of the captives was thus decided not by legal or humanitarian principles, but by the luck of the draw. Even if the court found in favour of the slaves, this did not guarantee their freedom. Again, the location of the Mixed Commission was an important factor.

In Sierra Leone, the 'certificate of emancipation' certainly did mean that the slaves regained their freedom as registered subjects of the British Crown.[31] A 'Liberated African Department'[32] was set up for the purpose of supplying urgently needed clothing, food, shelter and, where necessary, medical assistance. The office then provided the new arrivals with building material and seeds, allowing them to settle around Freetown.[33] This resulted in ethnically mixed villages whose farming contributed to the colonisation of the territory. Others contributed to public works in the city as free labourers or served as messengers with the Mixed Commissions.[34] Many men enlisted with the Royal African Corps, the West India Regiments and the Royal Navy.[35] While in Sierra Leone, too, it happened that former slaves were abducted anew and sold into slavery illegally, being freed by the Freetown courts usually meant having avoided slavery.[36]

By contrast, in Rio de Janeiro and Havana the so-called *emancipados*,[37] although officially freed by the local Mixed Commission, were forced into several years of indentured labour under the guise of 'apprenticeship'.[38] The Spanish and Portuguese (later Brazilian) authorities leased the new workers, initially for a period of seven years, to the highest bidder, with the going rates in Cuba ranging, according to the British consul Turnbull, 'from three to six ounces of gold for women, and from six to ten ounces for men'.[39] Locally powerful figures would often be given the pick of the crop, with the aforementioned Spanish judges Herrera y Herrera and Buenaventura Esteva receiving 35 and 400 *emancipados* respectively for their own use, having previously 'freed' them in their Mixed Commission.[40] This practice brought tremendous profits to the colonial authorities, profits that were further increased by arbitrarily extending the period of 'apprenticeship' by another seven years and once more leasing out the surviving 'freed' slaves.[41] In the severest cases, *emancipados* in Cuba and Brazil were declared officially dead before being sold into regular slavery under false names and with false papers.[42]

By finding in favour of slaves, the Mixed Commissions in Rio de Janeiro and Havana did not restore their freedom, but in fact condemned them to slavery by another name and with official connivance. Being neither free nor officially slaves – and therefore stripped even of the solidarity of the slave population – the *emancipados* existed outside firm legal categories.[43] Consul Turnbull found them to be even worse off than ordinary slaves 'because the term of their apprenticeship is for seven years only, and because the parties to whom they are bound have therefore no interest in their existence after the period for which their services have been purchased'.[44] Their physical labour was thus exploited with no consideration for their long-term health, and in many cases they were worked to death.[45] James Hudson, the British ambassador to Rio de Janeiro, described the situation of the *emancipados* in Brazil in the following terms: 'The position of these Africans is most wretched: they are ill-used, ill-fed, beaten without mercy and without reason, sold, false certificates given of their death and, in short, every man's hand seems to be raised against them; they have no chance of real freedom in Brazil.'[46] Britain repeatedly intervened with the Spanish and Brazilian governments to stop these abuses. Where Spain was concerned, Britain went so far as to add a special clause to the 1835 treaty intended to strengthen abolitionist measures. The clause demanded slaves freed by the Mixed Commissions were to be handed over not to the country in whose territory the Mixed Commission was located, but to that whose navy had apprehended the slave ship.[47] Since by far the most seizures were made by the Royal Navy, this provision effectively denied the Spanish authorities access to the *emancipados*. From Britain's perspective, this came with the additional advantage of making the freed slaves available as much-needed labourers in its Caribbean possessions.[48]

To enforce this clause, the British government in 1836 created the post of 'Superintendent of Liberated Africans', based in Cuba and responsible for matters concerning freed slaves.[49] Its first holder was Richard Robert Madden, an avowed abolitionist who was undeterred by the resistance of the Spanish authorities.[50] Madden persuaded the Admiralty to order a retired warship, HMS *Romney*, into Havana harbour, where it served as a provisional shelter for freed slaves prior to their removal to the British West Indies.[51] In April 1840, HMS *Crescent* was sent to Rio de Janeiro for the same purpose.[52]

The crew of the hulk[53] moored off Havana consisted of Royal Marines belonging to the West Indian regiments who were themselves freed slaves or the descendants of slaves. This was not insignificant. Not only did the Spanish authorities find the symbolism provocative; they also held the presence of the British warship manned with soldiers of colour to constitute a security risk and forbade them from coming ashore. The government in Madrid backed down[54] only once the British side had pledged special caution, not least 'that every care will be taken on our part to prevent as much as possible any such contact between the soldiers of Her Britannic Majesty and the slaves of the island, as might lead to dangerous consequences'.[55]

Consul Turnbull was Madden's successor as superintendent and no less committed to the cause of the *emancipados*, on whose behalf he repeatedly intervened with the Spanish authorities. For their part, the *emancipados* increasingly considered the British officials to be their advocates and began to appeal to them directly for help.[56] This exacerbated lingering tensions with the island's authorities, so much so that in February 1842 the British government was compelled to recall Turnbull following credible threats against his life and considerable diplomatic pressure.[57]

British efforts notwithstanding, the situation of the *emancipados* in both Cuba and Brazil remained an unsolved problem and the cause of repeated diplomatic tensions. In December 1846, as on several occasions before and after, the government in London asked its counterpart in Madrid truly to free the Africans

> who having been adjudged to be free by the decree of the Mixed Tribunal, have, nevertheless, for many years continued to suffer the most degrading slavery, aggravated, if possible, by the circumstances of their bearing the name of Emancipados, in derision, as it were, of the cruel and oppressive bondage in which they have been illegally retained.[58]

Successive British enquiries into the whereabouts and general situation of freed slaves went unanswered by the authorities in Rio de Janeiro.[59] It took a long time for continuous British pressure on the Spanish and Brazilian governments to produce tangible results. In 1853, Juan de la Pezuela, the Spanish captain general in Cuba, declared all *emancipados* free upon completing their term of service – a decision which led to his swift recall and was soon rescinded by his successor.[60] In Brazil, the official liberation of all *emancipados* occurred another eleven years later, in September 1864.[61] Agreements under international law notwithstanding, the slaves freed by the Mixed Commissions in Rio were denied their freedom for decades. In the national interest of the slaveholding societies of Cuba and Brazil, they were forced into organised servitude, which many of them did not survive.[62]

Aside from these obvious shortcomings, the principal flaw in the global machinery for enforcing an end to the Atlantic slave trade lay in the fact that the mandate itself was insufficient. The treaties of 1817 and 1818 allowed only for the seizure and condemnation of ships that were actually carrying slaves. Ships that may have been used for slave trading but were found empty at the time of inspection were allowed to continue their journeys unimpeded. What was more, the treaty regime covered only four nations, Britain, the Netherlands, Spain and Portugal, with the latter exempted below the equator. Slave traders needed only to change the flag under which they sailed in order to place themselves out of reach of the navies of the signatory states and thereby to thwart the entire machinery of implementation.

The British commissioners in particular could not help becoming aware of these flaws in the course of performing their duties and kept suggesting improvements. In 1821, only two years after the Mixed Commissions were set up, the first British commissioner of arbitration in Havana, Robert Jameson, made his concerns public. In an account entitled *Letters from the Havana* and based on his experiences in Cuba, he called on 'all civilized nations' to redouble their efforts against the slave trade.[63] He made no bones about criticising such major nations as France and the United States for staunchly refusing to participate in the system of the Mixed Commissions and putting their national interest first. As long as so much as a single nation refused to endorse complete abolition, England was unable to prevent the slave trade from wreaking destruction in Africa and abusing 'humanity':[64] 'Till the principle of abolition is written in the code of nations as it is in that of nature, we must expect humanity to be outraged.'[65] Indeed, the Atlantic slave trade continued to thrive in spite of international efforts to stop it, and every year thousands of Africans were abducted and sold into slavery in the Americas.[66] The goal of British foreign policy must therefore in future be to extend the reach of the existing treaties in international law, to close loopholes and to persuade as many countries as possible to participate in an international treaty regime.[67]

The Long Road to the International Treaty Regime

The need to accommodate a new treaty partner presented itself in September 1822, when Brazil declared its independence from Portugal. This was only the culmination of a lengthy process of emancipation that had gained pace when the entire Portuguese court fled the Napoleonic invasion from Lisbon to Rio de Janeiro in 1807.[68] Overnight, the Portuguese slave market, which besides Cuba had been the principal destination of transatlantic slave transports, became that of independent Brazil. This development naturally raised questions in London concerning the continuing validity of the Anglo-Portuguese treaties and the future of the Mixed Commission in Rio de Janeiro. With a view to its own consolidation, meanwhile, the new Brazilian state gave top priority to securing its recognition in international law, an opportunity which the British government wasted no time in exploiting.[69]

At the Congress of Verona in 1822 Canning, the foreign secretary, said of his government's diplomatic imperative vis-à-vis the nascent states of Latin America 'that no state in the New World will be recognised by Great Britain which has not frankly and completely abolished the trade in slaves'.[70] A comprehensive ban on the slave trade was thus set as the price that Britain demanded for recognition under international law. This was no great obstacle to the majority of South American republics, which had professed abolition during the revolutionary phase and enshrined it in their respective constitutions.[71] National laws, for instance in Colombia and in the Argentine Federation, put slave trading on a level with piracy and made involvement in either a capital offence.[72] At the international level, the Argentine Federation, Columbia and Mexico signed treaties of friendship with Great Britain in which they affirmed their willingness to cooperate in measures against the slave trade, thereby swelling the ranks of the international alliance.[73]

In the Brazilian case, however, negotiations proved far more difficult since its plantation economy depended on a steady flow of fresh labour and the slave trading lobby was influential domestically. Nonetheless, soon after independence the new government in Rio de Janeiro under Emperor Dom Pedro I saw no choice but to recognise the treaties against the slave trade between Britain and Portugal.[74] This allowed the Royal Navy to stop slave ships sailing under the Brazilian flag north of the equator, and the Mixed Commission was able to continue its work. Yet the British government was not satisfied with this arrangement and took advantage of Brazil's weak international position to push for more comprehensive agreements.[75] The British side made it clear on several occasions that a ban on the slave trade was the condition for recognising Brazil's independence.[76] These lengthy negotiations resulted in the treaty of 23 November 1826, in which Brazil undertook to fulfil the Anglo-Portuguese treaties against the slave trade in accordance with international law and to set up Anglo-Brazilian Mixed Commissions in Freetown and Rio de Janeiro.[77] In addition, the Brazilian government pledged to outlaw the slave trade completely three years after ratification of the treaty and henceforth to treat it as piracy.[78] In return, Britain recognized Brazil's independence and signed a trade agreement with it.[79]

The British government thus took advantage of another country's international weakness to induce it to join the treaty regime against the slave trade and the implementation mechanism associated with it. Recognition of a new state and its concomitant adoption as a member of the community of international law were made to depend on the willingness to adopt active measures for the protection of 'humanity' and a humanitarian norm. Yet this strategy of exerting diplomatic pressure was likely to work only with regard to new states of uncertain international standing, such as the South American republics. It was rather harder to maintain against such powerful and firmly established countries as France and the United States,[80] both of which firmly rejected any British projects for international cooperation. They remained implacably opposed to participation in a treaty regime under the leadership of the hegemonic maritime power and particularly to any 'right to visit' their ships in peacetime, in which they saw an unconscionable infringement of their sovereign rights.[81]

In April 1818 the government in London first proposed to its counterpart in Washington – which, as already mentioned, had imposed a national ban on the slave trade in 1807 – that it join the treaty system under the same terms as the treaties that had just been concluded with Spain, Portugal and the Netherlands.[82] The United States were likewise asked to agree to a mutual 'right to search' of suspicious ships in peacetime and to seized slave ships being submitted to the international jurisdiction of the Mixed Commissions. This British proposal met with considerable resistance in the United States and was roundly rejected.[83] In his instructions to the ambassador to London, the secretary of state, John Quincy Adams, cited constitutional obstacles which, although the United States was in sympathy with the goal of abolishing the slave trade, precluded them joining the proposed international regime.[84] One problem was participating in the international jurisdiction of the Mixed Commissions, which would conflict with the constitutional position of the Supreme Court as the highest judicial body in the land.[85] Adams was therefore doubtful 'whether the power of the Government of The United States is competent to institute a Court, for carrying into execution their penal Statutes beyond the Territories of The United States, a Court consisting partly of Foreign Judges, not amenable to impeachment for corruption, and deciding upon the Statutes of the United States without appeal'.[86] Another problem, according to Adams, was that the federal government was unable to guarantee the freedom of slaves liberated by the Mixed Commissions, since the status of black people in American territory was regulated by state and not by federal law. Added to which, Adams left no doubt that neither Congress nor the public would ever agree to granting foreign officers the right to search US ships in peacetime.[87]

This steadfast refusal of a 'right to search' and the emotive nature of the issue was rooted above all in painful memories of recent history. During the Napoleonic wars, the Royal Navy had repeatedly interfered with American shipping. Although the United States were neutral, the Stars and Stripes did not protect ships from being stopped, searched and, on the pretext of supplying contraband to France, confiscated. The obstruction and damage to American overseas trade were considerable. British captains also claimed the right to search US ships for supposed British deserters and, in their constant need for crews, were not above impressing American sailors into service on board His Majesty's ships. This practice, which forced American sailors into military service for another country, produced violent confrontations and caused several deaths, with the incident of USS *Chesapeake* the most notorious. As well as impeding trade, it raised tensions between the two countries,[88] with the US government increasingly viewing it as a direct attack and not least as blatant disregard of national sovereignty on the part of the former colonial overlord. These were two compelling reasons for President James Madison to declare war on Great Britain in June 1812.[89] Other considerations aside, the slogan 'A Free Trade and Sailors' Rights' proved exceedingly popular in the war, which lasted until 1815.[90]

Coming only three years after peace was concluded at Ghent, the British proposal for a right to search as part of its efforts against the slave trade was bound to be received with some distrust in Washington. Recent experience suggested that, whatever safeguards might be put in place, the world's leading naval power would once again take such a right as a pretext for infringing on the sovereign rights of the United States.[91] These fears were only exacerbated by the persistent British refusal to reach an agreement over the unsolved question of the impressment of sailors.[92] Yet to the United States in particular, this was an urgent and highly emotive issue. Following the collapse of negotiations, the American ambassador to Britain, Richard Rush, even went so far as to claim that Britain's pursuit of this practice was 'more afflicting to humanity, as far as the scale extends, than was ever the African Slave Trade, and in the highest degree insulting to the rights and dignity of an independent and powerful nation'.[93]

Britain's efforts, tirelessly continued from 1818 to 1822, to get Washington to agree to a right of search in the struggle against the slave trade, were thus doomed to failure.[94] For its part, the US government rejected any such initiatives, pointing to Britain's refusal to make concessions on the question of impressment. John Quincy Adams, the secretary of state, phrased the American position in no uncertain terms: 'Unless Britain would bind herself by an article, as strong and explicit as language can make it, never again in time of war to take a man from an American vessel, we never for a moment could listen to a proposal for allowing a right of search in times of peace.'[95] For Adams, US foreign policy's priority lay not in combating the slave trade, but rather in securing his country's interests and above all in preserving the sovereign rights hard won in the American revolution. The maxims of what he called the 'general extra-European policy of the United States'[96] were to apply in this matter, too. Accordingly, he categorically refused to countenance his government's accession to the proposed treaty, arguing that its members 'could neither sacrifice the individual rights of their citizens, by subjecting them to trial for offence against their municipal Statues, before Foreign Judges, in Countries beyond the Seas; nor the rights of

National Independence, by authorizing Foreign Naval Officers to search and seize any American Vessel'.[97] Adams left no doubt as to the American position, restating it in further talks with Stratford Canning, the British ambassador. To Canning's question whether he could imagine a greater and more heinous evil than the slave trade, Adams replied: 'Yes: admitting the right of search by foreign officers of our vessel upon the seas in time of peace; for that would be making slaves of ourselves.'[98]

Yet this attitude of staunch refusal on the part of the US government should not lead us to assume that there was no strong abolitionist movement in the country. These political forces were strong enough to induce Congress to expand and strengthen decisively existing national legislation against the slave trade. On 3 March 1819, Congress voted in favour of the Act in Addition to the Acts Prohibiting the Slave Trade, which reaffirmed national implementation measures and extended the US Navy's mandate to cover operations in African waters.[99] The navy was now empowered to seize American slavers, regardless of whether they were carrying slaves or merely equipped to do so, as legal prizes. Moreover, by charging US government agents with looking after freed slaves in West Africa, the act also laid the foundation for the state of Liberia.[100] In December, President Monroe specified what had been a vague provision by announcing that freed slaves would be settled on the West African coast and that two ships would be dispatched to find a suitable spot.[101] This marked the beginning of the United States' more or less enthusiastic efforts to combat the slave trade itself and on its own terms. By founding, under the patronage of the American Colonization Society, a first settlement – later to be named Monrovia – at Cape Mesurado, the United States also acquired a base on the African continent as well as establishing a safe haven for freed slaves modelled on the British colony of Sierra Leone.[102] To ensure that the new settlement was protected and provisioned, US naval squadrons increased their presence in nearby coastal waters, although between 1822 and 1841 they moved only sporadically and with notable lack of success against slave ships operating in the area.[103]

In May 1820, Congress enacted further legislation in the United States' national struggle against the slave trade. It declared direct involvement in the slave trade to be tantamount to piracy and hence punishable by death.[104] Even compared to Great Britain, which enacted a corresponding law only in March 1824,[105] the United States now possessed the strictest laws against human trafficking. Although its actual effects were negligible – the US Navy achieved little, and only one person was ever executed for involvement in the slave trade, in February

1862[106] – these measures provided Adams with further arguments for resisting British pressure for international cooperation. Much like France, which was equally reluctant to compromise its sovereignty and submit to an abolition regime dominated by Britain, its great rival, the United States used its own national measures as a handy alibi. In the ongoing negotiations with Canning, Adams was in the habit of citing French reservations[107] while also making much of his country's own purported successes in fighting for the cause of humanity and against the slave trade.[108]

Negotiations over a mutual right to search were deadlocked until spring 1823, when Charles F. Mercer, a representative from Virginia, proposed a resolution that the House adopted by a resounding majority. In this resolution, the House of Representatives called upon the president to resume negotiations with European countries for an effective implementation of abolition and to ensure that slavery was equated with piracy under international law.[109] Domestic pressure was now such that Adams, the secretary of state, offered to reopen talks with the British government conditional upon British agreement to the piracy clause.[110] In the decisive cabinet meeting, Adams explained the importance of this principle to his fellow members of government by pointing out that a right to search was already in place where pirates – outlaws under international law – were concerned:

To piracy, by the law of nations, search is incident of course, since wherever there is a right to capture there must be a right to search. The end desired by the resolution of the House of Representatives cannot be obtained without conceding the right so far of search, and all that is left us is to keep it still inflexibly within the class of belligerent rights, as exercised only against pirates, the enemies of all mankind.[111]

By thus declaring slave traders pirates under international law, it was possible to acquire a right to search without admitting such a right as fundamental even in peacetime. Subtle though this distinction may seem, it enabled Adams to follow the demands of his own parliament without being seen as surrendering his own original position and giving in to British demands. The path was clear for international cooperation without surrendering sovereign rights – and above all without losing face diplomatically.

To the British government, Adams once more laid out in full the familiar arguments against a general right of search and placing US citizens under the jurisdiction of the Mixed Commissions before stating his government's conditions for an agreement.[112] Henceforth, arrested slave traders were to be delivered for trial to their own country's courts.

A limited right of search was to be granted only when both countries had declared human trafficking to be piracy. In his instructions to the ambassador to London, the secretary of state laid out the rationale behind these alternative proposals:

> To meet, explicitly and fully, the call so earnestly urged by the British Government, that in declining the proposals pressed by them upon us of conceding a mutual and qualified right of search we should offer a substitute for their considerations. The substitute, by declaring the crime piracy, carries with it the right of search for the pirates existing in the very nature of the crime. But to the concession to the right of search, distinct from the denomination of the crime, our objections remain in all their original force.[113]

Adams' proposals, which President Monroe mentioned in his celebrated 'state of the union' address at the end of 1823,[114] were broadly accepted by the British side and formed the basis for a convention signed, after further negotiation, in London in March 1824.[115] However, when the treaty came before Congress to be ratified, various factions formed to oppose the treaty that Adams had negotiated. The old resentment of Great Britain welled up and, with a presidential election looming, there was political capital to be gained from resisting a settlement.[116] In the event, Congress gave its approval only on condition of an amendment exempting US waters from the right to search.[117] Since Great Britain could not possibly accept this unilateral change to the treaty, what had seemed a done deal was nonetheless scuppered.[118] Subsequent negotiations between London and Washington were likewise inconclusive, and a joint approach to fighting the slave trade was postponed for another eighteen years.[119]

Aside from a treaty with the Kingdom of Sweden and Norway in November 1824,[120] the project of an international abolitionist treaty regime made no meaningful advances in the 1820s. Resistance came not only from the United States, but above all from France. In the French government's view, its former enemy and long-standing maritime rival had engineered the system to bolster its own naval supremacy and curtail French sovereignty, a point made by French delegates at the London ambassadors' conferences beginning in 1816 as well as at the congresses of the great powers of Europe in Aachen (1818) and Verona (1822).[121] While the British government pointed to the slave trade that was carried on unabated by French ships and pressed for international cooperation to stop it, the French government, like that of the United States, cited its own abolition laws and the implementation measures with which they were backed up.[122]

These measures included warships, which France dispatched to its West African possessions in June 1818.[123] Based at Saint-Louis in Senegal and the island of Gorée, their mission was to enforce the

French ban against the slave trade by stopping slave ships sailing under the French flag. Given that the squadron initially consisted of only four small ships with a total crew of 186, this task may seem overly ambitious.[124] As far as the French side was concerned, however, these ships fulfilled an important purpose, albeit a political rather than a humanitarian one: Their presence testified to France's own geostrategic ambitions in West Africa – a message intended above all for Britain – while lending support to France's continued rejection of diplomatic attempts to draw it into an international system of anti-slavery measures.[125] The French squadron shared the humanitarian mission of the Royal Navy in name only, and relations between the two reflected this discrepancy. Far from cooperating in a common cause, the French and British squadrons, particularly in the early stages of operations, approached each other in a spirit of mutual suspicion and national rivalry, which is barely surprising in view of their recent and profound hostility during the Napoleonic wars.

An actual rapprochement between the two countries only began in the mid-1820s, when France tightened its own abolition laws – involvement in the slave trade was now punishable by transportation and five years' imprisonment – and thereby increased the political credibility of its efforts against the slave trade.[126] The British government viewed this as expressing 'the sincere desire of the King, the Government, and the people of France to repress a practice so replete with evils to humanity'.[127] The French government backed up its tougher line by sending more ships to patrol western African waters, thereby making a significant improvement to its success rate. In January and February 1827 alone, the French navy apprehended eleven slave ships.[128] Moreover, French and British officers began to cooperate, exchanging information and even undertaking joint patrols. In the spring of 1827, the French warship *L'Alcibiade* and HMS *North Star* went on their first joint patrol of the waters between Cape St Paul (modern Ghana) and Fernando Pó (Equatorial Guinea).[129] From the French viewpoint, this procedure came with the considerable advantage of adding effectiveness to efforts against the slave trade without granting a mutual right to search and thereby compromising French sovereignty. Such French captains as Alexis Villaret de Joyeuse, whose frigate *L'Aurore* was operating in western African waters, were vocal advocates of joining forces with the Royal Navy for that reason.[130] In a memorandum addressed to the French Admiralty in April 1828, Villaret put the fact that the two squadrons could now operate in a spirit of trust down not least to the memory of the victory at Navarino, which France and Britain had won jointly.[131] In the Battle of Navarino on 20 October 1827, the French and British navies, acting in alliance with Russia, had intervened in the Greek war of independence and achieved a decisive victory for the Greek cause by destroying the Ottoman fleet almost completely. Officers of both countries clearly regarded such a success in another part of the world as a model for their nations' successful cooperation and referred to it as such.

A treaty establishing Anglo-French cooperation was finally signed in 1831, helped in large part by domestic upheaval in France.[132] The July Revolution of 1830 and the installation of a liberal government under the new king, Louis Philippe I, also brought leading abolitionists into high office. Achille-Léon-Victor de Broglie, a member of the Société de la morale chrétienne, held various important government posts.[133] French laws against the slave trade were further tightened[134] and, at the international level, negotiations with Great Britain resumed.[135] On 30 November 1831, the French and British governments signed a convention granting each other the right to search for the purpose of suppressing the slave trade.[136] Within zones precisely defined by degrees of longitude and latitude off the coasts of Brazil and West Africa and around the islands of Madagascar, Cuba and Puerto Rico, warships of both navies carrying a special permit were entitled to stop ships sailing under the other country's flag and examine them for involvement in the slave trade.[137] After more than a decade, the French government had abandoned its resistance to a right to search in peacetime, although it remained firm on the question of bringing seized slave ships to justice. According to the convention, these ships were subject to their respective national judiciaries, to which they must be delivered without delay.[138] As far as the French government was concerned, there was still no question of joining the international system of Mixed Commissions. This qualification aside, the convention, which was strengthened by a supplementary convention in 1833,[139] provided the cooperation of both countries with a solid foundation, ultimately putting an end to the slave trade under the French flag.[140]

These cooperation agreements formed the basis of a diplomatic initiative launched by France and Great Britain in early 1834. In a joint memorandum, they invited the governments of Austria, Prussia, Russia, Sardinia and Naples as well as the United States of America to join the Anglo-French treaty and combine forces to fight the slave trade effectively.[141] France, which had long presented one of the major obstacles to international cooperation in this area, now emerged as an increasingly valuable partner in British efforts.[142] This change of policy was not enough, however, to dispel misgivings across the Atlantic. The US government flatly rejected the joint initiative emanating from London and Paris, holding fast to its position that it would under no circumstances accept a treaty extending a mutual right of search to its own territorial waters in peacetime.[143]

While the United States continued to refuse international cooperation and the great powers of Europe remained hesitant, smaller countries were stung into action by the Anglo-French initiative. Denmark and Sardinia joined the treaty in 1834,[144] setting off something of a wave of signatures over the course of the next six years, with Tuscany, Naples, Haiti, Texas and the Hanse cities of Germany (Hamburg, Bremen and Lübeck) following their example.[145] During this time, Great Britain also succeeded in strengthening existing treaties and mending some of their faults. The new agreements with Spain, Brazil, Portugal and the Netherlands now also contained an 'equipment clause', according to which ships that, while not transporting slaves at the time, were clearly fitted out for the slave trade could be condemned as lawful prizes by the Mixed Commissions.[146] The new treaty signed with Spain in 1835 in particular served the republics of South America as a model for their treaties with Great Britain. The number of Mixed Commissions in Sierra Leone grew accordingly, with Chile, the Argentine Federation, Uruguay, Bolivia and Ecuador now represented – at least nominally.[147] In practice, these new signatories tended to shy away from the expense of sending their own representatives to Africa and left judicial decision-making powers in the hands of the British commissioners.[148]

Although individual treaties differed in individual points – particularly in agreeing to a Mixed Commission or insisting on the jurisdiction of their own courts over seized ships – depending on whether they followed the 'Spanish' or 'French' model, they formed a solid foundation for international cooperation in the fight against the slave trade. In a memorandum to the British government composed in March 1839 James Bandinel, the first superintendent of the Foreign Office's newly founded Slave Trade Department,[149] underscored the key importance of these treaties with 'Foreign Civilized Powers'.[150] Bandinel accordingly urged the expansion of this treaty regime to include such important powers as Prussia, Austria and the United States, citing the treaty with Spain and the convention with France as exemplary cases.[151] The measures he proposed included better equipment of the navy – including steamships – but also ideas for maintaining relations with the so-called Native Powers. Referring explicitly to the successful conclusion of treaties with Madagascar and the sultan of Muscat,[152] Bandinel now argued in favour of concluding similar agreements with indigenous rulers in East and West Africa:

I therefore venture, on this part of the subject, to suggest the usefulness of issuing a circular instruction to several British Commanders, naval, military, and civil, along the whole line of the Coast of Africa, enjoining that whenever they may have directions to make a compact with a Native Prince, they shall include in it a stipulation for stopping the Slave Trade; and that whenever occasion offers for making with effect a stipulation for that purpose only, they shall take advantage of it to make overtures for such a stipulation.[153]

This idea of cooperating with African rulers and drawing them into the treaty system against the slave trade matched up with the ideas of Sir Thomas Fowell Buxton, a leading abolitionist who had frequently argued in his writings in favour of such an approach.[154] Buxton was instrumental in setting up the British expedition to colonise the Niger delta in 1841,[155] in the course of which several such agreements were concluded between British commissioners and local princes.[156] Besides the general establishment of amicable political and economic relations, these agreements contained a strict ban on the slave trade and gave the Royal Navy the unlimited right to stop, confiscate and try any slave ship found off the coast of these territories. They also entitled the British Crown to send representatives, to be placed under the protection of the local ruler, to ensure observance of the treaty.[157]

Tropical diseases in particular led to a high mortality rate among the white participants and meant that the Niger expedition ended in disaster, being recalled by the British government in March 1842.[158] It nonetheless acted as a catalyst to the expansion of the treaty regime against the slave trade, for the agreements concluded during the expedition set a precedent for contractually involving African rulers in the battle against the slave trade. A detailed memorandum drawn up by Bandinel for Lord Aberdeen, the foreign secretary, gives a flavour of the official language in which such plans were framed:

The British Governors in the several settlements in Africa, and the commanders of the British naval forces, have Her Majesty's commands to take advantage of every favourable opportunity for entering into negotiations with the several native chiefs having power or influence in Africa, to secure the suppression of the Slave Trade in places within their influence, and to propose to them, instead thereof, legitimate commerce; and provision is to be made, that the advantages, to be secured conditionally to the native chiefs, shall be withholden, if the agreements as to Slave trade are not carried into effect: and that Great Britain shall be authorized to take more stringent measures, where necessary, for ensuring the fulfilment of the contracts entered into.[159]

It followed from these proposals that a breach of humanitarian agreements against the slave trade gave Britain the right to intervene unilaterally in the internal affairs of African rulers. A new strategic focus on the part of the British government meant that no fewer than ninety-three such agreements with 'native chiefs' were concluded between 1841 and 1856 alone.[160] Taken together, these developments show how between

1834 and the mid-1850s one of the first international treaty regimes emerged, with Great Britain at its centre and extending from the Arabian Peninsula via East and West Africa to Europe and the Americas. Its stated purpose was to enforce a humanitarian norm.[161] The idea of intervention, whether as a right of search on the high seas or by direct action on African soil, was key to this system, which reserved the use of military force in peacetime to ensure the effective enforcement of the ban on the slave trade.

Yet it should also be noted that these measures initially left slavery as an institution existing at the global level unaffected. In many of the states signatory to this regime, slavery was abolished and slaves emancipated only much later, often decades after they had committed themselves by treaty to suppressing the trade and sometimes taken active steps to implement this prohibition. Only in 1833 was slavery legally abolished in the British colonies, even though the United Kingdom had taken the lead in the fight against the slave trade with the 1807 Slave Trade Act.[162] It is therefore essential to distinguish between the fight against the slave trade on the one hand and the institution of slavery on the other and always to keep this distinction in mind.

As contemporary standards of international law would have it, the treaty regime against the slave trade covered states both 'civilised' and not. This did not, however, mean that the treaty partners met on an equal footing and as such were members of a community of international law. On the contrary, the distinction between 'civilised' and 'uncivilised' was maintained and stated in these agreements, which were expressly not to be referred to as treaties.[163] Drafting the model agreement for use on the Niger expedition of 1841, Lord Palmerston left no doubt that

the compacts to be made with the African chiefs should be described as 'arrangements or agreements', or by some other word which would exclude them from the class of Diplomatic Conventions. The distinction is not verbal or trivial. It means to reserve to the Secretary of State for Foreign Affairs his own exclusive power of negotiating Treaties, and it is also meant to mark the distinction between agreements with barbarous Chiefs and the international compacts of Civilized States.[164]

The British side set the greatest possible store by this distinction and was keen to avoid anything that might be perceived as undue diplomatic honour being given to African rulers. The word 'treaty' was hence to be avoided in favour of 'agreement' or 'engagement'. By the same token, the Admiralty issued separate rules of engagement to the officers involved in operations against the slave trade – one set of 'Instructions relating to States other than Uncivilized African States' and another of 'Instructions relating to Uncivilized African States', all the while emphasising that:

The powers committed to you for the purpose of suppressing the Slave Trade carried on by inhabitants of Uncivilized African States are of a different character; they include powers which may be exercised not only over suspected Vessels, but likewise on shore, and that irrespectively of the consent of the Native Government.[165]

The distinction was not, then, a matter of mere nomenclature, but manifest in the different principles on which the agreements were based. In recognition of and out of respect for equal sovereign rights, treaties with European and American countries were always founded on the principles of reciprocity and equality. In such cases, the two 'civilised' signatories had, under international law, equal rights, such as an equal right to search each other's ships and to participate equally in subsequent legal proceedings, whether in the Mixed Commissions or their own courts. The 'agreements' with African rulers, on the other hand, were entirely one-sided, entitling Britain alone to conduct searches, take legal proceedings, dispatch envoys to ensure observance of agreements, declare sanctions and intervene in support of its policies. It should therefore be noted that the international treaty regime established in the course of the first humanitarian intervention and in order to enforce a humanitarian norm contributed materially to establishing the double standards of nineteenth-century international law.[166]

'By the Almost Universal Consent of Nations': The 1840s as an International Breakthrough

For weaker European and South America states, enjoying a privileged position as an equal and 'civilised' member of the community of international law did not always mean that their incorporation into the treaty regime came about altogether consensually and in the spirit of international mechanisms of cooperation. Writing around the time of the Congress of Verona and in view of the uncooperative attitude of Portugal and Brazil, Canning, the foreign secretary, had contemplated the scope of 'justifiable violence':

If it be true that no combination of great Powers can justify an infliction of injury upon a smaller Power; it may be affirmed on the other hand that no power has the right (nor has it at all the more for being insignificant in strength) to interrupt by its single act, the consenting policy of all the civilized world on a matter on which the dictates of Christianity and morality are clear; and to perpetuate to a large portion of their fellow creatures misery and suffering which all other Powers are conspiring to heal.[167]

From Britain's perspective, the conduct of weaker states, particularly their unilateral obstruction of humanitarian efforts directed against the slave trade, could serve to legitimise direct intervention in their sovereign rights. To this extent, it was possible for the broad recognition of a humanitarian norm on the part of the 'civilised world' to override the protections of sovereignty, an idea which in this context referred no longer just to rights, but also to obligations towards the international community.[168] In 1839, Portugal became the first country to feel the effects of this shift. Beginning in 1834, the British government, seeking to extend the international treaty regime, entered into new negotiations with Portugal over an enhanced agreement that would do away with grace periods and the restriction of searches to north of the equator as well as containing an 'equipment clause'. This was an attempt on the part of the British government effectively to eliminate what was still a flour-ishing slave trade carried on by Portuguese ships between southern Africa – particularly the Portuguese colonies of Angola and Mozambique – and Brazil.[169] After these negotiations had dragged on for years, with Portugal remaining steadfast in its refusal to allow inter-ference in its domestic affairs, the prime minister, Palmerston, decided to act unilaterally. Arguing that Portugal was not only failing to meet its treaty obligation to fight the slave trade but was in fact continuing to support it on a large scale, he authorised the Royal Navy by act of parliament in August 1839 to seize Portuguese slavers as they saw fit and to deliver for trial not to the Mixed Commissions, but to the British Courts of Vice Admiralty.[170] The 'Palmerston Act', as it became known, constituted a severe interference in Portugal's internal affairs and met with correspondingly strong diplomatic protests.[171] The government in Lisbon, however, was in so much weaker a position that it could do nothing whatsoever to oppose British measures, instead seeing no option but to sign the new treaty in 1842 and thereby largely to end the slave trade under the Portuguese flag.[172] So complete was this about-turn that in 1843 Portuguese ships began to join patrols off the coast of Angola.[173]

Yet even in Britain, considerations of international law were raised in criticism of this unilateral approach. On signing the new treaty with Portugal, at which the 'Palmerston Act' was suspended, Lord Aberdeen, now prime minister, lost no time in qualifying the measure taken by his predecessor as 'an act very little consistent with the friendly relations that subsisted between England and Portugal; indeed, it was rather an act of hostility, and one which might have led to an intermin-able war, had it been directed against any power of greater weight, and better able to cope with us'.[174] This critical stance did not, however, stand in the way of Aberdeen's pursuit of virtually the same strategy with regard to Brazil. When in the spring of 1845 the government in Rio de Janeiro announced its intention of letting the existing treaties lapse without an option for their renewal,[175] the British prime minister once again brought in legislation for unilateral action.[176] Based on the piracy clause of the 1826 treaty, the 'Aberdeen Act' unreservedly authorised the Royal Navy to seize Brazilian slave ships and bring them to trial in Courts of Vice Admiralty.[177] Upon returning to the office of prime minister, Palmerston further extended the law's remit by authorising the Royal Navy in 1850 to act against slave ships in Brazilian waters, conduct landing operations against slave traders' shore installations on Brazilian territory and to seize ships moored in Brazilian ports.[178] The enormous pressure created by these military interventions and the threat of all-out war with Great Britain, the dominant global power, combined to persuade the government in Rio de Janeiro finally to make a serious commitment to abolition. This ushered in the irreversible demise of what at the time was still a thriving trade in Brazil.[179]

Both the Palmerston Act and the Aberdeen Act give impressive testimony to the fact that, from the early 1840s onwards, Britain was unafraid of carrying out unilateral interventions in the fight against the slave trade and made targeted use of the imbalance of power to bring weaker states into line.[180] What is striking is that, although this course of action had many government figures in London worried about the implications under international law, it drew no meaningful criticism from other countries. Whereas at the end of the Napoleonic wars the seizure of individual ships contrary to international law had caused an outcry, none was now to be heard.[181] When, in August 1839, the Portuguese government addressed a circular to the states signatory to the final act of the Congress of Vienna accusing Britain of a severe breach of international law and of violating the sovereign rights of an independent nation, no diplomatic support was forthcoming.[182] On the contrary, the British government was successful in making its position plausible to the other European powers by presenting them with selected papers documenting the unsatisfactory and inconclusive course taken by Anglo-Portuguese negotiations over the preceding years.[183] Britain further sought to dispel fears that it was overreaching its powers by giving assurances – as a letter from Palmerston to the British ambassador to Paris illustrates – that the Royal Navy would not use its unilateral action against Portuguese ships as a pretext for claiming a right to search ships of other nations, but instead continued strictly to be bound by existing treaties.[184] While Russia, Prussia and Austria had very little to say on the matter either way, a brief remark from Paris merely indicated that Britain's commitment to suppressing the 'crime' of human trafficking had been duly noted.[185]

The extreme restraint with which the other great powers of Europe reacted to Britain's unilateral use of force is a clear indication of changing attitudes to the struggle against the slave trade in international politics in the 1840s.[186] The 'consenting policy of all the civilized world' that Canning, as foreign secretary, had proclaimed at the time of the Congress of Verona (1822) had now become a reality. By concentrated diplomatic efforts over a period of more than twenty-five years the United Kingdom had succeeded in winning over other countries to the idea of abolition and bringing them into an international mechanism of cooperation for the enforcement of a humanitarian norm. An international moral consensus thus emerged, in which human trafficking was branded as a despicable crime against which active and, if necessary, unilateral intervention was justified. Such nations as Brazil and Portugal that stubbornly refused to join this consensus fell into the role of pariah states unworthy of meaningful support from any side – all the more so once the highest moral instance of the Catholic world spoke out against the slave trade. Out of consideration for Spain, Portugal and Brazil, three important Catholic countries, the Roman curia had long avoided a clear commitment to abolition, which after all was a cause identified with Protestant Great Britain. Now Rome found itself compelled to take notice of the changed climate of international politics.[187] In an apostolic letter entitled 'In supremo Apostolatus' and issued on 3 December 1839, Pope Gregory XVI condemned the slave trade as unchristian and strictly forbade both the laity and the clergy from defending the practice as in any way legitimate.[188] It took thirty-two years from the British Slave Trade Act of 1807 for the supreme head of Catholic Christianity to find his way to a moral condemnation of the slave trade – and it seems that fundamental changes in international politics left him with little choice in the matter.

This new international moral consensus was also documented in such core texts of contemporary international law as those of Henry Wheaton, a leading American legal scholar. In the first edition of his classic treatise *Elements of International Law* (1836), Wheaton confidently stated that: 'The African slave trade, once considered not only a lawful, but desirable branch of commerce, a participation in which was made the object of wars, negotiations, and treaties between different European states, is now denounced as an odious crime by the almost universal consent of nations.'[189] Wheaton supported this claim with explicit reference to national laws prohibiting the trade and to such international accords as the final act of the Congress of Vienna and the first treaties made by Great Britain with Spain, Portugal and Brazil. Wheaton went on to discuss the subject elsewhere, in a later treatise even calling the slave trade a 'crime against humanity'[190] and, in so doing, coining a phrase that would become a key legal norm in twentieth-century international criminal law.[191]

In spite of classifying it as a severe crime and recognising an international moral consensus against it, Wheaton clearly positioned himself against the opinion that held the slave trade to be proscribed under international law and the 'right of visitation and search' of ships in peacetime that was derived from this.[192] By staunchly denying such a right of intervention and assigning measures against the slave trade to the realm of strictly national responsibilities, Wheaton gave support to the position of the US government, which would brook no concessions in this matter.

Wheaton's stance within the theory of international law was, however, squarely contradicted by the practice of international politics. More and more states acceded to the treaty regime set up by Great Britain and expressly accepted a right to search in peacetime, thereby increasing the recognition of this new idea of intervention under international law. This principle received a strong boost from an accord between the five great powers of Europe. In December 1838, the British and French governments began new talks with their counterparts in Russia, Prussia and Austria with a view to continuing the process towards a universal abolition of the slave trade that had begun in 1815 at the Congress of Vienna.[193] Great Britain was the driving force and strongly canvassed the support of the other governments, as a letter from Palmerston to the Austrian government shows. Palmerston's proposal was 'to engage all the Powers of Christendom, both on the old and in the new world, in a general League by Treaty to put down the atrocious System of Piracy against the Natives of Africa, which has so long been carried on, to the disgrace of the civilized world, under the Name of the Slave Trade'.[194] He called upon the other countries 'for the Interests of Humanity' to join this international league.[195]

After three years of negotiations, the five powers signed a treaty in London on 20 December 1841.[196] In what was known as the 'Quintuple Treaty', Austria, Prussia and Russia committed themselves to a complete ban on their subjects engaging in the slave trade and declared it an act of piracy.[197] To enforce the ban, the five powers granted each other the right of search in an area extending from the eastern coast of the Americas to the eastern coast of India.[198] Within these waters, their warships were permitted to seize ships suspected of involvement in the slave trade and deliver them to the courts of the country under whose flag they were sailing. As a condition for this, Article 3 of the treaty stipulated that the other treaty partners must be notified in advance of the ships to be dispatched on such missions as well as their commanders, and for each of these ships to carry search warrants authorising them in in the name of the five powers to search suspected vessels.[199] These 'cruising warrants', as one might call them, were limited to the duration of a ship's mission and were to be cancelled as soon as its operations against the slave trade ceased.[200]

This commitment to mutual information and consent was an attempt to equip the treaty with a kind of control mechanism, the purpose of which was to create a degree of transparency with regard to military operations and to counteract suspicions that warrants might be abused to search any merchant ship at will. The traditional continental powers, Russia, Austria and Prussia, had always had far smaller navies than France and Great Britain and, as far as they were concerned, a mutual right to search on the high seas was at most a theoretical benefit. In the event, it was only the Royal Navy that solicited warrants from other countries and was responsible for the treaty's practical enforcement.[201] This does not, however, diminish the importance of the Quintuple Treaty as the first time the Concert of Europe committed itself, in the form of a treaty binding under international law, to the complete abolition of the slave trade. This was a major step that the Congress of Vienna and all its successor conferences had failed to achieve.[202]

This agreement among the Concert of Europe was heard across the Atlantic and gave new life to negotiations between Britain and the United States, which had been deadlocked for eighteen years.[203] On the day the Quintuple Treaty was signed, the foreign secretary, Lord Aberdeen, informed the US government of its provisions. With regard to a possible right to search, he stressed:

[T]he right thus claimed by Great Britain is not exercised for any selfish purpose. It is asserted in the interest of humanity, and in mitigation of the sufferings of our fellow-men. The object has met with the concurrence of the whole civilized world, including the United States of America; and it ought to receive universal assistance and support.[204]

By invoking 'the concurrence of the whole civilized world' in opposing slavery, Aberdeen hoped to win American support for and perhaps even participation in this alliance of Christian powers. Yet a diplomatic rapprochement and ultimately a treaty were achieved only once the principal stumbling-block – the United States' continued rejection of a right to search as an unconscionable infringement of its sovereignty[205] – was omitted from the proposed compromise. The 'Webster–Ashburton Treaty' of 9 August 1842, which begins by settling frontier disputes on the American continent, including between the state of Maine and the British territory of New Brunswick, also included an article in which Britain and America agreed each to put up a naval squadron of no fewer than eighty guns to patrol the African coast.[206] Although each squadron was to be under entirely independent command, the two governments committed themselves 'to give such orders to the officers commanding their respective forces, as shall enable them most effectually to act in concert and co-operation, upon mutual consultation, as exigencies may arise, for the attainment of the true object of this Article'.[207]

This treaty, which was the brainchild of Daniel Webster, the secretary of state, enhanced the American government's standing internationally while leaving it with enough room for manoeuvre domestically. Amid a growing international consensus opposing the slave trade, Washington astutely avoided diplomatic isolation without having to abandon a key principle of its foreign policy. With regard to other countries, particularly Great Britain, the United States could point to its dispatch of a naval squadron as a sign of its active cooperation in the fight against human trafficking. At the same time, any right to search American ships on the part of foreign countries remained taboo, which was of tremendous importance domestically. To an enquiry from the Senate concerning possible consequences of the Quintuple Treaty for the United States, President John Tyler answered that the agreement struck with Great Britain was fundamentally different from the Quintuple Treaty. Above all, it provided for no mechanism of intervention against the United States. Tyler instead repeatedly stressed

that those articles had their origin in a desire on the part of the Government of the United States to fulfil its obligations, entered into by the treaty of Ghent, to do its utmost for the suppression of the African slave-trade, and to accomplish this object, by such means as should not lead to the interruption of the lawful commerce of the United States, or any derogation from the dignity and immunity of their flag.[208]

While recognising the United States' international obligations in principle, such as the cooperation with Great Britain against the slave trade agreed at Ghent in 1814,[209] Tyler left no doubt that such recognition must not come at the expense of American sovereign rights, the protection of which continued to be accorded absolute priority.

This stance was equally in evidence in the rules of engagement issued by the Department of the Navy to the squadrons preparing to sail to West Africa. 'The rights of our citizens engaged in lawful commerce are under the protection of our flag', began Secretary Abel P. Upshur, 'and it is the chief purpose, as well as the chief duty, of our naval power, to see that these rights are not improperly abridged or invaded.'[210] His conclusion was no less emphatic:

It is to be borne in mind that while the United States sincerely desire the suppression of the slave trade, and design to exert their power in good faith for the accomplishment of that object, do not regard the success of their efforts as their paramount interest, nor as their paramount duty. They are not prepared to sacrifice to it any of their rights as an independent nation, nor will the object in view justify the exposure of their own people to injurious and vexatious interruptions in the prosecution of their lawful pursuits. Great caution is to be observed on this point.[211]

With this as the official line, it will come as no great surprise that the United States' African Squadron, which kept a permanent presence in western African waters from 1843 to 1861, did not accomplish much.[212] Over the course of eighteen years, the US Navy seized a mere thirty-six US-flagged slavers.[213] Instead of taking the fight to slave traders, it conceived of its mission rather as protecting American commercial interests in and off West Africa and defending American sovereign rights more generally.[214]

In making such concessions to American reservations against the right of search, the compromise struck with the United States had significant repercussions for the treaty between the five players in the Concert of Europe. The negotiations between Britain and the United States did not go unnoticed in France, where the question of a mutual right of search in peacetime, although it had seemingly been settled, was now revisited. Owing not least to the propagandistic efforts of the US ambassador, Lewis Cass, voices in France again were heard to suggest that granting a right of search to the old rival had been too great a surrender of sovereign rights and that the French government ought to reverse its policy on this matter.[215] Amid an anti-British mood that had spread in France, particularly following its diplomatic defeat in the Oriental Crisis of 1839–41 and increasing economic competition with Britain in West Africa, such criticism fell on fertile ground, culminating in massive resistance to the entire Quintuple Treaty.[216] In the French public sphere, Britain's efforts against the slave trade were once again decried as a humanitarian cloak for British efforts to cement its hegemony at sea and impede French commerce.[217] Faced with such pressure, the French government in November 1842 saw no choice but to decline ratification of the treaty it had signed in London nearly a year earlier and to withdraw its support for the agreement.[218]

Far from putting an end to domestic debates, the French decision only served to strengthen demands for a thoroughgoing revision of the agreements with Great Britain of 1831 and 1833, which remained in force and provided for a mutual right of search. The Webster–Ashburton Treaty was repeatedly cited as a desirable alternative for supposedly allowing the slave trade to be combated without compromising France's sovereign rights.[219] Public pressure was such that the French government reopened negotiations with Britain. A joint commission was appointed to work out a compromise, with naval officers from both countries brought in to contribute military expertise on the practical nature of anti-slavery operations.[220] The upshot of these consultations was a new convention, signed on 29 May 1845 and valid for ten years, which superseded the previous agreements and, with them, the mutual right of search they had granted.[221] Instead, in an obvious echo of the treaty between Britain and the United States, the two parties each pledged to dispatch a squadron of at least twenty-six ships to western African waters.[222]

On the whole, however, the new treaty amounts to a clear avowal of partnership and cooperation, of which Article 2 is only one expression: 'The said British and French naval forces shall act in concert for the suppression of the Slave Trade.'[223] Besides exchanging information and coordinating operations, this also meant that if either country signed an agreement against the slave trade with any African ruler, the other reserved the right to join it.[224] Moreover, it was agreed that the use of force in implementing the convention and any occupation of sections of the western African coast this might entail required the other country's consent.[225] What may at first have appeared as a setback – the abandonment of the mutual right of search – in fact turned out to open up new opportunities. Not only did the new convention serve to intensify cooperation between the two countries off the coast of West Africa; it also contributed to a marked improvement in Anglo-French relations overall.[226]

This resurgence of the debate over the right of search in the early 1840s once more illustrates the principal dilemma faced by the decades-long struggle against the slave trade. As the Napoleonic wars ended, Britain realised that a system of human trafficking that operated across oceans and continents could not be effectively suppressed by national but only by international measures, and accordingly tried to involve other countries in this project directly. Yet these efforts often collided with national sensibilities and the demands of realpolitik, often foundering on the question of sovereign rights.

It was this very constellation that between 1815 and 1845 left Great Britain with no choice but to be adaptable in implementing its foreign policy paradigm of abolition, to explore the possibilities of international cooperation and to find mechanisms by which it might be established on a steady footing.[227] Conferences and commissions as forums for communication were as much a part of this new repertoire of political action as were military cooperation with other countries' navies, establishing a normative order by means of the first international treaty regime and setting up an early form of international judiciary in the form of the Mixed Commissions. In the light of these developments, the struggle against the slave trade that had begun with the Congress of Vienna must be regarded as an important catalyst in the emergence of internationalism – which is to say that a development usually associated with the second half of the nineteenth century can be conclusively traced to the first.[228]

Great Britain, by diplomatic efforts pursued over decades, succeeded in establishing by the 'almost universal consent of nations'[229] that the slave trade was indeed a gross violation of the principles of humanity. No country – not even such stubborn adversaries as Portugal, Brazil and the United States – could in the long run exempt itself from this consensus.[230] Among its early expressions was one of the first international treaty regimes, which extended from the Arab world and East and West Africa via Europe to the Americas and which must overall be seen as a key development in the 'juridification of international relations'.[231] The various treaties were all founded on the idea of using military might to enforce a humanitarian norm and thereby to add to its power. There was no general agreement as to the shape such interventions ought to take, making it imperative to adapt and find flexible solutions. Measures thus ranged from direct and unlimited intervention in the realms of African rulers at sea and on land via the mutual granting by 'civilised states' of the right to search ships in peacetime to coordinated operations by national naval squadrons. This last type of intervention in particular, which persuaded even such reluctant partners as France and the United States to cooperate, meant that from the 1840s onwards, an impressive fleet of some sixty ships drawn from the navies of Great Britain, France, Portugal and the United States were on active duty against the slave trade off the coast of West Africa.[232]

This is not to say that the international military operation launched under British leadership was from the outset a resounding success and that it marked the beginning of a steady and uninterrupted progression leading to the abolition of the Atlantic slave trade. On the contrary, between the end of the Napoleonic wars, which marked the beginning of international efforts, and the late 1820s the slave trade saw a notable increase.[233] And set against the enormous figure of 3.5 million Africans sold into slavery in the Americas throughout the nineteenth century, the number of 200,000 liberated slaves may indeed seem paltry.[234] Building an effective system against the slave trade took decades of diplomatic wrangling, and the effectiveness of measures agreed on was dependent in large part on the willingness of the countries involved to participate in genuine international cooperation. The 1840s marked a breakthrough in this respect, which was reflected in a distinct drop in the number of slaves transported across the Atlantic.[235]

Aside from the unimpressive balance sheet, however, the practical efforts made against the slave trade in the period between 1815 and

1845 combined to produce a new understanding of intervention in which enforcing a humanitarian norm by military means became an instrument of international politics in the nineteenth century. Abolitionism thus became the guiding international norm for humanitarian action and indeed the 'gold standard of "civilization"'.[236] This was elementary to an emerging idea of a European civilising mission, in which the flag of humanity conferred unassailable legitimacy on projects of colonial and imperial expansion. It was from this wider constellation that a distinctive triangular relationship between humanitarianism, interventionism and colonialism (or, later, imperialism) began to emerge.

Part III

Humanitarian Intervention and Its Solidification as an Imperial and Colonial Practice

In all these varied ways it does seem to us that the British squadron has rendered important service to the cause of humanity. It has put down piracy on the African seas, has restored peace and tranquility to a line of sea-coast of more than 2,000 miles; has called into existence a large and flourishing commerce, and, at the same time, has thrown the shield of its protection over the cause of Christian missions, and all the varied agency that has been employed to promote the cause of humanity and civilisation among the benighted inhabitants of this great continent.[1]   J. Leighton Wilson
                                    (American missionary on the Gabon river), 1850

There is a country in Europe ... whose foreign policy is to let other nations alone. ... Any attempt it makes to exert influence over them, even by persuasion, is rather in the service of others, than of itself: to mediate in the quarrels which break out between foreign States, to arrest obstinate civil wars, to reconcile belligerents, to intercede for mild treatment of the vanquished, or finally, to procure the abandonment of some national crime and scandal to humanity, such as the slave-trade.[2]   John Stuart Mill, 1859

7   The Fight against the Slave Trade as a Vehicle for the Colonial and Imperial Penetration of Africa

Abolition and the Idea of Colonising West Africa

The abolitionist campaign against the slave trade played a decisive part in the formation of colonial and imperial designs for penetrating the African continent. It acted as both spur and catalyst. Abolitionism and colonialism were by no means contradictory concepts, but proved altogether complementary and indeed were symbiotically connected at many levels.[1] This connection is in evidence early on, vividly so in the plan hatched in 1787 by Granville Sharp, a leading British abolitionist, to found a 'Province of Freedom' for freed slaves in Sierra Leone, thereby resettling them on African soil.[2] To many abolitionists, this project, centred on the port of Freetown, gave concrete expression to their conviction that the successful colonisation of West Africa would bring a flourishing trade in African agricultural products and raw materials in its wake, thereby making the slave trade economically redundant.[3] Aside from the establishment of a legal economy, the introduction of European 'civilisation' and Christianity in particular were to ensure this project's success.[4] By the end of the eighteenth century, it was abolitionist voices in particular that could be heard to call for increased efforts at colonising West Africa.[5]

A particularly prominent voice in this chorus was that of Carl Bernhard Wadström, a Swede by birth who on his return from an expedition to the Guinea coast joined the circle around Granville Sharp, Thomas Clarkson and William Wilberforce. He provided the abolitionist movement with eyewitness accounts of the horrors of the slave trade that were valuable in rallying support both among the public and in parliament.[6] Yet Wadström also contributed to the abolitionist debate by laying out detailed plans for the colonisation of further African territories, along with the expansion of legitimate commerce to replace the slave trade and, more generally, the spread of European civilisation.[7] In *An Essay on Colonization, Particularly Applied to the Western Coast of Africa*, published in 1792, Wadström developed his programme, which was based on the assumption that

Societies may be divided into the *civilized* and the *uncivilized*; and the duties of the former to the latter are similar to those of parents to children; ... If we feel within ourselves a principle which teaches us to seek our own happiness in that of our offspring; ascending from particulars to generals, we shall also find, that civilized nations ought, for their own advantage, sincerely to promote the happiness of the uncivilized. As the tutelage of children is a state of subjection; so it would seem that civilized nations have perhaps some right to exercise a similar dominion over the uncivilized, provided that this dominion be considered and exercised as a mild paternal yoke; provided also that it be strictly limited to acts conducive to their happiness, and that it ceases when they arrive at maturity.[8]

This paternalistic guardianship under which Wadström wished to see the African population placed was not, however, to be solely in British hands, but rather called for international coordination. Having moved once more, this time to France, Wadström made a public appeal to the revolutionary government to join Britain in taking effective measures against the slave trade.[9] These were to consist of a joint naval squadron, which was to enforce abolition along the coast of West Africa by military power.[10] Moreover, the two countries were to take the lead in an international alliance that would assume responsibility for particular sections of the coastline and 'spread civilisation' there as well as ensuring that the slave trade was suppressed for good.[11] Already existing colonies, such as Sierra Leone, were to enjoy a special status on account of their abolitionist and civilising mission, ensuring their neutrality and protecting from attack even in the case of war breaking out between Britain and France.[12]

Wadström's plans for intensified efforts at colonisation and placing West Africa under supranational European trusteeship did not survive his death in 1799. That they were given no further consideration, let alone implemented, was due above all to the ongoing military conflict between Britain and France, the Napoleonic wars by now being under way. But although for the time being no further abolitionist attempts at colonisation were made, the battle against the slave trade did increasingly come to dominate the European view of West Africa and gradually led to ever deeper engagement, particularly on the part of Britain.[13] In August 1807 the British government assumed direct control of what had been a private settlement project, founded on abolitionist principles, from the Sierra Leone Company and made it a crown colony, officially absorbing it into the empire. Securing Britain's geostrategic position in West Africa against France was of course a factor in this decision,[14] but it must also be seen against the backdrop of the Slave Trade Act, which was passed in the same year and in which the government committed itself to enforcing the ban. The Crown's new possession, with Freetown as its capital and port, provided the West Africa Squadron with a valuable base from which to give chase to slavers. Freetown also became the seat of the judicial bodies set up to try seized slave ships, first the Court of Vice Admiralty under British control and later the various international Mixed Commissions. A further boost to the colony's development came from the fact that Sierra Leone was where more than 40 per cent of the slaves freed by the Royal Navy were landed and settled, thereby providing it with a stable and indeed growing population.[15] The British government's intervention against the slave trade thus contributed in several ways to establishing British rule in African territory, which in the case of Sierra Leone went as far as the assumption of formal sovereignty. More gener-ally, the Royal Navy's missions in pursuit of slave ships led to an increased British presence along the western African coast and hence to increased interaction between Britain and the wider region.[16]

The founding of the colony of Sierra Leone 'as a consequence of humanitarian intervention of the British government and of philan-thropic societies'[17] remained an exception however. Although it estab-lished smaller bases in the Gambia and along the Gold Coast as well as a short-lived outpost on the island of Fernando Pó,[18] Britain displayed no further interest in colonial expansion and assuming the responsibilities of direct rule in West Africa. Here, as elsewhere in the world, the guiding principle of British foreign policy – in the interest of fiscal prudence and under the influence of free trade ideas – was caution in acquiring new territory and a reluctance to make formal annexations.[19] Measures against the slave trade thus consisted largely of the Royal Navy's deploy-ment against slave ships on the high seas; with very few exceptions, they did not include operations on the African continent that would have constituted interference in the domestic affairs and violations of the sovereignty of indigenous rulers. When, after the end of the Napoleonic wars, it set about building an international alliance to enforce the ban on the slave trade, the British government was particularly keen to stress that the military measures under discussion did not have the colonisation of the African continent for their ultimate purpose. As discussed previously, the plan Castlereagh presented to the ambassadors of Russia, Prussia, Austria and France assembled in London in August 1816[20] proposed the creation of a temporary maritime league for the purpose of both combating piracy in North Africa and abolishing the slave trade for good.[21] Of the alliance's purpose and principles, Castlereagh declared that, 'as any attempt at African colonization or conquest might give rise to political as well as military difficulties of considerable magnitude, ... the proposed defensive concert should be purely maritime'.[22] This 'crusade' against the evil of slavery was to be fought in the Atlantic Ocean and not on the African continent, where competing ambitions on the part of other countries might involve Britain in costly foreign policy adventures as well as in political disputes in Africa itself.

This remained Britain's basic position for more than two decades. Yet in the late 1830s, the abolitionist movement revived its ideas for colonising West Africa in an attempt to suppress the slave trade. In so doing, it ushered in a change in British policy towards the region more generally.[23] Sir Thomas Fowell Buxton, a longstanding member of the House of Commons and a leading abolitionist, vigorously argued that a lasting victory against the slave trade could be achieved only by fostering legal economic relations. These were to serve as an alternative to human trafficking and involve the large-scale exploitation of Africa's hitherto untapped resources, such as palm oil.[24] Buxton stated his case in an influential treatise entitled *The African Slave Trade and Its Remedy*, in which he argued for close cooperation with African rulers and held out the prospect of a 'league between England and Africa, – for the suppression of the Slave Trade, – for the spread of commerce, – and for the development of those vast resources which are buried in the African soil'.[25] The book called for a broader change in British policy towards West Africa, as Buxton explained:

It appears to me worth while to adopt an entirely new line of policy, and to establish, to the utmost extent possible, a confederacy with the chiefs, from the Gambia on the West, to Begharmi on the East; and from the Desert on the North, to the Gulf of Guinea on the South. Thus, I have suggested two distinct kinds of preparatory measures. 1st. An augmentation of the naval force employed in the suppression of the Slave Trade, and the concentration of that force on the coast of Africa, thus forming a chain of vessels from Gambia to Angola. 2ndly. A corresponding chain of treaties with native powers in the interior, pledging them to act in concert with us; to suppress the Slave Trade in their own territory; to prevent slaves from being carried through their dominions, and, at the same time, to afford all needful facility and protection for the transport of legitimate merchandise.[26]

As far as these proposals were concerned, Buxton emphasised that the change of tactics – adding to the West Africa Squadron and drawing local rulers directly into the abolition regime – was only to be a temporary expedient, serving the long-term goal of securing the conditions for the wider strategy he had in mind.[27] The 'true remedy' that would ensure victory in the battle against the slave trade was colonisation, which would bring civilisation to African territories and set up a system of legal commerce.[28] With these proposals, Buxton may be seen as having anticipated a theme that would play a key part in debates on humanitarian intervention in the twentieth and twenty-first centuries: the relationship between and compatibility of military and civilian measures, with Buxton giving clear preference to the latter in solving the problem permanently.[29]

In order to put his ideas into practice, Buxton co-founded the Society for the Extinction of the Slave Trade and for the Civilization of Africa,[30] which in the summer of 1841 organised a British expedition to the Niger delta with a view to mapping the region, setting up a model agricultural colony and making treaties with local rulers.[31] Buxton had obtained support for his project from the government, which contributed funds to the expedition as well as dispatching commissioners to the Niger delta, who were to ensure that indigenous princes were incorporated into the nascent international treaty regime against the slave trade.[32] However, the high mortality rate among its white participants – West Africa was at the time notorious as the 'white man's grave' – meant that the expedition soon proved a disaster and was cancelled by the British government in March 1842, after only a few months.[33] The model colony that Buxton and his fellow campaigners had hoped to found as the seedbed for civilising the entire region was never realised. Indeed, the horrible failure of the whole enterprise served as a warning to Britain to avoid further attempts at direct colonisation in West Africa, at least for some years.

Yet the key role of the Niger expedition in changing British policy towards West Africa should not be underestimated, for it truly did mark an important step 'toward a general "forward policy" in West Africa, reversing the established doctrine of minimum commitments',[34] and as such was symbolic of the United Kingdom's 'new African policy'.[35] Although the project for colonisation had been a complete failure, measures that had been much discussed previously and which Buxton had demanded as key elements of an 'entirely new line of policy'[36] began to be implemented: naval operations off the coast of West Africa were ramped up and increasing numbers of treaties signed with African rulers. The turn to a more active British policy towards West Africa heralded by the Niger expedition did not mean an embrace of formal colonialism and the official annexation of territory, but instead employed the techniques of 'informal empire',[37] of which intervention in African affairs based on humanitarian claims was a major part.

Humanitarian Interventionism as Informal Imperialism

Indeed, in 1839 the Admiralty began to reinforce the West Africa Squadron, not least because the Palmerston Act demanded a more aggressive approach to Portuguese slavers. The effectiveness of the Royal Navy in the battle against the slave trade was also enhanced by a change in tactics.[38] Instead of cruising and patrolling the high seas, hoping to encounter a slave ship – which often resembled the proverbial search for the needle in a haystack – British captains began to move their ships to coastal waters close to known slave ports, seeking to put them out of business by means of a naval blockade.[39] In these hubs of human trafficking, slaves were often held for weeks or months in prisons known as barracoons, where they were forced to endure horrifying conditions before being transported to the Americas. It was to these ports, which were often located on estuaries, that the Royal Navy now directed its attentions and which, like the notorious Gallinas river[40] in November 1840, now became the new theatres of the war on the slave trade.

Having blockaded the estuary for several months, Joseph Denman, in command of HMS *Wanderer*, took an official order to liberate an African woman abducted from the crown colony of Sierra Leone and her child as grounds for performing a landing operation with his forces.[41] The amphibious assault succeeded in freeing not just the two British subjects, but a total of 841 slaves from the various barracoons in the port.[42] Denman also forced the local ruler, King Siacca, to sign a treaty agreeing to the demolition of all slaving bases on his territory and the surrender to the British of any slaves held there. The king also expressly pledged to banish all white slave traders from his realm and to prevent their return.[43] On signing the treaty, Denman took immediate action by setting fire to eight large barracoons, dealing the Spanish slave traders a crippling blow by depriving them of their operating bases. The slaves freed by Denman and his men were taken by ship to Freetown and the safety of British territory.

Denman's resounding success at the Gallinas river acted as something of a wake-up call to the other commanders of the West Africa Squadron. The change in tactics marked by the amphibious operation that Denman had undertaken on his own initiative promised a far more successful approach to suppressing the slave trade. Instead of chasing slave ships across the seas with highly uncertain results, this new approach made targeted attacks on slavers at their shore bases, the destruction of which would hamper their activities considerably. These tactics were thus willingly adopted by other commanders, who – like Captain H. W. Hill at the Shebar river and Commander Henry James Matson at Kabenda (Cabinda) and Ambriz – directly attacked the barracoons, liberating the slaves and then burning them down.[44]

The authorities in London endorsed their officer's actions after the fact, expressly praising his innovative approach to furthering the 'interests of humanity'.[45] Commander Denman was promoted to the rank of captain and paid a reward for his efforts.[46] On the whole, the British government welcomed the effectiveness of the new tactics and recommended their widespread adoption, as Lord John Russell, at the time secretary of state for war and the colonies, stressed in a letter written in April 1841 to the governor of Sierra Leone: 'Upon this Subject generally you will understand that HM. Govt. are of the opinion that operations similar to those undertaken by Comr. Denman at the Gallinas, should be executed against all piratical Slave Trade Estabts. which may be met with on all parts of the Coast not belonging to any civilized power.'[47] This was indeed a watershed in the British fight against the slave trade. Military operations that previously had taken place in international waters now shifted to African territorial waters and ultimately to the African continent itself.

The enthusiasm with which Denman's success was received in London was, however, short-lived, for the new tactics raised the question of the lawfulness of such unilateral interventions in African affairs. Considerations of international law and the prospect of criticism from other countries moved Lord Aberdeen, who took over at the foreign office following a change in government, to have the Royal Navy's new approach subjected to legal scrutiny by the Queen's Advocate.[48] On examining the evidence, the Queen's Advocate concluded that:

[B]lockading the rivers, landing and destroying buildings, and carrying off persons held in slavery in countries with which Great Britain is not at war, cannot be considered as sanctioned by the law of nations, or by the provisions of any existing treaties; and that however desirable it may be to put an end to the slave trade, a good, however eminent, should not be attained otherwise than by lawful means.[49]

Britain's new practice of intervention was thus found to be at odds with international law and hence in need of being placed on a solid legal foundation. Until it was, Lord Aberdeen in no uncertain terms asked the Admiralty in May 1842 to instruct its officers deployed to fight the slave trade

to abstain from destroying slave factories and carrying off persons held in slavery, unless the power upon whose territory or within whose jurisdiction the factories or the slaves are found, should by treaty with Great Britain, or by formal written agreement with British officers, have empowered Her Majesty's naval forces to take steps for the suppression of the slave trade.[50]

At first sight, Aberdeen's instructions would seem to have put a stop to the West Africa Squadron's new tactics, and it was indeed open to a fundamental misinterpretation that at first hampered a continuation of effective intervention. To add to the uncertainty of naval commanders, Juan Tomás Burón, one of the slave traders who lost his assets at the Gallinas, sued Captain Denman in person for damages amounting to £180,000.[51] However, in 1848 the court found in Denman's favour, setting a precedent after a trial that had dragged on for years. For its part, the government clarified certain previously misconstrued passages of Aberdeen's directive[52] and in doing so revealed its guiding policy. The idea was not to put an end to the new tactics, but rather to win diplomatic support and to make them unimpeachable under international law. An idea that Buxton had mooted before the Niger expedition – to conclude a 'chain of treaties with native powers'[53] – thus became hugely important. Bringing African rulers into the treaty regime against the slave trade was to provide the crucial legal foundation for Britain's new policy of intervention, and naval officers were accordingly tasked with concluding as many such agreements as possible along the African coast.[54] Between 1841 and 1856 – and particularly in 1847 and 1848 – representatives of the Crown signed a total of ninety-three such agreements with African rulers.[55]

Over the course of this period, the provisions of these agreements were subject to change, for instance with regard to indemnities paid to African rulers in exchange for their signature.[56] At the heart of these agreements, however, were the complete ban on the slave trade in and the promotion of legal commerce with the African territories concerned. Moreover, Britain always reserved the right to impose sanctions and take other measures in case of breach of agreement. This included not only permission for British forces to attack and destroy slave bases in the respective territories,[57] but also the formula exemplified here by Article 3 of the agreement of 25 May 1848 with the chiefs of Camma:

> If at any time it shall appear that Slave Trade has been carried on through or from the territory of the Chiefs of Camma the Slave Trade may be put down by Great Britain by force upon that territory, and British officers may seize the boats of Camma found anywhere carrying on the Slave Trade; and the Chiefs of Camma will be subject to a severe act of displeasure on the part of the Queen of England.[58]

In the name of the humanitarian proscription of the slave trade, these provisions gave Britain the non-reciprocal right to intervene in the sovereign affairs of African rulers on land and at sea.

Committing to this policy of intervention did not, however, mean an end to political debates on the Royal Navy's further operations. Far from it: During the 1840s, more and more voices could be heard questioning the West Africa Squadron's mission, pointing to its lack of effectiveness in stopping the slave trade overall, the burden on the Treasury and the losses among the crews. These 'anti-coercionists'[59] formed a heterogeneous group. Among their supporters were such important Quakers as Joseph Sturge, a founding member of the British and Foreign Anti-Slavery Society, who objected to military intervention on pacifist principles.[60] But particularly prominent were free traders, who saw in the Royal Navy's use of force against foreign ships and now against trading posts on the African coast a severe infringement of peaceful international commerce that placed Britain at constant risk of being drawn into wars with other countries. Accordingly, it was a leading advocate of free trade, William H. Hutt, who was among the fiercest parliamentary critics of measures founded on a sense of 'mistaken humanity'.[61] Demanding the squadron's immediate withdrawal, Hutt brought the following motion to the House of Commons:

That the course pursued by Great Britain, since 1814, for the suppression of the Slave Trade, has been attended by large expenditure of the public money, and by serious loss of life to the Naval Forces of the Country, and that it has not mitigated the horrors of the middle passage, nor diminished the extent of the traffic in Slaves.[62]

Hutt's motion sparked a debate on the future of the West Africa Squadron that was carried on in the public sphere and in parliament for several years.[63] Prominent among the supporters of a policy of intervention were such veterans of the squadron as Denman and Matson, who were eager to defend their actions in West Africa from the criticism that was beginning to rear its head at home. They issued pamphlets to justify their actions and to campaign for the Royal Navy's operations to be continued.[64] They claimed that without such a military presence, the slave trade would quickly revive and bring misery to the African continent. This would also mean that all the advances made by the navy at great cost and over several decades would be undone at the stroke of a pen.[65] These tangible effects on the situation in West Africa aside, Commander Matson viewed withdrawing the squadron as an act of surrender to the system of the slave trade that would have far-reaching ramifications in foreign policy. Suddenly to cast aside so central a policy tenet as the active struggle against the Atlantic slave trade, a paradigm of British foreign policy for nearly forty years, threatened the United Kingdom's standing and credibility abroad. Matson's warning was correspondingly stark:

The security of an Englishman, in his travels and mercantile transactions in Africa, consists in the *prestige* attached to his name. ... It enables the Englishman to go where no other man dare go; it enables the missionary to propagate the doctrines of Christianity, and the trader to extend the arts of civilization over the whole continent. If this feeling be once destroyed, by our retiring before the slave traders, these people will take our place. ... Our dominion in India was at first firmly established by brilliant successes of the British arms, but it is not maintained by the power of those arms alone; it is not an empire of bayonets, but an empire of opinion. May our power in Africa be based on the same solid foundation, and may future generations in that country have reason to bless, and not to curse the name of Britain.[66]

In this political dispute, the naval officers were not content with simply defending the actions of the West Africa Squadron and demanding that its operations continue. Instead they took advantage of the public attention their cause was now attracting in order to make heard their own proposals for improving the effectiveness of operations.[67] The parliamentary select committees set up in the course of debates provided forums well suited to making the case for tactical reforms and better equipment. Whenever he spoke or wrote, Captain Denman was tireless in advocating the model of coastal blockade and direct assault on 'slave factories' that he had pioneered. He consistently emphasised the importance of agreements with African rulers.[68] A debate that had originally threatened to stop the West Africa Squadron's mission was thus recast as being concerned with the means at its disposal and the effectiveness of its measures.[69]

In large part thanks to the support of Russell, by now prime minister, and Palmerston, the foreign secretary, the interventionist side carried the day against a parliamentary motion of the anti-coercionists, again led by Hutt, calling for the squadron to be permanently withdrawn.[70] The political debate left the proponents of a policy of active intervention strengthened, not least by the report of a House of Lords select committee.[71] Having heard the testimony of a number of naval officers, the Lords concluded that the Royal Navy's mission had indeed been effective and that to withdraw it would not only lead to a revival of the slave trade, but would also have deleterious effects on budding trade relations between Britain and Africa and more generally for the spread of Christianity and civilisation on the continent.[72] The report recommended that Britain should strengthen its position by acquiring Danish bases on the Gold Coast and setting up new consulates while also working to foster commercial relations along the western African coast more generally.

To maintain a military presence in the form of the West Africa Squadron was, according to the report, nothing less than an 'essential condition towards the success of every other effort'.[73] The stated goal was thus to make the measures already in place more effective. As well as a tactical dimension, this had a material one, equipping the squadron with the latest steam ships. The committee came out in favour of 'inshore cruising' and the direct assault on slave bases as demonstrated so successfully by Denman. With that case in mind, the committee strongly demanded that officers be given better legal protection against subsequent compensation claims from third parties.[74] The report also stressed the importance of agreements with African rulers in providing operations with a legal basis:

The Treaties concluded with the native Chiefs of Africa are of great value, from the power which they give us of enforcing their stipulations upon the Slave-Trader. Where they have been concluded, no questions can be raised as to the lawfulness of the destruction of the goods stored in the barracoons for the prosecution of the trade – a course of action which (as the evidence of all competent Witnesses proves) strikes the greatest blow at the trade.[75]

In conclusion, the select committee rejected as exaggerated the arguments brought against the squadron's deployment and restated the grave consequences that a withdrawal would have for Britain's international standing: 'That to abandon the suppression of the Trade, to which, in the face of the whole civilized world, Great Britain is solemnly and repeatedly pledged, would be a fatal blow to her national honour.'[76]

These recommendations of the Lords' select committee did much to set the course of future policy, heralding as they did not a reduction of Britain's commitments in West Africa but rather their strengthening, a consequence of which was increased intervention in African affairs. In practice, this meant that the Royal Navy concentrated its efforts on the remaining centres of the slave trade on the African coast, which it attacked with renewed determination. Already in February 1849, Commodore Sir Charles Hotham sailed once more for the Gallinas river at the head of a squadron of seven ships. He performed a landing operation with 300 men to destroy the 'slave factories' that had been rebuilt since Denham's assault – and this time for good.[77] To justify this intervention, Holtham invoked – having assured himself of the support of the Queen's Advocate in London – the violation of the humanitarian provisions in the treaty signed with the local rulers in 1840, which had outlawed the slave trade.[78]

British military interventions were not, however, sparked only by breaches of treaty, but by the stubborn refusal of a number of African rulers to submit to the treaty regime against the slave trade in the first place. Two interconnected examples offer a vivid illustration of this problem.[79] The rulers of the kingdom of Dahomey on the Bight of Benin, which profited enormously from the slave trade and regularly raided its neighbours to take new captives, remained firm in their refusal to commit to abolition even after several years of tough negotiations with British emissaries.[80] Renewed negotiations between King Gezo and the new British consul for the region, John Beecroft, having failed, Palmerston, the foreign secretary, in December 1851 decided to order a comprehensive naval blockade of the port of Whydah (Ouidah), Dahomey's principal slave port and the hub of its economy.[81] The ostensible reason for the blockade was the threat posed by Gezo's raids to British subjects in neighbouring Abeokuta. By means of the blockade, Britain succeeded in forcing the king of Dahomey to sign a treaty in which he banned the export of slaves from his territory.[82] Britain's show of force also persuaded other smaller territories in the region to conclude similar treaties.[83]

More or less simultaneously and under pressure from British settlers and missionaries in the region, the government in London addressed the second area of concern in neighbouring Lagos.[84] Beecroft astutely exploited local rivalries by playing the parties in the kingdom off against one another and using them to advance British goals. To King Akitoye, who had been banished in a coup d'état, he offered British support against his rival on condition of the exiled king acceding to the treaty regime against the slave trade. The new incumbent, King Kosoko, repeatedly rejected British advances, but in December 1851 units of the Royal Navy and allied African troops – after a failed attempt in the previous month – succeeded in capturing the city, which was situated on an island.[85] This victory reinstated King Akitoye to his throne, in return for which he signed the previously agreed treaty on board HMS *Penelope* in January 1852, thereby sealing Lagos' long withheld accession to the treaty regime.[86] This direct intervention in a domestic conflict and the regime change won by force secured an agreement that, in the aforementioned standard phrasing of Article 3, contractually entitled Britain to intervene in the affairs of the kingdom of Lagos in case of breach of the humanitarian ban on the slave trade.[87] This agreement did much to strengthen the British position in the region, both politically and economically, not least because a newly created British consulate in Lagos was tasked with ensuring compliance.[88]

Yet back at home, Britain's policies in the Bight of Benin were far from being uncontroversial even at the highest levels of government. Before the intervention had begun, the First Lord of the Admiralty, Sir Francis Baring, had – with reference to the precedent set on the Gallinas – pointed out the fundamental difference that, in the case of Lagos, no breach of treaty could be adduced to justify military action.[89] Such critical voices were also to be heard in the British press, where serious doubts as to the legitimacy of military action were forcefully expressed.[90] Defenders of the intervention tried to turn the principles of international law, as invoked by the critics, to their advantage. An anonymous apologetic published under the title *The Destruction of Lagos* gave a detailed account of the criminal practices in which the rulers of Dahomey and Lagos had engaged, specifically their incursions into neighbouring regions to capture slaves, which also threatened the property and safety of British subjects.[91] In the light of such conditions, the pamphlet raised the basic question:

whether, on the general principles of the law of nations, such places as Lagos can be deemed to possess rights as States, or be entitled to the observances of international law. It is by the habitual violation of every principle of the law of nations that they exist at all, and the whole civilised world is interested in putting down criminal communities which devote themselves to ruin of every country within their reach.[92]

By acting as a base for slave raids and a hub of human trafficking, the African polity of Lagos had, the pamphlet argued, forfeited its right to be considered a state under international law and the rights associated with that status. This ultimately meant that:

As a nest of piracy and plunder, the destruction of Lagos was a duty owing by civilised nations to themselves, in vindication of the laws of nations, and the principles so long ago laid down by the highest international authorities with regard to the Barbary States, in every respect hold good when applied to Lagos.[93]

Seen in this light, British intervention, far from constituting a breach of international law, was wholly in accordance with the obligations undertaken by 'civilised nations' when they began to fight the Barbary pirates of North Africa in the early nineteenth century. The British squadron was thus making an important contribution 'to the cause of humanity'[94] in Africa – nothing less.

The evident success of the Lagos operation as a fait accompli soon silenced the critics and strengthened the government's resolve to pursue its policy. The combination of military intervention and treaties in the name of the humanitarian cause of abolition thus succeeded in overcoming domestic resistance and became established as an instrument of foreign policy. For the kingdom of Lagos, this meant that it increasingly came under the informal influence of Great Britain and in the end formally lost its independence. Since the slave trade had not been wholly suppressed in the region and raids from neighbouring Dahomey continued to pose a threat, calls were heard – not least from British consuls on the ground – for a tougher line to be taken in the 'cause of humanity, peaceful commerce, and Christian civilization'.[95] Under the impression of these developments and in spite of its general policy of avoiding territorial acquisitions in West Africa, the British in the summer of 1861 decided to annex Lagos officially. In justification of this move, Lord John Russell, the foreign secretary, argued that:

[T]he permanent occupation of this important point in the Bight of Benin is indispensable to the complete suppression of the slave trade in the Bight, whilst it will give great aid and support to the development of lawful commerce, and will check the aggressive spirit of the King of Dahomey, whose barbarous wars, and encouragement to slave-trading, are the chief cause of disorder in that part of Africa.[96]

The government having thus left its position in no doubt, a British delegation backed up by a ship of the Royal Navy set out to convince the reigning King Docemo that it was to his advantage to give up his country's independence.[97] With a warship off the coast and under pressure from an ultimatum, Docemo boarded HMS *Prometheus* on 6 August 1861 to sign a treaty ceding his kingdom to Great Britain.[98] For the better protection of his own subjects and 'to put an end to the Slave Trade in this and the neighbouring counties, and to prevent the destructive wars so frequently undertaken by Dahomey and others for the capture of the slaves',[99] he transferred sovereignty over his realm to the British Crown. After Sierra Leone, this was the second West African territory to be incorporated into the British Empire in its fight against the slave trade, and it soon became something of an 'imperial bridgehead' for the United Kingdom's future political and territorial ambitions.[100] Britain's role of a force for order on the African continent, which had originally been defined decisively by abolitionist motives, was now reframed in view of economic interests and not least because France, too, was increasing its military and commercial presence in the region.[101] With a 'struggle between English and French interest in West Africa'[102] looming in the 1860s, Britain was not going to be left behind.

Seen in a broader perspective, the case of Lagos vividly illustrates the ambiguous aspect of the policy of intervention on humanitarian grounds that Britain began to pursue with regard to African rulers from the middle of the nineteenth century onwards: the use of informal techniques of rule backed up by local military interventions in combination with a well-developed diplomatic machine operating with treaties – and, if this combination failed, formal annexation with scant concern for international law.[103] Whatever the formal and informal aims may have been, however, the period between the first successful operation on the Gallinas river in 1840 and the annexation of Lagos in 1861 marked a decisive phase in relations between Europe's leading power and the

African continent. Under the humanitarian flag of fighting the slave trade, Britain came to pursue a policy of active intervention in African affairs, gradually eroding and ultimately pushing aside its previous paradigm of avoiding such commitments. Or, as David Eltis puts it, 'in the official mind the legal and moral barriers to the European partition of Africa were cleared away in the twenty years after 1840'.[104] The beginnings of 'humanitarian imperialism', which is often associated mostly with the late nineteenth century, are thus to be found somewhat earlier. In the mid-nineteenth century, we see paternalistic patterns of action emerging that were to prove definitive for future relations between Europe and Africa as a whole.[105] Since the emerging pattern of combining military intervention with diplomatic treaties was carried over to the coast of East Africa, the battle against the slave trade must indeed be regarded as the decisive catalyst of European expansionism in Africa.[106]

'When Will the English Come?': The Expansion of 'Humanitarian Imperialism' across the African Continent

In 1863 Dr David Livingstone, a Scottish missionary who had become something of a national hero in Great Britain by exploring uncharted regions of Africa, wrote a memorandum concerning an expedition to the Zambezi river supported by the British government. Based on his own experiences as an eyewitness, Livingstone described the cruel slave hunts in East Africa and the leading role played by Portuguese slavers.[107] The Portuguese authorities, he continued, were apparently unwilling or unable to take action against the slave trade, which continued unabated in Portuguese East Africa.[108] Against the Portuguese government's failure to remedy this state of affairs, Livingston set the model of intervention that Britain had developed in West Africa:

The squadron was expected by keeping the Slave trade in check for a time, to allow Christianity and civilization to put forth their influence, and thus indirectly to eradicate the evil. In the West Coast a large amount of success has followed. ... Stability has been given to various settlements on the coast. Missions have been protected and their efficiency promoted by the countenance and respect shown by the officers; the country dialects have been reduced, and the way paved to the interior by the blessings of peace to millions there, who, before the cruisers came, could only expect marauders from the coast. On this coast [of East Africa], however, the same repressive measures have not influenced in the least the paltry peddling in ivory and gold-dust, which constitutes the trade on the Zambesi; and in addition to the general respect for the English name, we have only the common cry at the whipping post of Tette, 'Oh, for the English!' 'When will the English come?' increasing the rage of the masters.[109]

This no doubt fictitious cry for help, supposedly issuing from Tete (in modern Mozambique), a centre of slave hunts in the Zambezi valley, served for Livingstone to underscore the urgent need for action in the most dramatic manner possible. By means of such accounts, Livingstone and other missionaries and explorers – Richard F. Burton and Henry Morton Stanley among them[110] – succeeded in redirecting the attention of the British government and the wider public, raising awareness of the slave trade in another part of the world. The Atlantic slave trade having been largely suppressed by the 1860s, it was due to the writings not least of such well-known figures that East Africa, where slaves continued to be captured and traded, moved into the focus of international attention.[111] Rather than providing slaves for plantations in European colonies, the slave raids in East Africa supplied the 'Arab' slave market, where demand was as strong as ever.[112] Slaves were captured in the African interior and brought to the coast in caravans before being loaded onto sailing dhows, which usually took them to the island of Zanzibar. From this notorious centre of the East African slave trade, an average of 20,000 African slaves were sold every year to destinations throughout the Arab world and Ottoman Empire.[113] Thousands of Africans were killed in the brutal raids on their villages, by the privations suffered on the long march to the coast or in the cramped conditions on board the dhows, causing entire regions of the East African interior to be threatened with depopulation.

Livingstone's many expeditions had acquainted him with this system of the slave trade, and he regarded it as his foremost duty 'to bring before my countrymen, and all others interested in the cause of humanity, the misery entailed by the slave-trade in its inland phases – a subject on which I and my companions are the first who have had any opportunities of forming a judgement'.[114] However, Livingstone was not content with merely describing the horrific consequences of these raids on the East African population. Since Portugal, the established colonial power in the region, did virtually nothing to alleviate the situation, Livingstone began to call on the government in London to assume the role of a force for order in the interest of humanity. Having defeated the Atlantic slave trade, it was time for Britain to turn its attention to East Africa. Livingstone proposed adopting the model successfully tested in West Africa and accordingly dedicated his lengthy report of the Zambezi expedition to the prime minister, Lord Palmerston, 'as a token of admiration ... of that policy which he has so long labored to establish on the West Coast of Africa; and which, in improving that region, has most forcibly shown the need of some similar system on the opposite side of the continent'.[115] To which he added, in the introduction to the book, a concrete proposal:

I propose to go inland, north of the territory which the Portuguese in Europe claim, and endeavor to commence that system on the East which has been so eminently successful on the West Coast – a system combining the repressive efforts of H.M. cruisers with lawful trade and Christian Missions, the moral and material results of which have been so gratifying.[116]

To Livingstone's mind, the recipe for successfully dealing with the slave trade in East Africa, too, was a combination of military intervention with political action to promote legal commerce and missionary efforts to spread Christianity and civilisation.[117] Another pamphlet, *The Slave Trade of East Africa*, issued by the Church Missionary Society in 1869,[118] likewise treated British policy in West Africa as its key point of reference and wholeheartedly endorsed Livingstone's demands. Here, too, Zanzibar was identified as the heart of the problem. The Arab sultanate was the dominant power in the region, its influence extending along much of the coast of East Africa and its hinterland up to the Arabian Peninsula. As the uncontested hub of the East African slave trade, it was also the single greatest political obstacle to its suppression.[119] The Church Missionary Society's pamphlet accordingly – and quoting from Livingstone's letters to that effect – called on the British government to adopt a stronger line with the sultan and to oblige him by treaty to take effective action against the slave trade.[120]

The idea of bringing East Africa and the nearby Arabian Peninsula into the treaty regime initiated by Great Britain was by this time far from new. In fact, the British government had set a precedent by making a treaty with Madagascar in 1817 and subsequently with several Arab principalities on the Persian Gulf.[121] One such agreement had even been signed in 1822 with the sultan of Muscat, who counted Zanzibar among his possessions and had moved his capital there. This treaty, which was renewed and expanded in 1839 and 1845, was to limit the slave trade overall.[122] Adherence to its provisions, however, depended entirely on the presence of the Royal Navy and its ability to enforce it, if necessary by military power. With British attention focused on fighting the Atlantic slave trade into the 1860s, the Admiralty sent only a few ships to patrol East African waters. Some 6,000 miles of coastline, extending from the Arabian Peninsula to the Cape of Good Hope and with numerous offshore islands and estuaries, were policed by no more than five to eight ships at a time.[123]

Needless to say, this was nowhere near enough for such an enormous task, much to the frustration of the officers deployed on these missions, who had few successes to report and all the more cause to complain of lack of resources. The figures confirm that the sailors were fighting an unequal battle: While an average of 20,000 slaves per year continued to be brought to (and largely sold from) the notorious Zanzibar slave market, the Royal Navy between 1867 and 1869 was able to stop only 116 Arab dhows and free 2,645 African captives.[124] The fact that, after Aden, another Vice-Admiralty Court was set up in Zanzibar in 1866 to try seized ships more efficiently[125] was not enough to conceal that the fight against the East African slave trade for a long time was given low priority in London, far behind the campaign against its Atlantic counterpart.

This situation changed in the early 1870s, when Livingstone and other explorers published accounts of their travels that awakened public awareness of the humanitarian disaster continuing in eastern Africa and decisively contributed to building up political pressure.[126] In consequence, the government in London found itself compelled to take the problem of the slave trade in East Africa far more seriously than had hitherto been the case.[127] As it had done years before in the case of West Africa, it now set up a select committee, which would consult naval officers and government officials familiar with the situation and come up with concrete recommendations for improving the enforcement of abolition in East Africa.[128] The tenor of these expert opinions was that attention should be directed at closing loopholes in the existing treaties with the sultan of Zanzibar, to increase the strength of the naval squadron deployed in the region and to focus on the centres of the slave trade and blockade them.

Looking back at his earlier experience off the coast of West Africa, Rear Admiral Charles F. Hillyar, who had commanded British operations in the Indian Ocean for eighteen months, found a clear lesson to be drawn:

> The death blow to the slave trade on the West Coast of Africa was the capture and retention of Lagos ... I have no doubt that the occupation of Zanzibar, or the cession of Zanzibar to the British Government, would very materially tend to suppress the slave-trade on the East Coast. I think it is the focus of the slave trade on the East Coast much the same as Lagos was on the West Coast.[129]

Hillyar's immediate successor at the head of the squadron, Sir Leopold G. Heath, himself a veteran of the West African campaign, likewise spoke in favour of assuming direct control of the island – as part, moreover, of a wider project: 'But I still hold that the only radical cure will be making Zanzibar a centre from which British civilization can radiate into that part of Africa.'[130] Drawing on their personal experience of the fight against the Atlantic slave trade and the successful occupation of Lagos in 1861, both these naval commanders now testified in favour of taking the same approach towards the East African sultanate.[131]

In the event, the select committee's recommendations fell short of the blunt demands for annexation made by Hillyar and Heath. Diplomatic considerations were the main obstacle. Another major European power – France – had made its own political and commercial interest in the region known and in 1862 itself signed a treaty with the sultan guaranteeing Zanzibar's independence. This all but precluded British action along the lines established at Lagos. The recommendations of the select committee therefore included not only sending more and better equipped ships to East Africa, but also entering into new negotiations with Sultan Barghash bin Said with the aim of securing a more effective treaty and, in the medium term, an end to the slave trade.[132] The select committee also drew attention to the other countries that had economic interests in the sultanate – not only France, but also Germany, Portugal and the United States – and recommended involving them in an international effort against human trafficking.[133] Particularly once the Suez Canal had been opened in 1869, the wider East African region came to take a more prominent role in the economic and geopolitical calculations of all these states – but particularly Great Britain, which had an overwhelming strategic interest in securing the sea route to India, the empire's 'crown jewel'.[134]

The man sent on this delicate diplomatic mission to Zanzibar was Sir Henry Bartle Frere, who as a former governor of Bombay was well acquainted with the problem of the slave trade in the Indian Ocean and was himself an avowed abolitionist.[135] In January 1873 he sailed into Stone Town at the head of four British warships to begin negotiations on a new treaty with the sultan.[136] Talks dragged on for several weeks without getting closer to a compromise acceptable to the British side. Arguing that abolishing the slave trade would spell economic ruin for the island and rouse the Arab ruling class to revolt against his rule, Barghash bin Said refused to make concessions of any kind and categorically refused to sign the draft treaty set before him.[137] Bartle Frere had no choice but to leave Zanzibar empty-handed, although he did instruct the units of the Royal Navy to take an aggressive approach to any suspected slave ships and above all to blockade such notorious coastal slave ports as Kilwa. He argued that Britain, 'seeing no other means open for securing [its] just and righteous demands in the interests of civilization and humanity', had no choice but to resort to such drastic measures.[138]

The government in London soon came out in support of its special envoy's unilateral decision to push for a military solution by officially setting the sultan an ultimatum, threatening to place the entire island under naval blockade if he continued to withhold his signature to the treaty.[139] In view of such a serious military threat, Barghash bin Said was left with no choice but to give in and on 5 June 1873 he signed the treaty.[140] In it, the sultan pledged to outlaw the slave trade in his realm completely and immediately to close the public slave markets. To the Royal Navy he conceded the right to seize slave ships as it saw fit and to have them tried by suitable courts.

Unlike in the case of Lagos, however, and against the vocal demands of two such experienced naval officers as Hillyar and Heath, intervention in Zanzibar did not culminate in its annexation. In combating the East African slave trade, Britain initially refrained from territorial expansion and the formal assumption of sovereignty. Bartle Frere, the special envoy to Zanzibar, gave an accurate account of the British view:

There is a tempting opening for an Empire in East Africa at the disposal of any great naval power; but common honesty forbids us to undertake a great philanthropic enterprise of this kind, and to find in it the coarse material reward of extended dominion; and, if we may not ourselves step in and undertake to do over again, in Africa, what we have done for the good of India, we are bound not to leave the country a prey to anarchy nor open to filibustering operations either of Northern Arabs or any one else. We have succeeded without seeking it, and almost without knowing it, to a dominant position and immense commercial interest in East Africa. We have taken the Arab ruler into the circle of western diplomacy, and made ourselves responsible with another great European power for mutually respecting the independence of Zanzibar and Muscat, and we are now bound to exercise the influence we have thus acquired, for the permanent benefit of the country and its ruler.[141]

To have withstood – as Bartle Frere put it – the temptation of making territorial and hence material gains in East Africa did not, in his view, acquit Britain of further responsibility for the region. Britain's efforts against the slave trade had greatly increased its power and thus imposed an obligation to use its newly won political influence to the (supposed) advantage of the sultanate. In practice, this meant nothing else than making Zanzibar a virtual showcase for informal imperialism. Under the humanitarian banner of abolition, Britain used a combination of military and diplomatic means to compel a sovereign ruler to accede to a treaty reflecting its own policy, thereby exercising decisive influence over his realm's domestic affairs and gradually hollowing out his sovereignty. Since the prohibition of the slave trade had the disastrous economic effects on the island's Arab ruling class that the sultan had anticipated, by signing the treaty Barghash bin Said made his own position dependent on British protection and goodwill. Britain's envoy, Sir John Kirk, a naturalist who had travelled to Africa with Livingstone, was accordingly placed in a powerful position, which he soon used to direct policy in Zanzibar in the British interest.[142]

The struggle against the slave trade continued to form a key area for intervention in the sultanate's affairs. For although the treaty of 1873 had dealt a decisive blow to the slave trade in East African waters, largely ending it but for small-scale smuggling between the mainland and such offshore islands as Pemba, it did not solve the problem as such.[143] The sea now being effectively closed to human trafficking, the Arab slave trade moved to the mainland,[144] with tens of thousands of slaves now being taken northwards on caravans to the slave markets of Arabia. The caravans were crueller still than the sea passage, the forced marches across hundreds of miles exacting a death toll of 30 per cent and sometimes more.[145] Sick and ailing slaves were left to die by the wayside, and the new slave routes were often lined with corpses.

In view of this worrying development, the British government repeatedly tried to bring its influence on the sultan to bear and to persuade him to take steps against the slave trade in his mainland territories.[146] Kirk, the consul general, was well aware of the sultan's difficult position with regard to the slave traders and his own governors on the mainland and assured him of Britain's full support in asserting his authority.[147] Safe in the knowledge of British backing, Barghash bin Said in April 1876 issued two proclamation, banning all trade in slaves on land and placing any involvement in slave caravans under penalty.[148] When open resistance to these decrees broke out in Kilwa, a centre of the slave trade, Kirk dispatched HMS *Thetis* to sail into the town's harbour. This show of force deterred hundreds of slavers from storming the town and allowed the government of Zanzibar to reassert its authority. The ringleaders were arrested in the name of the sultan.[149] Similar disturbances having erupted in Mombasa and elsewhere, the British consul advised Barghash bin Said to put up a military force of his own along European lines, the better to respond to such threats in future. Trained by British officers and equipped with modern British arms, this new intervention force, which ultimately comprised several thousand troops recruited from among both Zanzibarian slaves and Africans freed from slave ships, contributed to stabilising the sultan's regime. Commanded by Lloyd William Matthews, an officer of the Royal Navy deputised to Zanzibar who ultimately entered the sultan's service, it also formed a powerful force against the slave trade, while British troops were spared what were, on account of tropical diseases, highly dangerous missions.[150]

By taking a long-term interest in the affairs of Zanzibar, which in 1890 officially became a British protectorate, the United Kingdom in the early 1880s established itself as the key force for order in East Africa – just as Livingstone and his allies had so forcefully demanded. This position was consolidated by treaties against the Arab slave trade with

Egypt (1877) and the Ottoman Empire (1880). Having triumphed in West Africa, 'humanitarian imperialism' now gained ground at the other end of the continent.[151] Humanitarian intervention against the slave trade, in which Britain had taken the lead, set in motion and ultimately acted as the catalyst for a policy of expansion across Africa, both formal and informal, in which other European powers gradually joined.[152] The idea of abolition paved the way for and legitimised colonial and imperial projects whose motivation was altogether different. 'Anti-slavery ideology', as the historian Richard Huzzey so pithily put it, 'were one of the principal ways that commercial, strategic, spiritual, and moral objectives could be combined.'[153] Such humanitarian motives as the abolition of the slave trade, framed as part of a broader Western civilising mission, became increasingly fused with European countries' commercial and geopolitical interests, which became ever more distinct as the 'scramble for Africa' gained momentum.[154] The symbiotic relationship into which they had entered could be clearly observed at two international conferences that were to have far-reaching conferences for Africa's future.[155]

The International Conferences of Berlin (1884–85) and Brussels (1889–90)

In November 1884 the German chancellor, Otto von Bismarck, invited delegates from twelve European states, the Ottoman Empire and, for the first time, the United States to a conference in Berlin. Its purpose was to regulate the uncontrolled expansion of European countries in Africa and to find peaceful solutions to territorial disputes, which were breaking out not least with regard to the Congo Basin, an area particularly rich in natural resources.[156] In keeping with the style of nineteenth-century internationalism,[157] the participating nations – no African representatives had been asked – agreed to the diplomatic coordination of their future involvement in Africa and to establish shared principles governing European colonialism in the continent. The provisions of the conference's General Act, signed on 26 February 1885, included the freedom of commerce across the Congo Basin, the freedom of navigation on the Congo and Niger rivers, and the terms on which possession might be taken of African territory.[158] Besides obliging countries to notify other signatory powers of their claims, these terms included, as set down in Article 35 of the General Act, the principle of 'effective occupation', according to which territorial claims derived not from the discovery and exploration of previously unknown areas, but by establishing functioning authority within them.[159] In their deliberations, the participants also confirmed the private claims of Leopold II, king of (neutral)

Belgium, to a vast expanse of territory in Central Africa, not omitting to make frequent reference to the monarch's supposedly humanitarian and 'civilisational' intentions.[160] This wide international approval led to the founding, under Leopold's patronage, of a formally independent country, the Congo Free State.[161] The Italian ambassador, Count Edouard de Launay, welcomed it in the most effusive terms: 'The whole world [he said] could not but express its sympathy and admiration for this great work of humanity and civilisation, which was an honour to the nineteenth century and would continue ever more to redound to the benefit of its general humanitarian interests.'[162] Such far-reaching political and economic agreements aside, the Final Act itself contained some consequential humanitarian provisions,[163] which Britain in particular was instrumental in introducing. Great Britain was keen to underscore its claim to leadership at the international level and to use the Berlin Conference for its own diplomatic advantage.[164] In Article 6, the signatories pledged themselves not only to the protection of indigenous populations and the spread of civilisation, but also to the suppression of slavery and the slave trade.[165] In Article 9, they recognised that the slave trade at sea and on land was proscribed under the commonly recognised principles of international law and that by the same token the Congo Basin was not to be used for such purposes, neither as a market nor as a trade route for slaves. It also declared that '[e]ach of these Powers engages itself to employ all the means in its power to put an end to this commerce and to punish those who are occupied in it'.[166] The fact that a core paradigm of its foreign policy, for which Britain had campaigned for much of the nineteenth century – ever since the Congress of Vienna – was now firmly enshrined in a multilateral treaty under international law was an important diplomatic achievement for the United Kingdom.[167] However, the Final Act of the Berlin Conference did not go beyond this statement of intent. Owing to the concerns of certain signatories, including France and Germany, it made no provision for enforcing the international ban it proclaimed.

The Final Act hence had no immediate consequences for the slave trade, which continued in much of the African interior and in some parts even thrived. That the problem did not once more slip from view but instead reappeared on the international agenda with renewed force was due to the efforts of a French cardinal. Charles Martial Lavigerie, who as a priest had already coordinated humanitarian aid for the civilian population during the Western intervention in Lebanon in 1860,[168] was now archbishop of Algiers and Carthage. In this capacity and as founder of a colonial missionary order, the *Pères blancs*, he well knew the horrors of the African slave trade.[169] In the summer of 1888 – fittingly in the same year that Catholic Brazil became the last 'Western' state to officially abolish slavery – the cardinal undertook, with the explicit approval of Pope Leo XIII, a lecture tour of European capitals, where he summoned audiences to a veritable 'crusade' against the Arab slave trade.[170]

In his speeches, one of which he delivered in London in July 1888 at the invitation of the British Anti-Slavery Society, Lavigiere confronted his audiences with detailed accounts of the slave trade from his missionaries in the field, vivid depiction of the horrors of slavery which were calculated to produce an emotional effect.[171] The cardinal also used his platform to remind European governments of the commitment they had made at Berlin and the duty of care they had undertaken, calling on them to act at last:

> It is true that the European governments think of Africa; but up to the present time, they seem to have thought of it only to take possession of it. It is easy to meet in Congress in order to draw lines upon a map, and to parcel out empires; but Christian States cannot forget that duty corresponds with right. The chief nations of Europe, England, Belgium, France, Germany, and Portugal have settled and proclaimed by common consent their present and future rights over Africa. From that moment they had duties towards her.[172]

The prelate left no doubt that, in his view, the responsibility that the states of Europe had assumed for Africa imposed an obligation to act: 'I repeat in one word and very distinctly: to use force for the destruction of African slavery … The evil is too deeply rooted, and too widely spread, to be cured henceforward in any other way until it has finished its work.'[173] Although he continued to advocate charity as the guiding maxim for his missionaries and supported the widespread practice of buying slaves' freedom, Lavigiere was equally convinced that this was not enough to address the problem as a whole and reiterated his call to arms: 'I say again, it is force that is needed, a pacific force certainly, and intended only for defence, but an armed force.'[174] In favour of such a course, the cardinal cited the success of naval operations to stop the seaborne slave trade, while admitting that they had failed to achieve a comparable success on land. This was all the more reason to dispatch ground troops, armed volunteers who were to be sent to Africa to take the fight to the slavers.[175]

Aside from the brief and unsuccessful existence of a military order, the *Frères armés du Sahara*,[176] Lavigiere's idea for an abolitionist volunteer force was never put into practice, chiefly because of the objections of pacifist abolitionists to such a scheme. Nor did the leading European powers have the least interest in allowing an independent force of armed volunteers to operate on African soil. The cardinal's campaign was, however, successful in mobilising a broad section of the European public, and with lasting effect: New abolitionist committees were founded across the continent and the British government in particular felt the pressure to act.[177] One response was military cooperation between Britain and Germany in putting East Africa under naval blockade. Although this was carried out under the abolitionist banner, both countries were guided above all by the suppression of revolts in the region and hence by the prospect of consolidating their own respective interests.[178] Britain also took the initiative at the diplomatic level, suggesting that King Leopold II call an international conference under his patronage to find a solution in international law.[179]

The Belgian king, keen to bolster his reputation for humanitarian involvement in Africa, adopted the British proposal. On 18 November 1889 the signatories to the General Act of the Berlin Conference, joined by delegates from the nominally independent Congo Free State and the sultan of Zanzibar, met in Brussels.[180] The conference was widely hailed in Europe even before it began, with Lord Salisbury, the British prime minister, praising it in the highest terms: 'I do not think any Conference in the history of the world has ever before met for the purpose of promoting a matter of pure humanity and goodwill.'[181] Diplomatic talks lasted several months and were frequently overshadowed by colonial rivalries and conflicts of interest. In the end, however, the assembled representatives signed the General Act for the Repression of the African Slave Trade (the Brussels Act) on 2 July 1890.[182] In the act's preamble, the states expressed their common 'intention of putting an end to the crimes and devastations engendered by the traffic in African slaves, of effectively protecting the aboriginal populations of Africa, and of assuring to that vast continent the benefits of peace and civilization'.[183] To that end, they agreed on an extensive catalogue of measures in 100 articles, amounting to a veritable charter for colonial intervention.[184]

Article 1 of the General Act determined that the most effective means of combating human trafficking in the African interior was the creation of administrative structures, a judiciary, and religious and military outposts 'under the sovereignty or Protectorate of civilized nations' as well as the development of infrastructure in the form of roads, railways and telegraphs. The importation of firearms and ammunition to Africa was to be strictly regulated.[185] Besides providing for the criminal prosecution of slave hunters and traders[186] and for the protection of indigenous populations, the General Act also stipulated the closer monitoring of known trading routes and, where appropriate, the liberation of slaves by force.[187]

Owing above all to Britain's insistence, the fight against the seaborne slave trade continued to feature prominently, and the relevant provisions contain familiar measures of the kind typical of humanitarian interventions from the early nineteenth century on.[188] For instance, the General Act defined an area of sea extending from the Persian Gulf and the Red Sea along the coast of East Africa to the southern tip of Madagascar in which the signatories granted each other a mutual right to search and to seize slave ships.[189] Suspicious ships were to be escorted to the nearest port, where the search was to be conducted by a representative of the country under whose flag the ship was sailing. Detailed stipulations were made to prevent the abuse of flags and concerning inspection procedures, and the signatories also committed themselves to setting up an 'International Maritime Bureau' in Zanzibar, to which each contracting party was entitled to send one delegate. The purpose of this bureau was to ensure the documentation of proceedings under the treaty and to facilitate cooperation between the parties by the exchange of information.[190] From the battle against the slave trade thus emerged an international organisation that was based on African soil and was active from 1891 to 1914.

Many contemporary observers were elated at the outcome of the Brussels Conference, including Alfred Le Ghait, the Belgian ambassador to Washington:

The General Act of Brussels has been resolved upon in the cause of a supreme interest of humanity and justice. It is the expiation of the gloomy errors of past centuries, a renewed affirmation of the principle of freedom of all men; it is, above all, a promise of material and moral civilization for the unfortunate African population.[191]

The ambassador's comments seem to bear out the advance praise from Lord Salisbury who, as quoted above, had heralded the Brussels Conference as 'promoting a matter of pure humanity and goodwill'[192] before the delegates had even met. Even twentieth-century historians can be found praising the General Act as nothing less than the 'Magna Carta of the African Peoples'[193] or the 'Magna Carta of the African slave'.[194]

Such accolades, however, were far removed from reality. For one thing, the General Act left the institution of slavery largely untouched, allowing it to continue even once European government had been formally established in many African colonies and even taking on new forms, such as the exploitation of Africans for forced or indentured labour.[195] The most drastic case of such a 'new slavery' was Leopold II's supposedly 'humanitarian' project in the Congo, which soon turned into a reign of terror that itself became the object of an international humanitarian campaign led by such individuals as E. D. Morel and Sir Roger Casement. Only when the Belgian government assumed direct control of the Congo in 1908 was an end put to the atrocities of the 'Free State'.[196]

Moreover, with its many provisions against the slave trade, the General Act gave sanction to an active policy of intervention on the part of European states under the humanitarian banner of 'abolition'. In effect, it virtually gave them carte blanche under international law to interfere in the affairs of African states or, as Suzanna Miers put it, 'the treaty enabled the colonial powers to justify the entire conquest of Africa in humanitarian terms'.[197] The close interrelation between humanitarian concepts on the one hand and colonial or imperial projects on the other, to which recent scholarship has done so much to draw attention, is thus particularly evident in the practice of humanitarian intervention against the slave trade, in which elements of humanitarianism, interventionism, internationalism, colonialism and imperialism combine to form a highly distinctive amalgam.[198] This is true, however, not only of relations between Europe and Africa, but can equally be observed in other parts of the world and other political constellations.

The Protection of Christian Minorities
in the Ottoman Empire as a Selective
Practice of Imperial Intervention

The Greek Revolution and the 'Eastern Question'

On 22 February 1821 the Russian general Alexander Ypsilantis, at the
head a small band of men, crossed the river Prut, which at the time
marked the boundary between the Russian and Ottoman empires.
Ypsilantis, a scion of an influential family of the Greek nobility and highly
decorated veteran of the Napoleonic wars, was entering the Danubian
Principalities of Moldavia and Wallachia not in the official capacity of an
envoy of the tsar but rather as the leader of the secret 'society of friends',
the Filiki Eteria.[1] Founded in the Greek diaspora, in Odessa, by three
merchants in 1814, the organisation's aim was to liberate, by armed
struggle, the Greeks and other Christian peoples in the Balkans from
the centuries-long Muslim rule of the sultan in Constantinople.
Ypsilantis' scheme was to foment revolt in the Danubian Principalities,
which was to spread like wildfire to Greek lands and other parts of the
Balkans.[2] The timing seemed propitious, Ottoman authority being
weakened and challenged by the separatist ambitions of Tepedelenli Ali
Pasha of Ioannina, ruler of southern Albania, Thessaly, Epirus and
southern Macedonia.

While Ypsilantis' expedition came to a disastrous end – it had been
poorly prepared and Ypsilanti had miscalculated the political constellation, relying on military support from the tsar that never came – with the
defeat of his volunteer army at the battle of Drăgăşani in June 1821, the
situation in the Peloponnese was quite different. There, with the blessing
of the Orthodox metropolitan Germanos of Patras, Greeks had risen in
revolt on 25 March 1821.[3] In the subsequent guerrilla war, they inflicted
heavy defeats on Ottoman forces, capturing a number of important
military bases and thereby bringing large parts of the peninsula under
their permanent control. They soon laid the foundations for statehood.
The first Greek national assembly met in the village of Nea Epidavros
and in January 1822 proclaimed the independence of the Hellenes and a
provisional republican constitution.[4]

These military and political successes allowed the Greek independence movement to consolidate and the uprising to turn into a revolution that posed a serious threat to Sultan Mahmud II's claim to rule throughout the wider region. This, in turn, meant that the Greek war of independence was more than a regional conflict, but one whose geostrategic ramifications made it a highly sensitive international problem.[5] It exacerbated the 'Eastern Question', which was to remain a diplomatic challenge throughout the nineteenth century and even beyond the First World War.[6] The term 'Eastern Question' first emerged in or around 1821 and stands for the intricate international debates surrounding the future of the Ottoman Empire, which was repeatedly shaken by crises of domestic and foreign policy, and the conflicting imperial interests of the great powers of Europe which followed in their wake.[7] So charged was this issue that several times it threatened to blow up the edifice of the Vienna settlement and lead to war between the European powers – as it did, once, in the Crimean War of 1853–56.

A mixture of economic, strategic, and religious and ideological grounds had led the Russian tsars to pursue, beginning in the eighteenth century, a policy of aggressive expansion, which brought considerable territorial gains in the Caucasus and along the northern shore of the Black Sea. The government in St Petersburg attempted to exploit the Ottoman Empire's weakness in order to extend Russian influence in the Balkans and allow Russian shipping access to the Mediterranean through the Bosporus and Dardanelles.[8] Russia's role as patron and protector of the Christian Orthodox minorities, enshrined in the Treaty of Küçük Kaynarca (1774), provided Russia with welcome grounds for repeatedly bringing considerable influence to bear on the domestic affairs of the Ottoman Empire.[9] For their part, Austria, France and Great Britain had a strong interest in preserving the sovereignty and integrity of the Ottoman Empire, albeit weakened, as a strategic buffer against Russian expansion.[10] The collapse of the multi-ethnic empire and the power vacuum it would leave in the eastern Mediterranean were to be prevented at all costs. Britain and France already had conflicting commercial and particularly imperial interests in the region, as Napoleon's Egyptian expedition (1798–1801) and Britain's tough action to suppress it had already proved.[11] Britain's main interest lay in securing the shortest route of communications with India, the 'crown jewel' of its empire, which passed through Ottoman territory. The opening of the Suez Canal in 1869 gave renewed urgency to such considerations.

In spite of these strongly competing interests, the great powers of Europe at first succeeded in finding a shared position with regard to the 'Greek question' and to maintain strict neutrality in the matter. Even the many direct appeals by the Greek provisional government asking the Christian monarchs to come to the aid of their co-religionists oppressed by 'Muslim barbarians' in the name of religion, peace and humanity did nothing to sway the Concert of Europe.[12] A series of diplomatic talks succeeded, above all owing to the intense effort of Britain and Austria, in averting the threat of unilateral Russian intervention. Russia, as already indicated, was connected to Greece by close political and religious ties, not least in the person of Ioannis Kapodistrias, the Russian foreign minister and later the first president of Greece.[13] Tsar Alexander I's decision not to intervene was guided above all by the desire not to threaten existing alliances and amicable relations with the other major powers by stepping out of line on the Greek question.[14] As a member of the Holy Alliance, Russia had only recently, in November 1820, signed the Troppau Protocol with Austria and Prussia, committing the three powers to a paradigm of anti-revolutionary intervention that was rigorously applied against the liberal revolutions in Italy and Spain.[15] Against this background, Russian intervention on behalf of the insurgent Greeks, who after all were in revolt against what conservative monarchs could only consider the legitimate rule of the sultan of Constantinople, could only have discredited the Russian stance.

Historians have tried to interpret the fact that Russia, France and Great Britain did finally give up their neutrality and in various ways intervened jointly in the Greek war of independence at the Battle of Navarino in October 1827. Geostrategic factors have long been known to have played a large part, but recent historical scholarship has increasingly focused on humanitarian aspects. Gary Bass and Davide Rodogno have interpreted the naval intervention of the three great powers as the birth of the modern concept of humanitarian intervention. The purpose of this first appearance of the new practice in international politics had accordingly been to put an end to an increasingly savage war and the attendant massacres of the Christian population.[16]

What is left open by these interpretations, however, is the question of how these humanitarian impulses came about in the first place and were able to set off this mechanism of reaction. What had prepared the ground – both nationally and internationally, both in politics and the military – for the idea of collective military intervention for humanitarian ends, allowing it to spread and establish itself? The answer to this question lies in the new understanding of intervention that had taken hold since the early nineteenth century and that had been shaped by abolitionist campaigns. The idea of a humanitarian intervention in Greece did not appear out of nowhere, but grew from the meaningful alliance which humanitarianism and interventionism had formed in the struggle against the slave trade. The problem of enslavement and human trafficking was connected to the bloody conflict in the Levant in manifold ways.

Humanitarian Mobilisation and the Stigmatisation of the Ottoman Empire

One of the distinctive traits of the Greek war of independence was the extreme brutality and cruelty with which it was fought by both sides. Violence spiralled out of control and numerous massacres were perpetrated against the civilian population, often wiping out entire settlements. Having besieged and then captured Tripolitsa, the strategically important capital of the Peloponnese, Greek forces murdered the larger part of the Muslim and Jewish population. An orgy of violence continued for three days and claimed more than 8,000 lives. The insurgents left a trail of destruction as they advanced across the peninsula. Often encouraged by Orthodox priests, they showed no mercy to Muslims, killing more than 20,000 in the first months of the war alone.[17] Male prisoners were usually put to death immediately, while any women and children who had survived the attacks were enslaved. Anyone who could escape did so, and the Muslim population took flight across the Peloponnese.[18] On the Ottoman side, news of the revolt and the atrocities accompanying it led to savage retaliation against Greek Christians living elsewhere in the Ottoman Empire. The most prominent victim was Gregory V, patriarch of Constantinople, who was arrested on the orders of Sultan Mahmud II as he left the cathedral after the Easter mass. He was hanged in his robes from the gate of the episcopal residence for two days and his mutilated corpse thrown into the Bosporus. The Muslim population in Constantinople and in Greek communities elsewhere – in Smyrna (Izmir) in Asia Minor, in Salonika, Cyprus and Crete – committed a number of brutal massacres on Christians.[19]

Although neither side was to be outdone in terms of sheer brutality and showed no compunction in attacking civilians to the point of complete destruction – Jürgen Osterhammel has described these events as 'a harbinger of later ethnic cleansing in the region'[20] – the European public took notice almost exclusively of the atrocities against the Christian population, while Muslim suffering barely registered. Numerous articles in the press and the reports of European consuls in the region provided detailed if one-sided information and began to turn public interest towards the plight of the Greek Christians. Of critical importance in rallying public opinion was the massacre of Chios, one of the bloodiest episodes of the entire war.[21] After Greek insurgents had landed on this prosperous island in the eastern Aegean, only a few kilometres offshore from the mainland of Asia Minor, bringing parts of it under their control, the Sublime Porte in April 1822 sent a naval force of 4,000 men to recapture it. Ottoman retaliation was of the utmost brutality, with troops plundering and burning Greek villages, murdering an estimated 25,000 Greeks and abducting another 45,000, most of them women and children, and taking them to the slave markets of the Ottoman Empire. In a letter to the foreign secretary, Lord Castlereagh, the British ambassador to the Porte, Lord Strangford, described the situation in the following terms:

My Lord, The Transactions at Scio appear to have been of a most horrible description, and the ferocity of the Turks to have been carried to a pitch which makes humanity shudder. The whole of the Island with the exception of the Twenty-four Mastic Villages, presents one mass of ruin. The unfortunate Inhabitants have paid with their lives, the price of their ill-advised rebellion – The only persons who have been spared are the women and children, who have been sold as slaves.[22]

News of these horrific events in the islands, supposed by many to be the birthplace of Homer and with commercial ties across Europe as a major producer of mastic, caused an outcry throughout the capitals of Europe. At the diplomatic level, Lord Strangford registered his protest against the brutality of its forces with the Sublime Porte and demanded mercy for innocent civilians. Gianib Effendi, the head of the Ottoman foreign ministry, staunchly rejected such appeals as interference in his country's internal affairs, citing Muslim law, according to which the prisoners of Chios, as rebels, were lawfully condemned to slavery.[23] He did not omit to mention that the Christian states of Europe had themselves engaged in and profited from the trade for centuries. Britain, he added, had outlawed the trade only a few years ago, while half the countries still practised it.[24] Gianib Effendi refused to countenance any criticism of slavery as a punishment, accusing the European powers of double standards: 'Why do not the Christian Sovereigns interfere to prevent the Emperor of Russia from sending his subjects into Siberia? Because they know very well what answer they would receive! Thus there is one law of humanity for Turkey and another for Russia!'[25]

Throughout the summer of 1822, British and French newspapers kept their readers up to date on events in the eastern Aegean. *The Times* published an urgent appeal from the Greeks of Constantinople, in which the atrocities in Chios were described in some detail. The plight of the survivors, their enslavement by Muslims, was also discussed in evocative terms: 'The Slavery of so many respectable women, young people, and children of both sexes, sent off to different parts of Asia – the markets of

this city and Smyrna filled with women and young people of the first
rank, and who have received the best education! What can be more
dreadful than this?'[26] The Reverend Thomas S. Hughes, a Cambridge
don who had published accounts of his travels in Greece before the war,
now produced a pamphlet in which this theme also figured prominently.
It was scandalous, Hughes wrote, to find the daughters of Homer's native
island being sold 'at a price less than cattle in a market to Asiatic
barbarians and to African Moors'.[27] In view of such a catastrophe, he
called all readers to immediate action – particularly the abolitionists,
whose cause was directly affected:

> And you, the advocates of philanthropy in our senate, who have so often
> proclaimed the sorrows and vindicated the rights of suffering humanity, who
> have extended the arm of power to the relief of the captive African, why are ye
> now silent? I would be the last person to suppress generous feelings for human
> misery under any shape; but what are the pains of hunger, of captivity, or of death
> itself, what are the suffering of the Indian slave, or Irish peasant, compared with
> those horrors which overwhelm the wretched daughters of unfortunate Greece?
> Speak out therefore in this cause, or boast no more your philanthropic
> sentiments![28]

A parliamentary motion in Westminster put the massacre of Chios on the
agenda of both houses.[29] In the Commons, William Wilberforce, the
eminent veteran of many an abolitionist campaign, demanded military
action on the part of the British government to preserve the Greeks from
slavery and destruction. Wilberforce went so far as to demand that
the Ottomans, as a 'nation of barbarians' and ancient enemy of
Christendom, be pushed back into Asia.[30] Speaking in the House of
Lords, Earl Grosvenor likewise spoke in favour of active British intervention. Given that Britain had abolished the slave trade and was doing its
best to persuade other nations to follow suit, Grosvenor hoped 'that their
lordships would not think it unworthy of their dignity to consider the
state of unfortunate Christian slaves, on whom cruelties had been committed, which had excited the greatest horror throughout the country'.[31]

Speaking from the government benches, Castlereagh rebuffed such
demands and reminded the advocates of intervention that the Greek
insurgents were fighting no less brutal a campaign.[32] The prime minister,
Lord Liverpool, added that atrocities were being visited by the Sublime
Porte on its own subjects, in which case Britain had no right to intervene.
Liverpool instead warned that interfering in the domestic affairs of the
Ottoman Empire would set a dangerous precedent for arbitrary interven-
tion. Other countries – such as Spain or France – might conceivably take
it as justification for intervening in an armed conflict in Great Britain.[33]
Against parliamentary demands for a more active policy of intervention,

the British government stuck to its policy of non-intervention, from geostrategic considerations and with a particular view to the 'Eastern Question'. Whereas Russia broke off diplomatic relations with the Porte, Castlereagh left it at a note of protest, threatening to withdraw the British legation from Constantinople if such an atrocity were to be repeated.[34]

Such massacres as that of Chios were far from triggering an automatism of intervention. Like Great Britain, France and Russia withheld direct military action and limited themselves to diplomatic protests. Yet while the great powers, from strategic considerations, remained guarded in their response to the Greek question, civil society throughout Europe rallied to the cause of Greek independence almost from outset. Enthusiasm for ancient Greece as the cradle of European civilisation, as it grew in art, literature and scholarship from the late eighteenth century onwards, provided the foundation on which political philhellenism could take hold.[35] In this intellectual climate, news of such horrific events as those in Chios acted as a catalyst. In many European countries – in Spain and Switzerland, in the German and Italian states, in Denmark, Sweden, Hungary, Britain, France and Russia – and even in the United States, philhellenic committees were set up. These committees formed an international network, and exchange between them was often very lively.[36] They solicited donations to buy guns, ammunition, food and medicine, which were sent to the insurgents. Russian philhellenes not only took charge of feeding and housing the many refugees arriving in Russia, but also made efforts to buy the freedom of enslaved Greek Christians in the Ottoman slave markets.[37]

In western Europe, too, various philhellenic societies organised relief efforts for displaced Greeks. Above all, however, they recruited volunteers to fight for the cause. Somewhere between 1,000 and 1,200 philhellenes of various social backgrounds and nationalities sailed for Greece from such ports as Marseille, Trieste and Ancona to fight the Ottomans at the side of the Greek insurgents.[38] The most colourful character among them was no doubt George Gordon, Lord Byron. The romantic poet, something of a 'European media celebrity' of his age,[39] answered the philhellenic call, but died of a fever soon after arriving at Missolonghi in April 1824. Byron's importance was hence not of a directly military nature – he had no relevant experience and participated in no major operation – but lay in his propagandistic value. On his untimely death, he was declared a symbol of and a martyr for Greek independence, and as such mobilised immense enthusiasm throughout Europe.[40]

The philhellenes provided not only practical and material support, but tried to rally a wider public to the Greek cause. The point was not just to increase donations, but also to exert political pressure on the hesitant governments of the Concert of Europe and to force them finally to intervene on behalf of the insurgents. To this end, philhellenic authors across Europe wrote countless newspaper and magazine articles as well as pamphlets and handbills, some of which were translated and distributed abroad through international networks of like-minded campaigners.[41] The concepts of humanity, Christianity and freedom – '*l'humanité, le christianisme, et la liberté*', as the first Greek committee of Geneva had put it in its 1821 appeal – were the key recurring tropes in an intense publicity campaign.[42] They formed the conceptual frame of reference by which the philhellenes sought to justify their efforts on behalf of the Greeks and win supporters. At the same time, campaigners foregrounded Ottoman atrocities such as massacres and the enslavement of Christians, thereby framing the Greek war of independence as an elemental struggle between Western Christian civilisation on the one hand and Islamic or 'oriental' barbarism on the other.[43] The events in the island of Chios, situated as it was at the geographical boundary between Europe and Asia, was thus eminently suitable as a potent symbol of 'Turkish atrocities' in the European public sphere. This contributed to a general stigmatisation of the Ottoman Empire as an uncivilised, despotic and hence 'oriental' state, against which it was the duty of all Christian nations to act jointly.[44]

Although they adopted certain humanitarian practices, such as refugee relief or buying slaves' freedom, and in their published writings repeatedly invoked the concept of humanity, it would be mistaken to categorise the philhellenes as a genuinely humanitarian movement. Nor were they, as Gary Bass has claimed with particular reference to the British philhellenes, one of the first human rights organisations and as such the 'unmistakable ancestors of Amnesty International and Human Rights Watch'.[45] The activists' goal was not to advance general humanitarian norms or universal human rights – certainly not for the Muslim population – but to support the Greeks' armed struggle against Ottoman rule. To this end, the philhellenes chose a political strategy that was to prove characteristic of national independence movements and their supporters, particularly in the twentieth century and indeed to this day. They connected the goal of national independence with a humanitarian cause in order to enhance the appeal of their campaigns and thereby to increase the pressure on political decision-makers to act accordingly.[46]

Especially in Britain and France, where such philhellenic groups as the London Greek Committee and the Société de la morale chrétienne were also strongly supported by abolitionists, the international humanitarian campaign against the slave trade served as a model.[47] From this successful example, activists adopted such proven mobilisation devices as pamphlets, handbills and parliamentary petitions. They also understood the value of potent visual images. Everyday objects such as inkwells, vases, jewellery boxes, wine flasks and clocks were decorated with images of dying warriors and Greek maidens in distress, images that also appeared in lithographs and large-scale historical paintings.[48]

Among the many contemporary works explicitly depicting the suffering of Greek civilians caused by the war, those of the French painter Eugène Delacroix deserve particular mention, both for their artistic significance and for their immediate impact. Inspired by dramatic tales of the massacre of Chios, Delacroix painted a large canvas with the descriptive title 'Scènes des massacres de Scio; familles grecques attendent la mort ou l'esclavage'.[49] It depicted a group of captive and dying Greek islanders – men, women and children – at the mercy of Ottoman soldiers and their blind fury. When in 1824 the painting was first exhibited before a large audience at the Paris Salon, it created a stir even beyond France. Two years later Delacroix presented another painting, 'La Grèce sur les ruines de Missolonghi', at a charity event for the benefit of the Greek cause.[50] The subject matter now was the dramatic siege of the town of Missolonghi, from which the Greeks had tried to break out only to be massacred by Ottoman troops. As an allegory of the Greek nation in distress, Delacroix placed at the centre of his painting a woman, who, kneeling on the town's ruins with her native costume dishevelled, lifts her arms in a plea for help. A dark-skinned Ottoman soldier is discernible in the background. The symbolism of white Christian women being pursued and enslaved by 'black Muslim barbarians', with its subtext of sexual violence and exploitation, was highly emotive to contemporary European viewers.[51] Yet the imagery was also related to the tradition of the humanitarian visual narratives that had emerged in abolitionist campaigns against the slave trade. By vividly depicting the suffering of innocent victims, they sought to elicit sympathy for the plight of the Greeks and thus served as direct appeals for the mobilisation of help and support.

Alongside these tried and tested abolitionist devices, British and French philhellenes also became increasingly adept at linking the substance of their own cause to what was fast emerging as the humanitarian gold standard in international relations, the prohibition of the slave trade. Decades of public agitation and controversy had created a climate of public and political opinion in Britain – but also in France – of which the philhellenes tried to take advantage. Some British activists accordingly made much of the image of Greek Christians being enslaved by Muslims and drawing a direct parallel with the African slave trade. An example was Charles Brinsley Sheridan, whose father had been a friend of Lord Byron's. In 1822 Sheridan published a pamphlet entitled *Thoughts in the*

Greek Revolution and complaining of a lack of support for the Greeks – even though, in Sheridan's view, theirs was a cause 'which, like the abolition of African slavery, need not incur the imputation of party-feeling or interest, but might be advocated on the purest grounds of universal philanthropy'.[52] Sheridan drew a direct compassion between the plight of enslaved Greek women and children with African slavery, a comparison that informed his final plea:

> When we abolished the slave trade, we sacrificed avarice and prejudice at the altar of mercy, and we have not yet talked of relieving the Greeks. Unless all feeling is paralyzed, and numbness has crept over our souls, this disgraceful apathy must end; but it may last till we have earned disgrace, which regret will not wash away; and have given the foreigners, who envy and hate our pre-eminence, the triumph of seeing all, that they calumniously said of our mercantile selfishness, miraculously verified.[53]

Sheridan was here referring to accusations, repeatedly brought from abroad, that the United Kingdom was pursuing its strict paradigm of international abolition not from altruistic, humanitarian motives, but rather in its own commercial interest and to weaken its colonial competitors.[54] In his view, British wavering could only help to confirm such critics and was as damaging to the credibility of Britain's foreign policy as it was to its reputation as a sincere humanitarian actor.

In a pamphlet purporting to be an open letter to Lord Liverpool, Thomas Erskine, Baron Erskine, a renowned legal scholar and former Lord Chancellor, even went so far as to suggest that the horrors of the African slave trade paled in comparison to those of the Greek war.[55] This was, he argued, because, unlike the Africans, who as 'savages' subsisted in a state of nature, the Greeks were brutally torn from civilization and many of them carried off to the East for horrific sexual exploitation.[56] The stance Britain had taken against the slave trade obliged the country to act in this case, too:

> It appears to me, indeed, that the abolition of the Slave Trade, which raised this nation above all created beings since the beginning of the world, cannot be said to be complete not only whilst such monstrous abuses of slavery are predominant, but whilst any traffic in human beings whatsoever is suffered to exist.[57]

The former Lord Chancellor thus deftly linked the key foreign policy paradigm of abolition with intervention on behalf of the Greeks. Erskine also reminded his readers that in fighting the African slave trade, Britain had not been content to pass national legislation, but had also tirelessly worked to persuade other countries to do likewise – and had not been afraid to use compulsion if needed.[58] At a time when Britain was making a concerted diplomatic effort to bring as many countries as possible under an international treaty regime against the slave trade, Erskine decided to measure his government by the standard of this foreign policy paradigm in the interest of the Greek cause, which he had made his own.[59]

A pamphlet published in 1825 under the pseudonym of 'Ricardus Incognitus' followed this line of argument, explicitly linking the plight of the Greeks with that of African slaves.[60] The pamphlet also made much of the alleged sexual exploitation of enslaved Greek women and children by the 'barbarous' Turks and came to a somewhat startling conclusion:

> These tyrannical, cruel, degrading, and abominable scenes of slavery, above-mentioned, far exceeds what the natives of Africa have to suffer, when enslaved, in any part of America or Europe; he is not subjected to these abominable cruelties, as the law prevents him from suffering under any of the before-mentioned modes, by inflicting punishment upon the aggressors. The black slaves are free in comparison to the Greeks.[61]

From Britain's commitment to fighting the slave trade, 'Ricardus Incognitus' deduced an obligation to intervene on behalf of the oppressed Christian Greeks, whose civilization stood far above that of the indigenous Africans:

> It is my sincere wish that the slave-trade may be totally abolished. But, as there has much been done by this country, both for the civilization of the native Africans and many other people of the world, besides the abolishing of the slave-trade, which is nearly effected at present on the coast of Africa; but how much more reason have we to turn our attention to the case of the Greeks and commisserate [sic] their feelings? How much more must he feel than the native of Africa, who never knew the blessings of liberty, and whose feelings are not hurt by slavery?[62]

Beyond the Channel, too, prominent French philhellenes consciously began to establish a link between the trades in 'black' and 'white' slaves. In March 1826 François-René de Chateaubriand, his country's former foreign minister and known outside politics as one of the founding figures of literary romanticism in France, spoke before the Chambre des Pairs, the upper house of the French parliament. Chateaubriand, who in the previous year had already published a *Note sur la Grèce* arguing in favour of an intervention of the great powers in the Greek cause,[63] now proposed that the phrase 'trafic connu sous le nom de la traite des noirs' in the French abolition act of 1818 be replaced with the broader 'trafic des ésclaves'.[64] The reason he gave was that under French law, French subjects were prohibited from trading in black, but not in white slaves – a monstrous anomaly in view of the fact that

Christian women and children were being enslaved every day and sold in the slave markets of the East.[65] The protection of fellow Christians, Chateaubriand argued, must not take second place under French law to that of African slaves.

The proposed amendment was criticised for implying French participation in the white slave trade, which Chateaubriand vehemently refuted.[66] He very much hoped, he said, that none of his compatriots were involved. And the legal consequences of the change would indeed have been negligible, which is why Chateaubriand stressed its symbolic importance. He read from a letter supposedly written by a fifteen-year-old boy, several times wounded in defence of the besieged Greek city of Missolonghi.[67] Since French officers were participating in the siege on the Ottoman side, the boy criticised France heavily, accusing it of betraying the Greek cause. The proposed amendment would do much to counter such charges, Chateaubriand argued, and concluded his speech with an appeal to the assembled peers and ministers: If France would not help Greece by force of arms, the least it could do was to signal its disapproval of the crimes perpetrated against it by passing appropriate legislation. France should set a noble example and lead Europe on the path to a more humane policy.[68] The former foreign minister was thus able to use the debate over his proposed amendment to raise the Greek question in the highest body of the French legislature and bring to its attention the sufferings of the Greek people.

In both Britain and France, philhellenic campaigning succeeded in lodging the Greek struggle for freedom in the public imagination and mobilised both goodwill and material support for the cause. The activists, who counted among their number such celebrated writers and artists as Byron and Delacroix as well as members of the political establishment, from Wilberforce to former cabinet ministers such as Erskine and Chateaubriand, whose voices were heard in the highest echelons of parliament and government. Between them, they increased political pressure on the governments in London and Paris, gradually eroding their resistance to intervention in Greece.[69] Moreover, by deliberately linking the Greek question with the abolition of the slave trade, the philhellenes were able to give humanitarian weight to their cause and thereby make intervention seem both plausible and acceptable. For the United Kingdom in particular, which at the time was unflagging in its campaign to secure international abolition through diplomatic channels, the question soon became one of the integrity and credibility of its foreign policy. Amid such a political climate, a well-placed rumour concerning an alleged 'barbarisation plan' was apt to trigger a chain reaction among the great powers.

International Intervention in the Greek
War of Independence as a Precedent

The year 1825 marked a watershed in the Greek war of independence. While the Concert of Europe was still holding talks with the aim of reaching a diplomatic solution to the Greek question and securing lasting peace on the continent,[70] Sultan Mahmud II pushed for a decision on the battlefield. Having suffered military defeats and severe setbacks against his Greek subjects, he sought help from one of his most powerful vassals, the governor of the Ottoman province of Egypt, Muhammad Ali Pasha. Muhammad Ali ruled largely independently of the government in Constantinople and had built a powerful modern army and navy along European lines with the help of French officers, drawn mostly from the ranks of Napoleon's expeditionary force.[71] In return for the sultan's promise to make his son Ibrahim governor of the Greek territories, Muhammad Ali mobilised his forces for their reconquest. A huge armada of nearly 400 ships carrying some 17,000 men sailed under the command of Ibrahim Pasha and, after quelling revolts in Crete, landed in the Peloponnese late in February 1825.[72] The Greek insurgents, greatly weakened by an internecine war between rival factions, were no match for a disciplined and well-trained army under a seasoned and strategically astute commander. Ibrahim captured one Greek stronghold after another, reconquering the Peloponnese with savage cruelty, leaving a trail of destruction in his wake and carrying prisoners off to Egypt as slaves.[73] A few holdouts aside, large parts of the peninsula were thus brought back under Ottoman control. By the autumn of 1825, the Greek cause was looking quite hopeless and the insurgents, although Britain had twice loaned them money, were exhausted both financially and militarily as well as being divided among themselves. Hopes for a free and independent nation of the Hellenes seemed to recede ever further.

Yet in spite of his apparently resounding military success, Ibrahim's advance across the Peloponnese was something of mixed blessing for the sultan. The dramatic reversal undergone by Greek fortunes shook up the great powers of Europe and forced them to reconsider and ultimately overturn their position. Russia in particular was opposed to Egyptian rule in Greece, which the sultan in Constantinople supported, and now pressed its European partners to abandon their position of neutrality and to intervene in the conflict.[74] While Metternich, speaking for Austria and thus laying the policy that Prussia would follow, remained committed to a policy of non-intervention and secretly hoped that the Greek question would soon be resolved for good by a victory of Egyptian arms, Great Britain was quite willing to consider the Russian démarche.

The governments in London and St Petersburg were finding new common ground.[75] As part of Russian efforts to persuade Britain of the need to take joint action, the Russian ambassador to London, Christopher Lieven, in 1825 turned to George Canning, who had become foreign secretary after Castlereagh's suicide in 1822. In private conversation, Lieven told Canning of a supposed deal between the sultan and his Egyptian satrap, according to which the Sublime Porte had promised Ibrahim Pasha not only rule over all reconquered Greek territory, but also support for his plan 'to remove the whole Greek population, carrying them off into slavery in Egypt, or elsewhere; and to re-people the country with Egyptians, and others of the Mahometan religion'.[76] This story of Christian slavery and population exchange was planted by Russia at a time when the British government was trying to win international support for its foreign policy paradigm of abolition and soon had the desired effect. On the day that he had spoken to Lieven, Canning passed the news on to the prime minister, Lord Liverpool, adding: 'I begin to think that the time approaches when *something* must be done.'[77] He used even clearer terms when writing, in January 1826, to his cousin Stratford Canning, who had been appointed British ambassador to the Porte.[78] The struggle between the Greeks and the Ottoman Empire had reached a level of brutality that called for a change in approach:

I think I see ... a new ground of interference much higher than any that we have yet had open to us, – I mean the manner in which the war is now carried on in the Morea [Peloponnese] – the character of barbarism and *barbarization* which it has assumed. Butchering of captives we have long witnessed on both sides of the contest. ... But the selling into slavery – the forced conversions – the dispeopling of Christendom – the recruiting from countries of Islamism – the erection in short of a new Puissance Barbaresque in Europe – these are (not topics merely but) facts new in themselves, new in their principle, new and strange and hitherto inconceivable in their consequences, which I do think may be made the foundation of a new mode of speaking *if not* acting.[79]

Aside from isolated suggestions and highly generalised reports of the continuing practice of enslaving Greek prisoners, however, no firm evidence of a supposed 'barbarisation plan' was found.[80] Both Ibrahim Pasha, who had been interviewed by an officer of the Royal Navy sent for that express purpose and the sultan himself firmly refuted the existence of any such scheme.[81] Although many in the British government doubted the accuracy of Russian claims, Canning nevertheless issued an unambiguous warning to the Sublime Porte, stressing that Britain would tolerate neither the implementation of a 'system of depopulation' nor the creation of a 'new Barbary State' at the heart of European

Christendom.[82] To underscore Britain's resolve, Canning explicitly referred to the recent actions of the Royal Navy against the 'Barbary State' in North Africa, of which the sultan was officially the overlord, and threatened similar measures against the Sublime Porte itself.[83]

With regard to Russia, the foreign secretary finally committed to making common cause with Russia and sent the Duke of Wellington, an experienced negotiator as well as the hero of Waterloo, as special envoy to St Petersburg. There, Wellington was to discuss joint action on the Greek question with the new tsar, Nicholas I, who had recently succeeded to the throne on the sudden death of Alexander I. In his instructions to Wellington, Canning once more explicitly referred to the 'barbarisation plan' and described Britain's position as follows:

> Our information is not sufficient, indeed, to authorize a positive averment of the fact: but it is such as to preclude the possibility of our altogether doubting it. Supposing the fact true, it may surely be questioned, whether a warfare of such a nature can be tolerated by christian nations. It may be questioned whether, if the introduction of such a system of warfare into Greece were known and believed in this country, it would be possible for us to justify to the country a continued abstinence from all interposition; or whether, if we still so abstained, we could hope hereafter to interpose, with the consent of the country, any effectual resistance to whatever enterprize Russia (alone) might undertake at the impulse, and under the pretext, of so enormous a moral, as well as political provocation.[84]

The very possibility of such a plan existing and its likely consequences for British policy at home and abroad did much to influence the foreign secretary's decision in favour of cooperation with Russia and a policy of intervention. Yet it was not alone in making up Canning's mind – a variety of reasons coincided and proved compatible. For one thing, the conflict had, over the many years of its duration, already done much to harm Britain's important trade with the Levant as well as affecting shipping in the whole region (the Ionian Islands had been a British protectorate since the Congress of Vienna) by allowing the revival of piracy.[85] What was more, the expansion of Egyptian power in the eastern Mediterranean was as little in Britain's geostrategic interest as the creation of an independent Greece as a Russian client state, which was the likely outcome of any unilateral action on the tsar's part. Both these undesirable scenarios were to be circumvented by close cooperation with Russia.

Yet British intervention in the Greek question was due not only to commercial and imperial or geostrategic considerations.[86] There was also a moral, humanitarian dimension, of which Canning was well aware and which is discernible in his instructions to Wellington, even though the 'barbarisation plan' had been a piece of Russian disinformation. Canning realised that the British public had already been rallied to the Greek cause by philhellenic agitation and would countenance no further delay when the enslavement of an entire Christian people was at stake.[87] The British government was, so to speak, hostage to its own foreign policy paradigm of abolition, which it had spent the last decade and more trying to implement internationally. Humanitarian factors decisively influenced British policy, not least because they were well suited to justifying an interventionist stance and to reinforcing the credibility of British foreign policy. Concerning the Greek question, geostrategic and imperial goals on the one hand and humanitarian principles on the other now overlapped to such a degree that an interventionist policy was the logical consequence.

Wellington's special mission to the Russian court resulted in the Protocol of St Petersburg, signed in March 1826, in which the two countries agreed that Britain should seek to mediate between the conflicting parties.[88] The aim of the coordinated Anglo-Russian diplomatic effort was to be a resolution of the conflict based on the principles of 'religion, justice, and humanity' and to make peace on lasting terms.[89] Britain and Russia assumed that Greece would remain part of the Ottoman Empire, accepting the sultan's suzerainty, but be placed under a generous statute of autonomy. In order to avoid violent clashes between the two populations, the protocol proposed the 'complete separation between Individuals of the two Nations', in consequence of which Turkish property on both the Greek mainland and the islands was to fall into Greek hands.[90] This was, in effect, a scheme for the banishment of the entire Muslim population from Greece, the first time the idea of a population transfer appeared in the history of international diplomacy. Its consequences were to prove disastrous for both Greece and Turkey around a century later.[91] In Article 5 of their agreement, Britain and Russia furthermore agreed to seek no territorial gains or other national advantage from their involvement.[92] The other members of the Concert of Europe – Austria, Prussia and France – were invited to support this diplomatic initiative.

While this invitation was rejected in Vienna and Berlin, the French government signalled its willingness to cooperate. In view of a new Anglo-Russian alliance, France saw its own political influence and imperial designs in the eastern Mediterranean, especially with regard to Egypt, under threat. France was also home, as already mentioned, to an influential philhellenic movement, which counted even King Charles X among its supporters.[93] In the Treaty of London, signed on 6 July 1827, Britain, France and Russia accordingly agreed to make common cause in seeking a resolution to the Greco-Ottoman conflict: 'They have resolved to combine their efforts, and to regulate the operation thereof, by a formal Treaty, for the object of re-establishing peace between the Contending Parties, by means of an arrangement called for, no less by sentiments of humanity, than by interests for the tranquility of Europe.'[94] Considerations of realpolitik, of European peace and stability, were thus fused with concern for the 'sentiments of humanity'. In other respects, too, the treaty largely followed the model of the Protocol of St Petersburg: It proposed a joint role as mediators between the conflicting parties linked to the demand for an immediate ceasefire, and adopted the earlier proposals for the future status of Greece and the separation of the two populations[95] as well as the assurance on the part of the contracting parties to seek neither territorial gains nor other national advantage.

Yet a secret amendment opened up completely new possibilities for action.[96] If the Sublime Porte did not agree to negotiations within a month, the allied powers declared that they would enter into commercial and diplomatic relations with the Greek insurgents. They also agreed to enforce the ceasefire, if need be, by armed force against the resistance of one side and instructed their naval squadrons in the Levant accordingly. The three great powers thus arrogated to themselves a mandate to take collective measures to force an end to the war and thereby to the ongoing humanitarian crisis in Greece. Joint policy towards Greece was henceforth to be coordinated and negotiations with the warring parties to be conducted at conferences involving the three countries' ambassadors.[97]

While the Greek insurgents, who by now were fighting for their mere survival, instantly agreed to allied calls for a ceasefire, Mahmud II once more rejected them as interference in his realm's domestic affairs. Its successful advance across the Peloponnese had brought the Sublime Porte within striking distance of its final victory and, far from ordering a retreat, reinforcements were dispatched to the front for the decisive push.[98] According to the Treaty of London, however, this meant that the naval squadron in the Mediterranean composed of British, French and Russian ships was now under orders to start a blockade, cutting off Ottoman supply lines and forcing an end to hostilities.[99] In so doing, the great powers of Europe avoided formally declaring war on the Ottoman Empire and risking an unpredictable escalation of the conflict. Instead, they chose to use military force, but below the threshold of all-out war. Naval blockades – also a key element in the struggle against the Atlantic slave trade – were now being established as an instrument of intervention.[100]

Direct negotiations between the three allied admirals – Edward Codrington, Louis de Heiden and Henri de Rigny – and Ibrahim Pasha failed to bring about an end to Ottoman fighting: 'a species of warfare more destructive and exterminating than before', as the allied commanders put it.[101] The blockade was therefore escalated on 20 October 1827. In the Bay of Navarino (Pylos) in the south-eastern Peloponnese, a sea battle broke out between the allied squadron and the Egyptian-Ottoman fleet that was anchored there. The Battle of Navarino lasted several hours and resulted in the destruction of the entire Ottoman fleet and the loss of more than 6,000 men.[102] This overwhelming victory for the allied side, which lost no ships and a comparatively modest 174 crew, dealt a crippling blow to Ibrahim Pasha. Having now lost all his ships, his forces were cut off from supplies from home and thereby lost their strategic advantage on land. In his subsequent report, Admiral Codrington blamed the escalation entirely on the enemy, stating that sailing into the Bay of Navarino had been a joint decision on the part of the three allied admirals for the purpose of persuading Ibrahim Pasha to withdraw and keeping his forces from continuing their 'brutal war of extermination'.[103]

The allied success at sea did not, however, bring about an immediate end to hostilities on land. An Egyptian army of more than 24,000 men was still on Greek soil and controlled large swathes of the Peloponnese. Nor was Mahmud II any more willing to agree to the terms of the Treaty of London. He refused any further negotiations, to which the allies responded by severing diplomatic relations with the Porte.[104] Russia took advantage of the escalation to declare war on the Ottoman Empire in April 1828 and invade the Danubian Principalities.[105] Notwithstanding this unilateral action on the tsar's part, of which the other allies both disapproved, the three powers stuck to their common policy regarding Greece and extended their naval blockade to the strait of the Dardanelles and the Egyptian port of Alexandria.[106] The new instructions jointly issued to the three allied commanders now made explicit mention of the plight of the many Greek women and children who had been carried off for sale in the slave market of Alexandria. The naval squadron was accordingly under orders to prevent any such transports from taking place. Any captives found in the search of a ship were to be freed and returned to a part of Greece not under enemy occupation. The instructions to the allied naval squadron thus clearly contained a humanitarian and abolitionist element reminiscent of operations in West African waters against the Atlantic slave trade.[107] Documents in the French naval archive prove, moreover, that successful cooperation in the Mediterranean had a positive effect on the cooperation between French and British ships off West Africa.[108]

Faced with Ibrahim's intransigence, the allied powers came to realise that naval measures alone would not be enough to ensure compliance with the Treaty of London and that the use of their own ground troops was fast becoming inevitable.[109] On 11 August 1828 Britain, France and Russia jointly announced the deployment of an expeditionary force that was to enforce the ceasefire on land and the full withdrawal of the Egyptian-Ottoman army.[110] The mandate for intervention was issued in the name of all three powers to France, and the force's mission was explicitly defined as being not the conquest of Greece, but solely the re-establishment of peace in the region. Accordingly, the French army was to withdraw immediately its mission had been fulfilled.[111] In the event, however, the three allied admirals succeeded in persuading Muhammad Ali Pasha, with whom negotiations had resumed in Alexandria, to pull out his sick and starving troops from Greece even before the first French soldier had landed in the Peloponnese.[112] In personal talks with the pasha, Admiral Codrington persuaded him to promise 'to do every thing in his power towards obtaining the liberty of as many Greeks as possible' and to recognise 'that His Highness was aware how loud the cry had been, both in England and France, on this subject'.[113] In exchange for allied assurances of an honourable capitulation and a secure retreat for his troops, Muhammed Ali promised that his army would not force any Greeks to accompany them back to Egypt.[114]

In this radically changed situation, the allied squadron was now charged with supporting the safe return and transport of the Egyptian army across the Mediterranean to Alexandria and to ensure that it happened as quickly as possible.[115] Orders were once again given to prevent, under all circumstances, 'the embarkation from the ports of the Morea, of any Greek Christians, who may have been made prisoners or enslaved'.[116] For the 14,000-strong French expeditionary force, which had landed in the Peloponnese led by General Nicolas-Joseph Maison and with orders to drive out the Egyptian-Ottoman occupying army, all that was now left to do was supervise the retreat of Ibrahim Pasha's forces.[117] French soldiers and commissioners of the three allied powers were present at the troops' embarkation to ensure that no Greek women and children were being abducted.[118] Although the main French force soon withdrew, a brigade remained in Greece until 1833, accompanied by a delegation of artists, architects, archaeologists and scientists.[119] French troops gave vital assistance to the suffering Greek population, ensuring the return of enslaved Greeks to their homes, helping to rebuild infrastructure destroyed in the war, and taking on both policing and administrative tasks.[120] The operations of the French expeditionary force, which increasingly acted as an 'army of pioneers',[121] assumed certain features of what today would be called a 'stabilisation operation', combining the pacification of a war-torn region with the reconstruction of a state apparatus.

By their diplomatic and military intervention, the three great powers of Europe put an end to the Greco-Ottoman conflict. The London Protocol of 3 February 1830 proclaimed the independence of the Greek state, but it was made effective only in 1833 when, after long and tough diplomatic negotiations, the Bavarian Prince Otto was placed on the throne of the Kingdom of Greece.[122] There was, however, another level of significance to the allied intervention in Greece, which created a precedent for the future approach on the part of the great powers of Europe to the internal crises of the Ottoman Empire and for a policy of intervention for the protection of Christian minorities.[123] In the context of the 'Eastern Question' and the geostrategic rivalry between the great powers that played into it, the combination of imperial and humanitarian motives is striking indeed.

This did not, however, mark the much-proclaimed birth of the modern concept of humanitarian intervention as the first genuine instance of this novel practice. The mechanism of the great powers' reaction was instead based on a notion of intervention that had begun to take shape in the early nineteenth century in the struggle against the slave trade. Especially in the light of such momentous events as the large-scale enslavement of Chios' Greek population and the Ottomans' supposed 'barbarisation plan', abolitionist themes surfaced, in Britain and France, in public and parliamentary debates on the Greek question, but also in direct diplomatic negotiations with the Sublime Porte. The joint intervention measures – searching Egyptian-Ottoman ships, buying enslaved Greeks' freedom and returning them home, and strict supervision of the Egyptian army's retreat – also resembled anti-slavery operations in many respects.

The abolitionist tone set by the governments in London and Paris seems not to have gone completely unnoticed in Constantinople, for it was surely no accident that the first significant steps towards the abolition of slavery and the slave trade in the Ottoman Empire coincided with the end of the Greek war of independence and the intervention of the great powers. What had previously been standard Ottoman practice – to make slaves of rebels and prisoners-of-war – was now largely abandoned, and a decree issued by Mahmud II in 1830 effectively granted amnesty and hence their freedom to Christians enslaved in the course of the recent insurgency.[124] Although slavery was not abolished in the Ottoman Empire until later in the nineteenth century – again under massive British pressure – these steps did mark the beginning of a longer-term process of emancipation.[125]

One of the first appraisals of the peculiar character of the allied intervention in Greece under international law was provided by the eminent jurist Henry Wheaton. In his influential *Elements of International Law*, published in 1836, Wheaton argued that the Greek case had been exceptional in that policy had not only followed the national security interests of particular states, but also 'the general interests of humanity', which had been violated 'by the excesses of a barbarous and despotic government'.[126] Following an extensive analysis of the Treaty of London and the subsequent events – the Battle of Navarino and the occupation of the Peloponnese by the French expeditionary force – Wheaton concluded:

> Still more justifiable was the interference of the christian powers of Europe to rescue a whole nation, not merely from religious persecution, but from the cruel alternative of being transported from their native land into Egyptian bondage, or exterminated by their merciless oppressors. The rights of human nature, wantonly outraged by this cruel warfare, prosecuted for six years against a civilized and Christian people, to whose ancestors, mankind are so largely indebted for the blessings of arts and letters, were but tardily and imperfectly vindicated by this measure.[127]

Wheaton also, with reference to the 'barbarisation plan', picked up on the abolitionist aspect and linked it to the protection of Christian minorities. It was precisely this combination of two spheres of action – abolition and the protection of minorities – as providing grounds for intervention that emerged in the course of intervention in Greece.

Yet for a humanitarian understanding of intervention, this meant a narrow and selective focus. Whereas in the fight against the slave trade, all countries – Christian or otherwise, 'civilised' or not – were potentially affected by measures taken to implement abolition, this new paradigm of intervention was limited to the protection of Christian minorities and framed explicitly against the Muslim ruler of Constantinople. The displacement, enslavement and destruction of Muslim populations, which also took place on a large scale in the Greek war, were entirely disregarded. Abolitionist impulses can here be seen to have produced a selective notion of intervention that was apt to be mobilised against the Ottoman Empire on the pretext of the protection of Christian minorities.[128]

The Greek Legacy: European Intervention in the Lebanon, 1860–1861

The end of the Greco-Turkish conflict and Greek independence did not make the 'Eastern Question' disappear from the political agenda. It remained a hot topic of international diplomacy and gave the great powers repeated cause to interfere directly in the domestic affairs of the

Ottoman Empire.[129] All that shifted was its geographical focus, away from Greece and towards the empire's Syrian province, which extended from the Red Sea to Anatolia. Having sent his army, albeit unsuccessfully, to quell the Greek rebellion, the Egyptian governor Muhammad Ali Pasha now demanded his reward from the sultan in the form of this strategically valuable territory. Although his own position was much weakened, Mahmud II refused, in response to which forces led by Ibrahim Pasha occupied Syria in October 1831. The Egyptian governor had extended his sphere of influence to the point of posing a serious threat to central authority in Constantinople.[130] In order to consolidate his power, Ibrahim Pasha used the politics of 'divide and rule', playing the religious communities of the Druze and Maronites, who lived mostly in the area around Mount Lebanon, off against one another.[131] Egyptian rule lasted for nine years and produced social and political divisions that were to leave lasting traces in relations between ethnic and religious groups.[132] Only in 1840 did the Sublime Porte succeed in reasserting its sovereignty over the region, this time with the aid of Britain, Russia, Austria and Prussia, which were all keen to stabilise the Ottoman Empire and put a check on Egyptian ambitions. Eight thousand Ottoman, British and Austrian troops landed at the Lebanese coast, drove out Ibrahim Pasha and restored authority to the sultan in Constantinople.[133]

The reinstated Ottoman authorities tried to defuse the open rivalry that had erupted between Druze and Maronites during the Egyptian interregnum by creating, in 1842, a separate administrative unit for each population group. This placing of the Mount Lebanon area under this so-called dual caimacamate did little to resolve the lingering conflict, which erupted in severe clashes in 1845.[134] On the contrary, it was exacerbated by British and French attempts to use the two groups as proxies for their own rival interests in the region. France assumed the role of protector of the Maronite Christians, while Britain strengthened its ties with the Druze in order to counter France's growing influence in the region.[135] The terrible massacres of 1860, which ultimately brought about a collective humanitarian intervention on the part of the great powers of Europe, must therefore also be considered as resulting from repeated interference on the part of imperial actors – Egyptian, French and British – in Lebanese affairs, and particularly the manner in which local communities were made proxies for outside interests.[136]

Another destabilising factor turned out to be the reforms begun in 1839 by the Ottoman rulers under the heading of *Tanzimāt*, which were an attempt to modernise the empire politically, break up supposedly obsolete social structures and enforce new legal standards.[137] An example is the decree of 1856 known as *hatt-ı hümâyûn*, in which the sultan – not least under the influence of the Crimean War and the Paris peace negotiations that followed it – proclaimed the legal equality of his Christian subjects, a move to which Muslims were openly hostile and put up active resistance.[138] Existing tensions between Druze and Maronites were further exacerbated by questions of land and property privileges that arose in connection with the reforms, leading both ethnic groups to prepare for an armed confrontation.[139] After a series of skirmishes and sectarian killings, civil war between the two communities erupted in late May 1860, with Maronite militias targeting mixed-population villages and expelling or murdering their Druze inhabitants.[140] Although numerically inferior, the Druze were better organised and prepared and soon gained the upper hand. Their retaliation was no less brutal. In the following weeks, Druze raiders set fire to churches and monasteries, attacked Maronite villages and, in such places as Hasbaya and Deir al-Qamar, perpetrated massacres costing the lives of several thousand Christians. The surviving Maronites sought refuge in the coastal cities of Beirut and Sidon or inland in Damascus.[141]

There, too, however, the refugees were attacked, with local Muslims joining in the aggression. The violence culminated when, on 9 July, a frenzied mob of Bedouins, Druze and Muslims raided the Christian quarter of Damascus, which was crowded with Christian refugees. Homes and churches were burned, and the next two days were a veritable bloodbath claiming at least 3,000 lives.[142] It was only thanks to the bold intervention by Abd al-Qādir, who as emir of Mascara had led the embittered resistance to French colonisation of Algeria from 1830 to 1847 and had gone into exile in Damascus, that there were any survivors to speak of.[143] Their number included native Christians as well as missionaries and other Europeans, including consuls and their families, for the consulates of European states including Prussia, Russia and Austria were also attacked. These attacks suggest that behind this massive eruption of violence lay pent-up resentment of growing imperial interference by foreign powers in the region.[144]

The European consuls were visible representatives of the Western presence and influence, but they assumed a variety of other roles in the course of the civil war. As the flow of refugees increased and a humanitarian emergency threatened, they began to coordinate aid to displaced Maronites and, in various ports along the Lebanese coast, placed them under the direct protection of the Austrian, Russian, British and French warships that were docking there.[145] On several occasions small units of sailors landed in order protect Christians from attacks or to take them to safety. The envoys of the five great powers also made several collective representations, both to the local Ottoman authorities and to those in

Constantinople, to persuade Sultan Abdulmejid I to intervene and prevent further bloodshed.[146] They also tried to mediate in the civil war,
seeking contact with Druze leaders, initiating talks and even brokering a
temporary ceasefire.[147] With Britain and France in the lead, the envoys
of the European states involved themselves in various ways in a civil war
taking place within the borders of another sovereign state, the Ottoman
Empire. This policy of interference preceded that of outright
military intervention.

Much as in the case of Chios in the Greek war of independence,
however, the consuls' principal role was to gather information and documentation, and to send dispatches to their respective capitals.[148] The
many reports of massacres and the details of atrocities they sent were
often exaggerated, or at least one-sided in portraying the Maronites as
innocent victims of frenzied Druze aggression and 'barbarism'. An
example is that of Niven Moore, the British consul at Beirut. Writing
to Sheikh Ismail al-Atrash, Moore expressed his horror at the 'barbarous
cruelties' perpetrated by the sheikh's Druze fighters against Christians
and threatened serious consequences for Anglo-Druze relations if they
continued.[149] Al-Atrash replied that he had indeed ordered his forces to
retreat, but that it had been the Maronites who were the aggressors and
who had begun hostilities, leaving the sheikh no alternative but to act in
protection of his own people.[150] Not persuaded by this line of argument,
Moore drew up a list of all losses suffered in the civil war. While exact
figures were given for burned Maronite villages and killed Christians,[151]
his estimate of losses on the other side seems rather unconcerned: 'The
Druze losses are comparatively insignificant. They have had about the
same number of killed in warfare as the Christians while their losses in
burnt houses … is very inconsiderable.'[152] The roles of innocent victim
and brutal aggressor had thus been assigned, and this was the one-sidedly
pro-Maronite view of the Lebanese civil war that found its way to
Europe. It was picked up by the press, which made much of the incoming
reports, writing them up according to the familiar pattern of Christians as
the victims of 'oriental barbarism'. This one-dimensional picture
inflamed the European public. British and French newspapers such as
The Times, *Le Moniteur*, *Le Siècle* and *Le Constitutionnel* gave much room
to such incidents and contributed to the development of a public mood
that demanded European intervention.[153]

At the government level it was France – which as the self-appointed
protector of the Maronite community was particularly concerned with
the dramatic escalation of events – that pushed hardest for international
intervention. Directly on receiving the first consular reports of massacres
in the Lebanon, Édouard Antoine de Thouvenel, the French foreign

minister, informed the British ambassador to Paris. Thouvenel had spent many years as ambassador to Constantinople and was well acquainted with conditions in the Levant. Speaking to the British ambassador, he gave a detailed account of events and called for joint action on the part of the Concert of Europe.[154] This, he argued, was a clear-cut case, a fundamental '*question d'humanité*' that brooked no disagreement between the cabinets of Europe's leading powers.[155] In a letter addressed simultaneously to the envoys of Britain, Austria, Russia and Prussia, Thouvenel proposed sending a commission composed of one representative of each of the great powers and with Ottoman involvement to the Lebanon, where it was to establish the causes of the civil war, name those responsible, set compensation for the victims and finally determine a new settlement for the region that would prevent such conflicts from flaring up again.[156] The project was motivated – as Thouvenel stressed in a letter to the French ambassador to the Sublime Porte – not by political machinations or rivalry for influence in the region, but by humanity alone, which demanded immediate intervention.[157] Accordingly, at the order of Emperor Napoleon III himself, units of the French navy were dispatched to the Lebanese coast in preparation for their '*mission d'humanité*'.[158]

At Thouvenel's urging, France, which sought to find a collective solution to the crisis in cooperation with the other great powers, succeeded in persuading Russia, Austria and Prussia of the necessity of a joint intervention in the Levant.[159] Only Great Britain was at first wary of the French initiative and sceptical of the humanitarian arguments coming from Paris. Although Britain, too, dispatched additional ships to the eastern Mediterranean as well as Royal Marines that could come to the aid of imperilled Christians on land if necessary,[160] the tacit hope in London was that the Ottoman authorities would manage to regain control of the situation without support from abroad. The British government was guided largely by geostrategic considerations and the assumption that another foreign military intervention would further weaken the Ottoman Empire while strengthening the French position in the region, even leading to its permanent French occupation. Britain was also afraid that Russia in its turn might take an international intervention in the Lebanon as a precedent for an intervention of its own on behalf of Christians in the Balkan provinces of Bosnia and Bulgaria.[161] The British ambassador to Paris expressed these concerns in conversation with Thouvenel:

I mentioned to his Excellency, that he must admit that the landing of a foreign force in Syria would add to the complications already existing in that unfortunate country, and that, moreover, it might establish a precedent that might soon be taken advantage of by Russia, who could raise disturbances in the European Provinces of Turkey whenever it might suit her purposes.[162]

Such fears were nourished by Russia's (temporary) refusal to agree to any international convention on the Syrian question 'unless a Secret Article were added to it, obliging the Powers to consent to a similar armed intervention in the European Provinces of Turkey, should it become necessary'.[163]

What ultimately changed the British position was the news of the massacres at Damascus, which seemed to support Thouvenel's arguments. The three days of murderous attacks on Christians, including members of European delegations and missionaries, increased the pressure on the British government to act decisively.[164] Yet Britain still saw itself in a foreign policy dilemma, which Lord John Russell, the foreign secretary, expressed in concise terms in a letter to the prime minister, Lord Palmerston:

I am not blind to the danger of French intervention in Syria, but I weigh that danger against the opposite dangers which are there: ... That the conduct of the Turks being according to all our official reports quite indefensible the public opinion of Europe would be against us, if we were to forbid the French intervention to Syria.[165]

Another serious concern cited by Russell was the possibility of a Franco-Russian alliance, which, if joined by Austria and Prussia, would lead to Britain being isolated.[166] In order to avoid the censure of European public opinion and isolation from the other European powers, the British government ultimately, and in spite of its geostrategic concerns, gave the go-ahead for a joint intervention.[167] Britain's involvement in the Lebanese crisis thus appears to have been guided less by humanitarian considerations than by realpolitik.

At the invitation of the French foreign minister, the envoys of the United Kingdom, Russia, Prussia and Austria convened in Paris to discuss what form a joint intervention might take and how it was to proceed.[168] Also at the table was the Ottoman ambassador, Ahmed Vefik Effendi – a clear indication of the Ottoman Empire's international standing, which had improved since it had fought in the Crimean War on the side of Britain and France. Unlike the case of the Greek intervention, the great powers of Europe now intended to involve the Sublime Porte in its decision-making and to carry out any intervention not against its stated will, but with its approval. In a protocol signed by all parties and subsequently ratified as a convention, on 3 August the six delegates approved sending a European force of 12,000 men to Syria for the purpose of preventing further bloodshed and restoring peace.[169] France was to put up half the expeditionary force, the commander of which was to coordinate its actions in close conjunction with the Ottoman special commissioner upon arrival in the Levant. The four other states committed themselves to dispatching naval forces sufficient to safeguard the operation at sea and to provide active support off the Lebanese and Syrian coast. Syria's occupation by European forces charged with pacifying the Ottoman province was limited in advance to six months. In another protocol, the parties also agreed that they would not seek to exploit the intervention for their territorial or one-sided commercial advantage.[170] Explicit reference was also made to an article inserted in the peace treaty of 30 March 1856, by which the Crimean War had been settled. In that article, the Sublime Porte had pledged to make substantial administrative reforms with the aim of improving the situation of Christians in the Ottoman Empire.[171]

On the day the Paris Protocol was signed, the situation in Syria was also the subject of heated debate in Westminster. The British government, led by Palmerston and Russell, informed parliament of the international agreements that had just been made.[172] Strikingly, many of the members who favoured intervention invoked the Greek case, which by now lay more than thirty years in the past. Henry Rich, the member for Richmond, is reported to have responded to the news of atrocities in the Levant as follows: 'He recollected the massacres of Chios and the atrocities in the Morea, which had in like manner led to a European intervention to rescue the Greeks from the abominable rule of Turkey, and he should rejoice to see a similar result in Syria.'[173] Meanwhile, in the House of Lords, the marquess of Clanricarde condemned the Ottoman government in no uncertain terms:

It was not to be tolerated that this feeble, effete Government was to have a right to hold in a state of barbarism some of the finest districts in the world. All diplomatic conventionalities were broken through in the case of Greece; the Governments of that day interfered on the ground of the broad rights of humanity; and in this case we must do a good deal more than merely sign protocols and send Commissioners and a body of troops to remain there six months. ... The question must be met by a union among the Great Powers, to take upon themselves to see that the country was better governed in future.[174]

The French government, in accordance with the international agreement, prepared an expeditionary force of 6,000 men to sail for Syria.[175] Addressing some of these troops at Camp de Châlons, Emperor Napoleon III reminded them of the special character of their mission, which was not a war as they might know it:

You are about to sail for Syria and France wishes you well on this expedition, which has but one goal: to bring about the triumph of justice and humanity.

You are indeed not making war on any particular power, but rather going to the aid of the sultan in bringing back under his authority those among his subjects who have been blinded by the fanaticism of another century.[176]

This rhetoric also appeared in the orders issued to the troops, which emphasised that France was fighting in the name of '*l'Europe civilisée*' and of Christendom at large, even tracing a line back to Godfrey of Bouillon and the first crusade.[177] The expeditionary force was placed under the command of Brigadier-General Charles-Marie-Napoléon de Beaufort d'Hautpoul, who had been Ibrahim Pasha's chief of staff for three years during the latter's occupation of Syria and knew conditions on the ground there well.[178] While the other great powers were dispatching their ships to sail for the Lebanese coast – an operation in which they were joined by warships from several smaller states, including the Netherlands, the Kingdom of Sardinia and even Greece[179] – Beaufort took his ground troops to Beirut, where on 16 August 1860 they were received with wild enthusiasm by the city's Christian population.[180]

Beaufort soon discovered, however, that his mission's principal goal – to restore peace and order in the province – had already been largely achieved even without the aid of the expeditionary force he was leading. The decisive factor had been the decision made by the Sublime Porte in mid-July – about a month before the French contingent arrived – to send Mehmed Fuad Pasha to the province equipped with special powers and more than 15,000 troops. Fuad Pasha was the Ottoman foreign minister and a leading exponent of the *Tanzimāt* reforms, and the stated aim of his mission was to put an end to the civil war and the massacres associated with it under the sultan's own sovereign authority, while also providing humanitarian aid to the affected populations.[181] Fuad Pasha went about his tasks as special commissioner with great energy and indeed ferocity. Alleged troublemakers and participants in massacres were arrested by the hundreds, among them high-ranking officials, and tried by hastily convened tribunals before being publicly executed.[182] There was a twofold thrust to this policy. At home, it served Fuad Pasha in breaking resistance to the *Tanzimat* reforms associated with him and to advance the cause of modernisation throughout the region. To the great powers of Europe, it sent the clear message that the Ottoman Empire was capable of dealing with crises in its sovereign territory without the interference of third parties and that collective interventions from abroad were obsolete and unnecessary. By means of an internal intervention, the Ottoman foreign minister had hoped to outmanoeuvre an intervention from outside – or to take, as it were, the wind out of its sails.[183]

The Ottoman side having already accomplished so much in its plan for pacification before the French had even arrived, there apparently remained little to do in military terms for the expeditionary force. Its scope for action was further narrowed by the international agreement signed in Paris, which committed Beaufort to close cooperation at all times with the Ottoman special commissioner as well as requiring the approval of the other European powers. The brigadier-general found it difficult to accept this highly circumscribed role and the sharing of responsibility demanded by it. This made for extremely tense relations with Fuad Pasha, who did all he could to neutralise European influence and protect the sovereign rights of the Sublime Porte.[184] Whereas Beaufort had expected to restore peace by force, his troops ultimately found themselves limited to stabilising measures. As in the Greek case some thirty years earlier, French soldiers became involved above all in rebuilding ruined villages, supervising the return of displaced Christians to their homes, distributing supplies and undertaking small-scale policing operations in support of Ottoman forces.[185] The government in Paris having invoked the spectre of a recrudescence of hostilities and urged the other powers to agree to extending the expeditionary force's remit, it remained in the country for another three months, being formally withdrawn on 5 June 1861.[186]

Besides its military aspect, there was, however, another element to this European intervention 'in the name of humanity' which really did represent a fundamental innovation. In the form of an international ad hoc commission, which Thouvenel had already proposed in his first letter to the great powers, one representative each of Britain, France, Austria, Prussia and Russia was to join the Ottoman special commissioner on location to examine recent events and work to find solutions.[187] Lord John Russell, the foreign secretary, provided a concise summary of this shared agenda in his instructions to Lord Dufferin, who had been appointed British commissioner:

Your first care, after putting yourself in relation with the Commissioner of the Porte, and with those of Austria, France, Prussia, and Russia will be to inquire, in concert with them, into the origin and causes of the late deplorable events, to determine the share of responsibility incurred by the chiefs of the insurrection and the agents of the administration, and to call for the punishment of the guilty. ... It will be your duty, on the other hand, to appreciate the extent of the disasters which have been suffered by the Christians, and to consider of the means best fitted to alleviate, and even to indemnify, as far as possible, the losses which have been sustained. There is another point which equally deserves attention; I mean the arrangements which it may be useful to make in order to establish for the future order and security in Syria, and prevent the return of similar calamities.[188]

Beyond reacting to the most urgent necessities, there were three key points to be addressed by the international commission: to coordinate acute humanitarian relief for the suffering Christian population, to identify and bring to justice those responsible for the massacres, and to plan a viable political order for the Ottoman province that would be able to prevent such disturbances in the future. Lord Dufferin was explicitly tasked with pursuing these aims 'in the spirit of harmony'[189] together with his fellow commissioners, who came with similar briefs from their respective governments.

In early October the six commissioners, with Fuad Pasha having been asked to preside, first assembled in Beirut and, in regular meetings that were held until May 1861, tried to work their way through their copious agenda.[190] In view of the disastrous conditions in the country, with hundreds of destroyed villages and thousands of displaced refugees, the most urgent task of the commission was to deal with the humanitarian consequences of the civil war and provide effective relief for the desperate situation in which many people found themselves.[191] To this end, the European commissioners began to observe and examine the Ottoman efforts initiated by Fuad Pasha, to reveal any flaws they identified and suggest improvements, thereby putting pressure on local authorities.[192] It was also imperative, they recognised, to coordinate the activities of the various European relief committees,[193] most of which had been started by Western diplomats and missionaries, in order to increase the effectiveness of their efforts. The Comité Directeur was the body set up for this purpose, which channelled the various disparate efforts and ensured the effective distribution of relief goods.[194] Donations arrived especially from Great Britain and France, where Charles Martial Lavigerie, a clergyman already known for his part in the abolitionist movement, had launched a successful campaign for the benefit of Christians in the Levant.[195] The international committee was indeed successful in providing aid, especially to Christian refugees in coastal towns. Since this was above all a humanitarian effort for the benefit of the civilian population, Fuad Pasha allowed these European activities to proceed largely unimpeded.[196]

A far more delicate problem was posed by the commission's intention, which had been stated in its first session, to involve itself in identifying and prosecuting those responsible for the massacres.[197] Since this constituted a direct infringement on the authority of the Ottoman legal system and hence the sultan's sovereignty, such advances met with considerable reserve from the Ottoman side. Fuad Pasha's special tribunals and the swift (if rough) justice they administered had after all been established to pre-empt any such outside intervention and to preserve the Sublime Porte's judicial independence. Following lengthy discussions,

Fuad Pasha finally agreed to allow the European commissioners to send deputies of their own to observe the proceedings.[198] In practice, this even meant that Fuad Pasha submitted the verdicts made by the special tribunals against Ottoman officials in Beirut and Druze in Moukhtara to the commissioners for their approval.[199] The international commission thereby assumed the role of a kind of international appellate court, allowing the European commissioners to interfere in Ottoman jurisdiction and influence it as they saw fit.[200] Particularly under the aspect of a system of international criminal justice, which began to be established only in the mid-twentieth century, this role of an international ad hoc commission in conducting legal proceedings in cases of massacres and atrocities committed in a situation of civil war is nothing short of remarkable.

Yet the commissioners were far from agreeing among themselves who should be taken to task for the massacres and what their punishment should be.[201] The French in particular pushed for a severe punishment of the Druze, whom they held to be solely responsible for the massacre and hence accountable collectively for the crimes committed against the Maronites. But this was not merely about bringing justice to the Druze. The idea underpinning this stance was that tough action against the Druze would strengthen the Maronites and, since the French considered the Maronites to be their allies, ultimately the French interest in the region itself.[202] Lord Dufferin meanwhile tried to reach a more balanced view of responsibilities, emphasising the character of the conflict as a civil war and the fact the Christians had provoked its outbreak and hence must share in the responsibility.[203] He vehemently opposed any collective punishment of the Druze population and warned against the '*désir d'exterminer la nation druse*' in vengeance.[204] Sir Henry Bulwer, the British ambassador to Constantinople, criticised any such excessive and one-sided punishment of the Druze, laying out his position in a letter to Lord John Russell:

> The Druses were formerly considered under British protection, as the Maronites were under French. It would have been disgraceful to England to have made this protection a shield against the consequences of murder and rapine, but I think it would also be an humiliation to England if she so far abandoned such protection as not to interpose it against the extremes of cruelty and injustice. This language I have held from the first, and I am glad to see that Lord Dufferin is acting in conformity with it.[205]

Britain, whose own geostrategic interests in the Levant inclined it to take the side of the Druze, succeeded in persuading the other great powers to take a more moderate line. Even Thouvenel ultimately came out against a collective execution of Druze leaders – which, incidentally, he referred to as a 'holocaust'[206] to be avoided – and demanded that of the two principal ringleaders.[207]

This question of holding the perpetrators to account, which was the subject of long debates and much controversy, illustrates the fact that the international commission in Beirut was far from being just a site of inter-state cooperation and conflict mediation. It was instead marked by the rival interests of the European powers in the Levant and divided along the lines of competing imperial claims. This was particularly true of the last point on the commission's agenda, the search for a new and sustainable ordering of the Ottoman province, in which the Anglo-French antagonism was thrown into stark relief, making it all but impossible to reach a solution that was acceptable to all parties.[208] Whereas France favoured a privileged, virtually independent position for the province's Christians, Britain was adamant that Ottoman sovereignty over the region must be preserved in full.[209] As Lord John Russell wrote to Earl Cowley, the British ambassador to Paris: 'I am convinced the French wish to deprive the Sultan permanently of Syria.'[210] The foreign secretary was wary of French motives: 'Humanity in France extends only to Maronites, whereas we think it should cover all men, women & children in Syria.'[211] Debates within the commission were accordingly hard-fought. A number of different plans – for instance independence for the province under the suzerainty of one of the smaller European powers or even its renewed annexation by Egypt – were discussed without any common denominator being found.[212] Britain's insistence on Ottoman sovereignty was guided by the concern, expressed early on and many times after, that 'European occupation would be a precedent for other occupations in Bulgaria, in Bosnia, and other Provinces, and thus lead the way to a partition of the Turkish Empire'.[213]

One question to which the five European commissioners could agree on a solution, at least in principle, was that of how to prevent future massacres between Druze and Maronites. To this end, they returned to an idea that had first been discussed in the context of the Greek war of independence and set down in the Protocol of St Petersburg, signed in March 1826: the complete geographical separation of the rival communities along ethnic lines.[214] Druze and Christian populations were to be kept apart and areas that had seen centuries of mixed settlement were to be divided into ethnically homogeneous zones.[215] This so-called *mesure de désagrégation*[216] was to be carried out under the supervision of a commission made up of local authorities and representatives of the five powers, with assurances given that the interests of both communities would be given equal consideration. Owing to a lack of political will and above all the massive resistance of the local population,[217] however, this resettlement plan, although developed in detail,[218] was never imple-mented. Yet it highlights, as the intervention in Greece did before, how the idea of population transfers – which was to create severe ruptures in the history of Greco-Turkish relations, but also in that of Europe at large in the twentieth century – arose in international diplomacy in the train of humanitarian interventions throughout the long nineteenth century.

The political reorganization of the Lebanon would ultimately be settled not by the international commission in Beirut, but at a conference of ambassadors in Constantinople. On 9 June 1861 the Sublime Porte and the five great powers of Europe signed the '*Règlement et protocole relatifs à la réorganisation du Mont Liban*',[219] in which the future administration of the Ottoman Empire was set down. Its governor was to be a Christian appointed by and answerable to the sultan himself, with a three-year term of office and far-reaching powers.[220] The governor was to be advised and supported by a twelve-member administrative council, to which all reli-gious groups would send delegates in proportion to their share of the population.[221] Alongside a host of other regulations, the new statute also empowered the governor to put up a police corps, again to be staffed by members of all religions, which must not, however, exceed a strength of seven policemen per 1,000 inhabitants.[222] What the '*Règlement du Mont Liban*' offered was above all a compromise between rival solutions. It strengthened the position of Christians without excluding other groups while leaving no doubt as to the ultimate sovereignty of the Sublime Porte. With minor changes, it remained the foundation of the province's admin-istration for more than fifty years and contributed to the peaceful coexist-ence of the various communities inhabiting the area around Mount Lebanon until the outbreak of the First World War in 1914.[223]

Aside from these palpable effects on Lebanon itself, the European military intervention left its mark at the international level, too. The actions of the Concert of Europe did much to reinforce both the vilifica-tion of the Ottoman Empire as 'barbaric' and 'uncivilised' and the acceptance of intervention under the banner of humanity for the benefit of Christian minorities. Rather less attention was paid to the fact that the special commission under Fuad Pasha dispatched by the Porte itself had done much to restore peace and order even before the arrival of the French expeditionary force and the European commission. Instead, the great powers of Europe dressed up their intervention as a glorious humanitarian and 'civilising' mission, which had put a check on 'oriental barbarism'. Especially in France, there was heavy emphasis on the idea that the pacification of the province had been guided solely by the '*pensée d'humanité*'.[224] In view of the attacks on one another by Druze and Maronites and the massacre of Damascus, humanitarian motives surely had a part to play in setting the European powers on a course of collective intervention, but they were by no means alone in doing so. Rather, imperial interests and rivalries in the Levant – above all that between France and Great Britain – strongly influenced the decision to intervene and illustrate how strongly considerations of humanity and realpolitik were intertwined in addressing the situation in the Lebanon.[225]

In the aftermath of the Lebanese intervention, the Sublime Porte found its capacity for responsible government and the effective protection of Christian minorities increasingly questioned by the great powers of Europe. The consequence of this somewhat condescending attitude was that the Lebanese case and the reforms enacted in consequence of it were cited as a precedent in subsequent crises affecting Christians in other parts of the empire, notably in Crete and the Balkans. This paved the way for an increasing tendency on the part of the European powers to interfere in the internal affairs of the Ottoman Empire.[226] Russia in particular welcomed the occasion repeatedly (if selectively) to highlight the plight of Christians in the empire's European provinces and draw artful parallels. Even as the intervention in the Lebanon was still taking place, Britain observed Russia's revived interest in the protection of Christian minorities with mounting concern, as expressed in a letter from Russell to Cowley:

> But the question naturally arises, if Turkish authority is unfit to rule in Syria now, why should it be fit at the end of two months, or of six months? Again, if it is unfit to rule in Syria, why in Bulgaria or in Bosnia? It is obvious … that this last question will be raised by the Representative of Russia. Nay more: if it is once admitted that, apart from the horrible events which occasioned the foreign occupation of Syria, the Turks cannot be trusted with the government of Christians, the wide application of this dogma asserted by the Russian Government must be admitted.[227]

Russell's fear, voiced early on, that the European occupation of the Lebanon might set a precedent for intervention in other Ottoman provinces, such as Bulgaria or Bosnia,[228] was indeed prophetic and borne out by events some years later.

The Great Eastern Crisis (1875–1878), the 'Bulgarian Horrors' and the Concept of Humanitarian Intervention in International Law

When parts of the Christian population of Herzegovina, driven by mounting economic hardship caused by poor harvests and high taxation, rose up against Ottoman rule in July 1875, they set off a chain reaction throughout the Balkans and caused a crisis of international proportions. What began as a local rebellion soon engulfed neighbouring Bosnia and threatened Ottoman authority there, with the insurgents reiving crucial support from their Slavic co-religionists in neighbouring Serbia and Montenegro.[229] This show of weakness on the part of the Sublime Porte, which struggled to contain the revolts in both regions, encouraged the Bulgarian nationalist movement to rise up in its turn, seeking to shake off the Ottoman yoke and gain independence for their country. Towards the end of April 1876 Bulgarian insurgents targeted Ottoman officials in a number of places and began a campaign of violence against the Muslim population, murdering or expelling Muslims on a large scale.[230] However, the Bulgarian revolt was poorly prepared and coordinated, and collapsed only a few weeks later under an Ottoman assault.[231] A key part in the empire's retaliation was played by the *bashi-bouzouks*, irregular forces in the sultan's pay, which visited harsh retribution on the Christian population and killed thousands, notably in Batak, a rebel stronghold.[232] This was a worrying turn of events for the Christian-Slavic side and led to the autonomous principalities of Serbia and Montenegro declaring war on the Ottoman Empire in June 1876 and thereby further exacerbating the crisis.

These new developments in the 'Eastern Question' were closely watched in the capitals of Europe. Russia and Austria in particular stepped up their diplomatic efforts in an attempt to influence events.[233] What became known as the 'Great Eastern Crisis' did not, however, reach wider public attention until the summer of 1876, when news of 'Turkish atrocities' against Christians in Bulgaria caused an outcry throughout Europe. In June, Edwin Pears and Januarius A. MacGahan, correspondents for the London *Daily News*, began a series of articles describing such massacres as that at Batak in horrifying detail.[234] Other similarly one-sided accounts followed, telling of Christian villages that had been razed and burned, women and children who had been violated, and brutally tortured men whose mutilated corpses lined the roads.[235] These stories found a particularly receptive audience in Russia, where pan-Slavism was gaining ground and descriptions of Balkan atrocities circulated widely, often linked to demands for intervention.[236] Elsewhere in Europe, too, these stories evoked reactions from a wide public and, as they had done in the cases of Greece and the Lebanon, triggered familiar anti-Ottoman reflexes. The massacres were taken as evidence of supposed 'oriental barbarism' visited on innocent Christians and luridly portrayed in both words and images. The *Illustrated London News* printed pictures of roads lined with scaffolds and the bodies of those that had been hanged from them. Another picture showed three mounted *bashi-bouzouks* in a burning village, riding over a priest carrying a cross to threaten a prostrate Christian woman and her child with their lances.[237] Similar themes were reproduced in other contemporary paintings, for instance in 'The Bulgarian Martyresses' by the Russian artist Konstantin E. Makovsky, which depicts two strikingly pale-complexioned Christian women (one with a babe-in-arms) being variously raped, murdered and abducted by three *bashi-bouzouks* with African and Asian features.[238]

At the government level, the news from the Balkans led to protests addressed to the Porte. Even the British government, now under the Conservative prime minister Benjamin Disraeli, who was concerned for the stability of the Ottoman Empire and rejected such accounts as wildly exaggerated, joined these protests and dispatched Walter Baring on a special diplomatic mission to Bulgaria to gather information and report home on the situation.[239] Although Baring's confidential report found some of the more lurid accounts to have been fabrications, he nonetheless concluded that some 12,000 Bulgarians had been killed and more than sixty villages destroyed in the violence.[240] However, these figures from Baring, who spoke no Bulgarian himself, were rough estimates rather than being based on concrete evidence.[241] Nor did the figures change the position of the British government, which stuck to Disraeli's policy of caution. His guiding policy was to put the national interest first or, as he declared to parliament: 'What our duty is at this critical moment is to maintain the Empire of England. Nor will we ever agree to any step, though it may obtain for a moment comparative quiet and a false prosperity, that hazards the existence of that Empire.'[242] From this it followed, in Disraeli's view, that the Ottoman Empire must be preserved as a geostrategic buffer and hence protected from any further destabilising interventions from without, especially from Russia.

Amid the outcry caused by the accounts of atrocities in the Balkans, however, Disraeli's position lost support among the British public and met with increasing resistance. In the late summer and autumn of 1876 a nationwide protest movement took shape, convening public meetings in various parts of the kingdom under such banners as 'Turkish Atrocities in Bulgaria'[243] and attacking the government's stance on the issue. In an echo of the abolitionist campaigns of earlier decades, more than 450 petitions were submitted to the government in London demanding that policy be reversed 'in the interest of humanity'.[244] The petitioners saw in the atrocities committed in Bulgaria, one term for which was 'crime against humanity',[245] further evidence of 'Turkish cruelty' to defenceless Christians and of the Porte's inability to govern its dominions in a just and civilised manner. Disraeli and his government were requested to stop British support for such a regime immediately and to reconsider Anglo-Turkish relations. Moreover, they were to make every effort to see the perpetrators brought to justice and to work towards a political solution, one aspect of which was to be a high degree of sovereignty for the afflicted provinces.[246]

The Liberal opposition encouraged such protests and sought to take advantage of them by turning this foreign policy question into a frontal assault on the Tory government's domestic record. William Gladstone, the former prime minister, was one of the leading voices of this campaign. Having withdrawn from politics following his electoral defeat two years earlier, Gladstone now returned to an active role at the urging of his friends and allies.[247] In September 1876 he published a pamphlet entitled *Bulgarian Horrors and the Question of the East*, which quickly sold more than 40,000 copies and some 200,000 in the longer term. In this bestseller, Gladstone drew on familiar accounts of what he termed 'Bulgarian Horrors', from which the Ottomans as a whole emerged as demons in human form, as 'one great anti-human specimen of humanity. Wherever they went, a broad line of blood marked the track behind them; and as far as their dominion reached, civilisation disappeared'.[248] His indictment of the Porte was directed at another of his longstanding rivals, Disraeli, on whose government he called to abandon its impassiveness and work with the other great powers of Europe to persuade the Porte to grant far-reaching autonomy to the troubled provinces of Bulgaria, Bosnia and Herzegovina, to ensure that such violent excesses might in future be prevented.[249]

In order to combine forces and keep up the protest movement's momentum, in December 1876 its leading figures convened a 'National Conference' in London, at which the Eastern Question Association was founded as an institutional framework. The association's purpose was to observe closely developments in the 'Eastern Question' and to shape public opinion by providing information.[250] To this end, the Eastern Question Association launched a lively publishing operation, quickly producing a number of pamphlets, all of which provided a distinctly one-sided view of the situation in the Ottoman Empire and fiercely attacked the Porte's supposedly chronic 'misrule'.[251]

A striking fact is that many of the association's members had close personal ties to the British anti-slavery movement – for instance, Frederick William Chesson, who was not only instrumental in initiating the 'Bulgarian atrocities' campaign, but at the same time was secretary of the Aborigines Protection Society.[252] Activists such as Chesson saw their cause as part of moral tradition that stretched back to the abolitionist movement, and the theme of slavery accordingly figured prominently in their attacks on the Porte.[253] Under the association's imprint, Chesson published a pamphlet on *Turkey and the Slave Trade*, which dealt not with recent events in the Balkans, but rather sought to show, drawing on numerous eyewitness reports, how slavery and the slave trade continued unabated in much of the Ottoman Empire in defiance of all international conventions to stop them. In Chesson's view, the Ottoman Empire had brought about its own isolation among the European powers by refusing to accept a minimum standard of civilisation that had become the international norm in the course of the last few decades: 'The Porte now stands alone among the Governments of Europe in its contemptuous defiance of that enlightened public opinion which was so emphatically expressed more than fifty years ago.'[254] By obstinately cleaving to the institution of slavery, the Ottoman Empire had proved its backwardness. It was, in Chesson's view, the main obstacle to the spread of civilisation in the sultan's dominions, preventing the extirpation of other evils:

If the African slave trade were effectually abolished – and this is a policy which certainly ought not to be beyond the power of united Europe to enforce – I believe that a deadly blow would be struck at two institutions [slavery and polygamy] which, so long as they exist, will absolutely prevent the superior class of Turks from making the slightest real approach either to civilisation or to civilised modes of thought. The gain to Turkey, if the great Powers were to decide upon adopting measures for the total extinction of the slave trade, would be incalculable.[255]

This motif of slavery as an expression of 'Turkish barbarism' was also used in the anti-Ottoman writings of other campaigners, a frequently occurring theme being the abduction of young Christian women into harems and hence sexual exploitation.[256]

Successful though it was in rallying public support, the protest movement and its campaign on the issue of 'Bulgarian atrocities' were by no means uncontroversial. Something of a countermovement formed in conservative circles to support Disraeli and defend the prime minister's stance. This camp, too, used public meetings and petitions – albeit rather fewer of both – to express its full confidence in the government's foreign policy.[257] The opposite side's agitation was attacked, as was Gladstone himself, who was accused of promoting a policy that was irresponsible and dangerous to British interests. A pamphlet mocked 'these full-blown humanitarians'[258] and accused such activists of persisting in the delusion

that the Russian Cabinet in her ambitious schemes is only animated by the sentiments of 'philanthropy', 'civilisation', and 'progress'. These meaningless and dangerous words, which Russia knows are of so much value in Europe, are only used by her to gild her infamous deeds, and to suit the palate and soothe the apprehensions of England, whose empire is to be wrecked and destroyed by the introduction of such insidious poisons. Finally, Russia uses the phrases *oppression of the Christians* in order to draw down the sympathy of Europe and to alienate the Christian provinces from the Porte under the mask of '*autonomy*' and '*independence*' which means, in the first place, handing them over to the tender mercies of the assassin of Poland and the jailor of Siberia. In the second place, it means also, and this is really what it does mean, transforming them from being bulwarks of defence against Muscovite ambition into instruments for the attack and downfall of Constantinople, and the destruction of the Ottoman Empire, as exemplified by the present attitude of Servia [Serbia], Montenegro, Bosnia, and Herzegovina.[259]

While Disraeli's and his own side's position were, of course, astute and guided by political realities, the opposition could only be naïve, their perspective skewed by 'humanitarian' ideals that prevented them from recognising the tsar's true motivation, which was to weaken the British Empire.

Although the British government's position did not lack a certain degree of support domestically, its hand nonetheless was eventually forced, above all by an escalation of the situation in the Balkans. A series of crushing defeats to the Serbian army had given Ottoman forces a clear march on Belgrade, threatening a renewed Ottoman occupation of the whole autonomous principality of Serbia. This was a disastrous prospect for pan-Slavists and compelled the tsar to threaten the Porte with war if it did not end hostilities.[260] The government of London was deeply concerned at the prospect of Russian intervention, which it feared would jeopardise European stability in general and British interests in the region in particular, and took diplomatic steps to contain the Russian threat.[261] Once the Porte had agreed to a temporary ceasefire in the Balkans, the foreign secretary, Lord Derby, made a proposal to the governments in Paris, Berlin, Vienna, St Petersburg, Rome and Constantinople for a joint conference to resolve the crisis.[262] Negotiations were to be held on the assumption that the Ottoman Empire's territorial integrity was inviolable. Derby also had recourse to a formula that had served as a common maxim for action in the international interventions in both Greece and the Lebanon, in which all the powers involved pledged to abstain from pursuing territorial gains or other one-sided advantages for themselves.[263] The Lebanese model in particular, with its emphasis on collective action and the creation of an international commission to oversee necessary reforms, was frequently cited as a point of reference and an example for a possible solution during the preliminary diplomatic talks.[264]

It was under these auspices that the envoys of Britain, France, Russia, Italy, Austria and Germany met in Constantinople in December 1876, first of all to discuss their respective positions with no involvement on the part of the Porte itself.[265] Although there was no hiding the antagonism between Britain and Russia, the six envoys managed to agree on a joint solution that would be proposed to the sultan.[266] Its key provision was autonomy for the provinces of Bosnia, Herzegovina and Bulgaria, together with an enhanced status for the Christian population there. A variety of other measures was also proposed. Besides fundamental structural, administrative and political reforms, the Porte was to rebuild houses and churches that had been destroyed, punish the perpetrators, compensate Christian victims (at the expense of the Muslim population) and ensure the return of refugees. Once more, the implementation of these proposals was to be overseen by an international commission, which would have an international police corps as its executive arm. Up to 4,000 policemen, to be drawn chiefly from such smaller, neutral states as Belgium, were to be deployed to Bulgaria and Bosnia to keep the peace, exert a stabilising influence and enforce the policies of the commission.[267]

The proposals of the six European powers obviously and massively impinged on the sovereignty of the new sultan, Abdul Hamid II. Unlike in the case of the Lebanon sixteen years earlier, the Porte now refused to accept any such far-reaching interference in its affairs. In order to under-score its willingness to cooperate and enact reforms, however – and above all to counter the reforms proposed by the European powers – it pointed to the first Ottoman constitution, which had just come into force and had introduced a parliamentary system for the first time in the empire's history.[268] The Constantinople Conference thus came to an end in January 1877 without having resolved the Great Eastern Crisis.[269]

Russia took the Porte's rejection of a subsequent diplomatic initia-tive[270] on the part of the six European powers as a pretext for declaring war on the Ottoman Empire on 24 April 1877, Tsar Alexander II having previously assured himself of Austrian neutrality and at least the tacit toleration of the other great powers. The tsar justified his resorting to military force by the continued oppression suffered by fellow Christians in the Balkan provinces:

Our faithful and beloved subjects know the lively interest which we have always devoted to the destinies of the oppressed Christian population of Turkey. Our desire to ameliorate and guarantee their condition has been shared by the whole of the Russian nation, which shows itself ready to-day to make fresh sacrifices to relieve the condition of the Christians in the Balkan Peninsula.[271]

Since the Porte had flatly rejected all reform proposals collectively advanced by the European powers and all attempts at a peaceful solution had been exhausted, the tsar now claimed to have no choice but to take up arms. Alexander II was thus able to dress his longstanding imperial ambitions in the region in humanitarian rhetoric and thereby ward off international criticism.[272] While they sustained heavy losses themselves during their advance, Russian forces inflicted a series of heavy defeats on the Ottoman Empire, which in March 1878 found itself with no choice but to sign the Treaty of San Stefano, in which it unconditionally accepted considerable territorial losses and the independence of Serbia, Montenegro and Romania as well as the autonomy of a territorially enlarged Bulgaria.[273]

These provisions, which promised to increase Russian power by giving it a greater Bulgarian principality as a client state on the Black Sea, shifted the geostrategic balance in the region in the tsar's favour, much to the concern of the other European powers. Calls were heard for a new and this time collective settlement, with tension between Russia on one side and Britain and Austria on the other bringing them to the brink of war.[274] It was against this background that the German chancellor, Otto von Bismarck, assumed the mantle of the honest broker and invited representatives of Britain, France, Russia, Austria, Italy and the Ottoman Empire to the Congress of Berlin, held in June and July 1878.[275] After a month of tough negotiations, the parties signed a treaty containing a number of territorial provisions, including the complete independence of Serbia, Montenegro and Romania.[276] Bulgaria's status was elevated to that of an autonomous principality, albeit smaller than originally envisaged for excluding Eastern Rumelia, a consciously placed check on Russian expansion. Austria, for its part, was permitted to occupy Bosnia and Herzegovina, which would turn out to be a heavy burden on Austro-Russian relations and more generally on future developments in the Balkans.[277]

Aside from this extensive redrawing of the map, a striking element of the Treaty of Berlin was that it made a humanitarian provision for each of the new territorial entities it created: religious discrimination was outlawed and the right to the free exercise of religion enshrined. In each instance, the text of the treaty contained a passage similar to this, quoted here according to the article concerning Bulgaria:

The difference of religious creeds and confessions shall not be alleged against any person as a ground for exclusion or incapacity in matters relating to the enjoyment of civil and political rights, admission to public employments, functions, and honours, or the exercise of the various professions and industries in any locality whatsoever. The freedom and outward exercise of all forms of worship are assured to all persons belonging to Bulgaria, as well as to foreigners, and no hindrance shall be offered either to hierarchical organization of the different communions, or to their relations with their spiritual chiefs.[278]

For its part, the Sublime Porte undertook to respect and implement these principles in all parts of the Ottoman Empire.[279] It also declared its willingness to enact reforms that would bring about lasting improvements to the security and living conditions of the Armenians and to inform the other signatories of such measures as it took.[280] The Treaty of Berlin thus firmly enshrined the principles of religious freedom and the protection of religious minorities in international law.

The historian Carole Fink has rightly judged these provisions of the Treaty of Berlin to mark an important step towards a system of the international protection of minorities, as it became established in the first half of the twentieth century.[281] She situates these developments above all in the context of the question of the protection of the Jewish minority in Romania, emphasising the key role of such prominent advocates for their cause as Gerson von Bleichröder, Bismarck's banker and close confidant. The 'Jewish question' and the various diplomatic initiatives associated with it in the nineteenth century no doubt had an important part to play, although Fink's analysis completely omits all mention of the various Western interventions for the protection of Christians in the Ottoman Empire, even claiming that 'when several thousand Maronite Christians were massacred in Lebanon in 1860 ... the western powers were silent'.[282] Considering the policies of the Concert of Europe since the Greek war of independence, however, such a claim hardly bears scrutiny: Far from standing by when Christians was massacred, the great powers several times intervened collectively for the benefit of particular minorities in the Ottoman Empire.[283] It was these repeated interventions and the diplomatic efforts associated with them – from Greece via the Lebanon to Bulgaria – that paved the way for the policy of protecting religious minorities that was ultimately enshrined in the Treaty of Berlin.

Overall, the Great Eastern Crisis acted as a catalyst for debates on intervention on humanitarian grounds that had already been initiated in the early nineteenth century by jurists such as James Stephen and Henry Wheaton, and contributed substantially to the development of scholarly opinion in the field.[284] This was particularly true of the circle of respected legal scholars who founded the Institut de droit international in Ghent in 1873 and whom the Finnish legal historian Martti Koskenniemi has called 'the "founders" of the modern international law profession'.[285] In October 1876, Gustave Rolin-Jaequemyns, the new institute's secretary general, published a long essay in the scholarly journal *Revue de droit international et de législation comparée*, in which he addressed the role of international law against the backdrop of the 'Eastern Question', which just then was poised to escalate.[286] He gave a detailed account of historical developments leading up to the present crisis, the revolts in Bosnia and Herzegovina, the massacres in Bulgaria, and the diplomatic negotiations that had begun in response to them. The Belgian jurist was highly critical of the Ottoman conduct of the war, accusing the Porte of having grievously and systematically violated the first Geneva Convention (1864), to which it had been a signatory.[287]

A central part in the essay was played by the question of the right or even the duty of the great powers of Europe to intervene collectively in the internal affairs of the Ottoman Empire.[288] To support such a right, Rolin-Jacquemyns adduced previous interventions of the great powers in Greece and Syria, and the international treaties that had been concluded in their train.[289] Systematically drawing connections between historical examples and the current situation, he was particularly critical of the hesitant attitude adopted by Britain under Disraeli, comparing it unfavourably to the '*politique d'intervention humaine*'[290] that his predecessor, Canning, had pursued in the Greek case. Rolin-Jacquemyns concluded:

> *The law*, as it emerges from history and treaties, is the collective intervention of Europe in the domestic affairs of Turkey *in the interest of general peace and of humanity. The fact* is the prolongation and aggravation of a state affairs that with each day is becoming *more dangerous to general peace* and ever more *contrary to humanity*. Under such conditions, it is no great effort to demonstrate that the great powers have not only the *right* but the *obligation* to intervene to whatever extent necessary and with all the resources at their disposal.[291]

As the Belgian jurist saw it, there existed a right and even a duty on the part of the Concert of Europe to intervene collectively, although this did not translate into the political reality of the day.[292]

In order to underpin his argument, Rolin-Jaequemyns reprinted in his journal a letter from Aegidius Arntz, a friend and colleague who taught law at the University of Brussels and had been a Prussian deputy in 1848–49. In this letter, which Rolin-Jaequemyns claimed to have received while working on his essay,[293] Arntz supported his friend's position with regard to the right of intervention and indeed went one step further in asking whether the classic principle of non-intervention in international law could still be upheld. In his own considerations on the lawfulness of interventions, Arntz concluded that they were permissible for securing the peaceful coexistence of nations and also in the following case:

> When a government, though acting within the limits of its sovereign rights, violates the rights of humanity – be it by measures contrary to the interest of

other states or be it by excesses of injustice and cruelty which are deeply wounding to our manners and our civilisation – the right of intervention is lawful. For, however worthy of respect the rights of sovereignty and the independence of states may be, there is something worthy of greater respect still, and that is the right of humanity, or of *human society*, which must not be insulted. Just as *within* the state the freedom of the *individual* is restrained and must be restrained by the *law* and by the *manners* of society, so the individual freedom of *states* must be limited by the law of human society.[294]

In order to bring this right of intervention into harmony with the guarantee of the independence of states – and thereby to guard against abuse – Arntz further proposed that it should be governed by the '*décision collective*' of the majority of 'civilised states', who were to adjudicate such cases in the form of an international tribunal or congress.[295] With this formula, Arntz provided something like a general definition of humanitarian intervention, limiting the legal protection of the sovereignty and independence of states by (or even subordinating it to) the 'law of humanity'. In the light of twenty-first-century debates on the 'responsibility to protect' vested in the community of states, which likewise is based on a limited concept of sovereignty, Arntz's deliberations from the 1870s are remarkable indeed.

Another of the Ghent institute's prominent members, Friedrich Fromhold Martens, added his opinion after the outbreak of the Russo-Ottoman war in 1877. Martens, a Russian diplomat and one of the most influential jurists of his time in the development of international humanitarian law, published an article (also in the *Revue de droit international*) justifying Russia's declaration of war under international law.[296] The tsar, Martens argued, had acted with no political or imperial interests of his own but solely '*au nom des intérêts de l'humanité*',[297] in order to improve the lot of the oppressed Christians in the Ottoman Empire. Martens' justification drew on the by now established precedents of Greece and Syria, but also referred explicitly to the negotiations at the Congress of Vienna in 1815.[298] Drawing a direct line between the Vienna declaration proscribing the slave trade and a note of protest from the tsar at the time concerning Ottoman atrocities against Christians in Serbia, he quoted from the latter document as follows:

It is by being based on what redounds to the benefit of the human race that the cause of the negroes was brought before the tribunal of the sovereigns, and it is by invoking these same principles that the heads of the European family claim the right to demand of the Porte the cessation of such atrocities.[299]

What Martens was trying to prove was that intervention – and ultimately armed intervention – on the part of the Concert in Europe to protect the Christians of the Ottoman Empire was supported by the same principles of civilisation as the great humanitarian project that was the battle against the slave trade.[300]

In arguing for this position, Martens was broadly following an understanding of the law that had been developed by the Swiss jurist Johann Caspar Bluntschli. Bluntschli, a co-founder of the Ghent institute and professor at the University of Heidelberg, was the author of an influential and indeed definitive work, *Das moderne Völkerrecht der civilisirten Staten*, the third edition of which was published in 1878 and took account of recent events.[301] In his preface to the new edition, Bluntschli stated that it was the key purpose of international law to safeguard the peaceful coexistence and freedom of states and that the principle of sovereignty was thus very precious indeed. Yet sovereignty was not an unlimited right, but subject to certain exceptions which justified, 'for the protection of certain human rights', interference in a country's domestic affairs.[302] The precedents he cited under the headings 'Penalties for Slavery' (*Massregeln gegen die Sclaverei*) and 'Religious Liberty' were European interventions, both military and diplomatic, against the slave trade and on behalf of fellow Christians in the Ottoman Empire.[303] Bluntschli hence argued that

When a violation of the law of nations is dangerous to the common good, then it is incumbent not only on the state thus violated, but on the other states, in whose power it stands to uphold the law of nations, to act against it and to vouch for the restoration and preservation of the legal order. Such violations dangerous to the common good pose a threat to the general world order and hence are apt to trouble all states.[304]

These dangerous violations included the oppression of other independent peoples, the introduction of slavery as well as 'flagrant and cruel tyranny against those of another faith'.[305] In such cases, the Swiss jurist argues, states were entitled

to set in motion their diplomatic representatives and demand redress of grievances, and they may, if need be, enter into an alliance, joining forces in order to ensure that justice is done and respect given to the law of nations and of man. In certain cases use of the diplomatic corps alone has sufficed to eradicate a violation of the law of nations. On other occasions the grievance was removed by the intercession of another power. Yet from time to time graver penalties may be called for, for instance such penalties as are jointly imposed for the punishment and prevention of piracy, to staunch the supply of slaves, ... to restrain inhumane cruelties. The European powers have repeatedly intervened in Turkey, chiefly for the protection of the Christian population, and likewise Austria in Romania to suppress the persecution of the Jews in 1867.[306]

The most recent example, Russia's war against the Ottoman Empire (1877–78), is explicitly mentioned elsewhere in the book.[307]

The arguments of such prominent and influential legal scholars as Rolin-Jaequemyns, Arntz, Martens and Bluntschli – all leading lights in their field – provided military interventions on humanitarian grounds with justification under international law, in which the struggle against the slave trade and the protection of Christian minorities in the Ottoman Empire served as precedents par excellence. In constantly referring back to these historical examples, they formulated as a theory in international law what had been a practice since the early nineteenth century. To this theory of humanitarian intervention, they gave a solid conceptual foundation and firmly anchored the resulting doctrine in international law. This development did not, however, proceed unopposed. A number of scholars of international law continued to reject any such right of intervention and demanded strict adherence to the principle of non-intervention.[308] Yet their numbers gradually diminished; from the later nineteenth century onwards, a majority of leading jurists supported the doctrine.[309] What this did not mean was that intervention now became automatic, that every severe humanitarian crisis was invariably met with a collective intervention on the part of the great powers. Such decisions continued to be made with political, geostrategic and imperial interests in mind as well as with a view to their military practicability. The massacres of several thousand Armenians in the interior of the Ottoman Empire between 1894 and 1896 are a case in point. While strong protests were made through diplomatic channels, no collective military intervention was ever launched.[310] What gradually happened instead was that the idea of humanitarian intervention became dissociated from its original motivations in the fight against the slave trade and the protection of Christian minorities. It now moved across the Atlantic, where it developed a new dynamism that would throw the double-sidedness of the practice of intervention into sharp relief.[311]

9 From Colonial Threat to 'Humanitarian' Example:

European Practices of Intervention and the United States of America

Perceptions of a European Threat and the Emergence of a Paradigm of American Non-Intervention

In the early nineteenth century the young republic that was the United States perceived intervention as it was practised by the monarchies of Europe as a serious threat to its interests and indeed its national security. These fears were sparked above all by the Holy Alliance's policy of intervention in the domestic affairs of sovereign states.[1] Under the impression of the wave of liberal revolutions that rocked the absolutist monarchies across southern Europe and threatened to spread elsewhere,[2] at the Congress of Troppau (1820) the Holy Alliance – the reactionary monarchies of Prussia, Russia and Austria – arrogated to itself a right of intervention.[3] Under the pretext of ensuring peace and political stability in Europe, the three great powers agreed to support legitimate (in their view) monarchies in neighbouring countries against revolutionary challenges of any kind, if necessary by force of arms. In direct consequence of this agreement the three powers undertook several repressive interventions between 1821 and 1823, dispatching troops to suppress liberal revolutions in Spain and the Italian peninsula.

These developments were registered with increasing concern on the other side of the Atlantic. For one thing, there was considerable sympathy in the United States for the revolutions in southern Europe, in which Americans were able to recognise their own nation's founding principles. The idea of monarchical restoration by the intervention of foreign powers was naturally abhorrent to them. Yet the government in Washington also had reason to fear that this policy of intervention might affect the American continent itself. Amid the turmoil of the Napoleonic wars, Spain's possessions in Central and South America had one by one declared their independence and embarked on a lengthy armed struggle for its recognition. Not unlike the 'Eastern Question' in the case of the Ottoman Empire, the waning of Spanish (and Portuguese) colonial rule gave rise to a 'Western Question'. The future of Latin America was at stake amid new geopolitical rivalries over spheres of political and commercial influence.[4] The United States, which had won its own independence in a long struggle within living memory, took the side of the nascent nations to its south. In 1822, the US government formally recognised the new republics of Buenos Aires, Chile, Gran Colombia, Mexico and Peru, considering them potential future allies.[5] In the light of the anti-revolutionary paradigm of intervention formulated at Troppau, however, Washington was worried that, having restored Ferdinand VII's absolutist rule, the Holy Alliance might support him in bringing the former colonies back under Spanish rule.

Itself still a young republic, the United States was at this point in its history concerned with consolidating its statehood at home and bolstering its standing as an independent nation abroad. Feeling itself still to be in a position of relative weakness, the US government was deeply mistrustful of the policies of the great powers of Europe and was accordingly wary of any changes in its own neighbourhood.[6] The idea that Spanish America might be recolonised and monarchic rule restored through the intervention of European powers posed a threat to the United States' own interests. There were, moreover, indications that a member of the Holy Alliance was seeking to expand its territory at the other end of the Americas. Already in September 1821 Tsar Alexander I had issued a decree (*Ukase*) proclaiming the north-western coast of North America – the coast, that is, of what is now the state of Alaska – as far south as 51° N latitude to constitute a Russian sphere of influence.[7] Trade in this area was to be the privilege of Russian merchants and foreign vessels were to keep 100 nautical miles away from the coast. Taken together with the scenario of a possible reassertion of European power in Latin America, this situation could only serve to heighten American concerns.

Amid this gathering international storm a surprising potential ally appeared in the shape of the United States' much-resented former colonial ruler and opponent in the war of 1812. Although Great Britain was perceived in Washington as a rival for the Oregon territory and, above all, the highly desirable Caribbean island of Cuba, its stance on the recolonisation of South America and the Holy Alliance's interventionist policy more generally was similar to that of the United States. As discussed previously, the British government had on several occasions taken a clear line opposing interference on the part of the reactionary monarchs and roundly rejected the Troppau Protocol.[8] Especially once the king of France, acting in the name of the Holy Alliance, had sent his forces to crush the liberal revolution in Spain, the intra-European conflict over an anti-revolutionary right of intervention became ever more acute.

Besides the consequences French action might have on the stability of the European system, another problem worried the British government. What aims across the Atlantic was France pursuing by allying itself with the absolutist king of Spain? Specifically, Britain was worried that France might not leave it at marching its troops across the Pyrenees and into the Iberian Peninsula, but might move on to Latin America in a bid to restore the rule of the Spanish Crown over its former possessions.[9] In return for its support, France might expect political and trading privileges in the Americas. This was a scenario that the government in London sought to avoid at all costs. By breaking out of Spain's sphere of influence, the newly formed Latin American republics had also broken out of their economic isolation and opened up entirely new commercial opportunities to nations other than Spain. As the world's leading commercial power, Britain stood to profit enormously from this development, whereas a restoration of Spanish rule would have closed off these emerging markets. With such benefits in mind, the British government considered giving diplomatic recognition to the new countries.[10]

This was the common ground between Britain and the United States: both were eager to avoid an intervention of the great powers of Europe in Latin America.[11] Britain, which was extending its own possessions in what is now Canada, was also opposed to southward Russian expansion along the coast of Alaska. In August 1823 Canning, the foreign secretary, seized the initiative and began talks with Richard Rush, the American ambassador to London, in order to establish whether the two governments might cooperate closely in addressing this sensitive issue.[12] The British idea was that such cooperation might begin with a joint declaration opposing all attempts and recolonisation and all forms of territorial expansion in the Americas. Canning underscored his government's commitment by adding that the United Kingdom would likewise desist from taking any such steps. Yet Canning was forced to note that this was where the American ambassador drew a line: 'Rush, in accepting my disavowal of any design upon Cuba, evades any reciprocal dis-avowal, on the part of his government in return.'[13] A condition of a joint declaration was a joint commitment to put one's own territorial expansion on hold, and this the American government was not prepared to make.

The British demarche sparked heated debates in Washington government circles regarding the benefits and drawbacks of a joint declaration. President James Monroe solicited the advice of two of his predecessors, Thomas Jefferson and James Madison, both of whom favoured cooperation with Britain, since the United States would have to fear no European power if it allied itself with the world's major naval power.[14] While Jefferson had always been a prominent advocate of acquiring

Cuba, he accepted the deferral of such territorial ambitions as a price worth paying for the alliance. The secretary of war, John C. Calhoun, although he had been cheerleader for war with Britain in 1812, now likewise urged President Monroe to accept the British offer. After the fall of Cadiz, the last stronghold of the Spanish revolutionaries, Calhoun feared that nothing stood in the way of French forces sailing from there to South America and hence that a European intervention was imminent.[15]

However, the secretary of state, John Quincy Adams, took a different view from Calhoun, holding fears of an imminent European intervention and the wholesale recolonisation of Spanish America to be vastly exaggerated.[16] To Adams' mind, the danger was rather that, by entering into an alliance with Britain, the United States might become embroiled in European disputes. Nor did he trust the sincerity of British motives. The British proposal, he argued, was directed 'ostensibly against the forcible interference of the Holy Alliance between Spain and South America; but really or especially against any acquisition to the United States themselves of any part of the Spanish-American possessions'.[17] There was, thought Adams, no particular diplomatic benefit to his country to be derived from a joint proclamation in which the United States acted only as a junior partner to Britain. Against this stood the real cost of forgoing America's own territorial ambitions in Texas and above all Cuba, which, alongside the general desirability of maintaining an independent foreign policy and the scope for action it entailed, militated against accepting the British proposal.[18] His advice to President Monroe was hence to take advantage of the forthcoming 'state of the union' address to Congress to define America's position clearly and without committing to an alliance with a foreign power.

President Monroe followed his secretary of state's advice. In the 'state of the union' address delivered on 2 December 1823 he gave a clear and bold outline of America's stance.[19] After announcing that negotiations with the governments of Russia and Britain would be entered into regarding their respective territorial claims on the north-western coast, Monroe asserted the principle 'that the American continents, by the free and independent condition which they have assumed and maintain, are henceforth not to be considered as subjects for future colonization by any European powers'.[20] This included Great Britain. The president added that the two hemispheres were fundamentally divided by their political systems – republics in the Americas, monarchies in Europe[21] – from which there followed Monroe's second principal claim:

We owe it, therefore, to candor and to the amicable relations existing between the United States and those powers to declare that we should consider any attempt on their part to extend their system to any portion of this hemisphere as dangerous to our peace and safety. With the existing colonies or dependencies of any European power we have not interfered and shall not interfere. But with the Governments who have declared their independence and maintain it, and whose independence we have, on great consideration and just principles, acknowledged, we could not view any interposition for the purpose of oppressing them, or controlling in any other manner their destiny, by any European power in any other light than as the manifestation of an unfriendly disposition toward the United States.[22]

Any European interference in the Americas was thus defined as constituting a potential threat to the security of the United States and hence rejected. Monroe took this opportunity to restate that it was a pillar of American policy to abstain from interfering in the domestic affairs of European states and that such abstention was expected in return from the European side: 'It is still the true policy of the United States to leave the parties to themselves, in hope that other powers will pursue the same course.'[23] The American president had thus formulated an independent foreign policy position for his country without binding it to Great Britain and abandoning its own plans for territorial expansion.

International responses to Monroe's declaration were varied. While the independence movements of Latin America were enthusiastic in their agreement,[24] the courts of Europe bristled at America's bold self-assertion. Such leading figures of the Holy Alliance as Metternich and Alexander I saw in Monroe's demands arrogance and presumption, although in common with the other European states their governments issued no notes of protest.[25] For one thing, there was little expectation that, in a crisis, the United States would have the capacity to act militarily on the foreign policy it had just proclaimed. Nor was there much inclination to dignify such effrontery with official responses, but rather to make a point of ignoring them. Meanwhile, the international crisis over the threat of European intervention in South America had receded and indeed had done so, unbeknown to Monroe, two months before he delivered his 'state of the union' address. In early October, Canning, the British foreign secretary, had discussed the problem in confidential talks with Prince Jules de Polignac, the French ambassador to London, who had assured Canning that France would neither support any attempts at recolonisation in South America nor make territorial claims of its own. As far as Canning was concerned, this removed any strategic need to cooperate with the United States.[26] The resulting 'Polignac Memorandum' left no doubt that Britain, in view of its own commercial interests, would not stand by and allow any European intervention in former Spanish America, while also making it clear that the Holy Alliance posed no acute threat in that regard.[27]

The American president's statement of principles, which acquired the name of 'Monroe Doctrine' only in the mid-nineteenth century, thus can be seen to have resulted from a misperception of imminent threats to American interests from European intervention.[28] Monroe's speech accordingly had few direct consequences or international repercussions. It was, however, a trailblazing statement of future American foreign policy as well as marking the United States' further emancipation as an independent power on the international scene.[29] The government in Washington declared its principled view on some of the urgent issues of the day, from which it derived the two key paradigms of its foreign policy, anti-colonialism and non-intervention. By unambiguously rejecting all colonial ambitions and attempts at interference in the western hemisphere, the United States defined its national security policy independently of the European powers while simultaneously raising the profile of its own foreign policy.[30] Yet the Monroe Doctrine arose above all from an awareness of America's own vulnerability and was defensive in character, as its commitment to non-intervention in European affairs clearly shows. Any kind of entanglement beyond the Atlantic that might affect America's own national security was thus to be precluded.

As a guideline for foreign policy, the Monroe Doctrine bore the unmistakable stamp of John Quincy Adams, the secretary of state,[31] who had asserted these principles on previous occasions, most prominently in a speech delivered to the House of Representatives on the occasion of Independence Day, 4 July 1821.[32] In this speech, Adams reaffirmed the United States' commitment to the republican ideals of freedom, justice and equality, while also pointing out that his country had

abstained from interference in the concerns of others, even when the conflict has been for principles to which she clings, as to the last vital drop that visits the heart. ... Wherever the standard of freedom and Independence has been or shall be unfurled, there will her heart, her benedictions and her prayers be. But she does not go abroad, in search of monsters to destroy. She is the well-wisher to the freedom and independence of all. She is the champion and vindicator only of her own.[33]

In support of this stance, Adams emphasised that a policy of intervention risked embroiling the United States 'in all the wars of interest and intrigue, of individual avarice, envy, and ambition' fought by other powers.[34] While assuring freedom and independence movements elsewhere of America's moral support, Adams made it equally clear that no active intervention was to be expected from the United States.

Yet a conflict in the south-eastern corner of Europe soon put this paradigm of American foreign policy to a severe test. From early 1821 onwards, the Greek war of independence not only threw relations between European states into increasing turmoil, but resounded even in political debates on the far side of the Atlantic. Soon after taking up arms against their Ottoman oppressors, the Greek insurgents addressed a petition directly to the United States,[35] emphasising that, the geographical distance between them notwithstanding, the Greek people felt much closer to America than to their European neighbours. The reason, as the petition put it, lay in the example set by America for the freedom of humankind more generally:

It is you, who first proclaimed these rights; it is you who have been the first again to recognize them, in rendering the rank of men to the Africans degraded to the level of brutes. It is by your example, that Europe has abolished the shameful and cruel trade in human flesh, from you that she receives lessons of justice, and learns to renounce her absurd and sanguinary customs.[36]

This was, needless to say, a gross distortion of the situation and rights of African slaves in the United States. Congress, it is true, had on 2 March 1807 and thus twenty-three days before the British parliament, passed a national ban on the Atlantic slave trade, forbidden the importation of new slaves into its territory and placed penalties on its own citizens' involvement of up to $20,000 in fines and ten years' imprisonment.[37] In practice, however, these measures were barely enforced, and successive US governments, as discussed previously, steadfastly refused to join an international system for the implementation of abolition, or put up resistance to any agreements that were made.[38] Moreover, slavery notoriously persisted in the South and divided the nation more than virtually any other issue.

For the Greeks, this manner of exalting the United States as the ultimate moral example served – along with the reference to abolition, the key humanitarian concern of the day – to obtain a hearing for their cause. It came with an appeal to the government in Washington to come to the aid of the Greek war of liberation from 'barbaric' Muslim occupation and in so doing to meet its obligations as a civilised nation. With a well-aimed jab at European inaction, the petition tried further to encourage America to intervene: 'You will not assuredly imitate the culpable indifference or rather the long ingratitude of some of the Europeans.'[39]

This Greek appeal to shared ideals and its stress on the United States' status as an example to other nations did not lack the desired effect among the American public. The State Department, however, was unswayed. Adams adhered to his policy, made no commitments to help the insurgents and brought all his political influence to bear for the purpose of preventing an American intervention in Greece.[40] His decisions were guided by consistent creed: 'The ground that I wish to take is that of earnest remonstrance against the interference of the European powers by force with South America, but to disclaim all interference on our part with Europe; to make an American cause, and adhere inflexibly to that.'[41] In debates within government circles in the run-up to the 1823 State of the Union, Adams even succeeded in persuading President Monroe to delete passages from his original draft that would have given official recognition to Greek independence and recommended sending an ambassador there.[42] In the address that ended up being delivered, Monroe expressed only general sympathy with the Greek cause and the hope that its struggle might succeed, without offering anything at all by way of concrete assistance.[43]

This was, at the time, a highly unpopular position for the Monroe administration and Secretary Calhoun in particular to take. As in Europe, the Greek struggle for independence was widely supported in the United States. The ideals of classical education encouraged many Americans to identify with the Greek cause, and between 1821 and 1824 philhellenic committees sprang up throughout the country. With their strongholds in Boston, New York and Philadelphia, these committees collected donations to buy arms and supplies for the insurgents and to rally the public to their support.[44] Accounts of the enslavement of women and children and of massacres and atrocities against civilians, indeed of a 'war of extermination' supposedly being fought by the Ottomans, were, as they were in Europe, instrumental in creating public pressure and channelling it towards the government.[45] Such eminent philhellenes as Robert Walsh, editor of the Philadelphia *National Gazette*, Albert Gallatin, the US ambassador to France, and Edward Everett, professor of Greek at Harvard University and editor of the *North American Review*, repeatedly demanded that the American government intervene in the conflict, with one proposed measure being to dispatch ships of the US Navy to the Mediterranean in support of the Greek war effort.[46] Support for the Greek cause extended into the highest political circles, its most prominent advocates being the former presidents Thomas Jefferson, James Madison and John Adams, father of none other than John Quincy Adams.

Nor did Monroe's statement of principles put an end to debates over the stance America should take. Only six days after the State of Union, a group of philhellenic congressmen led by Daniel Webster, the influential representative for Massachusetts, tabled a draft resolution recommending that the president nominate a special US envoy to Greece.[47] By introducing the notion of Greek independence at the parliamentary level, Webster sparked controversy ahead of the vote.[48] Webster's resolution, which was supported by such eminent representatives as Samuel Houston and Henry Clay, the speaker of the house, made a moral argument based on the United States' liberal and democratic traditions. To the House of Representatives, Webster spoke in favour of using 'moral force' of the kind expressed in public opinion and which most distinctly set the United States apart from the reactionary monarchies of Europe:

> There is a force in public opinion which, in the long run, will outweigh all the physical force that can be brought to oppose it. ... What is the soul, the informing spirit of our institutions, of our entire system of government? Public opinion. While this acts with intensity, and moves in the right direction, the country must ever be safe – let us direct the force, the vast moral force of this engine, to the aid of others. Public opinion is the great enemy of the Holy Alliance.[49]

Webster criticised the alliance of European monarchs for claiming to uphold Christian principles while doing nothing to stop the murder and enslavement of thousands of Greek Christians by the 'barbarian' Turks. After giving a vivid account of the massacre of Greek civilians in Chios, Webster concluded by emphasising that his draft resolution did not imply a departure from the United States' avowed foreign policy of non-intervention, but merely constituted a peaceful measure for the moral support of the Greeks:

> It will give them courage and spirit, which is better than money. It will assure them of the public sympathy, and will inspire them with fresh constancy. It will teach them that they are not forgotten by the civilized world, and to hope one day to occupy, in that world, an honorable station.[50]

Webster's opponents in the House were not, however, at all convinced that this initiative was as harmless as he claimed. It was, they argued, political dynamite, and in any case apt to harm the American interest by bringing the United States into direct conflict with both the Ottoman Empire and the great powers of Europe. While professing himself sympathetic to the Greek cause, Joel Poinsett, representative for South Carolina, considered it his foremost duty to protect his own country's security and not to expose it to the risk of war fought in pursuit of other than the United States' immediate interests.[51] Poinsett found the moral arguments to be outweighed by American security interests:

In whatever light we may regard a policy which sacrifices to its selfish views the rights of humanity and justice, and the claims of a suffering Christian people, in matters relating exclusively to Europe, we ought not to interfere. We cannot do so without departing from those principles of sound policy which have hitherto guided our councils, and directed our conduct. Any inference on our part, in favor of a cause which not even remotely affects our interests, could only be regarded in the light of a crusade, and might injure the Greeks by alarming the fears of the Allied Powers.[52]

A similar position was taken by John Randolph, representative for Virginia, who reminded the House that he and his fellow representatives had been elected to protect the rights not of foreign subjects, but of their own countrymen.[53] To intervene in the eastern Mediterranean would mean opening a 'Pandora's box of political evils',[54] the worst of which was a costly war with the Ottoman sultan and – a particularly sensitive issue in Washington – his clients, the Barbary pirates of North Africa. To this were added fears that armed conflict with the Ottoman Empire would put a stop to American trade with the port of Smyrna in Asia Minor, which was gaining in importance, and harm its Mediterranean commerce more generally.[55] The force of these counterarguments combined to defeat Webster's draft resolution by a clear majority. The opponents of intervention in Greece had won the day.[56]

Adams, who stood in close contact with the resolution's opponents and indeed supplied them with arguments,[57] was thus able to maintain his policy of American non-intervention. The US stance remained unchanged to the end of the Greek war of independence.[58] Aid to the Greek insurgents in the form money, arms and other supplies remained the preserve of numerous private organisations, which some historians have taken to mark the beginning of American humanitarian relief efforts overseas.[59] That Adams refused to countenance an official intervention was by no means due to a lack of warmth towards the Greek cause. When he himself became president, he several times expressed an interest in events and his own sympathy with the rebels.[60] In his 'state of the union' addresses of both 1827 and 1828 he expressly welcomed the intervention in the conflict of the great powers of Europe, paid tribute the part played by Tsar Nicholas I and gave voice to his hope that the 'triumph of humanity and of freedom' might now be assured.[61] Yet he remained staunchly opposed to an intervention by his own country, fearing entanglement in European affairs and the concomitant threat to American security. Like humanitarian considerations, republican ideals of liberty and independence were clearly subordinated to the interests of realpolitik.[62] Adams' priority was for America to pursue a foreign policy that would be wholly independent of European conflicts and constellations of powers, instead safeguarding above all its own funda-mental interests. The result was a foreign policy paradigm that was defensive in nature and prescribed non-intervention in European affairs.

An Expansionist Foreign Policy and the Strategic Importance of Cuba

Whereas President Monroe's statement of principle placed a bar on all new European colonial endeavours in the western hemisphere and any attempts at interference there, it left the United States with all options for expansion in the double continent. More still, in the following decades the Monroe Doctrine emerged as the foundation for the claim to contin-ental hegemony expressed by various US administrations.[63] Plans for territorial expansion concerned first of all the vast lands west of the Mississippi. As white settlers advanced and the Native American popu-lation was expelled, resettled or killed, the frontier moved steadily west-wards and US territory grew at an astonishing speed.[64]

This development sparked lively debates in the 1840s over both for-eign and domestic policy, the urgent issues being the annexation of Texas, which had broken loose from Mexico, and the vast Oregon Territory in the Pacific Northwest. The idea of a supposed 'manifest destiny' – the phrase was coined by a New York journalist, John L. O'Sullivan, in 1845 – by which the United States was virtually appointed by God to grow as a nation by taking possession of the entire North American continent, soon became a popular rallying call to a policy of unfettered expansion.[65] At the time, the president was James K. Polk, a Democrat and a vocal advocate of territorial expansion, a policy which he began increasingly to justify with reference to the prin-ciples of foreign policy proclaimed by his predecessor. In his December 1845 'state of the union' address, Polk discussed at some length the incorporation of the former Republic of Texas into the Union, which had, he stressed, taken place by violent conquest, but by the free and express desire of its citizens.[66] In this context, the president referred both to the rapid worsening of relations with Mexico and the failed attempts of Britain and France (both monarchies at the time) to prevent the acces-sion of Texas by diplomatic manoeuvring.[67] Against British ambitions, Polk restated the United States' claim to the Oregon Territory as an integral part of its interests in the continent of North America.[68] With regard to conflicts with European powers that might arise in the course of America's pursuit of rapid territorial expansion, Polk left no doubt that he would tolerate no form of European interference, not even in the interest of a 'balance of powers':

The people of the United States can not, therefore, view with indifference attempts of European powers to interfere with the independent action of the nations on this continent. The American system of government is entirely different from that of Europe. ... We must ever maintain the principle that the people of this continent alone have the right to decide their own destiny. Should any portion of them, constituting an independent state, propose to unite themselves with our Confederacy, this will be a question for them and us to determine without any foreign interposition.[69]

This claim and Polk's commitment to its practical implementation were underscored by a direct appeal to the principles stated by President Monroe twenty-two years previously.

While the Oregon question was settled peacefully – negotiations resulted in a treaty separating British and American claims along the forty-ninth parallel[70] – tensions over the annexation of Texas led to a two-year war with Mexico. The Mexican–American War ended in 1848 with a heavy Mexican defeat and enormous territorial gains for the United States. In the Treaty of Guadalupe Hidalgo, all of California and all territory north of the Rio Grande were ceded to the United States, definitively establishing it as the dominant power in North America.[71] By invoking the danger of European intervention in these conflicts – as he did so conspicuously in his 'state of the union' address – Polk made a deliberate appeal to old fears while offering his own policies by way of reassurance. The Monroe Doctrine played an important part in justifying his policies, but it is also worth noting how Polk reinterpreted principles that had originally been defensive in nature as setting the United States on an expansionist and increasingly even imperial course.[72]

A little-known episode from the Mexican–American War vividly illustrates this development: the *Guerra de Castas* or Caste War of Yucatan.[73] While US forces were occupying all of northern Mexico and preparing to advance on the capital, the country's socially and economically extremely disadvantaged indigenous majority rose up in the south-east in July 1847. The insurgents, descendants of the peninsula's native Maya population, soon brought large parts of the region under their control and came to pose such a threat to the white ruling class, descendants of the Spanish conquerors, that the provincial governor appealed to Britain, Spain and the United States for help.

The appeal to Washington, which in return for an American military intervention seemed to promise the transfer of sovereignty over the peninsula to the United States and ultimately its formal annexation, was referred by President Polk to Congress. Polk told Congress of the white population's increasingly perilous situation and indeed the prospect of its complete annihilation, according to the reports he had received, at the hands of the indigenous insurgents:

These communications present a case of human suffering and misery which can not fail to excite the sympathies of all civilized nations. From these and other sources of information, it appears that the Indians of Yucatan are waging a war of extermination against the white race. In this civil war they spare neither age nor sex, but put to death, indiscriminately, all who fall within their power. The inhabitants, panic stricken and destitute of arms, are flying before their savage pursuers toward the coast, and their expulsion from their country or their extermination would seem to be inevitable unless they can obtain assistance from abroad.[74]

The president made no secret of it that in this desperate situation, the white population had addressed similar appeals to the European colonial powers, Spain and the United Kingdom. It was at this point that Polk referred to the Monroe doctrine and his own 'state of the union' address of December 1845. He forcefully reiterated the principled refusal to admit any form of European interference in the western hemisphere. The Yucatan Peninsula, he continued, exposed as it was in the Gulf of Mexico and facing the south-western coast of the United States as well as Cuba, the largest island in the Caribbean, could pose a threat to national peace and security if it fell under the rule of a European state. Polk thus hoped that Congress would take measures 'to prevent Yucatan from becoming a colony of any European power, which, in no event, could be permitted by the United States, and, at the same time, to rescue the white race from extermination or expulsion from their country'.[75] In his call for action, the president shrewdly dressed American geostrategic interests in a purportedly humanitarian concern for a white population threatened with expulsion and destruction by indigenous 'savages'.

Polk's initiative was hotly debated between the various parties in Congress. While most Democrats supported their president's line and adopted his humanitarian rhetoric, the Whigs were opposed to taking action, fearing above all that it might jeopardise the peace treaty that had only just been negotiated with Mexico.[76] The debates dragged on for several weeks and ended only when the news reached Washington that the warring parties had begun talks. The argument for or against intervention was never settled. Although the Yucatan episode had no direct consequences for American policy, it can be seen representing Polk's reinterpretation of the Monroe Doctrine along expansionist and imperialist lines and his conception of the United States as the ultimate arbiter of order in the Americas, the right of intervention included. This manner of seizing on humanitarian and civilizational concerns and combining them with geostrategic interests give a suggestive foretaste of developments in US foreign policy that would only fully reveal themselves later in the nineteenth century.[77]

As the Yucatan crisis shows, Washington kept a watchful eye not only on the mainland, but included the Caribbean's largest island in its foreign policy planning. Cuba, which had been a Spanish colony since the sixteenth century, was an attractive prize for a variety of players on account of its large and profitable sugar and coffee plantations. Moreover, the island, situated a mere 180 kilometres off the coast of Florida and by virtue of its size and shape commanding both passages to the Gulf of Mexico, and which had a well-developed port in Havana, was considered the strategic key to the entire region. As the last bastion of Spanish rule, which once had dominated the Americas, Cuba became the site of competing imperial interests and particularly of the growing rivalry between Britain and the United States.[78] The governments of both countries were resolved not to let the other gain dominance on the island, let alone allow the rival to assume sovereignty over it. Cuba thus came to figure in the imperial designs and the foreign policy of both countries.

The issue of slavery and the slave trade was inextricably tied to and played a key role in these considerations.[79] Cuba's entire colonial economy and the tremendous wealth it generated were based on the forced labour of enslaved Africans. Even after Spain had signed the treaties of 1817 and 1835 and thereby acceded to the international ban on the slave trade, Cuba remained the centre of a thriving human traffic in which a further 400,000 slaves were brought to Cuba in defiance of the trade's international proscription.[80] This meant that the island was often the focus of British efforts at abolition. The government in London repeatedly used diplomatic channels to remind its counterpart in Madrid to abide by its treaty obligations while dispatching the Royal Navy to seize slave ships in the Caribbean. Unlike in the case of Brazil after 1850, however, when British ships had taken the fight to the country's territorial waters and even to installations on the coast, Britain did not escalate matters as far with regard to Cuba.[81] Britain's more cautious approach was driven by concerns that too aggressive an attack might cause the powerful slaveholders and plantation owners of Cuba to rise up against the Spanish government and drive them into the open arms of the United States – or at any rate give the Americans a compelling reason to intervene on the island.[82] Britain thus put its own geostrategic and imperial interests in the Caribbean ahead of the consistent implementation of its humanitarian foreign policy imperative.

The American side meanwhile saw only dangerous interference in any British attempt to implement abolition. British attempts to persuade the Republic of Texas to join the international treaty regime against the slave trade in exchange for diplomatic recognition of its independence from Mexico had already inflamed American opinion and encouraged latent Anglophobia.[83] There were concerns that British policy in Cuba might succeed in hastening the end of slavery in the American South, too. Talk of a supposedly imminent 'Africanization of Cuba' was calculated to appeal to fear of a bloody 'race war' along the lines of the Haitian Revolution, which would result in the emancipation of all Cuban slaves, the creation of a free 'black' republic in the island under British protection and all the threats that having such an entity close by posed to the system of slavery in the United States.[84] The idea that Cuba should be annexed by the United States was hence popular not only with many Cuban plantation owners and slave holders, but also to many in the American South. To arrest this development and preserve the institution of slavery in Cuba would be to make it a bulwark against further abolitionist encroachments.[85] Whereas British attempts at intervention were designed to put an end to the slave trade and ultimately to slavery in Cuba as such, those of the United States sought to accomplish the exact opposite, the preservation of the existing system.

The annexationist movement in the United States now supported any measures that might help to bring Cuba under US control. A series of so-called 'filibuster' expeditions were launched between 1849 and 1855, in which bands of irregular fighters from the United States landed in Cuba with the aim of toppling the government.[86] Wary on such goings-on, the governments of Britain and France in 1853 proposed a joint convention in which both countries promised to give up any claims of their own to Cuba if the United States likewise agreed to respect and preserve Spanish sovereignty over the island. This was rejected by the US government, which argued that the question of Cuba was above all an American matter.[87] Indeed, in the following year the administration of President Franklin Pierce made a new offer to Spain to buy the island, although it was no more successful than James Polk had been in 1848.[88] The American Civil War, which settled the issue of slavery in the United States, also put an end to the 'annexationist era'.[89] In spite of many foreign attempts at intervention, Cuba remained a Spanish possession.

In the years that followed, however, Spanish rule over Cuba was under threat from within rather than from foreign powers. For want of urgent political, social and economic reform, an independence movement grew and rose up in arms in October 1868.[90] Led by Antonio Maceo and Máximo Gómez, the insurgents fought a skilled campaign of guerrilla warfare, inflicting severe losses on Spanish forces and bringing large swathes of the remote eastern provinces under their control. Spain reacted to this threat to its authority by massively increasing its forces.

It also embarked on a policy of brutal repression which, in its reliance on such means as the resettlement and internment of Cuban civilians, anticipated core elements of the anti-insurgency tactics that would be fully developed later in the century by General Valeriano Weyler.[91]

The Cuban insurgents looked north in their search for allies, hoping for political and moral support from the United States. Although large sections of the US public were fundamentally in sympathy with the insurgents' struggle against Spanish rule, which was perceived as increasingly cruel and despotic, President Ulysses S. Grant's administration refused to accord them belligerent status and thereby give them valuable international recognition. With its own commercial interests in mind, the US government limited itself to diplomatic attempts at mediation and repeatedly called on the Spanish government to make basic political reforms in Cuba. Having recently fought a civil war to enforce abolition across its own country, the US government also stressed that slavery must end in Cuba, citing international standards of civilisation.[92]

The Ten Years' War ended in 1878 without the insurgents having achieved their goal of *Cuba libre*. Nor did a brief resurgence of the independence struggle, the *Guerra Chiquita* or 'little war' of 1879–80, change matters.[93] Spain held onto Cuba at the cost of an estimated 260,000 dead and an island ravaged by eleven years of warfare.[94] But the political, social and economic roots of the conflict had not been removed, and Cuban yearning for independence only continued to grow. Inspired by the writer José Marti, the movement regrouped in exile and tried to regain its revolutionary momentum. In 1892, Marti, alongside Cuban tobacco workers, founded the Partido Revolucionario Cubano in the United States as the movement's political arm and persuaded Maceo and Gomez, the Cuban leaders in the Ten Years' War, who by now were also living in American exile, to resume the armed struggle.[95]

After years of preparation the revolutionaries launched their campaign in February 1895, calling Cubans to rise up against Spanish rule. In spite of setbacks and Marti's early death in a gun battle, the rebellion spread across the island from east to west. Unlike in the Ten Years' War, the rebels were now able to take the fight into the wealthy western provinces, where the liberation army found support and new recruits among the rural population. The gates of Havana were soon in sight and with them the centre of political and economic power in Cuba.[96] Such bad news from the Caribbean alarmed the Spanish government, which was desperate to hold onto its remaining overseas possessions. In January 1896 it named General Valeriano Weyler the new captain general and sent him to Cuba with reinforcements to restore order and quell the insurgency.

Weyler was known as a particularly fierce and ruthless military leader, a reputation gained in the Ten Years' War in Cuba, in the Philippines and also in putting down unrest in Spain itself.[97] Since the revolutionary forces avoided pitched battles with the better-equipped Spanish army and instead relied on hit-and-run raids, Weyler's counter-insurgency strategy was to cut them off from their support among the civilian population and to prevent reinforcements, in both personnel and materiel, from reaching them. Combined with scorched-earth tactics, the Spanish captain general ordered the island's rural population to be 'reconcentrated' around fortified towns and villages and thereby to bring them under the close control of the authorities.[98] Some 400,000 people were forcibly resettled on Weyler's orders, mostly to completely overcrowded reconcentration centres with insufficient food and shocking sanitary conditions. Within a short period, this brutal policy of reconcentration claimed the lives of an estimated 170,000 civilians, around one in ten of the population at the time, who died of disease and malnutrition.[99] Yet even this radicalisation of violence did not achieve Weyler's goal of completely suppressing the anti-colonial revolt. His choice of strategy turned out to be completely misguided and indeed counterproductive, contributing as it did to the further alienation of Cubans from Spanish rule and driving large sections of the population into the arms of the revolutionaries. By heralding the end of centuries of Spanish rule in the Caribbean, Weyler's campaign was a disaster for his country's foreign policy, too.

The Spanish–American War of 1898: A Humanitarian Intervention?

Although the Spanish government made every effort at censorship, it was unable to conceal the worsening humanitarian situation in Cuba from the wider world. Foreign correspondents and diplomats sent home reports that caused an international outcry and protests against Spain's conduct of the war, with the American media taking a particular interest in the situation.[100] This was due not least to the effort of the 'Cuban Junta', based in New York and Washington, which acted as a kind of overseas branch of the Cuban independence movement. Under the leadership of Tomás Estrada Palma, the Junta sought to win both material and moral support for its armed campaign.[101] To this end, it built a network of supporters in the United States, setting up political clubs in various cities. It also held public 'sympathy meetings' to promote the revolutionary cause and raise funds for the purchase of much-needed supplies. In its efforts to sway American public opinion in its favour and thereby to force the government of Washington to intervene, it drew on its close links with major newspapers, feeding them information (sometimes daily) on the progress of the war that suited the Junta's own propagandistic purposes.[102]

Besides glorifying its revolutionary campaign as a heroic anti-colonial liberation struggle, a key issue in the Junta's appeals was General Weyler's policy of reconcentration. The activists constantly launched new 'atrocity stories' about Spanish measures, stories that were often exaggerated and sometimes outright fabrications. Yet these stories found willing takers in the American press, which made itself a participant in a well-orchestrated campaign.[103] Papers ran more and more stories under such headlines as 'The Cuban Horror' and 'Spanish Barbarities', telling of the deaths of hundreds of thousands of *reconcentrados* and focusing their attention in particular on Spain's 'barbaric' conduct of the war.[104] These tales of horror were visually underpinned by horrifying photographs and illustrations from the reconcentration centres, depicting Cubans starved to the bone.[105] Influential publishers such as William Randolph Hearst and Joseph Pulitzer, who competed for mass readerships, took up the issue and couched their papers' reporting on the war in sensationalist terms, thereby increasing the impact of the horrific stories even further.[106] Such stories were lapped up by a public of which large sections had long held latently anti-Spanish views.[107] The suffering of Cuban civilians was taken as further proof of Spain's cruel tyranny over America's Caribbean neighbour, and frequent comparisons were made with the 'Turkish despotism' of the Ottoman Empire.[108] Meanwhile General Weyler, styled the 'Butcher' on account of his savage pursuit of the war, came to figure as evil incarnate in the American press.[109]

These stories not only gave detailed accounts of Cuban suffering; they increasingly also made concrete demands. The American government was asked no longer to stand by while a 'war of extermination' was being waged against innocent civilians on its own doorstep, but to put an end to it by means of direct intervention.[110] In justifying such demands, writers repeatedly invoked the practice of European states, pointing to interventions on behalf of Christians (and against the Ottoman Empire) in Greece, the Lebanon and the Balkans as precedents for the kind of action they were demanding.[111] In this view, the United States was not only entitled to intervene, but indeed, as a civilised Christian nation, morally obliged to do so, as an article published in April 1898 argued with particular force:

Interference by one power with the sovereign rights of another power is always a proceeding fraught with danger, and the cases in which it is warranted are very few. But by common consent, if not under the rules of international law, it is warranted on humanitarian ground. Europe intervened to stop the slaughter in Greece in 1827. Russia intervened in Bulgaria in 1877, and, last year, the powers put a stop by force to Ottoman oppression in Crete. To-day, in Cuba, a situation has been reached which makes almost inevitable the extermination of the neutral population, and the reduction of the fertile island to a desert, unless the pacification of the island is soon effected. It is for this reason that intervention is needed, and for this object alone that it is made. President McKinley has been insistent in keeping before Congress and the country the humanitarian duty as the sole national justification of intervention. The situation in Cuba has become so intolerable that no self-respecting Christian Nation can permit its continuance. On the ground of simple humanity the duty of interference is imperative.[112]

This mood, created among the public by the press, was increasingly noted by political decision-makers in Washington, where it caused lively debates. While Grover Cleveland's administration had adopted a stance of strict neutrality and limited itself to occasional efforts at diplomatic arbitration,[113] his Republican successor, William McKinley, who took office in 1897, found such a policy increasingly difficult to maintain. As the war dragged on and its repercussions were felt ever more widely, the new president was subject to mounting pressure, both from the public and within government circles.[114] McKinley hence felt compelled to clarify US policy with regard to the Cuban independence struggle. American voices, led by McKinley himself, now came to emphasise not only the harm done by the war to commerce in general and American holdings in Cuba in particular, but also the humanitarian consequences of Spain's pursuit of the war.[115] In protest at the country's 'uncivilised' conduct, particularly its 'reconcentration' measures aimed at innocent civilians, McKinley addressed a note of protest to the Spanish government 'in the name of the American people and in the name of common humanity'.[116]

Spain recalled General Weyler, who had devised the policy of reconcentration, in the autumn of 1897. The appointment in his place of Rámon Blanco as captain general, along with the announcement of a statute of autonomy and fundamental reforms, reduced tensions, if only temporarily. The Spanish government also allowed shipments of US aid to enter Cuba for the first time, having previously refused to do so on the grounds that this would constitute an admission of its own failure as well as opening the door to foreign intervention. Under the auspices of Clara Barton, a well-known public figure who had founded and now chaired the American Red Cross, and the Cuban Relief Committee, which the president had set up for the purpose, a concerted effort was now made to collect clothing, medicine and above all food in the United States and send them to Cuba for the benefit of the civilian population.[117] The US government broadly approved of these encouraging developments. In his 'state of the union' address of December 1897, President McKinley praised the Spanish government for the steps it had taken so far and said that it should be given a chance to enact the reforms that it had announced. Yet McKinley also left no doubt that American forbearance was not limitless: 'If it shall hereafter appear to be a duty imposed by our obligations to ourselves, to civilization and humanity to intervene with force, it shall be without fault on our part and only because the necessity for such action will be so clear as to command the support and approval of the civilized world.'[118] Although willing to remain on good diplomatic terms with Spain, the president kept open the option of military intervention in the name of humanity.

Yet in early 1898 the two countries' bilateral relations took a turn for the worse, making a direct armed confrontation between the United States and Spain seem likelier than ever. First came a wave of public anger at the publication of a letter intercepted by the Cuban Junta, in which the Spanish ambassador to Washington, Enrique Dupuy de Lôme, expressed his disdain for President McKinley and US efforts to resolve the ongoing conflict.[119] Around the same time the cruiser USS *Maine*, which had been dispatched to Cuba to protect American citizens and their interests, sank in Havana harbour. An explosion on the night of 15 February 1898 completely destroyed the ship and killed 266 of the crew. Americans suspected an act of sabotage on the part of Spain, further stoking public indignation. 'Remember the Maine! To Hell with Spain!' became a patriotic rallying cry, and calls for military intervention could no longer be ignored.[120]

Irrespective of these two serious incidents, however, the US government's patience was wearing thin. Washington no longer believed that Spain would be able to regain control of the situation and restore lasting peace to Cuba in the foreseeable future.[121] The regular dispatches of Fitzhugh Lee, the US consul, who had been in favour of intervention from the moment he took office in Havana, suggested that the reforms initiated by Spain were ineffective, particularly with regard to the humanitarian plight of the *reconcentrados*.[122] This estimate was shared by Redfield Proctor, a Republican senator who had made his own way to Cuba to obtain a view of events unclouded by sensationalist reporting and public fury at home. During the two weeks of his fact-finding mission, Proctor met Spanish officials, including Captain-General Blanco himself, visited hospitals and reconcentration settlements, and accompanied Clara Barton on her mission to distribute relief supplies.[123]

Having returned to Washington, Proctor delivered a widely noticed speech to the Senate on 17 March 1898, in which he gave a detailed account of his travels. He discussed various aspects of the conflict, but was particularly affected by the tremendous suffering of the civilian population:

> Conditions are unmentionable in this respect. Torn from their homes, with foul earth, foul air, foul water, and foul food or none, what wonder that one-half have died and that one-quarter of the living are so diseased that they cannot be saved? A form of dropsy is a common disorder resulting from these conditions. Little children are still walking about with arms and chests terribly emaciated, eyes swollen, and abdomen bloated three times the natural size. The physicians say these cases are hopeless.[124]

Senator Proctor further claimed that, before visiting Cuba, he had been sure that the images and reports circulating in the press were exaggerations based on isolated incidents. Now, however, that he had witnessed the plight of the *reconcentrados* with his own eyes, he was able fully to confirm these accounts.[125] While Proctor acknowledged that, under Captain-General Blanco, the Spanish authorities had changed tack, he also remarked that the new measures had been largely ineffective, clashing as they did with continuing military imperatives.[126] Finally, he emphasised that he had at no point communicated with members of the Cuban Junta and that the account of his experiences was not to be taken as arguing for any particular measures. His fellow senators were to draw their own conclusions, although Proctor added:

> To me the strongest appeal is not the barbarity practiced by Weyler nor the loss of the *Maine*, if our worst fears should prove true, terrible as are both of these incidents, but the spectacle of a million and a half of people, the entire native population of Cuba, struggling for freedom and deliverance from the worst misgovernment of which I ever had knowledge.[127]

Such a statement made by the senator from Vermont, who was respected across party lines, did not fail to make an impact in Congress and in the US government itself.[128] President McKinley began to discuss armed intervention against Spain with his closest confidants, among whom was his personal friend John J. McCook. McCook, a Republican whom McKinley had even considered for the departments of justice and the interior in his first cabinet, was a successful corporate lawyer and accordingly well-connected in New York business and finance. He also had contacts in the Cuban Junta and was himself a strong advocate of Cuban independence – above all because of the island's potential for trade and investment.[129] Since the spring of 1897, McCook and Samuel M. Janney, an influential Wall Street banker, had been working on a plan to buy Cuba from Spain with the help of a financial syndicate, in return for which they were to receive treasury bonds from a newly independent republic of Cuba, offering a good rate of interest and guaranteed by the American treasury. McCook went about lobbying for support in Washington while soliciting potential investors, including among European bankers. Writing, for instance, to the Paris house of Perier Mercet & Co, McCook argued that his project could put an end to the savage war raging in the island, thereby promoting 'la cause de l'Humanité' while promising a highly attractive return on investment.[130]

McCook's friendship with McKinley also gave him direct access to the president, whom he worked to persuade of the legitimacy and necessity of American intervention in Cuba. To this end, McCook explicitly invoked the concept of humanitarian intervention, for instance in a memorandum dated 22 March 1898 and suitably entitled 'Intervention'.[131] McCook began his argument by referring to the principles established in the Monroe Doctrine, which, while committing the United States to a strict policy of non-intervention in European affairs, was no less firm in obliging it to intervene on behalf of American republics threatened by interference from the European powers. As for the case of Cuba, McCook cited US security interests, but above all the violation of the principle of 'humanity' as lawful grounds for intervention. To bolster his case, he quoted at length such noted authorities on international law as Vattel and Arntz, all of whom recognised a right of intervention under international law in case of violation of humanitarian principles. The prime example of such an 'intervention because of demands of humanity' was to be found in the actions of Britain, France and Russia, who had intervened in the Greek war of independence to stop bloodshed and restore order.[132]

Spain's cruelty and inhumanity in suppressing the Cuban revolt was, according to McCook, historically unprecedented, for no civilised European nation would ever have permitted such atrocities to occur. From this fact, he inferred an obligation on Cuba's closest neighbour to intervene, once more invoking the Monroe Doctrine as the central dogma of American foreign policy. According to the Monroe Doctrine, the Cuban question concerned only the Americas, and hence it was for the United States to deal with it – not least on account of the losses to trade caused by the war.[133] McCook's advice to the president thus concluded:

It seems unnecessary to recite the varied instances of intervention. They are all based on the rules, already referred to. In no case has there been such necessity for intervention, nor such strong grounds as in the case of Cuba. Intervention for the independence of the Cubans will be justified not only by policy and necessity, but by all laws, human and Divine.[134]

A last diplomatic effort, in the form of an ultimatum to Madrid demanding a ceasefire, having failed, McKinley's decision to intervene militarily was set.[135] On 11 April 1898, the president asked Congress to authorise any means necessary for the pacification of the Cuban conflict, placing humanitarian motives at the centre of his argument.[136] McKinley discussed both the economic costs of the continuing conflict and the sinking of the *Maine*, but above all Spain's policy of reconcentration and the suffering caused by it among Cuban civilians. In the process, he once again accused the Spanish government of pursuing not 'civilized warfare', but 'extermination'.[137] The US government's stated aim was thus to put an immediate stop to the war, to rescind the reconcentration order and to allow relief to reach suffering civilians. Several diplomatic initiatives having failed, the United States was now to bring about these changes by force: 'The forcible intervention of the United States as a neutral to stop the war according to the large dictates of humanity and following many historical precedents where neighboring States have interfered to check the hopeless sacrifices of life by internecine conflicts beyond their borders, is justifiable on rational grounds.'[138]

Like many stories in the press and his friend McCook before him, McKinley now likewise referred to historical precedent in his decisive statement. Besides preserving American commercial and security interests, he therefore gave this as his chief argument for intervention:

In the cause of humanity and to put an end to the barbarities, bloodshed, starvation, and horrible miseries now existing there, and which the parties to the conflict are either unable or unwilling to stop or mitigate. It is no answer to say this is all in another country, belonging to another nation, and is therefore none of our business. It is specially our duty, for it is right at our door.[139]

Only by force from outside, President McKinley concluded, could this conflict now be resolved:

The only hope of relief and response from a condition which can no longer be endured is the enforced pacification of Cuba. In the name of humanity, in the name of civilization, in behalf of endangered American interests which give us the right and the duty to speak and to act, the war in Cuba must stop.[140]

The president's arguments were echoed only two days later by the Senate Committee on Foreign Relations, which played a key part in all questions of foreign policy.[141] Its paper ran to more than twenty pages, not only discussing the sinking of the *Maine*, but also giving a detailed account of the suffering brought by the war to Cuba's civilian population.

The Spanish government was accused of using its policy of reconcentration to decimate the local population before resettling the island with
immigrants from Spain.[142] Spain was moreover accused of having grossly
violated the 'laws of civilized warfare' in its campaign. A state, the
memorandum concluded, that abused and perverted its power in such
a manner had forfeited its sovereign rights under both natural and
international law. From this followed a right to intervention, in
support of which the familiar precedents relating to the Ottoman
Empire were cited:

And this principle has been the foundation of the repeated interventions by the
States of Europe in the affairs of Turkey, who, abominable and atrocious as her
cruelty has been toward her subjects in Greece and in the northern part of her
dominions in Europe, and in Armenia, has not approached the eminence at
which Spain stands in solitary and unapproachable infamy.[143]

Yet the committee was no less adamant that any military action must be
taken in accordance with existing international law and hence gave a
précis of the relevant debates on the right to intervene.[144] Such a right
was clearly affirmed with reference to such authorities as Arntz, Vattel,
Wheaton and Bluntschli. From these scholars, the report's authors
derived the opinion that

Justification for intervention is strengthened in such cases as the present, where
the oppressions by a State of its subjects have been so inveterate, atrocious, and
sanguinary as to require intervention by other nations in the interest of humanity
and the peace of the world, for the purpose of overthrowing that Government and
establishing or recognizing another in its place as the only means of extirpating an
otherwise incurable and dangerous evil.[145]

The report again cited the interventions of the great powers of Europe in
the Ottoman Empire for support, drawing a direct comparison between
Ottoman massacres and those perpetrated by Spain in Cuba:

The cause of these great interventions was the cruelty of Turkey toward her own
subjects. The result was that the interventions secured their independence. The
cases of the Danubian provinces are so similar to that of Cuba as to be nearly
identical. The fact that the wrongs were inflicted by Mohammedans upon
Christians does not mitigate the responsibility of Spain or make intervention as
to her any less rightful. Surely Christian Spain, from the fact that she is a
Christian state, is not given greater warrant to exterminate her subjects than
Mohammedan Turkey possessed to extirpate hers.[146]

The conclusion was that the time had come to put an end to the war in
Cuba and at the same time to give the island its independence. To this
end, the Committee on Foreign Relations advised the president to use
such forces of the army and navy as were necessary to terminate Spanish

rule in Cuba.[147] Both houses of Congress approved these measures by a large majority on 19 April, together with the Teller Amendment, which forbade the outright annexation of Cuba by the United States.[148]

These were the events that led up to the outbreak of the Spanish–American War on 23 April 1898, which ended just over three months later with a crushing Spanish defeat.[149] Following a full-scale naval blockade, American forces landed in Cuba, where they were joined by Cuban independence fighters in their march on Santiago. The city and its port were put under siege. An ill-fated attempt by the Spanish Atlantic fleet to break out of Santiago Bay resulted in its near-total destruction, leaving Spain no choice but to surrender. Another US naval squadron attacked Puerto Rico and took that Spanish colony in a brief campaign. Operations were not, however, limited to the Caribbean theatre. In fact, the first skirmish in the Spanish–American War took place several thousand miles away in the western Pacific. On 1 May the US Navy's Asian squadron attacked and destroyed the Spanish pacific fleet in Manila Bay, which resulted in the United States replacing Spain as the colonial rulers of the Philippines. The loss of two fleets was more than a setback, it was a disaster for Spain. The government in Madrid sued for peace and a provisional peace treaty came into force on 12 August 1898.[150]

After several months of peace negotiations, in the Treaty of Paris, signed on 10 December 1898, the Spanish government surrendered it claims to Cuba, Puerto Rico, Guam and the Philippines.[151] Once Europe's greatest imperial power, Spain was now forced to abandon its remaining possessions in Asia and the Americas, becoming 'the real imperial loser of the nineteenth century'.[152] Yet for Spain's former colonies, this did not mean independent statehood, but rather absorption into the growing sphere of influence of a new imperial power. Against the payment of a $20 million indemnity, Spain ceded control of Guam and Puerto Rico – two smaller territories – to the United States, as well as the Philippines, which were highly desirable for the access they offered to the lucrative Chinese market. Cuba, although nominally independent, entered into a relation of complete political, military and economic dependence on the United States, which in 1901 passed the Platt Amendment, granting itself the unlimited right to intervene to secure its interests on the island.[153] Even Major-General Leonard Wood, US military governor in Cuba from 1899 to 1902, frankly confessed: 'There is, of course, little or no independence left Cuba under the Platt Amendment.'[154]

The Spanish–American War, described by John Hay, the American ambassador to London, with unabashed jingoism as 'a splendid little war; begun with highest motives' in a letter to Theodore Roosevelt,[155] led to a significant expansion of the United States' formal sphere of power. A political cartoon published in 1899 and captioned 'Ten thousand miles from tip to tip' illustrated the point with an American eagle whose wings stretched from Puerto Rico in the Caribbean to the Philippines in the Pacific.[156] Thus 1898 is often regarded as a pivotal year in the history of the United States, marking its adoption of an openly imperialist foreign policy and its ascent to the rank of an imperial global power.[157] This about-turn in foreign policy was driven – as was in the case for the European imperial powers – by a potent concatenation of commercial, geostrategic, 'civilisational' and humanitarian considerations, which had come ever more strongly to the fore from the early 1890s on. These were the reasons that ultimately guided McKinley's decision in favour of military intervention in Cuba.[158]

What is striking here is how, as far as the United States was concerned, outside intervention in the internal affairs of sovereign states as a foreign policy practice underwent a fundamental change of meaning in the course of the nineteenth century. As practised earlier in the century by the great powers of Europe, the United States had considered such intervention a serious threat to its own national security interests and, in response, developed the Monroe Doctrine as a paradigm of non-intervention. Yet as its own power and the ability to project it abroad grew, and against the backdrop of its own expansionist urges, the United States began, in its own distinctive fashion, to adapt the concept to its own purposes, beginning in the mid-nineteenth century. Historic instances of European interventions gradually took on an exemplary character. Before, during and even after the war, US jurists would cite them as precedent in justifying their own country's military intervention in both legal and moral terms.[159] The United States itself now assumed the mantle of the force for order in the western hemisphere, arrogating to itself the right to humanitarian intervention – to enforce by military means 'civilisational' standards and principles of humanity, unilaterally and, if need be, even against a Christian European state.

The war against Spain, which was fought with wide popular support at home, was consistently presented as a 'war for humanity', and as such both necessary and just, in a wide range of contemporary newspaper articles and other publications.[160] In one such treatise, published in 1898, H. Allen Tupper even went so far as to accuse the European states of having failed to rise to the challenge of the humanitarian catastrophe of Cuba just as they had failed to respond to the Armenian massacres. These were failures which the United States was not going to repeat:

Europe's attitude was that which it had assumed in the case of Armenia – a passive spectator of the application of the policy of extermination by famine and the sword, through which Spain hoped forever to settle the long-vexed 'Cuban question'. Then there came a time when our own free and favored nation, horrified at the great crime being enacted at its very doors, espoused Cuba's cause in the interest of humanity, and commanded Spain to put an end to the pitiless warfare which had made of the once beautiful and fertile island a wilderness of graves.[161]

Tupper exalted the role of the United States, which fought nothing less than a 'Battle for Humanity'[162] in Cuba, while it was the 'Good Samaritan'[163] to the island's suffering population by virtue of the relief it provided. President McKinley himself chimed into this chorus of glorification, making many speeches in which he claimed that the United States had fought the war not from a desire for territory, but solely in the service of humanity and civilisation.[164] Yet McKinley added that this military victory came with new obligations and a responsibility to which the United States must live up. Speaking in Atlanta in December 1898, he placed the victory over Spain in a line with other important battles of American history:

At Bunker Hill liberty was at stake; at Gettysburg the Union was the issue, before Manila and Santiago our armies fought not for gain or revenge, but for human rights. They contended for the freedom of the oppressed, for whose welfare the United States has never failed to lend a helping hand to establish and uphold, and, I believe, never will. The glories of the war cannot be dimmed, but the result will be incomplete and unworthy of us unless supplemented by civil victories, harder possibly to win, but in their way no less indispensable.[165]

McKinley made no bones about calling on his country to continue its struggle in the name of humanity in peacetime, in the form of an American civilising mission. He accordingly concluded his speech with a leading question: 'Shall we now, when victory won in war is written in the treaty of peace, and the civilized world applauds and waits in expectation, turn timidly away from the duties imposed upon the country by its own great deeds?'[166] In the president's view, his country was obliged to accept this duty as a 'civilised' nation – a duty which Rudyard Kipling, writing under the impression of the American conquest of the Philippines in February 1899, had memorably called 'the white man's burden'.[167]

McKinley used this kind of paternalistic rhetoric, which was fully the equal of its European imperialist counterpart, to promote acceptance at home of the Treaty of Paris and the colonial gains agreed therein.[168] Such campaigning was all the more necessary since the United States' long anti-colonial tradition meant that resistance to imperial expansion was not slow in expressing itself. Public figures from various spheres – the writer Mark Twain, the politician Carl Schurz and the industrialist Andrew Carnegie, to name but three – raised their voices in opposition to their government's imperialist turn.[169] The annexation of the Philippines in particular sparked intense political debate between opponents and supporters of acquiring colonies, so much so that ratification of the Treaty of Paris was highly doubtful. Only a narrow majority in the Senate approved the treaty in February 1899, thereby setting the course for the United States' colonial expansion.[170]

Yet the annexation of the Philippines also provides a particularly vivid example of how a military operation begun in the name of humanity and to stop a humanitarian crisis could segue directly into a brutal war of colonial conquest. The *Nation* accurately summarised this development in April 1899: 'This war is the most savage war which was ever known in the history of our republic. … The war of 1898 "for the cause of humanity" has degenerated in 1899 into a war of conquest, characterized by rapine and cruelty worthy of savages.'[171]

Having seen its own declaration of independence ignored and realising that the Treaty of Paris had merely substituted American for Spanish colonial masters, the Philippine independence movement launched a campaign of massive resistance to the new rulers. Led by Emilio Aguinaldo, who had still been an ally of the Americans against Spain when the US Navy brought him home from exile in Hong Kong, an armed uprising against US occupation began in February 1899.[172] The United States responded with brute force, which soon came also to be directed at the civilian population and sought to break its support for the independence movement. American forces maintained a racist attitude towards the local population, some going so far as to claim that the archipelago would not be pacified 'until the niggers are killed off like Indians'.[173] On the evidence of the widespread destruction of villages and the mass execution of prisoners, such sentiments appear to have been far from unusual. Torture was the order of the day, with the so-called 'water cure' gaining particular notoriety.[174] In this method, which became synonymous with torture itself and was a precursor to the more recent technique of waterboarding, the fear of drowning was exploited to make victims ingest large quantities of water or other fluids. Fear for their lives was meant to make prisoners compliant and reveal information.[175]

Nor did US forces shy away from measures that General Weyler had introduced in Cuba and which the United States had cited as justifying war against the Spanish. Scorched-earth tactics were used to lay waste to wide swathes of land, the local population being forcibly removed to reconcentration zones.[176] The *Philadelphia Ledger*, a broadly anti-imperialist paper, was mordant in its commentary on this turn of events:

Who would have supposed on 6th of December, 1897, when President McKinley stated in a formal message to Congress that 'the cruel policy of concentration pursued by Weyler in Cuba' was not civilized warfare, that the same policy would be, only four years later, adopted and pursued as the policy of the United States in the Philippines? Time does truly work wonders; but when and where has it worked a greater wonder than this?[177]

The United States' colonial war in the Philippines was to last until 1913 and claim at least 230,000 civilian lives – some estimates set the death toll at over 700,000.[178] Although the United States fought the Philippine war no less savagely than Spain had done in Cuba – and at the cost, most likely, of even more lives – no other government dared to remind the rising imperial power of the humanitarian norms it had itself so recently invoked or even to challenge it militarily. The practice of humanitarian intervention in the late nineteenth century remained the exclusive preserve of the dominant powers – now American as well as European – which used it as an instrument for enforcing their colonial and imperial interests against weaker states.

Epilogue:
Perspectives on the Twentieth and Twenty-First Centuries

It is too late in the day, after these precedents, to tell us that nations may not forcibly interfere with one another for the sole purpose of stopping mischief and benefiting humanity.[1]   John Stuart Mill, 1849

Finally, the situation in Biafra is one that would have been ideal for collective humanitarian intervention of the nineteenth century type.[2]   Richard B. Lillich, 1969

Anyone who poses the question of global responsibility will find themselves, then as now, faced with the temptations and dangers of colonialism. Back in the day, colonialism was known as colonialism, today it goes by 'humanitarian intervention'.[3]   Ulrich Beck, 2004

In June 1900 the Canadian historian William E. Lingelbach, who taught modern European history at the University of Pennsylvania, published an article entitled 'The Doctrine and Practice of Intervention in Europe'.[4] In this essay, Lingelbach examined the historical development of European practices of intervention and the various forms they had taken since the early modern age. With regard to the nineteenth century, Lingelbach found that 'On the other hand there is a feature of this kind of intervention which is peculiarly a growth of the present century. The moral sentiment of civilized peoples in modern times has been frequently aroused and governments have been forced to intervene in cases where intolerance has become apprehensive and cruel.'[5] In support of this conclusion, Lingelbach referred to the intervention of the great powers of Europe in the Greek war of independence in 1827. The practice of 'intervention on humanitarian grounds', he claimed, was now largely recognised, although he also noted that humanitarian concerns were not alone in deciding states on a course of action, but that political and commercial motives might be closely entwined with them and even tip the scales.[6] Lingelbach's general conclusion was:

These and other recent developments all show that intervention is becoming more and more recognized as the legal means by which the society of nations enforces its rights. This is true whether it is carried out by several states or by an individual state, acting in accordance with precedent and the consensus of international public opinion, although the modern practice shows a strong tendency towards action in concert. Intervention, therefore, instead of being outside the pale of the law of nations and antagonistic to it, is an integral and essential part of it; an act of police for enforcing recognized rights, and the only means, apart from war, for enforcing the rules of International Law.[7]

From his historical analysis, made with a particular focus on developments in the century that had only just ended, Lingelbach concluded that by 1900 the practice of intervention had become ever more firmly established as a legal instrument for the robust implementation of universally recognised principles of international law.

This was a pithy summary by a historian writing at the turn of the century. Yet this manner of looking back at historical precedents played a decisive role in forming the opinions of generations of jurists. Scholars of international law drew upon them throughout the twentieth century in order to formulate and advance their own concepts of humanitarian intervention. The nineteenth century, in the course of which both the theory and practice of humanitarian intervention had taken shape, thus assumed the function of a discursive frame of reference in legal debates. It served as a surface for reflection and projection, in which international lawyers could find their own ideas on international intervention mirrored, and based on which they could proceed to develop them further, adding such new elements as the increasingly prominent idea of human rights and the role of international organisations as instances or authorities ruling on intervention.

One of the first scholars to take a systematic approach to the question in the early twentieth century was the French jurist Antoine Rougier, who in 1910 published his *Theorie de l'intervention humaine*.[8] Rougier cited the familiar historical examples – the European interventions in the Ottoman Empire, that of the United States in Cuba – while also drawing on the existing theoretical approaches of such eminent jurists as Bluntschli, Rolin-Jaequemyns and Arntz.[9] Unlike them, however, he was not content merely to invoke the hitherto rather abstract 'lois de l'humanité' and 'droits humains' and their violation as legitimate grounds for intervention. Rougier was keen to examine the specific content of these laws and rights, regarding their vagueness as constituting a deficit of legitimation and posing the threat of an arbitrary practice of intervention.[10] It was in this context that he identified violation of the fundamental individual 'droits de l'homme' (human rights) as the only legitimate grounds for intervention. These rights were to be sharply distinguished from and accorded primacy over 'droits du citoyen' (civil rights). Human rights alone were to be guaranteed by and subject to the protection of all nations.[11] Rougier cited three such fundamental human rights: the 'droit à la vie', the 'droit à la liberté' and the 'droit à la légalité'. A look back at the nineteenth century revealed these fundamental rights in particular to have been in grave jeopardy time and again. The 'right to life and physical inviolability' had been threatened above all by massacres of civilians and prisoners of war and by the inhuman treatment of the wounded in the Ottoman Empire, the 'right to freedom' by slavery and the slave trade, and the 'right to the rule of law' by harsh laws and 'barbaric' forms of punishment.[12] The purpose of any 'intervention d'humanité' must therefore be, according to Rougier, to ensure that these fundamental rights were respected. In linking the idea of humanitarian intervention to the protection of specific and well-defined human rights, which occupied the central position, Rougier's scheme truly was innovative.

After the First World War, this issue of the protection of human rights became joined to the fundamental question of who was to carry out such interventions and by whose mandate they were to be authorised. For their part, exhausted as they were by the costly war they had just fought, the great powers had no interest in taking up arms for supposedly humanitarian reasons.[13] Increasingly, the hope was that, in place of the pre-war Concert of Europe and regional hegemons, the newly founded League of Nations might assume the role of international arbiter of order and intervention.[14] In a study on humanitarian intervention in international law, Malbone W. Graham, an American jurist and political scientist, put this potential role of the League of Nations at the centre of his reflections. Graham found a sea change to have occurred since the pre-war era:

Yet the fundamental fact remains that the pre-war European Concert of Power, or the Continental Paramountcy of the United States in the new world were the only vehicles for the enforcement of a humanitarian intervention. There was still lacking a definitely coherent, organized Society of Nations capable of both formulation and enforcement of international law. That is why the creation of the League of Nations has so fundamentally altered the question of humanitarian intervention ... In brief, while hitherto collective interventions have tended to assume the form of actions taken by a self-appointed committee of the family of states in the interest of all members of that family, the creation of an organized Society of Nations has given the sanction of social solidarity, on an objective basis, to the hitherto purely sporadic, isolated acts of altruistic nations acting as enforcers of the law of nations.[15]

In contrast to the nineteenth century, the role of the international authority able to issue a mandate for and thereby legitimise humanitarian intervention was no longer to fall to the Concert of Europe or to the

United States, dominant in the western hemisphere, but rather to the new international organisation in Geneva. In Graham's view, nor could the right to intervene any longer be deduced from a subjective understanding of natural law or even a 'sentimental law of Humanity', but rather drew its legitimacy from a substantially new grounding in international law.[16] Looking to the future, Graham was certain that isolated interventions without the approval of the international community would become increasingly unfeasible: 'Rather will they occur as the express result of the action of the League in selecting the appropriate country to act as its mandatory, its agent, in enforcing the terms of the mandate given for the purpose of removing unfortunate conditions violative of the most elementary human rights.'[17] Graham here also referred to the United States, whose intervention in Cuba had proved its political commitment to the principle of humanitarian intervention as well as its practical capacity for putting it into action.[18] In line with the Monroe Doctrine, the United States might after all act as a responsible and effective bearer of mandates for humanitarian intervention in the western hemisphere – if only it abandoned isolationism and joined the international system of the League of Nations.[19]

This idea of collective implementation mechanisms under the aegis of the League of Nations was likewise taken up by André N. Mandelstam, a Russian jurist and diplomat who had been a pupil and friend of Friedrich Fromhold Martens, another important figure in the development of international law. Mandelstam, who had gone into exile in Paris when the Bolsheviks seized power in 1917, became a leading figure in the international struggle for the establishment of universal human rights in the inter-war period. As a member of the famous Institut de droit international, he was involved in several initiatives to promote the cause.[20] He was instrumental in drafting the *Déclaration des droits internationaux de l'homme*,[21] proclaimed at the institute's New York congress in October 1929 and used his platform as a writer to make it widely known. In one such account of the significance of the New York declaration, Mandelstam discussed the aspect of the active international protection of human rights in some detail, again referring explicitly to the various interventions by European powers in the Ottoman Empire over the course of the nineteenth century.[22] In spite of the competing interests of the great powers involved, he found them nonetheless to have constituted 'an "intervention in the name of humanity" – an "Intervention d'Humanité"',[23] which had brought lasting benefits to the protection of minorities.

With regard to the coming struggles for international human rights, Mandelstam rejected humanitarian interventions that were based on the division, so widespread in the nineteenth century, between 'civilised' and 'uncivilised' nations. In his view, the founding of the League of Nations and the tendency to universality it embodied meant that all states, equally and without exception, were now obliged to protect human rights around the world.[24] To this end, Mandelstam proposed enshrining 'the principle of the universal protection of human rights in a global treaty'.[25] The New York declaration, he hoped, would set the requisite process in motion.

The idealistic hopes projected onto the League of Nations as a new arbiter of international intervention by such actors as Graham and Mandelstam were not realised in practice. Although the League took an active role on such humanitarian issues as the question of slavery and the protection of minorities, and had successes to show for its efforts, it lacked the robust mechanisms of implementation that would have allowed it to enforce the proposed 'world treaty' for the protection of universal human rights. While such non-European states as Abyssinia, Siam and Japan had been admitted to the League, it nonetheless remained in thrall to an imperialist hierarchy with its European members at the top.[26] Indeed, the League's dominant powers, Britain and France, reached the zenith of their imperial expansion between the two world wars and were accordingly not in the least interested in building an international system that would have allowed for interference in internal affairs for the implementation of universal human rights.

Paradoxically enough, it was above all fascist dictatorships in the 1930s who seized upon the two core motives for humanitarian intervention in the nineteenth century – the abolition of slavery and the slave trade, and the protection of minorities – and used them to justify their own aggressive foreign policy.[27] Benito Mussolini presented Italy's attack on Abyssinia in October 1935 to the international community as a response to a humanitarian emergency, pointing to the persistence of slavery and the slave trade in the East African country. Italy's international propaganda campaign fused the rhetoric of abolition and civilisation, while concealing the Duce's true motives – imperial expansionism – from the public.[28] For its part, between 1937 and 1939 Nazi Germany could often be found invoking the protection of German minorities in justification of Hitler's aggressively interventionist policy towards its eastern neighbours Czechoslovakia and Poland.[29] It was this instrumentalisation by the two fascist regimes that did much to put a lasting taint on an ostensibly humanitarian practice of intervention in international politics. In combination with the weaknesses of the League of Nations already described, this led to the 1930s being regarded as a crisis in or even 'the eclipse of humanitarian intervention'.[30]

Yet controversy over the concept of humanitarian intervention and its possible implementation by no means disappeared. In 1938 Philip C. Jessup, an American jurist and diplomat, published an article in the *American Journal of International Law* warning against hasty US intervention on behalf of oppressed populations in a variety of contemporary crisis scenarios.[31] Although Jessup found active support for the republican side in the Spanish Civil War, for the Chinese against Japanese aggression and for the Ethiopians against that of Italy, as well as for the Jews in Palestine, largely to be both morally and even legally justifiable, he nonetheless in each case rejected it, citing concerns of realpolitik and foreign policy.[32] An American scholar of international law, Ellery C. Stowell, published an essay in the same journal in October 1939 – the month after the outbreak of the Second World War – arguing in favour of the concept of humanitarian intervention in light of recent attacks on the Jewish populations of several European states.[33] Against this backdrop, however, Stowell's conclusion may seem to have been unduly hopeful:

Humanitarian intervention is of recent, but very vigorous, growth and tends to bind the whole world closer together in defense of elementary principles of justice. It is as yet a toddling infant that becomes stronger every day with the spread of communications. Even if the great development of national self-sufficiency and isolation should continue, this growth of humanitarian intervention will undoubtedly still go on, although it may be at a slower pace.[34]

In 1945, after the devastation of two world wars and the loss of millions of lives, the United Nations enshrined a strict proscription of force and intervention in its Charter. Aside from the right to self-defence, which remained in place, any threat or use of force in international relations was now prohibited according to Article 2 (4) of the Charter, while Article 2 (7) prohibited intervention in the domestic affairs of another sovereign state.[35] These provisions are at the core of the Charter of the United Nations and may be abrogated only in an emergency: When peace is threatened or breached, the Security Council is entitled to authorise such measures, including direct intervention and military force, as are necessary 'to maintain or restore international peace and security'.[36]

This marked a clear restriction in international law of the idea of military intervention, but there were still scholars who created a direct link between the idea of humanitarian intervention, the international protection of human rights and the emerging system of the United Nations. Among them was no less an authority than Hersch Lauterpacht, professor of international law at the University of

Cambridge and, as a member of the United Nations' International Law Commission and a judge of the International Court of Justice in The Hague, one of the twentieth century's most influential jurists. Lauterpacht, who was born to a Jewish family in Galicia, then part of the Habsburg Empire, was an outspoken proponent of firmly embedding human rights in international law. This commitment was no doubt strengthened by his personal history and the loss of most of his family in the Holocaust.[37] Already during the Second World War, in December 1942, he delivered a lecture to the British Grotius society, arguing in terms derived from the natural law tradition in favour of drawing up an 'International Bill of Rights' backed up by effective protections.[38] In connection with this, Lauterpacht also expressly referred to the theory and practice of humanitarian intervention in the nineteenth century and the international treaty regime against slavery and for the protection of minorities that emerged from it.[39] He presented these historical examples as valuable cues for the further development of effective mechanisms for the protection of individual rights:

This, then, is the past contribution of the law of nations to the idea and the actual protection of the rights of man. It has expressed itself in the work and in the influence of the great publicists, in the practice of safeguarding the rights of man through humanitarian intervention and through a variety of treaties, and in the recognition of the rights of aliens. However, in relation to the rights of man the true part of international law lies not in its contribution in the past, but in the potentialities of its function in the future.[40]

Lauterpacht continued to pursue this idea of effective human rights protections after the Second World War. In such influential publications as *An International Bill of the Rights of Man*, he situated them within the emerging system of the United Nations.[41] Rather than individual states, Lauterpacht assumed that the organisation would now assume the role of the supreme global authority, both guaranteeing and enforcing his proposed international bill of rights. He considered various means by which the UN might promote, supervise and peacefully implement international human rights standards.[42] However, should political means be exhausted, the use of force might be unavoidable:

However, in the last resort, ... there must remain with the highest political authority of the Organization of States the legal power to give effect to the Bill of Rights by means of coercive action. Such action will be exceptional, but it is that ultimate power which will give to the Bill of Rights the impress of an organic part of the international legal order.[43]

For the United Nations to enforce human rights, by coercion if necessary, marked, to Lauterpacht, a crucial step in creating an effective international human rights regime. This was a position equally expressed in his new edition of Lassa Oppenheim's classic treatise on international law.[44] Having once again cited the humanitarian interventions in the nineteenth century as precedent and pointed to the potential for abuse by individual states, Lauterpacht praised the principle of collective intervention in the United Nations system as a milestone:

> The Charter of the United Nations, in recognizing the promotion of respect for fundamental human rights and freedoms as one of the principal objects of the Organization, marks a further step in the direction of elevating the principle of humanitarian intervention to a basic rule of organised international society. This is so although under the Charter as adopted in 1945 the degree of enforceability of fundamental human rights is still rudimentary and although the Charter itself expressly rules out intervention in matters which are essentially within the domestic jurisdiction of the State.[45]

Lauterpacht was, of course, well aware of the restriction the UN had imposed on itself in Article 2 (7) of its Charter with regard to interference in the domestic affairs of sovereign states. Nonetheless, he had high hopes for the exercise of political influence within the existing framework of the UN and especially for its potential to grow into an effective system for the international protection of human rights.[46]

At least in the immediate post-war era, however, these hopes remained unfulfilled. The deepening rift between East and West and the violent conflicts surrounding decolonisation militated against the further development of a robust human rights regime.[47] Instead of the implementation and additional elaboration of mechanisms of protection, as favoured by Lauterpacht, governments now barricaded themselves behind the UN Charter's non-intervention clause and categorically rejected any form of humanitarian intervention. In so doing, they could cite scholars of international law in their support, for instance Ian Brownlie, a British jurist who was fundamentally opposed to the very concept of humanitarian intervention. In a study of international law and the deployment of force by states, Brownlie pointedly dismissed the topic under the rubric of 'Other Justifications for Resort to Force of Doubtful Validity'.[48] Brownlie did not deny that a majority of legal scholars in the late nineteenth century had recognised a right to 'intervention d'humanité', nor did he omit to discuss its concrete instances, the military intervention of the great powers of Europe in Greece and Syria, and that of the United States in Cuba. What he emphasised in these cases, however, was how humanitarian rhetoric had been put to the service of justifying the use of force by great powers against weaker states, of which Brownlie cited the German occupation of Bohemia and Moravia in March 1939, ostensibly for the protection of German minorities, as a particularly egregious example. Brownlie's position was clear enough: He was only too glad to see the back of so-called humanitarian intervention.

The state practice justifies the conclusion that no genuine case of humanitarian intervention has occurred, with the possible exception of the occupation of Syria in 1860 and 1861. With the embarrassing exception provided by Germany, the institution has disappeared from modern state practice. As a matter of legal and international policy this is a beneficial development. The institution did not conspicuously enhance state relations and was applied only against weak states. It belongs to an era of unequal relations.[49]

Like Lauterbach, Brownlie cast a historical glance back at the theory and practice of humanitarian intervention in the nineteenth century – but what they saw and the conclusions they drew were diametrically opposed. Brownlie expressly referred to Lauterpach as an outlier, arguing that the majority of contemporary scholars of international law either ignored the question of humanitarian intervention or denied that any such right existed.[50] Brownlie further doubted that this form of intervention could even continue to exist after the non-intervention clause and the general proscription of force were enshrined in the Charter of the United Nations.[51] This view seemed to be confirmed when, in December 1965, the UN General Assembly passed a 'Declaration on the Inadmissibility of Intervention in the Domestic Affairs of States and the Protection of Their Independence and Sovereignty', in which any such interference, whether direct or indirect, was condemned and the paradigm of non-intervention bolstered.[52]

Yet Brownlie's prediction that the concept of humanitarian intervention would disappear proved premature. Instead, and notwithstanding the UN resolution to the contrary, it once again became the subject of much debate among scholars of international law and human rights activists. Against the backdrop of the two human rights covenants adopted by the UN in 1966 and the International Year of Human Rights declared by UNESCO in 1968, culminating in the first International Conference on Human Rights in Tehran, the question gained new momentum. Fundamental questions concerning robust and concrete protection mechanisms were once again posed. At its congress in Helsinki in 1966, the influential International Law Association (ILA) passed a resolution announcing that it would refocus its work in the field of universal human rights, from a question of mere definitions to aspects of their concrete implementation.[53]

Key contributions to this debate came from a member of the ILA, Richard B. Lillich, an eminent American jurist and director of the

Procedural Aspects of International Law Institute, an eminent body based in Washington, DC. In his articles, Lillich argued vehemently in favour of a concept of humanitarian intervention within the system of the United Nations. As cases in point, Lillich was able to cite pressing political concerns of the day, such as the 1964 Congo Crisis, the 1965 US intervention in the Dominican Republic and the looming humanitarian crisis in the territory of Biafra, which had declared its independence from Nigeria.[54]

It was the Biafran conflict of 1967–70 in particular that re-established the lasting relevance of these questions in international law.[55] In view of the rapidly deteriorating humanitarian situation faced by the Igbo civilian population in the region, Michael Reisman, an American jurist associated with the influential New Haven School, submitted a petition in September 1968 asking the United Nations to intervene without delay.[56] In the midst of a severe humanitarian crisis, to interfere in a sovereign state's domestic affairs did not conflict with the UN's principles, Reisman argued. The situation in Biafra proved the need to place the concept of intervention on a firmer footing:

Whether or not a U.N. humanitarian intervention in Nigeria will lay the groundwork for an institutionalized pattern of humanitarian intervention in the future, the United Nations must consider the creation of such an institution as soon as possible. … We have waited too long and have already lost our innocence; if we cannot perfect, as a minimum, a system of humanitarian intervention, we have lost our humanity. If we sit passively by while the Ibos [sic] suffer genocide, we have forfeited our right to regain it.[57]

The memorandum, which did not omit to cite the historical cases of intervention in the nineteenth century,[58] having been submitted to the UN, Reisman sent copies to a wide range of scholars of international law in the United States and elsewhere. His bid to add momentum to the debate was successful: The Procedural Aspects of International Law Institute launched its own research project under the heading 'Humanitarian Interventions through the United Nations'. Its stated aim was 'to recommend new or revised procedures whereby the United Nations, which has not been especially effective in devising international machinery to protect human rights generally, might intervene in certain crisis situations to protect the most basic right of all – the right to live'.[59] This research project in turn led to a two-day conference at the University of Virginia in March 1972, at which some of the leading legal minds in the field gathered to discuss the past, present and future of the concept of humanitarian intervention.[60] Added urgency was given to discussions by events a few months previously. In December 1971,

India, responding not least to severe war crimes perpetrated by the Pakistani army against the civilian population of what was then East Pakistan, launched a decisive intervention in that country's civil war, leading to the eastern province's independence under the name of Bangladesh.

The conference by no means settled the debate, which continued – and vigorously so – among scholars of international law.[61] Further instances of intervention fed into it, notably by Vietnam in Cambodia in 1978 to end the Khmer Rouge reign of terror and in 1979 of Tanzania against Uganda, where Idi Amin's regime had become ever more bloodthirsty and unpredictable.[62] Humanitarian intervention, then, was a topic never far from the international agenda. Since the mid-1960s, leading experts in international law had been arguing over whether intervention by force in the internal affairs of a sovereign state for the protection of universal human rights was sanctioned by international law and might be carried out within the framework of the existing system of the UN.[63] This debate must be considered in the broader historical context of the development of the idea of human rights in the twentieth century. Beginning in the early 1970s, human rights came to figure ever more prominently in the study of international law in the West and in the United States in particular. The question was addressed by research institutes, congresses and journals, and took a prominent place on the syllabi of leading universities – but also in wider public and political discourse.[64]

In view of these theoretical debates and sometimes dramatic events, the period between 1945 and 1989 turns out to be misrepresented if it is seen, as it often still is, as marking a lull or indeed a complete standstill in the pursuit of humanitarian intervention, overshadowed by the Cold War. The question of military intervention for the protection of universal rights and the role the UN might play in it did not arise out of the blue in the 1990s.[65] To this broadened perspective may be added recent studies that have more firmly situated the practice of UN peacekeeping by means of its 'Blue Helmet' missions in the overall context of the history of humanitarian intervention and revealed a multi-layered development in the process.[66] The transition from classic Cold War-era peacekeeping to the humanitarian interventions of the post-1989 era was neither linear nor frictionless, but proceeded by fits and starts, often accompanied by setbacks and extreme tensions. The failure of the UN missions in Somalia, Rwanda and Bosnia–Herzegovina in the early 1990s illustrate this point with sad clarity.[67]

Yet it was this abject failure on the part of the United Nations to protect basic human rights, most glaringly in the organisation's non-intervention in the genocide of some 800,000 Tutsi in Rwanda in 1994 and the massacre of more than 8,000 Bosnian Muslims in the supposed UN-protected zone of Srebrenica in the following year that provided the impetus for reform.[68] These debates were launched above all by Kofi Annan, the UN secretary general, who in turn was able to build on the principles of conflict avoidance formulated by his predecessor, Boutros Boutros-Ghali, in his 1992 'Agenda for Peace'.[69] The idea of active crisis prevention now came to stand at the centre of debates, a programmatic reorientation that bore Annan's stamp. In a report delivered to the UN Security Council in June 2001, Annan argued that it was time 'to move the United Nations from a culture of reaction to a culture of prevention'.[70] In support of this demand, Annan cited the moral responsibility incurred by the international community after its failures in Rwanda and the former Yugoslavia effectively to prevent such atrocities from occurring in the future. Annan also pointed out that efficient crisis prevention was a far more cost-effective policy than full-scale military operations launched once a crisis had already escalated. He pointed to a study by the Carnegie Commission on Preventing Deadly Conflict, which had found that the international community could have saved some $70 billion in the 1990s if it had taken preventive measures rather than launching seven major military interventions.[71] The UN secretary general accordingly proposed fostering 'a culture of conflict prevention'.[72]

The International Commission on Intervention and State Sovereignty (ICISS) was founded on the initiative of the Canadian government in response to Annan's proposal and began to develop concepts for reforming humanitarian intervention. In its final report, delivered in December 2001, the committee of experts put forward the concept of the Responsibility to Protect (R2P),[73] which was officially adopted by the UN General Assembly on the organisation's sixtieth anniversary in 2005.[74] The new concept held that in cases of sovereign states no longer being able to guarantee their population's fundamental rights, the responsibility for their protection passed to the international community. There were three distinct dimensions to the R2P formula: The 'responsibility to prevent'[75] refers to the obligation to anticipate threats to human rights and to take suitable preventive measures, whereas the 'responsibility to react'[76] refers to intervention measures, including the use of military force, and the 'responsibility to rebuild'[77] refers to the reconstruction efforts to be undertaken after the conflict. While in earlier formulations, the concept of humanitarian intervention had been limited to its military dimension, the R2P doctrine was framed as a holistic concept that pointedly included both prevention and post-conflict care.

Nor did the ICISS report leave any doubt as to where it saw the priority: 'Prevention is the single most important dimension of the responsibility to protect: prevention options should always be exhausted before intervention is contemplated, and more commitment and resources must be devoted to it.'[78] From the deep political crisis of humanitarian intervention had thus emerged a reformed concept that differed from its predecessor not only in name, but crucially in the emphasis it placed on the idea of prevention in international politics.[79]

The new R2P formula was first put to the test in 2011, when the UN Security Council authorised the organisation's member states to intervene in the Libyan civil war, a brief picked up by NATO, which launched air strikes against the country's leader, Muammar Gaddafi, and his forces.[80] Although R2P was often heralded as a normative breakthrough, its application to the Libyan case was no less controversial among both scholars and the public at large. Critics emphasised that NATO's intervention, which soon brought about Gaddafi's downfall, had been motivated by the Western desire to see a regime change in Libya and ultimately by geopolitical considerations, with scant attention (if any) paid to the core aspects of R2P: prevention and rebuilding. If the Libyan example is anything to go by, the viability of R2P as a strategy offering effective prevention against looming humanitarian crises and grave violations of human rights in the early twenty-first century looks questionable.[81]

It seems appropriate instead to heed cautious voices such as that of the sociologist Ulrich Beck, who soon after the turn of the millennium, and under the impression of the invasion of Iraq in particular, warned against 'human rights wars' and a kind of 'military humanism'.[82] Beck drew attention to the human rights regime's double-edged nature, which, he argued, not only made it easier to resolve conflicts across borders:

It also opens the gates to 'humanitarian interventions' in other countries. Its effects may be said to resemble those of an erupting volcano, covering the world in the fiery lava of armed conflict. It is precisely because enforcing human rights overcomes and must overcome national resistance that the promise of pacification and stability by means of human rights – the 'perpetual peace' heralded by Kant – may so easily lapse into de-pacification and de-stabilisation through perpetual wars.[83]

What Beck saw in the military protection of universal human rights in an ever-increasing number of countries and regions – for example in Kosovo, Afghanistan and Iraq – was the danger of a thoroughgoing 'human rights colonialism', the vehicle of which would be 'UN protectorates'.[84] Within the question of global responsibility lay concealed the dangers and temptations of a new colonialism cloaked in the idea of humanitarian intervention.[85] Beck warned that 'the defence of human rights on foreign soil may well be entwined with geostrategic, commercial and hegemonic interests. The outcome is a new post-national politics of *military humanism*'.[86]

In view of such an analysis of our present situation and the warning it contains against 'human rights colonialism' and 'military humanism', a careful historical look back at the emergence and development of the concept of humanitarian intervention in the long nineteenth century may indeed promise to shed some light on its subsequent career in the twentieth and twenty-first centuries. The retrospective view should not, however, mislead us into treating historical examples as constituting a guide to or even a lesson in political decision-making today, or to follow Gary Bass in believing that the 'nineteenth century shows how the practice of humanitarian intervention can be *managed*'.[87] This is precisely not what a look at the nineteenth century may teach us. On the contrary, it ought rather to sharpen our view of the danger of military intervention under the banner of humanity coalescing with colonial and imperial projects – and all that may follow from it.

Even the scholarly *Supplementary Volume to the Report of the ICISS*, produced as part of the R2P project and weighing in at over 400 pages,[88] cites the standard examples from the nineteenth century – although it devotes no more than a single page to them and hence leaves little room for historical context. Yet particularly when it comes to developing viable global concepts for the international protection of human rights, it is essential to deepen our historical perspective on the phenomenon of humanitarian intervention and the manifold ways in which it has been linked to colonial and imperial projects. Such a perspective can help us better to understand the risks posed by intervention to the very concept of human rights that it claims to protect. The experience of Western intervention in Africa, Asia and the Americas is a case in point.[89] For humanitarian intervention is not a new concept or a new phenomenon that appeared out of nowhere and with no meaningful of history of its own as the twentieth century gave way to the twenty-first. Instead, it emerged in the course of the long nineteenth century from a highly distinctive interaction of theory and practice, the many ambivalent consequences of which were still being felt in various parts of the world.

Notes

Introduction

1 Kofi Annan, *Interventions: A Life in War and Peace*, New York 2012, XI.
2 Kofi Annan, 'We the Peoples': The Role of the United Nations in the 21st Century. Report of the Secretary-General, New York 2000.
3 Ibid., 46f.
4 Ibid., 48.
5 How strongly these experiences influenced Annan's subsequent position is clear from his autobiography, which is aptly entitled *Interventions*. See Annan, *Interventions*, 29–133, esp. 78, 84.
6 The United Nations' complete failure is evident from the reports of two inquiries published in 1999: Report of the Secretary-General Pursuant to General Assembly Resolution 53/35. The Fall of Srebrenica, 15 November 1999, UNGA A/54/549; Report of the Independent Inquiry into the Actions of the United Nations during the 1994 Genocide in Rwanda, 16 December 1999, UNSC/1999/1257.
7 On the 1999 Kosovo crisis and the NATO strikes without a UN mandate, see the exemplary work by Albrecht Schnabel/Ramesh Thakur, eds., *Kosovo and the Challenge of Humanitarian Intervention: Selective Indignation, Collective Action, and International Citizenship*, Tokyo 2000; Aidan Hehir, *Humanitarian Intervention after Kosovo: Iraq, Darfur and the Record of Global Civil Society*, Basingstoke 2008.
8 This dimension of sovereignty as responsibility, which underpinned the ICISS report, was first proposed in 1996 by Francis M. Deng/Sadikiel Kimaro/Terrence Lyons/Donald Rothchild/I. William Zartman, *Sovereignty as Responsibility: Conflict Management in Africa*, Washington, DC 1996.
9 International Commission on Intervention and State Sovereignty, ed., *The Responsibility to Protect*, Ottawa 2001, XI.
10 On the development of the concept of R2P, see Gareth Evans, *The Responsibility to Protect: Ending Mass Atrocity Crimes Once and For All*, Washington, DC 2008; James Pattison, *Humanitarian Intervention and the Responsibility to Protect: Who Should Intervene?*, Oxford 2010; Anne Orford, *International Authority and the Responsibility to Protect*, Cambridge 2011; Ramesh Thakur, *The Responsibility to Protect: Norms, Laws, and the Use of*

Force in International Politics, London 2011; Aidan Hehir, *The Responsibility to Protect: Rhetoric, Reality and the Future of Humanitarian Intervention*, Basingstoke 2012; Manuel Fröhlich, The Responsibility to Protect: Foundation, Transformation, and Application of an Emerging Norm, in Fabian Klose, ed., *The Emergence of Humanitarian Intervention: Ideas and Practice from the Nineteenth Century to the Present*, Cambridge 2016, 299f.

11 Resolution 60/1, 2005 World Summit Outcome, 24 October 2005, UNGA A/RES/60/1, 30.

12 In its earlier Resolution 1970, the UN Security Council had already admonished the Libyan regime to abide by its responsibility to protect its population. See Resolution 1970 (2011), 26 February 2011, in UNSC S/RES/1970; Resolution 1973 (2011), 17 March 2011, in UNSC S/RES/1973.

13 'Srebrenica-Moment': Der künftige UN-Vizechef über gute Gründe für Interventionen, *Die Zeit* (22 March 2012). For a similar interpretation see also Brendan Simms, Road to Libya Runs through Srebrenica, *The Independent* (29 May 2011). On the intervention in Libya, see Karin Wester, *Intervention in Libya: The Responsibility to Protect in North Africa*, Cambridge 2020.

14 On these contemporary debates, see Ramesh Thakur, R2P after Libya and Syria: Engaging Emerging Powers, *Washington Quarterly* 36/2 (Spring 2013), 61–76; C. A. J. Coady/Ned Dobos/Sagar Sanyal, eds., *Challenges for Humanitarian Intervention: Ethical Demand and Political Reality*, Oxford 2018; Alex J. Bellamy/Stephen McLoughlin, *Rethinking Humanitarian Intervention*, London 2018; Yasmine Nahlawi, *The Responsibility to Protect in Libya and Syria: Mass Atrocities, Human Protection, and International Law*, Abingdon 2020.

15 On the notion of the 'long nineteenth century', a term originally coined by Eric Hobsbawm, and the debates over this periodisation, see e.g. Christopher A. Bayly, *The Birth of the Modern World, 1780–1914*, New York 2004, 1–22; Jürgen Osterhammel, Auf der Suche nach einem 19. Jahrhundert, in Sebastian Conrad et al., eds., *Globalgeschichte, Theorie, Ansätze, Themen*, Frankfurt a. M. 2007, 109–130; Jürgen Osterhammel, The *Transformation of the World: A Global History of the Nineteenth Century*, Princeton, NJ 2014, 45–49.

16 Jeff L. Holzgrefe, The Humanitarian Intervention Debate, in Jeff L. Holzgrefe/Robert O. Keohane, eds., *Humanitarian Intervention: Ethical, Legal, and Political Dilemmas*, Cambridge 2004, 18. This definition is closely related to that of R. J. Vincent, according to whom intervention was to be understood 'as that activity undertaken by a state, a group within a state, a group of states or an international organization which interferes coercively in the domestic affairs of another state'. On this, see R. J. Vincent, *Nonintervention and International Order*, Princeton, NJ 1974, 3–13 at 13.

17 Sean D. Murphy, *Humanitarian Intervention: The United Nations in an Evolving World Order*, Philadelphia, PA 1996, 8–20; Adam Roberts, *Humanitarian Action in War: Aid, Protection and Impartiality in a Policy Vacuum*, Oxford 1996, 19–31; Francis Kofi Abiew, *The Evolution of the Doctrine and Practice of Humanitarian Intervention*, The Hague 1999, 18; Nicolas J. Wheeler, *Saving Strangers: Humanitarian Intervention in*

International Society, Oxford 2003, 1f.; Jennifer M. Welsh, ed., *Humanitarian Intervention and International Relations*, Oxford 2006, 3; Simon Chesterman, *Just War or Just Peace? Humanitarian Intervention and International Law*, Oxford 2003, 2f.; Taylor B. Seybolt, *Humanitarian Military Intervention: The Conditions for Success and Failure*, Oxford 2007, 5f.; Aidan Hehir, *Humanitarian Intervention: An Introduction*, Basingstoke 2010, 11–21; Thomas G. Weiss, *Humanitarian Intervention: Ideas in Action*, Cambridge 2012, 6–15.

18 On these forms of humanitarian action, see Larry Minear, *The Humanitarian Enterprise: Dilemmas and Discoveries*, Bloomfield, NJ 2002; Fabrice Weissman, ed., *In the Shadow of 'Just Wars': Violence, Politics, and Humanitarian Action*, London 2004; David P. Forsythe, *The Humanitarians: The International Committee of the Red Cross*, Cambridge 2005; Michael Barnett/Thomas G. Weiss, eds., *Humanitarianism in Question: Politics, Power, Ethics*, Ithaca, NY 2008; Johannes Paulmann, Conjunctures in the History of International Humanitarian Aid during the Twentieth Century, *Humanity* 4/2 (Summer 2013), 215–238; Johannes Paulmann, ed., *Dilemmas of Humanitarian Aid in the Twentieth Century*, Oxford 2016.

19 On this, see Minear, *Humanitarian Enterprise*, 99–118; Didier Fassin/Mariella Pandolfi, Introduction: Military and Humanitarian Government in the Age of Intervention, in Didier Fassin/Mariella Pandolfi, eds., *Contemporary States of Emergency: The Politics of Military and Humanitarian Intervention*, New York 2010, 9–25; Didier Fassin, *Humanitarian Reason: A Moral History of the Present*, Berkeley, CA 2012, 223–242; Johannes Paulmann, The Dilemmas of Humanitarian Aid: Historical Perspectives, in Paulmann, ed., *Dilemmas*, 1–31 at 4–11.

20 On the concept of intervention and its definition, see Vincent, *Nonintervention and International Order*, 13; Hedley Bull, ed., *Interventions in World Politics*, Oxford 1986, 1–6; Jürgen Osterhammel, Krieg im Frieden: Zu Formen und Typologie von Interventionen, in Jürgen Osterhammel, ed., *Geschichtswissenschaft jenseits des Nationalstaats: Studien zu Beziehungsgeschichte und Zivilisationsvergleich*, Göttingen 2001, 288–294; Martha Finnemore, *The Purpose of Intervention: Changing Beliefs about the Use of Force*, Ithaca, NY 2003, 7–11. On the conceptual history of intervention, see Percy H. Winfield, The History of Intervention in International Law, *British Yearbook of International Law* 130 (1922–23), 130–149; David J. Trim, Intervention in European History c. 1520–1850, in Stefano Recchia/Jennifer M. Welsh, eds., *Just and Unjust Military Intervention: European Thinkers from Vitoria to Mill*, Cambridge 2013, 21–47 at 23–25; Davide Rodogno, European Legal Doctrines on Intervention and the Status of the Ottoman Empire within the 'Family of Nations' throughout the Nineteenth Century, *Journal of the History of International Law* 18 (2016), 1–37 at 11–14.

21 On these new approaches, see Michael Barnett, *Empire of Humanity: A History of Humanitarianism*, Ithaca, NY 2011, 49–94; Silvia Salvatici, *A History of Humanitarianism, 1755–1989: In the Name of Others*, Manchester 2019, 35–48; Amalia Ribi Forclaz, *Humanitarian Imperialism: The Politics of Anti-Slavery Activism, 1880–1940*, Oxford 2015; James Heartfield, *The Aborigines' Protection Society: Humanitarian Imperialism in Australia, New Zealand, Fiji, Canada, South Africa, and the Congo, 1836–1909*, New York 2011; Alan

Lester/Fae Dussart, *Colonization and the Origins of Humanitarian Governance: Protecting Aborigines across the Nineteenth-Century British Empire*, Cambridge 2014; Rob Skinner/Alan Lester, Humanitarianism and Empire: New Research Agendas, *Journal of Imperial and Commonwealth History* 40/5 (December 2012), 729–747; Ian Tyrrell, *Reforming the World: The Creation of America's Moral Empire*, Princeton, NJ 2010, 98–145; Caroline Shaw, *Britannia's Embrace: Modern Humanitarianism and the Imperial Origins of Refugee Relief*, Oxford 2015; Johannes Paulmann, Humanity – Humanitarian Reason – Imperial Humanitarianism: European Concepts in Practice, in Fabian Klose/Mirjam Thulin, eds., *Humanity: A History of European Concepts in Practice from the Sixteenth Century to the Present*, Göttingen 2017, 287–311. For an important early study, see Andrew Porter, Trusteeship, Anti-Slavery, and Humanitarianism, in Andrew Porter, ed., *The Oxford History of the British Empire*, vol. III: *The Nineteenth Century*, Oxford 1999, 198–221. Exceptions that explicitly consider violent imperial interventions as part of the history of humanitarianism include Johannes Paulmann, Humanitarianism and Empire, in John M. MacKenzie, ed., *The Encyclopedia of Empire*, vol. II: *D–J*, Malden, MA 2016, 1112–1123 at 1112–1117; Andrew Thompson, Humanitarian Interventions, Past and Present, in Klose, ed., *Emergence of Humanitarian Intervention*, 331–356. On the broader intellectual history of a so-called liberal imperialism, see Jennifer Pitts, *A Turn to Empire: The Rise of Liberal Imperialism in Britain and France*, Princeton, NJ 2005.

22 For this legal-historical perspective, see Murphy, *Humanitarian Intervention*, 33–64; Wilhelm G. Grewe, *The Epochs of International Law*, Berlin 2000, 487–496; Abiew, *Evolution of the Doctrine*, 21–59; Chesterman, *Just War*, 7–44; Mark Swatek-Evenstein, *A History of Humanitarian Intervention*, Cambridge 2020 (Originally published in German as *Geschichte der 'Humanitären Intervention'*, Baden-Baden 2008); Hans Köchler, *The Concept of Humanitarian Intervention in the Context of Modern Power Politics: Is the Revival of the Doctrine of 'Just War' Compatible with the International Rule of Law?*, Vienna 2001; Stephen Kloepfer, The Syrian Crisis, 1860–1861: A Case Study in Classic Humanitarian Intervention, *Canadian Yearbook of International Law* 23 (1985), 246–260; Istvan Pogany, Humanitarian Intervention in International Law: The French Intervention in Syria Re-Examined, *International and Comparative Law Quarterly* 35/1 (January 1986), 182–190; Christian Hillgruber, Humanitäre Intervention, Grossmachtpolitik und Völkerrecht, *Der Staat* 40/21 (2001), 165–191; Stefano Recchia/Jennifer M. Welsh, eds., *Just and Unjust Military Intervention: European Thinkers from Vitoria to Mill*, Oxford 2013; Fernando R. Tesón/Bas van der Vossen, *Debating Humanitarian Intervention: Should We Try to Save Strangers?*, New York 2017.

23 Fernando R. Tesón, *Humanitarian Intervention: An Inquiry into Law and Morality*, Ardsley, NY 2005; Thakur, *Responsibility to Protect*; Ramesh Thakur, *The United Nations, Peace and Security: From Collective Security to the Responsibility to Protect*, Cambridge 2017; Orford, *International Authority*.

24 Louis Henkin, Kosovo and the Law of 'Humanitarian Intervention', *American Journal of International Law* 93/4 (October 1999), 824–828; Jonathan I. Charney, Anticipatory Humanitarian Intervention in Kosovo, *American*

Journal of International Law 93/4 (October 1999), 834–841; Richard A. Falk, Kosovo, World Order, and the Future of International Law, *American Journal of Law* 93/4 (October 1999), 847–857; Sean D. Murphy, The Intervention in Kosovo: A Law-Shaping Incident?, *Proceedings of the Annual Meeting* (American Society of International Law) 94/5–8 (April 2000), 302–304; Allen Buchanan, Reforming the International Law of Humanitarian Intervention, in Jeff L. Holzgrefe/Robert O. Keohane, eds., *Humanitarian Intervention: Ethical, Legal, and Political Dilemmas*, Cambridge 2004, 130–173; Ryan Goodman, Humanitarian Intervention and Pretexts for War, *American Journal of International Law* 100/1 (January 2006), 107–141; Katariina Simonen, *The State versus the Individual: The Unresolved Dilemma of Humanitarian Intervention*, Leiden 2011; Ciarán Burke, *An Equitable Framework for Humanitarian Intervention*, Oxford 2013.

25 Particularly good examples of this multidimensional approach include: Wheeler, *Saving Strangers*; Jeff L. Holzgrefe/Robert O. Keohane, eds., *Humanitarian Intervention: Ethical, Legal, and Political Dilemmas*, Cambridge 2004; Anne Orford, *Reading Humanitarian Intervention: Human Rights and the Use of Force in International Law*, Cambridge 2003; Elizabeth M. Bruch, *Human Rights and Humanitarian Intervention: Law and Practice in the Field*, London 2016. The various dimensions of the question of humanitarian intervention are likewise considered in a four-volume compilation of previously published texts: Alex J. Bellamy, ed., *Humanitarian Intervention*, vol. I: *Law, Ethics, and Theories*, London 2017; Alex J. Bellamy, ed., *Humanitarian Intervention*, vol. II: *Humanitarian Intervention in History*, London 2017; Alex J. Bellamy, ed., *Humanitarian Intervention*, vol. III: *Humanitarian Intervention in Contemporary Practice*, London 2017; Alex J. Bellamy, ed., *Humanitarian Intervention*, vol. IV: *Beyond Humanitarian Intervention: The Responsibility to Protect*, London 2017.

26 Weiss, *Humanitarian Intervention*, 3. For an exemplary instance of this focus from the 1990s onwards: S. Neil MacFarlane, *Intervention in Contemporary World Politics*, New York 2002, 49–83; Michael C. Davis/Wolfgang Dietrich/Bettina Scholdan/Dieter Sepp, *International Intervention in the Post-Cold War World: Moral Responsibility and Power Politics*, Armonk, NY 2004; Seybolt, *Humanitarian Military Intervention*; John Janzekovic, *The Use of Force in Humanitarian Intervention: Morality and Practicalities*, Aldershot 2006; Aiden Warren/Damian Grenfell, eds., *Rethinking Humanitarian Intervention in the 21st Century*, Edinburgh 2017; Peter J. Hoffman/Thomas G. Weiss, *Humanitarianism, War, and Politics: Solferino to Syria and Beyond*, Lanham, MD 2018, 57–94.

27 For an overview and on the rise of UN military operations since 1990, see Weiss, *Humanitarian Intervention*, 46. On this new role of the UN see also Elizabeth G. Ferris, *The Challenge to Intervene: A New Role for the United Nations?*, Uppsala 1992; Murphy, *Humanitarian Intervention*; Thomas G. Weiss/David P. Forsythe/Roger A. Coate, *The United Nations and Changing World Politics*, Boulder, CO 2004, 47–92; Adam Roberts, The United Nations and Humanitarian Intervention, in Welsh, ed., *Humanitarian Intervention*, 71–97; Martin Binder, *The United Nations and the Politics of Selective Humanitarian Intervention*, Cham 2017.

28 Typical examples include Martha Finnemore, Constructing Norms of Humanitarian Intervention, in Peter J. Katzenstein, ed., *The Culture of National Security: Norms and Identity in World Politics*, New York 1996, 153–185 at 161–172; Rajan Menon, *The Conceit of Humanitarian Intervention*, New York 2016, 78–82. For exceptions from the field of political science that explicitly draw upon historical precedent, see Chaim D. Kaufmann/Robert A. Pape, Explaining Costly International Moral Action: Britain's Sixty-Year Campaign against the Atlantic Slave Trade, *International Organization* 53/4 (Autumn 1999), 631–668; Oded Löwenheim, 'Do Ourselves Credit and Render a Lasting Service to Mankind': British Moral Prestige, Humanitarian Intervention, and the Barbary Pirates, *International Studies Quarterly* 47/1 (March 2003), 23–48; Nicolas Onuf, Humanitarian Intervention: The Early Years, *Florida Journal of International Law* 16/4 (2004), 753–787; Tonny Brems Knudsen, The History of Humanitarian Intervention: The Rule or the Exception?, Paper for the 50th ISA Annual Convention, 15–18 February 2009; Ibrahim Seaga Shaw, The Politics of Humanitarian Intervention: A Critical Analogy of the British Response to End the Slave Trade and the Civil War in Sierra Leone, *Journal of Global Ethics*, 6/3 (2010), 273–285; Chris Brown, Humanitarian Intervention and International Political Theory, in Alexander Mosley/Richard Norman, eds., *Human Rights and Military Intervention*, London 2018, 153–169. The second volume of Alex Bellamy's four-volume compilation also addresses these historical antecedents – without, however, including the struggle to suppress the Atlantic slave trade: Bellamy, *Humanitarian Intervention*, vol. II.

29 Evans, *Responsibility to Protect*, 15–19. For a similar line of argument see also Ian Brownlie, *International Law and the Use of Force by States*, Oxford 1963, 338–342.

30 On the conflation of motives for humanitarian intervention, see Michael Walzer, *Just and Unjust Wars: A Moral Argument with Historical Illustrations*, New York 2000, 101; Wheeler, *Saving Strangers*, 37–39, 47; Shaw, Politics, 273–285; Brown, Humanitarian Intervention, 156; Menon, *Conceit of Humanitarian Intervention*, 78–82; Jürgen Osterhammel, Schutz, Macht und Verantwortung. Protektion im Zeitalter der Imperien und danach, in Jürgen Osterhammel, *Die Flughöhe der Adler: Historische Essays zur globalen Gegenwart*, Munich 2017, 160–182 at 174f.

31 As it is used here, the term 'humanitarian revolution' denoted the emergence of a humanitarian sensibility and the activities associated with it. It is not intended to imply, as Steven Pinker would have it, a broader decline in violence. On this, see Steven Pinker, *The Better Angels of Our Nature: Why Violence Has Declined*, New York 2011, 129–188.

32 For a typical example, see Thomas Haskell, Capitalism and the Origins of Humanitarian Sensibility, pt. 1, *American Historical Review* 90/2 (April 1985), 339–361; Thomas Haskell, Capitalism and the Origins of Humanitarian Sensibility, pt. 2, *American Historical Review* 90/3 (June 1985), 547–566; Thomas Laqueur, Bodies, Details, and the Humanitarian Narrative, in Lynn Hunt, ed., *The New Cultural History*, Berkeley, CA 1989, 176–204; Samuel Moyn, Empathy in History: Empathizing with Humanity, *History*

and Theory 45 (2006), 397–415; Lynn Hunt, *Inventing Human Rights: A History*, New York 2007; Richard D. Brown/Richard Wilson, eds., *Humanitarianism and Suffering: The Mobilization of Empathy*, Cambridge 2009; Lynn Festa, Humanity without Feathers, *Humanity* 1/1 (Autumn 2010), 3–27; Fabian Klose/Mirjam Thulin, eds., *Humanity: A History of European Concepts in Practice from the Sixteenth Century to the Present*, Göttingen 2017.

33 Carole Fink, *Defending the Rights of Others: The Great Powers, the Jews, and International Minority Protection*, Cambridge 2004, 3–38 at 9.

34 Paul G. Lauren, *The Evolution of International Human Rights: Visions Seen*, Philadelphia, PA 2011, 71–76. Jan Eckel, too, in his recent history of human rights, cursorily places the phenomenon of nineteenth-century humanitarian intervention in the prehistory of international human rights policy, emphasising that the European powers' military interventions had been solely for the benefit of persecuted Ottoman Christians. Jan Eckel, *Die Ambivalenz des Guten: Menschenrechte in der internationalen Politik seit den 1940ern*, Göttingen 2014, 38–41.

35 Matthias Schulz, *Normen und Praxis: Das Europäische Konzert der Großmächte als Sicherheitsrat 1815–1860*, Munich 2009, 73–88, 524–531, 577–620; Osterhammel, Krieg im Frieden, 283–321, esp. at 315–321. More recent historical approaches to the subject of intervention can be found in: Miloš Vec, Intervention/Nichtintervention: Verrechtlichung der Politik und Politisierung des Völkerrechts im 19. Jahrhundert, in Ulrich Lappenküper/ Reiner Marcowitz, eds., *Macht und Recht: Völkerrecht in den internationalen Beziehungen*, Paderborn 2010, 135–160.

36 Mark Mazower, *Governing the World: The History of an Idea*, London 2012, ch. 13.

37 Gary Bass, *Freedom's Battle: The Origins of Humanitarian Intervention*, New York 2008. The two essays by Davide Rodogno and Michael Marrus appeared almost simultaneously with Bass' book. See on this: Davide Rodogno, Réflexions liminaires à propos des intervention humanitaires des Puissances européenes aux XIXe siècle, *Relations Internationales* 131 (July–September 2007), 9–25; Michael R. Marrus, International Bystanders to the Holocaust and Humanitarian Intervention, in Richard Ashby Wilson/Richard D. Brown, eds., *Humanitarianism and Suffering: The Mobilization of Empathy*, Cambridge 2009, 156–174.

38 Bass, *Freedom's Battle*, 360.

39 For a critical take on the work of Gary Bass, see also Samuel Moyn, *Human Rights and the Uses of History*, London 2014, 35–51.

40 Davide Rodogno, *Against Massacre: Humanitarian Interventions in the Ottoman Empire 1815–1914*, Princeton, NJ 2012.

41 'Nineteenth-century humanitarian intervention took place in a clearly defined geographical area of the globe – the Ottoman Empire – and proved to be a selective practice as far as humanity on behalf of whom it took place was concerned.' Ibid., 264. Keith David Watenpaugh also emphasises the region's particular importance as – in his view – the cradle of modern humanitarianism in the inter-war period. Keith David Watenpaugh, *Bread from Stones: The Middle East and the Making of Modern Humanitarianism*, Oakland, CA 2015 at 1–29.

42 Brendan Simms/David J. B. Trim, eds., *Humanitarian Intervention: A History*, Cambridge 2011. The interdisciplinary collection of essays entitled *The History and Practice of Humanitarian Intervention and Aid in Africa* turns its gaze to a different part of the world, sub-Saharan Africa. However, the volume blurs the definition of humanitarian intervention by conflating it with other forms of humanitarian action. It also fails to make good on its promise to deliver a long-term historical perspective, with most contributions emphasising developments from the mid-1960s on. See on this Bronwen Everill/Josiah Kaplan, eds., *The History and Practice of Humanitarian Intervention and Aid in Africa*, Basingstoke 2013.

43 David J. B. Trim, Conclusion: Humanitarian Intervention in Historical Perspective, in Simms/Trim, eds., *Humanitarian Intervention*, 381.

44 Brendan Simms/David J. B. Trim, Towards a History of Humanitarian Intervention, in Simms/Trim, eds., *Humanitarian Intervention*, 21f.

45 Alexis Heraclides/Ada Dialla, *Humanitarian Intervention in the Long Nineteenth Century: Setting Precedent*, Manchester 2015.

46 Even in the copious literature on abolitionism, there is hardly ever any mention of a connection between the struggle against the slave trade and the concept of humanitarian intervention. For the rare exceptions, see Maeve Ryan, The Price of Legitimacy in Humanitarian Intervention: Britain, the Right of Search, and the Abolition of the West African Slave Trade 1807–1867, in Simms/Trim, eds., *Humanitarian Intervention*, 231–256; Marcel van der Linden, Unanticipated Consequences of 'Humanitarian Intervention': The British Campaign to Abolish the Slave Trade, 1807–1900, *Theory and Society* 39/3–4 (2010), 281–298; Löwenheim, 'Do Ourselves Credit'; Shaw, Politics of Humanitarian Intervention; Brown, Humanitarian Intervention, Kaufmann/Pape, Explaining Costly International Moral Action.

47 For this new approach, which avoids geographical and thematic strictures, see also the author's edited volume: Klose, ed., *Emergence of Humanitarian Intervention*.

48 The term 'Concert of Europe' is a contemporary coinage that became established in the nineteenth century as denoting the cooperation of the European great powers. On its conceptual history, see Schulz, *Normen und Praxis*, 36–39.

49 Bass, *Freedom's Battle*, ch. 1 'Humanitarianism or Imperialism?', 11–24.

Part I

1 Giuseppe Mazzini, On Nonintervention (1851), in Stefano Recchia/Nadia Urbinati, eds., *A Cosmopolitanism of Nations: Giuseppe Mazzini's Writings on Democracy, Nation Building, and International Relations*, Princeton, NJ 2009, 217f.

Chapter 1

1 Leonard S. Woolf, *International Government: Two Reports Prepared for the Fabian Research Department*, New York 1916, 4f., 148f.

2 Ibid., 150.
3 Ibid., 141.
4 For Woolf's detailed account of the history and structure of this for international cooperation, see esp. part II of his report, ibid., 137–388. For the section 'Morals and Crime', see ibid., 260–265.
5 For the Greek case study, see ibid., 40–47.
6 Ibid., 43. To describe a naval battle fought for several hours and with thousands killed – most of them on the Ottoman side – as 'pacific' would not seem to do justice to the true character of events in Navarino Bay.
7 Ibid., 43.
8 Ibid., 45.
9 On this, see Peter Wilson, *The International Theory of Leonard Woolf: A Study in Twentieth-Century Idealism*, New York 2003, 54–55.
10 The pathbreaking and still crucial book on this is Francis S. L. Lyons, *Internationalism in Europe 1815–1914*, Leiden 1963. For important new studies, see Martin H. Geyer/Johannes Paulmann, eds., *The Mechanics of Internationalism: Culture, Society, and Politics from the 1840s to the First World War*, Oxford 2001; Madeleine Herren, *Hintertüren zur Macht: Internationalismus und modernisierungsorientierte Außenpolitik in Belgien, der Schweiz und den USA, 1865–1914*, Munich 2000; Johannes Paulmann, Reformer, Experten und Diplomaten: Grundlagen des Internationalismus, in Hillard von Thiessen/Christian Windler, eds., *Akteure der Außenbeziehungen: Netzwerke und Interkulturalität im historischen Wandel*, Cologne 2010, 173–197; Daniel Laqua, *The Age of Internationalism and Belgium, 1880–1930: Peace, Progress and Prestige*, Manchester 2013; Mazower, *Governing the World*, Part 1 'The Era of Internationalism', 3–188; though Glenda Sluga's book deals mainly with the twentieth century, it does begin by discussing the strong international currents of the late nineteenth century. On this, see Glenda Sluga, *Internationalism in the Age of Nationalism*, Philadelphia, PA 2013, 11–32.
11 On this significant process of compression and interconnection, see esp. Bayly, *Birth of the Modern World*, esp. at 19f., 41, 236–244 and 455–462; Osterhammel, *Transformation of the World*, 505–513.
12 Paulmann, Reformer, Experten und Diplomaten, 174–182.
13 'The word international, it must be acknowledged, is a new one – though, it is hoped, sufficiently analogous and intelligible. It is calculated to express, in a more significant way, the branch of law which goes commonly under the name of the law of nations.' Jeremy Bentham, *An Introduction to the Principles of Morals and Legislation*, printed in the year 1780, and now first published, London 1789, cccxxiv. On the conceptual history of 'internationalism', see Peter Friedemann/Lucian Hölscher, Internationale, International, Internationalismus, in Otto Brunner/Werner Conze/Reinhart Koselleck, eds., *Geschichtliche Grundbegriffe: Historisches Lexikon zur politisch-sozialen Sprache in Deutschland*, vol. 3, Stuttgart 1982, 367–397; Mazower, *Governing the World*, 19–23. On different concepts of internationalisation, see Fred Halliday, Three Concepts of Internationalism, *International Affairs* 64/2 (Spring 1988), 187–198.

14 Paulmann, Reformer, Experten und Diplomaten, 187. It is on this definition of 'internationalism' that the volume edited by Johannes Paulmann and Martin H. Geyer was originally based. On this, see Geyer/Paulmann, *Mechanics of Internationalism*, 1–7.

15 Geyer/Paulmann, *Mechanics of Internationalism*; Lyons, *Internationalism in Europe*, Mazower, *Governing the World*, 13–115.

16 See e.g. Miloš Vec, Das Prinzip der Verkehrsfreiheit im Völkerrecht: Die Rheinschifffahrt zwischen dem Frieden von Lunéville (1801) und der Mannheimer Akte (1868), *Zeitschrift für Neuere Rechtsgeschichte* 30/3/4 (2008), 221–241; Lyons, *Internationalism in Europe*, 38–88; Bob Reinalda, *Routledge History of International Organizations: From 1815 to the Present Day*, London 2009, 28–30, 85–90.

17 Martin H. Geyer, One Language for the World: The Metric System, International Coinage, Gold Standard, and the Rise of Internationalism, in Geyer/Paulmann, eds., *Mechanics of Internationalism*, 55–92.

18 Miloš Vec, *Recht und Normierung in der Industriellen Revolution: Neue Strukturen der Normsetzung in Völkerrecht, staatlicher Gesetzgebung und gesellschaftlicher Selbstnormierung*, Frankfurt a. M. 2006, 21. On this, see also Lyons, *Internationalism in Europe*, 215–222; Jörg Fisch, Völkerrecht, in Jost Dülffer/Wilfried Loth, eds., *Dimensionen internationaler Geschichte*, Munich 2012, 151–168 at 160f.; Jost Dülffer, Recht, Normen und Macht, in Dülffer/Loth, eds., *Dimensionen internationaler Geschichte*, 169–188 at 175–180.

19 Vec, *Recht und Normierung*, 104–126. For the legalisation of international relations in general, see Vec, Intervention/Nichtintervention, 135–160; Matthias Schulz, Macht, internationale Politik und Normenwandel im Staatensystem des 19. Jahrhunderts, in Lappenküper/Marcowitz, eds., *Macht und Recht*, 113–134; Klaus Schlichte, Das formierende Säkulum: Macht und Recht in der internationalen Politik des 19. Jahrhunderts, in Lappenküper/Marcowitz, eds., *Macht und Recht*, 161–177.

20 Martti Koskenniemi, *The Gentle Civilizer of Nations: The Rise and Fall of International Law 1870–1960*, Cambridge 2001, 11–97.

21 Johann Caspar Bluntschli, *Das moderne Völkerrecht der civilisirten Staaten als Rechtsbuch dargestellt*, Nördlingen 1868.

22 On this, see Gerrit W. Gong, *The Standard of 'Civilization' in International Society*, Oxford 1984, 54–93; Jörg Fisch, Internationalizing Civilization by Dissolving International Society: The Status of Non-European Territories in Nineteenth-Century International Law, in Geyer/Paulmann, eds., *Mechanics of Internationalism*, 235–257 esp. at 246–255; Koskenniemi, *Gentle Civilizer*, 98–152; Brett Bowden, *The Empire of Civilization: The Evolution of an Imperial Idea*, Chicago, IL 2009, 117–128. On the concept of civilisation as the international guiding category of so-called liberal imperialism in general, see Gong, *Standard of 'Civilization'*; Bowden, *Empire of Civilization*; Mark B. Salter, *Barbarians and Civilization in International Relations*, London 2002; Eric D. Weitz, From the Vienna to the Paris System: International Politics and the Entangled Histories of Human Rights, Forced Deportations, and Civilizing Missions, *American Historical Review* 113/5 (December 2008), 1313–1343; Mark Mazower, Ende der Zivilisation und Aufstieg der

Menschrechte: Die konzeptionelle Trennung Mitte des 20. Jahrhunderts, in Stefan-Ludwig Hoffmann, ed., *Moralpolitik: Die Geschichte der Menschenrechte im 20. Jahrhundert*, Göttingen 2010, 41–62 at 42–48; Jo-Anne Claire Pemberton, The So-Called Right of Civilisation in European Colonial Ideology, 16th to 20th Centuries, *Journal of the History of International Law* 15/1 (2013), 25–52; Pitts, *A Turn to Empire*.

23 Bluntschli, *Moderne Völkerrecht*, § 280, 166.

24 James Lorimer, *The Institutes of International Law: A Treatise of the Jural Relations of Separate Political Communities*, vol. I, Edinburgh 1883, 101.

25 Ibid., 101f.

26 Ibid., 102.

27 On the pronounced connection between developments in international law and the growth of imperial power, see Koskenniemi, *Gentle Civilizer*, 98–178; Antony Anghie, *Imperialism, Sovereignty and the Making of International Law*, Cambridge 2005; Duncan S. A. Bell, Empire and International Relations in Victorian Political Thought, *Historical Journal* 49/1 (March 2006), 281–298 at 289–291; Lauren Benton, From International Law to Imperial Constitutions: The Problem of Quasi-Sovereignty, 1870–1900, *Law and History Review* 26/3 (Autumn 2008), 595–619; Turan Kayaoğlu, *Legal Imperialism: Sovereignty and Extraterritoriality in Japan, the Ottoman Empire, and China*, Cambridge 2010. Yet Andrew Fitzmaurice has also drawn attention to opposition to imperial expansion from among scholars of international law and outlines debates that sometimes were highly contentious. On this, see Andrew Fitzmaurice, Liberalism and Empire in Nineteenth-Century International Law, *American Historical Review* 117/1 (February 2012), 122–140.

28 On Sir Travers Twiss, see Andrew Fitzmaurice, The Justification of King Leopold II's Congo Enterprise by Sir Travers Twiss, in Shaunnagh Dorsett/ Ian Hunter, eds., *Law and Politics in British Colonial Thought: Transpositions of Empire*, New York 2010, 109–126.

29 Koskenniemi, *Gentle Civilizer*, 121–127, 143–152; Mazower, *Governing the World*, 67f. On the Africa Conference, see generally the edited collection: Stig Förster/Wolfgang J. Mommsen/Ronald Robinson, eds., *Bismarck, Europe, and Africa: The Berlin Africa Conference 1884–1885 and the Onset of Partition*, Oxford 1988, and in particular the chapter on international law: Jörg Fisch, Africa as terra nullius: The Berlin Conference and International Law, in Förster et al., eds., *Bismarck, Europe, and Africa*, 347–375. More generally on the subject of treaties between African and European states between the sixteenth and nineteenth centuries and the emergence of a particular colonial law, see Charles Henry Alexandrowicz, *The European–African Confrontation: A Study in Treaty Making*, Leiden 1973; Michael Mulligan, Nigeria, the British Presence in West Africa and International Law in the 19th Century, *Journal of the History of International Law* 11 (2009), 273–301.

30 On this, see Gustave Moynier, ed., *L'Afrique explorée et civilisée* 1–15 (1879–1894), periodical publihed in Geneva between 1879 and 1894; Gustave Moynier, *La question du Congo devant l'Institut de droit international*, Genf 1883; Gustave Moynier, *La fondation de l'État indépendant du Congo au point de vue juridique*, Paris 1887; Albert Wirz, Die humanitäre Schweiz im Spannungsfeld zwischen Philantrophie und Kolonialismus: Gustave

Moynier, Afrika und das IKRK, *Traverse: Zeitschrift für Geschichte/Revue d'histoire* 5/2 (1998), 95–111 at 104–108.

31 Jennifer Pitts, Boundaries of Victorian International Law, in Duncan Bell, ed., *Victorian Visions of Global Order: Empire and International Relations in Nineteenth-Century Political Thought*, Cambridge 2007, 67–88.

32 On the proscription of such ordnance, see 'Declaration (IV, 2) Concerning Asphyxiating Gas' and 'Declaration (IV, 3) Concerning Expanding Bullets', in Adam Roberts/Richard Guelff, eds., *Documents on the Laws of War*, Oxford 2000, 60f., 64f.

33 On this, see Edward M. Spiers, The Use of the Dum Dum Bullet in Colonial Warfare, *Journal of Imperial and Commonwealth History* 4/1 (1975), 3–14.

34 Mazower, *Governing the World*, 74–79.

35 A phrase from Kipling's poem 'The White Man's Burden' from 1899, in which the author describes colonialism as a civilising mission. On this, see Rudyard Kipling, *Rudyard Kipling's Verse: Definitive Edition*, New York 1929, 321–323.

36 On these various areas of and movements for social and political reform, see Lyons, *Internationalism in Europe*, 135–190, 263–361; Mazower, *Governing the World*, 31–64.

37 Bayly, *Birth of the Modern World*, 484. On the emergence and importance of publicity and the public sphere in the eighteenth and nineteenth centuries, see ibid., 94–104; James van Horn Melton, *The Rise of the Public in Enlightenment Europe*, Cambridge 2001; Osterhammel, *Transformation of the World*, 596–598; Paulmann, Reformer, Experten und Diplomaten, 194f.

38 On the nineteenth-century revolution in communications, see Hannah Barker/Simon Burrows, eds., *Press, Politics and the Public Sphere in Europe and North America, 1760–1820*, Cambridge 2002; Osterhammel, *Transformation of the World*, 35–37; Peter J. Hugill, *Global Communications since 1844: Geopolitics and Technology*, Baltimore, MD 1999; Roland Wenzlhuemer, *Connecting the Nineteenth-Century World: The Telegraph and Globalization*, Cambridge 2013.

39 Lyons, *Internationalism in Europe*, 263–274 at 263.

40 Ibid., 263–307 at 295–299.

41 Paulmann, Reformer, Experten und Diplomaten, 187.

42 Lyons, *Internationalism in Europe*, 13–18; Herren, *Hintertüren zur Macht*, 12, 507; Laqua, *Age of Internationalism*, 5–7; Osterhammel, *Transformation of the World*, 505, 510.

43 On the founding of international organisations and institutions in this period in particular, see Matthias Schulz, Internationale Institutionen, in Dülffer/Loth, eds., *Dimensionen*, 213–232 at 216–218; Craig N. Murphy, *International Organization and Industrial Change: Global Governance since 1850*, Cambridge 1994; John Boli/George M. Thomas, eds., *Constructing World Culture: International Nongovernmental Organizations since 1875*, Stanford, CA 1999; Akira Iriye, *Global Community: The Role of International Organizations in the Making of the Contemporary World*, Berkeley, CA 2002, 9–36.

44 For exemplary studies of the Congress of Vienna, see Harold Nicolson, *The Congress of Vienna: A Study in Allied Unity 1812–1822*, London 1947; Adam Zamoyski, *Rites of Peace: The Fall of Napoleon and the Congress of Vienna*,

New York 2007, 260–441; Brian E. Vick, *The Congress of Vienna: Power and Politics after Napoleon*, Cambridge 2014; Glenda Sluga, 'Who Hold the Balance of the World?' Bankers at the Congress of Vienna, and in International History, *American Historical Review* 122/5 (December 2017), 1403–1430.

45 Paul W. Schroeder, *The Transformation of European Politics 1763–1848*, Oxford 1994, at esp. 517–582.

46 'Le système politique qui s'est établi en Europe depuis 1814 et 1815 est un phénomène inouï dans l'histoire du monde. Au principe de l'équilibre ou, pour mieux dire, des contre-poids formés par des alliances particulières, principe qui a gouverné, et trop souvent aussi troublé et ensanglanté l'Europe pendant trois siècles, a succédé un principe d'union générale, réunissant la totalité des États par un lien fédératif, sous la direction des cinq principales Puisssances.' Dispatch by Friedrich von Gentz, 24 March 1818, in Comte Anton Prokesch-Osten, ed., *Dépêches inédites du Chevalier de Gentz aux hospodars de Valachie: Pour servir à l'histoire de la politique européene (1813 à 1828)*, vol. I, Paris 1876, 354–356.

47 In his seminal study, Paul Schroeder argues that the Congress of Vienna, rather than heralding a return to the old system of the 'balance of powers', established a cooperative hegemony of Great Britain and Russia, which was cloaked in the idea of political equilibrium for the benefit of the other major powers. On this, see Paul W. Schroeder, Did the Vienna Settlement Rest on a Balance of Power?, *American Historical Review* 97/3 (June 1992), 683–706; Schroeder, *Transformation of European Politics*. Matthias Schulz has criticised this idea of a cooperative hegemony while supporting the overall idea of a political equilibrium. On this, see Schulz, *Normen und Praxis*, 46–53, 70–72. On the subject of 'hegemony and balance' more generally, see Wolfram Pyta, Hegemonie und Gleichgewicht, in Dülffer/Loth, eds., *Dimensionen*, 373–388 at esp. 380–385.

48 On this role and function of the 'Concert of Europe', see Carsten Holbraad, *The Concert of Europe: A Study in German and British International Theory 1815–1914*, London 1970; Wolfram Pyta, ed., *Das europäische Mächtekonzert: Friedens- und Sicherheitspolitik vom Wiener Kongress 1815 bis zum Krimkrieg 1853*, Cologne 2009.

49 Martin H. Geyer/Johannes Paulmann, Introduction: The Mechanics of Internationalism, in Geyer/Paulmann, eds., *Mechanics of Internationalism*, 11; Lyons, *Internationalism in Europe*, 12f.

50 Mazower, *Governing the World*, viv. Political science has settled on the term 'global governance' to refer to this kind of internationalism. For an example focusing on the nineteenth century, see Kalevi J. Holsti, Governance without Government: Polyarchy in Nineteenth-Century European International Politics, in James N. Rosenau/Ernst-Otto Czempiel, eds., *Governance without Government: Order and Change in World Politics*, Cambridge 1992, 30–57; Margaret P. Karns/Karen A. Mingst, *International Organizations: The Politics and Process of Global Governance*, Boulder, CO 2010 at 65–68; Jennifer Mitzen, *Power in Concert: The Nineteenth-Century Origins of Global Governance*, Chicago, IL 2013.

51 Schulz, *Normen und Praxis*. On this, see also Wolfram Pyta, Konzert der Mächte und kollektives Sicherheitssystem: Neue Wege zwischenstaatlicher Friedenswahrung in Europa nach dem Wiener Kongress 1815, *Jahrbuch des Historischen Kollegs 2*, Munich 1997, 133–173; Beatrice de Graaf/Ido de Haan/Brian Vick, eds., *Securing Europe after Napoleon: 1815 and the New European Security Culture*, Cambridge 2019.

52 Osterhammel, *Transformation of the World*, 510f; Paul W. Schroeder, International Politics, Peace, and War, 1815–1914, in T. C. W. Blanning, ed., *The Nineteenth Century: The Short Oxford History of Europe*, Oxford 2000, 158–209; Richard J. Evans, *The Pursuit of Power: Europe 1815–1914*, London 2016, 20–28.

53 The Crimean War (1853–56) is widely regarded as a watershed marking the undoing of the Concert of Europe and the Vienna settlement. On this, see Paul W. Schroeder, *Austria, Great Britain, and the Crimean War: The Destruction of the European Concert*, Ithaca, NY 1972; Osterhammel, *Transformation of the World*, 398, 470f.; Matthias Schulz disagrees, arguing that the period between 1853 and 1871 was that 'in which the Concert worked at its most intense pitch yet, measured in the frequency of its conferences and mediation efforts' and that, accordingly, 'it was only in the permanent state of crisis between 1847 and 1867 that the Concert's institutional character took on stable form'. On this, see Matthias Schulz, Internationale Politik und Friedenskultur: Das Europäische Konzert in politikwissenschaftlicher Theorie und historischer Empirie, in Pyta, ed., *Europäisches Mächtekonzert*, 41–57 at 56; Schulz, *Normen und Praxis*, 348–357. On the Crimean War generally, see Winfried Baumgart, *The Crimean War 1853–1856*, London 1999.

54 Paulmann, Reformer, Experten und Diplomaten, 191. Madeleine Herren and Daniel Laqua have convincingly argued that internationalism opened completely new spheres for international action and influence to such smaller countries as Belgium and Switzerland, which were not members of the Concert of Europe, as well as to the up-and-coming great power, the United States, particularly in the late nineteenth century. On this, see Herren, *Hintertüren zur Macht*; and Madeleine Herren, Governmental Internationalism and the Beginning of a New World Order in the Late Nineteenth Century, in Geyer/Paulmann, eds., *Mechanics of Internationalism*, 121–144; Laqua, *Age of Internationalism*.

55 Mazower, *Governing the World*, viv.

56 Holbraad, *Concert of Europe*, 22f., 124–126; Schulz, *Normen und Praxis*, 73–88, 584–588; Holsti, Governance without Government, 37–38; Mazower, *Governing the World*, 6f.

57 The question of an anti-revolutionary intervention mechanism was hotly debated at congresses between 1818 and 1822 and was partly responsible for there being no further congresses after that of Verona in 1822. On this, see Schulz, *Normen und Praxis*, 76–88; Wolfram Pyta, Kulturgeschichtliche Annäherung an das europäische Mächtekonzert, in Pyta, ed., *Europäisches Mächtekonzert*, 5; Mitzen, *Power in Concert*, 105–123.

Chapter 2

1 On the definition of 'intervention', see Vincent, *Nonintervention and International Order*, 13; Bull, *Interventions*, 1–6; Osterhammel, Krieg im Frieden, 288–294; Finnemore, *Purpose of Intervention*, 7–11.

2 On the conceptual history of 'intervention', see Winfield, History of Intervention, 130–149; Trim, Intervention in European History, 23–25.

3 Osterhammel, Krieg im Frieden, 320. On this, see also Brownlie, *International Law*, 44f.; Wilhelm G. Grewe, *Epochen der Völkerrechtsgeschichte*, Baden-Baden 1984, 212; Finnemore, *Purpose of Intervention*, vii, 9; Walzer, *Just and Unjust Wars*, 86–108; MacFarlane, *Intervention*, 15; Stephen C. Neff, *War and the Law of Nations: A General History*, Cambridge 2007, 215–225.

4 William Vernon Harcourt, *Letters by Historicus on Some Questions of International Law*, London 1863, 46–47. 'Historicus' was the name under which William Vernon Harcourt published his newspaper column.

5 On the question of intervention in the early modern era, see David J. Trim, 'If a prince use tyrannie towards his people': Interventions on Behalf of Foreign Populations in Early Modern Europe, in Simms/Trim, eds., *Humanitarian Intervention*, 29–66; Patrick Milton, Intervening against Tyrannical Rule in the Holy Roman Empire during the Seventeenth and Eighteenth Centuries, *German History* 33/1 (2015), 1–29; Edward Keene, International Hierarchy and the Origins of the Modern Practice of International Intervention, *Review of International Studies* 39/5 (December 2013), 1077–1090.

6 On this, see Christoph Kampmann, Das 'Westfälische System', die Glorreiche Revolution und die Interventionsproblematik, *Historisches Jahrbuch* 131 (2011), 65–92; Christoph Kampmann, The English Crisis, Emperor Leopold, and the Origins of the Dutch Intervention in 1688, *Historical Journal* 55/2 (June 2012), 521–532; Antje von Ungern-Sternberg, Religion and Religious Intervention, in Bardo Fassbender/Anne Peters, eds., *The Oxford Handbook of the History of International Law*, Oxford 2012, 294–316 at 308–310. For a broader historical perspective on the notion of 'protection', see Osterhammel, Schutz, Macht und Verantwortung, 160–182; Lauren Benton/Adam Clulow/Bain Attwood, eds., *Protection and Empire: A Global History*, Cambridge 2017.

7 For a detailed analysis of the question in the classic texts from the early modern age to the nineteenth century, see especially the volume edited by Recchia/Welsh, *Just and Unjust Military Intervention*. For a philosophical and intellectual-historical account which, although it covers the period from the sixteenth to the eighteenth century as well as contemporary debates, completely ignores the fundamental historical and international legal developments in the matter of intervention, see Sebastian Laukötter, *Zwischen Einmischung und Nothilfe: Das Problem der 'humanitären Intervention' aus ideengeschichtlicher Perspektive*, Berlin 2014, 166f.

8 Hugo Grotius, *On the Law of War and Peace* (Student edition), ed. Stephen C. Neff, Cambridge 2012, 317–318 (book II, ch. 25, sec. 8).

9 Ibid., 285 (book II, ch. 20, sec. 40).

10 On Grotius and his ideas on intervention, see also R. J. Vincent, Grotius, Human Rights, and Intervention, in Hedley Bull/Benedict Kingsbury/Adam Roberts, eds., *Hugo Grotius and International Relations*, Oxford 2003, 241–256; Richard Tuck, Grotius, Hobbes, and Pufendorf on Humanitarian Intervention, in Recchia/Welsh, eds., *Just and Unjust Military Intervention*, 96–112. Earlier jurists and contemporaries such as Francisco de Vitoria, Alberico Gentili and Francisco Suarez also addressed the issue and influenced some of Grotius' ideas. On this, see Theodor Meron, Common Rights of Mankind in Gentili, Grotius and Suarez, *American Journal of International Law* 85/1 (January 1991), 110–116; Chesterman, *Just War or Just Peace*, 8–22; Gustaaf P. van Nifterik, Religious and Humanitarian Intervention in Sixteenth and Early Seventeenth-Century Legal Thought, in Randall Lesaffer/Georges Macours, eds., *Sovereignty and the Law of Nations (16th–18th Centuries)*, Brussels 2006, 35–60; James Muldoon, Francisco de Vitoria and Humanitarian Intervention, *Journal of Military Ethics* 5/2 (2006), 128–143; William Bain, Vitoria: The Law of War, Saving the Innocent, and the Image of God, in Recchia/Welsh, eds., *Just and Unjust Military Intervention*, 70–95; Stephen C. Neff, *Justice among Nations: A History of International Law*, Cambridge, MA 2014, 124f.

11 Chesterman, *Just War or Just Peace*, 16–20; Tuck, Grotius, Hobbes, and Pufendorf, 96–112.

12 § 255 'By nature no nation has the right to any act which belongs to the exercise of the sovereignty of another nation. For sovereignty, as it exists in a people or originally in a nation, is absolute', in Christian Wolff, *Jus gentium methodo scientifica pertractatum*, vol. II, 1749, trans. Joseph H. Drake, Oxford 1934, 130; § 256 'To interfere in the government of another, in whatever way indeed that may be done, is opposed to the natural liberty of nations, by virtue of which one is altogether independent of the will of other nations in its action', ibid., 131. For a rejection of the intervention paradigm even in cases of most grievous oppression, see § 258, ibid., 132.

13 Samuel von Pufendorf, *Of the Law of Nature and Nations: Eight Books*, Oxford 1710: 'But then we are not to imagine that every Man, even they that live in a Liberty of Nature, hath a Right to correct and punish with War any Person that hath done Another an Injury'. Book VIII, ch. VI, sec. XIV, p. 693; Emer de Vattel, *The Law of Nations, Or, Principles of the Law of Nature, Applied to the Conduct and Affairs of Nations and Sovereigns, with Three Early Essays on the Origin and Nature of Natural Law and on Luxury*, ed. and intro. Béla Kapossy and Richard Whatmore, Indianapolis, IN 2008: 'no foreign power has a right to interfere in them, nor ought to intermeddle with them otherwise than by its good offices', book I, ch. III, § 37, p. 96; 'that no state has the smallest right to interfere in the government of another. Of all the rights that can belong to a nation, sovereignty is, doubtless, the most precious, and that which other nations ought the most scrupulously to respect', ibid., book II, ch. IV, § 54, p. 155.

14 'The wrong therefore Another Man suffers, is not reason sufficient to engage one in his Quarrel, unless he calls me particularly to his Assistance, so that Whatever I undertake to do, is not to be charg'd upon me, but upon the person that desires my help. But whether it be lawful to take Arms in Defence

of the Subjects of a Foreign Common-wealth, against the Invasions and Oppressions of their Sovereign, is a Question; for the Solution of which I refer you to the opinion of Grotius, the safest Answer that can be given to it seems to me to be this, that we cannot Lawfully undertake to defend the Subjects of a Foreign Common-wealth in any other case than when they Themselves may Lawfully take Arms to repress the insupportable Tyranny and Cruelties of their own Governours', in von Pufendorf, *Of the Law of Nature and Nations*, book VIII, ch. VI, sec. XIV, p. 693.

15 De Vattel, *The Law of Nations*, book II, ch. IV, § 56, p. 156. In the case of continuing civil war and after the failure of all efforts at arbitration, de Vattel granted the right actively to enter into the conflict on the side of one party. On this, see ibid., book III, ch. XVIII, § 296, p. 648f.

16 Jennifer Pitts, Intervention and Sovereign Equality: Legacies of Vattel, in Recchia/Welsh, eds., *Just and Unjust Military Intervention*, 132–153; Stéphane Beaulac, *The Power of Language in the Making of International Law: The Word Sovereignty in Bodin and Vattel and the Myth of Westphalia*, Leiden 2004, 150–166. On the subject of 'sovereignty' see esp. James J. Sheehan, The Problem of Sovereignty in European History, *American Historical Review* 111/1 (February 2006), 1–15; Lauren Benton, *A Search for Sovereignty: Law and Geography in European Empires, 1400–1900*, Cambridge 2010.

17 Historians increasingly have come to criticise and indeed largely reject the concept of the 'Westphalian System', which has gained currency in political and legal studies, for its overly close fixation on the year 1648 and its attendant blindness to longer-term processes and developments. On this, see Heinz Duchhardt, 'Westphalian System': Zur Problematik einer Denkfigur, *Historische Zeitschrift* 269/2 (October 1999), 305–315.

18 Stephen D. Krasner, Westphalia and All That, in Judith Goldstein/Robert O. Keohane, eds., *Ideas and Foreign Policy: Beliefs, Institutions, and Political Change*, Ithaca, NY 1993, 235–264; Derek Croxton, The Peace of Westphalia of 1648 and the Origins of Sovereignty, *International History Review* 21/3 (September 1999), 569–591; Andreas Osiander, Sovereignty, International Relations, and the Westphalian Myth, *International Organization* 55/2 (Spring 2001), 251–287.

19 Brendan Simms, 'A false principle in the law of Nations': Burke, State Sovereignty, [German] Liberty, and Intervention in the Age of Westphalia, in Simms/Trim, eds., *Humanitarian Intervention*, 89–110 at 92.

20 On this, see the cases outlined in Andrew C. Thompson, The Protestant Interest and the History of Humanitarian Intervention, c. 1685–c. 1756, in Simms/Trim, eds., *Humanitarian Intervention*, 67–88.

21 Stephen D. Krasner, Sovereignty and Intervention, in Gene M. Lyons/ Michael Mastanduno, eds., *Beyond Westphalia? State Sovereignty and International Intervention*, Baltimore, MD 1995, 228–249 at 234–236.

22 For Burke's fierce attack on the French Revolution, see esp. Edmund Burke, *Reflections on the Revolution in France*, London 1790; Edmund Burke, *A Letter from Mr. Burke to a Member of the National Assembly*, London 1791; Edmund Burke, *Thoughts on French Affairs*, London 1791.

23 On Burke's anti-revolutionary idea of intervention, see Iain Hampsher-Monk, Edmund Burke's Changing Justification for Intervention, *Historical Journal* 48/1 (March 2005), 65–100; Jerome S. Handler, Burke's Counter-revolutionary Writings, in David Dwan/Christopher M. Insole, eds., *The Cambridge Companion to Edmund Burke*, Cambridge 2012, 209–220; Simms, 'A false principle', 100–110; Jennifer M. Welsh, Edmund Burke and Intervention: Empire and Neighborhood, in Recchia/Welsh, eds., *Just and Unjust Military Intervention*, 219–236.

24 On the key role played by the Congress of Vienna and the post-war settlement agreed on there, see e.g. Nicolson, *Congress of Vienna*; Schroeder, *Transformation*, 517–582; Zamoyski, *Rites of Peace*, 260–441; Mazower, *Governing the World*, 3–12.

25 Paul W. Schroeder, ed., *Systems, Stability, and Statecraft: Essays on the International History of Modern Europe*, New York 2004, 37–57, 223–241; Schulz, *Normen und Praxis*, 46–72; Schroeder, International Politics, 158–209.

26 On this, see Thomas G. Otte, Of Congresses and Gunboats: Military Intervention in the Nineteenth Century, in Andrew M. Dorman/Thomas G. Otte, eds., *Military Intervention: From Gunboat to Humanitarian Intervention*, Aldershot 1995, 19–52; Osterhammel, Krieg im Frieden, 295–298; Finnemore, *Purpose of Intervention*, 108–124; Schulz, *Normen und Praxis*, 577–580; Reinhard Stauber/Florian Kerschbaumer, Revolution, Restauration und Intervention: Beobachtungen zum Politikraum Europa in der Zeit des Wiener Kongresses, in Christoph Kampmann/Ulrich Niggemann, eds., *Sicherheit in der Frühen Neuzeit: Norm, Praxis, Repräsentation*, Cologne 2013, 156–174.

27 Osterhammel, *Krieg im Frieden*, 298.

28 On the history and significance of the Holy Alliance, see Johannes Paulmann, Searching for a 'Royal International': The Mechanics of Monarchical Relations in Nineteenth-Century Europe, in Paulman/Geyer, eds., *Mechanics of Internationalism*, 146–158.

29 On the liberal movement in Spain, see Charles W. Fehrenbach, Moderados and Exaltados: The Liberal Opposition to Ferdinand VII, 1814–1823, *Hispanic American Historical Review* 50/1 (February 1970), 52–69.

30 On the origins of and courses taken by these various revolutions, see Robert Gildea, *Barricades and Borders: Europe 1800–1914*, Oxford 2003, 65–69; John A. Davis, *Naples and Napoleon: Southern Italy and the European Revolutions 1780–1860*, Oxford 2006, 296–317; Martyn Lyons, *Post-Revolutionary Europe, 1815–1856*, Basingstoke 2006, 42–48; Richard Stites, *The Four Horsemen: Riding to Liberty in Post-Napoleonic Europe*, Oxford 2014; Evans, *Pursuit of Power*, 36–46.

31 On Metternich's attitude and the anti-revolutionary strategy, see Paul W. Schroeder, *Metternich's Diplomacy at Its Zenith 1820–1823*, Austin, TX 1962, 25–60; Alan Sked, Metternich's Enemies or the Threat from Below, in Alan Sked, ed., *Europe's Balance of Power 1815–1848*, London 1979, 164–189; Günther Heydemann, The Vienna System between 1815 and 1848 and the Disputed Antirevolutionary Strategy: Repression, Reforms, or

Constitutions?, in Peter Krüger/Paul W. Schroeder, eds., *The Transformation of European Politics, 1763–1848: Episode or Model in Modern History?*, Münster 2002, 187–203.

32 Alan Reinerman, Metternich, Italy, and the Congress of Verona, 1821–1822, *Historical Journal* 14/2 (June 1971), 263–287; Otte, Of Congresses and Gunboats, 24–28.

33 For the 'Protocole pour déterminer le droit d'intervention des grandes Puissances' of 19 November 1820, see Wilhelm G. Grewe, ed., *Fontes Historiae Iuris Gentium*, vol. 3/1, 1815–1945, Berlin 1992, 110–113. On the Troppau Protokoll, see also Rudolf Kurzweg, Die Heilige Allianz und das Interventionssystem des Vertrages von Troppau, *Jahrbücher für Geschichte Osteuropas*, new series 3/2 (1955), 141–160; Pyta, Konzert der Mächte, 168–173.

34 Kurzweg, Heilige Allianz, 141, 151; Johannes Paulmann, Europäische Monarchien in der Revolution von 1848/49: 'Die erste wahrhafte Internationale'?, in Dieter Langewiesche, ed., *Demokratiebewegung und Revolution 1847 bis 1849: Internationale Aspekte und europäische Verbindungen*, Karlsruhe 1998, 109–139 at 112; Paul W. Schroeder, Alliances, 1815–1945: Weapons of Power and Tools of Management, in Schroeder, ed., *Systems, Stability, and Statecraft*, 199f.

35 Schulz, *Normen und Praxis*, 81, 584–591. The pro-interventionist writings of von Kamptz, later Prussian minister of justice, from 1821 and of Friedrich von Gentz, Metternich's close adviser, from 1831 must also be considered in this context. On this, see Karl Christoph Albert Heinrich von Kamptz, *Völkerrechtliche Erörterungen des Rechts der Europäischen Mächte in die Verfassungen eines einzelnen Staats sich zu mischen*, Berlin 1821; Friedrich von Gentz, Bemerkungen über das Interventions-Recht, März 1831, in Gustav Schlesier, ed., *Schriften von Friedrich von Gentz: Ein Denkmal*, vol. 5, Mannheim 1840, 181–185. For a contemporary interpretation of the right of intervention from the perspective of international law, see Henry Wheaton, *Elements of International Law with a Sketch of the History of the Science*, Philadelphia, PA 1836, 82–88; Henry Wheaton, *History of the Law of Nations in Europe and America from the Earliest Times to the Treaty of Washington, 1842*, New York 1845, 518–563.

36 On the suppression of the revolution and the restoration in Italy, see Schroeder, *Metternich's Diplomacy*, 104–163; Otte, Of Congresses and Gunboats, 24–28; Stites, *Four Horsemen*, 164–185.

37 On the negotiations at the Congress of Verona and the various countries' positions, see Schroeder, *Metternich's Diplomacy*, 195–236; Reinerman, Metternich, 263–287; Irby C. Nichols, Jr, *The European Pentarchy and the Congress of Verona, 1822*, The Hague 1971, 84–136.

38 On the policies of the great powers and the French intervention in Spain, see Roger Bullen, The Great Powers and the Iberian Peninsula, 1815–1848, in Alan Sked, ed., *Europe's Balance of Power 1815–1848*, London 1979, 54–78; Schroeder, *Transformation*, 621–628; Stites, *Four Horsemen*, 98–120.

39 State Paper by Castlereagh dated 5 May 1820, in Harold Temperley/Lillian M. Penson, eds., *Foundations of British Foreign Policy: From Pitt (1792) to*

Salisbury (1902), Cambridge 1966, 48–63 at 61. On the British stance under Castlereagh, see also Charles K. Webster, *The Foreign Policy of Castlereagh 1815–1822: Britain and the European Alliance*, London [1925] 1963, 215–256; Vincent, *Nonintervention*, 73–83; D. L. Hafner, Castlereagh, the Balance of Power, and 'Non-Intervention', *Australian Journal of Politics and History* 26/1 (1980), 71–84; for a nineteenth-century account, see Augustus Granville Stapleton, *Intervention and Non-Intervention or the Foreign Policy of Great Britain from 1790 to 1865*, London 1866, 27–31.

40 State Paper by Castlereagh dated 5 May 1820, in Temperley/Penson, eds., *Foundations of British Foreign Policy*, 63.

41 Circular by Castlereagh to British diplomatic missions, 19 January 1821, in British and Foreign State Papers (BFSP) 8, 1160–1162.

42 Ibid., 1162.

43 Speech by Castlereagh to the House of Commons, 21 June 1821, in T. C. Hansard, ed., *The Parliamentary Debates from the Year 1803 to the Present Time*, vol. 5, new series, London 1822 (New York 1970), 1256–1257.

44 Ibid., 1257.

45 Harold Temperley, *The Foreign Policy of Canning 1822–1827: England, the Neo-Holy Alliance, and the New World*, London 1966, 42–49; Vincent, *Nonintervention and International Order*, 84–90; Temperley/Penson, eds., *Foundations of British Foreign Policy*, 47f.

46 Temperley, *Foreign Policy of Canning*, 81–91; Bullen, Great Powers and the Iberian Peninsula, 64f.

47 On this, see Vincent, *Nonintervention and International Order*, 70–102; Webster, *Foreign Policy of Castlereagh, 1815–1822*, 215–256; Hafner, Castlereagh, 71–84; Klaus Hildebrand, *No Intervention. Die Pax Britannica und Preußen 1865/66–1869/70: Eine Untersuchung zur englischen Weltpolitik im 19. Jahrhundert*, Munich 1997; Schulz, *Normen und Praxis*, 76–78, 82–84.

48 John Bew, 'From an Umpire to a Competitor': Castlereagh, Canning and the Issue of International Intervention in the Wake of the Napoleonic Wars, in Simms/Trim, eds., *Humanitarian Intervention*, 117–138 at 123–128.

49 On Britain's leading role, especially vis-à-vis the Ottoman Empire, see Holbraad, *Concert of Europe*, 162–176; Osterhammel, Krieg im Frieden, 302.

50 Declaration des 8 Cours, relative à l'Abolition Universelle de la Traite des Nègres, 8 February 1815, in BFSP 3, 971–972. On this, see also Helmut Berding, Die Ächtung des Sklavenhandels auf dem Wiener Kongress 1814/15, *Historische Zeitschrift* 219/2 (October 1974), 266–269, 285; Ian Clark, *International Legitimacy and World Society*, Oxford 2007, 37–60.

51 On this, see also Fabian Klose, 'To maintain the law of nature and of nations' – Der Wiener Kongress und die Ursprünge der humanitären Intervention, *Geschichte in Wissenschaft und Unterricht* 65/3–4 (March/April 2014), 217–237.

52 Jürgen Osterhammel, *Sklaverei und die Zivilisation des Westens*, Munich 2009, 64f.; Osterhammel, Krieg im Frieden, 318f.

53 David Trim has argued that 'the British intervention in Savoy is perhaps the first to which the term "humanitarian" could reasonably be applied'. On this, see Trim, Intervention in European History, 37; and also Trim, 'If a prince

use tyrannie', 53–66. By contrast, Christoph Kampmann claims that the concept of 'humanitarian intervention' can be applied only in a very limited sense to these seventeenth-century instances. On this, see Kampmann, 'Westfälische System', 65–92 at 80f.

54 In formulating his Théorie de l'intervention d'humanité in 1910, the French jurist Antoine Rougier was quite clear on this matter: 'L'intervention en matière de religion est chose nettement différente de l'intervention d'humanité.' On this, see Antoine Rougier, La théorie de l'intervention d'humanité, *Revue générale de droit internationale public* XVII (1910), 468–526 at 472.

55 Osterhammel, *Transformation of the World*, 451.

Chapter 3

1 The noun 'humanitarianism' and the adjective 'humanitarian', although they are not terms found in the eighteenth- and nineteenth-century sources, are now accepted analytical concepts. Only in the late nineteenth century do we find the British social reformer Henry S. Salt, founder of the Humanitarian League, giving the following definition: '[B]y humanitarianism I mean nothing more and nothing less than the study and practice of humane principles – of compassion, love, gentleness, and universal benevolence.' Henry S. Salt, *Humanitarianism: Its General Principles and Progress*, London 1891, 3; Henry S. Salt, What Is Humanitarianism?, *Humane Review* 8 (October 1907), 178–188. On Salt's Humanitarian League, which existed from 1891 to 1919 and campaigned for social reform in a number of fields, see George Hendrick, *Henry Salt, Humanitarian Reformer and Man of Letters*, Urbana, IL 1977, 56–86; Dan Weinbren, Against All Cruelty: The Humanitarian League, 1891–1919, *History Workshop* 38 (1994), 86–105. On the history of the words 'humanitarianism' and 'humanitarian' see also Raymond Williams, *Keywords: A Vocabulary of Culture and Society*, New York 1976, 121–124; Peter Redfield/Erica Bornstein, An Introduction to the Anthropology of Humanitarianism, in Peter Redfield/Erica Bornstein, eds., *Forces of Compassion: Humanitarianism between Ethics and Politics*, Santa Fe, NM 2010, 3–30.

2 The term 'humanitarian revolution' as it is used here denotes the emergence of a humanitarian sensibility and the activities associated with it. It is not to be understood, as Steven Pinker would have it, as referring to an overall decline in violence. On this, see Pinker, *Better Angels*, 129–188.

3 David Owen, *English Philanthropy 1660–1960*, Cambridge, MA 1964, 11–133; Michael Kraus, *The Atlantic Civilization: Eighteenth-Century Origins*, Ithaca, NY 1966, 123–158; M. J. Heale, Humanitarianism in the Early Republic: The Moral Reformers of New York, 1776–1825, *Journal of American Studies* 2/2 (October 1968), 161–175; Shelby T. McCloy, *The Humanitarian Movement in Eighteenth-Century France*, New York 1972; Randall McGowen, A Powerful Sympathy: Terror, the Prison, and Humanitarian Reform in Early Nineteenth-Century Britain, *Journal of British Studies* 25/3 (July 1986), 312–334; Hugh Cunningham/Joanna Innes,

eds., *Charity, Philanthropy, and Reform: From the 1690s to 1850*, Basingstoke 1998; M. J. D. Roberts, *Making English Morals: Voluntary Associations and Moral Reform in England, 1787–1886*, Cambridge 2004; Helen Rogers, Kindness and Reciprocity: Liberated Prisoners and Christian Charity in Early Nineteenth-Century England, *Journal of Social History* 47/3 (Spring 2014), 1–25; Daniel Laqua, Inside the Humanitarian Cloud: Causes and Motivations to Help Friends and Strangers, *Journal of Modern European History* 12/2 (2014), 175–185; Norbert Götz, Rationales of Humanitarianism: The Case of British Relief to Germany, 1805–1815, *Journal of Modern European History* 12/2 (2014), 186–199; Salvatici, *Humanitarianism*, 20–34.

4 Christopher L. Brown, Christianity and the Campaign against Slavery and the Slave Trade, in Stewart J. Brown/Timothy Tackett, eds., *The Cambridge History of Christianity*, vol. VII: *Enlightenment, Reawakening and Revolution 1660–1815*, Cambridge 2006, 517–535.

5 Michael Kraus, Eighteenth Century Humanitarianism: Collaboration between Europe and America, *Pennsylvania Magazine of History and Biography* 60/3 (July 1936), 270–286; Huw T. David, Transnational Advocacy in the Eighteenth Century: Transatlantic Activism and the Anti-Slavery Movement, *Global Networks* 7/3 (2007), 367–382. On the significance and function of networks of activists generally, see Margaret E. Keck/Kathryn Sikkink, *Activists beyond Borders: Advocacy Networks in International Politics*, Ithaca, NY 1998, for a historical perspective esp. pp. 39–78.

6 Frank J. Klingberg, The Evolution of the Humanitarian Spirit in Eighteenth-Century England, *Pennsylvania Magazine of History and Biography* 66/3 (July 1942, 260–278 at 267–270; Kraus, Eighteenth Century Humanitarianism, 278f.; J. R. Oldfield, *Transatlantic Abolitionism in the Age of Revolution: An International History of Anti-slavery, c. 1787–1820*, Cambridge 2013.

7 De Vattel, *The Law of Nations*, book II, ch. I, § 2, p. 134f. With reference to the mutual obligations of nations, however, de Vattel reaffirms the prohibition of intervention by force and his rejection of Grotius' position. On this, see book II, ch. I, § 7, p. 137.

8 Ibid., book II, ch. I, § 5, p. 136. On the significance and consequences of the earthquake, see Thomas D. Kendrick, *The Lisbon Earthquake*, London 1956; Russel R. Dynes, The Lisbon Earthquake of 1755: The First Modern Disaster, in Theodore E. D. Braun/John B. Radner, eds., *The Lisbon Earthquake of 1755: Representation and Reactions*, Oxford 2005, 34–49.

9 On shipments of foreign aid, see Kendrick, *Lisbon Earthquake*, 142–144; Malcolm Jack, Destruction and Regeneration: Lisbon, 1755, in Braun/Radner, eds., *Lisbon Earthquake*, 7–20 at 14. Peter Walker and Daniel Maxwell connect the 1755 earthquake and the subsequent foreign relief with the beginnings of the system of humanitarian aid. On this, see Peter Walker/Daniel Maxwell, *Shaping the Humanitarian World*, New York 2009, 16f; Salvatici, *Humanitarianism*, 15f.

10 Haskell, Capitalism and the Origins of Humanitarian Sensibility, pt. 1, 339–361; Haskell, Capitalism and the Origins of Humanitarian Sensibility, pt. 2, 547–566. For a critical discussion of Haskell's claims, see John

Ashworth, The Relationship between Capitalism and Humanitarianism, *American Historical Review* 92/4 (October 1987), 813–828.

11 G. J. Barker-Benfield, *The Culture of Sensibility: Sex and Society in Eighteenth-Century Britain*, Chicago, IL 1992; Janet Todd, *Sensibility: An Introduction*, London 1986.

12 Ronald S. Crane, Suggestions toward a Genealogy of the 'Man of Feeling', *Journal of English Literary History* 1/3 (December 1934), 205–230; Frans de Bruyn, Latitudinarianism and Its Importance as a Precursor of Sensibility, *Journal of English and Germanic Philology* 80/3 (July 1981), 349–368.

13 A. R. Humphreys, 'The Friend of Mankind' (1700–60): An Aspect of Eighteenth-Century Sensibility, *Review of English Studies* 24/95 (July 1948), 203–218; Chester Chapin, Shaftesbury and the Man of Feeling, *Modern Philology* 81/1 (August 1983), 47–50; Norman S. Fiering, Irresistible Compassion: An Aspect of Eighteenth-Century Sympathy and Humanitarianism, *Journal of the History of Ideas* 37/2 (April–June 1976), 195–218; Barker-Benfield, *Culture of Sensibility*, 105–141; Karen Halttunen, Humanitarianism and the Pornography of Pain in Anglo-American Culture, *American Historical Review* 100/2 (April 1995), 303–334 at 304–307; Ildiko Csengei, *Sympathy, Sensibility, and the Literature of Feeling in the Eighteenth-Century*, Basingstoke 2012, 29–62.

14 On the concept of 'sympathy' and its significance in the works of Hume and Smith, see Glenn R. Morrow, The Significance of the Doctrine of Sympathy in Hume and Adam Smith, *Philosophical Review* 32/1 (January 1923), 60–78; John B. Radner, The Art of Sympathy in Eighteenth-Century British Moral Thought, *Studies in Eighteenth-Century Culture* 9 (1979), 189–210; John Mullan, *Sentiment and Sociability: The Language of Feeling in the Eighteenth Century*, Oxford 1990, 18–56. For a distinction between the contemporary term 'sympathy' and that of 'empathy', which is preferred today, see Moyn, Empathy in History, 397–415.

15 David Hume, *Enquiries Concerning the Human Understanding and Concerning the Principles of Morals*, ed. L. A. Selby-Bigge, 2nd ed., Oxford, 1902, 219f. n. 1

16 Adam Smith, *The Theory of Moral Sentiments; or, An Essay towards an Analysis of the Principles by which Men Naturally Judge Concerning the Conduct and Character, First of their Neighbours, and afterwards of Themselves. To which Is Added, A Dissertation on the Origins of Languages. New Edition. With a Biographical and Critical Memoir of the Author, by Dugald Stewart*, London, 1853, 3.

17 On this broadening performed by Smith, see also Morrow, Significance, 69–73; Fiering, Irresistible Compassion, 210–212; Halttunen, Humanitarianism, 307.

18 Smith, *Theory of Moral Sentiments*, 4.

19 Ibid.

20 Geoffrey Atkinson, *The Sentimental Revolution: French Writers of 1690–1740*, Seattle, WA 1965. On this era's sentimental literature and its effects, see also Robert F. Brissenden, *Virtue in Distress: Studies in the Novel of Sentiment from Richardson to Sade*, London 1974; Mullan, *Sentiment*; Markman Ellis, *The*

Politics of Sensibility: Race, Gender and Commerce in the Sentimental Novel, Cambridge 1996; Lynn Festa, *Sentimental Figures of Empire in Eighteenth-Century Britain and France,* Baltimore, MD 2006.

21 Samuel Richardson, *Pamela: Or Virtue Rewarded,* London 1741; Samuel Richardson, *Clarissa: Or, the History of a Young Lady,* London 1748.

22 Hunt, *Inventing Human Rights,* 35–69.

23 David J. Denby, *Sentimental Narrative and the Social Order in France, 1760–1820,* Cambridge 1994; Brissenden, *Virtue in Distress,* 56–65; in this context, William Reddy has pointed out that the influence of sentimentalism markedly waned in France after 1794. On this, see William M. Reddy, Sentimentalism and Its Erasure: The Role of Emotions in the Era of the French Revolution, *Journal of Modern History* 72/1 (March 2000), 109–152.

24 Hunt, *Inventing Human Rights,* 35–112.

25 Ibid., 58. On this, see also Lynn Hunt, The Paradoxical Origins of Human Rights, in Jeffrey N. Wasserstrom/Greg Grandin/Lynn Hunt/Marilyn B. Young, eds., *Human Rights and Revolution,* Lanham, MD 2007, 3–20.

26 The strongest critique of the genealogy proposed by Hunt is that of Samuel Moyn, On the Genealogy of Morals, *The Nation* (16 April 2007), 25–31; Samuel Moyn, *The Last Utopia: Human Rights in History,* Cambridge, MA 2010, 11–43. On the genealogy of human rights generally, see Stefan-Ludwig Hoffmann, Einführung: Zur Genealogie der Menschenrechte, in Stefan-Ludwig Hoffmann, ed., *Moralpolitik. Geschichte der Menschenrechte im 20. Jahrhundert,* Göttingen 2010, 7–37; Samuel Moyn, Die neue Historiographie der Menschenrechte, *Geschichte und Gesellschaft* 38/4 (October–December 2012), 545–572; Stefan-Ludwig Hoffman, Human Rights and History, *Past & Present,* 232/1 (2016), 279–310; Eric Weitz, *A World Divided: The Global Struggle for Human Rights in the Age of Nation-States,* Princeton, NJ 2019.

27 Richard Ashby Wilson/Richard D. Brown, Introduction, in Richard Ashby Wilson/Richard D. Brown, eds., *Humanitarianism and Suffering: The Mobilization of Empathy,* Cambridge 2009, 1–28 at 12.

28 Whereas basic rights play no meaningful part in historical research on humanitarianism, which goes back a long way, studies of human rights – like that of Paul Gordon Lauren – annex this neighbouring territory, thereby contributing to the 'blurred boundary'. See Lauren, *Evolution of Interventional Human Rights,* chs. 1 and 2. On the controversy over the relationship of humanitarianism and human rights, see Wilson/Brown, Introduction, 4–18; Moyn, Historiographie der Menschenrechte, 557–561; Abigail Green, Humanitarianism in Nineteenth-Century Context: Religious, Gendered, National, *Historical Journal* 57/4 (December 2014), 1157–1175; Michael Geyer, Humanitarianism and Human Rights: A Troubled Rapport, in Klose, ed., *Emergence of Humanitarian Intervention,* 31–55; Michael Barnett, ed., *Humanitarianism and Human Rights: A World of Differences?,* Cambridge 2020. For the specific framing of humanitarian intervention in both research areas, see Fabian Klose, Humanitarian Intervention as an Entangled History of Humanitarianism and Human Rights, in Barnett, ed., *Humanitarianism and Human Rights,* 127–139.

29 For this reason, most studies situate eighteenth- and nineteenth-century abolitionism in the field of humanitarianism and not of human rights. For exceptions, see Jenny Martinez, *The Slave Trade and the Origins of International Human Rights Law*, Oxford 2012; Robin Blackburn, *The American Crucible: Slavery, Emancipation, and Human Rights*, London 2011; Eckel, *Ambivalenz des Guten*, 35–38; Weitz, *World Divided*, 122–158.

30 Speech by Wilberforce in the parliamentary debate of 18/19 April 1791, in Great Britain, Parliament, House of Commons, ed., *The Debate on a Motion for the Abolition of the Slave-Trade, in the House of Commons on Monday and Tuesday, April 18 and 19, 1791*, London 1791, 37.

31 William Mulligan, The Anti-Slave Trade Campaign in Europe, 1888–1890, in William Mulligan/Maurice Bric, eds., *A Global History of Anti-Slavery Politics in the Nineteenth Century*, Basingstoke 2013, 149–169 at 156f. Joyce E. Chaplin has pointed out that slaveholders in the American South might also acknowledge the fundamental humanity of their slaves and the concomitant obligation to treat them in a 'humanitarian' fashion while simultaneously denying them basic rights. On this, see Joyce E. Chaplin, Slavery and the Principle of Humanity: A Modern Idea in the Early Lower South, *Journal of Social History* 24/2 (Winter 1990), 299–315 esp. at 299–303; Joanna Bourke has argued that the kneeling position of the slave depicted on the celebrated Wedgwood medallion, an icon of the abolitionist movement, expressed subordination and thereby precluded a claim to full equality. On this, see Joanna Bourke, *What It Means to Be Human: Historical Reflections from the 1800s to the Present*, Berkeley, CA 2011, 120.

32 Festa, Humanity without Feathers, 3–27.

33 Samuel Johnson's pathbreaking mid-seventeenth-century *Dictionary* defines four senses of the word 'humanity': '1. The nature of a man', '2. Human kind; the collective body of mankind', '3. Benevolence; tenderness' and '4. Philology; grammatical studies'. On this, see Humanity, in Samuel Johnson, *A Dictionary of the English Language in Which the Words are Deduced from Their Originals, and Illustrated in Their Different Significations by Examples from the Best Writers*, vol. 1, London 1755. For the conceptual history, see Hans Erich Bödeker, Menschheit, Humanität, Humanismus, in Otto Brunner/Werner Conze/Reinhart Koselleck, eds., *Geschichtliche Grundbegriffe: Historisches Lexikon zur politisch-sozialen Sprache in Deutschland*, vol. 3, Stuttgart 1982, 1063–1128. On the historical development of the concept and practices of 'humanity', see Fabian Klose/Mirjam Thulin, Introduction: European Concepts and Practices of Humanity in Historical Perspective, in Fabian Klose/Mirjam Thulin, eds., *Humanity: A History of European Concepts in Practice from the Sixteenth Century to the Present*, Göttingen 2017, 9–25.

34 Wilberforce accordingly considered it a success: 'Already we have gained one victory: we have obtained, for these poor creatures, *The recognition of their human nature*, which, for a while, was most shamefully denied.' Speech by Wilberforce in the parliamentary debate of 18/19 April 1791, in Great Britain, Parliament, House of Commons, ed., *The Debate on a Motion for the Abolition of the Slave-Trade, in the House of Commons on Monday and Tuesday, April 18 and 19, 1791*, London 1791, 42.

35 Speech by Lord Grenville in the House of Lords on 24 June 1806, in Great Britain, Parliament, ed., *Substance of the Debates on a Resolution for Abolishing the Slave Trade, Which Was Moved in the House of Commons on the 10th June, 1806, and in the House of Lords, on the 24th June, 1806*, London 1806, 90.

36 For the normative development of the concept of 'humanity', especially with regard to the twentieth century, see Ruti G. Teitel, For Humanity, *Journal of Human Rights* 3/2 (June 2004), 225–237; Ilana Feldman/Miriam Ticktin, eds., *In the Name of Humanity: The Government of Threat and Care*, Durham, NC 2010.

37 Following the brief appearance of the concept of human rights in the course of the late-eighteenth-century Atlantic revolutions, Stefan-Ludwig Hoffman sees a 'disappearance of human rights after 1800'. On this, see Hoffmann, Einführung, 14–22. With regard to the dual impact of the anti-slavery and women's rights movements in the nineteenth-century United States, Ana Stevenson has found that while the rhetoric of human rights was in evidence, it was only ever used sporadically and not deployed systematically. See Ana Stevenson, The 'Great Doctrine of Human Rights': Articulation and Authentication in the Nineteenth-Century U.S. Antislavery and Women's Rights Movements, *Humanity* 8/3 (Winter 2017), 413–439.

Part II

1 Letter from Wellington to Henry Wellesley, 29 July 1814, in Arthur Wellesley Wellington, *Supplementary Despatches, Correspondence, and Memoranda*, vol. 9, London 1862, 165.

Chapter 4

1 W. E. B. Du Bois, *Black Reconstruction in America: An Essay toward a History of the Part Which Black Folk Played in the Attempt to Reconstruct Democracy in America, 1860–1880*, New York 1966, 727.

2 The first scientifically reliable statistics on the Atlantic slave trade were compiled by Philip D. Curtin in his seminal study *The Atlantic Slave Trade: A Census*, Madison, WI 1969. Many subsequent scholars have built on this study, and it is now assumed that some 11–12 million Africans were enslaved between 1519 and 1867. On this see e.g. David Eltis, The Volume and Structure of the Transatlantic Slave Trade: A Reassessment, *William and Mary Quarterly* 58/1 (January 2001), 17–46. A group of researchers led by David Eltis has produced an impressive database containing details of particular slave transports; it can be consulted at www.slavevoyages.org. On this see also David Eltis/David Richardson, A New Assessment of the Transatlantic Slave Trade, in David Eltis/David Richardson, eds., *Extending Frontiers: Essays on the New Transatlantic Slave Trade Database*, New Haven, CT 2008, 1–60; David Eltis/David Richardson, *Atlas of the Transatlantic Slave Trade*, New Haven, CT 2010.

3 Robin Blackburn, *The Making of New World Slavery: From the Baroque to the Modern, 1492–1800*, London 1997, 339; Blackburn, *American Crucible*, 29–96.

4 For a comparison and contextualisation of the Atlantic slave trade with other crimes against humanity, see Seymour Drescher, The Atlantic Slave Trade and the Holocaust: A Comparative Analysis, in Alan S. Rosenbaum, ed., *Is the Holocaust Unique? Perspectives on Comparative Genocide*, Boulder, CO 1996, 65–85.

5 Joseph E. Inikori, Slavery and Atlantic Commerce, 1650–1800, *American Economic Review* 82/2 (May 1992), 151–157; Herbert S. Klein, *The Atlantic Slave Trade*, Cambridge 2010, 17–29; Patrick Manning, *Slavery and African Life: Occidental, Oriental, and African Slave Trade*, Cambridge 1990, 30–32.

6 Roger Anstey, *The Atlantic Slave Trade and British Abolition, 1760–1810*, London 1975, 3–4; Curtin, *Atlantic Slave Trade*, 15 and 210–211; Eltis, Volume and Structure, 20 and 24.

7 On the 'sugar revolution' and its significance, see e.g. Philip D. Curtin, *The Rise and Fall of the Plantation Complex: Essays in Atlantic History*, Cambridge 1999, 73–85; B. W. Higman, The Sugar Revolution, *Economic History Review* 53/2 (May 2000), 213–236.

8 Higman, Sugar Revolution, 213, 226. On the importance of sugar in the history of the world, see Sidney W. Mintz, *Sweetness and Power: The Place of Sugar in Modern History*, New York 1985.

9 European slave traders also rounded the Cape of Good Hope to purchase slaves in south-east Africa. On the principal centres of the slave trade, see Anstey, *Atlantic Slave Trade*, 58; Eltis, Volume and Structure, 33–35.

10 Anstey, *Atlantic Slave Trade*, 4f., 10.

11 Herbert Klein has criticised the model of the 'Atlantic triangular slave trade' as largely a myth, pointing out that the slave ships generally returned from the Caribbean to Europe without cargo and that special merchant vessels were used instead used to transport colonial merchandise. He also argues that Brazilian slavers plied only the route between the African and American continents. On this, see Klein, *Atlantic Slave Trade*, 309; Gilman M. Ostrander, The Making of the Triangular Trade Myth, *William and Mary Quarterly* 30/4 (October 1973), 635–644.

12 Jochen Meissner/Ulrich Mücke/Klaus Weber, *Schwarzes Amerika: Eine Geschichte der Sklaverei*, Bonn 2008, 67, 89–98.

13 The first recorded use of the phrase 'white man's grave' is by F. Harrison Rankin, *The White Man's Grave: A Visit to Sierra Leone in 1834*, London 1836. On this, see also Kenneth F. Kiple, *The Caribbean Slave: A Biological History*, Cambridge 1984, 13–22.

14 Paul E. Lovejoy, *Transformation in Slavery: A History of Slavery in Africa*, Cambridge 2000; Stephanie Smallwood, *Saltwater Slavery: A Middle Passage from Africa to American Diaspora*, Cambridge 2007, 31; John Thornton, *Africa and Africans in the Making of the Atlantic World, 1400–1800*, Cambridge 1998, 116–125.

15 Hugh Thomas, *The Slave Trade: The History of the Atlantic Slave Trade, 1440–1870*, London 2006, 796.

16 Klein, *Atlantic Slave Trade*, 113.

17 Ibid., 75.

18 The process by which human beings were transformed into commodities is described in a particularly vivid manner by Smallwood, *Saltwater Slavery*, 33–64. On this, see also Emma Christopher, *Slave Ship Sailors and Their Captive Cargoes, 1730–1807*, Cambridge 2006, 163–170. On the dehumanisation of slaves generally, see David Brion Davis, *The Problem of Slavery in the Age of Emancipation*, New York 2014, 15–35.

19 Davis, *The Problem of Slavery*, 65–72; Marcus Rediker, *The Slave Ship: A Human History*, New York 2007, 268.

20 Klein, *Atlantic Slave Trade*, 315. On the debates over likely profits, see Joseph E. Inikori, Market Structure and the Profits of the British African Trade in the Late Eighteenth Century, *Journal of Economic History* 41/4 (December 1981), 745–776; B. L. Anderson/David Richardson, Market Structure and the Profits of the British African Trade in the Late Eighteenth Century: A Comment, *Journal of Economic History* 43/3 (September 1983), 713–721.

21 Raymond L. Cohn, Deaths of Slaves in the Middle Passage, *Journal of Economic History* 45/3 (September 1985), 685–692; Herbert S. Klein/ Stanley L. Engerman, Long-term Trends in African Mortality in the Transatlantic Slave Trade, *Slavery & Abolition* 18/1 (1997), 36–48; Herbert S. Klein/Stanley L. Engerman/Robin Haines/Ralph Shlomowitz, Transoceanic Mortality: The Slave Trade in Comparative Perspective, *William and Mary Quarterly* 58/1 (January 2001), 93–118.

22 James Oldham, Insurance Litigation Involving the *Zong* and Other British Slave Ships, 1780–1807, *Journal of Legal History* 28/3 (2007), 299–318; Michael Lobban, Slavery, Insurance and the Law, *Journal of Legal History* 28/3 (2007), 319–328.

23 Christopher, *Slave Ship Sailors*, 178.

24 Jane Webster, The Zong in the Context of the Eighteenth-Century Slave Trade, *Journal of Legal History* 28/3 (2007), 285–298.

25 On the trial itself, see Oldham, Insurance Litigation Involving the Zong, 310–315.

26 Prince Hoare, *Memoirs of Granville Sharp*, London 1820, 237–239.

27 Smallwood, *Saltwater Slavery*, 158–161; Christopher, *Slave Ship Sailors*, 198f.

28 Alexander Falconbridge, *An Account of the Slave Trade on the Coast of Africa*, London 1788, 29.

29 Letter from William Wilberforce, 1807, quoted in Thomas Fowell Buxton, *The African Slave Trade and Its Remedy*, London 1840, 122.

30 For a detailed account of these degrading examinations, see Theophilus Conneau, *A Slaver's Log Book or 20 Years' Residence in Africa*, Englewood Cliffs, NJ 1976, 71.

31 Falconbridge, *Account of the Slave Trade*, 19f.

32 Paul Edwards, ed., *Equiano's Travels. His Autobiography: The Interesting Narrative of the Life of Olaudah Equiano or Gustavus Vassa the African, Written by Himself*, London [1789] 1967, 28, 31; Jerome S. Handler, Survivors of the Middle Passage: Life Histories of Enslaved Africans in British America, *Slavery & Abolition* 23/1 (April 2002), 25–56 at 35;

William D. Pierson, White Cannibals, Black Martyrs: Fear, Depression, and Religious Faith as Causes of Suicide among New Slaves, *Journal of Negro History* 62/2 (April 1977), 147–159 at 147f.; Mark Stein, Who's Afraid of Cannibals? Some Uses of the Cannibalism Trope in Olaudah Equiano's Interesting Narrative, in Carey/Ellis/Salih, eds., *Discourses of Slavery and Abolition*, 96–107.

33 Smallwood, *Saltwater Slavery*, 52–64. The classic account of the social impact of enslavement more generally is Orlando Patterson, *Slavery and Social Death: A Comparative Study*, Cambridge, MA 1982.

34 Anstey, *Atlantic Slave Trade*, 28.

35 Falconbridge, *Account of the Slave Trade*, 23f.; John Newton, *Thoughts upon the African Slave Trade*, London 1788, 20; Christopher, *Slave Ship Sailors*, 188–191.

36 Vincent Carretta, Olaudah Equiano or Gustavus Vassa? New Light on an Eighteenth-Century Question of Identity, *Slavery & Abolition* 20/3 (December 1999), 96–105; Alexander X. Byrd, Eboe, Country, Nation, and Gustavus Vassa's Interesting Narrative, *William and Mary Quarterly* 63/1 (January 2006), 123–148; Paul Lovejoy, Autobiography and Memory: Gustavus Vassa, alias Olaudah Equiano, the African, *Slavery & Abolition* 27/3 (December 2006), 317–347; Vincent Carretta, *Equiano, the African: Biography of a Self-Made Man*, Athens, OH 2005.

37 Edwards, *Equiano's Travels*, 28f.

38 Richard H. Steckel/Richard A. Jensen, New Evidence and Crew Mortality in the Atlantic Slave Trade, *Journal of Economic History* 46/1 (March 1986), 57–77; Kiple, *Caribbean Slave*, 57–75; Smallwood, *Saltwater Slavery*, 135–137; Newton, *Thoughts upon the African Slave Trade*, 34–36.

39 Klein, *Atlantic Slave Trade*, 310; Rediker, *Slave Ship*, 273–276; Kenneth F. Kiple/Brian T. Higgins, Mortality Caused by Dehydration during the Middle Passage, *Social Science History* 13/4 (Winter 1989), 421–437.

40 Falconbridge, *Account of the Slave Trade*, 25.

41 Ibid., 27f.

42 Ibid., 31; Rediker, *Slave Ship*, 38–40.

43 On this, see esp. Smallwood, *Saltwater Slavery*, 140f., 152.

44 Daniel P. Mannix/Malcolm Cowley, *Black Cargoes: A History of the Atlantic Slave Trade, 1518–1865*, New York 1962, 104–130; Darold D. Wax, Negro Resistance to the Early American Slave Trade, *Journal of Negro History* 51/1 (January 1966), 1–15; Okon E. Uya, Slave Revolts in the Middle Passage: A Neglected Theme, *Calabar Historical Journal* 1/1 (June 1976), 65–88; Eugene D. Genovese, *From Rebellion to Revolution: Afro-American Revolts in the Making of the Modern World*, Baton Rouge, LA 1979; Winston McGowan, African Resistance to the Atlantic Slave Trade in West Africa, *Slavery & Abolition* 11/1 (May 1990), 5–29; Sylviane A. Diouf, ed., *Fighting the Slave Trade, West African Strategies*, Athens, GA 2004.

45 On this debate, see esp. Seymour Drescher/Pieter C. Emmer, eds., *Who Abolished Slavery? Slave Revolts and Abolitionism. A Debate with Joao Pedro Marques*, New York 2010.

46 On this, see esp. Richard Rathbone, Resistance to Enslavement in West Africa, in Patrick Manning, ed., *Slave Trades, 1500–1800: Globalization of Forced Labour*, Aldershot 1996, 183–194.

47 Ibid., 187f.; Antonio T. Bly, Crossing the Lake of Fire: Slave Resistance during the Middle Passage, 1720–1842, *Journal of Negro History* 83/3 (Summer 1998), 178–186 at 180–182; Piersen, White Cannibals, 150–151; Rediker, *Slave Ship*, 284–291; Edwards, *Equiano's Travels*, 67f.

48 On shipboard revolts, see Eric Robert Taylor, *If We Must Die: Shipboard Insurrections in the Era of the Atlantic Slave Trade*, Baton Rouge, LA 2006; David Richardson, Shipboard Revolts: African Authority, and the Atlantic Slave Trade, *William and Mary Quarterly* 58/1 (January 2001), 69–92; Rediker, *Slave Ship*, 291–301; Bly, Crossing the Lake of Fire, 183f.

49 Richardson, Shipboard Revolts, 72; Christopher, *Slave Ship Sailors*, 184–186.

50 See e.g. Conneau, *A Slaver's Log Book*, 208–210; Taylor, *If We Must Die*, 85–103.

51 David Richardson has argued that the shipboard revolts and increased costs associated with them meant that 10 per cent fewer slaves – about a million – were able to be transported to the Americas. Richardson, Shipboard Revolts, 74f., 88f. On this, see also Stephen D. Behrendt/David Eltis/David Richardson, The Costs of Coercion: African Agency in the Pre-Modern Atlantic World, *Economic History Review* 54/3 (August 2001), 454–476.

52 On the various slave revolts, see e.g. Joao José Reis, Slave Resistance in Brazil: Bahia, 1807–1835, *Luso-Brazilian Review* 25/1 (Summer 1988), 111–144; Michael Craton, The Passion to Exist: Slave Rebellions in the British West Indies 1650–1832, *Journal of Caribbean History* 13 (Summer 1980), 1–20; Joao Pedro Marques, Slave Revolts and the Abolition of Slavery: An Overinterpretation, in Drescher/Emmer, eds., *Who Abolished Slavery?*, 3–40; Genovese, *From Rebellion to Revolution*, 1–50.

53 On this, see e.g. Franklin W. Knight, The Haitian Revolution, *American Historical Review* 105/1 (February 2000), 103–115; David Patrick Geggus, *Haitian Revolutionary Studies*, Bloomington, IN 2002; David Patrick Geggus, ed., *The World of the Haitian Revolution*, Bloomington, IN 2009; Laurent Dubois, *Avengers of the New World: The Story of the Haitian Revolution*, Cambridge, MA 2004; David Geggus, Slave Resistance and Emancipation: The Case of Saint-Domingue, in Drescher/Emmer, eds., *Who Abolished Slavery?*, 112–119; Blackburn, *American Crucible*, 173–219; David Brion Davis, *Inhuman Bondage: The Rise and Fall of Slavery in the New World*, Oxford 2006, 157f.

54 David Brion Davis, Slave Revolts and Abolitionism, in Drescher/Emmer, eds., *Who Abolished Slavery?*, 163–168.

55 Curtin, *Atlantic Slave Trade*, 265; Blackburn, *Making of New World Slavery*, 384; Klein, *Atlantic Slave Trade*, 198.

56 On the origins of the abolitionist movement, see also Robin Blackburn, *The Overthrow of Colonial Slavery 1776–1848*, London 1988, 33–66; Joel Quirk, *The Anti-Slavery Project: From the Slave Trade to Human Trafficking*, Philadelphia, PA 2011, 31–34; Blackburn, *American Crucible*, 145–169.

57 Anstey, *Atlantic Slave Trade*, 200.

58 Germantown Friends' Protest against Slavery, 1688, in Roger Bruns, ed., *Am I Not a Man and a Brother? The Antislavery Crusade of Revolutionary America 1688–1788*, New York 1977, 3–5. In Quaker abolitionism, see e.g. David

Brion Davis, *The Problem of Slavery in Western Culture*, Ithaca, NY 1966, 291–332; David Brion Davis, *The Problem of Slavery in the Age of Revolution, 1770–1823*, Ithaca, NY 1975, 213–254; Brycchan Carey, *From Peace to Freedom: Quaker Rhetoric and the Birth of American Antislavery, 1657–1761*, New Haven, CT 2012.

59 Miles Mark Fisher, Friends of Humanity: A Quaker Anti-Slavery Influence, *Church History* 4/3 (September 1935), 187–202.

60 On Anthony Benezet, see esp. Maurice Jackson, *Let This Voice Be Heard: Anthony Benezet, Father of Atlantic Abolitionism*, Philadelphia, PA 2009.

61 Roger A. Bruns, Anthony Benezet and the Natural Rights of the Negro, *Pennsylvania Magazine of History and Biography* 96/1 (January 1972), 104–113; David L. Crosby, Anthony Benezet's Transformation of Anti-Slavery Rhetoric, *Slavery & Abolition* 23/3 (December 2002), 39–58 at 42, 54–56.

62 Srividhya Swaminathan, *Debating the Slave Trade: Rhetoric of British National Identity, 1759–1815*, Farnham 2009, 52–61; Crosby, Benezet's Transformation, 46–49.

63 Anthony Benezet, *Observations on the Inslaving, Importing and Purchasing of Negroes*, Germantown 1760, 3.

64 Ibid., 4–8.

65 Ibid., 8.

66 Ibid., 9.

67 This argument in particular was emphasised by Benezet in his subsequent writings, e.g. in Anthony Benezet, *A Caution and Warning to Great Britain and Her Colonies, in a Short Representation of the Calamitous State of the Enslaved Negroes in the British Dominions*, Philadelphia, PA 1766, 5.

68 Anthony Benezet, *Some Historical Account of Guinea, Its Situation, Produce and the General Disposition of Its Inhabitants. With an Inquiry into the Rise and Progress of the Slave Trade, Its Nature and Lamentable Effects*, Philadelphia, PA 1771.

69 On this, see Michael Kraus, Slavery Reform in the Eighteenth Century: An Aspect of Transatlantic Intellectual Cooperation, *Pennsylvania Magazine of History and Biography* 60/1 (January 1936), 53–66; Betty Fladeland, *Men and Brothers: Anglo-American Antislavery Cooperation*, Urbana, IL 1972, 17–20; Christopher Leslie Brown, *Moral Capital: Foundations of British Abolitionism*, Chapel Hill, NC 2006, 402–411.

70 On 'Somerset's Case', see Steven M. Wise, *Though the Heavens May Fall: The Landmark Trial That Led to the End of Human Slavery*, Cambridge, MA 2006; George van Cleve, 'Somerset's Case' and Its Antecedents in Imperial Perspective, *Law and History Review* 24/3 (Autumn 2006), 601–645.

71 Brown, *Moral Capital*, 98–100; Seymour Drescher, *Capitalism and Antislavery: British Mobilization in Comparative Perspective*, Oxford 1986, 37–41; Seymour Drescher, *Abolition: A History of Slavery and Antislavery*, Cambridge 2009, 100–105.

72 See e.g. Letter from Sharp to Benezet dated 21 August 1772, in Bruns, *Am I Not a Man and Brother*, 196–199; Letter from Benezet to Sharp dated 29 March 1773, in ibid., 262–267; Swaminathan, *Debating the Slave Trade*, 71–73.

73 Davis, *Problem of Slavery*, 213–254. On the significance of the collaboration between Benezet and Sharp, see also David Turley, *The Culture of English Antislavery, 1780–1860*, London 1991, 197f., 200f.; James Walvin, *England, Slaves and Freedom, 1776–1838*, Jackson, MS 1986, 101f. On the transatlantic and transnational nature of the abolitionist network, see esp. Oldfield, *Transatlantic Abolitionism*, here esp. 13–99; William Mulligan/Maurice Bric, eds., *A Global History of Anti-Slavery Politics in the Nineteenth Century*, Basingstoke 2013.

74 Brown, *Moral Capital*, 105–153, 456–459; Fladeland, *Men and Brothers*, 27–43.

75 Quaker Petition to the Continental Congress dated 4 October 1783, in Bruns, *Am I Not a Man and a Brother*, 493–502.

76 Judith Jennings, *The Business of Abolishing the British Slave Trade 1783–1807*, London 1997, 22–26; Drescher, *Capitalism and Antislavery*, 62f.; Brown, *Moral Capital*, 414–424.

77 *The Case of Our Fellow-Creatures, the Oppressed Africans, Respectfully Recommended to the Serious Consideration of the Legislature of Great Britain, by the People Called Quakers*, London 1784.

78 Ibid., 5, 8.

79 [Joseph Woods], *Thoughts on the Slavery of the Negroes*, London 1784.

80 Ibid., 5.

81 Ibid., 15.

82 Ibid., 23, 31f.

83 Brown, *Moral Capital*, 432f., 442; Adam Hochschild, *Bury the Chains: The British Struggle to Abolish Slavery*, Basingstoke 2005, 2, 78f.

84 Drescher, *Capitalism and Antislavery*, 64.

85 On the life and role of Thomas Clarkson, see Ellen Gibson Wilson, *Thomas Clarkson: A Biography*, New York 1990.

86 On the influence of Benezet's writings on Clarkson, see Jackson, Let This Voice Be Heard, 160–164.

87 A detailed account of this is given in Thomas Clarkson, *The History of the Rise, Progress, and Accomplishment of the Abolition of the African Slave-Trade by the British Parliament*, vol. 1, London 1808, 205–210.

88 Thomas Clarkson, *An Essay on the Slavery and Commerce of the Human Species, Particularly the African, Translated from a Latin Dissertation*, London 1786.

89 Brown, *Moral Capital*, 434–436; Wilson, *Clarkson*, 15–18.

90 Clarkson, *History*, 249–251; Robert I. Wilberforce/Samuel Wilberforce, eds., *The Life of William Wilberforce*, vol. 1, London 1838, 151–153; Walvin, *England, Slaves and Freedom*, 106.

91 Clarkson, *History*, 255–258; Frank J. Klingberg, *The Anti-Slavery Movement in England: A Study in English Humanitarianism*, New Haven, CT 1926, 73; Quirk, *Anti-Slavery Project*, 34f.

92 Turley, *Culture of English Antislavery*, 91; Anstey, *Atlantic Slave Trade*, 246f.

93 The nine Quaker founders were William Dillwyn, Samual Hoare, George Harrison, John Lloyd, Joseph Woods, Richard Phillips, John Barton, Joseph Hooper and James Phillips. Only Philip Sanson, Thomas Clarkson and Granville Sharp were Anglicans. Wilberforce was not a founding member,

but was informed immediately of the founding of the committee. On this, see Clarkson, *History*, 256–258.

94 Davis, *Problem of Slavery*, 220f.; Brown, *Moral Capital*, 443f.; Drescher, *Abolition*, 214.

95 Jennings, *Business of Abolishing*, 36f.; Thomas, *Slave Trade*, 492.

96 Clarkson, *History*, 284–286; David Beck Ryden, *West Indian Slavery and British Abolition, 1783–1807*, Cambridge 2009, 164–166.

97 Clarkson, *History*, 286f.

98 Ibid., 287.

99 *Circular Letter of the 1787 Committee Appended to the Pamphlet by Thomas Clarkson, A Summary View of the Slave Trade and of the Consequences of Its Abolition*, London 1787, 3.

100 Ibid.

101 On Wilberforce and the 'Clapham Sect', see Stephen Tomkins, *The Clapham Sect: How Wilberforce's Circle Transformed Britain*, Oxford 2010.

102 On the religious motivations of many abolitionists, see Anstey, *Atlantic Slave Trade*, 157–235; Davis, *Problem of Slavery*, 291–390; Brown, *Moral Capital*, 333–450. For a stronger emphasis on other social forces and concerns, see Nicholas Hudson, 'Britons Never Will Be Slaves': National Myth, Conservatism, and the Beginning of British Antislavery, *Eighteenth-Century Studies* 34/4 (Summer 2001), 559–576.

103 Seymour Drescher, Public Opinion and the Destruction of British Slavery, in James Walvin, ed., *Slavery and British Society 1776–1846*, London 1982, 22–25; Seymour Drescher, History's Engines: British Mobilization in the Age of Revolution, *William and Mary Quarterly* 66/4 (October 2009), 737–756; Anstey, *Atlantic Slave Trade*, 255–257. For the role of petitioning in political culture more generally, see Richard Huzzey/Henry Miller, Petitions, Parliament, and Political Culture: Petitioning the House of Commons, 1780–1918, *Past & Present*, No. 248 (August 2020), 123–164.

104 It was the poet Samuel Taylor Coleridge who called Clarkson, on account of his tireless dedication to abolition, a 'moral steam-engine, or the Giant with one idea'. Qtd. in Wilson, *Clarkson*, 1.

105 On this role of Clarkson's, see J. R. Oldfield, *Popular Politics and British Anti-Slavery: The Mobilization of Public Opinion against the Slave Trade 1787–1807*, Manchester 1995, 70–95.

106 Turley, *Culture of English Antislavery*, 54, 58.

107 For a detailed account of his travels, see Clarkson, *History*, chs. 14–19, 292–440.

108 On the treatment of crews, see Falconbridge, *Account of the Slave Trade*, 37–50.

109 On this, see esp. Thomas Clarkson, *An Essay on the Impolicy of the African Slave Trade*, London 1788; Christopher, *Slave Ship Sailors*, 91f.

110 Clarkson, *History*, 409f.

111 Clarkson incorporated his findings into such works of his as *An Essay on the Impolicy of the African Slave Trade*.

112 Clarkson, *History*, 374–377. After obtaining these items in a Liverpool ironmonger's shop, Clarkson wrote an outraged letter to *The Times* giving

a detailed account of their purpose and functioning. See *The Times* (22 November 1787).

113 Clarkson, *History*, 441–457; Fladeland, *Men and Brothers*, 41f.; Oldfield, *Transatlantic Abolitionism*, 13–41. The abolitionists also sought out like-minded campaigners in Spain. On this, see Christopher Schmidt-Nowara, Wilberforce Spanished: Joseph Blanco White and Spanish Antislavery, in Christopher Schmidt-Nowara/Josep M. Fradera, eds., *Slavery and Antislavery in Spain's Atlantic Empire*, New York 2013, 158–175.

114 On the Société des Amis des Noirs and its activities, see Daniel P. Resnick, The Société des Amis des Noirs and the Abolition of Slavery, *French Historical Studies* 7/4 (Autumn 1972), 558–569; Jean-Pierre Barlier, *La Société des Amis des Noirs 1788–1791: Aux origines de la première abolition de l'esclavage (4 février 1794)*, Paris 2010.

115 Lawrence C. Jennings, *French Anti-Slavery: The Movement for the Abolition of Slavery in France 1802–1848*, Cambridge 2000, 1f.

116 Seymour Drescher, British Way, French Way: Opinion Building and Revolution in the Second French Slave Emancipation, *American Historical Review* 96/3 (June 1991), 709–734 at 711–715.

117 Resnick, *Société des Amis des Noirs*, 567; Drescher, Public Opinion, 42.

118 Drescher refers to a particular form of 'Anglo-American antislavery'. On this, see Drescher, British Way, French Way, 714.

119 On the key role played by the London Committee, see J. R. Oldfield, The London Committee and Mobilization of Public Opinion against the Slave Trade, *Historical Journal* 35/2 (June 1992), 331–343; Drescher, *Abolition*, 213f.

120 Oldfield, *Popular Politics*, 44f., 64, 104; Turley, *Culture of English Antislavery*, 50f.; James Walvin, The Propaganda of Anti-Slavery, in James Walvin, ed., *Slavery and British Society 1776–1846*, London 1982, 57–61.

121 On this, see esp. Brycchan Carey, *British Abolitionism and the Rhetoric of Sensibility: Writing, Sentiment, and Slavery, 1760–1807*, New York 2005; Swaminathan, *Debating the Slave Trade*, 101f.; Festa, Humanity without Feathers, 3–27; Blackburn, *American Crucible*, 153–159.

122 On this, see James Field Stanfield, *Observations on a Guinea Voyage in a Series of Letters Addressed to the Rev. Thomas Clarkson*, London 1788; James Field Stanfield, *The Guinea Voyage: A Poem in Three Books*, London 1789.

123 Ibid., 30. The reference is to William Robertson, a historian and leading figure of the Scottish Enlightenment.

124 Turley, *Culture of English Antislavery*, 49f.

125 Clarkson, *History*, 450. British abolitionists first used an image of an African woman in the same pose and with the legend 'Am I Not a Woman and a Sister?' in 1828. On this, see Philip Lapsansky, Graphic Discord: Abolitionist and Antiabolitionist Images, in Jean Fagan Yellin/John C. Van Horne, eds., *The Abolitionist Sisterhood: Women's Political Culture in Antebellum America*, Ithaca, NY 1994, 201–20 at 203–206; Jean Fagan Yellin, *Women and Sisters: The Antislavery Feminists in American Culture*, New Haven, CT 1989, 3–26. Joanna Bourke has argued that the slave's attitude of supplication indicated his continued subordination. On this, see Bourke, *What It Means to Be Human*, 120.

126 On the significance of the medallion, see esp. Mary Guyatt, The Wedgwood Slave Medallion: Values in Eighteenth-Century Design, *Journal of Design History* 13/2 (2000), 93–105; Hugh Honour, *The Image of the Black in Western Art*, vol. 4: *From the American Revolution to World War I: Slaves and Liberators*, Cambridge, MA 1989, 62–64.

127 Thomas Clarkson, *The History of the Rise, Progress, and Accomplishment of the Abolition of the African Slave-Trade by the British Parliament*, vol. 2, London 1808, 191f.

128 Oldfield, *Popular Politics*, 156–163; Drescher, *Capitalism and Antislavery*, 73; Jennings, *Business of Abolishing*, 39f.

129 Plymouth Committee, ed., *Plan of an African Ship's Lower Deck with Negroes in the Proportion of Only One to a Ton*, Plymouth 1788.

130 Clarkson, *History*, vol. 2, 111.

131 [London Committee], *Plan and Sections of a Slave Ship*, London 1789.

132 Clarkson, *History*, vol. 2, 187.

133 On the various images of the *Brookes* and their distribution, see Rediker, *Slave Ship*, 308–342.

134 On the special role of the *Brookes* in the abolitionists' public campaigns, see Oldfield, *Popular Politics*, 163–166; Lapsansky, Graphic Discord, 202–205; Marcus Wood, *Blind Memory: Visual Representation of Slavery in England and America 1780–1865*, Manchester 2000, 16–29.

135 Both paintings are well reproduced in Honour, *Image of the Black*, 67–71.

136 On the significance of these images, see ibid., 66–73; Oldfield, *Popular Politics*, 169–172; Wood, *Blind Memory*, 36–38.

137 On the key importance of making human suffering visible to mobilising public support, see also Laqueur, Bodies, Details, and the Humanitarian Narrative, 176–204; Thomas W. Laqueur, Mourning, Pity, and the Work of Narrative in the Making of 'Humanity', in Richard Ashby Wilson/Richard D. Brown, eds., *Humanitarianism and Suffering: The Mobilization of Empathy*, Cambridge 2009, 31–57.

138 Joseph Priestley, *A Sermon on the Subject of the Slave Trade; Delivered to a Society of Protestant Dissenters, at the New Meeting, in Birmingham; and Published at Their Request*, Birmingham 1788, 7.

139 For this stress on the slaves' humanity and their belonging to humankind, see also the contemporary pamphlet by Peter Packard, *Am I Not a Man and a Brother? With All Humility Addressed to the British Legislature*, Cambridge 1788.

140 Festa, *Sentimental Figures of Empire*, 60 and 153–155.

141 Wilson/Brown, Introduction, 1–3 at 18–21. The abolitionist movement must therefore be considered in the context of other humanitarian reform projects, among which it was certainly dominant. On this, see Turley, *Culture of English Antislavery*, 108–154.

142 Already in 1787 the former slave Ottobah Cugoano had published an appeal against slavery, which however did not meet with anything close to the success of Equiano's autobiography. On this, see Ottobah Cugoano, *Thoughts and Sentiments on the Evil and Wicked Traffic of the Slavery and Commerce of the Human Species*, London 1787.

143 On the significance of Equiano and his autobiography to the abolitionist cause, see James Walvin, *The Trader, the Owner, the Slave: Parallel Lives in the Age of Slavery*, London 2007, 247–255; Carretta, *Equiano, the African*, 270–302, 330–367; Swaminathan, *Debating the Slave Trade*, 121–124.

144 Festa, *Sentimental Figures of Empire*, 32–135.

145 Drescher, *Capitalism and Antislavery*, 66.

146 On this direct link between publicity campaigns and petitioning, see Davis, *Problem of Slavery*, 101; Turley, *Culture of English Antislavery*, 48–52; Drescher, Public Opinion, 25–26.

147 On this, see James E. Bradley, *Religion, Revolution, and English Radicalism: Nonconformity in Eighteenth-Century Politics and Society*, Cambridge 1990, 316–330.

148 Drescher, *Capitalism and Antislavery*, 80.

149 Turley, *Culture of English Antislavery*, 63.

150 Drescher, History's Engines, 739–740; Oldfield, *Popular Politics*, 110–113.

151 Clarkson, *History*, 415f.; Walvin, *England, Slaves and Freedom*, 109f.; Jennings, *Business of Abolishing*, 43.

152 Seymour Drescher in particular sees this as an important indicator for the direct connection between the emergence of capitalism and the abolitionist movement. On this, see Drescher, *Capitalism and Antislavery*, 67f., 80.

153 Oldfield, London Committee, 337–339.

154 Drescher, *Abolition*, 219–221.

155 J. R. Oldfield has accordingly spoken of 'abolition at the grass-roots level'. On this, see Oldfield, *Popular Politics*, 125–154.

156 For the content typical of such petitions, see e.g. R. Hamilton, An Address Intended to Have Been Delivered at a Meeting of the Inhabitants of Ipswich for the Purpose of Considering the Propriety of Petitioning Parliament for an Abolition of the Slave Trade, Ipswich, 17 February 1792; Thomas Clarkson, A *Short Address Originally Written to the People of Scotland on the Subject of the Slave Trade with a Summary View of the Evidence Delivered before a Committee of the House of Commons on the Part of the Petitioners for Its Abolition*, Shrewsbury 1792; *Address & Petition to His Majesty from the Inhabitants of the Town and Neighbourhood of Sheffield*, Sheffield 1794; Seymour Drescher, People and Parliament: The Rhetoric of the British Slave Trade, *Journal of Interdisciplinary History* 20/4 (Spring 1990), 561–58 at 566f.

157 Walvin, *England, Slaves and Freedom*, 110f.; Drescher, *Abolition*, 216.

158 William Cobbett, ed., *The Parliamentary History of England from the Earliest Period to the Year 1803, Parliamentary Debates*, vol. 27: *14 February 1788 to 4 May 1789*, London 1816, 495.

159 Ibid., 496.

160 Ibid., 503f.

161 On the parliamentary debates, see Cobbett, *Cobbett's Parliamentary History*, vol. 27, 573–599, 649–652. See also James W. LoGerfo, Sir William Dolben and 'The Cause of Humanity': The Passage of the Slave Trade Regulation Act of 1788, *Eighteenth-Century Studies* 6/4 (Summer 1973), 431–451.

162 Jennings, *Business of Abolishing*, 47f.

163 See the illustration of the *Brooks* under the heading 'Stowage of the British Slave Ship Brookes under the Regulated Slave Trade Act of 1788' in Clarkson, *History*, vol. 2, 114f.

164 Wilberforce, *Life of Wilberforce*, vol. 1, 218–220; Klingberg, *Anti-Slavery Movement*, 86f.

165 William Cobbett, ed., *The Parliamentary History of England from the Earliest Period to the Year 1803, Parliamentary Debates*, vol. 28: *9 May 1789 to 15 March 1791*, London 1816, 42.

166 For Wilberforce's speech of 12 May 1789 see ibid., 41–67.

167 Speech of Charles James Fox, 23 June 1789, in ibid., 100.

168 For the entirety of the debate, see ibid., 67–101.

169 In January 1790 Wilberforce succeeded in forcing parliament to set up a Select Committee to consider the slave trade. On this, see Cobbett, *Parliamentary History*, vol. 28, 311–315; Klingberg, *Anti-Slavery Movement*, 88f.

170 On the debate of 18 and 19 April 1791 on Wilberforce's bill, see William Cobbett, ed., *The Parliamentary History of England from the Earliest Period to the Year 1803, Parliamentary Debates*, vol. 29: *22 March 1791 to 13 December 1792*, London 1817, 250–359; Wilberforce, *Life of Wilberforce*, vol. 1, 298f.

171 Wilberforce, *Life of Wilberforce*, vol. 1, 300.

172 William Bell Crafton, *A Sketch of the Evidence Delivered before a Committee of the House of Commons for the Abolition of the Slave-Trade: To Which Is Added, a Recommendation of the Subject to the Serious Attention of People in General*, London 1792.

173 Jennings, *Business of Abolishing*, 68f.; Hochschild, *Bury the Chains*, 181–198.

174 William Fox, *An Address to the People of Great Britain on the Propriety of Abstaining from West India Sugar and Rum*, Birmingham 1791. On this, see also *Considerations Addressed to Professors of Christianity of Every Denomination, on the Impropriety of Consuming West-India Sugar and Rum, as Produced by the Oppressive Labour of Slaves*, London 1792.

175 Wilberforce, *Life of Wilberforce*, vol. 1, 338f.

176 Wilson, *Clarkson*, 72f.

177 Clarkson, *History*, vol. 2, 349f. On the means, especially children's books, by which the abolitionist movement appealed to children, see Oldfield, *Popular Politics*, 142–148; Johanna M. Smith, Slavery, Abolition, and the Nation in Priscilla Wakefield's Tour Books for Children, in Brycchan Carey/Markman Ellis/Sara Salih, eds., *Discourses of Slavery and Abolition: Britain and Its Colonies, 1760–1838*, London 2004, 175–193.

178 On this, see Linda Colley, *Britons: Forging the Nation 1707–1837*, London 2003, 278; Turley, *Culture of English Antislavery*, 79. On the very active role taken by women in mobilising support for the abolitionist cause, see Clare Midgley, *Women against Slavery: The British Campaigns, 1780–1870*, London 1992, 9–40; Oldfield, *Popular Politics*, 135–142.

179 Clarkson, *History*, vol. 2, 355. On the anti-abolitionist efforts of the West Indian interest, see Anstey, *Atlantic Slave Trade*, 286–296; Ryden, *West Indian Slavery and British Abolition*, 189–195.

180 For Wilberforce's speech and bill, see Cobbett, *Parliamentary History*, vol. 29, 1055–1074.

181 For the entire parliamentary debate, see ibid., 1055–1158.
182 On this, see ibid., 1204–1293.
183 Clarkson, *History*, vol. 2, 486–488; Wilberforce, *Life of Wilberforce*, vol. 1, 350f.
184 On this, see Cobbett, Parliamentary History, vol. 29, 1349–1355.
185 Robert I. Wilberforce/Samuel Wilberforce, eds., *The Life of William Wilberforce*, vol. 2, London 1838, 20; David Patrick Geggus, The British Government and the Saint Domingue Slave Revolt, 1791–1793, *English Historical Review* 96/379 (April 1981), 285–30 at 293; David Patrick Geggus, British Opinion and the Emergence of Haiti, 1791–1805, in Walvin, ed., *Slavery and British Society*, 123–14 at 124–128; Turley, *Culture of English Antislavery*, 164, 174–177.
186 Klingberg, *Anti-Slavery Movement*, 99f.
187 For Abingdon's speech of 11 April 1793, see William Cobbett, ed., *The Parliamentary History of England from the Earliest Period to the Year 1803, Parliamentary Debates*, vol. 30: *13 December 1792 to 10 March 1794*, London 1817, 654f.
188 Ibid., 657f.
189 Wilberforce, *Life of Wilberforce*, vol. 2, 18f.; Anstey, *Atlantic Slave Trade*, 277f.
190 A detailed account of Wilberforce's annual proposed bills can be found in Klingberg, *Anti-Slavery Movement*, 109–114; Jennings, *Business of Abolishing*, 80–93.
191 Hochschild, *Bury the Chains*, 241–247; Oldfield, *Transatlantic Abolitionism*, 103–161.
192 Wilson, *Clarkson*, 79–90.
193 Wilberforce, *Life of Wilberforce*, vol. 2, 19.
194 Oldfield, *Popular Politics*, 187.

Chapter 5

1 See most notably James Stephen, *The Crisis of the Sugar Colonies or an Enquiry into the Objects and Probable Effects of the French Expedition to the West Indies, and Their Connection with Colonial Interest of the British Empire*, London 1802.
2 On Stephen's role and strategy, see Anstey, *Atlantic Slave Trade*, 349–357, 362f., 367f.; David Brion Davis, *Slavery and Human Progress*, New York 1984, 170–173; Ryden, *West Indian Slavery and British Abolition*, 180f.; Lauren Benton, Abolition and Imperial Law 1790–1820, *Journal of Imperial and Commonwealth History* 39/3 (September 2011), 355–337 at 357–360.
3 James Stephen, *War in Disguise or the Frauds of the Neutral Flags*, London 1805.
4 'Prize' derives from the French *prendre*, 'to take (away), to seize'. According to maritime law, states in wartime were permitted to capture enemy ships as prizes of war. Once legal sanction had been given to the seizure, the value of the captured ship and cargo was partitioned among the officers and crew according to fixed rules. For a contemporary account of prize law, see Henry Wheaton, *A Digest of the Law of Maritime Captures and Prizes*, New York 1815.

For a historical account of the prize system, see Richard Hill, *The Prizes of War: The Naval Prize System in the Napoleonic Wars, 1793–1815*, Stroud 1998.

5 See the debate in the House of Commons, 31 March 1806, in T. C. Hansard, ed., *The Parliamentary Debates from the Year 1803 to the Present Time*, vol. 6, London 1806 (New York 1970), 597–599.

6 See the debate in the House of Lords, May 1806, in T. C. Hansard, ed., *The Parliamentary Debates from the Year 1803 to the Present Time*, vol. 7, London 1812 (New York 1970), 31–33 at 32.

7 An Act to Prevent the Importation of Slaves, by any of His Majesty's Subjects, into any Islands, Colonies, Plantations, or Territories, Belonging to any Foreign Sovereign, State, or Power, 23 May 1806, *House of Commons Parliamentary Papers*, http://parlipapers.chadwyck.co.uk/fulltext/fulltext.do?area=hcpp&id=1806-000868&pagenum=1&backto=FULLREC. On this, see also African Institution, ed., *Abstract of the Acts of Parliament for Abolishing the Slave Trade, and of the Orders in Council Founded on Them*, London 1810, 1–16.

8 See the debate in the House of Commons, 31 March 1806, in Hansard, *Parliamentary Debates*, vol. 6, 397.

9 On the political debates surrounding the bill and the abolitionists' role more broadly, see Davis, *Slavery and Human Progress*, 170–173; Quirk, *Anti-Slavery Project*, 47f.; Oldfield, *Transatlantic Abolitionism*, 179–182.

10 On the debate on the resolution in the House of Commons on 10 June 1806, see James Philips, ed., *Substance of the Debates on a Resolution for Abolishing the Slave Trade, Which Was Moved in the House of Commons on the 10th June, 1806, and in the House of Lords on the 24th June, 1806*, London 1806, 1–85. On the debate on the resolution in the House of Lords on 24 June 1806 see ibid., 87–154.

11 Stephen Farrell, 'Contrary to the Principle of Justice, Humanity and Sound Policy': The Slave Trade, Parliamentary Politics and the Abolition Act 1807, in Stephen Farrell/Melanie Unwin/James Walvin, eds., *The British Slave Trade: Abolition, Parliament and People*, Edinburgh 2007, 141–171; Quirk, *Anti-Slavery Project*, 48f.; Boyd Hilton, 1807 and All That: Why Britain Outlawed Her Slave Trade, in Derek R. Peterson, ed., *Abolitionism and Imperialism in Britain, Africa, and the Atlantic*, Athens, OH 2010, 63–83.

12 Act of the British Parliament for the Abolition of the Slave Trade, 25 March 1807, in BFSP 5, 559–568. This is sometimes referred to as the 'Abolition Act', although it should not be confused with the Slavery Abolition Act of 1833.

13 Ibid., 559f.

14 The fine was set at £100 per insurance policy. Ibid., 562.

15 Ibid., 567.

16 Ibid., 564. The act was extremely vague in its provisions for dealing with the freed slaves, suggesting only that male captives join the British forces as volunteers or become 'apprentices' of some form or another. On this, see ibid., 563f. On the system of prizes for seized slave ships, see also Hill, *Prizes of War*, 195f.; Padraic Xavier Scanlan, The Rewards of their Exertions: Prize Money and British Abolitionism in Sierra Leone, 1808–1823, *Past & Present* 225/1 (November 2014), 113–142.

17 Slave Trade Act, 565.
18 An Act to Prohibit the Importation of Slaves Into Any Port or Place Within the Jurisdiction of the United States, 2 March 1807, in Yale Law School, ed., *The Avalon Project: Documents in Law, History, and Diplomacy*, http:// avalon.law.yale.edu/19th_century/sl004.asp. On the political debates surrounding the US law and its background in domestic politics, see Don E. Fehrenbacher, *The Slaveholding Republic: An Account of the United States Government's Relation to Slavery*, Oxford 2001, 144–147. Denmark became the first country to issue a national ban on slavery on 16 March 1792, although it only came into force on 1 January 1803. On this, see Edict of the King of Denmark and Norway, concerning the Slave Trade, 16 March 1792, in BFSP 1, pt. II, 971f.
19 W. E. B. Du Bois, *The Suppression of the Atlantic Slave-Trade to the United States of America 1638–1870*, New York 1965, 109.
20 Christopher Lloyd, *The Navy and the Slave Trade: The Suppression of the African Slave Trade in the Nineteenth Century*, London 1968, 61; W. E. F. Ward, *The Royal Navy and the Slavers: The Suppression of the Atlantic Slave Trade*, London 1969, 43; Robert Blyth, Britain, the Royal Navy and the Suppression of the Slave Trade in the Nineteenth Century, in Douglas Hamilton/Robert L. Blyth, eds., *Representing Slavery: Art, Artefacts and Archives in the Collection of the National Maritime Museum*, Aldershot 2007, 76–91; Siân Rees, *Sweet Water and Bitter: The Ships That Stopped the Slave Trade*, London 2009, 7–25.
21 Letter concerning 'Sierra Leone Settlers' by Lord Sydney to the Lords Commissioners of the Admiralty, 7 December 1786, in C. W. Newbury, ed., *British Policy towards West Africa: Select Documents 1786–1874*, Oxford 1965, 182. On the foundation of Sierra Leone and the link with abolition see Mary Louise Clifford, *From Slavery to Freetown: Black Loyalists after the American Revolution*, Jefferson, TX 1999; Cassandra Pybus, 'A Less Favourable Specimen': The Abolitionist Response to Self-Emancipated Slaves in Sierra Leone, 1793–1808, *Parliamentary History* 26 (Supplement 2007), 97–112. Drawing inspiration from this idea, in 1816 American abolitionists founded Liberia, their own colony for freed slaves from the United States. On this, see Bronwen Everill, *Abolition and Empire in Sierra Leone and Liberia*, Basingstoke 2013, 17–22; Mary Wills, *Envoys of Abolition: British Naval Officers and the Campaign against the Slave Trade in West Africa*, Liverpool 2020.
22 On British plans in West Africa from 1780, see Philip D. Curtin, *The Image of Africa: British Ideas and Action, 1780–1850*, vol. 1, Madison, WI 1973, 88–139; Christopher Fyfe, Freed Slave Colonies in West Africa, in John E. Flint, ed., *The Cambridge History of Africa*, vol. 5: *From c. 1790 to c. 1870*, Cambridge 1976, 170–199; J. F. Ade Ajayi/B. O. Oloruntimehin, West Africa in the Anti-Slave Trade Era, in Flint, ed., *Cambridge History of Africa*, vol. 5, 200–221; Christopher Leslie Brown, Empire without America: British Plans for Africa in the Era of the American Revolution, in Derek R. Peterson, ed., *Abolitionism and Imperialism in Britain, Africa, and the Atlantic*, Athens, OH 2010, 84–100. On the idea of establishing legal trading relations, see Suzanne Schwarz, Commerce, Civilization and Christianity: The Development of the

Sierra Leone Company, in David Richardson/Suzanne Schwarz/Anthony Tibbles, eds., *Liverpool and Transatlantic Slavery*, Liverpool 2007, 252–276; Robin Law, ed., *From Slavery to 'Legitimate' Commerce: The Commercial Transition in Nineteenth-Century West Africa*, Cambridge 2002.

23 Tara Helfman, The Court of Vice-Admiralty at Sierra Leone and the Abolition of the West African Slave Trade, *Yale Law Journal* 115/5 (March 2006), 1122–1115 at 1130f.

24 Seymour Drescher, Emperors of the World: British Abolitionism and Imperialism, in Derek R. Peterson, ed., *Abolitionism and Imperialism in Britain, Africa, and the Atlantic*, Athens, OH 2010, 129–49 at 135–139.

25 Rees, *Sweet Water and Bitter*, 16–18.

26 Helfman, Court of Vice-Admiralty, 1143.

27 'Then, and in every such case, the Person or Persons so offending, and their Counsellors, Aiders, and Abettors, shall be, and are, hereby, declared to be Felons, and shall be transported beyond seas for a term not exceeding 14 years, or shall be confined and kept to hard labour for a term not exceeding 5 years, nor less than 3 years, at the discretion of the Court before whom such Offender or Offenders shall be tried and convicted', in Act of the British Parliament, for rendering more effectual an Act made in the 47th Year of His Majesty's Reign, intituled, 'An Act for the Abolition of the Slave-trade', 14 May 1811, in BFSP 5, 571–57 at 572.

28 On the operations of the West Africa Squadron generally, see Lloyd, *Navy and the Slave Trade*; Ward, *Royal Navy and the Slavers*; Rees, *Sweet Water and Bitter*; Blyth, Britain, the Royal Navy; Wills, *Envoys of Abolition*.

29 Kaufmann/Pape, Explaining Costly International Moral Action, 633.

30 To put this figure into perspective, the average proportion of aid given by members of the OECD between 1975 and 1996 was a mere 0.23 per cent of gross national income. On the cost and this comparison, see ibid., 634–637. On the cost of the British operation, see also David Eltis, *Economic Growth and the Ending of the Transatlantic Slave Trade*, Oxford 1987, 97.

31 For details of this historiographical debate, see Thomas Bender, ed., *The Antislavery Debate: Capitalism and Abolitionism as a Problem in Historical Interpretation*, Berkeley, CA 1992; Heather Cateau/Selwyn H. Carrington, eds., *Capitalism and Slavery: Fifty Years Later*, New York 2000.

32 Eric E. Williams, *Capitalism and Slavery*, Chapel Hill, NC 1944. For a good overview of the influence of Williams' work, see Barbara Lewis Solow/Stanley L. Engerman, eds., *British Capitalism and Caribbean Slavery: The Legacy of Eric Williams*, Cambridge 1987.

33 On this, see esp. Seymour Drescher, *Econocide: British Slavery in the Era of Abolition*, Chapel Hill, NC 2010; Eltis, *Economic Growth and the Ending of the Atlantic Slave Trade*.

34 On the debate on the resolution in the House of Commons on 10 June 1806, see Philips, *Substance of the Debates on a Resolution for Abolishing the Slave Trade*, 1–85. On the debate on the resolution in the House of Lords on 24 June 1806 see ibid., 87–154. See also Farrell, 'Contrary to the Principle of Justice, Humanity and Sound Policy', 141–171.

35 On this fusion of motives, see, see Ralph A. Austen/Woodruff D. Smith, Images of Africa and British Slave-Trade Abolition: The Transition to an

Imperialist Ideology, 1787–1807, *African Historical Studies* 2/1 (1969), 69–83 at 82f.; Matthew Mason, Keeping Up Appearances: The International Politics of Slave Trade Abolition in the Nineteenth-Century Atlantic World, *William and Mary Quarterly* 66/1 (January 2009), 809–832; Philip D. Morgan, Ending the Slave Trade: A Caribbean and Atlantic Context, in Derek R. Peterson, ed., *Abolitionism and Imperialism in Britain, Africa, and the Atlantic*, Athens, OH 2010, 101–128; Richard Huzzey, *Freedom Burning: Anti-Slavery and Empire in Victorian Britain*, Ithaca, NY 2012. Lauren Benton has argued that the legal measures taken against the slave trade were primarily 'a project of consolidating the legal authority of empires'. On this, see Benton, Abolition and Imperial Law, 355–374.

36 Drescher, *Abolition*, 233.

37 Williams, *Capitalism and Slavery*, 175–176; Paul Michael Kielstra, *The Politics of Slave Trade Suppression in Britain and France, 1814–48: Diplomacy, Morality and Economics*, London 2000, 12.

38 Chaim Kaufmann and Robert Pape have stressed the importance of domestic policy. See Kaufmann/Pape, Explaining Costly International Moral Action, 649–661. See also Brown, Humanitarian Intervention, 156.

39 Robert Huzzey has accordingly referred to Great Britain as 'The Anti-Slavery State'. On this, see Huzzey, *Freedom Burning*, 40–74.

40 On Britain's naval hegemony from 1805 onwards and the Royal Navy's key political role, see Bernard Semmel, *Liberalism and Naval Strategy: Ideology, Interest, and Sea Power during the Pax Britannica*, Boston, MA 1986; Barry Gough, *Pax Britannica: Ruling the Waves and Keeping the Peace before Armageddon*, Basingstoke 2014.

41 Colley, *Britons*, 359.

42 It was Hugo Grotius who, in his treatise *Mare Liberum* of 1609, became the first jurist to develop this idea of the 'freedom of the seas'. On this, see Robert Feenstra, ed., *Hugo Grotius Mare Liberum 1609–2009*, Leiden 2009. The idea subsequently became the object of debates in international law and in the eighteenth century became increasingly established in the customary law of nations. On this development, see Grewe, *Epochen*, 300–322, 481–68 at 647f.

43 On the complicated relation between abolitionary measures and maritime law, see Jean Allain, The Nineteenth Century Law of the Sea and the British Abolition of the Slave Trade, *British Yearbook of International Law* 78/1 (2007), 342–388.

44 Letters patent 'Establishing a Court of Vice Admiralty at Sierra Leone', 2 May 1807, in TNA, ADM 5/51. For the history of the court, see Christopher Fyfe, *A History of Sierra Leone*, Aldershot 1993, 97f., 107–109, 115f. and the seminal essay by Helfman, Court of Vice-Admiralty, 1122–1156.

45 Maeve Ryan, The Price of Legitimacy in Humanitarian Intervention: Britain, the Right of Search, and the Abolition of the West African Slave Trade 1807–1867, in Simms/Trim, eds., *Humanitarian Intervention*, 231–25 at 234f.; Holger Lutz Kern, Strategies of Legal Change: Great Britain, International Law, and the Abolition of the Transatlantic Slave Trade, *Journal of the History of International Law* 6/2 (2004), 233–25 at 234f.

46 Tara Helfman has accordingly called the Court of Vice Admiralty an 'early and bold judicial experiment in humanitarian intervention'. See Helfman, Court of Vice-Admiralty, 1124. On this clear aim of Thorpe's, see ibid., 1132–1138, 1142.

47 For Thorpe's precise legal reasoning, see esp. ibid., 1138–1142.

48 On the history and the work of the African Institution, see Wayne Ackerson, *The African Institution (1807–1827) and the Antislavery Movement in Great Britain*, Lewiston, ME 2005.

49 *Report of the Committee of the African Institution, Read to the General Meeting on the 15th July 1807, Together with the Rules and Regulations which were then adopted for the Government of the Society*, London 1807, 65–67. On this, see also Oldfield, *Transatlantic Abolitionism*, 196f.; Kern, Strategies of Legal Change, 237f.; David Turley, Anti-Slavery Activists and Officials: 'Influence', Lobbying and the Slave Trade, 1807–1850, in Keith Hamilton/Patrick Salmon, eds., *Slavery, Diplomacy and Empire: Britain and the Suppression of the Slave Trade, 1807–1975*, Eastbourne 2009, 81–92.

50 *Report of the Committee of the African Institution, Read to the General Meeting on the 15th July 1807, Together with the Rules and Regulations which Were then Adopted for the Government of the Society*, London 1807, 68f.

51 'Besides making the necessary representations, from time to time, to his Majesty's Government, they have taken measures for communicating to the Officers of the Royal Navy distinct information respecting the provisions of the Legislature on this point ...; as well as to point out the pecuniary advantages which would accrue to them from a vigorous enforcement of the Abolition Laws', in *Fourth Report of the Directors of the African Institution, Read at the Annual General Meeting on 23rd of March, 1810*, London 1810, 3–5.

52 For these summaries, see ibid., 31–71; *Fifth Report of the Directors of the African Institution, Read at the Annual General Meeting on 27th of March, 1811*, London 1811, 40f., 116–121; *Sixth Report of the Directors of the African Institution, Read at the Annual General Meeting on 25th of March, 1812*, London 1812, 6–9, 30–57.

53 *Sixth Report of the Directors*, 9.

54 On these cases involving seized foreign slave ships, see Allain, Nineteenth Century Law, 348–354; Hugo Fischer, The Suppression of Slavery in International Law I, *International Law Quarterly* 3/1 (January 1950), 28–5 at 32–37. In a contemporary account of prize law, the eminent American scholar of international law Henry Wheaton discussed the singular legal status of captured ships while giving voice to the hope that abolition would soon be an integral part of the 'conventional law of nations'. On this, see Wheaton, *Digest of the Law*, 227–230.

55 While Portugal in the Anglo-Portuguese treaty of 1810 consented to a restriction and gradual abolition of its slave trade, it refused to allow the Royal Navy to interfere with its ships. On this, see Treaty of Friendship and Alliance between His Britannic Majesty and His Royal Highness the Prince Regent of Portugal, 19 February 1810, in BFSP 1, pt. I, 547–55 at 555f.

56 Only in the abolition treaties of 1817 did Great Britain grant compensation of £300,000 to Portugal and £400,000 to Spain. On this, see Additional

Convention for the Purpose of Preventing Their Subjects from Engaging in Any Illicit Traffic in Slaves between Great Britain and Portugal, 28 July 1817, in TNA, FO 84/2; and Tratado Para la Abolicion del Trafico de Negros between Spain and Great Britain, 23 September 1817, in AGI, ULTRAMAR, Legajo 32, N. 20.

57 On this development, see Helfman, Court of Vice-Admiralty, 1146–1149; J. P. van Niekerk, British, Portuguese, and American Judges in Adderley Street: The International Legal Background to and Some Judicial Aspects of the Cape Town Mixed Commissions for the Suppression of the Transatlantic Slave Trade in the Nineteenth Century (pt. 1), *Comparative and International Law Journal of Southern Africa* 37/1 (March 2004), 1–3 at 7–15. In a letter dated 28 June 1816 the king's advocate, Christopher Robinson, expressly warned Earl Bathurst, the secretary of war, that in his opinion there was no right to search foreign ships under maritime law any longer applied. On this, see Letter from C. Robinson to Earl Bathurst, 28 June 1816, in Newbury, ed., *British Policy*, 139.

58 Kern, Strategies of Legal Change, 239–241; Allain, Nineteenth Century Law, 351–354.

59 For the full legal account of the case of *Le Louis*, see John Dodson, ed., *Reports of Cases Argued and Determined in the High Court of Admiralty; Commencing with the Judgments of the Right Hon. Sir William Scott (Lord Stowell), Trinity Term 1811*, vol. 2: *1815–1822*, London 1828, 210–264.

60 Ibid., 243f.

61 Ibid., 244.

62 Ibid., 257.

63 Some of the issues raised in this section have already been discussed in my essay: Klose, 'To maintain the law of nature and of nations', 217–237.

64 Letter from Wilberforce to William Hey, April 1814, in Robert I. Wilberforce/ Samuel Wilberforce, eds., *The Life of William Wilberforce*, vol. 4, London 1839, 173.

65 Ibid., 180–184; Reginald Coupland, *The British Anti-Slavery Movement*, London 1964, 153f.; Betty Fladeland, Abolitionist Pressures on the Concert of Europe, 1814–1822, *Journal of Modern History* 38/4 (December 1966), 355–37 at 356f.; Martha Putney, The Slave Trade in French Diplomacy from 1814 to 1815, *Journal of Negro History* 60/3 (July 1975), 411–42 at 412.

66 Speech by Wilberforce, 2 May 1814, in T. C. Hansard, ed., *The Parliamentary Debates from the Year 1803 to the Present Time*, vol. 27, London 1814, 637–640.

67 Ibid., 640.

68 Address of the House of Commons to the Prince Regent of Great Britain, 3 May 1814, in BFSP 3, 893.

69 Ibid., 894.

70 Address of the House of Lords to the Prince Regent of Great Britain, 5 May 1814, in ibid., 895f.

71 On this, see Wilberforce/Wilberforce, *Life of William Wilberforce*, vol. 4, 172, 184.

72 On the Paris peace treaty of 1814, see also Zamoyski, *Rites of Peace*, 197–202.
73 Report from Castlereagh to Liverpool, 19 May 1814, in Charles K. Webster, ed., *British Diplomacy 1813–1815: Select Documents Dealing with the Reconstruction of Europe*, London 1921, 183f.
74 Additional Article to the Definitive Treaty of Peace between Great Britain and France, 30 May 1814, in BFSP 3, 890f.
75 On this, see Letter from Castlereagh to Talleyrand, 26 May 1814, in Arthur Wellesley of Wellington, ed., *Supplementary Despatches, Correspondence, and Memoranda of Field Marshal Arthur Duke of Wellington*, vol. 9, London 1862, 110; Letter from Castlereagh to Talleyrand, 27 May 1814, in ibid., 112f.; Letter from Talleyrand to Castlereagh, 27 May 1814, in ibid., 113.
76 Report from Castlereagh to Liverpool, 19 May 1814, in Webster, ed., *British Diplomacy*, 184f.
77 Letter from Castlereagh to the governments of Austria, Prussia and Russia, 31 May 1814, in BFSP 3, 887.
78 Parliamentary minutes concerning the peace treaty, 6 June 1814, in Hansard, *Parliamentary Debates*, vol. 27, 1078.
79 Diary entry by Wilberforce, 4 June 1814, in Wilberforce/Wilberforce, *Life of William Wilberforce*, vol. 4, 186.
80 Speech by Wilberforce, 6 June 1814, in Hansard, *Parliamentary Debates*, vol. 27, 1079.
81 Ibid., 1078–1082.
82 Wilberforce/Wilberforce, *Life of William Wilberforce*, vol. 4, 192.
83 On this, see *Observations on That Part of the Late Treaty of Peace with France Which Relates to the African Slave Trade, Extracted from a Periodical Work for June 1814*, London 1814.
84 Ibid., 8f.
85 Ibid., 10.
86 A good example is the petition of 17 June 1814, in ibid., 11f.
87 James Walvin, The Public Campaign in England against Slavery, 1787–1834, in David Eltis/James Walvin, eds., *The Abolition of the Atlantic Slave Trade: Origins and Effects in Europe, Africa, and the Americas*, Madison, WI 1981, 67f.; Seymour Drescher, Whose Abolition? Popular Pressure and the Ending of the British Slave Trade, *Past & Present* 143/1 (May 1994), 136–16 at 160–162; Kielstra, *Politics of Slave Trade Suppression*, 30f.; for the various petitions to parliament, see T. C. Hansard, ed., *The Parliamentary Debates from the Year 1803 to the Present Time*, vol. 28, London 1814, 372–374, 417, 655f., 700.
88 Letter from Wellington to Henry Wellesley, 29 July 1814, in Wellington, *Supplementary Despatches*, vol. 9, 165.
89 Presentation and speech by Wilberforce, 27 June 1814, in Hansard, *Parliamentary Debates*, vol. 28, 267f.
90 On this, see Address of the House of Commons to the Prince Regent of Great Britain, 27 June 1814, in BFSP 3, 896–899; and Address of the House of Lords to the Prince Regent of Great Britain, 30 June 1814, in ibid., 899f.
91 Letter from George, prince regent, to Louis XVIII, 5 August 1814, in BFSP 3, 900.

92 On these negotiations, see Letter from Castlereagh to Wellington, 6 August 1814, in ibid., 891–893; Letter from Wellington to Castlereagh, 25 August 1814, in ibid., 901f.

93 Letter from Castlereagh to Wellington, 6 August 1814, in BFSP 3, 901.

94 Letter from Wellington to Talleyrand, 26 August 1814, in MAE, MD A 23.

95 Drescher, Whose Abolition?, 163; Bernard H. Nelson, The Slave Trade as a Factor in British Foreign Policy 1815–1862, *Journal of Negro History* 27/2 (April 1942), 192–20 at 195–197.

96 Fladeland, Abolitionist Pressures, 132f.; Kern, Strategies of Legal Change, 242f.

97 On this, see Letter from Wellesley to Castlereagh, 6 July 1814, in BFSP 3, 920f.; Letter from Castlereagh to Wellesley, 30 July 1814, in ibid., 923–926; Letter from Wellesley to Castlereagh, 25 August 1814, in ibid., 926f.; Letter from Duque de Fernán Nunez, 30 July 1814, in AGS, ESTADO, Legajo 8176, N. 493; Letter from Duque de Fernán Nunez, 2 August 1814, in AGS, ESTADO, Legajo 8176, N. 499.

98 Clark, *International Legitimacy*, 47–51; Oldfield, *Transatlantic Abolitionism*, 203–210.

99 Diary entry by Wilberforce, 11 June 1814, in Wilberforce/Wilberforce, *Life of William Wilberforce*, vol. 4, 190, 198f.; Lettre à Son Excellence Monseigneur Le Prince de Talleyrand Périgord au sujet de la traite des nègres par Wm. Wilberforce, à Londres Octobre 1814 (de l'imprimerie de Schulze et Dean).

100 See e.g. the German version: *Eine summarische Uebersicht der vor dem Ausschuß des Unterhauses des Großbritannischen Parlaments abgelegten Zeugnisse über den Gegenstand des Sclaven-Handels den verschiedenen Regenten in der christlichen Welt zugeeignet von Thomas Clarkson*, London 1814, 5.

101 Ibid., 33.

102 Letter from Liverpool to Wellington, 2 September 1814, in Charles Petrie, *Lord Liverpool and His Times*, London 1954, 198f.

103 Nelson, Slave Trade as a Factor, 194; Coupland, *British Anti-Slavery Movement*, 154.

104 On this, see also Ethan A. Nadelmann, Global Prohibition Regimes: The Evolution of Norms in International Society, *International Organization* 44/4 (Autumn 1990), 479–52 at 491–494.

105 On the Congress of Vienna and its importance, see e.g. Nicolson, *Congress of Vienna*; Zamoyski, *Rites of Peace*, 260–441; Mark Jarrett, *The Congress of Vienna and Its Legacy: War and Great Power Diplomacy after Napoleon*, London 2014; Vick, *Congress of Vienna*; Evans, *Pursuit of Power*, 20–28.

106 It must at this point be recalled that another controversial issue besides abolition was the protection of Jewish communities in Germany under humanitarian aspects. On this, see Vick, *Congress of Vienna*, 166–192; Sluga, 'Who Hold the Balance of the World?', 1403–1430.

107 Letter from Castlereagh to Bathurst, 9 October 1814, in BFSP 3, 939; Letter from Castlereagh to Liverpool, 25 October 1814, in Webster, ed., *British Diplomacy*, 215f.

108 Letter from Talleyrand to Castlereagh, 5 November 1814, in BFSP 3, 940–941; Letter from Wellington to Castlereagh, 5 November 1814, in ibid., 913f. On the French negotiating position at the Congress of Vienna, see also Instruction de Prince de Talleyrand pour les plénipotentiaires français au congrès de Vienne, 10 September 1814, in MAE, MD F 677.

109 Jerome Reich, The Slave Trade at the Congress of Vienna: A Study in English Public Opinion, *Journal of Negro History* 53/2 (April 1968), 129–14 at 136; Putney, Slave Trade in French Diplomacy, 422.

110 Propositions du Plénipotentiare de France, 10 December 1814, in BFSP 3, 576f.

111 Protocole de la Conférence entre les Plénipotentiaires d'Autriche, d'Espagne, de France, de la Grande Bretagne, de Portugal, de Prusse, de Russie, et de Suède, 16 January 1815, in ibid., 946–949. The collected proceedings of the sessions addressing the slave trade may also be found in Johann Ludwig Klüber, ed., *Acten des Wiener Congresses in den Jahren 1814 und 1815*, vol. 8, Erlangen 1818, 3–52.

112 For a more detailed account of these negotiations, see Charles K. Webster, *The Foreign Policy of Castlereagh 1812–1815: Britain and the Reconstruction of Europe*, London 1931, 413–424. One of the first accounts of these negotiations from a French perspective was Histoire et Apologie du Congrés de Vienne, Livre IV, par M. de Flassan, Historiographe des Affaires étrangères, Paris 1817, in MAE, MD F 689.

113 Protocole de la 1ère Séance Particulière Entre les Plénipotentiares des 8 Cours, 20 January 1815, in BFSP 3, 949–951.

114 Ibid., 952.

115 Protocole de la 2de Conférence Particulière Entre les Plénipotentiares des 8 Cours, 28 January 1815, in ibid., 960. On Britain's negotiating strategy, see also Memorandum as to the Mode of Conducting the Negotiations in Congress for the Final Abolition of the Slave Trade, 1814, in MAE, MD F 685.

116 Protocole de la 2de Conférence, in BFSP 3, 961f.

117 Protocole de la 3ème Conférence Particulière Entre les Plénipotentiares des 8 Cours, 4 February 1815, in ibid., 964f.

118 Ibid., 967.

119 Separate Article to the Treaty between Great Britain and Sweden, 3 March 1813, in ibid., 886.

120 On this, see Convention between Great Britain and Portugal Relative to the Indemnification of Portuguese Subjects for Certain Detained Slave-Trade Vessels, 21 January 1815, in BFSP 2, 345–348.

121 Treaty between Great Britain and Portugal for the Restriction of the Portuguese Slave Trade; and for the Annulment of the Convention of Loan of 1809 and Treaty of Alliance of 1810, 22 January 1815, in ibid., 348–354; Leslie Bethell, *The Abolition of the Brazilian Slave Trade: Britain, Brazil and the Slave Trade Question 1807–1869*, Cambridge 1970, 13; João Pedro Marques, *The Sounds of Silence: Nineteenth-Century Portugal and the Abolition of the Slave Trade*, New York 2006, 42.

122 Protocole de la 1ère Séance, 20 January 1815, in BFSP 3, 956–958; Protocole de la 3ème Conférence, 4 February 1815, in ibid., 965.

123 Letter from Wellesley to Castlereagh, 26 January 1815, in ibid., 934f.; Les Plénipotentiaires Portugais aux Plénipotentiaires des Puissances Signataires du Traite de Paris, 6 February 1815, in ibid., 972–974; Les Plénipotentiaires Portugais au Vicomte Castlereagh, 11 February 1815, in ibid., 974.

124 Declaration des 8 Cours, relative à l'Abolition Universelle de la Traite des Nègres, 8 February 1815, in ibid., 971f.

125 Letter from Liverpool to Canning, 16 February 1815, in Wellesley, *Supplementary Despatches*, 565f.

126 In the Commons debate on the Congress of Vienna, 'Mr. Wilberforce expressed his satisfaction at what had been done respecting the Slave Trade', 20 March 1815, in T. C. Hansard, ed., *The Parliamentary Debates from the Year 1803 to the Present Time*, vol. 30, London 1815, 305.

127 The declaration was appended to the final act as Appendix 15 in Article 118. On this, see Johann Ludwig Klüber, ed., *Schluß-Acte des Wiener Congresses of 9 June 1815*, Erlangen 1818, 111.

128 Berding, Ächtung des Sklavenhandels, 266–269, 285; Clark, *International Legitimacy*, 42, 55–57.

129 Berding, Ächtung des Sklavenhandels, 285; Paul Gordon Lauren, *Power and Prejudice: The Politics and Diplomacy of Racial Discrimination*, Boulder, CO 1996, 27f.

130 Putney, Slave Trade in French Diplomacy, 424; Kielstra, *Politics of Slave Trade Suppression*, 56f.

131 Dècret Impérial Français, qui abolit la Traite des Noirs, 29 March 1815, in BFSP 3, 196.

132 On this, see Letter from Castlereagh to Stuart, 14 June 1815, in Arthur Wellesley of Wellington, ed., *Supplementary Despatches, Correspondence, and Memoranda of Field Marshal Arthur Duke of Wellington*, vol. 10, London 1863, 498; Letter from Liverpool to Castlereagh, 7 July 1815, in ibid., 677f.; Protocole de la 15ème Conférence entre les Plénipotentiaires des 4 Cours Alliées, 20 July 1815, in BFSP 3, 196f.; Letter from Castlereagh to Talleyrand, 27 July 1815, in ibid., 197f.

133 Letter from Talleyrand to Castlereagh, 30 July 1815, in ibid., 198f.; Putney, Slave Trade in French Diplomacy, 426.

134 Article Additionnel au Traite Définitif, 20 November 1815, in MAE, MD A 23.

135 Fladeland, Abolitionist Pressures, 367. On this, see also the memorandum by Don Pedros Cevallos on the criticism of the Spanish crown in the British press, 10 November 1815, in AGS, ESTADO, Legajo 8176.

136 James Stephen, *An Inquiry into the Right and Duty of Compelling Spain to Relinquish Her Slave Trade in Northern Africa*, London 1816, 13, 20, 59.

137 Ibid., 18–20, 33.

138 Ibid., 50.

139 Ibid., 69f.

140 Ibid., 71f., 78f.

141 Ibid., 82.

142 Ibid., 94.

143 On the history of piracy and the slave trade along the 'Barbary Coast', see Daniel Panzac, *Barbary Corsairs: The End of a Legend 1800–1820*, Leiden 2005; Robert C. Davis, *Christian Slaves, Muslim Masters: White Slavery in the Mediterranean, the Barbary Coast, and Italy, 1500–1800*, Basingstoke 2003; John B. Wolfe, *The Barbary Coast: Algiers under the Turks 1500 to 1830*, New York 1979.

144 Robert C. Davis, Counting European Slaves on the Barbary Coast, *Past & Present* 172/1 (August 2001), 87–12 at 118.

145 To this end, Admiral Smith also founded a philanthropic organisation, the 'Society of Knights Liberators of White Slaves in Africa'. On his activities, see Edward Howard, *Memoirs of Admiral Sir Sidney Smith*, vol. 2, London 1839, 194–203, 313–366; John Barrow, *The Life and Correspondence of Admiral Sir William Sidney Smith*, vol. 2, London 1848, 365–379; Tom Pocock, *Breaking the Chains: The Royal Navy's War against White Slavery*, London 2006, 5–23.

146 William Sidney Smith, Mémoire sur la nécessité et les moyens de faire cesser les pirateries des états barbaresques, 31 August 1814, in MAE, MD A 5. Other individuals also made appeals to the princes gathered in Vienna, among them Friedrich Hermann, a native of Lübeck who published a pamphlet calling for a joint intervention of the European powers against the Barbary pirates. Friedrich, too, linked the issue of Christian with that of African slaves. On this, see Friedrich Herrmann, *Ueber die Seeräuber im Mittelmeer und ihre Vertilgung: Ein Völkerwunsch an den erlauchten Kongress in Wien*, Lübeck 1815. Johann Smidt, a senator of Bremen, also demanded such a joint intervention against the *Barbaresken*. On this, see Wilhelm von Bippen, *Johann Smidt ein hanseatischer Staatsmann*, Stuttgart 1921, 155.

147 Circular from Smith to the 'Consuls of the Nations at Peace with the Barbaric Regencies, Resident at those Regencies Respectively', 20 January 1815, in Howard, *Memoirs*, 325–328; William Sidney Smith, Relation des atrocités commises par les corsaires barbaresques dans l'adriatique et autres parties de la méditerranée, 1815, in MAE, MD A 5; Pamphlet 'Circulaire à Messieurs les souscripteurs au fonds charitabale pour l'abolition de l'esclavage des blancs aussi-bien que celui des noirs en Afrique', 20 April 1816, in ibid.; William Sidney Smith, Souscription pour operer l'abolition de esclavage des blancs aussi-bien que des noirs en Afrique, 22 June 1816, in ibid. On Smith's campaign at the Congress of Vienna, see Florian Kerschbaumer, Sir Sidney Smith und die Barbaresken-Frage am Wiener Kongress, in Reinhard Stauber/Florian Kerschbaumer/Marion Koschier, eds., *Mächtepolitik und Friedenssicherung: Zur politischen Kultur Europas im Zeichen des Wiener Kongresses*, Berlin 2014, 89–105; Brian Vick, Power, Humanitarianism and the Global Liberal Order: Abolition and the Barbary Corsairs in the Vienna Congress System, *International History Review* 40/4 (2018), 939–960.

148 Wolfe, *Barbary Coast*, 224, 242.

149 J. L. Anderson, Piracy and World History: An Economic Perspective on Maritime Predation, *Journal of World History* 67/2 (Autumn 1995), 175–19 at 186–188.

150 James A. Field, *America and the Mediterranean World 1776–1882*, Princeton, NJ 1969, 32–37; Seton Dearden, *A Nest of Corsairs: The Fighting Karamanlis of Tripoli*, London 1976, 151f.

151 The conflict between the United States and the Barbary states was largely put to rest in a peace treaty signed in 1815. On this, see Treaty of Peace and Amity between the United States of America and the Dey of Algiers, 30 June 1815, in BFSP 3, 45–51. On the 'Barbary wars' generally, see Frank Lambert, *The Barbary Wars: American Independence in the Atlantic World*, New York 2005; Frederick C. Leiner, *The End of Barbary Terror: America's 1815 War against the Pirates of North Africa*, Oxford 2006.

152 On this, see esp. Löwenheim, 'Do Ourselves Credit', 23–48.

153 Webster, *The Foreign Policy of Castlereagh 1815–1822*, 463; S. C. Northcote Parkinson, *Edward Pellew, Viscount Exmouth, Admiral of the Red*, London 1934, 423f.

154 Letter from Cevallos to the British government, 7 April 1816, in TNA, FO 84/1; Letter from Castlereagh, 7 June 1816, in ibid.

155 On Spanish debates on the utility of abolishing the slave trade, see Proceedings of the Council of the Indies of Spain, relative to the expediency of the Abolition, by His Catholic Majesty, of the Slave Trade carried on by Spanish Subjects, February 1816, in BFSP 4, 516–549.

156 Letter from Castlereagh to Cathcart, British ambassador to St Petersburg, 28 May 1816, in Charles Vane, ed., *Correspondence, Despatches and Other Papers of Viscount Castlereagh*, vol. 11, London 1853, 255. On this, see also Extract from the Confidential Memorandum, 28 May 1816, in TNA, FO 84/1.

157 Parkinson, *Edward Pellew*, 426–432; Roger Perkins/K. J. Douglas-Morris, *Gunfire in Barbary: Admiral Exmouth's Battle with the Corsairs of Algiers in 1816 – the Story of the Suppression of White Slavery*, Homewell 1982, 67–71.

158 For the various treaties, see Treaties between Great Britain and the Barbary States 1816, in BFSP 3, 509–516; Treaties of Peace between Sicily and the Barbary States (Concluded under the Mediation of Great Britain), in ibid., 521–548; Treaties of Peace and Friendship between Sardinia and the Barbary States (Concluded under the Mediation of Great Britain), in ibid., 173–193.

159 Declaration of the Bey of Tripoli Relative to the Abolition of Christian Slavery, 29 April 1816, in ibid., 515f.; Declaration of the Bey of Tunis Relative to the Abolition of Christian Slavery, 17 April 1816, in ibid., 513.

160 *The Times*, 29 June 1816.

161 See parliamentary debate of 19 June 1816, in T. C. Hansard, ed., *The Parliamentary Debates from the Year 1803 to the Present Time*, vol. 34, London 1816, 1147.

162 Ibid., 1149–1150.

163 Order of Admiralty to Lord Exmouth, 18 July 1816, in TNA, FO 84/1; Parkinson, *Edward Pellew*, 437; Perkins/Morris, *Gunfire in Barbary*, 74f.

164 On the particulars of the attack, see Parkinson, *Edward Pellew*, 457–464; Perkins/Morris, *Gunfire in Barbary*, 107–132; Leiner, *End of Barbary Terror*, 164–170; Panzac, *Barbary Corsaires*, 284–288.

165 Treaty of Peace between Great Britain and Algiers, 28 August 1816, in
    BFSP 3, 516; Letter from Exmouth to the Admiralty, 28 August 1816, in
    ibid., 517f.; Letter from Exmouth to Dey of Algiers, 28 August 1816,
    in ibid., 518f.; General memorandum from Exmouth, 30 August 1816, in
    ibid., 519.
166 Declaration of the Dey of Algiers Relative to the Abolition of Christian
    Slavery, 28 August 1816, in ibid., 517; Notification of the Admiralty,
    24 September 1816, in ibid., 519–521.
167 There were a mere eighteen British subjects among the liberated slaves, the
    majority of whom were from the Kingdom of the Two Sicilies, Sardinia and
    Spain. An exact tally can be found in Perkins/Morris, *Gunfire in
    Barbary*, 147.
168 For details of these honours, see Parkinson, *Edward Pellew*, 469f.; Perkins/
    Morris, *Gunfire in Barbary*, 155, 165–171.
169 Personal letter from Castlereagh to Exmouth, 30 September 1816, in
    Parkinson, *Edward Pellew*, 467.
170 Speech of Castlereagh to the House of Commons, 3 February 1817, T. C.
    Hansard, ed., *The Parliamentary Debates from the Year 1803 to the Present
    Time*, vol. 35, London 1817, 177–179. Another contemporary publication
    adopted a similarly rapturous tone: J. Gleave, ed., *The Triumph of Justice, or
    British Valour Displayed in the Cause of Humanity: Being an Interesting
    Narrative of the Recent Expedition to Algiers*, Manchester 1816.
171 Löwenheim, 'Do Ourselves Credit', 42–44; Vick, Power, 939–960.
    Seymour Drescher has even called the 1816 attack on Algiers 'the largest
    armed humanitarian intervention in British military history'. Drescher,
    Emperors of the World, 142.
172 Protocole No. 1 des Conférences pour l'abolition de la Traite des Nègres,
    28 August 1816, in TNA, FO 84/1; Minutes of the individual sessions,
    which were continued until 1819, can be found in TNA, FO 84/1 and
    TNA, FO 84/2.
173 Annexe au Protocole de la 7éme Conférence, 20 September 1816, in TNA,
    FO 84/1; Memorandum 'Abolition de la traite des négres' by the French
    ambassador to London, 1 November 1816, in MAE, MD A 15; Webster,
    Foreign Policy of Castlereagh 1815–1822, 457f.; Kielstra, *Politics of Slave Trade
    Suppression*, 64–67; Brian Vick, The London Ambassadors' Conferences
    and Beyond: Abolition, Barbary Corsairs and Multilateral Security in the
    Congress of Vienna System, in Brian Vick/Beatrice de Graaf/Ido de Haan,
    eds., *Securing Europe after Napoleon: 1815 and the New European Security
    Culture*, Cambridge 2019, 114–129.
174 Annexe au Protocole de la 7éme Conférence, 20 September 1816, in TNA,
    FO 84/1.
175 Note sur le projet d'une ligue maritime pour assurer l'abolition de la traite et
    la repression de la piraterie des Barbaresques, n.d., in MAE, MD A 15.
176 Memorandum from Castlereagh, February 1818, in BFSP 8, 299–30 at 302.
177 Protocole de la Conférence entre les Plénipotentiaires des 5 Cours, Aix-la-
    Chapelle, 24 October 1818, in ibid., 58f.; Letter from Castlereagh to
    Bathurst, 2 November 1818, in ibid., 57f.; Protocole de la Conférence entre

les Plénipotentiaires des 5 Cours, Aix-la-Chapelle, 4 November 1818, in ibid., 64f.; Webster, *Foreign Policy of Castlereagh 1815–1822*, 462–464.

178 Letter from Castlereagh to the Duc de Richelieu with attached memorandum, 27 October 1818, in MAE, MD A 24.

179 Letter from Castelereagh to Bathurst, 23 November 1818, in BFSP 6, 65f.

180 Opinion du Cabinet d'Autriche sur la Question de la Traite des Nègres, in ibid., 75f.

181 Opinion du Cabinet de Russie sur la Question de la Traite des Nègres, 7 November 1818, in MAE, MD A 24.

182 Memorandum of the British Government, in BFSP 6, 79.

183 Opinion du Cabinet de Prusse sur la Traite des Nègres, in ibid., 76.

184 Mémoire Français sur la Traite des Nègres, in ibid., 69–75. On the French position, see also Note sur la traite des noirs, October 1818, in MAE, MD A 15.

185 Mémoire Français sur la Traite des Nègres, in BFSP 6, 69–74. On the French naval squadron's operations against the slave trade, see Serge Daget, *La répression de la traite des Noirs au XIXe siècle: L'action des croisières françaises sur les côtes occidentales de l'Afrique (1817–1850)*, Paris 1997.

186 Projet de Lettre de Cabinet des Souverains d'Autriche, de France, de la Grande Bretagne, de Prusse et de Russie à Sa Majesté le Roi de Portugal, in BFSP 6, 85f.

187 Protocole de la Conférence entre les Plénipotentiaires des 5 Cours, Aix-la-Chapelle, 19 November 1818, in ibid., 86f.

188 This aspect may serve to qualify claims that these talks were inconclusive or simply useless. On this, see Berding, Ächtung des Sklavenhandels, 281; Suzanne Miers, *Britain and the Ending of the Slave Trade*, New York 1975, 13f.; Ryan, Price of Legitimacy, 237.

189 I have previously published key findings of this section in Fabian Klose, Humanitäre Intervention und internationale Gerichtsbarkeit – Verflechtung militärischer und juristischer Implementierungsmaßnahmen zu Beginn des 19. Jahrhunderts, *Militärgeschichtliche Zeitschrift* 72/1 (2013), 1–21. See Allain, Nineteenth Century Law, 357–376; Kern, Strategies of Legal Change, 246–249.

190 Separate Article to the Treaty between Great Britain and Sweden, 3 March 1813, in BFSP 3, 886.

191 See Article 9 of the Convention between Great Britain and the Netherlands, Relative to the Dutch Colonies; Trade with the East and West Indies, 13 August 1814, in BFSP 2, 374f. On the negotiations between Great Britain and the Netherlands that preceded the treaty, see Letter from Clancarty to Castlereagh, 17 June 1814, in BFSP 3, 888f.; Decree of the Sovereign Prince of the Netherlands Relative to the Abolition of the Slave Trade, 15 June 1814, in ibid., 889f.

192 Treaty between Great Britain and Denmark, 14 January 1814, in ibid., 886.

193 On this, see Mason, Keeping Up Appearances, 813; Edward Keene, A Case Study of the Construction of International Hierarchy: British Treaty-Making against the Slave Trade in the Early Nineteenth Century, *International Organization* 61/2 (Spring 2007), 311–33 at 320–323.

194 Leslie Bethell, Britain, Portugal and the Suppression of the Brazilian Slave Trade: The Origins of Lord Palmerston's Act of 1839, *English Historical Review* 80/317 (October 1965), 761–78 at 763; Robert E. Conrad, *World of Sorrow: The African Slave Trade to Brazil*, Baton Rouge, LA 1986, 58–61.

195 Additional Convention for the Purpose of Preventing Their Subjects from Engaging in Any Illicit Traffic in Slaves between Great Britain and Portugal, 28 July 1817, in TNA, FO 84/2.

196 Form of Passport for Portuguese Vessels Destined for the Lawful Traffic in Slaves, in ibid. See also its Spanish equivalent, Form of Passport for Spanish Vessels Destined for the Lawful Traffic in Slaves, in AGI, ULTRAMAR, Legajo 32, N. 20. Spanish and Portuguese ships were hence permitted to continue their brisk trade in slaves between Africa and South America below the equator.

197 Tratado Para la Abolicion del Trafico de Negros between Spain and Great Britain, 23 September 1817, in AGI, ULTRAMAR, Legajo 32, N. 20; David R. Murray, *Odious Commerce: Britain, Spain and the Abolition of the Cuban Slave Trade*, Cambridge 1980, 50–71.

198 *The Times*, 13 October 1817.

199 On this, see the documents 'Expediente de escuadra rusa', in AHN, ESTADO, Legajo 8029; Murray, *Odious Commerce*, 69f.

200 Treaty for Preventing Their Subjects from Engaging in Any Illicit Traffic in Slaves between Great Britain and the Netherlands, 4 May 1818, in BFSP 5, 125–135.

201 Pieter C. Emmer, Abolition of the Abolished: The Illegal Dutch Slave Trade and the Mixed Courts, in David Eltis/James Walvin, eds., *The Abolition of the Atlantic Slave Trade: Origins and Effects in Europe, Africa, and the Americas*, Madison, WI 1981, 177–19 at 179f.

202 An informative overview of these commonalities can be found in the Memoranda for the Guidance of the Commissions des FO, 20 February 1819, in BFSP 8, 25–36; Regulations for the Guidance of the Commissions Appointed for Carrying Into Effect the Treaties for the Abolition of the Slave Trade, in TNA, FO 313/1.

203 On this, see also Henry Brougham's speech in the parliamentary debate of 9 July 1817, in T. C. Hansard, ed., *The Parliamentary Debates from the Year 1803 to the Present Time*, vol. 36, London 1817, 1334.

204 Letter from Viscount Castlereagh to Wellesley, 24 July 1817, in TNA, FO 72/196.

205 Article 5 of the Additional Convention, 28 July 1817, in TNA, FO 84/2; Article 9 of the Tratado, 23 September 1817, in AGI, ULTRAMAR, 32, N. 20; Article 2 of the Treaty, 4 May 1818, in BFSP 5, 127. In Article 3 of their treaty, Britain and the Netherlands agreed to mutual rights of visit in the Mediterranean and north European waters. For a contemporary account of conditions on these ships seized as prizes by the Royal Navy, see Robert Burroughs, Eyes on the Prize: Journeys in Slave Ships Taken as Prizes by the Royal Navy, *Slavery & Abolition* 31/1 (March 2010), 99–115.

206 Instructions Intended for the British and Portuguese Ships of War Employed to Prevent the Illicit Traffic in Slaves, in TNA, FO 84/2;

Instructions for the British and Spanish Ships of War Employed to Prevent the Illicit Traffic in Slaves, ibid.

207 Articles 7 and 5 of the Instructions, in ibid.

208 Form of Declaration of the State of the Vessel at the Time of Capture, in TNA, FO 313/1.

209 Articles 8 and 6 of the Instructions, in TNA, FO 84/2.

210 Article 8 of the Additional Convention, 28 July 1817, in TNA, FO 84/2; Article 12 of the Treaty, 23 September 1817, in AGI, ULTRAMAR, 32, N. 20; Article 7 of the Treaty, 4 May 1818, in BFSP 5, 130.

211 They have also been known as 'Mixed Courts of Justice' and 'Courts of Mixed Commission'.

212 Both the Jay Treaty of 19 November 1794 and the peace treaty with France of 20 November 1815 provided for the establishment of such commissions to settle claims to territory and compensation. On this, see Treaty of Amity, Commerce, and Navigation between Great Britain and the United States, 19 November 1794, in Miller Hunter, ed., *Treaties and Other International Acts of the United States of America*, vol. 2: *1976–1818*, Washington, DC 1931, 245–264; Convention between Great Britain, Austria, Prussia, and Russia, and France, Relative to the Claims of the Subjects of the Allied Powers upon France, 20 November 1815, in BFSP 3, 315–340.

213 For a highly detailed account of the workings of the Mixed Commission, see also Van Niekerk, British, Portuguese, and American Judges, 196–209.

214 For example, in a legal dispute with his Portuguese colleague on the Mixed Commission, the British commissioner Edmund Gabriel can be found to have made explicit use of the term 'international courts': 'That the Mixed Commissions ... being international Courts, created for a definite and special purpose, and existing solely in consequence of precise treaty stipulations, cannot be constituted or governed by the laws of either country', in Edmund Gabriel, Opinion of Her Majesty's Acting Commissioner, 20 December 1856, Foreign Office, ed., *Correspondence with the British Commissioners at Sierra Leone, Havana, the Cape of Good Hope, and Loanda; and Reports from British Naval Officers, Relating to the Slave Trade, from April 1, 1857, to March 31, 1858*, London 1858, 60; Klose, Humanitäre Intervention und internationale Gerichtsbarkeit; Drescher, *Abolition*, 237. Eugene Kontorovich has also considered the special tribunals under the aspect of international jurisdiction, while concentrating on the position of the United States and the constitutional arguments made there for not participating in this system. Eugene Kontorovich, The Constitutionality of International Courts: The Forgotten Precedent of Slave Trade Tribunals, *University of Pennsylvania Law Review* 158/1 (December 2009), 39–115. See also Mark Lewis, *The Birth of the New Justice: The Internationalization of Crime and Punishment, 1919–1950*, Oxford 2014, 14f.; Seymour Drescher/ Paul Finkelman, Slavery, in Bardo Fassbender/Anne Peters, eds., *The Oxford Handbook of the History of International Law*, Oxford 2012, 890–916 at 904; Cornelis G. Roelofsen, International Arbitration and Courts, in Fassbender/Peters, eds., *Oxford Handbook*, 144–116 at 162f.

215 Article 2 of the Regulations for the Mixed Commissions, in TNA, FO 84/2. On the role of the commissions' members, see Fabian Klose, Legal Practitioners –

Nineteenth Century International Jurisdiction and the Ambiguous Roles of the Members of the Mixed Commissions, in Marcus M. Payk/Kim Christian Priemel, eds., *Crafting the International Order: Practitioners and Practices of International Law since c. 1800*, Oxford 2021, 48–65.

216 Article 11 of the Regulations for the Mixed Commissions, see in TNA, FO 84/2.

217 An exception were the Mixed Commissions in Freetown, a third of which were funded by Great Britain, with Portugal, Brazil, Spain and the Netherlands coming up for a sixth each. See Farida Shaikh, Judicial Diplomacy: British Officials and the Mixed Commission Courts, in Hamilton/Salmon, eds., *Slavery, Diplomacy and Empire*, 42–64 at 43. According to Foreign Office estimates, British spending alone on all four Mixed Commissions amounted to £16,850 in 1831. On this, see Estimates for 1831: Slave Trade Restriction Commission, in TNA, FO 96/34. For an exemplary breakdown of costs for the Mixed Commission in Freetown between 1820 and 1842, see Contingent Expenses of Mixed Commissions, in TNA, FO 315/37.

218 Dennis A. Lypka, The Slave Trade Department of the British Foreign Office and the Suppression of the Transatlantic Slave Trade (MA diss., University of Calgary 1977), 126f.

219 To put these figures into perspective, a British commissary judge and commissioner of arbitration in Havana earned £1,850 and £1,200 respectively, £1,500 and £1,000 in Suriname and £1,200 and £800 in Rio de Janeiro. Slave Trade Restriction Commission, in TNA, FO 96/34.

220 On members of the commissions dying, see e.g. Letter from the British commissioner Hamilton in Sierra Leone to Canning, 15 January 1825, in BPP, vol. 10, Class A, 17; Letter from the British commissioners in Sierra Leone to Viscount Palmerston, 30 June 1834, in BPP, vol. 14, Class A, 63; Letter from British Commissioner Macaulay in Sierra Leone to Viscount Palmerston, 14 August 1834, ibid.

221 Article 14 of the Regulations for the Mixed Commissions, in TNA, FO 84/2.

222 Article 3 of the Regulations for the Mixed Commissions, in ibid.; Form of Proceedings, and Steps to Be Taken on Arrival in Port, in BFSP 8, 30; Mode of Process, or Form of Procedure for the Mixed Court at Surinam, in BFSP 10, 473–475.

223 On this, see Interrogatories for the Use of the British Commissioners, to Be Administered to the Witnesses Belonging to the Vessel Taken, 1819, in TNA, FO 313/1.

224 Article 1 of the Regulations for the Mixed Commissions, in TNA, FO 84/2.

225 Article 3 of the Regulations for the Mixed Commissions, in ibid.

226 Article 6 of the Regulations for the Mixed Commissions, in ibid.

227 Article 8 of the Regulations for the Mixed Commissions, in ibid.

228 'Though all but forgotten today, these slave trade courts were the first international human rights courts.' Martinez, *Slave Trade*, 6. The claim was first made in an essay, Jenny S. Martinez, Antislavery Courts and the Dawn of International Human Rights Law, *Yale Law Journal* 117/4 (January 2008), 550–641.

229 On this, see esp. ch. 8, 'A Bridge to the Future: Links to Contemporary International Human Rights Law', in Martinez, *Slave Trade*, 148–157.
230 Article 7 of the Regulations for the Mixed Commissions, in TNA, FO 84/2.
231 Lloyd, *Navy and the Slave Trade*, 71–73.
232 Conneau, *A Slaver's Log Book*, 178.
233 Leslie Bethell, The Mixed Commissions for the Suppression of the Slave Trade in the Nineteenth Century, *Journal of African History* 7/1 (1966), 79–93 at 88; Fyfe, *History of Sierra Leone*, 197.
234 Numerous corresponding bills of sale issued by the Mixed Commissions, including that of the captured Brazilian schooner *Calliope*, can be found in TNA, FO 84/273.
235 Article 7 of the Regulations for the Mixed Commissions, in TNA, FO 84/2.
236 Eugene Kontorovich also briefly alludes to the aspect in the summary of his essay, Kontorovich, Constitutionality of International Courts, 114.

Chapter 6

1 Instructions of the Lords Commissioners of the Admiralty to Commodore Collier, 3 November 1819, in Newbury, *British Policy*, 139f.; Rees, *Sweet Water and Bitter*, 50–64. For an exemplary, vivid description of this mission, see Second Annual Report on the Coast of Africa by Commodore Sir George Collier, Bart. to the Admiralty, 16 September 1820, in National Museum of the Royal Navy, Portsmouth (NMRN), Manuscript Collection, NMRN, MSS 45; Survey by HMS Tartar Captain Sir George Ralph Collier, on the Gold Coast, made to the Admiralty between 1821 and 1824, on settlements and slaving, in National Maritime Museum, Greenwich, Archives (NMM), NMM WEL/10.
2 On this mission in the wider context of British naval strategy, see Semmel, *Liberalism and Naval Strategy*, 31–50; Gough, *Pax Britannica*, 165–188.
3 Rees, *Sweet Water and Bitter*, 35.
4 On this, see the documents 'Expediente de escuadra rusa', in AHN, ESTADO, Legajo 8029; Murray, *Odious Commerce*, 69f.
5 A vivid description of the many dangers and difficulties of these missions in West Africa can be found in the diary of Henry Cheesman Binstead, an ensign serving in HMS *Owen Glendower*: Memorandum of Remarks on Board HM Ship Owen Glendower, 1823, in NMRN, 2005.76/1; and Remark Book off the River Congo Coast of Africa, 1823–24, in NMRN, 2005.76/2.
6 Letter from Commissary Judge Thomas Gregory to Viscount Castlereagh, Sierra Leone, 21 June 1819, in BFSP 8, 52f.; Notification Concerning the Appointment of the Mixed Commission, Surinam, 3 November 1819, in BFSP 8, 198f.; Protocol of the Installation of the Mixed Commission at Rio de Janeiro, 18 December 1819, in ibid., 191f.; Letter from J. Kilbee to Viscount Castlereagh, Havanna, 12 November 1819, in TNA, FO 313/9.
7 Letter from Commissary Judge Thomas Gregory to Viscount Castlereagh, Sierra Leone, 21 June 1819, in BFSP 8, 53. See also Letter from Viscount

Castlereagh to Commissary Judge Thomas Gregory, 19 February 1819, in TNA, FO 315/1.

8 Luis Martínez-Fernandéz, The Havana Anglo-Spanish Mixed Commission for the Suppression of the Slave Trade and Cuba's Emancipados, *Slavery & Abolition* 16/2 (August 1995), 205–22 at 207; Bethell, Mixed Commissions, 85f.; Shaikh, Judicial Diplomacy, 51; Klose, Legal Practitioners.

9 For a good example, see List of Slave Ships and Slaves Arrived at Rio de Janeiro during the Months of January, February and March 1823, in TNA, FO 84/23; Result of Voyages of 32 Vessels Which Sailed from the Port of Havannah for the Coast of Africa during the Year 1825, in BFSP 15, 229.

10 For a good example, see 'Memorandum of the Present Actual State of the Slave Trade on the Coast of Africa' by Charles MacCarthy, Sierra Leone, 14 January 1822, in BFSP 9, 164–166; Report of the British commissioners in Sierra Leone to Foreign Secretary Canning, 15 May 1824, in BFSP 12, 56–71; Report of the British commissioners in Sierra Leone to Foreign Secretary Canning, 10 April 1825, in BFSP 13, 30–40; Report of John Tasker Williams, Commissary Judge in Sierra Leone to Foreign Secretary Canning, 30 March 1826, in BFSP 14, 21.

11 Letter from the Marquess of Londonderry to Lionel Hervey, 10 March 1822, in BFSP 9, 61. For an example of the forgery of licences by the Portuguese authorities, see Report of the British commissioners in Sierra Leone to Viscount Palmerston, 2 January 1836, in BFSP 24, 10; Report of the British commissioners in Sierra Leone to Viscount Palmerston, 5 January 1837, in BFSP 25, 17f.

12 Letter from Palmerston, 17 March 1834, in TNA, FO 313/4.

13 A fine example of this lively flow of information is a letter from Palmerston to the British commissioners, to which are appended the latest reports on the state of the slave trade in various locations. On this, see Letter from Viscount Palmerston to British commissioners, 11 August 1841, in BPP 21 pt. I, 217. On the network and this aspect of the commissioners' duties, see also Lypka, Slave Trade Department, 136; Huzzey, *Freedom Burning*, 45f., 49–51.

14 David Turnbull, *Travels in the West: Cuba with Notices of Puerto Rico and the Slave Trade*, London 1840, 77f.; Klose, Legal Practitioners.

15 Luis Martínez-Fernández, *Fighting Slavery in the Caribbean: The Life and Times of a British Family in Nineteenth Century Havana*, Armonk, NY 1998, 47.

16 Letter from Viscount Palmerston to H. L. Bulwer, 14 August 1846, in BFSP 35, 402.

17 Letter from Viscount Palmerston to H. L. Bulwer, 10 December 1846, in ibid., 408.

18 Prime examples include: Report of the British commissioners in Sierra Leone to Foreign Secretary Canning, 15 May 1824, in BFSP 12, 58; Report of the British commissioners in Sierra Leone to Viscount Palmerston, 14 December 1833, in BPP 14 Class A, 10f.; Report of the British commissioners in Sierra Leone to Viscount Palmerston, 5 January 1837, in BFSP 25, 16; Murray, *Odious Commerce*, 76f.

19 Letter from Kilbee to Foreign Secretary Canning, 1 January 1825, in BPP 10 Class A, 143.

20 Ibid.

21 Report of the British commissioners in Havana to Canning, 1 January 1827, in TNA, FO 313/10. On this, see also the Report of the British commissioners in Havana to Dudley, 1 January 1828, in ibid.

22 Report of the British commissioners in Havana to Canning, 1 January 1827, in TNA, FO 313/10.

23 Murray, *Odious Commerce*, 80.

24 Bethell, Mixed Commissions, 84. No doubt a special case was the Anglo-Dutch Commission in Suriname, which during its entire existence conducted only one trial, condemning the slaver *La Nueve of Snauw* in March 1823. See Emmer, Abolition of the Abolished, 180–192; Pieter C. Emmer, *The Dutch Slave Trade*, New York 2006, 119–125.

25 Bethell, *Abolition of the Brazilian Slave Trade*, 131.

26 These statistics refer to the 1831–41 period. On this, see Shaikh, Judicial Diplomacy, 51.

27 Bethell, Mixed Commissions, 79. For a map giving an overview of the slaves freed in the 1808–67 period and their geographic distribution, see Eltis/Richardson, *Atlas of the Transatlantic Slave Trade*, 289.

28 Report of the British commissioners in Sierra Leone to Foreign Secretary Canning, 15 May 1824, in BFSP 12, 57.

29 Report of the British commissioners in Sierra Leone to Foreign Secretary Canning, 10 April 1825, in BFSP 13, 31.

30 Turnbull, *Travels in the West*, 41.

31 Bethell, Mixed Commissions, 89; Shaikh, Judicial Diplomacy, 48. Some freed slaves were also settled in the Cape Colony in modern South Africa. On this, see Christopher Saunders, Liberated Africans in Cape Colony in the First Half of the Nineteenth Century, *International Journal of African Historical Studies* 18/2 (1985), 223–239 at 236f. On the Mixed Commissions in Cape Town, see van Niekerk, British, Portuguese, and American Judges; Christopher Saunders, A Nineteenth Century Farce: The Anglo-Portuguese Mixed Commission at the Cape of Good Hope, *Quarterly Bulletin of the South African Library* 37 (1983), 298–302.

32 Originally named the 'Captured Negro Department', for political reasons it was renamed the 'Liberated African Department' in August 1822.

33 Letter from Governor Charles Turner to Earl Bathurst, 25 January 1826, in Newbury, *British Policy*, 185f. On this, see also Richard Meyer-Heiselberg, *Notes from Liberated African Department*, Uppsala 1967; Christopher Fyfe, *A Short History of Sierra Leone*, London 1979, 39–44, 48–55; Maeve Ryan, 'A Most Promising Field for Future Usefulness': The Church Missionary Society and the Liberated Africans of Sierra Leone, Mulligan/Bric, eds., *Global History*, 37–58.

34 Letter from the British commissioners in Sierra Leone to Viscount Palmerston, 20 September 1841, in BPP 21 Class A, 31.

35 Ibid., 219, 224f., 230; Further Papers Relating to Captured Negroes Enlisted, and to the Recruiting of Negro Soldiers in Africa for the West India Regiments, in BPP 61, 611–628.

36 On these abductions, see Meyer-Heiselberg, *Notes*, XI; Fyfe, *History of Sierra Leone*, 183f.

37 The Portuguese term used in Brazil was *africanos livres*.

38 Robert Conrad, Neither Slave nor Free: The Emancipados of Brazil, 1818–1868, *Hispanic American Historical Review* 53/1 (February 1973), 50–70 at 51f.

39 Turnbull, *Travels in the West*, 162.

40 Martínez-Fernández, Havana Anglo-Spanish Mixed Commission, 210f.; Letter from Viscount Palmerston to Bulwer, 3 August 1846, in AHN, Estado, Esclavitud, Legajo 8040.

41 Turnbull, *Travels in the West*, 161f.; William Dougal Christie, *Notes on Brazilian Questions*, London 1865, 47–49; Conrad, Neither Slave nor Free, 61.

42 Martínez-Fernández, Havana Anglo-Spanish Mixed Commission, 213; Conrad, Neither Slave nor Free, 59–61; Letter from Crawford to Lord Clarendon, 3 January 1855, in BPP 41 Class B, 563; Letter from Crawford to Lord Clarendon, 1 June 1855, in AHN, Estado, Esclavitud, Legajo 8048; Letter from Stephen to Backhouse, 19 January 1839, in BPP 17 Class A, 124; Letter from Strangways to Stephen, 4 February 1839, in ibid., 125.

43 Ibid., 214.

44 Turnbull, *Travels in the West*, 75.

45 Ibid., 76; Conrad, *World of Sorrow*, 160–166.

46 Letter from Hudson to Palmerston, 11 November 1850, quoted in Christie, *Notes on Brazilian Questions*, 35.

47 See Article 13 of the treaty between Great Britain and Spain, 28 June 1835, in TNA, FO 93/99/18A.

48 Murray, *Odious Commerce*, 120f.

49 Turnbull, *Travels in the West*, 42; Martínez-Fernández, Havana Anglo-Spanish Mixed Commission, 207. The office of the Superintendent of Liberated Africans was abolished in 1843. On this, see Murray, *Odious Commerce*, 158.

50 David R. Murray, Richard Robert Madden: His Career as a Slavery Abolitionist, *Studies: An Irish Quarterly Review* 61 (1972), 41–53 at 48; Turnbull, *Travels in the West*, 164. For Madden's views on slavery in Cuba, see Richard Robert Madden, *Address on Slavery in Cuba Presented to the General Anti-Slavery Convention*, London 1840.

51 Murray, Madden, 49; Murray, *Odious Commerce*, 123–127. HMS *Romney* served in this function till 1845, when it was sold to Spain.

52 On this, see Letter from Viscount Palmerston to the British commissioners, 26 April 1839, in BPP 17 Class A, 146; Letter from Quseley to Viscount Palmerston, 14 April 1840, in BPP 20 Class B, 155; Letter from Quseley to Viscount Palmerston, 24 September 1840, in ibid., 188f.

53 *Hulk* denotes a ship that has been decommissioned and can no longer move unaided. Hulks were moored offshore and used as dwellings and prisons or for storage.

54 Letter from Captain General Ezpeleta to the British commissioners in Havana, 20 December 1838, in BPP 17 Class A, 101; Letter from Evaristo Perez de Castro to Henry Southern, 3 April 1839, in BPP 17 Class B, 11.

55 Letter from the British commissioners in Havana to the Spanish captain general, 17 December 1838, in BPP 17 Class A, 100.

56 On this, see also the role of George Backhouse, commissary judge in Havana from 1852 to 1855. Martínez-Fernández, *Fighting Slavery*, 54f.

57 Luis Martínez-Fernández, *Torn between Empires: Economy, Society, and Patterns of Political Thought in the Hispanic Caribbean, 1840–1878*, Athens, OH 1994, 14–16; Murray, *Odious Commerce*, 133–158.

58 Letter from Viscount Palmerston to Bulwer, 14 December 1846, in BFSP 35, 409.

59 For a detailed account of British efforts, see Christie, *Notes on Brazilian Questions*, 1–50.

60 Martínez-Fernández, Havana Anglo-Spanish Mixed Commission, 217–220; Martínez-Fernández, *Torn between Empires*, 34f.

61 Conrad, *World of Sorrow*, 166–170; Bethell, *Abolition of the Brazilian Slave Trade*, 383.

62 This manner of the Mixed Commissions in Havana and Rio de Janeiro clearly refutes Jenny Martinez's claim that these tribunals had been 'the first international human rights courts'. On this, see Martinez, *Slave Trade*, 6.

63 Robert Jameson, *Letters from the Havana during the Year 1820; Containing an Account of the Present State of the Island of Cuba and Observations on the Slave Trade*, London 1821, 25.

64 Ibid., 26f.

65 Ibid., 35.

66 According to estimates by Paul Lovejoy, the number of captured Africans even increased, to 599,600 for the 1811–20 period and 694,000 for 1821–30. On this, see Lovejoy, *Transformations in Slavery*, 146. Other estimates, such as those by David Eltis and David Richardson, confirm the picture. They reach a figure of 603,000 abductees between 1808 and 1817 and 795,000 between 1818 and 1827. On this, see Eltis/Richardson, *Atlas of the Transatlantic Slave Trade*, 274.

67 For the creation of an international abolitionist regime, see Nadelmann, Global Prohibition Regimes, 491–498; Renee de Nevers, Imposing International Norms: Great Powers and Norm Enforcement, *International Studies Review* 9/1 (Spring 2007), 53–80.

68 On Brazilian independence, see Roderick J. Barman, *Brazil: The Forging of a Nation, 1798–1852*, Stanford, CA 1988.

69 Canning's Memorandum for the Cabinet, 15 November 1822, in Charles K. Webster, ed., *Britain and the Independence of Latin America 1812–1830*, vol. 2, New York 1970, 397f.

70 Letter from Canning to Wellington, 27 September 1822, ibid., 74.

71 Webster, *Britain and the Independence of Latin America*, vol. 1, 54, 76; James Ferguson King, The Latin-American Republics and the Suppression of the Slave Trade, *Hispanic American Historical Review* 24/3 (August 1944), 387–411 at 388f.

72 Law of Buenos Ayres, of November 15, 1824, declaring Slave Trade Piracy, in AHN, ESTADO, Legajo 8047/8, N. 22; Act of the Congress of Colombia, of February 14, 1825, declaring Slave Trade Piracy, in AHN, ESTADO, Legajo 8047/8, N. 24.

73 King, Latin-American Republics, 392f. On this, see also Letter from Viscount Strangford to Viscount Castlereagh, 30 November 1814, in TNA, FO 63/169.

See Article 14 of the Treaty of Amity, Commerce, and Navigation, between His Majesty and the United Provinces of Rio de la Plata, 2 February 1825, in Lewis Hertslet, ed., *A Complete Collection of the Treaties and Conventions, and Reciprocal Regulations at Present Subsisting between Great Britain and Foreign Powers*, vol. 3, London 1841, 49. See Article 13 of the Treaty of Amity, Commerce, and Navigation, between Great Britain and Colombia, 18 April 1825, in ibid., 61. See Article 15 of the Treaty of Amity, Commerce, and Navigation, between Great Britain and Mexico, 26 December 1826, in ibid., 254.

74 On this, see Confidential Brazil Slave Trade Bill Memorandum, 3 July 1845, in TNA, FO 881/318, 2f.

75 On the negotiations between Great Britain and Brazil, see Leslie Bethell, The Independence of Brazil and the Abolition of the Brazilian Slave Trade: Anglo-Brazilian Relations, 1822–1826, *Journal of Latin American Studies* 1/2 (November 1969), 115–147.

76 On this, see Secret Letter from Canning to Chamberlain, 15 February 1823, in Webster, *Britain and the Independence of Latin America*, vol. 1, 220f.; Secret Letter from Chamberlain to Canning, 31 December 1823, in ibid., 232–234.

77 Articles 2 and 4 of the Convention between Great Britain and Brazil for the Abolition of the African Slave Trade, 23 November 1826, in BFSP 14, 610f. For a detailed account of these lengthy negotiations, see Bethell, *Abolition of the Brazilian Slave Trade*, 47–61.

78 Article 1 of the Convention between Britain and Brazil, in BFSP 14, 610.

79 Mason, Keeping Up Appearances, 814; Allain, Nineteenth Century Law, 365–367.

80 De Nevers, Imposing International Norms, 65–68.

81 Allain, Nineteenth Century Law, 361f.; Keene, Case Study of the Construction of International Hierarchy, 321f.

82 Letter from Rush to Adams, 15 April 1818, in BFSP 7, 376f.; Letter from Castlereagh to Rush, 20 June 1818, in ibid., 378f.

83 Charles Francis Adams, ed., *Memoirs of John Quincy Adams, Comprising Portions of His Diary 1795–1848*, vol. 4, New York 1969, 150–152.

84 For the official rejection of the British proposal, see Letter from Rush to Castlereagh, 21 December 1818, in BFSP 7, 381–383; Letter from Adams to Rush and Gallatin, 2 November 1818, in ibid., 220–222. See also Negotiation between Great Britain and the United States for the Extinction of the Slave Trade, *The National Recorder* (4 September 1819).

85 For constitutional misgivings about joining the Mixed Commission system, see Kontorovich, Constitutionality of International Courts, 39–115. With reference to the nineteenth century, Kontorovich also draws analogies with the United States' present stance on international courts.

86 Letter from Adams to Rush and Gallatin, 2 November 1818, in BFSP 7, 221.

87 'That the admission of a right in the Officers of Foreign Ships of War to enter and search the Vessels of The United States in time of Peace, under any circumstances whatever, would meet with universal repugnance in the public opinion of this Country. That there would be no prospect of a Ratification by advice and consent of the Senate, to any Stipulation of that nature.' Ibid., 222.

88 Robert E. Cray, Jr, Remembering the USS Chesapeake: The Politics of Maritime Death and Impressment, *Journal of the Early Republic* 25/3 (Autumn 2005), 445–474.

89 On the official reasons for going to war given by James Madison, see his message to Congress of 1 June 1812, in Annals of Congress, House of Representative, 12th Congress, 1st Session, 1624–1630. Mlada Kukovansky, American Identity and Neutral Rights from Independence to the War of 1812, *International Organization* 51/2 (Spring 1997), 209–243.

90 Paul A. Gilje, 'Free Trade and Sailors' Rights': The Rhetoric of the War of 1812, *Journal of the Early Republic* 30/1 (Spring 2010), 1–23. On the background to and course of the 1812–15 war, see e.g. Bradford Perkins, ed., *The Causes of the War of 1812: National Honor or National Interest?*, New York 1976; J. C. A. Stagg, *The War of 1812: Conflict for a Continent*, Cambridge 2012.

91 Matthew E. Mason, The Battle of the Slaveholding Liberators: Great Britain, the United States, and Slavery in the Early Nineteenth Century, *William and Mary Quarterly* 59/3 (July 2002), 665–696 at 670f.

92 For the negotiations over impressment, see Letter from Rush to Adams, 26 June 1818, in Message from the President of the United States Transmitting the Correspondence between the Government of the United States and Great Britain Relating to the Negotiation of the Convention of 20th October 1818, Washington 1823, 65–71; Letter from Adams to Rush and Gallatin, 2 November 1818, in BFSP 7, 217–220.

93 Letter from Rush to Adams, 26 June 1818, in Message from the President of the United States Transmitting the Correspondence between the Government of the United States and Great Britain Relating to the Negotiation of the Convention of 20th October 1818, Washington 1823, 67.

94 On these negotiations, see Hugh G. Soulsby, *The Right of Search and the Slave Trade in Anglo-American Relations 1814–1862*, Baltimore, MD 1933, 17–26; Samuel F. Bemis, *John Quincy Adams and the Foundation of American Foreign Policy*, New York 1949, 424f.

95 Adams' reply to Ambassador Canning, 4 December 1821, in Adams, ed., *Memoirs of John Quincy Adams*, vol. 5448.

96 Adams' justification for rejecting the British proposal in discussion with Canning, 2 October 1820, in ibid., 182.

97 Letter from Adams to Canning, 15 August 1821, in BFSP 9, 82.

98 Adams' reply to Ambassador Canning, 29 June 1822, in Adams, ed., *Memoirs of John Quincy Adams*, vol. 6, 37.

99 An Act in Addition to the Acts Prohibiting the Slave Trade, 3 March 1819, in Edward Ingersoll, ed., *A Digest of the Laws of the United States of America from March 4th, 1789, to May 15th, 1820*, Philadelphia, PA 1821, 804–806.

100 See ibid., sec. II, 805.

101 Message from the President of the United States to Congress, relative to the execution, on the Coast of Africa of the Acts of Congress, prohibiting the Slave Trade, 17 December 1819, in BFSP 6, 1120–1122.

102 On this, see Fehrenbacher, *Slaveholding Republic*, 153–155; Donald L. Canney, *Africa Squadron: The U.S. Navy and the Slave Trade,*

1842–1861, Washington, DC 2006, 8–12; Everill, *Abolition and Empire*, 22–29, 55–78.

103 On this, see e.g.: Report of the Secretary of the Navy, 7 February 1821, in BFSP 9, 71. On the operations of the US Navy in this period, see Lloyd, *Navy and the Slave Trade*, 50–52, 176; Canney, *Africa Squadron*, 8–27.

104 Act of Congress of the United States, to continue in force 'An Act to protect the Commerce of The United States and punish the Crime of Piracy', and also to make Provisions for punishing the Crime of Slave Trading, as Piracy, 15 May 1820, in BFSP 7, 824–826.

105 On this, see Act for the More Effectual Suppression of the African Slave Trade, 31 March 1824, in BFSP 11, 122f.

106 Nathaniel Gordon, the American captain of the seized slaver *Erie*, was executed in New York on 21 February 1862. On this, see Letter from Consul Archibald to Russell, 24 February 1862, in TNA, FO 881/4196.

107 Conversation between Adams and Canning, 2 October 1820, in Adams, *Memoirs of John Quincy Adams*, vol. 5, 184.

108 See e.g. Letter from Adams to Canning, 30 December 1820, in BFSP 8, 398f.; Letter from Adams to Canning, 15 August 1821, in BFSP 9, 82f.; Conversation between Adams and S. Canning, 29 June 1822, in Adams, *Memoirs of John Quincy Adams*, vol. 6, 36.

109 On the resolution and the subsequent debate of 28 February 1823, see Annals of Congress, House of Representatives, 17th Congress, 2nd Session, 1147–1155.

110 Letter from Adams and S. Canning, 30 March 1823, in BFSP 10, 261–263. On the further course of negotiations, see Soulsby, *Right of Search*, 27–35.

111 Adams' statements to the cabinet, 19 June 1823, in Adams, *Memoirs of John Quincy Adams*, vol. 6, 148f.

112 Letter from Adams to S. Canning, 24 June 1823, in BFSP 11, 416–420.

113 Letter from Adams to Rush, 24 June 1823, in Ashbury Dickins/James C. Allen, eds., *American State Papers: Documents, Legislative and Executive of the Congress of the United States*, vol. 5, Washington, DC 1858, 335.

114 'In compliance with a resolution of the House of Representatives, adopted at their last session, instructions have been given to all the Ministers of the United States accredited to the Power of Europe and America, to propose the proscription of the African slave trade, by classing it under the denomination, and inflicting on its perpetrators the punishment of piracy. Should this proposal be acceded to, it is not doubted that this odious and criminal practice will be promptly and entirely suppressed.' Monroe's State of the Union Address, 2 December 1823, quoted in Annals of Congress, Senate, 18th Congress, 1st Session, 15.

115 On the substance of the convention of 13 March 1824, which contained all the points proposed by Adams, see BFSP 12, 838–844.

116 On the dimension of domestic politics, see Adams' diary entries of 7 May 1824 and 23 May 1824, in Adams, *Memoirs of John Quincy Adams*, vol. 6, 321f., 350f.; Soulsby, *Right of Search*, 35–38; Bemis, *John Quincy Adams*, 434f.

117 On the vote and the changes made to the convention, see Dickins/Allen, *American State Papers*, vol. 5, 359–362; Letter from Adams to Rush, 29 May 1824, in ibid., 362f.

118 Letter from Canning to Rush, 27 August 1824, in ibid., 364f.; Letter from Rush to Adams, 30 August 1824, in ibid., 364.

119 Allain, Nineteenth Century Law, 368–371; Kern, Strategies of Legal Change, 246–249.

120 Treaty between His Britannick Majesty and His Majesty the King of Sweden and Norway, for Preventing their Subjects from Engaging in any Traffick in Slaves, 6 November 1824, in BFSP 12, 3–14.

121 On this, see e.g. Note sur le projet d'une ligue maritime pour assurer l'abolition de la traite et la repression de la piraterie des Barbaresques, n. d., in MAE, MD A 15; Mémoire Français sur la Traite des Nègres, in BFSP 6, 69–75; Note sur la traite des noirs, October 1818, in MAE, MD A 15; Kielstra, Politics of Slave Trade Suppression, 86–95, 119–124.

122 Mémoire Français sur la Traite des Nègres, in BFSP 6, 69–75; Confidential letter from the French navy office to the French foreign ministry, 3 March 1824, in MAE, MD A 26. For British charges against France for continuing the slave trade under its own flag, see e.g. Annual Report von Commodore Collier, 16 September 1820, in Newbury, ed., British Policy, 140–142; Letter from the French consul in London to the French naval minister, 7 November 1820, in MAE, MD A 24; Letter from Canning to Percy, 13 November 1824, in BFSP 12, 330–333; Letter from Granville to Baron de Damas, 20 November 1824, in TNA, ADM 1/5123/11; Letter from Baron de Damas to Granville, 23 November 1824, in ibid.; Letter from Granville to Baron de Damas, 4 June 1825, in MAE, MD A 26; Letter from Canning to Granville, 8 September 1825, in BFSP 13, 261f.

123 Ordinance of the King of France, 24 June 1818, in BFSP 8, 315f.; Letter from the Duc de Richelieu to Charles Stuart, 9 July 1818, in ibid., 317.

124 On the operations of the French naval squadron, see esp. Daget, La répression de la traite des Noirs, 211–246; Serge Daget, Tactiques, stratégies et effets du droit de visite, in Serge Daget, ed., De la traite à l'esclavage: Actes du Colloque international sur la traite des Noirs, Nantes 1988, 343–358.

125 Mason, Keeping Up Appearances, 819. For the French perspective on these operations, see Note sur les dispositions qui ont été faites ou provoquées par le départment de la Marine avant et depuis les conventions de November 1815 pour la repression du trafic connu sous le noms de Traite des Noirs, February 1820, in MAE, MD A 24; Observations confidentielles à l'occassion des communications faites au Ministre de la Marine, 23 January 1821, in MAE, MD A 25; Confidential letter from the naval office to the foreign ministry, 3 February 1821, in ibid.

126 Loi relative à la Répression de la Traite des Noirs, 25 April 1827, in BFSP 15, 451f.; Serge Daget, The Abolition of the Slave Trade by France: The Decisive Years 1826–1831, in David Richardson, ed., Abolition and Its Aftermath: The Historical Context, 1790–1916, London 1985, 141–167.

127 Letter from Dudley to Hamilton, 8 May 1827, in BFSP 15, 452.

128 Daget, La répression de la traite des Noirs, 330–338. For an overview and appraisal of French naval operations between 1815 and 1831 see ibid., 363–407.

129 Ibid., 346.

130 Ibid., 358f.
131 'Le souvenir de Navarin ne peut manquer de rendre plus intimes les rap-
     ports qui, jusqu' à present, ont existé entre les deux stations.' Quoted from a
     report by Villaret de Joyeuse to the French naval office, 12 January 1828, in
     SHD, Marine, BB 4/504.
132 Jennings, *French Anti-Slavery*, 24–47.
133 Kielstra, *Politics of Slave Trade Suppression*, 148. For the role of the French
     abolitionists associated with the Société de la morale chrétienne, see
     Lawrence C. Jennings, French Anti-Slavery under the Restoration: The
     Société de la morale chrétienne, *Revue française d'histoire d'outre-mer*, 81/
     304 (1994), 321–331.
134 On this, see Loi de France, concernant la Répression de la Traite des Noirs,
     4 March 1831, in MAE, MD A 27.
135 For the French perspective on these negotiations, see Correspondance
     relative à la déclaration du gouvernement au sujet de la traite comme gage
     d'entente entre La France et l'Angleterre, 29 November 1831, in MAE, CP
     A 635.
136 Convention between Great Britain and France, for the More Effectual
     Suppression of the Traffic in Slaves, 30 November 1831, in BFSP 18,
     641–644.
137 See Article 1 of the Convention, in ibid., 642.
138 See Article 7 of the Convention, in ibid., 644.
139 Supplementary Convention between His Majesty and the King of the
     French, for the More Effectual Suppression of the Traffic in Slaves,
     22 March 1833, in BFSP 20, 286–301.
140 Kielstra, *Politics of Slave Trade Suppression*, 179; Daget, Abolition of the
     Slave Trade, 162.
141 Letter from Palmerston to Granville, 23 January 1834, in BFSP 23, 102f.;
     Letter from Duc de Broglie to Granville, 1 February 1834, in ibid., 103f.;
     Letter from Talleyrand to Broglie 'au sujet des négociations anglo-
     américaine visant les États-Unies à adhérer aux conventions abolissant la
     traite', 13 May 1833, in MAE, CP A 641; Letter from Palmerston to
     Metternich, 7 May 1834, in HHStA, MdÄ AR F39 1.
142 Kielstra, *Politics of Slave Trade Suppression*, 163f.
143 Letter from M'Lane to Vaughan, 24 March 1834, in BFSP 23, 139f.; Letter
     from Vaughan to Serurier, 21 August 1834, in ibid., 143; Letter from
     Serurier to Forsyth, 12 September 1834, in ibid., 144f.; Letter from
     Forsyth to Vaughan, 4 October 1834, in MAE, MD A 18.
144 Treaty between Great Britain and France and Denmark containing the
     Accession of Denmark to the Conventions of 1831 and 1833, between
     Great Britain and France, for the More Effectual Suppression of the Slave
     Trade, 26 July 1834, in BFSP 22, 218–222; Treaty between Great Britain
     and France, and Sardinia, for the More Effectual Suppression of the Slave
     Trade, 8 December 1834, in ibid., 1059–1067.
145 The diplomatic correspondence of the accession negotiations and the final
     treaties can be found e.g. in MAE, MD A 19; Kielstra, *Politics of Slave Trade
     Suppression*, 164–171.

146 The treaties with Spain, Brazil and the Netherlands stipulate in addition that captured slave ships were to go on public sale not in their entirety, but broken up into their component parts. The idea was to prevent slave traders from simply buying back their ships and returning them to use in the slave trade. On this, see e.g. Treaty between His Majesty and the Queen Regent of Spain, during the Minority of Her Daughter, Donna Isabella the Second, Queen of Spain, for the Abolition of the Slave Trade, 28 June 1835, in BFSP 23, 343–355. For the equipment clause see Article X, 351–353 and for provisions concerning the breaking-up of ships see Article XII, 354.

147 The treaties with the Argentine Federation, Uruguay, Bolivia and Ecuador were based directly on the treaty of 1835, while Peru, Chile, Venezuela and Mexico signed similar treaties.

148 On this, see Letter from Aberdeen 'Commission of Appointment under the Treaty with the Oriental Republic of the Uruguay', 2 August 1842, in BFSP 32, 149f.; Letter from Aberdeen 'Commission of Appointment under Treaty with Chile', 13 October 1843, in ibid., 147f.; Letter from Aberdeen 'Commission of Appointment under Treaty with Bolivia', 13 October 1843, in ibid., 135f.; Letter from Mandeville to Aberdeen, 26 November 1842, in ibid., 310f.; Letter from Mandeville to Aberdeen, 18 July 1843, in ibid., 311f.

149 On the Slave Trade Department, see Lypka, Slave Trade Department; Keith Hamilton, Zealots and Helots: The Slave Trade Department of the Nineteenth-Century Foreign Office, in Hamilton/Salmon, eds., *Slavery, Diplomacy and Empire*, 20–41.

150 James Bandinel, Memorandum on the Means to Be Taken by Great Britain for Putting Down the Slave Trade, 30 March 1839, in TNA, FO 881/533.

151 Ibid., 5–9.

152 Britain signed such a treaty with Madagascar as early as 1817. On this, see Treaty between Great Britain and Madagsacar, 23 October 1817, in Lewis Hertslet, ed., *A Complete Collection of the Treaties and Conventions and Reciprocal Regulations at Present Subsisting between Great Britain and Foreign Powers*, vol. 1, London 1820, 354–356. A treaty with the sultan of Muscat followed in 1822 and was expanded in 1839. On this, see Treaty between Great Britain and Muscat, 10 September 1822, in T. R. Harrison, ed., *Treaties, Conventions and Engagements, for the Suppression of the Slave Trade*, London 1844, 274–276; Article XV of the Convention of Commerce between Her Majesty and the Imaum of Muscat, 31 May 1839, in ibid., 277f.

153 Bandinel, Memorandum on the Means to Be Taken by Great Britain for Putting Down the Slave Trade, 2.

154 Buxton, *African Slave Trade*, 283–300. On Buxton's life and work, see David Bruce, *The Life of Sir Thomas Fowell Buxton: Extraordinary Perseverance*, Plymouth 2014.

155 On the Niger expedition of 1841, see Howard Temperley, *White Dreams, Black Africa: The Antislavery Expedition to the Niger 1841–1842*, New Haven, CT 1991.

156 Lord John Russell, 'Instructions to Her Majesty's Niger Commissioners', 30 January 1841, in Newbury, ed., *British Policy*, 154–159.

157 Draft Agreement with African Chiefs, July 1840, in Newbury, ed., *British Policy*, 150–153; Keene, Case Study of the Construction of International Hierarchy, 326–329.

158 House of Commons, 'The Niger Expedition', 4 March 1842, in Newbury, ed., *British Policy*, 161f.

159 James Bandinel, *Some Account of the Trade in Slaves from Africa as Connected with Europe and America*, London 1842, 296f. For the Admirality guidelines, see Instructions for the Senior Officers of Her Majesty's Ships and Vessels on the African Stations, for Negotiating with Chiefs of Africa, 12 June 1844, in Both Houses of Parliament, ed., *Instructions for the Guidance of Her Majesty's Naval Officers Employed in the Suppression of the Slave Trade*, London, July 1844, 15–17, in TNA, FO 115/87.

160 All these agreements with African rulers made between 1827 and 1861 are reprinted in Her Majesty's Stationery Office, ed., *Supplement to the Slave Trade Instructions*, vol. II: *Engagements with Uncivilized African States*, London 1865. France, too, began to conclude such agreements with African rulers, albeit on a rather smaller scale. On this, see e.g. Treaty between France and Lahou, 6 July 1845, in BFSP 35, 682f.; Treaty between France and Grand Bassam, 10 July 1845, in ibid., 683f.

161 Nadelmann, Global Prohibition Regimes, 491–498; Quirk, *Anti-Slavery Project*, 60, 72–74. A good overview of the many legal documents, treaties and agreements concerning the slave trade between 1776 and 1863 can be found in: Slave Trade Suppression Tables; or A Chronologically arranged Statement of the Measures taken by different Nations for the Abolition of the Slave Trade, in Her Majesty's Stationery Office, ed., *Slave Trade Instructions, Being Instructions for the Guidance of the Commanders of Her Majesty's Ships of War Employed in the Suppression of the Slave Trade*, London 1865, 131–142.

162 On emancipation in the British colonies in the Americas, Mauritius and the Cape Colony in 1833, see Drescher, *Abolition*, 245–266. There are many other examples of this discrepancy, with France (1848), the United States (1862), Spain (Cuba; 1886) and Brazil (1888) ending slavery years or decades after abolition of the slave trade. On this, see Jennings, *French Anti-Slavery*, 281; Drescher, *Abolition*, 333–371; Laird W. Bergad, *The Comparative Histories of Slavery in Brazil, Cuba, and the United States*, Cambridge 2007, 251–290; Blackburn, *American Crucible*, 391–454.

163 On this distinction in international law, see Quirk, *Anti-Slavery Project*, 57f., 73f.; Robin Law, Abolition and Imperialism: International Law and the British Suppression of the Atlantic Slave Trade, in Derek R. Peterson, ed., *Abolitionism and Imperialism in Britain, Africa, and the Atlantic*, Athens, OH 2010, 150–174 at 166–170.

164 James Stephen, Colonial Office Minute, 6 September 1841, in TNA, CO 87/25.

165 On this, see Her Majesty's Stationery Office, *Slave Trade Instructions*, 5–7; Her Majesty's Stationery Office, ed., *Supplement to the Slave Trade Instructions*, vol. I: *Treaty Engagements with States other than Uncivilized African States*, London 1865; Her Majesty's Stationery Office, *Supplement to the Slave Trade Instructions*, vol. II.

166 On the construction of this hierarchy in international law, see also Keene, Case Study of the Construction of International Hierarchy, 311–339; Pitts, Boundaries, 67–88; Bell, Empire and International Relations, 289–291.

167 Letter from Canning to Wellington, 30 September 1822, in Arthur Wellesley of Wellington, ed., *Despatches, Correspondence, and Memoranda of Field Marshal Arthur Duke of Wellington*, vol. 1, London 1867, 329.

168 It is remarkable how this early-nineteenth-century view of sovereignty seems to prefigure the idea of a 'responsibility to protect' developed in the early twenty-first century.

169 On this, see Bethell, Britain, Portugal and the Suppression of the Brazilian Slave Trade; Bandinel, *Some Account of the Trade*, 214–226; Ryan, Price of Legitimacy, 242–247.

170 Act of the British Parliament, 'for the Suppression of the Slave Trade'; and the Seizure of Certain Portuguese and Other Vessels Engaged in Such Trade, 24 August 1839, in Lewis Hertslet, ed., *A Complete Collection of the Treaties and Conventions, and Reciprocal Regulations at Present Subsisting between Great Britain and Foreign Powers*, vol. 5, London 1840, 427–431. For the parliamentary debate and Palmerston's arguments, see 8 August 1839, in T. C. Hansard, ed., *The Parliamentary Debates from the Year 1803 to the Present Time*, vol. 50, London 1839 (New York 1970), cc. 117–132; Howard Hazen Wilson, Some Principal Aspects of British Efforts to Crush the African Slave Trade, 1807–1929, *American Journal of International Law* 44/3 (July 1950), 505–526 at 511–514; for the relevant instructions to the Royal Navy, see Letter from Palmerston to Admiralty, 15 August 1839, in TNA, FO 84/302. For this return to the Courts of Vice Admiralty and particularly that set up at St Helena, see J. P. van Niekerk, The Role of the Vice-Admiralty Court at St Helena in the Abolition of the Transatlantic Slave Trade: A Preliminary Investigation, pt. 1, *Fundamina: A Journal of Legal History* 15/1 (2009), 69–111; J. P. van Niekerk, The Role of the Vice-Admiralty Court at St Helena in the Abolition of the Transatlantic Slave Trade: A Preliminary Investigation, pt. 2, *Fundamina: A Journal of Legal History* 15/2 (2009), 1–56; Andrew Pearson, *Distant Freedom: St Helena and the Abolition of the Slave Trade, 1840–1872*, Liverpool 2016.

171 Allain, Nineteenth Century Law, 365–367; van Niekerk, British, Portuguese, and American Judges, pt. 1, 27–30.

172 Treaty between Her Majesty and the Queen of Portugal, for the Suppression of the Traffick in Slaves, 3 July 1842, in TNA, FO 312/1; Bethell, Britain, Portugal, 781–784.

173 Eltis, *Economic Growth*, 87, 95.

174 Lord Aberdeen, in the debate of 2 August 1842, quoted in T. C. Hansard, ed., *The Parliamentary Debates from the Year 1803 to the Present Time*, vol. 65, London 1842 (New York 1970), cc. 935–936.

175 Letter from Hamilton to Aberdeen, 22 March 1845, in TNA, FO 84/581.

176 Confidential Memorandum 'Brazil Slave Trade Bill of 1845', 7 July 1845, in TNA, FO 420/3; Note from the Earl of Aberdeen to Commander Marques Lisboa, 6 August 1845, in ibid.; Wilbur Devereux Jones, The Origins and Passage of Lord Aberdeen's Act, *Hispanic American Historical Review* 42/4 (November 1962), 502–520.

177   Act of the British Parliament, 'to amend an Act, intituled an Act to carry into execution a Convention between His Majesty and the Emperor of Brazil, for the Regulation and final Abolition of the African Slave Trade', 8 August 1845, in BFSP 34, 1216–1219; Bethell, *Abolition of the Brazilian Slave Trade*, 242–266.

178   Andrew Lambert, Slavery, Free Trade and Naval Strategy, 1840–1860, in Keith Hamilton/Patrick Salmon, eds., *Slavery, Diplomacy and Empire: Britain and the Suppression of the Slave Trade, 1807–1975*, Eastbourne 2009, 65–80 at 71–73; Rees, *Sweet Water and Bitter*, 278–280; Lloyd, *Navy and the Slave Trade*, 139–148.

179   Bethell, *Abolition of the Brazilian Slave Trade*, 327–363; Jeffrey D. Needell, The Abolition of the Brazilian Slave Trade in 1850: Historiography, Slave Agency and Statesmanship, *Journal of Latin American Studies* 33/4 (November 2001), 681–711.

180   Allain, Nineteenth Century Law, 367; de Nevers, Imposing International Norms, 65–67; Huzzey, *Freedom Burning*, 58–60.

181   Ryan, Price of Legitimacy, 247–250.

182   Le Baron da Ribiera de Sabrosa, Lettre Circulaire, 4 August 1839, in BFSP 28, 622–624.

183   Letter from Palmerston to General Alava, 30 September 1839, in ibid., 566f.

184   Letter from Palmerston to Earl Granville, 2 November 1839, in ibid., 795f.

185   Letter from Marshal Soult to Earl Granville, 29 November 1839, in ibid., 796f.

186   Ryan, Price of Legitimacy, 251–254. Joaquín Alcaide Fernández, Hostes Humani Generis: Pirates, Slavers, and Other Criminals, in Bardo Fassbender/Anne Peters, eds., *The Oxford Handbook of the History of International Law*, Oxford 2012, 120–144 at 130–132.

187   Kielstra, *Politics of Slave Trade Suppression*, 198f.

188   'We, therefore, by our Apostolic authority, reprobate all the above-mentioned practices as utterly unworthy of the Christian name; and by the same authority, we strictly prohibit and interdict any ecclesiastic or layman from presuming to defend the traffic in negroes as lawful.' Qtd. according to 'A Apostolic Letter of Our Most Holy Lord Gregory XVI, By Divine Providence Pope, Upon the Duty of Abstaining from the Traffic in Negroes', 3 December 1839, in TNA, FO 313/7. John F. Quinns, 'Three Cheers for the Abolitionist Pope!' American Reactions to Gregory XVI's Condemnation of the Slave Trade, 1840–1860, *Catholic Historical Review* 90/1 (January 2004), 67–93; Nicole Priesching, Die Verurteilung der Sklaverei unter Gregor XVI. im Jahr 1839: Ein Traditionsbruch?, *Saeculum. Jahrbuch für Universalgeschichte* 59/1 (2008), 143–162.

189   Wheaton, *Elements of International Law*, 114.

190   '[a] traffic so justly stigmatized by every civilized and Christian powers as a crime against humanity' and 'Public opinion stigmatizing the traffic as a crime against humanity', in Henry Wheaton, *Enquiry into the Validity of the British Claim to a Right of Visitation and Search of American Vessel Suspected to be Engaged in the African Slave Trade*, Philadelphia, PA 1842, 4, 16. For a further instance of the use of the term in this context, see Wheaton, *History*

of the Law of Nations, 594. Joseph Denman, who sailed against the slave trade with the Royal Navy, also used the term in 1850: 'Public opinion urged on an unwilling government all the efforts against the traffic at the Congress of Vienna; which, in declaring it a crime against humanity and universal morality, spoke the sentiments of the people of England.' On this, see Joseph Denman, *The Slave Trade, the African Squadron, and Mr. Hutt's Committee*, London [1850], 10. This evidence notwithstanding, Bruce Mazlish denies the abolitionist movement any part in this development, situating the context in the early twentieth century. On this, see Bruce Mazlish, *The Idea of Humanity in a Global Era*, New York 2009, 2, 15, 35–37.

191 The concept of a 'crime against humanity' is commonly associated with the Allied note of 28 May 1915 accusing the Ottoman Empire of atrocities against the Armenian population and with later instances of war crimes throughout the twentieth century. On the historical development of the concept, see Martinez, *Slave Trade*, 114–116; Kerstin von Lingen, Fullfilling the Martens Clause: Debating 'Crimes Against Humanity', 1899–1945, in Klose/Thulin, eds., *Humanity*, 187–208.

192 'The Slave Trade, though prohibited by the municipal laws of most nations, and declared to be piracy by the statues of Great Britain and the United States, is not such by the general international law, and its interdiction cannot be enforced by the exercise of the ordinary right of visitation and search. That right does not exist in time of peace, independently of special compact.' In Wheaton, *Elements of International Law*, 114–118 at 114. For Wheaton's staunch rejection of a right of visitation and search in peacetime, see esp. Wheaton, *Enquiry into the Validity*.

193 Protocol of a Conference held in London between Austria, France, Great Britain, Prussia, and Russia, relative to the Slave Trade, 12 December 1838, in BFSP 28, 1059–1060.

194 Letter from Palmerston to Hummelauer, 11 December 1839, in HHStA, MdÄ AR F39-1. On this, see also Letter from Palmerston to Estérhazy, 13 September 1839, in ibid.

195 Letter from Palmerston to Hummelauer, 11 December 1839, in ibid.

196 Treaty between Great Britain, Austria, France, Prussia, and Russia for the Suppression of the African Slave Trade, 20 December 1841, in TNA, FO 115/80.

197 See Article 1 of the treaty, in ibid., 5.

198 The area was set as extending from 32°N to 45°S latitude and the eastern coast of the Americas in the west and 80°E longitude in the east. The Mediterranean was expressly exempt from the right of search. See Article 2 of the treaty, in ibid., 5f.

199 'The names of the ships appointed for this purpose, and those of their Commanders, shall be communicated by each of the High Contracting Parties to the others; and they shall reciprocally apprize each other every time that a cruiser shall be placed on a station, or shall be recalled from thence, in order that the necessary Warrants may be delivered by the Governments authorizing the search, and returned to those Governments by the Governments which has received them, when those Warrants shall no

longer be necessary for the execution of the present Treaty.' See Article 3 of the treaty, in ibid., 6.

200 Numerous examples of such 'cruising warrants', in this case issued to British warships by the Austrian government, can be found in the files of the Haus-, Hof- und Staatsarchiv Vienna: HHStA, MdÄ AR F 39–3. For an example of an application for a 'cruising warrant', see British application to Austrian foreign ministry for 'H.M. Sloop "Prometheus", Commander N. B. Bedingfield', 25 November 1860, in ibid. For an example of an application for a 'cruising warrant' being rescinded, see British application to Austrian foreign ministry for 'HMS Buzzard, Commander P. H. Martin', 19 March 1866, in ibid.

201 Grewe, *Epochen*, 661f.

202 Belgium acceded to the Quintuple Treaty on 24 February 1848, as did the German Empire in its entirety on 29 March 1879. On the key role of the Quintuple Treaty in International Law, see Fischer, Suppression of Slavery, 45f.; Andrea Nicholson, Transformations in the Law Concerning Slavery: Legacies of the Nineteenth Century Anti-Slavery Movement, in Mulligan/ Bric, eds., *Global History*, 214–237 at 219f.

203 James C. Duram, A Study of Frustration: Britain, the USA, and the African Slave Trade, 1815–1870, *Social Science* 40/4 (October 1965), 220–225.

204 Letter from Aberdeen to Everett, 20 December 1841, in H. Doc. No. 192, 27th Congress, 3rd Session, 7–10 at 9.

205 Britain's alternative proposal to institute a 'right of visit' rather than a right of search – the visit having for its purpose only to ascertain the true nationality of the ship in question – made no difference to the American stance, being likewise flatly rejected by the US government. On the diplomatic arguments between Britain and the United States over these rights in the early 1840s, see e.g. Letter from Palmerston to Stevenson, 27 August 1841, in TNA, FO 881/164; Letter from Stevenson to Aberdeen, 10 September 1841, in ibid.; Letter from Aberdeen to Stevenson, 13 October 1841, in ibid.; Letter from Stevenson to Aberdeen, 21 October 1841, in ibid. On this, see also Richard W. van Alstyne, The British Right of Search and the African Slave Trade, *Journal of Modern History* 2/1 (March 1930), 37–47; Soulsby, *Right of Search*, 58–77. For a contemporary legal appraisal from an American perspective, see Wheaton, *Elements of International Law*, 347–351; Wheaton, *Enquiry into the Validity*; Wheaton, *History of the Law of Nations*, 585–699.

206 See Article 8 of the Treaty between Great Britain and the United States, to Settle and Define the Boundaries between the Possessions of Her Britannic Majesty in North America, and the Territories of the United States; for the final Suppression of the African Slave Trade; and for the Giving Up of Criminals, Fugitive from Justice, in Certain Cases, 9 August 1842, in BFSP 30, 365f.

207 Article 8 of the Treaty of 9 August 1842, in BFSP 30, 365f.

208 Message from the President of the United States, In compliance with a resolution of the Senate, on the subject of the communication of the Quintuple Treaty to the Government of the United States, 9 January 1843, in S. Doc. No. 52, 27th Congress, 3rd Session, 5. On this, see also

Message from the President of the United States Transmitting a Report from the Secretary of State, in Answer to the Resolution of the House of Representatives, 27 February 1843, in H. Doc. No. 192, 27th Congress, 3rd Session.

209 The Treaty of Ghent, signed on 24 December 1814, ended the war of 1812 (1812–15). Article 10 stated: 'Whereas the Traffic in Slaves is irreconcilable with the principles of humanity and Justice, and whereas both His Majesty and the United States are desirous of continuing their efforts to promote its entire abolition, it is hereby agreed that both the contracting parties shall use their best endeavours to accomplish so desirable an object.' See Treaty of Peace and Amity between His Britannic Majesty and the United States of America, 24 December 1814, http://avalon.law.yale.edu/19th_century/ghent .asp

210 Instructions from Upshur to Commander Perry, 15 March 1843, in BFSP 32, 456–462 at 457.

211 Ibid., 460.

212 On the mission of the US Navy's African Squadron, see Alan R. Booth, The United States African Squadron, 1843–1861, in Jeffrey Butler, ed., Boston University Paper in African History, vol. 1, Boston, MA 1964, 77–117; Calvin Lane, The African Squadron: The U.S. Navy and the Slave Trade, 1820–1862, Log of Mystic Seaport 50/4 (Spring 1999), 86–98; Canney, Africa Squadron. For a contemporary view from the perspective of John C. Lawrence, an officer in the US Navy, see C. Herbert Gilliland, Voyage to a Thousand Cares: Master's Mate Lawrence with the African Squadron, 1844–1846, Annapolis, MD 2004.

213 Canney, Africa Squadron, 222f.

214 Booth, United States African Squadron, 89–98; Canney, Africa Squadron, 56–58. Only the American Cicil War brought about a radical shift in US foreign policy, with President Lincoln signing a new treaty with the United Kingdom in April 1862. In Article 1, the United States agreed to a mutual right of search and, in Article 4, to setting up Mixed Commissions in Sierra Leone, Cape Town and New York, although no case was ever brought before any of them. See Treaty between the United States of America and Her Majesty the Queen of the United Kingdom of Great Britain and Ireland, for the Suppression of the African Slave Trade, 7 April 1862, in S.Ex.Doc. No. 57, 37th Congress, 2nd Session, 4–8.

215 Daget, La répression de la traite des Noirs, 487–528; Kielstra, Politics of Slave Trade Suppression, 207–233. On Ambassador Cass' propaganda efforts and American resistance to a mutual right of search, see Letter from Cass to Guizot, 13 February 1842, in MAE, MD A 18; Dépeche de Saint-Aulaire à Guizot relative à l'opposition des États-Unies au droit de visite mutuel des naivres et au traité sur l'abolition de la traite, 22 April 1842, in MAE, CP A 659.

216 Kielstra, Politics of Slave Trade Suppression, 217–221; Lawrence C. Jennings, France, Great Britain, and the Repression of the Slave Trade, 1841–1845, French Historical Studies 10/1 (Spring 1977), 101–125; Lawrence C. Jennings, Slave Trade Repression and the Abolition of French Slavery,

in Serge Daget, ed., *De la traite à l'esclavage: Actes du Colloque international sur la traite des Noirs*, Nantes 1988, 359–372. On France's growing commercial interests in West Africa, see e.g. Instructions from the French naval ministry to the commander of the African station, containing the points 'Protection du Commmerce' and 'Renseignements à fournir sur les opérations commerciales des anglais à la Côte Occidentales d'Afrique', 16 November 1842, in MAE, MD A 28.

217 Lawrence C. Jennings, The French Press and Great Britain's Campaign against the Slave Trade, 1830–1848, *Revue française d'histoire d'outre-mer* LXVII/246f. (1980), 5–24 at 9–20.

218 Protocole de la Conférence tenue au Foreign Office, 9 November 1842, in BFSP 30, 299f.

219 On this, see e.g. 'Par ces considérations de dignité et d'intérêt national, la France se croit en droit de proposer à l'Angleterre la conclusion d'un noveau traité sur les bases du traite conclu aves les États-Unis' Qtd. according to Le Duc De Valmy, Note sur le droit de visite, 23 December 1842, in MAE, MD A 15, 21–24 at 23.

220 On these negotiations, see Letter from de Broglie to Guizot, 31 March 1845, in MAE, MD A 22; Minutes des conférences tenues en présence de la Haute commission du Droit de Visite, April 1845, in ibid.; Confidential Memorandum from the Duke de Broglie, 4 May 1845, in TNA, FO 881/ 317; Daget, *La répression de la traite des Noirs*, 529–537. For the testimony of the British and French naval officers in particular, see Minutes of Evidence taken before the Duke de Broglie and the Rt. Hon. Stephen Lushington, 31 March 1845 and 1–4 April 1845, in TNA, FO 881/4178.

221 Convention between Her Majesty and the King of the French for the Suppression of the Traffic in Slaves, 29 May 1845, in TNA, FO 881/49.

222 Article 1 of the Convention, in ibid., 2.

223 Article 2 of the Convention, in ibid., 2. Another example: 'The officers ... having respectively the command of the squadrons of Great Britain and France, to be employed in carrying out this Convention, shall concert together as to the best means of watching strictly the parts of the African coast before described.' Article 3 of the Convention, in ibid., 3.

224 Article 5 of the Convention, in ibid., 3f. Once the convention had been concluded, the following stipulation was added to Article 5 of the standard agreement with the 'native chiefs': 'Power is hereby expressly reserved to his Majesty the King of the French to become a party to this Treaty, if he should think fit, agreeably to the provisions of the 5th article of the Convention between her Majesty and the King of the French, signed at London on the 29th of May, 1845.' See e.g. Article 5 of the 'Engagement between Her Majesty the Queen of England and the Chiefs of Jack Jacques for the Abolition of the Traffic in Slaves', 29 February 1848, in TNA, FO 93/6/3.

225 Article 6 of the Convention, in ibid., 4.

226 Kielstra, *Politics of Slave Trade Suppression*, 253–258.

227 Aberdeen's memorandum of December 1842 contains an exemplary statement of the need for international cooperation: 'Other nations must be induced to co-operate cordially with us, or the success of all our efforts will

be imperfect ... We must, by the perfect justice and openness of our proceedings, induce Foreign Powers to join Great Britain in the Christian and humane task, which, at immense coast and labour, she has imposed upon herself.' On this, see Earl of Aberdeen to Dr. Lushington, Mr. Bandinel, Captain Denman, and Mr. Rothery, Selected to Revise Instructions for Her Majesty's Naval Officers Employed in the Suppression of the Slave Trade, 14 December 1842, in TNA, FO 881/ 4175, 1f.

228 On this, see Lyons, *Internationalism in Europe*, 13–18; Herren, *Hintertüren zur Macht*, 12, 507; Laqua, *Age of Internationalism*, 5–7.

229 Wheaton, *Elements of International Law*, 114.

230 On this, see Fabian Klose, 'A War of Justice and Humanity': Abolition and Establishing Humanity as an International Norm, in Klose/Thulin, eds., *Humanity*, 169–186.

231 On the juridification of international relations in the nineteenth century generally, see Vec, Intervention/Nichtintervention, 135–160; Schulz, Macht, internationale Politik, 113–134.

232 Eltis, *Economic Growth*, 87; Serge Daget, The Abolition of the Slave Trade, in J. F. Ade Ajayi, ed., *General History of Africa*, vol. VI: *Africa in the Nineteenth Century until the 1880s*, Paris 1989, 64–89 at 70–73.

233 According to Paul Lovejoy's estimate, the number of enslaved Africans increased to 599,600 for the 1811–20 period and 694,400 between 1821 and 1830. On this, see Lovejoy, *Transformations in Slavery*, 146. Other estimates, such as that by David Eltis and David Richardson, point in the same direction. According to them, the numbers rose to 603,000 for the 1808–17 period and 795,000 for 1818–27. On this, see Eltis/Richardson, *Atlas of the Transatlantic Slave Trade*, 274.

234 For a precise balance sheet of these measures, see Eltis, *Economic Growth*, 97–101. According to Seymour Drescher's estimates, in spite of all measures against it, the overall volume of the Atlantic slave trade declined by only 5 per cent between 1826 and 1850. Drescher, *Abolition*, 245.

235 According to Paul Lovejoy's estimate, the number of enslaved Africans decreased from 435,300 for the 1841–50 period to 179,100 for 1851–60 and finally to 52,600 for 1861–67. On this, see Lovejoy, *Transformations in Slavery*, 146. Other estimates, such as that by David Eltis and David Richardson, point in the same direction. According to them, the numbers dropped from 643,000 for the 1838–47 period to 308,000 for 1848–57 and again to 135,000 for 1858–63. On this, see Eltis/Richardson, *Atlas of the Transatlantic Slave Trade*, 274.

236 Drescher, Emperors of the World, 146; Joel Quirk/David Richardson, Anti-Slavery, European Identity and International Society: A Macro-historical Perspective, *Journal of Modern European History* 7/1 (2009), 68–92 at 78–84.

Part III

1 J. Leighton Wilson, *The British Squadron on the Coast of Africa*, London 1850, 12f.

2 John Stuart Mill, A Few Words on Non-Intervention, December 1859, in John Stuart Mill, *Dissertations and Discussions Political, Philosophical, and Historical Reprinted Chiefly from the Edinburgh and Westminster Reviews*, vol. 3, London 1867, 153–178 at 153.

Chapter 7

1 On this, see Curtin, *Image of Africa*, 95–119; Basil Davidson, *Black Mother: Africa; the Years of Trial*, London 1961, 242f.; Austen/Smith, Images of Africa and British Slave-Trade Abolition, 69–83; Ronald Robinson/John Gallagher, *Africa and the Victorians: The Official Mind of Imperialism*, London 1981, 27–52; Ronald Hyam, *Britain's Imperial Century, 1815–1914: A Study of Empire and Expansion*, London 1993, 77–86; John Darwin, Imperialism and the Victorians: The Dynamics of Territorial Expansion, *English Historical Review* 112/447 (June 1997), 614–642 at 622–624; Ade Ajayi/ Oloruntimehin, West Africa in the Anti-Slave Trade Era, 200f. For another important connection between colonialism and humanitarianism in efforts to protect indigenous populations in the developing colonies, see Zoe Laidlaw, Investigating Empire: Humanitarians, Reform and the Commission of Eastern Inquiry, *Journal of Imperial and Commonwealth History* 40/5 (December 2012), 749–768; Penelope Edmonds, Travelling 'Under Concern': Quakers James Backhouse and George Washington Walker Tour the Antipodean Colonies, 1832–41, *Journal of Imperial and Commonwealth History* 40/5 (December 2012), 769–788; Alan Lester, Humanitarians and White Settlers in the Nineteenth Century, in Norman Etherington, ed., *Missions and Empire*, Oxford 2009, 64–85.

2 Letter re. the 'Sierra Leone Settlers' from Lord Sydney to the Lords Commissioners of the Admiralty, 7 December 1786, in Newbury, *British Policy*, 182. On the foundation of the Sierra Leone settlement and its connection to abolition, see Pybus, 'A Less Favourable Specimen', 97–112; Fyfe, Freed Slave Colonies in West Africa, 170–199.

3 On this, see esp. Law, *From Slavery to 'Legitimate' Commerce*.

4 On British plans after 1780 for West Africa in general and on abolitionist plans for Sierra Leone more specifically, see Curtin, *Image of Africa*, 88–139; Brown, Empire without America, 84–100. On the idea of establishing legal trade and spreading civilisation and Christianity, see Schwarz, Commerce, Civilization and Christianity, 252–276.

5 On this, see esp. Deirdre Coleman, *Romantic Colonization and British Anti-Slavery*, Cambridge 2005.

6 Carl Bernhard Wadström, *Observations on the Slave Trade, and a Description of Some Part of the Coast of Guinea, during a Voyage Made in 1787 and 1788, in Company with Doctor A. Sparrman and Captain Arrehenius*, London 1789.

7 Jonas Ahlskog, The Political Economy of Colonisation: Carl Bernhard Wadström's Case for Abolition and Civilisation, *Sjuttonhundratal: Nordic Yearbook for Eighteenth-Century Studies* 7 (2010), 146–167.

8 Carl Bernhard Wadström, *An Essay on Colonization, Particularly Applied to the Western Coast of Africa, with Some Free Thoughts on Cultivation and Commerce,*

London 1794, 19. For an earlier plan, see Carl Bernhard Wadström, *Plan for a Free Community at Sierra Leona, upon the Coast of Africa, under the Protection of Great Britain; with an Invitation to all Persons Desirous of Partaking the Benefits Thereof*, London 1792.

9 Carl Bernhard Wadström, *Adresse au corps législatif et au directoire exécutif de la République Française*, Paris 1795.

10 'Elle armeraient, à frais communs, une escadre dont l'objet serait de s' opposer à ce que toute nation qui aurait refusé de concourir à l'exécution d'un projet si noble et si utile, continuat la *traite d'esclaves* en Afrique.' On this, see ibid., 7.

11 'Les deux nations, et toutes autres qui feraient partie de cette association, indiqueraient celles des portions de la côte d'Afrique où elles se chargeraient de porter la civilization.' On this, see ibid., 7f.

12 '[D]'où il résulte que ces établissemens et tous autres semblables ne devront jamais être confondus avec les colonies qui ont été formées sur les principes d'un systéme commercial, et qu' en cas de guerre entre les deux nations, ils seront toujours respectés par l'une et par l'autre.' On this, see ibid., 8.

13 Austen/Smith, Images of Africa and British Slave-Trade Abolition, 80–83; Ade Ajayi/Oloruntimehin, West Africa in the Anti-Slave Trade Era, 207–221; Christopher Fyfe, Opposition to the Slave Trade as a Preliminary to the European Partition of Africa, in Christopher Fyfe, ed., *The Theory of Imperialism and the European Partition of Africa*, Edinburgh 1967, 129–143; Robinson/Gallagher, *Africa and the Victorians*, 27–41; J. F. Ade Ajayi, Africa at the Beginning of the Nineteenth Century: Issues and Prospects, in J. F. Ade Ajayi, ed., *General History of Africa*, vol. 6: *Africa in the Nineteenth Century until the 1880s*, Paris 1989, 1–22 at 6–8; E. J. Alagoa, The Niger Delta and the Cameroon Region, in Ade Ajayi, ed., *General History of Africa*, vol. 6, 724–748 at 729–731.

14 Helfman, Court of Vice-Admiralty at Sierra Leone, 1130f.; Drescher, Emperors of the World, 135–139.

15 Drescher, Emperors of the World, 136f.; Fyfe, Freed Slave Colonies in West Africa, 179–184.

16 Ade Ajayi/Oloruntimehin, West Africa in the Anti-Slave Trade Era, 207f.; Hyam, *Britain's Imperial Century*, 18; Quirk, *Anti-Slavery Project*, 90f.

17 Winfried Baumgart, *Imperialism: The Idea and Reality of British and French Colonial Expansion, 1880–1914*, Oxford 1982, 12.

18 It was the advantageous geographical position of Fernando Pó (now Bioko, Equatorial Guinea) in the Gulf of Guinea that encouraged the British authorities to move the Mixed Commissions there from Sierra Leone. The ships would have had a shorter distance to sail to their main theatre of operations and, importantly, seized ships would have been at sea for a shorter time before being brought to trial. The project failed, however, and was officially abandoned in 1834. On this, see Robert T. Brown, Fernando Po and the Anti-Sierra Leonean Campaign: 1826–1834, *International Journal of African Historical Studies* 6/2 (1973), 249–264.

19 Robinson/Gallagher, *Africa and the Victorians*, 13–15, 27–30; Drescher, Emperors of the World, 135–141. On the relationship between formal and

informal techniques of rule in the colonial context, see John Gallagher/Ronald Robinson, The Imperialism of Free Trade, *Economic History Review*, new series 6/1 (August 1953), 1–15; Darwin, Imperialism and the Victorians; Gregory A. Barton, *Informal Empire and the Rise of One World Culture*, Basingstoke 2014.

20 Protocole No. 1 des Confèrences pour l'abolition de la Traite des Négres, 28 August 1816, in TNA, FO 84/1.

21 Annexe au Protocole de la 7éme Confèrence, 20 September 1816, in TNA, FO 84/1; Memorandum 'Abolition de la traite des négres' from the French ambassador to London, 1 November 1816, in MAE, MD A15.

22 Annexe au Protocole de la 7éme Confèrence, 20 September 1816, in TNA, FO 84/1.

23 John Gallagher, Fowell Buxton and the New African Policy, 1838–1842, *Cambridge Historical Journal* 10/1 (1950), 36–58; Curtin, *Image of Africa*, 289–317.

24 Buxton's humanitarian activities were not limited to the matter of abolition or to the African continent; he was also active in the cause of protecting indigenous populations in British colonies elsewhere and was an important figure in a wide humanitarian network. On this, see Alan Lester, Thomas Fowell Buxton and the Networks of British Humanitarianism, in Helen Gilbert/Chris Tiffin, eds., *Burden or Benefit? Imperial Benevolence and Its Legacies*, Bloomington, IN 2008, 31–48.

25 Buxton, *African Slave Trade*, 289.

26 Ibid., 298f.

27 'I propose the two measures I have just named, not as a remedy, but as an expedient necessary for a time, in order that the real remedy may be applied in the most effectual manner.' Ibid., 300.

28 On this, see esp. pt. II, 'The Remedy', in ibid., 301–522.

29 On the uneasy relation between military and civilian intervention measures in the twentieth and twenty-first centuries, see Minear, *Humanitarian Enterprise*, 99–118; Fassin/Pandolfi, Introduction: Military and Humanitarian Government, 9–25.

30 Sir Thomas Buxton, Memorandum for the African Civilization Society, April 1839, in Newbury, *British Policy*, 147f.; Bruce, *Life of Sir Thomas Fowell Buxton*, 157–182.

31 On the Niger expedition of 1841, see John Murray, ed., *Report of the Committee of the African Civilization Society to the Public Meeting of the Society Held at Exeter Hall, on Tuesday, the 21st of June 1842*, London 1842.

32 Lord John Russell, Instructions to Her Majesty's Niger Commissioners, 30 January 1841, in Newbury, *British Policy*, 154–159.

33 House of Commons, 'The Niger Expedition', 4 March 1842, in Newbury, *British Policy*, 161–162.

34 Curtin, *Image of Africa*, 298.

35 Gallagher, Fowell Buxton and the New African Policy, 54f. Richard Huzzey has even called the Niger expedition 'a prelude to the scramble of Africa'. On this, see Huzzey, *Freedom Burning*, 211.

36 Buxton, *African Slave Trade*, 298.

37 The Cambridge historians John Gallagher and Ronald Robinson were instrumental in sparking the historiographical debate on this idea of 'informal empire' and informal imperialism. On this, see Gallagher/Robinson, Imperialism of Free Trade; Robinson/Gallagher, Africa and the Victorians; Ronald Robinson, The Excentric Idea of Imperialism, with or without Empire, in Wolfgang J. Mommsen/Jürgen Osterhammel, eds., Imperialism and After: Continuities and Discontinuities, London 1986, 267–289; Darwin, Imperialism and the Victorians; Barton, Informal Empire, 10–21; Andrew Thompson, Informal Empire: Past, Present and Future, in Matthew Brown, ed., Informal Empire in Latin America: Culture, Commerce and Capital, Malden, MA 2008, 229–241.

38 Lord Russell, Memorandum on the African Slave Trade, 23 September 1839, in Newbury, British Policy, 148f.; Letter from the Admiralty to CO, 25 March 1840, in TNA, CO 267/161.

39 The tactic of concentrating naval units at estuaries and close to the onshore slave bases was already discussed in 1825, but never adopted. On this, see Letter 'Plan for Gunboats' from Earl Bathurst to Governor Turner, 19 December 1825, in Newbury, British Policy, 142f. For a contemporary account by an officer of the Royal Navy of manning the naval blockade, see e.g. Lieutenant Forbes, Six Months' Service in the African Blockade, from April to October, 1848, in Command of H.M.S. Bonetta, London 1849.

40 The Gallinas river is now known as the Kerefe and is located in Sierra Leone's Southern Province.

41 Order from Governor Doherty to Commander Denman to free Fry Norman and her child, 30 October 1840, Appendix, No. 22, Correspondence Relative to the Slave Trade at the Gallinas, in BPP, vol. 3, Report from the Select Committee on the West Coast of Africa together with the Minutes of Evidence, Appendix, and Index, pt. II, 5 August 1842, 452. Commander Denman had already called for a more aggressive approach by the Royal Navy in a pamphlet published in 1839 on British policy towards Portugal. On this, see Joseph Denman, Practical Remarks on the Slave Trade, and on the Existing Treaties with Portugal, London 1839.

42 On the particular of the operation, see Report by Commander Denman, 28 November 1840, in Appendix, No. 22, Correspondence, BPP, vol. 3, 5 August 1842, 453–455; Report by Governor Doherty to Lord Russell, 7 December 1840, in ibid., 449f.

43 Treaty between King Siacca and Commander Denman, 21 November 1840, in ibid., 459f.

44 On the key role and exemplary nature of Denman's operation on the Gallinas, see Lloyd, Navy and the Slave Trade, 94–96; Rees, Sweet Water and Bitter, 202–214.

45 Letter on the 'Destruction of Slave Factories at Gallinas' from Lord Russell to Governor Jeremie, 15 April 1841: 'I have requested the L.C. of the Admy. to express to the Commr. the high sense which HM's Govt. entertain of his very spirited and able conduct & of his important results to the interest of humanity', in Newbury, British Policy, 161.

46 Lloyd, Navy and the Slave Trade, 97; Ward, Royal Navy and the Slavers, 174.

47 Letter from Lord Russell to Governor Jeremie, 15 April 1841, in Newbury, *British Policy*, 161.
48 Lloyd, *Navy and the Slave Trade*, 97f.; Ward, *Royal Navy and the Slavers*, 178–181.
49 Letter on the 'Blockade and the Destruction of Slave Factories' from Lord Aberdeen to the Lords Commissioners of the Admiralty, 20 May 1842, in Newbury, *British Policy*, 162f.
50 Ibid. On this, see also The Earl of Aberdeen to Dr. Lushington, Mr. Bandinel, Captain Denman, and Mr. Rothery, selected to revise Instructions for Her Majesty's Naval Officers employed in the Suppression of the Slave Trade, 14 December 1842, in TNA, FO 881/417.
51 Lloyd, *Navy and the Slave Trade*, 98f.; Law, Abolition and Imperialism, 155.
52 On this, see e.g. letter from Denman to Eddisbury, 4 August 1848, in TNA, ADM 7/606; letter from Addington to Deman, 16 September 1848, in ibid.
53 Buxton, *African Slave Trade*, 299.
54 On this, see Instructions for the Senior Officers of Her Majesty's Ships and Vessels on the African Stations, for Negotiating with Chiefs of Africa, 12 June 1844, in Both Houses of Parliament, ed., *Instructions for the Guidance of Her Majesty's Naval Officers Employed in the Suppression of the Slave Trade*, London, July 1844, 15–17, in TNA, FO 115/87; Ade Ajayi/Oloruntimehin, West Africa in the Anti-Slave Trade Era, 208–210, 218f.
55 All these agreements struck with African rulers between 1827 and 1861 can be found reprinted in Her Majesty's Stationery Office, *Supplement to the Slave Trade Instructions*, vol. II.
56 For example, Britain promised an annual payment in kind to the value of $10,000 for a period of five years to King Pepple of Bonny in return for signing the agreement. On this, see Agreement with the King and Chiefs of Bonny, 6 June 1844, in BFSP 45, 885–887. In later treaties, Britain largely refrained from making such payments. On this, see Newbury, *British Policy*, 134f.
57 '[A]nd if any such houses, stores, or buildings, shall at any future time be erected, and the Chiefs of Camma shall fail or be unable to destroy them, they may be destroyed by any British officers employed for the suppression of Slave Trade.' Article 2 of the 'Engagement between Her Majesty the Queen of England and the Chiefs of Camma for the Abolition of the Traffic in Slaves', 25 May 1848, in TNA, FO 93/6/3. This is only one example of many such agreements concluded with African rulers, which are to be found in TNA, FO 93/6/3, TNA, FO 93/6/7 and TNA, CO 879/35.
58 Article 3 of the 'Engagement between Her Majesty the Queen of England and the Chiefs of Camma for the Abolition of the Traffic in Slaves', 25 May 1848, in TNA, FO 93/6/3.
59 This term appears to have first been used by William L. Mathieson, *Great Britain and the Slave Trade 1839–1865*, London 1929, 48.
60 Sturge accordingly rejected the use of force in suppressing the slave trade. At the World Anti-Slavery Convention held in London in June 1840 he instead called for peaceful measures to be taken. On this, see Douglas H. Maynard, The World's Anti-Slavery Convention of 1840, *Mississippi Valley Historical*

Review 47/3 (December 1960), 452–471; Lyons, *Internationalism in Europe*, 290–292.

61 For Hutt's motion and the subsequent parliamentary debate on 24 June 1845, see T. C. Hansard, ed., *The Parliamentary Debates from the Year 1803 to the Present Time*, vol. 81, London 1845 (New York 1970), cc. 1156–1182, http://hansard.millbanksystems.com/commons/1845/jun/24/the-slave-trade

62 Ibid.

63 On this debate, see Lloyd, *Navy and the Slave Trade*, 106–114; Huzzey, *Freedom Burning*, 113–124.

64 Denman, *Slave Trade, the African Squadron*; Henry James Matson, *Remarks on the Slave Trade and African Squadron*, 4th ed., London 1848; J. Leighton Wilson, *The British Squadron on the Coast of Africa, by the Rev. J. Leighton Wilson, An American Missionary in the Gaboon River, West Coast of Africa, with Notes by Captain H. D. Trotter, Royal Navy*, London 1851. The case for the African Squadron was not, however, made solely by naval officers. On this, see Lord Thomas Denman, *A Letter from Lord Denman to Lord Brougham, on the Final Extinction of the Slave Trade*, London 1848; Henry Yule, *The African Squadron Vindicated*, London 1850; J. S. Mansfield, *Remarks on the African Squadron*, London 1851; George Smith, *The Case of Our West-African Cruisers and West-African Settlements Fairly Considered*, London 1848.

65 Denman, *Slave Trade, the African Squadron*, 56; Matson, *Remarks*, 6.

66 Matson, *Remarks*, 69.

67 See e.g.: Denman, *Slave Trade, the African Squadron*, 34–36; Matson, *Remarks*, 17–34.

68 See e.g.: Select Committee on the Slave Trade: Evidence of Captain the Hon. Joseph Denman, 1 April 1845, in Newbury, British Policy, 168–170; Letter from Denman to British admiralty , 20 May 1850, in TNA, ADM 7/606.

69 For officers' suggestions for increased effectiveness, see Reports from various Officers as to the best means to be adopted for the abolition of the African Slave Trade, 1850, in TNA, ADM 123/173.

70 Hutt's motion was defeated by 232 votes to 154. For this motion and the subsequent debate of 19 March 1850, see T. C. Hansard, ed., *The Parliamentary Debates from the Year 1803 to the Present Time*, vol. 109, London 1850 (New York 1970), cc. 1093–1184, http://hansard. millbanksystems.com/commons/1850/mar/19/slave-trade#S3V0109P0_18500319_ HOC_15

71 House of Commons, ed., *Report from the Select Committee of the House of Lords, Appointed to Consider the Best Means which Great Britain can Adopt for the Final Extinction of the African Slave Trade; and to Report thereon to the House; together with the Minutes of Evidence, 15 July 1850*, London 1850.

72 Ibid., 5.

73 Ibid., 6.

74 Ibid., 7.

75 Ibid., 3.

76 Ibid., 8.

77 Commodore Sir Charles Hotham to the Secretary to the Admiralty, Destruction of Slave Factories at Gallinas, 13 February 1849, in Newbury, *British Policy*, 172–174.

78 Treaty between König Siacca and Commander Denman, 21 November 1840, in Appendix, No. 22, Correspondence, Parliamentary Papers, 5 August 1842, 459f.

79 The entire correspondence on the cases of Dahomey and Lagos can be found in Houses of Parliament, ed., *Papers Relative to the Reduction of Lagos by Her Majesty's Forces on the West Coast of Africa*, London 1852.

80 On this, see Robin Law, An African Response to Abolition: Anglo-Dahomian Negotiations on Ending the Slave Trade, 1838–1877, *Slavery & Abolition* 16/3 (December 1995), 281–310 at 281–295; Rees, *Sweet Water and Bitter*, 270–278.

81 Letter from Palmerston to Lord Commissioners of the Admiralty, 27 September 1851, in Houses of Parliament, *Reduction of Lagos*, 135f. On the expedition against Dahomey and the blockade of Whydah, see also Lloyd, *Navy and the Slave Trade*, 152–156.

82 In the negotiations, King Gezo managed to prevent the standard formulation stipulating the destruction of the barracoons and a British right of intervention from being adopted. 'Engagement between Her Majesty the Queen of England and the King of Dahomey for the Abolition of the Traffic in Slaves', 13 January 1852, in Her Majesty's Stationery Office, ed., *Supplement to the Slave Trade Instructions*, vol. II, 90.

83 These included Porto-Novo, Grand Popo, Agoué and Little Popo. On this, see Law, Abolition and Imperialism, 159.

84 Letter from Palmerston to Lord Commissioners of the Admiralty, 27 September 1851, in Houses of Parliament, *Reduction of Lagos*, 135f.

85 On British policy and the military intervention in Lagos, see Report from Commodore Bruce to Secretary of the Admiralty, 2 January 1852, in Houses of Parliament, *Reduction of Lagos*, 193f.; Rees, *Sweet Water and Bitter*, 281–290; Robert S. Smith, *The Lagos Consulate 1851–1861*, London 1978, 18–33.

86 On this, see 'Engagement between Her Majesty the Queen of England and King and the Chiefs of Lagos for the Abolition of the Traffic in Slaves', 1 January 1852, in TNA, FO 93/6/7; Report by Commodore Bruce to Secretary of the Admiralty, 17 January 1852, in Houses of Parliament, *Reduction of Lagos*, 212–214.

87 See Article 3: 'If at any time it shall appear that Slave Trade has been carried on through or from the territory of the King and Chiefs of Lagos the Slave Trade may be put down by Great Britain by force upon that territory, and British officers may seize the boats of Lagos found anywhere carrying on the Slave Trade; and the King and Chiefs of Lagos will be subject to a severe act of displeasure on the part of the Queen of England.' Engagement between Her Majesty the Queen of England and King and the Chiefs of Lagos, in TNA, FO 93/6/7.

88 C. W. Newbury, *The Western Slave Coast and Its Rulers: European Trade and Administration among the Yoruba and Adja-Speaking Peoples of South-Western Nigeria, Southern Dahomey and Togo*, Oxford 1973, 49–76; Martin Lynn, Consul and Kings: British Policy, the 'Man on the Spot', and the Seizure of Lagos, 1851, *Journal of Imperial and Commonwealth History* 10/2 (1982), 150–167.

89 'In the Gallinas, we had a Treaty which had been broken – and we block-aded the coast because we had a right of war from their having neglected to carry out their treaty agreements …. I doubt that we have a right to make war against him [King Kosoko of Lagos] or to depose him if he carries on the slave trade.' Baring quoted in Eltis, *Economic Growth*, 121.

90 Law, Abolition and Imperialism, 163.

91 Anon., *The Destruction of Lagos*, London 1852, 16–19.

92 Ibid., 19f.

93 Ibid., 21.

94 As a supposedly impartial observer, the pamphlet at this point quotes the American missionary J. Leighton Wilson's publication *The British Squadron on the Coast of Africa*. Ibid., 23f.

95 On this, see e.g. letter from Konsul Brand to Lord Russell, 9 April 1860, in BFSP 51, 981f.

96 Letter from Russell to Consul Foote, 22 June 1861, in BFSP 52, 175–177 at 175.

97 Orders addressed to Rear-Admiral Sir B. Walker, 28 June 1861, in ibid., 178f.

98 On the negotiations and the ceremony marking the cession, see Report from Acting Consul McCoskry to Russell, 7 August 1861, in ibid., 179–181.

99 Treaty of Cession, 6 August 1861, in ibid., 181f. at 181.

100 On the significance of such 'bridgeheads' for imperial expansion, see Darwin, Imperialism and the Victorians, 614–642, esp. 629f., 640–642; Everill, *Abolition and Empire*, 148–172.

101 Letter from Foote to Russell, 9 January 1861, in TNA, FO 84/1141; Smith, *Lagos Consulate*, 108–110, 120f. On the economic background to annex-ation, see Antony G. Hopkins, Property Rights and Empire Building: Britain's Annexation of Lagos, 1861, *Journal of Economic History* 40/4 (December 1980), 777–798.

102 Letter from Burton to Russell, 10 January 1863, in TNA, FO 881/4197.

103 On the characteristic interplay between formal and informal techniques of British rule in Africa, see also Barton, *Informal Empire*, 71–94.

104 Eltis, *Economic Growth*, 122.

105 A similar interpretation is offered by Andrew Porter: 'By the 1840s, humani-tarianism had become a vital component of Britain's national or Imperial identity.' Porter, Trusteeship, 19. For an interpretation of 'humanitarian imperialism' beginning only in the late nineteenth and early twentieth cen-turies, see Ribi Forclaz, *Humanitarian Imperialism*.

106 Davidson, *Black Mother*, 242f.; Law, Abolition and Imperialism, 169f.; Huzzey, *Freedom Burning*, 146f.; Quirk, *Anti-Slavery Project*, 91. In this context, Marcel van der Linden refers to the 'unanticipated consequences of "humanitarian intervention"'. See van der Linden, Unanticipated Consequences, 290–293.

107 Memorandum by David Livingstone, 1863, in TNA, FO 881/4197.

108 Ibid. On Livingstone's criticism of the Portuguese authorities and their inaction, see Letter from Livingstone to Russell, 28 January 1863, in ibid.

109 Memorandum by David Livingstone, 1863, in ibid.

110 On this influential network of missionaries, businessmen and explorers, see Dorothy O. Helly, 'Informed' Opinion on Tropical Africa in Great Britain 1860–1890, *African Affairs* 68/272 (July 1969), 195–217.

111 On this key part played Livingstone and other public figures, see Curtin, *Image of Africa*, 319; Lovejoy, *Transformations in Slavery*, 262–267; Reginald Coupland, *The Exploitation of East Africa 1856–1890: The Slave Trade and the Scramble*, London 1968, 102–133, 147–151; Richard Huzzey, Minding Civilisation and Humanity in 1867: A Case Study in British Imperial Culture and Victorian Anti-Slavery, *Journal of Imperial and Commonwealth History* 40/5 (December 2012), 807–825 at 816–821.

112 For a contemporary account seeking to brand the East African slave trade as a specifically 'Arab' affair, see Daniel Laqua, The Tensions of Internationalism: Transnational Anti-Slavery in the 1880s and 1890s, *International History Review* 33/4 (December 2011), 705–726 at 716–719.

113 According to R. W. Beachey's estimates, more than 2 million Africans were captured as slaves in East Africa in the nineteenth century alone. On this, see R. W. Beachey, *The Slave Trade of Eastern Africa*, London 1976, 260–262. On the East African slave trade, see also Coupland, *Exploitation of East Africa*, 134–151; Robert Harms/Bernard K. Freamon/David W. Blight, eds., *Indian Ocean Slavery in the Age of Abolition*, New Haven, CT 2013; Matthew S. Hopper, *Slaves of One Master: Globalization and Slavery in Arabia in the Age of Empire*, New Haven, CT 2015.

114 David Livingstone/Charles Livingstone, *Narrative of an Expedition to the Zambesi and Its Tributaries; and of the Discovery of the Lakes Shirwa and Nyassa, 1858–1864*, London 1865, v. For Livingstone's account of the horrors of the East African slave trade see e.g. ibid., 411–413; report from Livingstone to Granville, 14 November 1871, in Both Houses of Parliament, ed., *Despatches Addressed by Dr. Livingstone, Her Majesty's Consul, Inner Africa, to Her Majesty's Secretary of State for Foreign Affairs, in 1870, 1871, and 1872*, London 1872, 10–15; Report from Livingstone to Granville, 20 February 1872, in ibid., 19–24.

115 Dedication by Livingstone to Lord Palmerston, in Livingstone/Livingstone, *Narrative of an Expedition*.

116 Ibid., vi.

117 On this, see also H. Alan C. Cairns, *Prelude to Imperialism: British Reactions to Central African Society 1840–1890*, London 1965, 192–230.

118 Church Missionary Society, ed., *The Slave Trade of East Africa*, London 1869, 6f.

119 Ibid., 8–20. For historical background, see Norman R. Bennett, *A History of the Arab State of Zanzibar*, London 1978.

120 Appendix, Note A, Extract from Pamphlet on the Slave Trade of East Africa, published by the Church Missionary Society in 1868, in Church Missionary Society, ed., *The Slave Trade of East Africa*, 24–30; Note B, Extracts from Dr. Livingstone's Report on the East African Slave Trade, June 11, 1866, in ibid., 30f.; Note B, Extract from Letter of Dr. Livingstone to the Earl of Clarendon, August 20, 1866, in ibid., 31f.

121 On this, see Treaty between Great Britain and Madagascar, 23 October 1817, in Hertslet, ed., *Complete Collection of the Treaties*, 354–356. For an

overview of treaties on the slave trade, see Slave Trade Suppression Tables; or a Chronologically arranged Statement of the Measures taken by different Nations for the Abolition of the Slave Trade, in Her Majesty's Stationery Office, *Slave Trade Instructions*, vol. II, 131–142. On British policy in the Indian Ocean in the early nineteenth century, see Edward A. Alpers, On Becoming a British Lake: Piracy, Slaving, and British Imperialism in the Indian Ocean during the First Half of the Nineteenth Century, in Harms/ Freamon/Blight, eds., *Indian Ocean Slavery in the Age of Abolition*, 45–58.

122 On this, see Treaty between Great Britain and Muscat, 10 September 1822, in Harrison, ed., *Treaties*, 274–276; Article XV of the Convention of Commerce between Her Majesty and the Imam of Muscat, 31 May 1839, in ibid., 277f.; Agreement with the Sultan of Muscat, 2 October 1845, in BFSP 35, 632f. On these treaties and the preceding negotiations, see Moses D. E. Nwulia, *Britain and Slavery in East Africa*, Washington, DC 1975, 41–76.

123 On the Royal Navy's operations against the East African slave trade, see Raymond Howell, *The Royal Navy and the Slave Trade*, London 1987; Lloyd, *Navy and the Slave Trade*, 185–274; Beachey, *Slave Trade of Eastern Africa*, 67–93; Lindsay Doulton, 'The Flag That Sets Us Free': Antislavery, Africans, and the Royal Navy in the Western Indian Ocean, in Harms/ Freamon/Blight, eds., *Indian Ocean Slavery in the Age of Abolition*, 101–119. For a detailed account of these missions from the perspective of an officer involved, see Captain G. L. Sulivan, *Dhow Chasing in Zanzibar Waters and on the Eastern Coast of Africa: Narrative of Five Years' Experiences in the Suppression of the Slave Trade*, London 1873; Captain Philip Howard Colomb, *Slave-Catching in the Indian Ocean: A Record of Naval Experiences*, London 1873.

124 Lloyd, *Navy and the Slave Trade*, 255f. For a statistical overview of the 1867–78 period, see Appendix B 'Captures from the Arab Slave Trade', in ibid., 278. Between 1860 and 1890 the Royal Navy seized around 1,000 slave dhows and freed more than 12,000 slaves in the process. On this, see Howell, *Royal Navy*, 220.

125 Nwulia, *Britain and Slavery*, 82f. The documents concerning the court's establishment are preserved under the heading 'Establishment of Vice-Admiralty Court at Zanzibar', 1867, in TNA, FO 96/294.

126 R. J. Gavin, The Bartle Frere Mission to Zanzibar, 1873, *Historical Journal* 5/ 2 (June 1962), 122–148 at 140–144; William Mulligan, British Anti-Slave Trade and Anti-Slavery Policy in East Africa, Arabia, and Turkey in the Late Nineteenth Century, in Simms/Trim, eds., *Humanitarian Intervention*, 257–280 esp. at 262–274. For an example of growing public awareness of the slave trade, see Captain H. A. Fraser/Bishop Tozer/James Christie, *The East African Slave Trade and the Measures Proposed for Its Extinction, as Viewed by Residents in Zanzibar*, London 1871; H. A. Fraser, *A Letter to the Honourable Members of the Select Committee of the House of Commons Appointed to Inquire into the Question of the Slave Trade on the East Coast of Africa*, Zanzibar 1872; Anon., East African Slave Trade, *Quarterly Review* 133/266 (October 1872), 521–557.

127 It testifies to Livingstone's influence even in the highest political circles that his accounts were prominently cited in official reports. See e.g. Both Houses of Parliament, ed., *Report Addressed to Earl of Clarendon by the Committee on the East African Slave Trade*, London, 24 January 1870.

128 For verbatim testimony, see Minutes of Evidence, in House of Commons, ed., *Report from the Select Committee on Slave Trade (East Coast of Africa); together with the Proceedings of the Committee, Minutes of Evidence*, Appendix and Index, London, 4 August 1871.

129 Statement by Hillyars, 25 July 1871, in ibid., 77–80 at 78.

130 Statement by Heath, 20 July 1871, in ibid., 52–56 at 54.

131 Coupland, *Exploitation of East Africa*, 167–169. Similar demands for territorial expansion to combat the East African slave trade were also made by Captain Philip Howard Colomb, who also invoked the success of the West African campaign: 'but I mean that by occupying territory, with precisely the same views as we occupied it on the West Coast, we might check the slave trade as cheaply and more permanently than we can by mere squadrons of cruisers.' Colomb, *Slave-Catching in the Indian Ocean*, 463.

132 Report from the Select Committee on Slave Trade (East Coast of Africa), 4 August 1871, in House of Commons, ed., *Report from the Select Committee on Slave Trade*, vi–viii.

133 'In view of the considerable commercial interest which Germany, France, America, and Portugal possess in commerce with Zanzibar and the surroundings, your Committee suggest that Her Majesty's Government invite the co-operation of these several Governments in the suppression of a traffic so subversive of these interest.' Ibid., v. Already in 1872 the British government had addressed a circular to Germany, France, the United States and Portugal which had unsuccessfully tried to win their support in making a joint appeal to the sultan of Zanzibar for the abolition of the slave trade. On this, see Circular Letter des FO, 16 February 1872, in TNA, FO 84/1386.

134 Richard D. Wolff, British Imperialism and the East African Slave Trade, *Science & Society* 36/4 (Winter 1972), 443–462 at 451–454; Darwin, Imperialism and the Victorians, 634–639.

135 On the part played by Sir Bartle Frere and his personality, see F. V. Emery, Geography and Imperialism: The Role of Sir Bartle Frere (1815–84), *Geographical Journal* 150/3 (November 1984), 342–350.

136 On the events of this mission, see Coupland, *Exploitation of East Africa*, 183–216; Gavin, Bartle Frere Mission, 122–148.

137 Letter from Bartle Frere to Granville, 13 February 1873, in Both Houses of Parliament, ed., *Correspondence Respecting Sir Bartle Frere's Mission to the East Coast of Africa, 1872–1873*, London 1873, 36f.

138 Bartle Frere, Memorandum on the Position and Authority of the Sultan of Zanzibar, 17 April 1873, in TNA, FO 84/1391, 19.

139 Letter from Granville to Kirk, 15 May 1873, in Both Houses of Parliament, ed., *Correspondence Respecting Sir Bartle Frere's Mission to the East Coast of Africa*, 88f.

140 Treaty between Her Majesty and the Sultan of Zanzibar for the Suppression of the Slave Trade, 5 June 1873, in ibid., 154f.

141 Bartle Frere, Memorandum on the Position and Authority of the Sultan of Zanzibar, 17 April 1873, in TNA, FO 84/1391, 16.

142 Reginald Coupland goes so far as to claim that '[t]he British consul-general became also a sort of unofficial prime minister of Zanzibar'. See Coupland, *Exploitation of East Africa*, 237–270 at 266.

143 On the direct consequences of the treaty on the seaborne slave trade see e.g. letter from Kirk to Granville, 22 July 1873, in Both Houses of Parliament, ed., *Correspondence with British Representatives and Agents, and Reports from Naval Officers, Related to the East African Slave Trade, from January 1 to December 31, 1873*, London 1874, 58.

144 Letter from Kirk to Granville, 6 September 1873, in ibid., 86f. On this geographical shift and the consequent boom in land-based slave trading, see Coupland, *Exploitation of East Africa*, 217–234; Beachey, *Slave Trade of Eastern Africa*, 114–120.

145 Coupland, *Exploitation of East Africa*, 221f.

146 See e.g. letter from Kirk to Derby, 20 April 1876, in Both Houses of Parliament, ed., *Communications from Dr. Kirk, Respecting the Suppression of the Land Slave Traffic in the Dominions of the Sultan of Zanzibar*, London 1876, 1–3.

147 As the consul general put it: 'I can promise the full support of the British authorities and of the Government, and assure your Highness at the same time ... that her Majesty's Government are fully aware of the difficult and delicate position you yourself occupy.' On this, see Letter from Kirk to the Sultan of Zanzibar, 1876, in ibid., 3f.

148 Letter from Kirk to Derby, 28 April 1876, in ibid., 5f.; Circular Letter to the Zanzibar Governors on the Coast Forwarding Proclamations, 20 April 1876, in ibid., 6; Letter Forwarding Two Proclamations Addressed to the Governor of Kilwa, 20 April 1876, in ibid., 6.

149 On this, see Coupland, *Exploitation of East Africa*, 226–229; Nwulia, *Britain and Slavery*, 143f.

150 Bennett, *History of the Arab State*, 99–101; Wolff, British Imperialism, 452f.

151 Mulligan, British Anti-Slave Trade, 257–280. On the treaties and abolition in the Ottoman Empire, see Ehud R. Toledano, *The Ottoman Slave Trade and Its Suppression: 1840–1890*, Princeton, NJ 1982, 224–248; Y. Hakan Erdem, *Slavery in the Ottoman Empire and Its Demise, 1800–1909*, Basingstoke 1996, 132–142.

152 Fyfe, Opposition to the Slave Trade, 129–134; Huzzey, *Freedom Burning*, 146f.; Quirk, *Anti-Slavery Project*, 91–94; Van der Linden, Unanticipated Consequences of 'Humanitarian Intervention', 290–293.

153 Huzzey, *Freedom Burning*, 174.

154 On the 'scramble for Africa' see e.g. Albert Wirz/Andreas Eckert, The Scramble for Africa: Icon and Idiom of Modernity, in Olivier Pétré Grenouilleau, ed., *From Slave Trade to Empire: Europe and the Colonisation of Black Africa 1780s–1880s*, London 2004, 133–153; John Darwin, *After Tamerlane: The Rise and Fall of Global Empires, 1400–2000*, London 2007, 304–318; Jane Burbank/Frederick Cooper, *Empires in World History: Power and the Politics of Difference*, Princeton, NJ 2010, 287–294, 312–321.

155 On the various and interconnected motives for and drivers of imperial and colonial expansion, see Darwin, *Imperialism and the Victorians*, 614–642 esp. at 627f., 640–642; Huzzey, *Freedom Burning*, 152–160 and 174–176; Mulligan, *Anti-Slave Trade Campaign*, 149–170.

156 The conference lasted from 15 November 1884 to 26 February 1885. The participating countries were Germany, Austria, Belgium, Denmark, Spain, France, Great Britain, Italy, the Netherlands, Portugal, Russia, Sweden and Norway, the Ottoman Empire and the United States of America. On the Berlin Conference of 1884–85 and its significance, see William Roger Louis, The Berlin Congo Conference, in William Roger Louis/Prosser Gifford, eds., *France and Britain in Africa: Imperial Rivalry and Colonial Rule*, New Haven, CT 1971, 167–220; Förster/Mommsen/Robinson, *Bismarck, Europe, and Africa*. For the minutes of the conference, see Frank Thomas Gatter, ed., *Protokolle und Generalakte der Berliner Afrika-Konferenz 1884–1885*, Bremen 1984.

157 On the conference under the aspect of nineteenth-century internationalism, see Lyons, *Internationalism in Europe*, 293f.; Laqua, *Age of Internationalism*, 46f.

158 For an English translation of the General Act, see 'General Act of the Conference of Berlin Concerning the Congo', *American Journal of International Law* 3/1, Supplement: Official Documents (January 1909), 7–25.

159 On articles 34 and 35, see ibid. On this, see also Fisch, *Africa as terra nullius*.

160 On this, see Protokoll Nr. 9 der Berliner Afrika-Konferenz, session of 23 February 1885, in Gatter, *Protokolle*, 446–454; Annex Nr. 1 zum Protokoll Nr. 9 'Abschriften der verschiedenen Verträge, durch welche die Internationale Assoziation des Kongo die Anerkennung der Regierung erlangt hat', in ibid., 475–519.

161 On the Congo Free State, see Adam Hochschild, *King Leopold's Ghost: A Story of Greed, Terror, and Heroism in Colonial Africa*, New York 1999.

162 De Launay, quoted in Protokoll Nr. 9, in Gatter, *Protokolle*, 451.

163 On the humanitarian aspects of the Berlin Conference, see L. H. Gann, The Berlin Conference and the Humanitarian Conscience, in Förster/Mommsen/Robinson, eds., *Bismarck, Europe, and Africa*, 321–331; Suzanne Miers, Humanitarianism at Berlin: Myth or Reality?, in ibid., 333–345; Kristina Lovrić-Pernak, *Morale internationale und humanité im Völkerrecht des späten 19. Jahrhunderts, Bedeutung und Funktion in Staatenpraxis und Wissenschaft*, Baden Baden 2013, 33–76.

164 Suzanne Miers, The Brussels Conference of 1889–1890: The Slave Trade in the Policies of Great Britain and Germany, in Prosser Gifford/William Roger Louis, eds., *Britain and Germany in Africa: Imperial Rivalry and Colonial Rule*, New Haven, CT 1967, 83–118 at 86f.

165 Article 6 of the General Act, 'General Act of the Conference of Berlin Concerning the Congo', 12–13.

166 Article 9 of the General Act, in ibid., 13–14.

167 Memorandum on the Bearing of International Law on the Slave Trade from FO, 15 November 1889, in TNA, FO 541/34; Miers, Humanitarianism at

Berlin, 342f.; Nicholson, Transformation in the Law Concerning Slavery, 220f.

168 On this, see François Renault, *Cardinal Lavigerie: Churchman, Prophet, and Missionary*, London 1994, 33–41.

169 On the life and work of Cardinal Lavigerie, see ibid. For a contemporary biography, see Richard F. Clarke, ed., *Cardinal Lavigerie and the African Slave Trade*, London 1889.

170 Lavigerie's crusading rhetoric was strong indeed. Speaking in Brussels, he called on modern-day Belgians to emulate the deeds of the medieval crusader, Godfrey of Bouillon. On this, see Mulligan, Anti-Slave Trade Campaign in Europe, 154; Laqua, Tensions of Internationalism, 716–719; 'The Pope's New Crusade. Cardinal Lavigerie on the Slave Trade', *Pall Mall Gazette* (1 August 1888); cartoon and poem 'The New Crusade, and the Five Champions of Christendom', *Punch, or the London Charivari* (11 August 1888), 70f.; cartoon and poem 'The New Crusade', *Punch, or the London Charivari* (30 November 1889), 258f.; on Lavigerie's abolitionist campaign more generally, see Renault, *Cardinal Lavigerie*, 367–385; François Renault, *Lavigerie, l'esclavage africain et l'Europe, 1868–1892, Tome II: Campagne antiesclavagiste*, Paris 1971, 73–120; Bertrand Taithe, Evil, Liberalism and the Imperial Designs of the Catholic Church, 1867–1905, in Bertrand Taithe/Tom Crook/Rebecca Gill, eds., *Evil, Barbarism and Empire: Britain and Abroad, c. 1830–2000*, Basingstoke 2011, 147–171.

171 Slavery in Africa: A Speech by Cardinal Lavigerie, 31 July 1888, Boston 1888.

172 Ibid., 12.

173 Ibid., 14.

174 Ibid., 5. On this, see also 'Charity … however great, will not suffice to save Africa. It requires a more speedy, more decided, more efficacious remedy. Our Holy Father, the Pope, after appealing to charity, then appeals to force, but a pacific force, which would be employed not for attack, but for defence.' Clarke, *Cardinal Lavigerie*, 338.

175 Slavery in Africa: A Speech by Cardinal Lavigerie, 15f. On the formation of these groups of armed volunteers, see also Clarke, *Cardinal Lavigerie*, 337–343.

176 Although in 1890 Laviegerie managed to assemble a force of several hundred men under the name *Frères armés du Sahara* and to provide them with arms, the fighting unit was dissolved upon the cardinal's death in November 1892. On this, see Renault, *Lavigerie, l'esclavage africain*, 392–407; Bertrand Taithe, Missionary Militarism? The Armed Brothers of the Sahara and Léopold Joubert in the Congo, in Owen White/J. P. Daughton, eds., *In God's Empire: French Missionaries and the Modern World*, Oxford 2012, 129–150 at 133–137.

177 On this, see esp. Laqua, Tensions of Internationalism, 705–726; Miers, Brussels Conference, 91f.; Mulligan, Anti-Slave Trade Campaign, 149–170 esp. at 164–166.

178 On the Anglo-German naval blockade, see Miers, *Britain and the Ending of the Slave Trade*, 209–216; Howell, *Royal Navy*, 195–209, 216f.

179 Letter from Salisbury to Vivian, 17 April 1889, in TNA, FO 541/37. On the British position regarding the Brussels Conference, see Francis William Fox, Memorandum on the Brussels African Slave Trade Conference, 17 October 1889, in TNA, FO 541/37; Memorandum by Lord Vivian on the Programme of the Brussels Anti-Slave Trade Conference, 2 November 1889, in ibid.

180 As already mentioned, the humorous British magazine *Punch* published a cartoon and a poem entitled 'The New Crusade' on the occasion of the Brussels Conference. The cartoon depicts the leading European monarchs and statesmen of the day in medieval armour alongside Cardinal Lavigerie, all wearing determined expressions and raising their swords (or, in the cardinal's case, his cross) against a demon lying prostrate, wearing Arab garb and bearing the legend 'Slavery'. On this, see *Punch, or the London Charivari* (30 November 1889), 258f.

181 Lord Salisbury, 9 November 1889, quoted in Gwendolen Cecil, *Life of Robert Marquis of Salisbury*, vol. IV: *1887–1892*, London 1932, 256.

182 On the negotiations and the various parties' positions, see Miers, Brussels Conference, 102–118. A leading role in formulating the agreement was taken by the well-respected Russian jurist and diplomat Friedrich Fromhold Martens. On this, see Jean Allain, Fydor Martens and the Question of Slavery at the 1890 Brussels Conference, in Jean Allain, ed., *The Law and Slavery: Prohibiting Human Exploitation*, Leiden 2015, 101–120.

183 Preamble, in General Act of the Brussels Conference relative to the African slave trade, signed at Brussels, July 2, 1890. Presented to both houses of Parliament by command of Her Majesty February 1892. London: Printed for H. M. Stationery Off. by Harrison and Sons, 1892, p. 35.

184 Besides concrete measures against the slave trade, the General Act also contained specific provisions limiting the trade in firearms and spiritous liquors in Africa. On this, see Articles 8–14 (ibid., pp. 40–42) and chapter IV (ibid., pp. 54–56) of the General Act. The importation of firearms was restricted with the purpose of impeding the native population's ability to resist European incursions and hence to stabilise European rule.

185 Article 1 of the General Act, in ibid. 37–38.

186 Articles 5 and 19 of the General Act, in ibid. 39, 43–44.

187 On this, see ch. II, 'Caravan Routes and Land Transport of Slaves', in ibid. 42–44.

188 On this, see ch. III, 'Repression of the Slave Trade by Sea', in ibid. 44–54.

189 Although France signed the General Act, it ratified the treaty in January 1892 only with reservations concerning the provisions for search. On this, see Allain, Nineteenth Century Law, 305–307.

190 For the International Maritime Bureau, see Article 27 (p. 45) and ch. V (pp. 56–60) of the General Act. A counterpart in Brussels was set up at the same time. On this, see Miers, *Britain and the Ending of the Slave Trade*, 284–286; Lyons, *Internationalism in Europe*, 293–295.

191 Alfred Le Ghait, The Anti-Slavery Conference, *North American Review* 154/424 (March 1892), 287–296 at 296.

192 Cecil, *Life*, 256.
193 Lloyd, *Navy and the Slave Trade*, 273.
194 Coupland, British Anti-Slavery, 224.
195 On this, see esp. Jan-Georg Deutsch, *Emancipation without Abolition in German East Africa c. 1884–1914*, Oxford 2006; Kevin Grant, *A Civilised Savagery: Britain and the New Slaveries in Africa, 1884–1926*, New York 2005.
196 On the 'moral hazards' established in the General Act with regard to Leopold's rule in the Congo, see esp. Mairi S. MacDonald, Lord Vivian's Tears: The Moral Hazards of Humanitarian Intervention, in Klose, ed., *Emergence of Humanitarian Intervention*, 121–141. On the humanitarian campaign against the 'Congo atrocities', see Kevin Grant, Christian Critics of Empire: Missionaries, Lantern Lectures, and the Congo Reform Campaign in Britain, *Journal of Imperial and Commonwealth History* 29/2 (May 2001), 27–58; Andrew Porter, Sir Roger Casement and the International Humanitarian Movement, *Journal of Imperial and Commonwealth History* 29/2 (May 2001), 59–74; Charles Laderman, The Invasion of the United States by an Englishman: E. D. Morel and the Anglo-American Intervention in the Congo, in Mulligan/Bric, eds., *Global History of Anti-Slavery*, 171–197.
197 Miers, Humanitarianism at Berlin, 344. Suzanne Miers has accordingly called the General Act a 'Magna Carta of the colonial powers'. On this, see Miers, *Britain and the Ending of the Slave Trade*, 318. For a similarly critical appraisal of the General Act, see Nwulia, *Britain and Slavery*, 163f.; Van der Linden, Unanticipated Consequences of 'Humanitarian Intervention', 293.
198 For the intimate and manifold connection between humanitarianism and imperialism or colonialism, see Ribi Forclaz, *Humanitarian Imperialism*; Lester/Dussart, *Colonization and the Origins of Humanitarian Governance*; Skinner/Lester, Humanitarianism and Empire, 729–747; Thompson, Humanitarian Interventions, 331–356; Barnett, *Empire of Humanity*, 29f., 47–94; Salvatici, *Humanitarianism*, 35–48.

Chapter 8

1 On the *Filiki Eteria* and the emergence of a Greek independence movement, see Christopher M. Woodhouse, *The Greek War of Independence: Its Historical Setting*, New York 1975, 42–50; Douglas Dakin, *The Greek Struggle for Independence 1821–1833*, Berkeley, CA 1973, 41–49; Theophilus C. Prousis, *Russian Society and the Greek Revolution*, DeKalb, IL 1994, 18–24; Misha Glenny, *The Balkans 1804–1999: Nationalism, War and the Great Powers*, London 1999, 22–39; David Brewer, *The Flame of Freedom: The Greek War of Independence 1821–1833*, London 2001, 26–35.
2 On Alexander Ypsilantis' mission, see Barbara Jelavich, *History of the Balkans: Eighteenth and Nineteenth Centuries*, vol. 1, Cambridge 1983, 204–214; Stites, *Four Horsemen*, 186–211.
3 Woodhouse, *Greek War of Independence*, 56f.; Dakin, *Greek Struggle*, 59.

4 Constitution Provisoire de l'Hellénie – Dont à Epidaure, 13 January 1822, in BFSP 9, 620–629; Proclamation d'Indépendance de l'Assemblée Nationale Hellénique – Epidaure, 27 January 1822, in ibid., 629–632; Brewer, *Flame of Freedom*, 124–134.

5 On this international dimension, see Schroeder, *Transformation of European Politics*, 614–621, 637–653; Schulz, *Normen und Praxis*, 89–102.

6 In his classic and still relevant account, Matthew Anderson situates the 'Eastern Question' as spanning the period between the treaties of Küçük Kaynarca (1774) and Lausanne (1923). Matthew S. Anderson, *The Eastern Question 1774–1923: A Study in International Relations*, Basingstoke 1991. On the 'Eastern Question' in relation to the Greek war of independence see ibid., 53–87; Oliver Schulz, *Ein Sieg der zivilisierten Welt? Die Intervention der europäischen Großmächte im griechischen Unabhängigkeitskrieg (1826–1832)*, Berlin 2011, 135–199. On more recent historiography concerning the 'Eastern Question', see Michelle Tusan, Britain and the Middle East: New Historical Perspectives on the Eastern Question, *History Compass* 8/3 (March 2010), 212–222; Stéphanie Prévost, New Perspectives on the Eastern Question(s) in Late-Victorian Britain, Or How 'the Eastern Question' Affected British Politics (1881–1901), in Catherine Delmas/Isabelle Gadoin, eds., *Représentations: 'Naming, Labelling and Addressing'*, June 2015, Grenoble University, https://representations.univ-grenoble-alpes.fr/IMG/pdf/8-prevost_eastern_question_s_final_def.pdf

7 Lawrence P. Meriage, The First Serbian Uprising (1804–1813) and the Nineteenth-Century Origins of the Eastern Question, *Slavic Review* 37/3 (September 1978), 421–439; M. Şükrü Hanioğlu, *A Brief History of the Late Ottoman Empire*, Princeton, NJ 2008, 6–71. Recent scholarship has contradicted the frequently heard claim that the Ottoman Empire had been in a state of irreversible decline for centuries, instead finding its later development to have been marked by ups as well as downs. On this, see e.g. Karen Barkey, *Empire of Difference: The Ottomans in Comparative Perspective*, Cambridge 2009.

8 On Russian expansion and its motives see esp. Barbara Jelavich, *Russia's Balkan Entanglements 1806–1914*, Cambridge 1991, 1–41; Alexander Bitis, *Russia and the Eastern Question: Army, Government, and Society 1815–1833*, Oxford 2006, 15–35; John C. K. Daly, *Russian Seapower and the 'Eastern Question' 1827–41*, Basingstoke 1991.

9 On the key role of the Treaty of Küçük Kaynarca (1774), see Christoph K. Neumann, Political and Diplomatic Developments, in Suraiya N. Faroqhi, ed., *The Cambridge History of Turkey*, vol. 3: *The Later Ottoman Empire, 1603–1839*, Cambridge 2006, 44–62 at 57–58.

10 On the respective positions and occasionally overlapping motives of the other great powers of Europe, see Jelavich, *History of the Balkans*, 186–188; Schroeder, *Metternich's Diplomacy*, 164–194.

11 Vernon John Puryear, *France and the Levant: From the Bourbon Restoration to the Peace of Kutiah*, Berkeley, CA 1968, 1–36; Robert Holland, *Blue-Water Empire: The British in the Mediterranean since 1800*, London 2013, 7–25; Gough, *Pax Britannica*, 104–116.

12 For an example of these appeals by the Greek provisional government, see Declaration of the Provisional Government of Greece to Christian Nations, 27 April 1822, in BFSP 9, 795–798; Declaration adressée aux Monarques réunis à Vérone, de la part du Gouvernement des Grecs, 29 August 1822, in BFSP 10, 1021f.

13 On this intense diplomatic activity, see the copious documentation contained in MAE, MD G 8 and TNA, FO 800/230. See also Irby C. Nichols, Jr, The Eastern Question and the Vienna Conference, September, 1822, *Journal of Central European Affairs* 21/1 (1961), 53–66; C. W. Crawley, *The Question of Greek Independence: A Study of British Policy in the Near East, 1821–1833*, New York 1973, 17–29.

14 On the Russian position, see Jelavich, *Russia's Balkan Entanglements*, 49–67; Prousis, *Russian Society and the Greek Revolution*, 26–33.

15 For the 'Protocole pour déterminer le droit d'intervention des grandes Puissances' of 19 November 1820, see Grewe, *Fontes Historiae*, 110–113.

16 Bass, *Freedom's Battle*; Rodogno, *Against Massacre*. The same approach has been taken by Hillgruber, Humanitäre Intervention, 169–176; Swatek-Evenstein, *History*, 9–10 and 45–75; Heraclides/Dialla, *Humanitarian Intervention*, 105–133.

17 On the Tripolitsa massacre and other Greek atrocities against the Muslim population, see George Finlay, *A History of Greece from the Conquest by the Romans to the Present Time*, vol. VI: *The Greek Revolution*, pt. I, Oxford 1877, 152f.; William St Clair, *That Greece Might Still Be Free: The Philhellenes in the War of Independence*, London 1972, 1f.; Justin McCarthy, *Death and Exile: The Ethnic Cleansing of Ottoman Muslims 1821–1922*, Princeton, NJ 1995, 10–12; Bass, *Freedom's Battle*, 64–66.

18 On the expulsion of Muslims from the Balkans generally, see Berna Pekesen, Vertreibung und Abwanderung der Muslime vom Balkan, *Europäische Geschichte Online* (EGO), hg. vom Institut für Europäische Geschichte (IEG), Mainz 2011-02-04, http://www.ieg-ego.eu/pekesenb-2011-de

19 On the murder of Patriarch Gregory V and Ottoman massacres of Christian populations, see Finlay, *History of Greece*, 186–193; Brewer, *Flame of Freedom*, 100–106.

20 Osterhammel, *Transformation of the World*, 140.

21 On the massacre of Chios, see Helen Long, *Greek Fire: Massacres of Chios*, London 1992; Brewer, *Flame of Freedom*, 154–167; Bass, *Freedom's Battle*, 67–73. For accounts of the massacre by European diplomats, see Philip P. Argenti, ed., *The Massacres of Chios: Described in Contemporary Diplomatic Reports*, London 1932.

22 Report from Strangford to Castlereagh, 25 May 1822, in Argenti, *Massacres of Chios*, 16–19 at 16.

23 On the practice of enslaving rebels and prisoners of war, considered lawful by the Ottomans, see Toledano, *Ottoman Slave Trade*, 15f.; Bernard Lewis, *Race and Slavery in the Middle East: An Historical Enquiry*, Oxford 1990, 3–15.

24 Report from Strangford to Castlereagh, 25 May 1822, in Argenti, *Massacres of Chios*, 18.

25 Gianib Effendi responded to a protest from the Prussian legation in similar terms. Ibid., 19.

26 Massacre of the Greeks at Constantinople and Scio, *The Times* (28 June 1822).

27 Thomas S. Hughes, *An Address to the People of England in the Cause of the Greeks, Occasioned by the Late Inhuman Massacres in the Isle of Scio, & c.*, London 1822, 32f.

28 Ibid., 33f.

29 Debate in the House of Commons, 15 July 1822, in T. C. Hansard, ed., *The Parliamentary Debates from the Earliest Period to the Year 1803*, vol. 7, London 1823, 1649–1653.

30 Ibid., 1651f.

31 Debate in the House of Lords, 17 July 1822, in ibid., 1665.

32 Debate in the House of Commons, in ibid., 1652f.

33 Debate in the House of Lords, in ibid., 1666f.

34 Letter from Castlereagh to Strangford, 9 July 1822, in Argenti, *Massacres of Chios*, 25f.

35 On the various currents of philhellenism and its political development, see Florian Kerschbaumer/Korinna Schönhärl, Der Wiener Kongress als 'Kinderstube' des Philhellenismus: Das Beispiel des Bankiers Jean-Gabriel Eynard, in Anne-Rose Meyer, ed., *Vormärz und Philhellenismus, Forum Vormärz Forschung, Jahrbuch* 18 (2012), 99–127.

36 On European philhellenism, see Virginia Penn, Philhellenism in Europe, 1821–1828, *Slavonic and East European Review* 16/48 (April 1938), 638–653; Jean Dimakis, La 'Société de la morale chrétienne' de Paris et son action en faveur des Grecs lors de l'insurrection de 1821, *Balkan Studies* 7/1 (1966), 27–48; Allan Cunningham, The Philhellenes, Canning and Greek Independence, *Middle Eastern Studies* 14/2 (May 1978), 151–181; Jean Dimakis, Le Philhellénisme en Europe pendant l'insurrection grecque et le rôle de la presse, *Études Slaves et Est-Européennes/Slavic and East-European Studies* 13 (1968), 46–53; Natalie Klein, 'L'humanité, le christianisme, et la liberté': Die internationale Philhellenische Vereinsbewegung der 1820er Jahre, Mainz 2000.

37 On this, see esp. Theophilus C. Prousis, Russian Philorthodox Relief during the Greek War of Independence, *Modern Greek Studies Yearbook* 1 (1985), 31–62; Klein, 'L'humanité, le christianisme, et la liberté', 43–50.

38 On the units of philhellenic volunteers, which scholars have often compared to the International Brigades that fought in the Spanish Civil War, see Douglas Dakin, *British and American Philhellenes during the War of Greek Independence, 1821–1833*, Thessaloniki 1955; Christopher M. Woodhouse, *The Philhellenes*, London 1969; Brewer, *Flame of Freedom*, 137–153.

39 Andreas Fahrmeir, *Europa zwischen Restauration, Reform und Revolution 1815–1850*, Munich 2012, 41f.

40 On Byron's role and his importance to the Greek struggle for independence, see St Clair, *That Greece Might Still Be Free*, 173–184; Bass, *Freedom's Battle*, 100–110.

41 On the philhellenic press and its international campaigns, see Dimakis, Le philhellénisme en Europe, 46–53; Jean Dimakis, *La guerre de l'indépendance greque vue par la presse française (Période de 1821 à 1824)*, Thessaloniki 1968; Carl R. Zimmermann, Philhellenism in the American Press during the Greek

Revolution, *Neo-Hellenika* 2 (1975), 181–211; Richard Clogg, Some Aspects of the Philhellenic Press in Britain during the Early Nineteenth Century, *Philhellenische Studien* 3 (1994), 19–30.

42 Klein, '*L'humanité, le christianisme, et la liberté*', 235–238, 292–306.

43 Outstanding examples of such 'atrocity propaganda' include Johann Friedrich Gottlieb Nagel, *Werden die türkischen Schlachtbänke noch länger von griechischem Blute rauchen? oder soll der Erbfeind des Kreuzes die Christenheit noch länger höhnen? Ein Wort zu seiner Zeit*, Braunschweig 1821; Anon., *Address in Behalf of the Greeks: Especially Those Who Have Survived the Late Massacre in Scio*, Edinburgh 1822; Sophia Mazro, translated by Mr Kelch, *Turkish Barbarity: An Affecting Narrative of the Unparalleled Suffering of Mrs. Sophia Mazro, A Greek Lady of Missolonghi*, Providence, RI 1828.

44 Thomas Scheffler, 'Wenn hinten, weit, in der Türkei die Völker aufeinander schlagen...': Zum Funktionswandel 'orientalischer' Gewalt in europäischen Öffentlichkeiten des 19. und 20. Jahrhunderts, in Jörg Requate/Martin Schulze Wessel, eds., *Europäische Öffentlichkeit: Transnationale Kommunikation seit dem 18. Jahrhundert*, Frankfurt a. M. 2002, 205–230 at 220–224; Jon Western, Prudence or Outrage? Public Opinion and Humanitarian Intervention in Historical and Comparative Perspective, in Klose, ed., *Emergence of Humanitarian Intervention*, 165–184 at 171–177.

45 Bass, *Freedom's Battle*, 48.

46 On the importance of humanitarian strategies by independence movements to gain international public support into the twenty-first century, see Thomas Scheffler, Ethnizität, symbolische Gewalt und internationaler Terrorismus im Vorderen Orient, in Thomas Scheffler, ed., *Ethnizität und Gewalt*, Hamburg 1991, 221–250 at 228–230; Fabian Klose, *Menschenrechte im Schatten kolonialer Gewalt: Die Dekolonisierungskriege in Kenia und Algerien 1945–1962*, Munich 2009, 256–275.

47 Klein, '*L'humanité, le christianisme, et la liberté*', 176–178, 190f.; Rodogno, *Against Massacre*, 72–74.

48 Nina Athanassoglou-Kallmyer, *French Images from the Greek War of Independence 1821–1830: Art and Politics under the Restoration*, New Haven, CT 1989.

49 Eugène Delacroix, 'Scènes des massacres de Scio; familles grecques attendent la mort ou l'esclavage', 1824. The oil painting, measuring 354 cm by 419 cm, is now on display at the Louvre in Paris. On the meaning and significance of the painting, see Athanassoglou-Kallmyer, *French Images*, 29–37; Paul Colin Joannides, Delacroix, Byron and the Greek War of Independence, *Burlington Magazine* 125/965 (August 1983), 495–500; Elisabeth A. Fraser, *Delacroix, Art and Patrimony in Post-Revolutionary France*, Cambridge 2004, 39–77.

50 Eugène Delacroix, 'La Grèce sur les ruines de Missolonghi', 1826. The oil painting, measuring 142 cm by 213 cm, is now on display at the Musée des Beaux-Arts de Bordeaux. On the meaning and significance of the painting, see Athanassoglou-Kallmyer, *French Images*, 87–107.

51 On the potent symbolism of white (Greek) women enslaved by (Turkish) Muslims, which reached as far as abolitionist circles in the United States, see

Yellin, *Women and Sisters*, 99–124. On the subtext of sexual violence against enslaved Christian women by Muslims in the paintings of Delacroix, see Fraser, *Delacroix*, 70–77. The motif of white Christian women abducted, raped and enslaved by 'black Muslim barbarians' was used by later artists in different contexts, e.g. by Jaroslav Čermák in his paintings 'Raid by Bachi-Bouzouks on a Christian Village in Herzegovina' and 'Abduction of a Herzegovinian Woman' (both 1861) and 'Spoils of War' (Herzegovina, 1862; Young Christian Women Abducted by Bachi-Bouzouks and Taken to Adrianople, There to Be Sold) (1868). On this, see Roger Diederen, Über die Grenzen: Ein Blick in die Ferne, in Roger Diederen/Davy Depelchin, eds., *Orientalismus in Europa: Von Delacroix bis Kandinsky*, Munich 2010, 35–53 at 51–53.

52 Charles Brinsley Sheridan, *Thoughts on the Greek Revolution*, London 1822, 16.

53 Ibid., 77f.

54 This was the precise line of argument adopted by Jean Joseph Paris, a former French commissioner in the Ionian Islands, in criticising British policy. In an 1821 pamphlet, which was translated into German (although not, it seems, into English), he accused Britain of concealing mercantilist ambitions under 'the sacred veil of humanity' and of opposing African slavery with such force and persistence 'only because it can rely on the bondage of the Indians' – a policy 'that drops the mask of philanthropy in making representations from court to court in favour of a barbarous people which connives at the trade in negroes as well as the trade in and murder of whites'. Jean Joseph Paris, *Considérations sur la crise actuelle de l'empire ottoman, les causes qui l'ont amenée, et les effets qui doivent la suivre*, Paris 1821, vii.

55 'I assert that the Negro Slave Trade was nothing in the scale of misery and debasement against the horrors which, during this sanguinary contest, must continue for ever.' Thomas Lord Erskine, *A Letter to the Earl of Liverpool on the Subject of the Greeks*, London 1823, 17.

56 Ibid., 18f

57 Ibid., 19.

58 Ibid., 20.

59 Ibid., 20–22.

60 Ricardus Incognitus, *An Address to the People of the British Dominions, on Behalf of Humanity, and of the Suffering Greeks*, London 1825, 1–9.

61 Ibid., 6.

62 Ibid., 7.

63 François-René de Chateaubriand, *Note sur la Grèce*, Paris 1825.

64 François-René de Chateaubriand, Opinion sur le projet de loi relative à la repression des délits commis dans les échelles du Levant, 13 March 1826, in François-René de Chateaubriand, *Œuvres completes de Chateaubriand*, vol. 5, Paris 1861, 56–62 at 57.

65 Ibid., 57f.

66 François-René de Chateaubriand, Discours en réponse à M. Le Garde des Sceaux, in François-René de Chateaubriand, *Œuvres completes de Chateaubriand*, vol. 5, Paris 1861, 63–66.

67 Ibid., 65f.
68 Ibid., 66.
69 Schulz, *Sieg der zivilisierten Welt*, 237–244; Rodogno, *Against Massacre*, 78.
70 On the diplomatic efforts to solve the Greek question by the European Concert of Powers between 1822 and 1825, see Temperley, *Foreign Policy of Canning*, 326–337; Crawley, *Question of Greek Independence*, 30–42.
71 On Muhammad Ali Pasha and his significance, see Khaled Fahmy, *Mehmed Ali: From Ottoman Governor to Ruler of Egypt*, Oxford 2009.
72 On the Egyptian invasion under Ibrahim Pasha, see Dakin, *Greek Struggle*, 132–141; Brewer, *Flame of Freedom*, 234–246.
73 A vivid account is given in the report from Stratford Canning to George Canning, 17 December 1825: '[Ibrahim] now acts on a system little short of extermination … he seems to spare no one, where the slightest show of resistance is made.' In TNA, FO 881/165.
74 Jelavich, *Russia's Balkan Entanglements*, 71–75.
75 Schroeder, *Transformation of European Politics*, 642–647; Crawley, *Question of Greek Independence*, 43–54.
76 Extract from the Memorandum of a Conference between Mr. Canning and Count Lieven, 25 October 1825, in TNA, FO 881/165. For the memorandum, see also Arthur Wellesley of Wellington, ed., *Supplementary Despatches, Correspondence, and Memoranda of Field Marshal Arthur Duke of Wellington*, vol. 2, London 1867, 547.
77 Letter from Canning to Liverpool, 25 October 1825, in Augustus Granville Stapleton, *George Canning and His Time*, London 1859, 465f.
78 On Stratford Canning's role as British ambassador in the diplomatic negotiations with the Porte, see Steven Richmond, *The Voice of England in the East: Stratford Canning and Diplomacy with the Ottoman Empire*, London 2014, 133–147, 164–200.
79 Letter from George Canning to Stratford Canning, 9 January 1826, in Stanley Lane-Poole, *The Life of the Right Honourable Stratford Canning: From His Memoirs and Private and Official Papers*, vol. 1, London 1888, 395. Augustus Granville Stapleton, Canning's private secretary and biographer, would later also describe this as the turning point: 'It was not until the mode in which hostilities were conducted by the Turkish general, Ibrahim Pacha, … that he entertained the idea of a forcible intervention. It was evident that the Pacha was carrying on a war of extermination – wherever there was the slightest resistance, he massacred all the males, and sent the women and children into slavery in Egypt. He was labouring to blot out of existence a whole Christian people, and to establish a new Barbary State on the shores of the Mediterranean, in the very midst of Europe. Mr. Canning held this to be a *casus belli*, giving all nations a right to interfere by force.' In Augustus Granville Stapleton, *Intervention and Non-Intervention or the Foreign Policy of Great Britain from 1790 to 1865*, London 1866, 32.
80 Besides Lieven's claims, Britain's purported knowledge of the 'barbarisation plan' stemmed largely from a memorandum written by Stratford Canning on 17 December 1825: 'There is room to apprehend that many of his prisoners have been sent into Egypt as slaves, the children, it is asserted, being even compelled to embrace the Mahometan faith.' In TNA, FO 881/165. On the

serious doubts concerning the existence of any such plan, see Letter from Lord Bathurst to Wellington, 17 February 1826, in Arthur Wellesley of Wellington, ed., *Supplementary Despatches, Correspondence, and Memoranda of Field Marshal Arthur Duke of Wellington*, vol. 3, London 1868, 119; Memorandum on Count Lieven's Paper of Queries von Wellington to Canning, 3 August 1826, in ibid., 362.

81 Instructions from Earl Bathurst to the Lords Commissioners of the Admiralty, 8 February 1826, in TNA, ADM 1/467; Letter from Canning to Lieven, 29 August 1826, in Wellington, *Supplementary Despatches*, vol. 3, 393–395.

82 Instructions from George Canning to Stratford Canning, 10 February 1826, in TNA, FO 881/165.

83 Ibid. Sir Robert Wilson also drew this parallel in the Commons debate on 21 November 1826: 'He could see no objection to the interference of this country between Greece and the Pacha of Egypt, who carried Greek women into slavery. The principle upon which this country attacked Algiers was, the carrying Europeans into slavery. Now was the time, or never. Every assistance ought to be given by our government to the Greeks.' In T. C. Hansard, ed., *The Parliamentary Debates from the Earliest Period to the Year 1803*, vol. 16, http://hansard.millbanksystems.com/commons/1826/nov/21/address-on-the-kings-speech-at-the.

84 Instructions Given to the Duke of Wellington, on Proceeding to St Petersburgh, in February 1826, Canning to Wellington, 10 February 1826, in TNA, FO 881/165.

85 On the question of piracy, see Apostolos E. Vacalopoulos, Piracy during the Last Years of the Greek War of Independence, in Apostolos E. Vacalopoulos/ Constantinos D. Svolopoulos/Belá K. Király, eds., *Southeast European Maritime Commerce and Naval Policies from the Mid-Eighteenth Century to 1914*, Boulder, CO 1988, 363–377.

86 John Bew has argued that Britain had been drawn into military intervention on behalf of Greece solely for strategic reasons, to preserve the balance of power, and that moral and humanitarian reasons had had no part to play. This argument fails, however, to consider that its foreign policy paradigm of abolition had years ago committed Britain to a policy of intervention that was decisively influenced by humanitarian impulses. On this, see Bew, 'From an Umpire to a Competitor', 117–138 at 117–119 and 128–134.

87 Instructions from Canning to Wellington, 10 February 1826, in TNA, FO 881/165. On the influence of public opinion, see also Temperley, *Foreign Policy of Canning*, 349f., 391f.

88 On negotiations between Britain and Russia see Wellington's memoranda in TNA, FO 800/231. See also Temperley, *Foreign Policy of Canning*, 351–356, 390–393; Crawley, *Question of Greek Independence*, 54–62.

89 Protocol of Conference, between the British and Russian Plenipotentiaries, Relative to the Mediation of Great Britain, between the Ottoman Porte and the Greeks, 23 March 1826, in BFSP 14, 629–632.

90 'In order to effect a complete separation between Individuals of the two Nations, and to prevent the collisions which must be the necessary

consequences of a conflict of such duration, the Greeks should purchase the property of Turks, whether situated on the Continent of Greece, or in the Islands.' Ibid., 630.

91 On the later policy of population transfer, see Weitz, From the Vienna to the Paris System, 1313–1343; Michelle Tusan, *Smyrna's Ashes: Humanitarianism, Genocide, and the Birth of the Middle East*, Berkeley, CA 2012.

92 See Article 5: 'That, moreover, His Britannick Majesty and His Imperial Majesty will not seek, in this arrangement, any increase of Territory, nor any exclusive influence, nor advantage in Commerce for their Subjects, which shall not be equally attainable by all other Nations.' BFSP 14, 632.

93 On the French position see e.g. Note du département sur les affaires d'Orient, 1826, in MAE, MD G 9; Note pour le Conseil, 5 December 1826, in ibid.; Notes adressées aux ambassadeurs de Russie et d'Angleterre par le baron de Damas, in ibid.

94 For the treaty in its original French, see TNA, FO 93/81/29. For its English translation, see Treaty between Great Britain, France, and Russia for the Pacification of Greece, 6 July 1827, in BFSP 14, 632–636 at 633. On the negotiations preceding the Treaty of London, see Abstracts of Proceedings in the Greek Question, to the Conclusion of the Treaty between England, Russia, and France, of July 6th 1827, in TNA, FO 421/2; Crawley, *Question of Greek Independence*, 73–78.

95 The Treaty of London also made explicit reference to the idea of separating the populations: 'In order to effect a complete separation between the individuals of the two Nations, and to prevent the collisions which would be the inevitable consequence of so protracted a struggle, the Greeks shall become possessors of all Turkish Property situated either upon the Continent, or in the Islands of Greece, on condition of indemnifying the former proprietors.' Treaty, 6 July 1827, in BFSP 14, 635.

96 For the 'Article Additionnel et Sécret', see TNA, FO 93/81/29. For its English translation, see 'Additional Article', 6 July 1827, in BFSP 14, 637–639.

97 On this, see Secret and Confidential, Abstract of Proceedings in the Greek Question Subsequent to the Treaty of the 6th July, 1827, in TNA, FO 421/3; Secret and Confidential, Protocols of Conferences Held at Constantinople, between the Representatives of Great Britain, France, and Russia, 1827, in TNA, FO 881/6A.

98 Proclamation of the Provisional Government of Greece, accepting the Armistice with the Ottoman Porte, proposed by the Mediating Powers, Great Britain, France, and Russia, 21 August 1827, in BFSP 14, 1048–1050; Manifesto of the Sublime Porte, declining the Pacification with the Greeks, proposed by the Mediating Powers, 9 June 1827, in ibid., 1042–1048; Christopher M. Woodhouse, *The Battle of Navarino*, London 1965, 55–60.

99 On this, see Premières Instructions communes aux Officiers commandans, dans les mers du Levant, les escadres respectives des Hautes Puissance Contractantes, 12 July 1827, in TNA, FO 881/6C; Seconde Instruction

commune aux Officiers commandans, dans les mers du Levant, les escadres respectives des Hautes Puissance Contractantes, 12 July 1827, in ibid.; Secret Instructions to be addressed to the Admirals commanding the squadrons of the three Powers in the Mediterranean, 15 October 1827, in ibid.

100 Will Smiley has described this 'pacific blockade' as practised in Greece as a significant precedent in international law. See Will Smiley, War without War: The Battle of Navarino, the Ottoman Empire, and the Pacific Blockade, *Journal of the History of International Law* 18/1 (2016), 42–69.

101 Protocol of the Admirals commanding the British, Russian, and French Squadrons, off Navarin, 18 October 1827, in BFSP 14, 1050f.

102 For a detailed account of the Battle of Navarino, the last naval battle to be fought only with sailing ships, see George Finlay, *A History of Greece from the Conquest by the Romans to the Present Time*, vol. VII: *The Greek Revolution*, pt. II, Oxford 1877, 16–20; Woodhouse, *Battle of Navarino*, 110–141; Brewer, *Flame of Freedom*, 325–336.

103 Report from Codrington to Stratford Canning, 20 October 1827, in TNA, FO 881/6A; report from Codrington to Croker, 21 October 1827, in TNA, FO 78/162. In an account written not long after the events, the naval historian James Ralfe sought to justify Codrington's actions at Navarino by equating it with, among others, that of Admiral Exmouth at Algiers in 1816, in each case blaming the outbreak of hostilities on the opposing side. On this, see James Ralfe, *The Battle of Navarin, Compared with Other Important Naval Events; Justifying, by Analogy, the Conduct of Sir Edward Codrington Shewing His Right to the Thanks of Parliament, and the Propriety of Granting Pecuniary Compensation to the Men*, London 1829, 27–32.

104 On this, see Copie d'une note addressée à Son Excellence le Reis Effendi, par les Ambassadeurs des trois Cours, 10 November 1827, in TNA, FO 881/6C; Letter from Stratford Canning to Wellesley, 11 November 1827, in ibid.

105 The war between Russia and the Ottoman Empire ended on 14 September 1829 with the Treaty of Adrianople, in which Russia made territorial gains in the Danube delta and in Armenia. On this, see Jelavich, *Russia's Balkan Entanglements*, 81–89; Anderson, *Eastern Question*, 67–73; Bitis, *Russia and the Eastern Question*, 274–377.

106 Protocole de la Conférence tenue au Foreign Office, 12 March 1828, in TNA, FO 881/6C; Letter from Dudley to Lieven, 12 March 1828, in ibid.; Instructions à adresser aux Amiraux commandant les Escadres des Hautes Puissances dans les Mers du Levant, 12 March 1828, in ibid.

107 Instructions à adresser aux Amiraux commandant les Escadres des Hautes Puissances dans les Mers du Levant, 12 March 1828, in ibid., 48–50. On the question of slaves, see also Letter from Barker to Stratford Canning, 20 May 1828, in TNA, FO 352/20A. Most accounts of Greece as the first instance of humanitarian intervention fail to consider this genuinely humanitarian aspect.

108 French report, 12 January 1828, in SHD, Marine, BB4/504.

109 Protocols of Conferences held in London, between the Plenipotentiaries of Great Britain, France, and Russia, relative to the Mediation between Turkey

and Greece, 19 July 1828, in BFSP 16, 1083–1086. After the Battle of Navarino the French diplomatist and archbishop Dominique Dufour de Pradt accused the naval measures of being insufficient to prevent Ibrahim Pasha from continuing his campaign on land and therefore of limited use in settling the conflict. On this, see Dominique Dufour de Pradt, *De l'intervention armée pour la pacification de la Grèce*, Paris 1828, 61–70.

110 Projet de Déclaration au sujet de l'envoi d'un coprs de troupes dans la Péninsule Grecque, 11 August 1828, in TNA, FO 881/6D.

111 On the French expeditionary force, see Tableau de la Composition du Corps destine pour la Morée, July 1828, in SHAT, D² 1; Instructions confidentielles, Ministère de la Guerre, 6 August 1828, in ibid.; Etat des Troupes Composant la Division Expeditionnaire, Embarqués à Toulon pour la Morée, n.d., in SHAT, D² 6.

112 Protocol of Conference between Vice-Admirals Sir Edward Codrington, De Rigny, and Count Heyden, 25 July 1828, in BFSP 17, 374f.

113 Memorandum of Conference between Vice-Admiral Sir Edward Codrington and the Pacha of Egypt, 6 August 1828, in BFSP 17, 376–380 at 379; Letter from Codrington to Croker, 9 August 1828, in ibid., 372–374.

114 Convention concluded by Sir Edward Codrington with the Pacha of Egypt, 6 August 1828, in ibid., 380–382.

115 Protocole de la Conférence tenue au Foreign Office, 18 August 1826, in TNA, FO 881/6D; Instructions for the Admirals, 18 August 1828, in ibid.

116 Instructions for the Admirals, 18 August 1828, in ibid.

117 For documents and reports concerning the deployment of the French expeditionary force between August 1828 and February 1833, see SHAT, D² 1; SHAT, D² 2; SHAT, D² 3; SHAT, D² 4; SHAT, D² 5. On the deployment of the French expeditionary force, see also Général de division Pellion, La Grèce et les Capodistrias pendant l'occupation française de 1828 à 1834, Paris 1855; Puryear, *France and the Levant*, 54–58.

118 'Des commissaires des trois puissances, accompagnés de personnages grecs, furent chargés de présider à l'embarquement de l'armée égyptienne, et d'empêcher que les Arabes n'enlevassent de force les femmes et les enfants.' Pellion, *La Grèce*, 92.

119 A comparable delegation of artists and scholars also accompanied Napoleon's Egyptian campaign. On this, see Note pour le Ministre, Ministère de la Guerre, 13 October 1829, in SHAT, XP 51.

120 'La brigade française devait, au nom de l'alliance, servir de sauvegarde au pays et y maintenir le bon ordre.' Pellion, *La Grèce*, 125–168 at 125; Rodogno, *Against Massacre*, 84–87; Finlay, *History of Greece*, pt. II, 27f.

121 Of these actions, George Finlay writes: 'The French troops transformed themselves into an army of pioneers; and these pestilential mediaeval castles were converted into habitable towns', Finlay, *History of Greece*, pt. II, 28.

122 Protocole, No. 1, de la Conférence tenue au Foreign Office, 3 February 1830, in TNA, FO 881/6AA. On the founding of the Greek state and the diplomatic negotiations surrounding it, see Woodhouse, *Greek War of Independence*, 141–155.

123 Rodogno, *Against Massacre*, 88–90; Hanioğlu, *Brief History*, 67–69.

124 'Affranchissement d'esclaves blancs. Firman du Sultan Mahmoud II aux
    Juges, Naibs, Muselims et autres gouverneurs de l'Empire', 1830, in George
    Young, *Corps de droit ottoman: Recueil des Codes, Lois, Règlements,
    Ordonnances et Actes les plus importants du Droit Intérieur, et d'Ètudes sur le
    Droit Coutumier de l'Empire Ottoman*, vol. 2, Oxford 1905, 171f. On this, see
    also Erdem, *Slavery in the Ottoman Empire*, 44–45, 59.
125 On this, see Bernard Lewis, *What Went Wrong? The Clash between Islam and
    Modernity in the Middle East*, London 2002, 98f.; Lewis, *Race and Slavery*,
    78–84.
126 Wheaton, *Elements of International Law*, vol. I, 125. The French diplomat
    Dominique Dufour de Pradt likewise referred to an 'intervention au nom de
    l'humanité', with 'l'humanité' as the key category. The driving force behind
    the intervention had been the progress of civilisation, which had also swept
    away the slave trade: 'C'est la civilisation qui … a poursuivi l'abolition de la
    traite des nègres.' On this, see Pradt, *De l'intervention armée*, 2, 11f.
127 Wheaton, *Elements of International Law*, 129.
128 On the protection of minorities as justification for intervention, see also
    Stefan Kroll, The Legal Justification of International Intervention:
    Theories of Community and Admissibility, in Klose, ed., *Emergence of
    Humanitarian Intervention*, 73–88 at 79–87.
129 On the position and interests of the great powers of Europe with regard to
    the 'Eastern Question' and the eastern Mediterranean after 1830 see e.g.
    Barry Dennis Hunt, The Eastern Question in British Naval Policy and
    Strategy, 1789–1913, in Apostolos E. Vacalopoulos/Constantinos
    D. Svolopoulos/Béla K. Király, eds., *Southeast European Maritime
    Commerce and Naval Policies from the Mid-Eighteenth Century to 1914*,
    Boulder, CO 1988, 52–75; Holland, *Blue-Water Empire*, 61–108;
    Puryear, *France and the Levant*, 147–218.
130 Caesar E. Farah, *The Politics of Interventionism in Ottoman Lebanon,
    1830–1861*, London 2000, 12–29; Anderson, *Eastern Question*, 88–109.
131 The Maronites are the oldest and largest Christian community in Lebanon
    and recognise the pope in Rome as the head of their church. The Druzes
    came into being as a religious community in their own right in the eleventh
    century as an offshoot of an Islamic denomination, Ismailism. On the history
    of these two religious communities, see Pierre Dib, *History of the Maronite
    Church*, Beirut 1971; Kais M. Firro, *A History of the Druzes*, Leiden 1992.
132 Maroun Kisirwani, Foreign Interference and Religious Animosity in
    Lebanon, *Journal of Contemporary History* 15/4 (October 1980), 685–700;
    Ussama Makdisi, *The Culture of Sectarianism: Community, History, and
    Violence in Nineteenth-Century Ottoman Lebanon*, Berkeley, CA 2000, 51–66.
133 In this constellation, which is often referred to as the 'second Egyptian crisis'
    or 'second oriental crisis' and which lasted from 1839 to 1841, Britain,
    Russia, Austria and Prussia took the side of the sultan, while France, looking
    to protect its own interests in the region, stood by its Egyptian ally
    Muhammad Ali Pasha. On the crisis and its international significance, see
    Farah, *Politics of Interventionism*, 30–51.
134 Makdisi, *Culture of Sectarianism*, 67–95. On the heavy clashes between Druze
    and Maronites in 1845, see Letter from Colonel Rose to Earl Aberdeen,

9 February 1845, in BFSP 36, 310–312; Statement respecting the Civil War in the Lebanon, 30 April 1845, in ibid., 338f.; Letter from Colonel Rose to Earl Aberdeen, 17 May 1845, in ibid., 346–349; E. Hertslet, Memorandum on the Affairs of Syria, 1841 to 1845, 2 August 1860, in TNA, FO 881/879.

135 On this, see Yann Bouyrat, *La France et les maronites du Mont-Liban: Nassiance d'une relation privilégiée (1831–1861)*, Paris 2013; Shakeed Salih, The British–Druze Connection and the Druze Rising of 1896 in the Hawran, *Middle Eastern Studies* 13/2 (May 1977), 251–257.

136 Farah, *Politics of Interventionism*, 76–78; Kisirwani, Foreign Interference and Religious Animosity, 685–700.

137 On the broad *Tanzimāt* programme of reforms from 1839 to 1876, see Roderic H. Davison, *The Reform in the Ottoman Empire 1856–1876*, Princeton, NJ 1963; Donald Quataert, *The Ottoman Empire 1700–1922*, Cambridge 2005, 65–68; Carter Vaugh Findley, The Tanzimat, in Reşat Kasaba, ed., *The Cambridge History of Turkey*, vol. 4: *Turkey in the Modern World*, Cambridge 2008, 11–37.

138 On the general response to the reform programme, see Davison, *Reform in the Ottoman Empire*, 52–80. For a special focus on the province of Syria, see Moshe Ma'oz, *Ottoman Reform in Syria and Palestine, 1840–1861: The Impact of the Tanzimat on Politics and Society*, Oxford 1968, 210–230.

139 Farah, *Politics of Interventionism*, 525f. For the origins of the conflict from a contemporary French perspective, see Mémoire sur les Causes et Origines des événements de 1860 au Mont-Liban, 25 July 1860, in MAE, MD T 62.

140 Letter from Moore to Bulwer, 30 May 1860, in TNA, FO 195/655.

141 For a detailed account of the fighting and the massacres Farah, *Politics of Interventionism*, 554–602; Leila Tarazi Fawaz, *An Occasion for War: Civil Conflict in Lebanon and Damascus in 1860*, Berkeley, CA 1994, 47–77. The artist Jean-Baptiste Huysmans in 1862 unveiled a historical painting entitled 'The Captive: Christian woman kidnapped by the Druze in Sidon' in which the prejudices of the time are strongly in evidence: A young Christian woman of strikingly pale complexion and wearing a white dress is shown in the process of being abducted by three dark-skinned Druze, while the city of Sidon can be seen burning in the background. On this, see Diederen, Über die Grenzen, 50.

142 Estimates of the number of victims claimed by the massacre vary greatly, from some 3,000 to well over 8,000. On the events in Damascus on 9 July 1860, see Farah, *Politics of Interventionism*, 587–593; Fawaz, *Occasion for War*, 78–100. For a contemporary European account, see Letter from Brant to Bulwer, 11 July 1860, in TNA, FO 78/1557; Letter from Blunt to Bulwer, 21 July 1860, in ibid.; Eyewitness report of the Irish missionary, Robson, Letter from Dufferin to Russell, 23 September 1860, in TNA, FO 406/10.

143 In recognition of his efforts, Abd al-Qādir received decorations from several European rulers including Napoleon III, who awarded him the grand cross of the Legion of Honour. Jean-Baptiste Huysmans memorialized his deeds in an 1861 painting entitled 'Mon salut d'amitié et de respect à tous ceux qui vous parleront de moi'. For Abd al-Qādir's efforts in Damascus, see Letter from Cowley to Russell, 25 July 1860, in TNA, FO 406/10.

144 Letter from Moore to Russell, 13 July 1860, in TNA, FO 78/1557; John P. Spagnolo, *France and Ottoman Lebanon 1861–1914*, London 1977, 31–33; Ma'oz, *Ottoman Reform*, 228–240.

145 Davide Rodogno, The 'Principles of Humanity' and the European Powers' Intervention in Ottoman Lebanon and Syria in 1860–1861, in Simms/Trim, eds., *Humanitarian Intervention*, 159–183 at 168; Farah, *Politics of Interventionism*, 583–585. For the protection given by the massed warships see e.g. Letter from Admiral Martin to Weckbecker, consul general of Austria, 14 September 1860, in HHSta, GKA KsA Beirut 4–1.

146 On this, see e.g. Letter from Moore to Bulwer, 1 June 1860, in TNA, FO 195/655; Letter from Moore to Bulwer, 3 June 1860, in ibid.; Joint note of protest of the foreign consuls to Fuad Pasha, 30 June 1860, in TNA, FO 78/1557.

147 On this, see Lettre Collective adressée par les Cinq Consuls des Grandes Puissances à Beyrout aux Cheiks Druzes, 27 June 1860, in TNA, FO 195/655; Report on a Mission to the Druzes Chiefs in Lebanon, 27 June 1860, in TNA, FO 78/1557; Translation of the Reply of the Druze Chiefs to the Collective Letter of the Five Consuls General, 9 July 1860, in ibid.; Treaty of Peace between the Christians and the Druzes, June 1860, in ibid.

148 For the numerous accounts by British and French diplomats of the massacres, see TNA, FO 78/1557 and TNA, FO 195/655; MAE, CPC B12. On the key role of the British consuls as political and humanitarian actors in the Levant more generally, see John Dickie, *The British Consul: Heir to a Great Tradition*, London 2007, 57–80.

149 'You know the good will of my Government towards the Druze Community and their Chiefs, and the advantages which these have often desired in their time of need and distress at the hands of that Government. Should you not comply with my desire you will have acted in a manner which will affect the interests of your community.' Letter from Moore to Sheikh al-Atrash, 16 June 1860, in TNA, FO 78/1557.

150 Letter from Sheikh al-Atrash to Moore, 23 June 1860, in ibid.

151 According to Moore's estimates, 150 Christian villages were destroyed and 6,000 Christians killed, with another 7,500 directly harmed by the conflict. Report from Moore to Bulwer, 30 June 1860, in ibid.

152 Ibid.

153 Rodogno, *Against Massacre*, 97f.; Bass, *Freedom's Battle*, 182–186.

154 Letter from Cowley to Russell, 5 July 1860, in TNA, FO 406/10.

155 'La question au surplus est une question d'humanité, et ne comporte aucune divergence d'opinion entre les cabinets. Leurs appréciations seront unanimes.' Le Ministre des Affaires Étrangères à M. le Marquis de Châteaurenard, 5 July 1860, in ibid., 193f. at 193.

156 'Cette commission serait envoyée dans le Liban pour rechercher les circonstances qui ont provoqué les derniers conflits, déterminer la part de responsabilité des chefs de l'insurrection et des agents de l'administration locale, ainsi que les réparations dues aux victimes, et enfin détudier, pour les soumettre à l'approbation de leurs Gouvernements et de la Porte, les dispositions qui pourraient être adoptees en vue de conjurer de noveaux malheurs.' Le Ministre des Affaires Étrangères, aux Représentants de

l'Empereur à Londres, Vienne, Saint-Pétersbourg et Berlin, 6 July 1860, in Ministère des Affaires Étrangères, ed., *Documents Diplomatiques 1861*, Paris 1862, 194–196 at 195; Letter from Thouvenel to Count Persigny, 16 July 1860, in TNA, FO 406/10.

157 'Il ne s' agit aujourd'hui ni de dissentiments politiques, ni de rivalitiés d'influence; l'humanité exige une prompte intervention et des disposition urgentes.' Le Ministre des Affaires Étrangères à M. le Marquis de Lavalette, 6 July 1860, in TNA, FO 406/10, 196f. at 196.

158 Le Ministre de la Marine à M. le Ministre des Affaires étrangères, 7 July 1860, in ibid., 197.

159 Letter from Cowley to Russell, 25 July 1860, in ibid.; Fawaz, *Occasion for War*, 112f.

160 Letter from Russell to Cowley, 6 July 1860, in TNA, FO 406/10; Letter from Russell to Bulwer, 10 July 1860, in ibid.

161 On this, see the conversation between the British ambassador, Erskine, and the Russian foreign minister, Alexander Gorchakov: 'He could scarcely conceal the triumph … and told me that he was sure the whole world would sooner or later admit that he had not at all overstated the grievances under which the Christian subjects of the Porte were now suffering. … I refrained from reminding his Excellency that the atrocities which had called forth animadversion of Her Majesty's Government had nothing in common with alleged state of normal misrule in Bulgaria, Bosnia.' Letter from Erskine to Russell, 11 July 1860, in ibid.

162 Letter from Cowley to Russell, 24 July 1860, in ibid.

163 Letter from Cowley to Russell, 25 July 1860, in ibid. The Russian proposal for such a secret additional article ultimately foundered on the opposition of the other great powers. On this, see Letter from Bloomfield to Russell, 11 August 1860, in ibid.

164 Letter from Cowley to Russell, 17 July 1860, in ibid.; Letter from Cowley to Russell, 25 July 1860, in ibid.; Rodogno, *Against Massacre*, 105.

165 Personal letter from Russell to Palmerston, 27 July 1860, in TNA, PRO 30/22/30.

166 'Russia would probably join France … If Austria and Prussia should leave us, we should be alone.' Ibid. On the danger of a Franco-Russian alliance, see also Letter from Bulwer to Russell, 25 July 1860, in TNA, PRO 30/22/88.

167 Letter from Cowley to Russell, 19 July 1860, in TNA, FO 406/10; Letter from Russell to Cowley, 23 July 1860, in ibid.

168 On the negotiations at the conference, see Fawaz, *Occasion for War*, 113f.; Bass, *Freedom's Battle*, 186–189.

169 Protocols of Conference between Great Britain, Austria, France, Prussia, Russia, and Turkey, respecting Measures to be taken for the Pacification of Syria, 3 August 1860, in BFSP 50, 8f. See also Convention between Great Britain, Austria, France, Prussia, Russia, and Turkey, respecting Measures to be taken for the Pacification of Syria, 5 September 1860, in ibid., 6–8.

170 Protocols of Conference between Great Britain, Austria, France, Prussia, Russia, and Turkey, respecting Measures to Be Taken for the Pacification of Syria, 3 August 1860, in ibid., 9.

171 Ibid.
172 House of Commons debate on 3 August 1860, in T. C. Hansard, ed., *The Parliamentary Debates from the Earliest Period to the Year 1803*, vol. 160, http:// hansard.millbanksystems.com/commons/1860/aug/03/question-2,   cc. 642–647 and cc. 651–653.
173 Arguments by Henry Rich in the House of Commons debate on 3 August 1860, in T. C. Hansard, ed., *The Parliamentary Debates from the Earliest Period to the Year 1803*, vol. 160, http://hansard.millbanksystems.com/com mons/1860/aug/03/observations#S3V0160P0_18600803_HOC_19,   cc. 632–635 at cc. 635.
174 Arguments by the Marquess of Clanricarde in House of Lords debate on 3 August 1860, in T. C. Hansard, ed., *The Parliamentary Debates from the Earliest Period to the Year 1803*, vol. 160, http://hansard.millbanksystems .com/lords/1860/aug/03/disturbances-in-stria-question,   cc. 622–623 at cc. 623. 'See' is unaccountably rendered as 'Bee' in this digitised version.
175 On the exact composition of the expeditionary force, see list 'Corps expéditionnaire de Syrie' by the Ministère de la Guerre, in SHAT, G4 2.
176 'Vous partez pour la Syrie et la France salue avec bonheur une expédition qui n'a qu'un but, celui de faire triompher les droits de la justice et de l'humanité. Vous n'allez pas, en effet, faire guerre à une Puissance quelcon que, mais vous allez aider le Sultan à faire rentrer dans l'obéissance des sujets aveuglés par un fanatisme d'un autre siècle.' Excerpt from the speech of Napoleon III, 7 August 1860, published in *Le Moniteur*. Letter from Bulwer to Russell, 8 August 1860, in TNA, FO 406/10. On the use of crusading rhetoric in the context of the intervention in the Lebanon, see Jonathan Phillips, *Heiliger Krieg: Eine neue Geschichte der Kreuzzüge*, Bonn 2012, 519f.
177 General de Beaufort d'Hautpoul, Ordre Général No. 1, 7 August 1860, in SHAT, G4 1. See also Letter from MAE to Admiral Hamelin, 4 August 1860, in ibid.
178 Ministère de la Guerre, Notification, 21 July 1860, in SHAT, G4 6; Ernest Louet, *Expédition de Syrie: Beyrouth, Le Liban – Jérusalem, 1860–1864*, Paris 1862, 8f.
179 Louet, *Expédition de Syrie*, 27f.; Bass, *Freedom's Battle*, 194. The king of Sweden made Britain an offer of troops as a contribution to this 'crusade': '[W]ere the Syrian affair to become a Crusade, he should like to take part in it.' Private letter from Jerningham to Russell, 9 August 1860, in TNA, PRO 30/22/78.
180 Letter from Moore to Russell, 16 August 1860, in TNA, FO 195/655; Letter from Moore to Russell, 22 August 1860, in ibid.; Bouyrat, *La France et les maronites*, 549–551; Bass, *Freedom's Battle*, 197–200. Beaufort's landing was commemorated in a painting by Jean-Adolphe Beaucé entitled 'Le Debarquement des troupes français en Syrie, à Beyrouth' (1875).
181 Translation of the Sultan's Firman Addressed to Fuad Pasha, 1860, in TNA, FO 195/655; Translation of Fuad Pasha's Proclamation, in ibid.; Letter from Moore to Bulwer, 21 July 1860, in TNA, FO 406/10.
182 On Fuad Pasha's mission and how he went about it, see Fawaz, *Occasion for War*, 105–108, 135–152; Farah, *Politics of Interventionism*, 603–619.

183 On this, see Makdisi, *Culture of Sectarianism*, 146–151; Ussama Makdisi, After 1860: Debating Religion, Reform, and Nationalism in the Ottoman Empire, *International Journal of Middle East Studies* 34/4 (November 2002), 601–617.

184 On their relations, see Fawaz, *Occasion for War*, 119–121; Yann Bouyrat, *Devoir d'intervenir? L'expédition 'humanitaire' de la France au Liban, 1860*, Paris 2013, 135–148.

185 Farah, *Politics of Interventionism*, 647–668; Bouyrat, *Devoir d'intervenir?*, 135–151. For a detailed account of the French expeditionary force, see Ernest Louet, *Expédition de Syrie;* Camille de Rochemonteix, *Le Liban et l'expédition française en Syrie (1860–1861)*, Paris 1921; Bouyrat, *Devoir d'intervenir?*, 127–152; Olivier Forcade/Frédéric Guelton, L'expédition en Syrie en août 1860 – juin 1861, *Revue internationale d'histoire militaire* 75 (1995), 49–62.

186 Convention Evacuation of Syria, 19 March 1861, in TNA, FO 93/110/17. On the heated debates on extending the period of occupation see e.g. Letter from Dufferin to Russell, 18 December 1860, in TNA, FO 406/10; Letter from Cowley to Russell, 4 January 1861, in ibid.

187 The sources refer to this international ad hoc commission by a variety of names, such as 'Mixed Commission' and 'Syrian Commission'. See e.g. Letter from Cowley to Russell, 2 August 1860, in TNA, FO 406/10.

188 Letter from Russell to Dufferin, 14 August 1860, in ibid.

189 Ibid.

190 The commission met a total of twenty-nine times between 5 October 1860 and 4 May 1861. Its members were the commissioners Weckenbecker (Austria), Beclard (France), Dufferin and later Claneboye (Great Britain), Rehfues (Prussia), Novikov (Russia) and Fuad Pasha and later Abro Efendi for the Ottoman Empire. See Collective Note addressed by European Commissioners to Fuad Pasha, 26 September 1860, in ibid.; Protocol of the First Meeting for the Syrian Commission, held at Beyrout, 5 October 1860, in ibid. The minutes of the commission's sessions can be found in BFSP 51, 293–490.

191 Letter from Dufferin to Brant, 27 September 1860, in TNA, FO 406/10.

192 Letter from Dufferin to Colonel Burnaby and Rev. Jules Ferrette, 24 October 1860, in ibid.; Letter from Dufferin to Bulwer, 26 October 1860, in ibid.

193 On the activities of these relief committees, see Farah, *Politics of Interventionism*, 632–636; Bouyrat, *Devoir d'intervenir?*, 158–179.

194 Protocol of the Third Meeting of the Syrian Commission, held in Beyrout, 11 October 1860, in TNA, FO 406/10; Letter 'Opérations du Comité de Secours à Beyrouth' to Thouvenel, 14 December 1860, in MAE, CPC B13.

195 On this, see Renault, *Cardinal Lavigerie*, 33–41.

196 Fawaz, *Occasion for War*, 201; Rodogno, *Against Massacre*, 109–111.

197 Protocol of the First Meeting for the Syrian Commission, held at Beyrout, 5 October 1860, in TNA, FO 406/10.

198 Protocol of the Sixth Meeting of the Syrian Commission, held at Beyrout, 26 October 1860, in ibid.; Letter from Russell to Dufferin, 2 November

1860, in ibid.; Farah, *Politics of Interventionism*, 619–612. For the Ottoman court files submitted to the commission see e.g. Judgements passed by the Extraordinary Tribunal at Beyrout on the Chief People inculpated in the late Disturbances in the Mountains, December 1860, in TNA, FO 406/10. 'Interrogatories of the Druse Chiefs tried by the Extraordinary Tribunal at Beyrout' appended to Letter from Bulwer to Russell, 3 April 1861, in TNA, FO 881/983; 'Untersuchungsakte gegen die Führer der Libanon Bewegung 1861' fol. 1–252, in HHSta, GKA KsA Beirut 5a-1.

199 Protocol of the Twentieth Meeting of the Syrian Commission, held at Beyrout, 24 January 1861, in TNA, FO 406/10; Protocol of the Twenty-first Meeting of the Syrian Commission, held at Beyrout, 29 January 1861, in ibid.; Protocol of the Twenty-third Meeting of the Syrian Commission, held at Beyrout, 28 February 1861, in ibid.; Farah, *Politics of Interventionism*, 627–629.

200 Bouyrat, *La France et les maronites*, 570.

201 On the respective positions taken by the commissioners and the controversies between them, see Bouyrat, *La France et les maronites*, 567–572; Letter from Dufferin to Bulwer, 7 March 1861, in TNA, FO 406/10; Letter from Russell to Loftus, 13 March 1861, in ibid.; Protocol of the Twenty-third Meeting of the Syrian Commission, held at Beyrout, 28 February 1861, in ibid.

202 On the French position, see Bouyrat, *La France et les maronites*, 566–568.

203 Substance of an Interpellation addressed by Lord Dufferin to Fuad Pasha 10 November 1860, in TNA, FO 406/10; Protocol of the Ninth Meeting of the Syrian Commission, held at Beyrout, 10 November 1860, in ibid. On the British position, see also Private letter from Russell to Dufferin, 8 September 1860, in TNA, PRO 30/22/116; Rodogno, *Against Massacre*, 112; Bass, *Freedom's Battle*, 208–212.

204 Protocol of the Sixteenth Meeting of the Syrian Commission, held at Beyrout, 29. December 1860, in TNA, FO 406/10; Letter from Dufferin to Bulwer, 30 December 1860, in ibid.

205 Letter from Bulwer to Russell, 8 January 1861, in TNA, FO 881/983.

206 Letter from Dufferin to Russell, 4 March 1861, in ibid.

207 Letter from Russell to Bulwer, 8 February 1861, in TNA, FO 406/10. The Porte ultimately proclaimed an amnesty for the entire Druze people. On this, see Farah, *Politics of Interventionism*, 631f.

208 Letter from Napier to Russell, 12 April 1861, in TNA, FO 881/983. Whereas Beclard, the French envoy, was often supported by the Prussian Rehfues, Dufferin and Fuad Pasha formed the opposite pole, with Weckenbecker (Austria) and Novikov (Russia) tending to adopt an intermediate position. On this, see Farah, *Politics of Interventionism*, 702–709; John P. Spagnolo, Constitutional Change in Mount Lebanon: 1861–1864, *Middle Eastern Studies* 7/1 (January 1971), 25–48 at 28–31.

209 Bouyrat, *Devoir d'intervenir?*, 215–250; 'It must always be borne in mind that England and Austria wish to preserve the Turkish Empire. France, Russia and I fear Prussia to destroy it.' Letter from Russell to Cowley, 16 January 1861, in TNA, PRO 30/22/104; Letter from Dufferin to Bulwer,

13 November 1860, in TNA, FO 406/10; Letter from Dufferin to Bulwer, 25 April 1861, in TNA, FO 881/983.

210 Letter from Russell to Cowley, 21 February 1861, in TNA, PRO 30/22/104.

211 Letter from Russell to Cowley, 9 March 1861, in ibid.

212 On the debates within the commission and the models proposed, see e.g. Letter from Dufferin to Bulwer, 18 November 1860, enclosed a 'Synoptic Table of the Various Schemes which have been proposed for the future Government of Syria and the Lebanon', in TNA, FO 406/10; Letter from Dufferin to Bulwer, 14 March 1861, in TNA, FO 881/983; Protocol of the Twenty-sixth Meeting of the Syrian Commission, held at Beyrout, 21 March 1861, in ibid.

213 Letter from Russell to Cowley, 7 November 1860, in TNA, FO 406/10. On this, see also Letter from Russell to Bulwer, 8 October 1860, in TNA, PRO 30/22/116.

214 'In order to effect a complete separation between Individuals of the two Nations, and to prevent the collisions which must be the necessary consequences of a conflict of such duration, the Greeks should purchase the property of Turks, whether situated on the Continent of Greece, or in the Islands.' Protocol of Conference, between the British and Russian Plenipotentiaries, relative to the Mediation of Great Britain, between the Ottoman Porte and the Greeks, 23 March 1826, in BFSP 14, 629–632 at 630.

215 Article 1 'Il sera procédé à la separation ethnographique des Chrétiens et des Druses.' Projet de Réorganisation de la Montagne, 20 March 1861, in TNA, FO 881/983.

216 Ibid.

217 Rodogno, *Against Massacre*, 113–114.

218 On this, see Letter from Dufferin to Bulwer, 11 May 1861, containing 'Maps showing the Proposed Division of the Lebanon into Kamakamiyehs and Circumscriptions, according to the Commissioners' First and Second Projects', in TNA, FO 881/983.

219 Protocol of Conference between the Representatives of the 5 Powers (Great Britain, Austria, France, Prussia, Russia) and Turkey, relative to the Administration of the Lebanon, 9 June 1861, in BFSP 51, 287f.

220 Article 1 'Le Liban sera administré par un Gouverneur Chrétien nommé par la Sublime Porte et relevant d'elle directement.' Règlement pour l'Admnistration du Liban, 9 June 1861, in ibid., 288.

221 Article 2, ibid.

222 Article 15, ibid., 291.

223 Spagnolo, Constitutional Change, 25–48; Farah, *Politics of Interventionism*, 695–698.

224 'Nos efforts à la pacification du Liban, nous avons été guides uniquement par une pensée d'humanité.' Letter from the MAE, 1 July 1861, in MAE, MD T142. Gorchakov, the Russian foreign minister, had likewise claimed 'that his sentiments and policy in the matter had no connection with political rivalries, but were solely governed by considerations of justice and humanity.' Letter from Napier to Russell, 12 April 1861, in TNA, FO 881/983.

225 Pogany, Humanitarian Intervention, 182–190; Rodogno, 'Principles of Humanity', 179–181.

226 On this exemplary character of the intervention in the Lebanon, see Rodogno, *Against Massacre*, 115f. The first application came in the Cretan crisis of 1866–69, which was triggered by a revolt of island's majority Christian population against Ottoman rule. This resulted not in a direct military intervention, but in the evacuation of Christian refugees by warships from France, Russia, Prussia, Austria and Italy (Britain remained strictly neutral). When it came to devising a political settlement, the European states made proposals along the lines of the 'Lebanese solution'. On this, see Rodogno, *Against Massacre*, 118–140; Ann Pottinger Saab, The Doctor's Dilemma: Britain and the Cretan Crisis 1866–69, *Journal of Modern History* 49/4 (December 1977), 1383–1407.

227 Letter from Russell to Cowley, 9 February 1861, in TNA, FO 406/10.

228 'European occupation would be a precedent for other occupations in Bulgaria, in Bosnia, and other Provinces.' Letter from Russell to Cowley, 7 November 1860, in ibid.

229 On the situation in Bosnia and Herzegovina and the revolts there, see Richard Millman, *Britain and the Eastern Question 1875–1878*, Oxford 1979, 13–26; Glenny, *Balkans*, 102–106.

230 What this one-sided contemporary account of events completely omitted to mention was that hundreds of thousands of Muslims were displaced or killed in the course of these insurrections. On this, see McCarthy, *Death and Exile*, 59–108.

231 On the Bulgarian revolt, see Jelavich, *History of the Balkans*, 346–348; Glenny, *Balkans*, 107–112; Millman, *Britain and the Eastern Question*, 121–145.

232 According to contemporary British and American estimates, between 12,000 and 15,000 people were killed in these massacres. However, Richard Millman points out that these estimates often lacked any concrete evidence and were instead decisively shaped by a fundamentally anti-Ottoman attitude. On this, see Richard Millman, The Bulgarian Massacres Reconsidered, *Slavonic and East European Review* 58/2 (April 1980), 218–231.

233 See e.g. Despatch from Count Andrassy to Count Beust, respecting the Insurrection in Bosnia and Herzegovina, and proposed Reforms, 30 December 1875, in Edward Hertslet, ed., *The Map of Europe by Treaty; showing the various Political and Territorial Changes which have taken place since the General Peace of 1814*, vol. IV: *1875 to 1891*, London 1891, 2418–2429. On these early diplomatic activities and the British position, see R. W. Seton-Watson, *Disraeli, Gladstone and the Eastern Question: A Study in Diplomacy and Party Politics*, London 1971, 16–50; Millman, *Britain and the Eastern Question*, 39–57; Matthias Schulz, The Guarantees of Humanity: The Concert of Europe and the Origins of the Russo-Ottoman War of 1877, in Simms/Trim, eds., *Humanitarian Intervention*, 184–204 at 189–192; Stéphanie Prévost, The Eastern Question and Britain's Foreign Policy (1876–1896), in Trevor Harris, ed., *Art, Politics and Society in Britain*

(1880–1914): Aspects of Modernity and Modernism, Newcastle upon Tyne 2009, 121–137.

234 Edwin Pears, The Assasinations at Constantinople, *Daily News* (23 June 1876), 5f.; Edwin Pears, The Moslem Atrocities in Bulgaria, *Daily News* (8 July 1876), 5f.; Januarius A. MacGahan, The War in the East: Atrocities in Bulgaria, *Daily News* (7 August 1876), 5; Januarius A. MacGahan, Turkish Atrocities in Bulgaria, *Daily News* (22 August 1876), 5f. For a collection of MacGahan's reports, see J. A. MacGahan, *The Turkish Atrocities in Bulgaria: Letters of the Special Commissioner of the 'Daily News'*, London 1876.

235 In the next eighteen months, some 3,000 articles about the massacres were published in 200 newspapers across Europe. On this, see David Harris, *Britain and the Bulgarian Horrors of 1876*, Chicago, IL 1939, 61–138; Miloš Ković, *Disraeli and the Eastern Question*, Oxford 2011, 122–125; R. T. Shannon, *Gladstone and the Bulgarian Agitation 1876*, Hassocks 1975, 23–48; For a large collection of French reports on the massacres, see MAE, MD T 131.

236 On the reports being picked up in the Russian press and the demands for intervention raised there, see Letter from Loftus to Derby, 28 June 1876, in TNA, FO 65/938; Letter from Loftus to Derby, 5 July 1876, in ibid.; Letter from Loftus to Derby, 1 August 1876, in TNA, FO 65/939; Report 'Opinions of "Russki Mir" as to the policy of non-intervention pursued by England in the regard to Turkey' by Loftus, 2 August 1876, in ibid.; Report 'Right of intervention in Turkish affairs' by Loftus, 23 August 1876, in ibid.

237 The War in Turkey: Executions of Bulgarians in the Streets of Philippopolis, *Illustrated London News* 1933/LXIX (12 August 1876); The War: Bashi-Bazouks Burning a Village, *Illustrated London News* 1934/LXIX (19 August 1876).

238 Konstantin E. Makovsky, 'The Bulgarian Martyresses' (1877), oil on canvas, 207 x 141 cm, now on display at the National Art Museum of the Republic of Belarus, Minsk.

239 On Walter Baring's special mission, see Millman, *Britain and the Eastern Question*, 148–164; Seton-Watson, *Disraeli*, 57–61.

240 On Baring's final report, see Letter from Elliot to Derby, 5 September 1876, in TNA, FO 881/2936A; Report by Mr. Baring on the Bulgarian Insurrection of 1876, 1 September 1876, in ibid. The report was finally published on 19 September 1876 in *The London Gazette*, the government's official journal. On this, see Report by Mr. Baring on the Atrocities Committed upon the Christians in Bulgaria, 19 September 1876, in TNA, FO 881/2936B.

241 On how these figures came about, see Millman, Bulgarian Massacres Reconsidered.

242 Speech by Disraeli in the House of Commons on 11 August 1876, in T. C. Hansard, ed., *The Parliamentary Debates*, vol. 231, http://hansard .millbanksystems.com/commons/1876/aug/11/turkey-the-alleged-atrocities-in, cc. 1146–1147.

243 For an example of such an appeal as made on a poster, see poster 'Turkish Atrocities in Bulgaria' calling for a public meeting of the citizens of

Worcester, 8 September 1876, in TNA, FO 78/2554. Posters making similar appeals can be found in TNA, FO 78/2551.

244 On this, see e.g. Petition of the citizens of Richmond, September 1876, in TNA, FO 78/2554.

245 On this, see Petition of the Stourbridge & District Bulgarian Relief Fund, 12 September 1876, in TNA, FO 78/2551.

246 Hundreds of petitions with lists of signatures appended to them are collected in TNA, FO 78/2551; TNA, FO 78/2552; TNA, FO 78/2553; TNA, FO 78/2554; TNA, FO 78/2555; TNA, FO 78/2556. R. T. Shannon gives the number of petitions filed with the government between September and December 1876 as 455. On this, see Shannon, *Gladstone and the Bulgarian Agitation*, 147–151. On this protest movement more generally, see Millman, *Britain and the Eastern Question*, 176–189; Ann Pottinger Saab, *Reluctant Icon: Gladstone, Bulgaria, and the Working Classes, 1856–1878*, Cambridge, MA 1991, 80–150.

247 For a detailed account of Gladstone's role and campaigning, see Shannon, *Gladstone and the Bulgarian Agitation*; Seton-Watson, *Disraeli*, 73–83; Saab, *Reluctant Icon*, 75–79, 89–95. Michelle Tusan has found this campaign in particular to mark a watershed in the emergence of a liberal 'humanitarian conscience' with regard to the Middle East in Britain. However, her analysis fails to take into account the earlier campaigns and interventions with regard to Greece and Syria. See Tusan, *Smyrna's Ashes*, 4–7, 16–30. Again, as in the case of the Lebanon, crusading rhetoric was deployed in this campaign. On this, see Stéphanie Prévost, W. T. Stead and the Eastern Question (1875–1911); or, How to Rouse England and Why?, *19: Interdisciplinary Studies in the Long Nineteenth Century* 16 (2013), 1–28 at 7–10, https://www.19.bbk.ac.uk/articles/10.16995/ntn.654/.

248 William E. Gladstone, *Bulgarian Horrors and the Question of the East*, London 1876, 9.

249 On this, see ibid., 25–32. Gladstone restated his sharp criticism of the Porte in a second pamphlet published in March 1877: William E. Gladstone, *Lessons in Massacre: The Conduct of the Turkish Government in and about Bulgaria*, London 1877. On Gladstone's Balkan policy more generally, see Richard T. Shannon, Gladstone and British Balkan Policy, in Ralph Melville/Hans-Jürgen Schröder, eds., *Der Berliner Kongress von 1878: Die Politik der Grossmächte und die Probleme der Modernisierung in Südosteuropa in der Zweiten Hälfte des 19. Jahrhunderts*, Wiesbaden 1982, 163–178.

250 'This Association was formed at the National Conference, December 8th, 1876, at St. James's Hall, for the purpose of watching events in the East, giving expression to public opinion, and spreading useful information.' Quoted from the preface to Eastern Question Association, ed., *Papers on the Eastern Question*, London 1877. On the National Conference and the founding of the Eastern Question Association, see also Eastern Question Association, ed., *Report of Proceedings of the National Conference at St. James's Hall*, London, December 8th, 1876; Shannon, *Gladstone and the Bulgarian Agitation*, 251–265; Seton-Watson, *Disraeli*, 110–115.

251 The Eastern Question Association published a total of twelve pamphlets in 1877, including some with very telling titles: Henry Richard, *The Evidences,*

of Turkish Misrule, Eastern Question Association, Papers on the Eastern Question, No. 1, London 1877; J. Llewelyn Davies, *The Religious Aspects of the Eastern Question,* Eastern Question Association, Papers on the Eastern Question, No. 2, London 1877; F. W. Chesson, *Turkey and the Slave Trade,* Eastern Question Association, Papers on the Eastern Question, No. 7, London 1877; M. G. Fawcett, *The Martyrs of Turkish Misrule,* Eastern Question Association, Papers on the Eastern Question, No. 11, London 1877.

252 It is no accident that the newly founded Eastern Question Association had its offices in the Canada Building, where the Aborigines Protection Society was already established. On this, see Shannon, *Gladstone and the Bulgarian Agitation,* 30. On the Aborigines Protection Society, which emerged from the British abolitionist movement, see Heartfield, *Aborigines' Protection Society.*

253 See also Thomas Fowell Buxton's speech to the National Conference: 'It is the fact that the Turkish system of government is based upon slavery and the slave trade.' Eastern Question Association, Report of Proceedings, 21–23. Gladstone, too, several times drew this connection with the abolition of slavery: '[H]e [Gladstone] is absorbed in the one strong feeling that the Turkish Government is so execrable and hopelessly vile and bad, that it must be put a stop to in the oppressed provinces at all hazards – just as slavery had to be abolished.' John Bailey, ed., *The Diary of Lady Frederick Cavendish,* vol. II, London 1927, 199; 'in time of the great negro conflict we were told just the same things that are told now about the Turks'. Speech by Gladstone, Mr. Gladstone and the Liberal Party, *The Times* (21 August 1877), 4. On link with the anti-slavery movement, see Shannon, *Gladstone and the Bulgarian Agitation,* 29f.

254 Chesson, *Turkey and the Slave Trade,* 4.

255 Ibid., 16.

256 'The oppression which the Bosnians and Herzegovinians most deeply and bitterly resent, is the forcible carrying off of girls and women to the Turkish harems.' Quoted from the pamphlet: Fawcett, *Martyrs of Turkish Misrule,* 10. On this, see also Malcolm MacColl, *The Eastern Question: Its Facts and Fallacies,* London 1877, 83–85 and 406f.

257 For an example of such a resolution passed at a public meeting, see Letter from the Conservative Working Mens Club, Grantham, to Derby, 25 October 1876, in TNA, FO 78/2556; Godmanchester Conservative Association, 28 October 1876, in ibid.; Petition des Foreign Affairs Committees of Cheshire and Lancashire, 5 November 1876, in ibid. Other such counter-resolutions, although distinctly fewer in number than in the atrocities campaign, may be found in TNA, FO 78/2555 and TNA, FO 78/2556. For what is above all a personal criticism of Gladstone, see Henry A. Munro Butler-Johnstone, *Bulgarian Horrors, and the Question of the East: A Letter Addressed to the Right Hon. W. E. Gladstone, M. P.,* London 1876; Henry de Worms, *England's Policy in the East,* London 1876.

258 The Bulgarian Atrocities: Protest of a Conference of the Foreign Affairs Committees of Keighley, Bingley, Shipley, Bradford, Cononley, Glusburn, and New Road Side, held at Keighley, September, 1876, in TNA, FO 78/2555.

259 Ibid.
260 Russian Ultimatum to the Porte, demanding the immediate conclusion of an Armistice between Turkey, Servia, and Montenegro, 31 October 1876, in Hertslet, ed., *Map of Europe*, vol. IV, 2502f.; Ković, *Disraeli and the Eastern Question*, 166f.
261 On these diplomatic efforts, see Letter from Derby to Loftus, 30 October 1876, in Ministère des Affaires Étrangères, ed., *Documents Diplomatiques: Affaires d'Orient. 1875–1876–1877*, Paris 1877, 213–228; Millman, *Britain and the Eastern Question*, 190–207.
262 Circular addressed to her Majesty's Representatives at Paris, Berlin, Vienna, St Petersburgh, Rome and Constantinople, from Derby, 4 November 1876, in BFSP 67, 293f. On this, see also Letter from Derby to Lyons, 4 November 1876, in MAE, MD T 101.
263 'A declaration that the Powers do not intend to seek for, and will not seek for, any territorial advantages, any exclusive influence, or any concession with regard to the commerce of their subjects which those of every other nation may not equally obtain.' Circular addressed, BFSP 67, 293.
264 On this, see e.g. 'The new form of administration in the Lebanon had been settled by a European Commission. ... the Porte would not object to the appointment of a European Commission to watch over the execution of the new great reform.' Letter from Lyons to Derby, 12 October 1876, in BFSP 67, 277–280 at 278; 'This occupation should be of European character, as in the case of Syria.' Letter from Loftus to Derby, 6 November 1876, in ibid., 299; 'An International Commission, for instance, somewhat similar to that which was employed in the affairs of the Lebanon, might be named to work out the details of a scheme of which the general principles might be laid down in the conference.' Letter from Derby to Elliot, 20 November 1876, in BFSP 68, 1081.
265 For a detailed account of these preliminary talks and the various states' positions, see Millman, *Britain and the Eastern Question*, 208–221; Ković, *Disraeli and the Eastern Question*, 176–182.
266 For minutes of each session, see Letter from Salisbury to Derby, enclosed: minutes of sessions one to four, 22 December 1876, in TNA, FO 881/3030; Letter from Salisbury to Derby, enclosed: minutes of sessions five to nine, 23 December 1876, in TNA, FO 881/3048.
267 For this proposal, jointly drafted by the six European powers, see Réunion Préparatoires, Séance du 21 Décembre 1876, in MAE, MD T 101; 8e Compte-Rendu – Séance du 21 Décembre, 1876, in TNA, FO 881/3048.
268 For the minutes and events of the conference from December 1876 to January 1877, see Protocols of Conference between Great Britain, Austria-Hungary, France, Germany, Italy, Russia and Turkey, respecting the Affairs of Turkey (Servia; Montenegro; Bulgaria; Bosnia; Herzegovina; Reforms), in BFSP 68, 1114–1207.
269 Despatch from Safvet Pasha to Musurus Pasha, explaining the Causes which led to the Close of the Conference at Constantinople without result, 25 January 1877, in Hertslet, ed., *Map of Europe*, vol. IV, 2545–2550.
270 On this, see Protocols of Conference between the Plenipotentiaries of Great Britain, Austria, France, Germany, Italy, and Russia, relative to the Affairs

of Turkey (Christian Population; Reforms in Bosnia; Herzegovina, and Bulgaria; Servia; Montenegro), 31 March 1877, in BFSP 68, 823f.

271 Manifesto of the Emperor of Russia announcing War with Turkey, 24 April 1877, in Hertslet, ed., *Map of Europe*, vol. IV, 2598f.

272 Schulz, Guarantees of Humanity, 200–204; Heraclides/Dialla, *Humanitarian Intervention*, 176–178. On Russian perecptions of the campaign as a kind of 'holy war' for the liberation of Slavic Christians from the 'Turkish yoke', see Stephen N. Norris, *A War of Images: Russian Popular Prints, Wartime Culture, and National Identity, 1812–1945*, DeKalb, IL 2006, 80–106.

273 On the treaty of San Stefano, see Preliminary Treaty of Peace between Russia and Turkey, 3 March 1878, in BFSP 69, 732–744. On the Russo-Ottoman war of 24 April 1877 to 3 March 1878, see Jelavich, *Russia's Balkan Entanglements*, 170–175.

274 Abstract of Secret and Confidential Correspondence on the Eastern Question by P. Currie, 18 January 1878, in TNA, FO 881/3451; Letter from Salisbury to British ambassadors, 1 April 1878, in BFSP 69, 807–814; Letter from Andrassy to Beust, 29 April 1878, in TNA, FO 881/3594. For the acute danger of war between the European powers, see Ković, *Disraeli and the Eastern Question*, 247–266; Millman, *Britain and the Eastern Question*, 403–432.

275 The Congress of Berlin lasted from 13 June to 13 July 1878. On the congress, see e.g. Melville/Schröder, *Berliner Kongress*; W. N. Medlicott, *The Congress of Berlin and After: A Diplomatic History of the Near Eastern Settlement 1878–1880*, London 1938.

276 The protocols of the conference (in the original French) may be found in MAE, MD T 108. For the treaty, see 'Treaty between Great Britain, Germany, Austria, France, Italy, Russia, and Turkey for the Settlement of Affairs in the East: Signed at Berlin, July 13, 1878.' *American Journal of International Law* 2/4, Supplement: Official Documents (October 1908), 401–424.

277 Although its territorial gains in Bessarabia and the Transcaucasus were confirmed, Russia considered the Treaty of Berlin a diplomatic defeat. For its long-term consequences, see Jelavich, *Russia's Balkan Entanglements*, 176–178; Glenny, *Balkans*, 143–151.

278 Article 5 of the Treaty of Berlin, in Treaty between Great Britain, Germany, Austria, France, Italy, Russia, and Turkey, 406. This formula was adopted for Montenegro (Article 27), Serbia (Article 35) and Romania (Article 44). Article 44 further states that 'The subjects and citizens of all the Powers, traders or others, shall be treated in Roumania, without distinction of creed, on a footing of perfect equality.' Ibid., 413, 416, 419.

279 These obligations were extended to Eastern Rumelia in Article 27 and for the Ottoman Empire in general in Article 62 of the Treaty of Berlin. On this, see ibid., 413, 423.

280 Article 12 of the Treaty of Berlin, ibid., 422.

281 Fink, *Defending the Rights of Others*, 3–38. On early attempts to protect minorities under international law, see also Patrick Thornberry,

International Law and the Rights of Minorities, Oxford 1991, 25–37; Janne E. Nijman, Minorities and Majorities, in Bardo Fassbender/Anne Peters, eds., *The Oxford Handbook of the History of International Law*, Oxford 2012, 95–119. Michelle Tusan and Eric Weitz situate this development in the context of a history of 'human rights'. See: Michelle Tusan, 'Crimes against Humanity': Human Rights, the British Empire, and the Origins of the Response to the Armenian Genocide, *American Historical Review* 119/1 (February 2014), 47–77 at 49–52; Weitz, *World Divided*, 159–205.

282 Fink, *Defending the Rights*, 9. For an analysis of diplomatic efforts in relation to the 'Jewish question' with explicit reference to the context of humanitarian interventions, see Abigail Green, Intervening in the Jewish Question, 1840–1878, in Simms/Trim, eds., *Humanitarian Intervention*, 139–158; Abigail Green, From Protection to Humanitarian Intervention? Enforcing Jewish Rights in Romania and Morocco around 1880, in Klose, ed., *Emergence of Humanitarian Intervention*, 142–161.

283 In practice, the great powers never intervened on behalf of Muslim minorities in the Ottoman Empire's European provinces, and Muslims ended being brutally expelled from these areas. On this, see esp. McCarthy, *Death and Exile*.

284 See Koskenniemi, *Gentle Civilizer of Nations*, 94f.; Daniel Marc Segesser, Humanitarian Intervention and the Issue of State Sovereignty in the Discourse of Legal Experts between 1830s and the First World War, in Klose, ed., *Emergence of Humanitarian Intervention*, 56–72; Heraclides/Dialla, *Humanitarian Intervention*, 57–67; Rodogno, European Legal Doctrines, 16f., 33–36; Swatek-Evenstein, *History*, 111–117.

285 Koskenniemi, *Gentle Civilizer of Nations*, 92.

286 Gustave Rolin-Jaequemyns, Le droit international et la phase actuelle de la question d'Orient, *Revue de droit international et de législation comparée* VIII (1876), 293–385. For another discussion by Rolin-Jaequemyns of the 'Eastern Question' and the Constantinople Conference, at which the European delegates had, in his view, acted 'dans un esprit d'humanité, de modération et de paix', see also Gustave Rolin-Jaequemyns, La Question d'Orient – L'Armistice – La conférence de Constantinople et ses suites (Octobre 1876–Janvier 1877), *Revue de droit international et de législation comparée* VIII (1876), 511–544 at 540.

287 Rolin-Jaequemyns, Le droit international, 343–346. The International Committee of the Red Cross also received a number of reports of Ottoman atrocities. For these reports to the ICRC from Serbia, see ACICR, AF 15.6, Courier reçu Serbie.

288 '[A]utant il y a, pour les puissances qui dirigent ou prétendent diriger l'ensemble de la politique international, un droit, et par consequent, une obligation d'intervention collective à exercer dans ces malheureses et intéressantes contrées. Ce droit se fonde sur l'histoire, sur les précédents diplomatiques, sur les évènements récents.' Rolin-Jaequemyns, Le droit international, 293.

289 For comparisons with the Greek case see ibid., 309–314; with that of Syria see ibid., 327f.

290 Ibid., 311. For further criticism of the British position see ibid., 357–361.

291 'Le droit, résultant de l'histoire et des traités, c'est l'intervention collective de l'Europe dans les affaires intérieures de la Turquie, dans un intérét de paix générale et d'humanité. Le fait, c'est la prolongation et l'aggravation d'un état de choses chaque jour plus dangereux pour la paix générale et plus contraire à l'humanité. Dans ces circonstances, il n'est pas difficile de démontrer que les grandes puissances ont, non seulement la faculté, mais l'obligation d'exercer l'intervention dans toute son étendue et avec toutes les ressources dont elles disposent.' Ibid., 367.

292 For a retrospective view taking into account Russia's declaration of war on the Ottoman Empire, see 'Si l'intervention collective en faveur des populations chrètiennes de la Turquie était un droit et un devoir, imposé par l'humanité et par des exigences supérieures aux convenances individuelles de chaque État, ce droit existait pour chacun comme pour tous, pour la Russie comme pour l'Angleterre.' Gustave Rolin-Jaequemyns, Chronique du droit international: L'année 1877 et les débuts de 1878 au point de vue du droit international, *Revue de droit international et de législation comparée* X (1878), 5–59 at 19.

293 Gustave Rolin-Jaequemyns, Note sur la théorie du droit d'intervention, a propos d'une lettre de M. le Professeur Arntz, *Revue de droit International et de legislation comparée* VIII (1876), 673–682.

294 'Lorsqu'un gouvernement, tout en agissant dans la limite des ses droits de souveraineté, viole les droits de l'humanité, soit par des mesures contraires à l'intérét des autres États, soit par des excès d'injustice et de cruauté qui blessent profondément nos mœurs et notre civilisation, le droit d'intervention est légitime. Car, quelque respectables que soient les droits de souveraineté et d'independance des États, il y a quelque chose de plus respectable encore, c'est le droit de l'humanité, ou de la société humaine, qui ne doit pas être outragé. De même que dans l'État la liberté de l'individu est restreinte et doit être restreinte par le droit et par les moeurs de la société, de même la liberté individuelle des États doit être limitée par les droits de la société humaine.' Ibid., 675.

295 '[C]e droit ne peut être exercé qu' au nom de l'humanité représentée par tous les autres États, ou tout au moins par le plus grand nombre des États civilisés, qui doivent se réunir en un congrès ou en un tribunal pour prendre une décision collective. De cette manière on peut concilier le droit d'intervention avec la garantie de l'independance des États.' Ibid.

296 Friedrich Martens, Étude historique sur la politique russe dans la question d'Orient, *Revue de droit international et de législation comparée* 9/1 (1877), 49–77.

297 Ibid., 50.

298 For references to the Greek and Syrian examples see ibid., 54–58, 62–64; for the Congress of Vienna see ibid., 53f.

299 Ibid., 54.

300 Martens went on to play a leading part in formulating the General Act of the Brussels Anti-Slavery Conference 1889–90. On this, see Allain, Fydor Martens, 101–120.

301 Bluntschli, *Das moderne Völkerrecht*. The first edition of this standard text was published in 1866.

302 Ibid., 20. Bluntschli here uses the term 'human rights' (*Menschenrechte*), but he does so without defining it, as Antoine Rougier has critically remarked: 'Le grand juriste allemand ne dit pas quels sont les droits individuels reconnus nécessaire à l'humanité.' Rougier, La théorie de l'intervention d'humanité, 493.
303 Bluntschli, *Das moderne Völkerrecht*, 21–24.
304 Ibid., 265.
305 Ibid., 266.
306 Ibid.
307 On this, see 'Werden in Folge der Verfassungskämpfe das allgemein als nothwendig anerkannte Menschenrecht oder das Völkerrecht verletzt, dann wird auch eine Intervention zum Schutze desselben aus denselben Gründen gerechtfertigt, wie das Einschreiten der civilsierten Staten überhaupt bei gemeingefährlichen Rechtsverletzungen. ... Die Christen in der Türkei haben das wiederholt mit Erfolg gethan. Zuletzt hat Russland 1877/78 zum Schutz derselben, zunächst der Bulgaren, den Krieg gegen die Türkei durchgeführt.' Ibid., 270. Éduoard Engelhardt, a French scholar of international law, also closely examined the case of the Ottoman Empire and came out in favour of a right of intervention on humanitarian grounds. On this, see Éduoard Engelhardt, Le droit d'intervention et la Turquie: Étude historique, *Revue de droit international et de législation comparée* XII (1880), 363–388 at 364f.
308 On these controversies, see Segesser, Humanitarian Intervention, 61–71; Alexis Heraclides, Humanitarian Intervention in International Law 1830–1939: The Debate, *Journal of the History of International Law* 16 (2014), 26–62. For a table listing advocates and opponents the doctrine of humanitarian intervention between 1830 and 1939, see Heraclides/Dialla, *Humanitarian Intervention*, 57–80 at 60–62.
309 On this, see Heraclides/Dialla, *Humanitarian Intervention*, 57–59, 63–73.
310 On this, see Tusan, 'Crimes against Humanity', 52–56; Watenpaugh, *Bread from Stones*, 62–69; Mark Toufayan, Empathy, Humanity and the 'Armenian Question' in the Internationalist Legal Imagination, *Revue québécoise de droit international* 24 (2011), 171–191; Charles Laderman, *Sharing the Burden: The Armenian Question, Humanitarian Intervention and Anglo-American Visions of Global Order*, New York 2019. One reason why the British government decided not to send military force for the relief of the Armenians was that the massacres occurred deep in the Anatolian interior and hence out of reach of the Royal Navy. Rodogno, *Against Massacre*, 185–211.
311 On this, see also Fabian Klose, Frieden durch Krieg? Zur Janusköpfigkeit militärischer Interventionspraxis im langen 19. Jahrhundert, in Sandrine Mayoraz/Frithjof Benjamin Schenk/Ueli Mäder, eds., *Hundert Jahre Basler Friedenskongress (1912–2012): Die erhoffte 'Verbrüderung der Völker'*, Basel 2015, 201–212.

Chapter 9

1 Mazower, *Governing the World*, 8.
2 On the causes of and courses taken by these revolutions, see Schroeder, *Transformation of European Politics*, 606–614; Lyons, *Post-Revolutionary Europe*, 42–48.

3 For the Troppauer Protocol of 19 November 1820, see Grewe, *Fontes Historiae Iuris Gentium*, vol. 3/1, 110–113.

4 Rafe Blaufarb, The Western Question: The Geopolitics of Latin American Independence, *American Historical Review* 112/3 (June 2007), 742–763.

5 Arthur Whitaker, *The United States and the Independence of Latin America, 1800–1830*, New York 1964, 370–395. On the American stance towards the independence struggles in Latin America, see esp. John J. Johnson, *A Hemisphere Apart: The Foundations of United States Policy toward Latin America*, Baltimore, MD 1990; James E. Lewis, *The American Union and the Problem of Neighborhood: The United States and the Collapse of the Spanish Empire, 1783–1829*, Chapel Hill, NC 1998.

6 Jay Sexton, *The Monroe Doctrine: Empire and Nation in Nineteenth-Century America*, New York 2011, 8–13, 28f.

7 On this *Ukase* of Alexander I, see W. P. Cresson, *The Holy Alliance: The European Background of the Monroe Doctrine*, New York 1922, 123–125; Dexter Perkins, *A History of the Monroe Doctrine*, London 1963, 30–32.

8 State Paper by Castlereagh dated 5 May 1820, in Temperley/Penson, eds., *Foundations of British Foreign Policy*, 48–63 at 61; circular from Castlereagh to British legations, 19 January 1821, in BFSP 8, 1160–1162. On Britain's position under Castlereagh, see also Leonard Axel Lewis, *The Relation of British Policy to the Declaration of the Monroe Doctrine*, New York 1922, 30–50; Webster, *Foreign Policy of Castlereagh*, 215–256; Hafner, Castlereagh, the Balance of Power, and 'Non-Intervention', 71–84.

9 Lewis, *Relation of British Policy*, 69–75; Temperley/Penson, *Foundations of British Foreign Policy*, 68–70.

10 Lewis, *Relation of British Policy*, 76–103. On the British stance towards the independence struggles in Latin America, see Webster, *Britain and the Independence of Latin America*, 3–79.

11 Johnson, *A Hemisphere Apart*, 114–129.

12 For a detailed account of the talks between Canning and Rush, see Bradford Perkins, *Castlereagh and Adams. England and the United States 1812–1823*, Berkeley, CA 1964, 316–323; Ernest R. May, *The Making of the Monroe Doctrine*, Cambridge, MA 1975, 1–8.

13 Canning to Liverpool, 26 August 1823, quoted in Perkins, *Castlereagh and Adams*, 321.

14 Ibid., 197; Lewis, *Relation of British Policy*, 126f.; Gale W. McGee, The Monroe Doctrine – A Stopgap Measure, *Mississippi Valley Historical Review* 38/2 (September 1951), 238f.

15 Perkins, *History of the Monroe Doctrine*, 41; May, *Making of the Monroe Doctrine*, 200f.

16 On John Quincy Adams's stance, see Bemis, *John Quincy Adams*, 384–390; May, *Making of the Monroe Doctrine*, 198–218; Walter A. McDougall, *Promised Land, Crusader State: The American Encounter with the World*, New York 1997, 69f.

17 Adams' argument of 7 November 1823, quoted in Perkins, *Castlereagh and Adams*, 333f.

18 On American policy against British interests in Cuba, see Edward H. Tatum, To Forestall Britain's Designs on Cuba and New World Markets, in Armin Rappaport, ed., *The Monroe Doctrine*, New York 1964, 22–33.

19 For the text of Monroe's 'state of the union' address of 2 December 1823, see Annals of Congress, Senate, 18th Congress, 1st Session, 12–24.

20 Ibid., 14.

21 On the idea of a 'western hemisphere', see Arthur P. Whitaker, *The Western Hemisphere Idea: Its Rise and Decline*, Ithaca, NY 1954; Gretchen Murphy, *Hemispheric Imaginings: The Monroe Doctrine and Narratives of U.S. Empire*, Durham, NC 2005.

22 State of the Union Address of 2 December 1823, in Annals of Congress, Senate, 18th Congress, 1st Session, 22f.

23 Ibid., 23. On the principle of non-intervention as enshrined in the Monroe Doctrine, see Vincent, *Nonintervention*, 107–113.

24 For the reactions on the part of the Latin American independence movements, see William Spence Robertson, South America and the Monroe Doctrine, 1824–1828, *Political Science Quarterly* 30/1 (March 1915), 82–105; Whitaker, *United States and the Independence*, 535–538; Gaston Nerval, A Latin American View: Egoistic from Its Pronouncement, in Rappaport, ed., *Monroe Doctrine*, 92–98.

25 On reactions in Europe, see Perkins, *History of the Monroe Doctrine*, 55–57; Mark T. Gilderhus, The Monroe Doctrine: Meanings and Implications, *Presidential Studies Quarterly* 36/1 (March 2006), 8.

26 On the talks between Canning and Polignac, see Temperley, *Foreign Policy of Canning*, 103–121.

27 On the 'Polignac Memorandum', see Temperley/Penson, *Foundations of British Foreign Policy*, 70–76.

28 W. F. Craven, Jr, The Risk of the Monroe Doctrine (1823–1824), *Hispanic American Historical Review* 7/3 (August 1927), 320–333.

29 On the considerable importance for foreign policy of the Monroe Doctrine, which has even been called a 'diplomatic declaration of independence', see Harry Ammon, *James Monroe: The Quest for National Identity*, Charlottesville, VA 1990, 491f.; Bradford Perkins, *The Cambridge History of American Foreign Relations*, vol. 1: *The Creation of a Republican Empire, 1776–1865*, Cambridge 1993, 169; George C. Herring, *From Colony to Superpower: U.S. Foreign Relations since 1776*, Oxford 2008, 151–158.

30 Cresson, *Holy Alliance*, 122–126; McDougall, *Promised Land*, 59, 72f.; Sexton, *Monroe Doctrine*, 57–60. The foundations of this isolationist tendency and the attempt to avoid entanglements with other powers are already discernible in American political thought at the time of the revolution. On this, see Reginald C. Stuart, *War and American Thought: From the Revolution to the Monroe Doctrine*, Kent, OH 1982, 35–39; Justin Raimondo, Defenders of the Republic: The Anti-Interventionist Tradition in American Politics, in John V. Denson, ed., *The Costs of War: America's Pyrrhic Victories*, New Brunswick, NJ 1997, 67–74.

31 On Adams' decisive influence on Monroe's speech, see Bemis, *John Quincy Adams*, 407f.; Worthington C. Ford, The Work of John Quincy Adams, in

Rappaport, ed., *Monroe Doctrine*, 40–48; Edward P. Crapol, John Quincy Adams and the Monroe Doctrine: Some New Evidence, *Pacific Historical Review* 48/3 (August 1979), 413–418.

32 Speech of Adams to the House of Representatives, 4 July 1821, in Walter LaFeber, ed., *John Quincy Adams and American Continental Empire: Letters, Papers, and Speeches*, Chicago, IL 1965, 42–46.

33 Ibid., 45.

34 Ibid.

35 An English translation of the Greek appeal for help of 25 May 1821 was printed, see *North American Review*, vol. XVII, Boston, MA 1823, 415f.

36 Ibid., 416.

37 An Act to Prohibit the Importation of Slaves into Any Port or Place within the Jurisdiction of the United States, 2 March 1807, in Yale Law School, ed., *The Avalon Project: Documents in Law, History, and Diplomacy*, http://avalon.law .yale.edu/19th_century/sl004.asp.

38 On the question of slavery and the slave trade in Anglo-American relations, see Mason, Battle of the Slaveholding Liberators.

39 *North American Review*, vol. XVII, 416.

40 Adams' stance is very much in evidence in his response to Andreas Luriottis, the Greek negotiator in London, of 18 August 1823, in BFSP 11, 301f.

41 Adams, *Memoirs of John Quincy Adams*, vol. 6, 197f.

42 May, *Making of the Monroe Doctrine*, 214–218; Edward M. Earle, Early American Policy Concerning Ottoman Minorities, *Political Science Quarterly* 42/3 (September 1927), 348–351; Paul C. Pappas, *The United States and the Greek War for Independence, 1821–1828*, New York 1985, 57–60; Lawrence S. Kaplan, The Monroe Doctrine and the Truman Doctrine: The Case of Greece, *Journal of the Early Republic* 13/1 (Spring 1993), 1-21 at 12–14.

43 State of the Union Address, 2 December 1823, in Annals of Congress, Senate, 18th Congress, 1st Session, 22.

44 On the American philhellenes and their mobilisation campaigns, see Edward M. Earle, American Interest in the Greek Cause, 1821–1827, *American Historical Review* 33/1 (October 1927), 44–63; Pappas, *United States and the Greek War*, 27–43; Angelo Repousis, 'The Cause of the Greeks': Philadelphia and the Greek War for Independence, 1821–1828, *Pennsylvania Magazine of History and Biography* 123/4 (October 1999), 333–363; Bass, *Freedom's Battle*, 88–99.

45 Earle, American Interest, 52f.; Repousis, 'The Cause of the Greeks', 349, 356.

46 Repousis, 'The Cause of the Greeks', 337f.; *North American Review*, vol. XVII, Boston, MA 1823, 413.

47 For Webster's draft resolution of 8 December 1823, see Annals of Congress, House of Representatives, 18th Congress, 1st Session, 805f.

48 On the debate in the House of Representatives, see Pappas, *United States and the Greek War*, 66–74. For the minutes of the debate, see Annals of Congress, House of Representatives, 18th Congress, 1st Session, 1084–1099, 1104–1178 and 1181–1213.

49 For Webster's speech of 19 January 1824, see Annals of Congress, House of Representatives, 18th Congress, 1st Session, 1084–1099 at 1093.

50 Ibid., 1097f.

51 Speech by Poinsett to the House of Representatives on 20 January 1824, in Annals of Congress, House of Representatives, 18th Congress, 1st Session, 1104–1111.

52 Ibid., 1108. Poinsett introduced an alternative resolution of his own, which expressed only general sympathy for the Greek cause without proposing any concrete measures. On Poinsett's draft resolution see ibid., 1111.

53 Speech by Randolph to the House of Representatives on 20 January 1824, in ibid., 1111–1113.

54 Ibid., 1112.

55 On these commercial considerations, see Earle, Early American Policy, 358–360; Field, *America and the Mediterranean World*, 125–140.

56 For the vote on Webster's draft resolution on 26 January 1824, see Annals of Congress, House of Representatives, 18th Congress, 1st Session, 1213f.

57 On this, see Adams, *Memoirs of John Quincy Adams*, vol. 6, 227, 230, 233, 240; Earle, Early American Policy, 361.

58 Only under the presidency of Martin Van Buren did the United States finally recognise Greek independence in November 1837. On this, see Pappas, *United States and the Greek War*, 122.

59 On this, see esp. Earle, American Interest, 60f.; Repousis, 'The Cause of the Greeks', 335, 341, 363.

60 In 1825 Adams even sent William C. Somerville to Greece as a secret envoy. Alas, Somerville died en route in France. On this, see Earle, Early American Policy, 362–364; Pappas, *United States and the Greek War*, 85–91.

61 State of the Union Address of 4 December 1827, in Annals of Congress, Senate, 20th Congress, 1st Session, 2779; State of the Union Address of 2 December 1828, in Annals of Congress, Senate, 20th Congress, 2nd Session, 6.

62 Stuart, *War and American Thought*, 166–170.

63 Herring, *From Colony to Superpower*, 151, 157.

64 On the United States' westward expansion, see e.g. Osterhammel, *Transformation of the World*, 324–327, 331–346, 448–450.

65 On the origins of the term, see John O'Sullivan, Annexation, *United States Magazine and Democratic Review* 17/1 (July–August 1845), 5–10; Julius W. Pratt, The Origin of 'Manifest Destiny', *American Historical Review* 32/4 (July 1927), 795–798. On the concept's association with US expansion, see e.g. Herring, *From Colony to Superpower*, 180–207; Sam W. Haynes/Christopher Morris, eds., *Manifest Destiny and Empire: American Antebellum Expansionism*, College Station, TX 2008.

66 James K. Polk, State of the Union Address, 2 December 1845, in James D. Richardson, ed., *A Compilation of the Messages and Papers of the Presidents, 1789–1897*, vol. IV, Washington, DC 1899, 385–416 at 387.

67 Ibid.

68 Ibid., 392–397.

69 Ibid., 398.

70 On the Oregon question, see Frederick Merk, *The Monroe Doctrine and American Expansionism, 1843–1849*, New York 1966, 65–104.

71 On the Mexican–American War and its consequences, see e.g. Michael Scott Van Wagenen, *Remembering the Forgotten War: The Enduring Legacies of the U.S.–Mexican War*, Amherst, MA 2012.

72 On this expansionist and imperial reinterpretation of the Monroe Doctrine under Polk, see esp. Merk, *Monroe Doctrine and American Expansionism* at 278–289; Sexton, *Monroe Doctrine*, 97–111.

73 Yucatan was already marked by instability, having declared itself an independent republic in 1841 and returned to the Mexican fold only in part and after a bloody struggle that ended in 1846. On the political situation in Yucatan before the Caste War, see Gilbert M. Joseph, From Caste to Class War: The Historiography of Modern Yucatán (c. 1750–1940), *Hispanic American Historical Review* 65/1 (February 1985), 111–134; Gilbert M. Joseph, The United States, Feuding Elites, and Rural Revolt in Yucatán, 1836–1915, Daniel Nugent, ed., *Rural Revolt in Mexico: US Intervention and the Domain of Subaltern Politics*, Durham, NC 1998, 173–206 at 178–191; Don E. Dumond, *The Machete and the Cross: Campesino Rebellion in Yucatan*, Lincoln, NB 1997, 83–149; Nelson A. Reed, *The Caste War of Yucatán*, Stanford, CA 2001, 59–186.

74 James K. Polk, To the Senate and House of Representatives of the United States, 29 April 1848, in Richardson, *Compilation*, 581–583 at 581.

75 Ibid., 583.

76 On this, see Mark J. White, The Case of the Yucatecan Request: American Foreign Policy at the Close of the Mexican War, *Mid-America: An Historical Review* 72/3 (October 1990), 169–190 at 181–190; Merk, *Monroe Doctrine and American Expansionism*, 209–232. The Democratic senator Edward A. Hannegan argued in favour of intervention by claiming that 'Yucatan appealed to this country, urging it, by every tie of humanity that binds man to man, to save her from destruction.' Quoted in White, Case of the Yucatecan Request, 182.

77 Merk, *Monroe Doctrine and American Expansionism*, 231f.; Perkins, *History of the Monroe Doctrine*, 89f.; Sexton, *Monroe Doctrine*, 94f.

78 Merk, *Monroe Doctrine and American Expansionism*, 233–277. On this, see also Foreign Office, Statement of what has taken place since 1815, between Great Britain and Spain, France, and the United States, about securing Cuba to Spain, 12 June 1850, in TNA, FO 881/218.

79 Harral E. Landry, Slavery and the Slave Trade in Atlantic Diplomacy, 1850–1861, *Journal of Southern History* 27/2 (May 1961), 184–207 at 195–207; Richard K. MacMaster, The United States, Great Britain and the Suppression of the Cuban Slave Trade, 1835–1860 (PhD diss., Georgetown University, Washington, DC 1968); Seymour Drescher, From Empires of Slavery to Empires of Antislavery, in Fradera/Schmidt-Nowara, eds., *Slavery and Antislavery*, 291–316 at 302f.; Louis A. Pérez, Jr, *Cuba between Reform and Revolution*, New York 2015, 80–86.

80 Philip S. Foner, *A History of Cuba and Its Relation with the United States*, vol. 1: *1492–1845: From Conquest of Cuba to La Escalera*, New York 1962, 184–200; Lambert, Slavery, 73f.

81 On British action taken against Brazil, see Mason, Keeping Up Appearances, 814f.; Ward, *Royal Navy and the Slavers*, 164–166; Lloyd, *Navy and the Slave Trade*, 139–148.

82 De Nevers, Imposing International Norms, 68; Lambert, Slavery, 74–77.

83 On this, see Fehrenbacher, *Slaveholding Republic*, 119–126; Sam W. Haynes, Anglophobia and the Annexation of Texas: The Quest for National Security, in Haynes/Morris, eds., *Manifest Destiny*, 115–145.

84 Foner, *History of Cuba*, vol. 1, 224–228; Philip S. Foner, *A History of Cuba and Its Relation with the United States*, vol. 2: *1845–1895: From the Era of Annexationism to the Outbreak of the Second War of Independence*, New York 1963, 9–40, 75–85; C. Stanley Urban, The Africanization of Cuba Scare, 1853–1855, *Hispanic American Historical Review* 37/1 (February 1957), 29–45.

85 Lester D. Langley, Slavery, Reform, and American Policy in Cuba, 1823–1878, Revista de Historia de América 65/66 (January–December 1968), 71–84 at 71–77; Lester D. Langley, *The Cuban Policy of the United States: A Brief History*, New York 1968, 23f.; Louis A. Pérez, Jr, *Cuba and the United States: Ties of Singular Intimacy*, Athens, OH 1997, 32–37.

86 The word *filibuster* derives from the Spanish *filibustero*, which in turn is a corruption of the Dutch *vrijbuiter* or 'freebooter'. In the nineteenth century it was applied to military operations carried out by irregular forces from the United States in Latin America. On this, see Robert E. May, Manifest Destiny's Filibusters, in Haynes/Morris, eds., *Manifest Destiny*, 146–179; Robert E. May, *Manifest Destiny's Underworld: Filibustering in Antebellum America*, Chapel Hill, NC 2002. On the filibuster raids on Cuba, see Foner, *History of Cuba*, vol. 2, 41–74.

87 On this diplomatic demarche and the subsequent negotiations, see Correspondence between the United States, Spain, and France Concerning Alleged Projects of Conquest and Annexation of the Island of Cuba, 11 April 1853, in TNA, FO 881/674. On its rejection, see 'The President does not covet the acquisition of Cuba for the United States. At the same time, he considers the condition of Cuba as mainly an American question, and to a limited extent only, a European question.' Letter from Everett to Crampton, 1 December 1852, in TNA, FO 115/124.

88 On the American attempts to buy Cuba from Spain, for $100 million in 1848 and $130 million in 1854, see Foner, *History of Cuba*, vol. 2, 20–29, 96–105; Pérez, Jr, *Cuba and the United States*, 43–47.

89 Foner, *History of Cuba*, vol. 2, 116–124.

90 On the Cuban war of independence (1868–1878), see ibid., 162–198, 224–239, 253–275; Ada Ferrer, *Insurgent Cuba: Race, Nation, and Revolution, 1868–1898*, Chapel Hill, NC 1999, 15–69.

91 Andreas Stucki, *Aufstand und Zwangsumsiedlung: Die kubanischen Unabhängigkeitskriege 1868–1898*, Hamburg 2012, 19–66; Andreas Stucki, Bevölkerungskontrolle in asymmetrischen Konflikten: Zwangsumsiedlung und spanische Antiguerilla auf Kuba, 1868–1898, in Tanja Bührer/ Christian Stachelbeck/Dierk Walter, eds., *Imperialkriege von 1500 bis heute: Strukturen, Akteure, Lernprozesse*, Paderborn 2011, 241–259.

92 On the American position and demands for political reform, including an end to slavery in Cuba, see Foner, *History of Cuba*, vol. 2, 198–223, 240–252; Langley, *Cuban Policy*, 53–81; Pérez, Jr, *Cuba and the United States*, 50–54. Only in 1886 was slavery finally abolished in Cuba.

93 On the 'little war' (1879–1880), see Foner, *History of Cuba*, vol. 2, 276–288; Ferrer, *Insurgent Cuba*, 70–89.

94 On the death toll and the widespread destruction in Cuba, see Stucki, *Aufstand*, 31f.; Alfonso W. Quiroz, Loyalist Overkill: The Socioeconomic Costs of 'Repressing' the Separatist Insurrection in Cuba, 1868–1878, *Hispanic American Historical Review* 78/2 (May 1998), 261–305.

95 On the Cuban national movement and the influence of the Cuban exiles, see Ferrer, *Insurgent Cuba*, 112–138; Gerald E. Poyo, Evolution of Cuban Separatist Thought in the Emigré Communities of the United States, 1848–1895, *Hispanic American Historical Review* 66/3 (August 1986), 485–507; Pérez, Jr, *Cuba between Reform and Revolution*, 100–121.

96 Ferrer, *Insurgent Cuba*, 141–186; Joseph Smith, *The Spanish–American War: Conflict in the Caribbean and the Pacific 1895–1902*, London 1994, 7–27.

97 See also an article on Weyler's arrival in Cuba: The Struggle in Cuba, *New York Observer and Chronicle* (27 February 1896); John Lawrence Tone, *War and Genocide in Cuba, 1895–1898*, Chapel Hill, NC 2006, 153–177.

98 Smith, *Spanish–American War*, 18–23; Philip S. Foner, *The Spanish–Cuban–American War and the Birth of American Imperialism 1895–1902*, vol. 1: *1895–1898*, New York 1972, 110–118; Tone, *War and Genocide*, 193–224.

99 For the death toll, see Stucki, *Bevölkerungskontrolle*, 243; Tone, *War and Genocide*, 209–216.

100 See e.g.: Report of the British consul in Havana to Salisbury, 8 August 1897, in: TNA, FO 72/2056; Stucki, *Aufstand*, 222–240.

101 On this, see George W. Auxier, The Propaganda Activities of the Cuban Junta in Precipitating the Spanish–American War, 1895–1898, *Hispanic American Historical Review* 19/3 (August 1939), 286–305; William J. Schellings, Florida and the Cuban Revolution, 1895–1898, *Florida Historical Quarterly* 39/2 (October 1960), 175–186 at 178f.; Ernest R. May, *Imperial Democracy: The Emergence of America as a Great Power*, New York 1961, 69–74; Foner, *Spanish–Cuban–American War*, vol. 1, 163–176.

102 Auxier, Propaganda Activities, 299–303; Smith, *Spanish–American War*, 33.

103 On the key role played by the US press in rallying public opinion in the run-up to the Spanish–American War, see George W. Auxier, Middle Western Newspapers and the Spanish–American War, 1895–1898, *Mississippi Valley Historical Review* 26/4 (March 1940), 523–534; Charles H. Brown, *The Correspondents' War: Journalist in the Spanish–American War*, New York 1967; Harold J. Sylvester, The Kansas Press and the Coming of the Spanish–American War, *The Historian* 31/2 (February 1969), 251–267; Carmen González López-Briones, The Indiana Press and the Coming of the Spanish–American War, 1895–1896, *Atlantis* 12/1 (June 1990), 165–176; Jules R. Benjamin, *The United States and the Origins of the Cuban Revolution: An Empire of Liberty in an Age of National Liberation*, Princeton, NJ 1990, 34f.

104 Some illustrative examples from a vast number of such articles include No more Butcheries: Spanish Barbarism on the Isle of Cuba Must Stop, *Daily News* (9 January 1897), 6; The Cuban Horror, *Friends' Intelligencer* (2 April 1898); Horrors of Cuba, *News and Observer* (24 March 1898), 1; Barbarities in Cuba, *The Sentinel* (25 March 1898), 5; Spanish Barbarities, *Weekly News and Courier* (13 April 1898), 2; Massacred by the Spanish Soldiers, *Rocky Mountain News* (30 November 1896), 1; An Island of Death, *Morning Oregonian* (22 November 1897), 1; A Vivid Picture of Spanish Cruelty, *Daily Picayune* (24 March 1898), 7; Cuban Horrors, *Weekly News* (24 March 1898), 5; Barbarities in Cuba, *Semi-Weekly Tribune* (25 March 1898), 2.

105 Examples of such images can be found in Tennyson F. Neely/Gilson Willets/Margherita Arlina Hamm, eds., *Greater America: Heroes. Battles. Camps. Dewey Islands, Cuba, Porto Rico*, New York 1898, 153 (picture on the left) and 156 (picture on the right). On this, see also Bonnie M. Miller, *From Liberation to Conquest: The Visual and Popular Cultures of the Spanish–American War of 1898*, Amherst, MA 2011, 19–54.

106 On the role of the so-called yellow press, see Marcus M. Wilkerson, *Public Opinion and the Spanish–American War: A Study in War Propaganda*, New York 1967; Joseph E. Wisan, *The Cuban Crisis as Reflected in the New York Press (1896–1898)*, New York 1965.

107 On the emergence of the 'black legend' and the anti-Spanish tenor of US public opinion, see María DeGuzmán, *Spain's Long Shadow: The Black Legend, Off-Whiteness, and Anglo-American Empire*, Minneapolis, MN 2005, 139–185; Gerald F. Linderman, *The Mirror of War: American Society and the Spanish–American War*, Ann Arbor, MI 1974, 119–127.

108 DeGuzmán, *Spain's Long Shadow*, 170–175, 181–185.

109 See e.g. The Butcher of Cuba: Weyler in His Ferocious and Frivolous Moods – Origin of Reconcentrado Plan, *Semi-Weekly Tribune* (5 April 1898).

110 On this, see e.g. President Says Spain Must End War in Cuba – If It Fails to Do So, the United States Will Forcibly Intervene on Humanitarian Ground, *Sunday Sentinel* (27 March 1898), 1; The Cuban Revolution and United States Intervention, *The Independent* (23 April 1896); Our Responsibility: Starvation at Our Doors Calls for Intervention, *Sunday Oregonian* (17 April 1898); Cuba and Intervention, *The Independent* (17 March 1898); Intervention of the United States in Cuba, *North American Review* (March 1898). See also the political cartoons depicting an armed Uncle Sam marching on Cuba carrying bread and relief supplies, e.g. the cartoon captioned 'If this is Intervention Let U.S. Intervene', 22 March 1898, in Journal Printing Company, ed., *Cartoons of the Spanish–American War by Bart with Dates of Important Events from the Minneapolis Journal*, Minneapolis, MN 1899, 22 and the cartoon 'For Starving Cuba', 9 May 1898, in ibid., 56.

111 Recognition of Cuba: Precedents for Intervention during the Past Century, *Washington Post* (22 December 1896); Must Help Cuba, *Milwaukee Journal* (22 December 1896); A Line of Precedents, *Salt Lake Semi-Weekly Tribune* (22 December 1896); Precedents for Intervention, *The Morning Oregonian*

(23 March 1898); National Interference, *The Sentinel* (3 April 1898). For a pithy formulation, see: 'This description of the Grecian struggle for independence from Turkish yoke needs only a change of words, "Turkish" to "Spanish" and "Greek race" to "Cuban people" faithfully and accurately to describe the Cuban situation to-day.' The U.S. Must Intervene. The Principles of Such Action Laid Down in Text Books – How They Apply to Cuba, *News and Observer* (20 March 1898).

112 The Object of Intervention, *New York Observer and Chronicle* (7 April 1898).
113 An example is the offer of arbitration made by Richard Olney, the secretary of state, to the Spanish ambassador, 4 April 1896, in Government Printing Office, ed., *Spanish Diplomatic Correspondence and Documents 1896–1900 Presented to the Cortes by the Minister of State*, Washington, DC 1905, 4–8; Reply of the Spanish foreign minister to the Spanish ambassador to Washington, 22 May 1896, in ibid., 8–13; Extracts from the Message of the President of the United States, December 7, 1896, relative to the Cuban Insurrection, in ibid., 14–19; Elbert J. Benton, *International Law and Diplomacy of the Spanish–American War*, Gloucester 1968, 21–64; David Healy, *The United States in Cuba 1898–1902: Generals, Politicians, and the Search for Policy*, Madison, WI 1963, 10–12; John L. Offner, *An Unwanted War: The Diplomacy of the United States and Spain Over Cuba, 1895–1898*, Chapel Hill, NC 1992, 17–36.
114 Western, Prudence or Outrage?, 180; Richard F. Hamilton, *President McKinley, War and Empire*, vol. 1: *President McKinley and the Coming of War, 1898*, New Brunswick, NJ 2006, 109–147.
115 Offner, *Unwanted War*, 48; Louis A. Pérez, Jr, *The War of 1898: The United States and Cuban in History and Historiography*, Chapel Hill, NC 1998, 40f.; Mike Sewell, Humanitarian Intervention, Democracy, and Imperialism: The American War with Spain, 1898, and After, in Simms/Trim, eds., Humanitarian Intervention, 303–322 at 303, 306–310.
116 On this, see e.g. Letter from Sherman to Dupuy de Lôme, 26 June 1897, in Government Printing Office, ed., *Spanish Diplomatic Correspondence*, 25f.
117 On this, see Declaration by John Sherman, Secretary of State, 24 December 1897, in ACICR, AF 5.2, Courrier reçu États-Unies 1893–1913; Declaration 'Relief of Suffering in Cuba' by Secretary John Sherman, 8 January 1898, in ibid. On US relief shipments and the part played by Clara Barton, see Clara Barton, Relieving the Cuban Reconcentrados, 1897, in LoC Manuscript Division, Clara Barton Papers 1822–1912, Microfilmed from the Sophia Smith Collection, Microfilm 23, 471; Letter from Barton to Moynier, 3 May 1898, in ACICR, AF 5.2, Courrier reçu États-Unies 1893–1913; Letter from Barton to Moynier, 8 April 1899, in ibid. Clara Barton, *A Story of the Red Cross: Glimpses of Field Work*, New York 1928, 115–163.
118 Extract from the Message of the President of the United States, Mr McKinley, December 6, 1897, Relative to the Cuban Insurrection, in Government Printing Office, ed., *Spanish Diplomatic Correspondence*, 44–51 at 50.
119 In this private letter, written in December 1897, de Lôme described President McKinley as 'weak and a bidder for the admiration of the crowd,

besides being a would-be politician (*politicastro*), who tries to leave a door open behind himself while keeping on good terms with the jingoes of his party'. De Lôme's Letter, December 1897, in Robert Dallek, *1898: McKinley's Decision. The United States Declares War on Spain*, New York 1969, 109–111. The translation was published on 9 February 1898 in the *New York Journal* under the heading 'Worst Insult to the United States in Its History'. On the de Lôme letter and its repercussions, see Offner, *Unwanted War*, 116–122; Foner, *Spanish–Cuban–American War*, vol. 1, 232–236.

120 The explosion was not in fact caused by a mine or torpedo, but most likely by the ignition of gases formed in the ship's coal bunker, causing a fire that spread to the ammunition magazines. On the sinking of the *Maine* and its aftermath, see Louis A. Pérez, Jr, The Meaning of the Maine: Causation and the Historiography of the Spanish–American War, *Pacific Historical Review* 58/3 (August 1989), 292–322; Pérez, Jr, *War of 1898*, 57–80; Offner, *Unwanted War*, 122–126.

121 Pérez, Jr, *War of 1898*, 12–18.

122 On these reports from Consul Fitzhugh Lee, see e.g. Letter from Lee to Day, 7 December 1897, in BFSP 90, 825f.; Letter from Lee to Day, 13 December 1897, in ibid., 826; Letter from Lee to Day, 14 December 1897, in ibid., 827; Letter from Lee to Day, 8 January 1898, in ibid., 830; Letter from Lee to Day, 10 February 1898, in ibid., 836–838. On this, see also Gerald G. Eggert, Our Man in Havana: Fitzhugh Lee, *Hispanic American Historical Review* 47/4 (November 1967), 463–485.

123 On Proctor's mission, see Benjamin, *United States*, 49f.; Linderman, *Mirror of War*, 37–59.

124 Condition of Cuba under Spanish Misrule: Speech of Hon. Redfield Proctor in the Senate of the United States March 17, 1898, in Chas. C. Haskell & Son, ed., *The American–Spanish War: A History by the War Leaders*, Norwich 1899, 541–553 at 545.

125 Ibid., 546.

126 Ibid., 547f.

127 Ibid., 552.

128 On the impact of Proctor's speech, see Offner, *Unwanted War*, 134f.; Linderman, *Mirror of War*, 49–59.

129 McCook signed a commercial treaty with the Cuban Junta on 5 August 1897. On this scheme and McCook's part in it, see Benjamin, *United States*, 44f.; Healy, *United States*, 14–16; Foner, *Spanish–Cuban–American War*, vol. 1, 220–222.

130 'Dans ces conditions, il m' a semblé que ce serait non seulement servir la cause de l'Humanité, mais encore faire une œuvre profitable' and 'une proposition de ce genre qui, s'ils veulent bien en tirer parti, devrait leur procurer des avantages et en même temps servir la cause de l'Humanité'. Letter from McCook to Perier Mercet & Co, 17 August 1897, in MAE, CPC E 17; Memorandum des MAE, 9 October 1897, in MAE, CPC E 18.

131 Letter from McCook to McKinley with appended memorandum 'Intervention', 22 March 1898, in LoC Manuscript Division, Papers of William McKinley, Series 1, Reel 3, 2297–2302.

132 Ibid., 2298–2300.
133 Ibid., 2300f.
134 Ibid., 2302.
135 On the ultimatum and the diplomatic manoeuvres surrounding it, see Foner, *Spanish–Cuban–American War*, vol. 1, 250–261; Offner, *Unwanted War*, 143–176.
136 Message of the President of the United States, Communicated to the Two Houses of Congress, on the Relations of the United States to Spain by Reason of Warfare in the Island of Cuba, 11 April 1898, in H.Doc. No. 405, 55th Congress, 2nd Session.
137 Ibid., 5.
138 Ibid., 10f.
139 Ibid., 11.
140 Ibid., 13.
141 Report of the Committee of Foreign Relations, United States Senate, Relative to Affairs in Cuba, 13 April 1898, in S.rp.885, 55th Congress, 2nd Session.
142 'There can be no doubt that the contriver of this unexampled scheme of atrocity intended to depopulate, to the full extent of an ability undeniably great in the conception and perpetration of colossal crime, the island of its native people and to repeople it by natives of Spain.' Ibid., X.
143 Ibid., XI.
144 Ibid., XIII–XVI.
145 Ibid., XVI.
146 Ibid., XVII.
147 Ibid., XXII.
148 Foner, *Spanish–Cuban–American War*, vol. 1, 275f.; Smith, *Spanish–American War*, 45–47.
149 For exemplary accounts of the war, see David F. Task, *The War with Spain in 1898*, Lincoln, NB 1996; Graham A. Cosmas, *An Army for Empire: The United States Army in the Spanish–American War, 1898–1899*, College Station, TX 1994. On the copious historiography, see Pérez, Jr, *War of 1898*. On European views, see Sylvia L. Hilton/Steve J. S. Ickringill, eds., *European Perceptions of the Spanish–American War of 1898*, Bern 1999.
150 Protocol of Agreement Embodying the Terms of a Basis for the Establishing of Peace Between the United States and Spain, 12 August 1898, in US Government Printing Office, ed., *Treaties, Conventions, International Acts, Protocols and Agreements between the United States of America and Other Powers, 1776–1909*, pt. II, vol. II, New York 1968, 1688f.
151 Treaty of Peace between the United States and Spain, Signed at Paris, December 10, 1898, in BFSP 90, 382–387. On the negotiations preceding the Treaty of Paris and its consequences, see Philip S. Foner, *The Spanish–Cuban–American War and the Birth of American Imperialism 1895–1902*, vol. 2: *1898–1902*, New York 1972, 406–421; Benton, *International Law*, 219–248.
152 Osterhammel, *Transformation of the World*, 418.
153 On the Platt Amendment and the Republic of Cuba's continued dependence on the United States, see Louis A. Pérez, Jr, *Cuba between Empires*,

1878–1902, Pittsburgh, PA 1983, 314–327; Langley, *Cuban Policy*, 115–152. On its supposed moral foundations, see Louis A. Pérez, Jr, Incurring a Debt of Gratitude: 1898 and the Moral Sources of United States Hegemony in Cuba, *American Historical Review* 104/2 (April 1999), 356–398.

154 Wood quoted in Jack McCallum, *Leonard Wood: Rough Rider, Surgeon, Architect of American Imperialism*, New York 2006, 187.

155 Hay quoted in Walter Millis, *The Martial Spirit: Being a Study of our War with Spain*, Boston, MA 1931, 340.

156 As a foil to its recent imperial expansion, the cartoonist added a smaller map showing the extent of the United States in 1798. The cartoon may be found at Cornell University Library Digital Collection, Persuasive Maps: PJ Mode Collection, https://digital.library.cornell.edu/catalog/ ss:3293830.

157 A contemporary observer, the American jurist Henry Wade Rogers summarised the consequences of the Spanish–American War thus: 'It cost Spain a colonial empire and advanced the United States to the position of a World-Power.' Henry Wade Rogers, International Law in the Late War, *Forum* 27 (July 1899), 578–591 at 578. On the wider debate on American imperialism, the significance of 1898 and the United States' rise as an imperial power, see e.g. May, *Imperial Democracy*; Walter LaFeber, *The New Empire: An Interpretation of American Expansion 1860–1898*, Ithaca, NY 1998; William Appleman Williams, *The Tragedy of American Diplomacy*, New York 2009, 27–57; Frank Ninkovich, *The United States and Imperialism*, Malden, MA 2001; Paul T. McCartney, *Power and Progress: American National Identity, the War of 1898, and the Rise of American Imperialism*, Baton Rouge, LA 2006.

158 For a summary of debates on American motives, see Pérez, Jr, *War of 1898*, 23–56. Even Philip S. Foner, who distinctly foregrounds economic considerations, concludes: 'There were political, social and psychological roots, too, and no analysis of the road to war can ignore humanitarian sentiments, the role of the press, the sinking of the Maine, the influence of the ideologists of expansionism.' Philip S. Foner, Why the United States Went to War with Spain in 1898, *Science & Society* 32/1 (Winter 1968), 39–65 at 65. For an emphasis on mixed motives in the case of US imperialism, see also Langley, *Cuban Policy*, 110–113; Sewell, Humanitarian Intervention, 306–312.

159 See e.g. Amos S. Hershey, Intervention and the Recognition of Cuban Independence, *Annals of the American Academy of Political and Social Science* 11 (May 1898), 53–80; Talcott H. Russell, The National Idea, *Yale Law Journal* 7/8 (May 1898), 346–351; Rogers, International Law, 579–581. From 1898 onwards the practice of intervention became firmly established in the repertoire of American policy. On this, see Lester D. Langley, *The Banana Wars: United States Intervention in the Caribbean 1898–1934*, Lexington, MA 1985.

160 For a selection of representative newspaper articles, see A War for Humanity, *Daily Picayune* (29 May 1898), 6; It Is a Just and Necessary War, *The Sentinel* (4 May 1898), 7; A War of Humanity: The Way the People in China View the Spanish–American War, *Macon Telegraph* (24 May 1898), 2; War of Humanity Applauded, *Denver Sunday Post* (14 August 1898), 20; John J. Ignalls, ed., *America's War for Humanity*

Related in Story and Picture, Embracing a Complete History of Cuba's Struggle for Liberty, and the Glorious Heroism of America's Soldiers and Sailors, New York 1898. On this, see also Pérez, Jr, *War of 1898,* 39–44.

161 H. Allen Tupper, Jr, *Columbia's War for Cuba: A Story of the Early Struggles of the Cuban Patriots, and of All the Important Events Leading Up to the Present War between the United States and Spain for Cuba Libre,* New York 1898, 11f.

162 Ibid., 67–78.

163 Ibid., 167–202.

164 On this, see e.g. 'We entered upon it [the war] for no other purpose but that of humanity – no desire for new territory, no motive of aggrandizement, but that we might stop the oppression of a neighboring people whose cry we could almost hear. … But whatever it is, whatever obligation shall justly come from this strife for humanity, we must take up and perform, and as free, strong, brave people, accept the trust which civilization puts upon us.' McKinley's speech in Columbus, 21 October 1898, in Doubleday & McClure, ed., *Speeches and Addresses of William McKinley, From March 1, 1897 to May 30, 1900,* New York 1900, 151–153. For a typical reference to purely humanitarian motives, see also McKinley's speech in Belle Plaine, 11 October 1898, in ibid., 89–90; McKinley's speech in Chicago, 18 October 1898, in ibid., 131; McKinley's speech in Indianapolis, 21 October 1898, in ibid., 144f.

165 McKinley's speech in Atlanta, 15 December 1898, in ibid., 159–164 at 162.

166 Ibid., 164.

167 Rudyard Kipling, The White Man's Burden: The United States and The Philippine Islands, 1899, in Kipling, *Rudyard Kipling's Verse,* 321–323. The poem was originally published in *McClure's Magazine* XII/4 (February 1899), 290f.

168 This paternalistic attitude to the newly conquered territories is expressed in many contemporary cartoons depicting Uncle Sam as teacher to Cuba, Puerto Rico, Guam and the Philippines, which are shown as children in need of instruction. On this, see Cartoons, 134; Miller, *From Liberation to Conquest,* 187–230 esp. at 212.

169 On the anti-imperialist movement in the US between 1898 and 1909, see e.g. Michael Patrick Cullinane, *Liberty and American Anti-Imperialism 1898–1909,* New York 2012.

170 On this heated political debate, see McCartney, *Power and Progress,* 224–257; Smith, *Spanish–American War,* 200–208.

171 Our Savage War 'for the Cause of Humanity', *The Nation* 68/1764 (20 April 1899), 288.

172 On the Philippine–American War see e.g. Brian McAllister Linn, *The Philippine War, 1899–1902,* Lawrence, TX 2000; Richard E. Welch, Jr, *Response to Imperialism, The United States and the Philippine–American War, 1899–1902,* Chapel Hill, NC 1979.

173 Letter from a US soldier, quoted in Fred Poole/Max Vanzi, *Revolution in the Philippines: The United States in a Hall of Cracked Mirrors,* New York 1984, 171.

174 On America's brutal warfare in the Philippines see esp. Richard E. Welch, Jr, American Atrocities in the Philippines: The Indictment and the

Response, *Pacific Historical Review* 43/2 (May 1974), 233–253; Paul A. Kramer, Race-Making and Colonial Violence in the U.S. Empire: The Philippine–American War as Race War, *Diplomatic History* 30/2 (April 2006), 169–210.

175 For a contemporary depiction of the 'water cure', see illustration in the *New York Evening Journal* of 15 April 1902 captioned 'Soldiers Trying "Water Cure" on Filipino', in David Brody, *Visualizing American Empire: Orientalism and Imperialism in the Philippines*, Chicago, IL 2010, 75.

176 Stucki, Bevölkerungskontrolle, 254f.; Welch, American Atrocities, 245f.

177 Quoted in General Bell's Reconcentration Policy, *Literary Digest* XXIV/5 (1 February 1902), 138f. at 138.

178 For the difficulties of reaching an accurate estimate of deaths, see John M. Gates, War-Related Deaths in the Philippines, 1898–1902, *Pacific Historical Review* 53/3 (August 1984), 367–378.

Epilogue

1 John Stuart Mill, Vindication of the French Revolution of February 1848, in John Stuart Mill, *Dissertations and Discussions Political, Philosophical, and Historical Reprinted Chiefly from the Edinburgh and Westminster Reviews*, vol. 2, London 1867, 380.

2 Richard B. Lillich, Intervention to Protect Human Rights, *McGill Law Journal* 15/2 (June 1969), 205–219 at 216.

3 Ulrich Beck, *Der kosmopolitische Blick oder: Krieg ist Frieden*, Frankfurt a. M. 2004, 84.

4 William E. Lingelbach, The Doctrine and Practice of Intervention in Europe, *Annals of the American Academy of Political and Social Science* 16 (July 1900), 1–32.

5 Ibid., 19.

6 Ibid., 25. On the concept of humanitarian intervention in international law around 1900, see also Swatek-Evenstein, *History*, 156–160. Such a position was by no means shared by all scholars of international law in the early twentieth century, some of whom continued to consider humanitarian intervention unlawful. For an overview of supporters and opponents, see Heraclides/Dialla, *Humanitarian Intervention*, 60f., 67–69.

7 Lingelbach, Doctrine and Practice, 31f.

8 Rougier, La théorie de l'intervention d'humanité, 468–526.

9 Ibid., 472–480.

10 'Pour affirmer sa légitimité, il faut donc préalablement démontrer l'existence des "lois de l'humanité" en tant que préceptes juridiques, et les préciser.' Ibid., 478. 'Le grand juriste allemand [Bluntschli] ne dit pas quels sont les droits individuels reconnus nécessaires à l'humanité. Si cette appréciation est laissée aux puissances intervenantes, elle sera arbitraire, variable suivant les circonstances.' Ibid., 493f.

11 'Les droits de l'homme seraient les droits antérieurs et supérieurs à toute organisation politique, placés sous la garantie de toutes les nations, s'imposant à chaque legislateur particullier. Ils se résumerait en deux idées

essentielles: droit à la vie et droit à la liberté. … Seule la violation de ces droits essentiels serait une juste cause d'intervention.' Ibid., 517.

12 Ibid., 489–497, 517–523.

13 Marrus, International Bystanders to the Holocaust, 164–168. In consequence of such hesitancy on the part of governments, the mantle of humanitarian action passed increasingly to NGOs in the inter-war period. Davide Rodogno has illustrated this process by the example of an American organisation, Near East Relief. On this, see Davide Rodogno, Non-State Actors' Humanitarian Operations in the Aftermath of the First World War: The Case of the Near East Relief, in Klose, ed., *Emergence of Humanitarian Intervention*, 185–207.

14 On the role and significance of the League of Nations in the inter-war period see e.g. Sluga, *Internationalism*, 45–78; Susan Pedersen, *The Guardians: The League of Nations and Crisis of Empire*, Oxford 2014.

15 Malbone W. Graham, Humanitarian Intervention in International Law as Related to the Practice of the United States, *Michigan Law Review* 22/4 (February 1924), 312–328 at 320f. On the role of the League of Nations, see also Ellery C. Stowell, La théorie et la pratique de l'intervention, Académie de droit international, ed., *Recueil des cours* II/40 (1932), 91–148 at 138–148; Swatek-Evenstein, *History*, 165–175.

16 'There exists now, therefore, not a subjective Law of Nature nor a sentimental Law of Humanity to sanction interventions of a humanitarian character, but a substantive Law of Nations defining the right of humanitarian intervention in a new light.' Graham, Humanitarian Intervention, 321f.

17 Ibid., 326.

18 Ibid., 327f.

19 Ibid., 328.

20 On Mandelstam's life and importance, see Herman Burger, André Mandelstam, Forgotten Pioneer of International Human Rights, in Fons Coomans/Fred Grünfeld/Ingrid Westendorp, eds., *Rendering Justice to the Vulnerable: Liber Amicorum in Honor of Theo van Boven*, The Hague 2000, 69–82; Helmut Philipp Aust, From Diplomat to Academic Activist: André Mandelstam and the History of Human Rights, *European Journal of International Law* 25/4 (2014), 1105–1121; Hülya Adak, The Legacy of André Nikolaievitch Mandelstam (1869–1949) and the Early History of Human Rights, *Zeitschrift für Religions- und Geistesgeschichte* 70/2 (2018), 117–130.

21 For the New York declaration of the Institut de droit international, see L'Institut de Droit international, Rapporteur André Mandelstam, 'Déclaration des droits internationaux de l'Homme', 12 October 1929, http://www.idi-iil.org/app/uploads/2017/06/1929_nyork_01_fr.pdf.

22 André N. Mandelstam, Der internationale Schutz der Menschenrechte und die New-Yorker Erklärung des Instituts für Völkerrecht, *Zeitschrift für ausländisches öffentliches Recht und Völkerrecht* 2 (1931), 335–377 at 340–346; Aust, From Diplomat to Academic Activist, 1115–1117. For Mandelstam's position on the international protection of human rights, see also André N. Mandelstam, La généralisation de la protection internationale des droits de l'homme, *Revue de droit international et de législation comparée* 3/XI (1930), 297–325 and 699–713.

23 Mandelstam, Internationale Schutz, 346.
24 Ibid., 367f.
25 Ibid., 375.
26 On this, see Mark Mazower, An International Civilization? Empire, Internationalism and the Crisis of the Mid-Twentieth Century, *International Affairs* 82/3 (May 2006), 553–566 at 559–563; Pedersen, *Guardians*, 107–194; Paul Betts, Universalism and Its Discontents: Humanity as a Twentieth-Century Concept, in Klose/Thulin, eds., *Humanity*, 51–70 at 53–58.
27 Ibid., 57f.
28 On this, see esp. Forclaz, *Humanitarian Imperialism*, 108–171; Jean Allain, Slavery and the League of Nations: Ethiopia as a Civilised Nation, in Jean Allain, *The Law and Slavery: Prohibiting Human Exploitation*, Leiden 2015, 121–158 at 147–158.
29 On this, see Jost Dülffer, Humanitarian Intervention as Legitimation of Violence – The German Case 1937–1939, in Klose, ed., *Emergence of Humanitarian Intervention*, 208–228; Goodman, Humanitarian Intervention, 113; Jörg Fisch, Adolf Hitler und das Selbstbestimmungsrecht der Völker, *Historische Zeitschrift* 290/1 (February 2010), 93–118 at 103–118, Swatek-Evenstein, *History*, 177–179.
30 Marrus, International Bystanders, 164–168.
31 Philip C. Jessup, The Defense of Oppressed Peoples, *American Journal of International Law* 32/1 (January 1938), 116–119.
32 Ibid., 116f.
33 On this, see Ellery C. Stowell, Humanitarian Intervention, *American Journal of International Law* 33/4 (October 1939), 733–736. For an earlier study by Stowell on the question of intervention, see Ellery Stowell, *Intervention in International Law*, Washington, DC 1921.
34 Stowell, Humanitarian Intervention, 736.
35 Articles 2 (4) and 2 (7) of the Charter of the United Nations, https://www.un.org/en/sections/un-charter/chapter-i/index.html.
36 Chapter VII of the Charter of the United Nations, 'Action with Respect to Threats to the Peace, Breaches of the Peace, and Acts of Aggression', Article 39, https://www.un.org/en/sections/un-charter/chapter-vii/index.html. On the use of force under international law after 1945 also see esp. Claus Kreß, Major Post-Westphalian Shifts and Some Important Neo-Westphalian Hesitations in the State Practice on the International Law on the Use of Force, *Journal on the Use of Force and International Law* 1/1 (2014), 11–54.
37 Martti Koskenniemi, Lauterpacht: The Victorian Tradition in International Law, *European Journal of International Law* 2/8 (1997), 215–263 at 244.
38 Hersch Lauterpacht, The Law of Nations, the Law of Nature and the Rights of Man, *Transactions of the Grotius Society* 29: Problems of Peace and War, Papers Read before the Society in the Year 1943, 1–33.
39 Ibid., 27f. For a reference to Hugo Grotius as the supposed originator of the idea of humanitarian intervention, see 'Finally, in assessing the place of Grotius in the matter of the fundamental rights of man we must not forget that it is to him that dates back the idea of international humanitarian

intervention for the protection of these rights.' Ibid., 24. For Lauterpacht's repeated references to the humanitarian interventions against slavery and for the protection of minorities in the nineteenth century, see also Hersch Lauterpacht, *International Law and Human Rights*, London 1950, 120f.

40 Lauterpacht, Law of Nations, 28.

41 Hersch Lauterpacht, *An International Bill of the Rights of Man*, New York 1945, 169–178.

42 Ibid., 194–213.

43 Ibid., 209f.

44 Hersch Lauterpacht, ed., *Lassa Oppenheim, International Law: A Treatise*, vol. I: *Peace*, London 1948.

45 Ibid., 280.

46 Ibid., 287. On his interpretation of Article 2 (7) of the UN Charter and the scope for intervention within the system of the UN, see also Lauterpacht, *International Law and Human Rights*, 166–173.

47 On this, see Fabian Klose, *Human Rights in the Shadow of Colonial Violence: The Wars of Independence in Kenya and Algeria*, Philadelphia, PA 2013.

48 Brownlie, *International Law*, 338–342.

49 Ibid., 340f.

50 Ibid., 341.

51 Ibid., 342.

52 Resolution 2131 (XX), Declaration on the Inadmissibility of Intervention in the Domestic Affairs of States and the Protection of Their Independence and Sovereignty, 21 December 1965, UNGA A/RES/20/2131.

53 On this, see International Law Association, *Report of the Fifty-Second Conference Held at Helsinki, August 14th to August 20th, 1966*, London 1967, 744–754.

54 Richard B. Lillich, Forcible Self-Help by States to Protect Human Rights, *Iowa Law Review* 53 (1967), 325–351; Lillich, Intervention to Protect Human Rights, 205–219. On these debates, see also David S. Bogen, The Law of Humanitarian Intervention: United States Policy in Cuba (1898) and in the Dominican Republic (1965), *Harvard International Law Club Journal* 7/2 (Spring 1966), 296–315; Howard L. Weisberg, The Congo Crisis 1964: A Case Study in Humanitarian Intervention, *Virginia Journal of International Law* 12/2 (1972), 261–276. On this, see also Swatek-Evenstein, *History*, 214–220.

55 Swatek-Evenstein, *History*, 222–228. On the Biafran conflict and the humanitarian disaster it caused see e.g. Dirk Moses/Lasse Heerten, eds., *Postcolonial Conflict and the Question of Genocide: The Nigeria–Biafra War, 1967–1970*, New York 2018; Lasse Heerten, *The Biafran War and Postcolonial Humanitarianism: Spectacles of Suffering*, Cambridge 2017.

56 Michael Reisman with the collaboration of Myers S. McDougal, Humanitarian Intervention to Protect the Ibos, in Richard B. Lillich, ed., *Humanitarian Intervention and the United Nations*, Charlottesville, NC 1973, 167–195. On the New Haven School and its influence, see Neff, *Justice among Nations*, 429–432.

57 Reisman, Humanitarian Intervention, 194f.

58 Ibid., 179–183.

59 Richard B. Lillich, Preface, in Lillich, ed., *Humanitarian Intervention*, vi.

60 This was indeed the conference's official agenda 'Part I: The Past', 'Part II: The Present' and 'Part III: The Future'. On this, see Conference Proceedings, in Lillich, ed., *Humanitarian Intervention*, 3–135. The preface to the conference's subsequently published papers was written by no less an eminence than John P. Humphrey, the Canadian jurist who in his capacity as director of the United Nations Division of Human Rights had been instrumental in drafting the Universal Declaration of Human Rights of 1948.

61 On this, see e.g. John M. Paxman/George T. Boggs, eds., *The United Nations: A Reassessment. Sanctions, Peacekeeping, and Humanitarian Assistance*, Charlottesville, VA 1973 esp. at 103–148; Ian Brownlie, Humanitarian Intervention, in John N. Moore, ed., *Law and Civil War in the Modern World*, Baltimore, MD 1974, 217–228; Richard B. Lillich, Humanitarian Intervention: A Reply to Ian Brownlie and a Plea for Constructive Alternatives, in ibid., 229–251; Laurie S. Wiseberg, Humanitarian Intervention: Lessons from the Nigerian Civil War, *Revue des droits de l'homme* 70/1 (1974), 61–98; B. de Schutter, Humanitarian Intervention: A United Nations Task, *California Western International Law Journal* 21/3 (1972), 21–36; Thomas M. Franck/Nigel S. Rodley, After Bangladesh: The Law of Humanitarian Intervention by Military Force, *American Journal of International Law* 67/2 (April 1973), 275–305; Jean-Pierre L. Fonteyne, The Customary International Law Doctrine of Humanitarian Intervention: Its Current Validity under the U.N. Charter, *California Western International Law Journal* 4 (1973), 203–270.

62 As in the case of East Pakistan, the intervening states justified their actions not in terms of the doctrine of humanitarian intervention, but on the principle of self-defence. On this, see Murphy, *Humanitarian Intervention*, 97–107.

63 Thomas E. Behuniak, The Law of Unilateral Humanitarian Intervention by Armed Force: A Legal Survey, *Military Law Review* 79/27 (Winter 1978), 157–191; Farooq Hassan, Realpolitik in International Law: After Tanzanian–Ugandan Conflict: 'Humanitarian Intervention' Reexamined, *Willamette Law Review* 17 (1981), 859–912; Michael J. Bazyler, Reexamining the Doctrine of Humanitarian Intervention in the Light of the Atrocities in Kampuchea and Ethiopia, *Stanford Journal of International Law* 23 (1987), 547–619. On this, see also Fabian Klose, Protecting Universal Rights through Intervention: International Law Debates from the 1930s to the 1980s, in Norbert Frei/ Daniel Stahl/Annette Weinke, eds., *Human Rights and Humanitarian Intervention: Legitimizing the Use of Force since the 1970s*, Göttingen 2017, 169–184.

64 The first genuine human rights law classes were set up at the law schools of Columbia and Harvard in 1971. On this, see Mark Philip Bradley, *The World Reimagined: Americans and Human Rights in the Twentieth Century*, New York 2016, 213–216. On the development of human rights in the 1970s more generally, see Barbara Keys, *Reclaiming American Virtue: The Human Rights Revolutuion of the 1970s*, Cambridge, MA 2014; Jan Eckel/Samuel Moyn, eds., *The Breakthrough: Human Rights in the 1970s*, Philadelphia, PA 2014.

On French debates on intervention from the 1970s on, see Eleanor Davey, *The Language of ingérence: Interventionist Debates in France, 1970s–1990s*, in Frei/Stahl/Weinke, eds., *Human Rights*, 46–63.

65 Klose, Protecting Universal Rights, 169–184; Klose, *Emergence of Humanitarian Intervention*; Jan Eckel, Humanitarian Intervention as Global Governance: Western Governments and Suffering 'Others' before and after 1990, in Frei/Stahl/Weinke, eds., *Human Rights*, 64–85.

66 On this, see esp. Norrie MacQueen, *Humanitarian Intervention and the United Nations*, Edinburgh 2011; Norrie MacQueen, Cold War Peacekeeping versus Humanitarian Intervention: Beyond the Hammarskjöldian Model, in Klose, ed., *Emergence of Humanitarian Intervention*, 231–252; Jan Erik Schulte, From the Protection of Sovereignty to Humanitarian Intervention? Traditions and Developments of United Nations Peacekeeping in the Twentieth Century, in Klose, ed., *Emergence of Humanitarian Intervention*, 253–277.

67 On this, see James Mayall, ed., *The New Interventionism, 1991–1994: The United Nations Experience in Cambodia, Former Yugoslavia, and Somalia*, Cambridge 1996; Stephen Wertheim, A Solution from Hell: The United States and the Rise of Humanitarian Interventionism, 1991–2003, *Journal of Genocide Research* 12/3–4, September–December 2010, 149–172; Yuki Abe, *Norm Dilemmas in Humanitarian Intervention: How Bosnia Changed NATO*, Abingdon 2019.

68 For the UN's complete failure in each case see the reports produced by the respective inquiries: Report of the Secretary-General Pursuant to General Assembly Resolution 53/35. The Fall of Srebrenica, 15 November 1999, UNGA A/54/549; Report of the Independent Inquiry into the Actions of the United Nations during the 1994 Genocide in Rwanda, 16 December 1999, UNSC S/1999/1257.

69 The core elements of Boutros-Ghali's 'Agenda for Peace' are in its title: 'preventive diplomacy', 'peacemaking' and 'peace-keeping'. On this, see Agenda for Peace: Preventive Diplomacy, Peacemaking, and Peace-keeping, 17 June 1992, UNGA A/47/277 – S/24111.

70 Prevention of Armed Conflict: Report of the Secretary-General on the Work of the Organization, 7 June 2001, UN General Assembly (UNGA) A/55/985 – S/2001/574, 1.

71 According to the Carnegie Foundation, the cost of the seven major military interventions in Bosnia and Herzegovina, Somalia, Rwanda, Haiti, the Persian Gulf, Cambodia and El Salvador in the 1990s amounted to $200 million, whereas preventive measures were estimated at a mere $130 billion. Ibid., 6.

72 Ibid., 36f.

73 ICISS, *Responsibility to Protect*, vi. In the introduction to its report, the ICISS cited the failure of the UN missions in Somalia, Bosnia and Rwanda as well as NATO's intervention in Kosovo 1999 (without a UN mandate). See ibid., vii, 1.

74 Resolution 60/1, 2005 World Summit Outcome, 24 October 2005, UNGA A/RES/60/1, 30.

75 ICISS, *Responsibility to Protect*, 19–27.

76 Ibid., 29–37.
77 Ibid., 39–45.
78 Ibid., vi.
79 On the relation between humanitarian intervention and preventive strategies, see Fabian Klose, Humanitäre Intervention und Prävention in der internationalen Politik vom 19. bis ins 21. Jahrhundert, in Nicolai Hannig/Malte Thiessen, eds., *Vorsorge in der Moderne: Akteure, Räume und Praktiken*, Berlin 2017 (Schriftenreihe der Vierteljahrshefte für Zeitgeschichte 115), 27–44.
80 See Resolution 1970 (2011), 26 February 2011, in UNSC S/RES/1970; Resolution 1973 (2011), 17 March 2011, in UNSC S/RES/1973. On the intervention in Libya, see also Wester, *Intervention*.
81 For current debates on R2P as an instriemnt of human rights protection in the twenty-first century see esp. Tesón/van der Vossen, *Debating Humanitarian Intervention*; Warren/Grenfell, *Rethinking Humanitarian Intervention*; Aidan Hehir/Robert W. Murray, eds., *Protecting Human Rights in the 21st Century*, London 2017; Bellamy/McLoughlin, *Rethinking Humanitarian Intervention*, 187–209; Hoffman/Weiss, *Humanitarianism*, 105–111; Cecilia Jacob/Martin Mennecke, eds., *Implementing the Responsibility to Protect: A Future Agenda*, Abingdon 2020.
82 Beck, *Kosmopolitische Blick*. For the terms 'human rights war' (*Menschenrechtskriege*) and 'military humanism' (*militärischer Humanismus*) see e.g. ibid., 193–196, 212–220 and 233.
83 Ibid., 75.
84 Ibid., 84f. Jürgen Osterhammel, too, has warned of a responsibility to protect in international politics leading to a 'return of the protectorate'. On this, see Osterhammel, Schutz, Macht und Verantwortung, 167–170.
85 Beck, *Kosmopolitische Blick*, 84.
86 Ibid., 208. Noam Chomsky is another observer who has warned against a 'new military humanism' and its abuse for neo-colonialist ends. On this, see Noam Chomsky, *A New Generation Draws the Line: 'Humanitarian' Intervention and the Standards of the West*, London 2012; Noam Chomsky, *The New Military Humanism: Lessons from Kosovo*, London 1999. For other critical voices, see also Wertheim, Solution from Hell, 149–172; Goodman, Humanitarian Intervention, 107–141; Menon, *Conceit of Humanitarian Intervention*; Nicholas J. Wheeler/Justin Morris, Justifying the Iraq War as a Humanitarian Intervention: The Cure is Worse than the Disease, in Ramesh Thakur/W. P. S. Sidhu, eds., *The Iraq Crisis and World Order: Structural, Institutional and Normative Challenges*, Tokyo 2006, 444–463; Philip Cunliffe, *Cosmopolitan Dystopia: International Intervention and the Failure of the West*, Manchester 2020; Marek Madej, ed., *Western Military Interventions after the Cold War: Evaluating the Wars of the West*, Abingdon 2019.
87 Bass, *Freedom's Battle*, 360.
88 On this, see International Commission on Intervention and State Sovereignty, ed., *The Responsibility to Protect: Research, Bibliography, Background. Supplementary Volume to the Report of the ICISS*, Ottawa 2001, 16f.
89 With this in mind, it should come as little surprise that countries of the Global South with colonial experiences of their own – such as South Africa, Brazil

and India – should be highly critical of the concept of R2P. On this, see also Ramesh Thakur, Global Norms and International Humanitarian Law: An Asian Perspective, *International Review of the Red Cross* 841 (31 March 2001), https://www.icrc.org/eng/resources/documents/article/other/57jqzd.htm; Dan Krause/Daniel Peters, eds., *Southern Democracies and the Responsibility to Protect: Perspectives from India, Brazil and South Africa*, Baden-Baden 2017.

Bibliography

Unpublished Sources

Archives du Comité International de la Croix-Rouge, Geneva, Switzerland
(ACICR)
Anciens Fonds (AF)
AF 5.2, Courrier reçu États-Unies 1893–1913
AF 15.6, Courier reçu Serbie

Archivo General de Indias, Seville, Spain (AGI)
ULTRAMAR
Legajo 32

Archivo General de Simancas, Valladolid, Spain (AGS)
ESTADO
Legajo 8176

Archivo Histórico Nacional, Madrid, Spain (AHN)
ESTADO
Legajo 8029
Legajo 8040
Legajo 8047
Legajo 8048

Library of Congress, Manuscript Division, Washington, DC, USA (LoC)
Clara Barton Papers 1822–1912, Microfilmed from the Sophia Smith
Collection, Microfilm 23, 471 Papers of William McKinley, Series
1, Reel 3

Ministère des Affaires Étrangères, Archives des Affaires Étrangères, Paris,
France (MAE)
Série Correspondence Politique, Angleterre (MAE CP A)
CP A 635
CP A 641
CP A 659
Série Correspondence politique des consuls, Beyrouth (MAE CP C B)
CP C B12
CP C B13

Série Correspondence Politique et Commerciale, Nouvelle Série 1897 à 1918, Espagne (MAE CP C E)
CP C E18
Série Mémoires et Documents, Afrique (MAE MD A)
MD A 5
MD A 15
MD A 18
MD A 19
MD A 22
MD A 23
MD A 24
MD A 25
MD A 26
MD A 27
MD A 28
Série Mémoires et Documents, France (MAE MD F)
MD F 677
MD F 685
MD F 689
Série Mémoires et Documents, Grèce (MAE MD G)
MD G 9
Série Mémoires et Documents, Turquie (MAE MD T)
MD T 62
MD T 101
MD T 108
MD T 131
MD T 142

National Maritime Museum, Manuscripts, Greenwich, UK (NMM)
WEL/10, Survey by Captain George Ralph Collier, on the Gold Coast made to the Admiralty between 1821–1824, on settlements and slaving, Two Parts

Haus-, Hof- und Staatsarchiv, Vienna, Austria (HHStA)
Diplomatie und Außenpolitik 1848–1918, Ministerium des Äußern 1735–1924, Fach 39 Sklavenhandel und Piraterie (MdÄ AR F39)
MdÄ AR F39-1: Sklavenhandel, Piraterie, Baraterie, Kaperei, Generalia (dabei: Verhandlungen wegen Abschlusses eines gemeinschaftlichen Traktates wegen Abschaffung des Handels mit Negersklaven), 1834–1847
MdÄ AR F 39-3: Sklavenhandel, Piraterie, Baraterie, Kaperei, Generalia (includes: Kreuzungsvollmachten), 1857–1866
Diplomatie und Außenpolitik 1848–1918, Gesandtschafts- und Konsulatsarchive 1617–1920, Konsulatsarchiv Beirut 1844–1912 (GKA KsA)
GKA KsA Beirut 4–1 Libanon-Akten: Libanon-Reglement, 1844–1861
Diplomatie und Außenpolitik 1848–1918, Gesandtschafts- und Konsulatsarchive 1617–1920, Konsulatsarchiv Beirut, 1861–1918 (GKA KsA)

GKA KsA Beirut 5a–1 Libanon-Akten: Reglement des Libanon und dessen Überwachung durch die Kommissare der Signatarmächte, 1860–1873

National Museum of the Royal Navy, Manuscript Collection, Portsmouth, Great Britain (NMRN)
MSS 45, Second Annual Report on the Coast of Africa, Commodore Sir George Collier, Bart.
2005.76/1, Diaries of Henry Cheesman Binstead (Midshipman on Owen Glendower, West Africa Squadron 1823–24)
2005.76/2, Diaries of Henry Cheesman Binstead (Midshipman on Owen Glendower, West Africa Squadron 1823–24)

Service historique de la défense, Vincennes, France (SHD/SHAT)
Departement Marine, Sous Série (BB 4)
SHD, Marine, BB 4/504
Ministère de la Guerre, État-Major de l'Armée, Archives Historiques, Corps Expéditionnaire de la Morée (SHAT D²)
SHAT D² 1
SHAT D² 2
SHAT D² 3
SHAT D² 4
SHAT D² 5
SHAT D² 6
Ministère de la Guerre, État-Major de l'Armée, Archives Historiques, Armée Expédition de Morée
(SHAT XP)
SHAT XP 51
Ministère de la Guerre, État-Major de l'Armée, Archives Historiques, Expédition de Syrie 1860–61 (SHAT G4)
SHAT, G4 1
SHAT, G4 2
SHAT, G4 6

The National Archives of the United Kingdom: Public Record Office, Kew, Great Britain, (TNA)
Records of the Admiralty, Naval Forces, Royal Marines, Coastguard, and Related Bodies (ADM)
ADM 1: Admiralty, and Ministry of Defence, Navy Department: Correspondence and Papers ADM 5: Admiralty and predecessors: Letters Patent, Navy Board, Transport Board, Vice-Admiralty and Commissions of Inquiry Appointments ADM 7: Admiralty: Miscellanea
ADM 123: Admiralty: Africa Station: Correspondence
Foreign Office: Records created and inherited by the Foreign Office (FO)
FO 63: Foreign Office and predecessor: Political and Other Departments: General Correspondence before 1906, Portugal

FO 65: Foreign Office and predecessor: Political and Other Departments: General Correspondence before 1906, Russian Empire

FO 72: Foreign Office and predecessor: Political and Other Departments: General Correspondence before 1906, Spain (formerly incorporating Spanish America)

FO 78: Foreign Office and predecessor: Political and Other Departments: General Correspondence before 1906, Ottoman Empire

FO 84: Foreign Office: Slave Trade Department and successors: General Correspondence before 1906

FO 93: Foreign Office and Foreign and Commonwealth Office: Protocols of Treaties

FO 96: Foreign Office and predecessors: Political and Other Departments: Miscellanea, Series II

FO 115: Embassy and Consulates, United States of America: General Correspondence

FO 195: Foreign Office: Embassy and Consulates, Turkey (formerly Ottoman Empire): General Correspondence

FO 312: Archives of Cape Town Slave Trade Commission

FO 313: Archives of Havana Slave Trade Commission

FO 315: Archives of Sierra Leone Slave Trade Commission

FO 352: Correspondence with Stratford Canning

FO 406: Foreign Office: Confidential Print Eastern Affairs

FO 420: Confidential Print America, South and Central

FO 421: Foreign Office: Confidential Print South-East Europe

FO 541: Foreign Office: Confidential Print Slave Trade

FO 880: Foreign Office: Consulate, Shiraz, Persia: General Correspondence

FO 881: Foreign Office: Confidential Print (Numerical Series)

Colonial Office: Records of the Colonial Office, Commonwealth and Foreign and Commonwealth Offices, Empire Marketing Board, and related bodies (CO)

CO 87: War and Colonial Department and Colonial Office: Gambia, Original Correspondence

CO 267: Colonial Office and Predecessors: Sierra Leone Original Correspondence

CO 879: War and Colonial Department and Colonial Office: Africa, Confidential Print

Domestic Records of the Public Record Office, Gifts, Deposits, Notes and Transcripts (PRO)

PRO 30/22/30: Correspondence: to the Queen and Lord Palmerston

PRO 30/22/78: Russia: embassy in London and miscellaneous. Private correspondence from British and foreign envoys, and others to Lord John (from 1861 earl) Russell, foreign secretary

PRO 30/22/88: Turkey (Ottoman Empire). Embassy in Constantinople Private correspondence. Sir Henry Lytton Bulwer, ambassador to Lord John Russell, foreign secretary

PRO 30/22/104: France, vol. 2: Embassy in Paris. Private correspondence (drafts). Lord John (from 1861 earl) Russell, foreign secretary, to Lord Cowley, ambassador and Hon. William Grey, embassy secretary

PRO 30/22/116: (a) Turkey. Embassy in Constantinople. (b) Persia. Legation in Teheran. Private correspondence (drafts). Lord John (from 1861 earl) Russell, foreign secretary to Sir Henry Bulwer, ambassador, Constantinople; to Lord Dufferin, special mission to Syria 1860; to Hon. W. Stuart, embassy secretary, Constantinople; to Musurus Bey, Turkish ambassador, London; to Aali Pasha, grand vizier, Turkey; to Charles Alison, minister, Teheran, and others

Published Sources

Official British Government Publications

British and Foreign State Papers (BFSP)

Foreign Office (ed.), British and Foreign State Papers, vol. 1, pt. I (1812–1814), London 1841.

BFSP, vol. 1, pt. II (1812–1814), London 1841.
BFSP, vol. 2 (1814–1815), London 1839.
BFSP, vol. 3 (1815–1816), London 1838.
BFSP, vol. 4 (1816–1817), London 1836.
BFSP, vol. 5 (1817–1818), London 1837.
BFSP, vol. 6 (1818–1819), London 1835.
BFSP, vol. 7 (1819–1820), London 1834.
BFSP, vol. 8 (1820–1821), London 1830.
BFSP, vol. 9 (1821–1822), London 1829.
BFSP, vol. 10 (1822–1823), London 1828.
BFSP, vol. 11 (1823–1824), London 1843.
BFSP, vol. 12 (1824–1825), London 1846.
BFSP, vol. 13 (1825–1826), London 1848.
BFSP, vol. 14 (1826–1827), London 1829.
BFSP, vol. 15 (1827–1828), London 1829.
BFSP, vol. 16 (1828–1829), London 1832.
BFSP, vol. 17 (1829–1830), London 1832.
BFSP, vol. 18 (1830–1831), London 1833.
BFSP, vol. 20 (1832–1933), London 1836.
BFSP, vol. 21, pt. I (1833–1834), London 1842.
BFSP, vol. 22 (1834–1835), London 1847.
BFSP, vol. 23 (1834–1835, London 1852.
BFSP, vol. 24 (1835–1836), London 1853.
BFSP, vol. 25 (1836–1837), London 1853.
BFSP, vol. 28 (1839–1840), London 1857.
BFSP, vol. 30 (1841–1842), London 1858.
BFSP, vol. 32 (1843–1844), London 1857.
BFSP, vol. 34 (1845–1846), London 1860.
BFSP, vol. 35 (1846–1847), London 1860.
BFSP, vol. 36 (1847–1848), London 1861.
BFSP, vol. 45 (1854–1855), London 1865.
BFSP, vol. 50 (1859–1860), London 1867.
BFSP, vol. 51 (1860–1861), London 1868.

BFSP, vol. 67 (1875–1876), London 1888.
BFSP, vol. 68 (1876–1877), London 1884.
BFSP, vol. 69 (1877–1878), London 1885.
BFSP, vol. 82 (1889–1890), London 1890.
BFSP, vol. 90 (1897–1898), London 1898.
Correspondence with the British Commissioners at Sierra Leone, Havana, The Cape of Good Hope, and Loanda; and Reports from British Naval Officers, Relating to the Slave Trade, From April 1, 1857, to March 31, 1858, London 1858.

British Parliamentary Papers (BPP)

The British Parliamentary Papers (BPP), vol. 3: Select committee on the West Coast of Africa together with the Minutes of Evidence, Appendix, and Index, pt. II, Dublin 1968.
BPP vol. 10: Correspondence with British Commissioners and Foreign Powers relating to the Slave Trade, 1825–1826, Dublin 1969.
BPP vol. 14: Correspondence with British Commissioners and Foreign Powers relating to the Slave Trade, 1835–1836 (Class A and Class B), Dublin 1969.
BPP vol. 17: Correspondence with British Commissioners and Foreign Powers relating to the Slave Trade, 1839, Dublin 1969.
BPP vol. 20: Correspondence with British Commissioners and Foreign Powers relating to the Slave Trade, 1841, Dublin 1970.
BPP vol. 21: Correspondence with the British Commissioners on the Slave Trade, 1842, Dublin 1969.
BPP vol. 41: Correspondence with the British Commissioners and British Ministers on the Slave Trade, 1854–1855, Dublin 1969.
BPP vol. 61: Papers relating to the Slave Trade, 1801–1815, Dublin 1971.

Great Britain, Houses of Parliament

Great Britain, Parliament, House of Commons (ed.), The Debate on a Motion for the Abolition of the Slave-Trade, in: the House of Commons on Monday and Tuesday, April 18 and 19, 1791, London 1791.
(ed.), Substance of the Debates on a Resolution for Abolishing the Slave Trade, which was moved in the House of Commons on the 10th June, 1806, and in the House of Lords, on the 24th June, 1806, London 1806.
(ed.), Report from the Select Committee of the House of Lords, Appointed to Consider the best Means which Great Britain can adopt for the final Extinction of the African Slave Trade; and to Report thereon to the House; together with the Minutes of Evidence, 15 July 1850, London 1850.
(ed.), Papers Relative to the Reduction of Lagos by Her Majesty's Forces on the West Coast of Africa, London 1852.
(ed.), Report from the Select Committee on Slave Trade (East Coast of Africa); together with the Proceedings of the Committee, Minutes of Evidence, Appendix and Index, 4 August 1871, London 1871.

(ed.), Despatches Addressed by Dr. Livingstone, Her Majesty's Consul, Inner Africa, to Her Majesty's Secretary of State for Foreign Affairs, in 1870, 1871, and 1872, London 1872.

(ed.), Correspondence Respecting Sir Bartle Frere's Mission to the East Coast of Africa, 1872–73, London 1873.

(ed.), Correspondence with British Representatives and Agents, and Reports from Naval Officers, Related to the East African Slave Trade, From January 1 to December 31, 1873, London 1874.

(ed.), Communications from Dr. Kirk, Respecting the Suppression of the Land Slave Traffic in the Dominions of the Sultan of Zanzibar, London 1876.

Hansard Parliamentary Debates

Cobbett, William (ed.), The Parliamentary History of England from the Earliest Period to the Year 1803, Parliamentary Debates, vol. 27: 14 February 1788 to 4 May 1789, London 1816.

(ed.), The Parliamentary History of England from the Earliest Period to the Year 1803, Parliamentary Debates, vol. 28: 9 May 1789 to 15 March 1791, London 1816.

(ed.), The Parliamentary History of England from the Earliest Period to the Year 1803, Parliamentary Debates, vol. 29: 22 March 1791 to 13 December 1792, London 1817.

(ed.), The Parliamentary History of England from the Earliest Period to the Year 1803, Parliamentary Debates, vol. 30: 13 December 1792 to 10 March 1794, London 1817.

Hansard, T. C. (ed.), The Parliamentary Debates from the Year 1803 to the Present Time, vol. 5, New Series, London 1822 (New York 1970).

(ed.), The Parliamentary Debates from the Year 1803 to the Present Time, vol. 6, London 1806 (New York 1970).

(ed.), The Parliamentary Debates from the Year 1803 to the Present Time, vol. 7, London 1812 (New York 1970).

(ed.), The Parliamentary Debates from the Year 1803 to the Present Time, vol. 27, London 1814 (New York 1970).

(ed.), The Parliamentary Debates from the Year 1803 to the Present Time, vol. 28, London 1814 (New York 1970).

(ed.), The Parliamentary Debates from the Year 1803 to the Present Time, vol. 30, London 1815 (New York 1970).

(ed.), The Parliamentary Debates from the Year 1803 to the Present Time, vol. 34, London 1816 (New York 1970).

(ed.), The Parliamentary Debates from the Year 1803 to the Present Time, vol. 35, London 1817 (New York 1970).

(ed.), The Parliamentary Debates from the Year 1803 to the Present Time, vol. 36, London 1817.

(ed.), The Parliamentary Debates from the Year 1803 to the Present Time, vol. 50, London 1839 (New York 1970).

(ed.), The Parliamentary Debates from the Year 1803 to the Present Time, vol. 65, London 1842 (New York 1970).

(ed.), The Parliamentary Debates from the Year 1803 to the Present Time, vol. 81, London 1842 (New York 1970).

(ed.), The Parliamentary Debates from the Year 1803 to the Present Time, vol. 109, London 1850 (New York 1970).

Her Majesty's Stationery Office (HMSO)

Her Majesty's Stationery Office (ed.), Supplement to the Slave Trade Instructions, vol. I: Treaty Engagements with States other than Uncivilized African States, London 1865.

(ed.), Supplement to the Slave Trade Instructions, vol. II: Engagements with Uncivilized African States, London 1865.

(ed.), Slave Trade Instructions, being Instructions for the Guidance of the Commanders of Her Majesty's Ships of War employed in the Suppression of the Slave Trade, London 1865.

Publications of the African Institution

African Institution (ed.), Abstract of the Acts of Parliament for Abolishing the Slave trade, and of the Orders in Council Founded on Them, London 1810.

(ed.), Report of the Committee of the African Institution, Read to the General Meeting on the 15th July 1807, Together with the Rules and Regulations which were then adopted for the Government of the Society, London 1807.

(ed.), Fourth Report of the Directors of the African Institution, Read at the Annual General Meeting on 23rdh of March, 1810, London 1810.

(ed.), Fifth Report of the Directors of the African Institution, Read at the Annual General Meeting on 27th of March, 1811, London 1811.

(ed.), Sixth Report of the Directors of the African Institution, Read at the Annual General Meeting on 25th of March, 1812, London 1812.

Official French Government Publications

Ministère des Affaires Étrangères (ed.), Documents Diplomatiques 1861, Paris 1862.

(ed.), Documents Diplomatiques. Affaires d'Orient. 1875–1876–1877, Paris 1877.

Official US Government Publications

Annals of Congress of the United States

Annals of Congress, House of Representative, 12th Congress, 1st Session.

Annals of Congress, House of Representatives, 17th Congress, 2nd Session.

Annals of Congress, House of Representatives, 18th Congress, 1st Session.

Annals of Congress, Senate, 18th Congress, 1st Session.

Annals of Congress, Senate, 20th Congress, 1st Session.

Annals of Congress, Senate, 20th Congress, 2nd Session.

Government Printing Office

Government Printing Office (ed.), Spanish Diplomatic Correspondence and Documents 1896– 1900 Presented to the Cortes by the Minister of State, Washington 1905.

(ed.), Treaties, Conventions, International Acts, Protocols and Agreements Between the United States of America and Other Powers, 1776–1909, pt. II, vol. II, New York 1968.

United States, Department of State

United States, Dept. of State, Message from the President of the United States Transmitting the Correspondence between the Government of the United States and Great Britain Relating to the Negotiation of the Convention of 20th October 1818, Washington, 1823.

United States Congressional Serial Set 1817–1980

Lord Aberdeen to Mr. Everett, 20 December 1841, in: H.Doc. No. 192, 27th Congress, 3rd Session.

Message from the President of the United States, In compliance with a resolution of the Senate, on the subject of the communication of the Quintupel treaty to the Government of the United States, 9 January 1843, in: S.Doc. No. 52, 27th Congress, 3rd Session.

Message from the President of the United States Transmitting a Report from the Secretary of State, in answer to the Resolution of the House of Representatives, 27 February 1843, in: H.Doc. No. 192, 27th Congress, 3rd Session.

Message of the President of the United States, Communicated to the Two Houses of Congress, on the Relations of the United States to Spain by Reason of Warfare in the Island of Cuba, 11 April 1898, in: H.Doc. No. 405, 55th Congress, 2nd Session.

Report of the Committee of Foreign Relations, United States Senate, Relative to Affairs in Cuba, 13 April 1898, in: S.rp.885, 55th Congress, 2nd Session.

Treaty between the United States of America and Her Majesty the Queen of the United Kingdom of Great Britain and Ireland, for the Suppression of the African Slave Trade, 7 April 1862, in: S.Ex.Doc. No. 57, 37th Congress, 2nd Session.

United Nations Publications

United Nations (ed.), Resolution 2131 (XX), Declaration on the Inadmissibility of Intervention in the Domestic Affairs of States and the Protection of Their Independence and Sovereignty, 21 December 1965, UNGA A/RES/20/ 2131.

(ed.), Agenda for Peace. Preventing Diplomacy, Peacemaking, and Peace-keeping, 17 June 1992, UNGA A/47/277.

(ed.), Report of the Secretary-General Pursuant to General Assembly Resolution 53/35. The Fall of Srebrenica, 15 November 1999, UNGA A/54/549.

(ed.), Report of the Independent Inquiry into the Actions of the United Nations during the 1994 Genocide in Rwanda, 16 December 1999, UNSC S/1999/1257.

(ed.), Prevention of Armed Conflict. Report of the Secretary-General on the Work of the Organization, 7 June 2001, UNGA A/55/985 – S/2001/574.

(ed.), Resolution 60/1, 2005 World Summit Outcome, 24 October 2005, UNGA A/RES/60/1.

(ed.), Resolution 1970 (2011), 26 February 2011, UNSC S/RES/1970.

(ed.), Resolution 1973 (2011), 17 March 2011, UNSC S/RES/1973.

Collections of Sources

Argenti, Philip P. (ed.), *The Massacres of Chios: Described in Contemporary Diplomatic Reports*, London 1932.

Dallek, Robert (ed.), *1898: McKinley's Decision: The United States Declares War on Spain*, New York 1969.

Dickins, Ashbury/James C. Allen (eds.), *American State Papers: Documents, Legislative and Executive of the Congress of the United States*, vol. 5, Washington, DC 1858.

Doubleday & McClure (ed.), *Speeches and Addresses of William McKinley, From March 1, 1897 to May 30, 1900*, New York 1900.

Gatter, Frank Thomas (ed.), *Protokolle und Generalakte der Berliner Afrika-Konferenz 1884–1885*, Bremen 1984.

Geiss, Imanuel (ed.), *Der Berliner Kongreß 1878: Protokolle und Materialen*, Boppard 1978.

Grewe, Wilhelm G. (ed.), *Fontes Historiae Iuris Gentium*, vol. 3/1, *1815–1945*, Berlin 1992.

Harrison, T. R. (ed.), *Treaties, Conventions and Engagements, for the Suppression of the Slave Trade*, London 1844.

Hertslet, Edward (ed.), *A Complete Collection of the Treaties and Conventions at Present Subsisting between Great Britain and Foreign Powers*, vol. 1, London 1820.

Hertslet, Edward *A Complete Collection of the Treaties and Conventions, and Reciprocal Regulations at Present Subsisting between Great Britain and Foreign Powers*, vol. 3, London 1841.

A Complete Collection of the Treaties and Conventions, and Reciprocal Regulations at Present Subsisting between Great Britain and Foreign Powers, vol. 5, London 1840.

The Map of Europe by Treaty; Showing the Various Political and Territorial Changes Which Have Taken Place since the General Peace of 1814, vol. IV, *1875 to 1891*, London 1891.

Klüber, Johann Ludwig (ed.), *Acten des Wiener Congresses in den Jahren 1814 und 1815*, vol. 8, Erlangen 1818.

LaFeber, Walter (ed.), *John Quincy Adams and American Continental Empire: Letters, Papers, and Speeches*, Chicago, IL 1965.

Lane-Poole, Stanley (ed.), *The Life of the Right Honourable Stratford Canning: From His Memoirs and Private and Official Papers*, vol. 1, London 1888.

Miller, Hunter (ed.), *Treaties and Other International Acts of the United States of America*, vol. 2: *1976–1818*, Washington, DC 1931.

Newbury, C. W. (ed.), *British Policy towards West Africa: Select Documents 1786–1874*, Oxford 1965.

Richardson, James D. (ed.), *A Compilation of the Messages and Papers of the Presidents, 1789–1897*, vol. IV, Washington, DC 1899.

Vane, Charles (ed.), *Correspondence, Despatches and Other Papers of Viscount Castlereagh*, vol. 11, London 1853.

Wellington, Arthur Wellesley of (ed.), *Despatches, Correspondence, and Memoranda of Field Marshal Arthur Duke of Wellington*, vol. 1, London 1867.

(ed.), *Supplementary Despatches, Correspondence, and Memoranda of Field Marshal Arthur Duke of Wellington*, vol. 2, London 1867.

(ed.), *Supplementary Despatches, Correspondence, and Memoranda of Field Marshal Arthur Duke of Wellington*, vol. 3, London 1868.

(ed.), *Supplementary Despatches, Correspondence, and Memoranda of Field Marshal Arthur Duke of Wellington*, vol. 9, London 1862.

(ed.), *Supplementary Despatches, Correspondence, and Memoranda of Field Marshal Arthur Duke of Wellington*, vol. 10, London 1863.

Literature

Abe, Yuki, *Norm Dilemmas in Humanitarian Intervention: How Bosnia Changed NATO*, Abingdon 2019.

Abiew, Francis Kofi, *The Evolution of the Doctrine and Practice of Humanitarian Intervention*, The Hague 1999.

Ackerson, Wayne, *The African Institution (1807–1827) and the Antislavery Movement in Great Britain*, Lewiston, ME 2005.

Adak, Hülya, The Legacy of André Nikolaievitch Mandelstam (1869–1949) and the Early History of Human Rights, *Zeitschrift für Religions- und Geistesgeschichte*, 70/2 (2018), 117–130.

Adams, Charles Francis (ed.), *Memoirs of John Quincy Adams, Comprising Portions of His Diary 1795–1848*, vol. 4, New York 1969.

(ed.), *Memoirs of John Quincy Adams, Comprising Portions of His Diary 1795–1848*, vol. 5, New York 1969.

(ed.), *Memoirs of John Quincy Adams, Comprising Portions of His Diary 1795–1848*, vol. 6, New York 1969.

Ade Ajayi, Jacob. F./B. O. Oloruntimehin, Africa at the Beginning of the Nineteenth Century: Issues and Prospects, in Jacob F. Ade Ajayi (ed.), *General History of Africa*, vol. 6: *Africa in the Nineteenth Century until the 1880s*, Paris 1989, 1–22.

West Africa in the Anti-Slave Trade Era, in John E. Flint (ed.), *The Cambridge History of Africa*, vol. 5: *From c. 1790 to c. 1870*, Cambridge 1976, 200–221.

Ahlskog, Jonas, The Political Economy of Colonisation: Carl Bernhard Wadström's Case for Abolition and Civilisation, *Sjuttonhundratal: Nordic Yearbook for Eighteenth-Century Studies* 7 (2010), 146–167.

Alagoa, E. J., The Niger Delta and the Cameroon Region, in Jacob F. Ade Ajayi (ed.), *General History of Africa*, vol. 6: *Africa in the Nineteenth Century until the 1880s*, Paris 1989, 724–748.

Alexandrowicz, Charles Henry, *The European–African Confrontation: A Study in Treaty Making*, Leiden 1973.

Allain, Jean, Fydor Martens and the Question of Slavery at the 1890 Brussels Conference, in Jean Allain, *The Law and Slavery: Prohibiting Human Exploitation*, Leiden 2015, 101–120.

The Nineteenth Century Law of the Sea and the British Abolition of the Slave Trade, *British Yearbook of International Law* 78/1 (2007), 342–388.

Slavery and the League of Nations: Ethiopia as a Civilised Nation, in Jean Allain, *The Law and Slavery: Prohibiting Human Exploitation*, Leiden 2015, 121–158.

Alpers, Edward A., On Becoming a British Lake: Piracy, Slaving, and British Imperialism in the Indian Ocean during the First Half of the Nineteenth Century, in Robert Harms/Bernard K. Freamon/David W. Blight (eds.), *Indian Ocean Slavery in the Age of Abolition*, New Haven, CT 2013, 45–58.

Ammon, Harry/James Monroe, *The Quest for National Identity*, Charlottesville, VA 1990.

Anderson, B. L./David Richardson, Market Structure and the Profits of the British African Trade in the Late Eighteenth Century: A Comment, *Journal of Economic History* 43/3 (September 1983), 713–721.

Anderson, J. L., Piracy and World History: An Economic Perspective on Maritime Predation, *Journal of World History* 6/2 (Autumn 1995), 175–199.

Anderson, Matthew S., *The Eastern Question 1774–1923: A Study in International Relations*, Basingstoke 1991.

Anghie, Anthony, *Imperialism, Sovereignty and the Making of International Law*, Cambridge 2005.

Annan, Kofi, *Interventions: A Life in War and Peace*, New York 2012.

'We the peoples': The Role of the United Nations in the 21st Century. Report of the Secretary-General, New York 2000.

Anonymous, *Address in Behalf of the Greeks: Especially Those Who Have Survived the Late Massacre in Scio*, Edinburgh 1822.

Address & Petition to His Majesty from the Inhabitants of the Town and Neighbourhood of Sheffield, Sheffield 1794.

Case of Our Fellow-Creatures, The Oppressed Africans, Respectfully Recommended to the Serious Consideration of the Legislature of Great Britain, By the People Called Quakers, London 1784.

Considerations Addressed to Professors of Christianity of Every Denomination, on the Impropriety of Consuming West-India Sugar and Rum, as Produced by the Oppressive Labour of Slaves, London 1792.

The Destruction of Lagos, London 1852.

East African Slave Trade, *Quarterly Review* 133/266 (October 1872), 521–557.

General Bell's Reconcentration Policy, *Literary Digest* XXIV/5 (1 February 1902), 138–139.

Observations on That Part of the Late Treaty of Peace with France Which Relates to the African Slave Trade, Extracted from a Periodical Work for June 1814, London 1814.

Slavery in Africa: A Speech by Cardinal Lavigerie (31 July 1888), Boston 1888.

Anstey, Roger, *The Atlantic Slave Trade and British Abolition, 1760–1810*, London 1975.

Ashworth, John, The Relationship between Capitalism and Humanitarianism, *American Historical Review* 92/4 (October 1987), 813–828.

Athanassoglou-Kallmyer, Nina, *French Images from the Greek War of Independence 1821–1830: Art and Politics under Restoration*, New Haven, CT 1989.

Atkinson, Geoffrey, *The Sentimental Revolution: French Writers of 1690–1740*, Seattle, WA 1965.

Aust, Helmut Philipp, From Diplomat to Academic Activist: André Mandelstam and the History of Human Rights, *European Journal of International Law* 25/4 (2014), 1105–1121.

Austen, Ralph A./Woodruff D. Smith, Images of Africa and British Slave-Trade Abolition: The Transition to an Imperialist Ideology, 1787–1807, *African Historical Studies* 2/1 (1969), 69–83.

Auxier, George W., Middle Western Newspapers and the Spanish–American War, 1895–1898, *Mississippi Valley Historical Review* 26/4 (March 1940), 523–534.

The Propaganda Activities of the Cuban Junta in Precipitating the Spanish–American War, 1895–1898, *Hispanic American Historical Review* 19/3 (August 1939), 286–305.

Bailey, John (ed.), *The Diary of Lady Frederick Cavendish*, vol. II, London 1927.

Bain, William, Vitoria: The Law of War, Saving the Innocent, and the Image of God, in Stefano Recchia/Jennifer M. Welsh (eds.), *Just and Unjust Military Intervention: European Thinkers from Vitoria to Mill*, Cambridge 2013, 70–95.

Bandinel, James, *Some Account of the Trade in Slaves from Africa as Connected with Europe and America*, London 1842.

Barker, Hannah/Simon Burrows (eds.), *Press, Politics and the Public Sphere in Europe and North America, 1760–1820*, Cambridge 2002.

Barker-Benfield, G. J., *The Culture of Sensibility: Sex and Society in Eighteenth-Century Britain*, Chicago, IL 1992.

Barkey, Karen, *Empire of Difference: The Ottomans in Comparative Perspective*, Cambridge 2009.

Barlier, Jean-Pierre, *La Société des Amis des Noirs 1788–1791: Aux origines de la première abolition de l'esclavage (4 février 1794)*, Paris 2010.

Barman, Roderick J., *Brazil: The Forging of a Nation, 1798–1852*, Stanford, CA 1988.

Barnett, Michael, *Empire of Humanity: A History of Humanitarianism*, Ithaca, NY 2011.

Barnett, Michael, (ed.), *Humanitarianism and Human Rights: A World of Differences?*, Cambridge 2020.

Barnett, Michael/Thomas G. Weiss (eds.), *Humanitarianism in Question: Politics, Power, Ethics*, Ithaca, NY 2008.

Barrow, John, *The Life and Correspondence of Admiral Sir William Sidney Smith*, vol. 2, London 1848.

Barton, Clara, *A Story of the Red Cross: Glimpses of Field Work*, New York 1904.

Barton, Gregory A., *Informal Empire and the Rise of One World Culture*, Basingstoke 2014.

Bass, Gary J., *Freedom's Battle: The Origins of Humanitarian Intervention*, New York 2008.

Baumgart, Winfried, *Imperialism: The Idea and Reality of British and French Colonial Expansion, 1880–1914*, Oxford 1982.

The Crimean War 1853–1856, London 1999.

Bayly, Christopher A., *The Birth of the Modern World, 1780–1914*, New York 2004.

Bazyler, M., Reexamining the Doctrine of Humanitarian Intervention in the Light of the Atrocities in Kampuchea and Ethiopia, *Stanford Journal of International Law* 23 (1987), 547–619.

Beachey, R. W., *The Slave Trade of Eastern Africa*, London 1976.

Beaulac, Stéphane, *The Power of Language in the Making of International Law: The Word Sovereignty in Bodin and Vattel and the Myth of Westphalia*, Leiden 2004.

Beck, Ulrich, *Der kosmopolitische Blick oder: Krieg ist Frieden*, Frankfurt a. M. 2004.

Behrendt, Stephen D./David Eltis/David Richardson, The Costs of Coercion: African Agency in the Pre-Modern Atlantic World, *Economic History Review* 54/3 (August 2001), 454–476.

Behuniak, Thomas E., The Law of Unilateral Humanitarian Intervention by Armed Force: A Legal Survey, *Military Law Review* 79/27 (Winter 1978), 157–191.

Bell, Duncan S., Empire and International Relations in Victorian Political Thought, *Historical Journal* 49/1 (March 2006), 281–298.

Victorian Visions of Global Order: Empire and International Relations in Nineteenth-Century Political Thought, Cambridge 2007.

Bellamy, Alex J. (ed.), *Humanitarian Intervention*, vol. I: *Law, Ethics, and Theories*, London 2017.

(ed.), *Humanitarian Intervention*, vol. II: *Humanitarian Intervention in History*, London 2017.

(ed.), *Humanitaran Intervention*, vol. III: *Humanitarian Intervention in Contemporary Practice*, London 2017.

(ed.), *Humanitarian Intervention*, vol. IV: *Beyond Humanitarian Intervention: The Responsibility to Protect*, London 2017.

Bellamy, Alex J./Stephen McLoughlin, *Rethinking Humanitarian Intervention*, London 2018.

Bemis, Samuel F., *John Quincy Adams and the Foundation of American Foreign Policy*, New York 1949.

Bender, Thomas (ed.), *The Antislavery Debate: Capitalism and Abolitionism as a Problem in Historical Interpretation*, Berkeley, CA 1992.

Benezet, Anthony, *A Caution and Warning to Great Britain and Her Colonies, in a Short Representation of the Calamitous State of the Enslaved Negroes in the British Dominions*, Philadelphia, PA 1766.

Observations on the Inslaving, Importing and Purchasing of Negroes, Germantown, PA 1760.

Some Historical Account of Guinea, Its Situation, Produce and the General Disposition of Its Inhabitants: With an Inquiry into the Rise and Progress of the Slave Trade, Its Nature and Lamentable Effects, Philadelphia, PA 1771.

Benjamin, Jules R., *The United States and the Origins of the Cuban Revolution: An Empire of Liberty in an Age of National Liberation*, Princeton, NJ 1990.

Bennett, Norman R., *A History of the Arab State of Zanzibar*, London 1978.

Bentham, Jeremy, *An Introduction to the Principles of Morals and Legislation*, London 1789.

Benton, Elbert J., *International Law and Diplomacy of the Spanish–American War*, Gloucester 1968.

Benton, Lauren, Abolition and Imperial Law 1790–1820, *Journal of Imperial and Commonwealth History* 39/3 (September 2011), 355–374.

From International Law to Imperial Constitutions: The Problem of Quasi-Sovereignty, 1870–1900, *Law and History Review* 26/3 (Autumn 2008), 595–619.

A Search for Sovereignty. Law and Geography in European Empires, 1400–1900, Cambridge 2010.

Benton, Lauren/Adam Clulow/Bain Attwood (eds.), *Protection and Empire: A Global History*, Cambridge 2017.

Berding, Helmut, Die Ächtung des Sklavenhandels auf dem Wiener Kongress 1814/15, *Historische Zeitschrift* 219/2 (October 1974), 265–289.

Bergad, Laird W., *The Comparative Histories of Slavery in Brazil, Cuba, and the United States*, Cambridge 2007.

Bethell, Leslie, Britain, Portugal and the Suppression of the Brazilian Slave Trade: The Origins of Lord Palmerston's Act of 1839, *English Historical Review* 80/357 (1965), 761–784.

The Mixed Commissions for the Suppression of the Slave Trade in the Nineteenth Century, *Journal of African History* 7/1 (1966), 79–93.

The Independence of Brazil and the Abolition of the Brazilian Slave Trade: Anglo-Brazilian Relations, 1822–1826, *Journal of Latin American Studies* ½ (November 1969), 117–147.

The Abolition of the Brazilian Slave Trade: Britain, Brazil and the Slave Trade Question 1807–1869, Cambridge 1970.

Betts, Paul, Universalism and Its Discontents: Humanity as a Twentieth-Century Concept, in Fabian Klose/Mirjam Thulin (eds.), *Humanity: A History of European Concepts in Practice from the Sixteenth Century to the Present*, Göttingen 2017, 51–70.

Bew, John, 'From an Umpire to a Competitor': Castlereagh, Canning and the Issue of International Intervention in the Wake of the Napoleonic Wars, in Brendan Simms/David J. B. Trim (eds.), *Humanitarian Intervention: A History*, Cambridge 2011, 117–138.

Binder, Martin, *The United Nations and the Politics of Selective Humanitarian Intervention*, Cham 2017.

Bitis, Alexander, *Russia and the Eastern Question: Army, Government, and Society 1815–1833*, Oxford 2006.

Blackburn, Robin, *The Overthrow of Colonial Slavery 1776–1848*, London 1988.

The Making of New World Slavery: From the Baroque to the Modern, 1492–1800, London 1997.

The American Crucible: Slavery, Emancipation, and Human Rights, London 2011.

Blanning, T. C. W. (ed.), *The Nineteenth Century: The Short Oxford History of Europe*, Oxford 2000.

Blaufarb, Rafe, The Western Question: The Geopolitics of Latin American Independence, *American Historical Review* 112/3 (June 2007), 742–763.

Bluntschli, Johann Caspar, *Das moderne Völkerrecht der civilisirten Staten als Rechtsbuch dargestellt*, Nördlingen 1868.

Das moderne Völkerrecht der civilisirten Staten als Rechtsbuch dargestellt: Dritte mit Rücksicht auf die neueren Ereignisse bis 1877 ergänzte Auflage, Nördlingen 1878.

Bly, Antonio T., Crossing the Lake of Fire: Slave Resistance during the Middle Passage, 1720–1842, *Journal of Negro History* 83/3 (Summer 1998), 178–186.

Blyth, Robert, Britain, the Royal Navy and the Suppression of the Slave Trade in the Nineteenth Century, in Robert Blyth/Douglas Hamilton (eds.), *Representing Slavery: Art, Artefacts and Archives in the Collection of the National Maritime Museum*, Aldershot 2007, 76–91.

Bödeker, Hans Erich, Menschheit, Humanität, Humanismus, in Otto Brunner/ Werner Conze/Reinhart Koselleck (eds.), *Geschichtliche Grundbegriffe: Historisches Lexikon zur politisch-sozialen Sprache in Deutschland*, vol. 3, Stuttgart 1982, 1063–1128.

Bogen, David S., The Law of Humanitarian Intervention: United States Policy in Cuba (1898) and in the Dominican Republic (1965), *Harvard International Law Club Journal* 7/2 (Spring 1966), 296–315.

Boli, John/Goerge M. Thomas (eds.), *Constructing World Culture: International Nongovernmental Organizations since 1875*, Stanford, CA 1999.

Booth, Alan R., The United States African Squadron, 1843–1861, in Jeffrey Butler (ed.), *Boston University Paper in African History*, vol. 1, Boston, MA 1964, 77–117.

Bourke, Joanna, *What It Means to Be Human: Historical Reflections from the 1800s to the Present*, Berkeley, CA 2011.

Bouyrat, Yann, *Devoir d'intervenir? L'expédition 'humanitaire' de la France au Liban, 1860*, Paris 2013.

La France et les maronites du Mont-Liban: Nassiance d'une relation privilégiée (1831–1861), Paris 2013.

Bowden, Brett, *The Empire of Civilization: The Evolution of an Imperial Idea*, Chicago, IL 2009.

Bradley, James E., *Religion, Revolution, and English Radicalism: Nonconformity in Eighteenth-Century Politics and Society*, Cambridge 1990.

Bradley, Mark Philip, *The World Reimagined: Americans and Human Rights in the Twentieth Century*, New York 2016.

Braun, Theodore E. D./John B. Radner (eds.), *The Lisbon Earthquake of 1755: Representation and Reactions*, Oxford 2005.

Brewer, David, *The Flame of Freedom: The Greek War of Independence 1821–1833*, London 2001.

Brissenden, Robert F., *Virtue in Distress: Studies in the Novel of Sentiment from Richardson to Sade*, London 1974.

Brody, David, *Visualizing American Empire: Orientalism and Imperialism in the Philippines*, Chicago, IL 2010.

Brown, Charles H., *The Correspondents' War: Journalists in the Spanish–American War*, New York 1967.

Brown, Chris, Humanitarian Intervention and International Political Theory, in Alexander Mosley/Richard Norman (eds.), *Human Rights and Military Intervention*, London 2018, 153–169.

Brown, Christopher Leslie, Christianity and the Campaign against Slavery and the Slave Trade, in Stewart J. Brown/Timothy Tackett (eds.), *The Cambridge History of Christianity*, vol. VII: *Enlightenment, Reawakening and Revolution 1660–1815*, Cambridge 2006, 517–535.

Moral Capital: Foundations of British Abolitionism, Chapel Hill, NC 2006.

Empire without America: British Plans for Africa in the Era of the American Revolution, in Derek R. Peterson (ed.), *Abolitionism and Imperialism in Britain, Africa, and the Atlantic*, Athens, GA 2010, 84–100.

Brown, Richard D./Richard Wilson (eds.), *Humanitarianism and Suffering: The Mobilization of Empathy*, Cambridge 2009.

Brown, Robert T., Fernando Po and the Anti-Sierra Leonean Campaign: 1826–1834, *International Journal of African Historical Studies* 6/2 (1973), 249–264.

Brownlie, Ian, *International Law and the Use of Force by States*, Oxford 1963.

Humanitarian Intervention, in John N. Moore (ed.), *Law and Civil War in the Modern World*, Baltimore, MD 1974, 217–228.

Bruce, David, *The Life of Sir Thomas Fowell Buxton: Extraordinary Perseverance*, Plymouth 2014.

Bruch, Elizabeth M., *Human Rights and Humanitarian Intervention: Law and Practice in the Field*, London 2016.

Bruns, Roger A., Anthony Benezet and the Natural Rights of the Negro, *Pennsylvania Magazine of History and Biography* 96/1 (January 1972), 104–113.

Am I Not a Man and a Brother: The Antislavery Crusade of Revolutionary America 1688–1788, New York 1977.

Buchanan, Allen, Reforming the International Law of Humanitarian Intervention, in Jeff L. Holzgrefe/Robert O. Keohane (eds.), *Humanitarian Intervention: Ethical, Legal, and Political Dilemmas*, Cambridge 2004, 130–173.

Bull, Hedley (ed.), *Interventions in World Politics*, Oxford 1986.

Bull, Hedley/Benedict Kingsbury/Adam Roberts (eds.), *Hugo Grotius and International Relations*, Oxford 2003.

Bullen, Roger, The Great Powers and the Iberian Peninsula, 1815–48, in Alan Sked (ed.), *Europe's Balance of Power 1815–1848*, London 1979, 54–78.

Burbank, Jane/Frederick Cooper, *Empires in World History: Power and the Politics of Difference*, Princeton, NJ 2010.

Burger, Herman, André Mandelstam, Forgotten Pioneer of International Human Rights, in Fons Coomans/Fred Grünfeld/Ingrid Westendorp (eds.), *Rendering Justice to the Vulnerable: Liber Amicorum in Honor of Theo van Boven*, The Hague 2000, 69–82.

Burke, Ciarán, *An Equitable Framework for Humanitarian Intervention*, Oxford 2013.

Burke, Edmund, *Reflections on the Revolution in France*, London 1790.

A Letter from Mr. Burke to a Member of the National Assembly, London 1791.

Burroughs, Robert, Eyes on the Prize: Journeys in Slave Ships Taken as Prizes by the Royal Navy, *Slavery and Abolition* 31/1 (March 2010), 99–115.

Butler-Johnstone, Henry A. Munro, *Bulgarian Horrors, and the Question of the East: A Letter Addressed to the Right Hon. W. E. Gladstone, M. P.*, London 1876.

Buxton, Thomas Fowell, *The African Slave Trade and Its Remedy*, London 1840.

Byrd, Alexander X., Eboe, Country, Nation, and Gustavus Vassa's Interesting Narrative, *William and Mary Quarterly* 63/1 (January 2006), 123–148.

Cairns, H. Alan C., *Prelude to Imperialism: British Reactions to Central African Society 1840–1890*, London 1965.

Canney, Donald L., *Africa Squadron: The U.S. Navy and the Slave Trade, 1842–1861*, Washington, DC 2006.

Carey, Brycchan, *British Abolitionism and the Rhetoric of Sensibility: Writing, Sentiment, and Slavery, 1760– 1807*, New York 2005.

From Peace to Freedom: Quaker Rhetoric and the Birth of American Antislavery, 1657–1761, New Haven, CT 2012.

Carey, Brycchan/Markman Ellis/Sara Salih (eds.), *Discourses of Slavery and Abolition: Britain and Its Colonies, 1760–1838*, Basingstoke 2004.

Carretta, Vincent, Olaudah Equiano or Gustavus Vassa? *New Light on an Eighteenth-Century Question of Identity, Slavery & Abolition* 20/3 (December 1999), 96–105.

Equiano, the African: Biography of a Self-Made Man, Athens, GA 2005.

Cateau, Heather/Selwyn H. Carrington (eds.), *Capitalism and Slavery: Fifty Years Later*, New York 2000.

Cecil, Gwendolen, *Life of Robert Marques of Salisbury*, vol. IV: *1887–1892*, London 1932.

Chapin, Chester, Shaftesbury and the Man of Feeling, *Modern Philology* 81/1 (August 1983), 47–50.

Chaplin, Joyce E., Slavery and the Principle of Humanity: A Modern Idea in the Early Lower South, *Journal of Social History* 24/2 (Winter 1990), 299–315.

Charney, Jonathan I., Anticipatory Humanitarian Intervention in Kosovo, *American Journal of International Law* 93/4 (October 1999), 834–841.

Chesterman, Simon, *Just War or Just Peace? Humanitarian Intervention and International Law*, Oxford 2003.

Chomsky, Noam, *The New Military Humanism: Lessons from Kosovo*, London 1999.

A New Generation Draws the Line: 'Humanitarian' Intervention and the Standards of the West, London 2012.

Christie, William Dougal, *Notes on Brazilian Questions*, London 1865.

Christopher, Emma, *Slave Ship Sailors and Their Captive Cargoes, 1730–1807*, Cambridge 2006.

Church Missionary Society (ed.), *The Slave Trade of East Africa*, London 1869.

Clark, Ian, *International Legitimacy and World Society*, Oxford 2007.

Clarke, Richard F. (ed.), *Cardinal Lavigerie and the African Slave Trade*, London 1889.

Clarkson, Thomas, *An Essay on the Slavery and Commerce of the Human Species, Particularly the African, Translated from a Latin Dissertation*, London 1786.

A Summary View of the Slave Trade and of the Consequences of Its Abolition, London 1787.

An Essay on the Impolicy of the African Slave Trade, London 1788.

A Short Address Originally Written to the People of Scotland on the Subject of the Slave Trade with a Summary View of the Evidence Delivered before a Committee of the House of Commons on the Part of the Petitioners for Its Abolition, Shrewsbury 1792.

The History of the Rise, Progress, and Accomplishment of the Abolition of the African Slave-Trade by the British Parliament, vol. 1, London 1808.

The History of the Rise, Progress, and Accomplishment of the Abolition of the African Slave-Trade by the British Parliament, vol. 2, London 1808.

Eine summarische Uebersicht der vor dem Ausschuß des Unterhauses des Großbritannischen Parlaments abgelegten Zeugnisse über den Gegenstand des Sclaven-Handels den verschiedenen Regenten in der christlichen Welt, London 1814.

Clifford, Mary Louise, *From Slavery to Freetown: Black Loyalists after the American Revolution*, Jefferson, TX 1999.

Clogg, Richard, Some Aspects of the Philhellenic Press in Britain during the Early Nineteenth Century, *Philhellenische Studien* 3 (1994), 19–30.

Coady, C. A. J./Ned Dobos/Sagar Sanyal (eds.), *Challenges for Humanitarian Intervention: Ethical Demand and Political Reality*, Oxford 2018.

Cohn, Raymond L., Deaths of Slaves in the Middle Passage, *Journal of Economic History* 45/3 (September 1985), 685–692.

Coleman, Deirdre, *Romantic Colonization and British Anti-Slavery*, Cambridge 2005.

Colley, Linda, *Britons: Forging the Nation 1707–1837*, London 2003.

Colomb, Captain Philip Howard, *Slave-Catching in the Indian Ocean: A Record of Naval Experiences*, London 1873.

Conneau, Theophilus, *A Slaver's Log Book or 20 Years' Residence in Africa*, Englewood Cliffs, NJ 1976.

Conrad, Robert E., *Neither Slave nor Free: The Emancipados of Brazil, 1818–1868*, Hispanic American Historical Review 53/1 (February 1973), 50–70.

World of Sorrow: The African Slave Trade to Brazil, Baton Rouge, LA 1986.

Cosmas, Graham A., *An Army for Empire: The United States Army in the Spanish-American War, 1898–1899*, College Station, TX 1994.

Coupland, Reginald, *The British Anti-Slavery Movement*, London 1964.

The Exploitation of East Africa 1856–1890: The Slave Trade and the Scramble, London 1968.

Crafton, William Bell, *A Sketch of the Evidence Delivered before a Committee of the House of Commons for the Abolition of the Slave-Trade: To Which Is Added, a Recommendation of the Subject to the Serious Attention of People in General*, London 1792.

Crane, Ronald S., Suggestions toward a Genealogy of the 'Man of Feeling', *Journal of English Literary History* 1/3 (December 1934), 205–230.

Crapol, Edward P., John Quincy Adams and the Monroe Doctrine: Some New Evidence, *Pacific Historical Review* 48/3 (August 1979), 413–418.

Craton, Michael, The Passion to Exist: Slave Rebellions in the British West Indies 1650–1832, *Journal of Caribbean History* 13 (Summer 1980), 1–20.

Craven, W. F., Jr, The Risk of the Monroe Doctrine (1823–1824), *Hispanic American Historical Review* 7/3 (August 1927), 320–333.

Crawley, C. W., *The Question of Greek Independence: A Study of British Policy in the Near East, 1821–1833*, New York 1973.

Cray, Robert E., Jr, Remembering the USS Chesapeake: The Politics of Maritime Death and Impressment, *Journal of the Early Republic* 25/3 (Autumn 2005), 445–474.

Cresson, W. P., *The Holy Alliance: The European Background of the Monroe Doctrine*, New York 1922.

Crosby, David L., Anthony Benezet's Transformation of Anti-Slavery Rhetoric, *Slavery & Abolition* 23/3 (December 2002), 39–58.

Croxton, Derek, The Peace of Westphalia of 1648 and the Origins of Sovereingty, *International History Review* 21/3 (September 1999), 569–591.

Csengei, Ildiko, *Sympathy, Sensibility, and the Literature of Feeling in the Eighteenth-Century*, Basingstoke 2012.

Cugoano, Ottobah, *Thoughts and Sentiments on the Evil and Wicked Traffic of the Slavery and Commerce of the Human Species*, London 1787.

Cullinane, Michael Patrick, *Liberty and American Anti-Imperialism 1898–1909*, New York 2012.

Cunliffe, Philip, *Cosmopolitan Dystopia: International Intervention and the Failure of the West*, Manchester 2020.

Cunningham, Alan, The Philhellenes, Canning and Greek Independence, *Middle Eastern Studies* 14/2 (May 1978), 151–181.

Cunningham, Hugh/Joanna Innes (eds.), *Charity, Philanthropy, and Reform: From the 1690s to 1850*, Basingstoke 1998.

Curtin, Philip D., *The Atlantic Slave Trade: A Census*, Madison, WI 1969.

The Image of Africa: British Ideas and Action, 1780–1850, vol. 1, Madison, WI 1973.

The Rise and Fall of the Plantation Complex: Essays in Atlantic History. Cambridge 1999.

Daget, Serge, The Abolition of the Slave Trade by France: The Decisive Years 1826–1831, in David Richardson (ed.), *Abolition and Its Aftermath: The Historical Context, 1790–1916*, London 1985, 141–167.

Tactiques, stratégies et effets du droit de visite, in Serge Daget (ed.), *De la traite à l'esclavage: Actes du Colloque international sur la traite des Noirs*, Nantes 1988, 343–358.

The Abolition of the Slave Trade, in Jacob F. Ade Ajayi (ed.), *General History of Africa*, vol. VI: *Africa in the Nineteenth Century until the 1880s*, Paris 1989, 64–89.

La répression de la traite des Noirs au XIXe siècle: L'action des croisières françaises sur les côtes occidentales de l'Afrique (1817–1850), Paris 1997.

Dakin, Douglas, *British and American Philhellenes during the War of Greek Independence, 1821–1833*, Thessaloniki 1955.

The Greek Struggle for Independence 1821–1833, Berkeley, CA 1973.

Daly, John C. K., *Russian Seapower and the 'Eastern Question' 1827–41*, Basingstoke 1991.

Darwin, John, Imperialism and the Victorians: The Dynamics of Territorial Expansion, *English Historical Review* 112/447 (June 1997), 614–642.

After Tamerlane: The Rise and Fall of Global Empires, 1400–2000, London 2007.

Davey, Eleanor, The Language of ingérence: Interventionist Debates in France, 1970s–1990s, in Norbert Frei/Daniel Stahl/Annette Weinke (eds.), *Human Rights and Humanitarian Intervention: Legitimizing the Use of Force since the 1970s*, Göttingen 2017, 46–63.

David, Huw T., Transnational Advocacy in the Eighteenth Century: Transatlantic Activism and the Anti-Slavery Movement, *Global Networks* 7/3 (2007), 367–382.

Davidson, Basil, *Black Mother Africa: The Years of Trial*, London 1961.

Davis, David Brion, *The Problem of Slavery in Western Culture*, Ithaca, NY 1966.

The Problem of Slavery in the Age of Revolution, 1770–1823, Ithaca, NY 1975.

Slavery and Human Progress, New York 1984.

Inhuman Bondage: The Rise and Fall of Slavery in the New World, Oxford 2006.

Slave Revolts and Abolitionism, in Seymour Drescher/Pieter C. Emmer (eds.), *Who Abolished Slavery? Slave Revolts and Abolitionism: A Debate with Joao Pedro Marques*, New York 2010, 163–168.

The Problem of Slavery in the Age of Emancipation, New York 2014.

Davis, John A., *Naples and Napoleon: Southern Italy and the European Revolutions 1780–1860*, Oxford 2006.

Davis, Michael C./Wolfgang Dietrich/Bettina Scholdan/Dieter Sepp, *International Intervention in the Post-Cold War World: Moral Responsibility and Power Politics*, Armonk, NY 2004.

Davis, Robert C., Counting European Slaves on the Barbary Coast, *Past & Present* 172/1 (August 2001), 87–124.

Christian Slaves, Muslim Masters: White Slavery in the Mediterranean, the Barbary Coast, and Italy, 1500–1800, Basingstoke 2003.

Davison, Roderic H., *The Reform in the Ottoman Empire 1856–1876*, Princeton, NJ 1963.

Dearden, Seton, *A Nest of Corsairs: The Fighting Karamanlis of Tripoli*, London 1976.

De Bruyn, Frans, Latitudinarianism and Its Importance as a Precursor of Sensibility, *Journal of English and Germanic Philology* 80/3 (July 1981), 349–368.

De Chateaubriand, *François-René, Note sur la Grèce*, Paris 1825.

Discours en réponse à M. Le Garde des Sceaux, in François-René de Chateaubriand, *OEuvres completes de Chateaubriand*, vol. 5, Paris 1861, 63–66.

Opinion sur le projet de loi relative à la repression des délits commis dans les échelles du Levant, 13 March 1826, in François-René de Chateaubriand, *OEuvres completes de Chateaubriand*, vol. 5, Paris 1861, 56–62.

De Graaf, Beatrice/Ido de Haan/Brian Vick (eds.), *Securing Europe after Napoleon: 1815 and the New European Security Culture*, Cambridge 2019.

DeGuzmán, María, *Spain's Long Shadow: The Black Legend, Off-Whiteness, and Anglo-American Empire*, Minneapolis, MN 2005.

De Nevers, Renee, Imposing International Norms: Great Powers and Norm Enforcement, *International Studies Review* 9/1 (Spring 2007), 53–80.

De Pradt, Dominique Dufour, *De l'intervention armée pour la pacification de la Grèce*, Paris 1828.

De Vattel, Emer, *The Law of Nations, Or, Principles of the Law of Nature, Applied to the Conduct and Affairs of Nations and Sovereigns, with Three Early Essays on the Origin and Nature of Natural Law and on Luxury*, edited and with an Introduction by Béla Kapossy and Richard Whatmore, Indianapolis, IN 2008.

De Worms, Henry, *England's Policy in the East*, London 1876.

Denby, David J., *Sentimental Narrative and the Social Order in France, 1760–1820*, Cambridge 1994.

Deng, Francis M./Sadikiel Kimaro/Terrence Lyons/Donald Rothchild/I. William Zartman, *Sovereignty as Responsibility: Conflict Management in Africa*, Washington, DC 1996.

Denman, Joseph, *Practical Remarks on the Slave Trade, and on the Existing Treaties with Portugal*, London 1839.

The Slave Trade, the African Squadron, and Mr. Hutt's Committee, London [1850].

Denman, Lord Thomas, *A Letter from Lord Denman to Lord Brougham, on the Final Extinction of the Slave Trade*, London 1848.

Deutsch, Jan-Georg, *Emancipation without Abolition in German East Africa c. 1884–1914*, Oxford 2006.

Dib, Pierre, *History of the Maronite Church*, Beirut 1971.

Dickie, John, *The British Consul: Heir to a Great Tradition*, London 2007.

Diederen, Roger, Über die Grenzen: Ein Blick in die Ferne, in Roger Diederen/ Davy Depelchin (eds.), *Orientalismus in Europa: Von Delacroix bis Kandinsky*, Munich 2010, 35–53.

Dimakis, Jean, La 'Société de la morale chrétienne' de Paris et son action en faveur des Grecs lors de l'insurrection de 1821, *Balkan Studies* 7/1 (1966), 27–48.

La guerre de l'indépendance greque vue par la presse française (Période de 1821 à 1824), Thessaloniki 1968.

Le Philhellénisme en Europe pendant l'insurrection grecque et le rôle de la presse, *Études Slaves et Est-Européennes/Slavic and East-European Studies* 13 (1968), 46–53.

Diouf, Sylviane A. (ed.), *Fighting the Slave Trade, West African Strategies*, Athens, OH 2004.

Dodson, John (ed.), *Reports of Cases Argued and Determined in the High Court of Admiralty; Commencing with the Judgments of the Right Hon. Sir William Scott (Lord Stowell), Trinity Term 1811*, vol. 2: *1815–1822*, London 1828.

Dorsett, Shaunnagh/Ian Hunter (eds.), *Law and Politics in British Colonial Thought: Transpositions of Empire*, New York 2010.

Doulton, Lindsay, 'The Flag That Sets Us Free': Antislavery, Africans, and the Royal Navy in the Western Indian Ocean, in Robert Harms/Bernard K. Freamon/David W. Blight (eds.), *Indian Ocean Slavery in the Age of Abolition*, New Haven, CT 2013, 101–119.

Drescher, Seymour, Public Opinion and the Destruction of British Slavery, in James Walvin (ed.), *Slavery and British Society 1776–1846*, London 1982, 22–48.

Capitalism and Antislavery: British Mobilization in Comparative Perspective, Oxford 1986.

People and Parliament: The Rhetoric of the British Slave Trade, *Journal of Interdisciplinary History* 20/4 (Spring 1990), 561–580.

British Way, French Way: Opinion Building and Revolution in the Second French Slave Emancipation, *American Historical Review* 96/3 (June 1991), 709–734.

Whose Abolition? Popular Pressure and the Ending of the British Slave Trade, *Past & Present* 143/1 (May 1994), 136–166.

The Atlantic Slave Trade and the Holocaust: A Comparative Analysis, in Alan S. Rosenbaum (ed.), *Is the Holocaust Unique? Perspectives on Comparative Genocide,* Boulder, CO 1996, 65–85.

History's Engines: British Mobilization in the Age of Revolution, *William and Mary Quarterly* 66/4 (October 2009), 737–756.

Abolition: A History of Slavery and Antislavery, Cambridge 2009.

Econocide: British Slavery in the Era of Abolition, Chapel Hill, NC 2010.

Emperors of the World: British Abolitionism and Imperialism, in Derek R. Peterson (ed.), *Abolitionism and Imperialism in Britain, Africa, and the Atlantic,* Athens, OH 2010, 129–149.

From Empires of Slavery to Empires of Antislavery, in Josep M. Fradera/ Christopher Schmidt-Nowara (eds.), *Slavery and Antislavery in Spain's Atlantic Empire,* New York 2013, 291–316.

Drescher, Seymour/Pieter C. Emmer (eds.), *Who Abolished Slavery? Slave Revolts and Abolitionism: A Debate with Joao Pedro Marques,* New York 2010.

Drescher, Seymour/Paul Finkelman, Slavery, in Bardo Fassbender/Anne Peters (eds.), *The Oxford Handbook of the History of International Law,* Oxford 2012, 890–916.

Du Bois, William Edward Burghardt, *The Suppression of the Atlantic Slave-Trade to the United States of America 1638–1870,* New York 1965.

Black Reconstruction in America: An Essay toward a History of the Part Which Black Folk Played in the Attempt to Reconstruct Democracy in America, 1860–1880, New York 1966.

Dubois, Laurent, *Avengers of the New World: The Story of the Haitian Revolution,* Cambridge, MA 2004.

Duchhardt, Heinz, 'Westphalian System': Zur Problematik einer Denkfigur, *Historische Zeitschrift* 269/2 (October 1999), 305–315.

Dülffer, Jost, Recht, Normen und Macht, in Jost Dülffer/Wilfried Loth (eds.), *Dimensionen internationaler Geschichte,* Munich 2012, 169–188.

Humanitarian Intervention as Legitimation of Violence – the German Case 1937–1939, in Fabian Klose (ed.), *The Emergence of Humanitarian Intervention: Ideas and Practice from the Nineteenth Century to the Present,* Cambridge 2016, 208–228.

Dülffer, Jost/Wilfried Loth (eds.), *Dimensionen Internationaler Geschichte,* Munich 2012 (Studien zur Internationalen Geschichte 30).

Dumond, Don E., *The Machete and the Cross: Campesino Rebellion in Yucatan,* Lincoln, NB 1997.

Duram, James C., A Study of Frustration: Britain, the USA, and the African Slave Trade, 1815–1870, *Social Science* 40/4 (October 1965), 220–225.

Dwan, David/Christopher M. Insole (eds.), *The Cambridge Companion to Edmund Burke*, Cambridge 2012.

Dynes, Russel R., *The Lisbon Earthquake of 1755: The First Modern Disaster*, in Theodore E. D. Braun/John B. Radner (eds.), *The Lisbon Earthquake of 1755: Representation and Reactions*, Oxford 2005, 34–49.

Earle, Edward M., Early American Policy Concerning Ottoman Minorities, *Political Science Quarterly* 42/3 (September 1927), 348–351.

American Interest in the Greek Cause, 1821–1827, *American Historical Review* 33/1 (October 1927), 44–63.

Eastern Question Association (ed.), *Report of Proceedings of the National Conference at St. James's Hall*, London 1876.

Papers on the Eastern Question, London 1877.

Eckel, Jan, *Die Ambivalenz des Guten: Menschenrechte in der internationalen Politik seit den 1940ern*, Göttingen 2014.

Humanitarian Intervention as Global Governance: Western Governments and Suffering 'Others' before and after 1990, in Norbert Frei/Daniel Stahl/ Annette Weinke (eds.), *Human Rights and Humanitarian Intervention: Legitimizing the Use of Force since the 1970s*, Göttingen 2017, 64–85.

Eckel, Jan/Samuel Moyn (eds.), *The Breakthrough: Human Rights in the 1970s*, Philadelphia, PA 2014.

Edmonds, Penelope, Travelling 'Under Concern': Quakers James Backhouse and George Washington Walker Tour the Antipodean Colonies, 1832–41, *Journal of Imperial and Commonwealth History* 40/5 (December 2012), 769–788.

Edwards, Paul (ed.), *Equiano's Travels: His Autobiography: The Interesting Narrative of the Life of Olaudah Equiano or Gustavus Vassa the African, Written by Himself*, London 1967.

Eggert, Gerald G., Our Man in Havana: Fitzhugh Lee, *Hispanic American Historical Review* 47/4 (November 1967), 463–485.

Ellis, Markman, *The Politics of Sensibility: Race, Gender and Commerce in the Sentimental Novel*, Cambridge 1996.

Eltis, David, *Economic Growth and the Ending of the Atlantic Slave Trade*, Oxford 1987.

The Volume and Structure of the Transatlantic Slave Trade: A Reassessment, *William and Mary Quarterly* 58/1 (January 2001), 17–46.

Eltis, David/David Richardson, *Atlas of the Transatlantic Slave Trade*, New Haven, CT 2010.

Eltis, David/David Richardson, (eds.), *Extending Frontiers: Essays on the New Transatlantic Slave Trade Database*, New Haven, CT 2008.

A New Assessment of the Transatlantic Slave Trade, in David Eltis/David Richardson (eds.), *Extending Frontiers. Essays on the New Transatlantic Slave Trade Database*, New Haven, CT 2008, 1–60.

Eltis, David/James Walvin (eds.), *The Abolition of the Atlantic Slave Trade: Origins and Effects in Europe, Africa, and the Americas*, Madison, WI 1981.

Emery, F. V., Geography and Imperialism: The Role of Sir Bartle Frere (1815–84), *Geographical Journal* 150/3 (November 1984), 342–350.

Emmer, Pieter C., Abolition of the Abolished: The Illegal Dutch Slave Trade and the Mixed Courts, in David Eltis/James Walvin (eds.), *The Abolition of the Atlantic Slave Trade: Origins and Effects in Europe, Africa, and the Americas*, Madison, WI 1981, 177–192.

The Dutch Slave Trade, 1500–1850, New York 2006.

Engelhardt, Éduoard, Le droit d'intervention et la Turquie: Étude historique, *Revue de droit international et de législation comparée* XII (1880), 363–388.

Erdem, Y. Hakan, *Slavery in the Ottoman Empire and Its Demise, 1800–1909*, Basingstoke 1996.

Erskine, Thomas Lord, *A Letter to the Earl of Liverpool on the Subject of the Greeks*, London 1823.

Evans, Gareth, *The Responsibility to Protect: Ending Mass Atrocity Crimes Once and For All*, Washington, DC 2008.

Evans, Richard J., *The Pursuit of Power, 1815–1914*, London 2016.

Everill, Bronwen, *Abolition and Empire in Sierra Leone and Liberia*, Basingstoke 2013.

Everill, Bronwen/Josiah Kaplan (eds.), *The History and Practice of Humanitarian Intervention and Aid in Africa*, Basingstoke 2013.

Fahmy, Khaled, *Mehmed Ali: From Ottoman Governor to Ruler of Egypt*, Oxford 2009.

Fahrmeir, Andreas, *Europa zwischen Restauration, Reform und Revolution 1815–1850*, Munich 2012.

Falconbridge, Alexander, *An Account of the Slave Trade on the Coast of Africa*, London 1788.

Falk, Richard A., Kosovo, World Order, and the Future of International Law, *American Journal of Law* 93/4 (October 1999), 847–857.

Farah, Caesar E., *The Politics of Interventionism in Ottoman Lebanon, 1830–1861*, London 2000.

Farrell, Stephen, 'Contrary to the Principle of Justice, Humanity and Sound Policy': The Slave Trade, Parliamentary Politics and the Abolition Act 1807, in Stephen Farrell/Melanie Unwin/James Walvin (eds.), *The British Slave Trade: Abolition, Parliament and People*, Edinburgh 2007, 141–171.

Farrell, Stephen/Melanie Unwin/James Walvin (eds.), *The British Slave Trade: Abolition, Parliament and People*, Edinburgh 2007.

Fassin, Didier, *Humanitarian Reason: A Moral History of the Present*, Berkeley, CA 2012.

Fassin, Didier/Mariella Pandolfi, Introduction: Military and Humanitarian Government in the Age of Intervention, in Didier Fassin/Mariella Pandolfi (eds.), *Contemporary States of Emergency: The Politics of Military and Humanitarian Intervention*, New York 2010, 9–25.

Fawaz, Leila Tarazi, *An Occasion for War: Civil Conflict in Lebanon and Damascus in 1860*, Berkeley, CA 1994.

Feenstra, Robert (ed.), *Hugo Grotius Mare Liberum 1609–2009*, Leiden 2009.

414   Bibliography

Fehrenbach, Charles W., Moderados and Exaltados: The Liberal Opposition to Ferdinand VII, 1814–1823, *Hispanic American Historical Review* 50/1 (February 1970), 52–69.

Fehrenbacher, Don E., *The Slaveholding Republic: An Account of the United States Government's Relation to Slavery*, Oxford 2001.

Feldman, Ilana/Miriam Ticktin (eds.), *In the Name of Humanity: The Government of Threat and Care*, Durham, NC 2010.

Fernández, Joaquín Alcaide, Hostes Humani Generis: Pirates, Slavers, and Other Criminals, in Bardo Fassbender/Anne Peters (eds.), *The Oxford Handbook of the History of International Law*, Oxford 2012, 120–144.

Ferrer, Ada, *Insurgent Cuba: Race, Nation, and Revolution, 1868–1898*, Chapel Hill, NC 1999.

Ferris, Elizabeth G., *The Challenge to Intervene: A New Role for the United Nations?*, Uppsala 1992.

Festa, Lynn, *Sentimental Figures of Empire in Eighteenth-Century Britain and France*, Baltimore, MD 2006.

Humanity without Feathers, *Humanity* 1/1 (Autumn 2010), 3–27.

Field, James A., *America and the Mediterranean World 1776–1882*, Princeton, NJ 1969.

Fiering, Norman S., Irresistible Compassion: An Aspect of Eighteenth-Century Sympathy and Humanitarianism, *Journal of the History of Ideas* 37/2 (April–June 1976), 195–218.

Findley, Carter Vaugh, The Tanzimat, in Reşat Kasaba (ed.), *The Cambridge History of Turkey, Volume 4, Turkey in the Modern World*, Cambridge 2008, 11–37.

Fink, Carole, *Defending the Rights of Others: The Great Powers, the Jews, and International Minority Protection, 1878–1938*, Cambridge 2004.

Finlay, George, *A History of Greece from the Conquest by the Romans to the Present Time*, vol. VI: *The Greek Revolution, pt. I*, Oxford 1877.

A History of Greece from the Conquest by the Romans to the Present Time, vol. VII: *The Greek Revolution, pt. II*, Oxford 1877.

Finnemore, Martha, Constructing Norms of Humanitarian Intervention, in Peter J. Katzenstein (ed.), *The Culture of National Security: Norms and Identity in World Poltics*, New York 1996, 153–185.

The Purpose of Intervention: Changing Beliefs about the Use of Force, Ithaca, NY 2003.

Firro, Kais M., *A History of the Druzes*, Leiden 1992.

Fisch, Jörg, Africa as Terra Nullius: The Berlin Conference and International Law, in Stig Förster/Wolfgang J. Mommsen/Ronald Robinson (eds.), *Bismarck, Europe, and Africa: The Berlin Africa Conference 1884–1885 and the Onset of Partition*, Oxford 1988, 347–375.

Internationalizing Civilization by Dissolving International Society. The Status of Non-European Territories in Nineteenth-Century International Law, in Martin H. Geyer/Johannes Paulmann (eds.), *The Mechanics of Internationalism: Culture, Society, and Politics from the 1840s to the First World War*, Oxford 2001, 235–257.

Adolf Hitler und das Selbstbestimmungsrecht der Völker, *Historische Zeitschrift* 290/1 (February 2010), 93–118.

Völkerrecht, in Jost Dülffer/Wilfried Loth (eds.), *Dimensionen internationaler Geschichte*, Munich 2012, 151–168.

Fischer, Hugo, The Suppression of Slavery in International Law I, *International Law Quarterly* 3/1 (January 1950), 28–51.

Fisher, Miles Mark, Friends of Humanity: A Quaker Anti-Slavery Influence, *Church History* 4/3 (September 1935), 187–202.

Fitzmaurice, Andrew, The Justification of King Leopold II's Congo Enterprise by Sir Travers Twiss, in Shaunnagh Dorsett/Ian Hunter (eds.), *Law and Politics in British Colonial Thought: Transpositions of Empire*, New York 2010, 109–126.

Liberalism and Empire in Nineteenth-Century International Law, *American Historical Review* 117/1 (February 2012), 122–140.

Fladeland, Betty, Abolitionist Pressures on the Concert of Europe, 1814–1822, *Journal of Modern History* 38/4 (December 1966), 355–373.

Men and Brothers: Anglo-American Antislavery Cooperation, Urbana, IL 1972.

Flint, John E. (ed.), *The Cambridge History of Africa*, vol. 5: *From c. 1790 to c. 1870*, Cambridge, MA 1976.

Foner, Philip S., A History of Cuba and Its Relation with the United States, vol. 1: *1492–1845: From Conquest of Cuba to La Escalera*, New York 1962.

A History of Cuba and Its Relation with the United States, vol. 2: *1845–1895, From the Era of Annexationism to the Outbreak of the Second War of Independence*, New York 1963.

Why the United States Went to War with Spain in 1898, *Science & Society* 32/1 (Winter 1968), 39–65.

The Spanish–Cuban–American War and the Birth of American Imperialism 1895–1902, vol. 1: 1895–1898, New York 1972.

The Spanish–Cuban–American War and the Birth of American Imperialism 1895–1902, vol. 2: 1898–1902, New York 1972.

Fonteyne, Jean-Pierre L., The Customary International Law Doctrine of Humanitarian Intervention: Its Current Validity under the U.N. Charter, *California Western International Law Journal* 4 (1973), 203–270.

Forbes, Frederick Edwyn ('Lieutenant Forbes'), *Six Months' Service in the African Blockade, from April to October, 1848, in Command of H.M.S. Bonetta*, London 1849.

Forcade, Olivier/Frédéric Guelton, L'expédition en Syrie en Août 1860–juin 1861, *Revue internationale d'histoire militaire* 75 (1995), 49–62.

Forclaz, Amalia Ribi, *Humanitarian Imperialism: The Politics of Anti-Slavery Activism, 1880–1940*, Oxford 2015.

Ford, Worthington C., The Work of John Quincy Adams, in Armin Rappaport (ed.), *The Monroe Doctrine*, New York 1964, 40–48.

Förster, Stig/Wolfgang J. Mommsen/Ronald Robinson (eds.), *Bismarck, Europe, and Africa: The Berlin Africa Conference 1884–1885 and the Onset of Partition*, Oxford 1988.

Forsythe, David P., *The Humanitarians: The International Committee of the Red Cross*, Cambridge 2005.

Fox, William, *An Address to the People of Great Britain on the Propriety of Abstaining from West India Sugar and Rum*, Birmingham 1791.

Franck, Thomas M./Nigel S. Rodley, After Bangladesh: The Law of Humanitarian Intervention by Military Force, *American Journal of International Law* 67/2 (April 1973), 275–305.

Fraser, Elisabeth A., *Delacroix, Art and Patrimony in Post-Revolutionary France*, Cambridge 2004.

Fraser, Captain H. A./Bishop Tozer/James Christie, *The East African Slave Trade and the Measures Proposed for Its Extinction, as Viewed by Residents in Zanzibar*, London 1871.

A Letter to the Honourable Members of the Select Committee of the House of Commons Appointed to Inquire into the Question of the Slave Trade on the East Coast of Africa, Zanzibar 1872.

Friedemann, Peter/Lucian Hölscher, Internationale, International, Internationalismus, in Otto Brunner/Werner Conze/Reinhart Koselleck (eds.), *Geschichtliche Grundbegriffe: Historisches Lexikon zur politisch-sozialen Sprache in Deutschland*, vol. 3, Stuttgart 1982.

Fröhlich, Manuel, The Responsibility to Protect: Foundation, Transformation, and Application of an Emerging Norm, in Fabian Klose (ed.), *The Emergence of Humanitarian Intervention: Ideas and Practice from the Nineteenth Century to the Present*, Cambridge 2016, 299–330.

Fyfe, Christopher, *A History of Sierra Leone*, London 1962.

Opposition to the Slave Trade as a Preliminary to the European Partition of Africa, in Christopher Fyfe (ed.), *The Theory of Imperialism and the European Partition of Africa*, Edinburgh 1967, 129–143.

Freed Slave Colonies in West Africa, in John E. Flint (ed.), *The Cambridge History of Africa*, vol. 5: *From c. 1790 to c. 1870*, Cambridge 1976, 170–199.

A Short History of Sierra Leone, London 1979.

Gallagher, John, Fowell Buxton and the New African Policy, 1838–1842, *Cambridge Historical Journal* 10/1 (1950), 36–58.

Gallagher, John/Ronald Robinson, The Imperialism of Free Trade, *Economic History Review*, New Series 6/1 (August 1953), 1–15.

Gann, L. H., The Berlin Conference and the Humanitarian Conscience, in Stig Förster/Wolfgang J. Mommsen/Ronald Robinson (eds.), *Bismarck, Europe, and Africa: The Berlin Africa Conference 1884–1885*, Oxford 1988, 321–331.

Gates, John M., War-Related Deaths in the Philippines, 1898–1902, *Pacific Historical Review* 53/3 (August 1984), 367–378.

Gavin, R. J., The Bartle Frere Mission to Zanzibar, 1873, *Historical Journal* 5/2 (June 1962), 122–148.

Geggus, David Patrick, The British Government and the Saint Domingue Slave Revolt, 1791–1793, *English Historical Review* 96/379 (April 1981), 285–305.

British Opinion and the Emergence of Haiti, 1791–1805, in James Walvin (ed.), *Slavery and British Society, 1776–1846*, London 1982, 123–149.

Haitian Revolutionary Studies, Bloomington, IN 2002.

The World of the Haitian Revolution, Bloomington, IN 2009.

Slave Resistance and Emancipation: The Case of Saint-Domingue, in Seymour Drescher/Pieter C. Emmer (eds.), *Who Abolished Slavery? Slave Revolts and Abolitionism: A Debate with Joao Pedro Marques*, New York 2010, 112–119.

Genovese, Eugene D., *From Rebellion to Revolution: Afro-American Revolts in the Making of the Modern World*, Baton Rouge, LA 1979.

Geyer, Martin H., One Language for the World: The Metric System, International Coinage, Gold Standard, and the Rise of Internationalism, in Martin H. Geyer/Johannes Paulmann (eds.), *The Mechanics of Internationalism: Culture, Society, and Politics from the 1840s to the First World War*, Oxford 2001, 55–92.

Geyer, Martin H./Johannes Paulmann (eds.), *The Mechanics of Internationalism: Culture, Society, and Politics from the 1840s to the First World War*, Oxford 2001.

Geyer, Michael, Humanitarianism and Human Rights: A Troubled Rapport, in Fabian Klose (ed.), *The Emergence of Humanitarian Intervention: Ideas and Practice from the Nineteenth Century to the Present*, Cambridge 2016, 31–55.

Gilbert, Helen/Chris Tiffin (eds.), *Burden or Benefit? Imperial Benevolence and Its Legacies*, Bloomington, IN 2008.

Gildea, Robert, *Barricades and Borders: Europe 1800–1914*, Oxford 2003.

Gilderhus, Mark T., The Monroe Doctrine: Meanings and Implications, *Presidential Studies Quarterly* 36/1 (March 2006), 5–16.

Gilje, Paul A., 'Free Trade and Sailors' Rights': The Rhetoric of the War of 1812, *Journal of the Early Republic* 30/1 (Spring 2010), 1–23.

Gilliland, C. Herbert, *Voyage to a Thousand Cares: Master's Mate Lawrence with the African Squadron, 1844–1846*, Annapolis, MD 2004.

Gladstone, William E., *Bulgarian Horrors and the Question of the East*, London 1876.

Lessons in Massacre: The Conduct of the Turkish Government in and about Bulgaria, London 1877.

Gleave, J., *The Triumph of Justice, or British Valour Displayed in the Cause of Humanity: Being an Interesting Narrative of the Recent Expedition to Algiers*, Manchester 1816.

Glenny, Misha, *The Balkans 1804–1999: Nationalism, War and the Great Powers*, London 1999.

Goodman, Ryan, Humanitarian Intervention and Pretexts for War, *American Journal of International Law* 100/1 (January 2006), 107–141.

Gong, Gerrit W., *The Standard of 'Civilization' in International Society*, Oxford 1984.

Götz, Norbert, Rationales of Humanitarianism: The Case of British Relief to Germany, 1805–1815, *Journal of Modern European History* 12/2 (2014), 186–199.

Gough, Barry, *Pax Britannica: Ruling the Waves and Keeping the Peace before Armageddon*, Basingstoke 2014.

Graham, Malbone W., Humanitarian Intervention in International Law as Related to the Practice of the United States, *Michigan Law Review* 22/4 (February 1924), 312–328.

Grant, Kevin, Christian Critics of Empire: Missionaries, Lantern Lectures, and the Congo Reform Campaign in Britain, *Journal of Imperial and Commonwealth History* 29/2 (May 2001), 27–58.

A Civilised Savagery: Britain and the New Slaveries in Africa, 1884–1926, New York 2005.

Green, Abigail, Intervening in the Jewish Question, 1840–1878, in Brendan Simms/David J. B. Trim (eds.), *Humanitarian Intervention: A History*, Cambridge 2011, 139–158.

Humanitarianism in Nineteenth-Century Context: Religious, Gendered, National, *Historical Journal* 57/4 (December 2014), 1157–1175.

From Protection to Humanitarian Intervention? Enforcing Jewish Rights in Romania and Morocco around 1880, in Fabian Klose (ed.), *The Emergence of Humanitarian Intervention: Ideas and Practice from the Nineteenth Century to the Present, Cambridge* 2016, 142–161.

Grewe, Wilhelm G., *Epochen der Völkerrechtsgeschichte*, Baden-Baden 1984.

The Epochs of International Law, Berlin 2000.

Grotius, Hugo, *On the Law of War and Peace (Student Edition)*, ed. Stephen C. Neff, Cambridge 2012.

Guyatt, Mary, The Wedgwood Slave Medallion: Values in Eighteenth-Century Design, *Journal of Design History* 13/2 (2000), 93–105.

Hafner, D. L., Castlereagh, the Balance of Power, and 'Non-Intervention', *Australian Journal of Politics and History* 26/1 (1980), 71–84.

Halliday, Fred, Three Concepts of Internationalism, *International Affairs* 64/2 (Spring 1988), 187–198.

Halttunen, Karen, Humanitarianism and the Pornography of Pain in Anglo-American Culture, *American Historical Review* 100/2 (April 1995), 303–334.

Hamilton, Douglas/Robert L. Blyth (eds.), *Representing Slavery: Art, Artefacts and Archives in the Collection of the National Maritime Museum*, Aldershot 2007.

Hamilton, Keith, Zealots and Helots: The Slave Trade Department of the Nineteenth-Century Foreign Office, in Keith Hamilton/Patrick Salmon (eds.), *Slavery, Diplomacy and Empire: Britain and the Suppression of the Slave Trade, 1807–1975*, Eastbourne 2009, 20–41.

Hamilton, Keith/Patrick Salmon (eds.), *Slavery, Diplomacy and Empire: Britain and the Suppression of the Slave Trade, 1807–1975*, Eastbourne 2009.

Hamilton, Richard F., *President McKinley, War and Empire*, vol. 1: *President McKinley and the Coming of War, 1898*, New Brunswick, NJ 2006.

Hamilton, Robert, An Address Intended to Have Been Delivered at a Meeting of the Inhabitants of Ipswich for the Purpose of Considering the Propriety of Petitioning Parliament for an Abolition of the Slave Trade, Ipswich, 17 February 1792.

Hampsher-Monk, Iain, Edmund Burke's Changing Justification for Intervention, *Historical Journal* 48/1 (March 2005), 65–100.

Handler, Jerome S., Survivors of the Middle Passage: Life Histories of Enslaved Africans in British America, *Slavery & Abolition* 23/1 (April 2002), 25–56.

Burke's Counter-Revolutionary Writings, in David Dwan/Christopher M. Insole (eds.), *The Cambridge Companion to Edmund Burke*, Cambridge 2012, 209–220.

Hanioğlu, M. Şükrü, *A Brief History of the Late Ottoman Empire*, Princeton, NJ 2008.

Harcourt, William Vernon, *Letters by Historicus on Some Questions of International Law*, London 1863.

Harms, Robert/Bernard K. Freamon/David W. Blight (eds.), *Indian Ocean Slavery in the Age of Abolition*, New Haven, CT 2013.

Harris, David, *Britain and the Bulgarian Horrors of 1876*, Chicago, IL 1939.

Haskell, Chas. C. & Son (ed.), *The American–Spanish War: A History by the War Leaders*, Norwich 1899.

Haskell, Thomas L., Capitalism and the Origins of Humanitarian Sensibility, pt. 1, *American Historical Review* 90/2 (April 1985), 339–361.

Capitalism and the Origins of Humanitarian Sensibility, pt. 2, *American Historical Review* 90/3 (June 1985), 547–566.

Hassan, Farooq, Realpolitik in International Law: After Tanzanian–Ugandan Conflict: 'Humanitarian Intervention' Reexamined, *Willamette Law Review* 17 (1981), 859–912.

Haynes, Sam W., Anglophobia and the Annexation of Texas: The Quest for National Security, in Sam W. Haynes/Christopher Morris (eds.), *Manifest Destiny and Empire: American Antebellum Expansionism*, College Station, TX 2008, 115–145.

Haynes, Sam W./Christopher Morris (eds.), *Manifest Destiny and Empire: American Antebellum Expansionism*, College Station, TX 2008.

Heale, M. J., Humanitarianism in the Early Republic: The Moral Reformers of New York, 1776–1825, *Journal of American Studies* 2/2 (October 1968), 161–175.

Healy, David, *The United States in Cuba 1898–1902: Generals, Politicians, and the Search for Policy*, Madison, WI 1963.

Heartfield, James, *The Aborigines' Protection Society: Humanitarian Imperialism in Australia, New Zealand, Fiji, Canada, South Africa, and the Congo, 1836–1909*, London 2011.

Heerten, Lasse, *The Biafran War and Postcolonial Humanitarianism: Spectacles of Suffering*, Cambridge 2017.

Hehir, Aidan, *Humanitarian Intervention after Kosovo: Iraq, Dafur and the Record of Global Civil Society*, Basingstoke 2008.

Humanitarian Intervention: An Introduction, Basingstoke 2010.

The Responsibility to Protect: Rhetoric, Reality and the Future of Humanitarian Intervention, Basingstoke 2012.

Hehir, Aidan/Robert W. Murray (eds.), *Protecting Human Rights in the 21st Century*, London 2017.

Helfman, Tara, The Court of Vice-Admiralty at Sierra Leone and the Abolition of the West African Slave Trade, *Yale Law Journal* 115/5 (March 2006), 1122–1156.

Helly, Dorothy O., 'Informed' Opinion on Tropical Africa in Great Britain 1860–1890, *African Affairs* 68/272 (July 1969), 195–217.

Hendrick, George, *Henry Salt: Humanitarian Reformer and Man of Letters*, Urbana, IL 1977.

Henkin, Louis, Kosovo and the Law of 'Humanitarian Intervention', *American Journal of International Law* 93/4 (October 1999), 824–828.

Heraclides, Alexis, Humanitarian Intervention in International Law 1830–1939: The Debate, *Journal of the History of International Law* 16 (2014), 26–62.

Heraclides, Alexis/Ada Dialla, *Humanitarian Intervention in the Long Nineteenth Century: Setting the Precedent*, Manchester 2015.

Herren, Madeleine, *Hintertüren zur Macht: Internationalismus und modernisierungsorientierte Außenpolitik in Belgien, der Schweiz und den USA, 1865–1914*, Munich 2000.

Governmental Internationalism and the Beginning of a New World Order in the Late Nineteenth Century, in Martin H. Geyer/Johannes Paulmann (eds.), *The Mechanics of Internationalism: Culture, Society, and Politics from the 1840s to the First World War*, Oxford 2001, 121–144.

Herring, George C., *From Colony to Superpower: U.S. Foreign Relations since 1776*, Oxford 2008.

Herrmann, Friedrich, *Ueber die Seeräuber im Mittelmeer und ihre Vertilgung: Ein Völkerwunsch an den erlauchten Kongress in Wien*, Lübeck 1815.

Hershey, Amos S., Intervention and the Recognition of Cuban Independence, *Annals of the American Academy of Political and Social Science* 11 (May 1898), 53–80.

Heydemann, Günther, The Vienna System between 1815 and 1848 and the Disputed Antirevolutionary Strategy: Repression, Reforms, or Constitutions?, in Peter Krüger/Paul W. Schroeder (eds.), *'The Transformation of European Politics, 1763–1848': Episode or Model in Modern History?*, Münster 2002, 187–203.

Higman, B. W., The Sugar Revolution, *Economic History Review* 53/2 (May 2000), 213–236.

Hildebrand, Klaus, *No Intervention: Die Pax Britannica und Preußen 1865/ 66–1869/70. Eine Untersuchung zur englischen Weltpolitik im 19. Jahrhundert*, Munich 1997.

Hill, Richard, *The Prizes of War: The Naval Prize System in the Napoleonic Wars, 1793–1815*, Stroud 1998.

Hillgruber, Christian, Humanitäre Intervention, Grossmachtpolitik und Völkerrecht, *Der Staat* 40 (2001), 165–191.

Hilton, Boyd, 1807 and All That: Why Britain Outlawed Her Slave Trade, in Derek R. Peterson (ed.), *Abolitionism and Imperialism in Britain, Africa, and the Atlantic*, Athens, OH 2010, 63–83.

Hilton, Sylvia L./Steve J. S. Ickringill (eds.), *European Perceptions of the Spanish–American War of 1898*, Bern 1999.

Hoare, Prince, *Memoirs of Granville Sharp*, London 1820.

Hochschild, Adam, *King Leopold's Ghost: A Story of Greed, Terror, and Heroism in Colonial Africa*, New York 1999.

Bury the Chains: The British Struggle to Abolish Slavery, Basingstoke 2005.

Hoffman, Peter J./Thomas G. Weiss, *Humanitarianism, War, and Politics: Solferino to Syria and Beyond*, Lanham, MD 2018.

Hoffmann, Stefan-Ludwig, Einführung: Zur Genealogie der Menschenrechte, in Stefan-Ludwig Hoffmann (ed.), *Moralpolitik: Geschichte der Menschenrechte im 20. Jahrhundert*, Göttingen 2010, 7–37.

Human Rights and History, *Past & Present*, 22 July 2016, https://academic.oup .com/past/article-abstract/232/1/279/1752430

Hoffmann, Stefan-Ludwig (ed.), *Moralpolitik: Geschichte der Menschenrechte im 20. Jahrhundert*, Göttingen 2010.

Holbraad, Carsten, *The Concert of Europe: A Study in German and British International Theory 1815–1914*, London 1970.

Holland, Robert, *Blue-Water Empire: The British in the Mediterranean since 1800*, London 2013.

Holsti, Kalevi J., Governance without Government: Polyarchy in Nineteenth-Century European International Politics, in James N. Rosenau/Ernst-Otto

Czempiel (eds.), *Governance without Government: Order and Change in World Politics*, Cambridge 1992, 30–57.

Holzgrefe, Jeff L., The Humanitarian Intervention Debate, in Jeff L. Holzgrefe/ Robert O. Keohane (eds.), *Humanitarian Intervention: Ethical, Legal, and Political Dilemmas*, Cambridge 2004.

Holzgrefe, Jeff L./Robert O. Keohane, *Humanitarian Intervention: Ethical, Legal, and Political Dilemmas*, Cambridge 2004.

Honour, Hugh, *The Image of the Black in Western Art*, vol. 4: *From the American Revolution to World War I: Slaves and Liberators*, Cambridge, MA 1989.

Hopkins, Antony G., Property Rights and Empire Building: Britain's Annexation of Lagos, 1861, *Journal of Economic History* 40/4 (December 1980), 777–798.

Hopper, Matthew S., *Slaves of One Master: Globalization and Slavery in Arabia in the Age of Empire*, New Haven, CT 2015.

Howard, Edward, *Memoirs of Admiral Sir Sidney Smith*, vol. 2, London 1839.

Howell, Raymond, *The Royal Navy and the Slave Trade*, London 1987.

Hudson, Nicholas, 'Britons Never Will Be Slaves': National Myth, Conservatism, and the Beginning of British Antislavery, *Eighteenth-Century Studies* 34/4 (Summer 2001), 559–576.

Hughes, Thomas S., *An Address to the People of England in the Cause of the Greeks, Occasioned by the Late Inhuman Massacres in the Isle of Scio & c.*, London 1822.

Hugill, Peter J., *Global Communications since 1844: Geopolitics and Technology*, Baltimore, MD 1999.

Hume, David, *Enquiries Concerning the Human Understanding and Concerning the Principles of Morals*, ed. L. A. Selby-Bigge, 2nd ed., Oxford 1902.

Humphreys, A. R., 'The Friend of Mankind' (1700–60): An Aspect of Eighteenth-Century Sensibility, *Review of English Studies* 24/95 (July 1948), 203–218.

Hunt, Barry Dennis, The Eastern Question in British Naval Policy and Strategy, 1789–1913, in Apostolos E. Vacalopoulos/Constantinos D. Svolopoulos/ Béla K. Király (eds.), *Southeast European Maritime Commerce and Naval Policies from the Mid-Eighteenth Century to 1914*, Boulder, CO 1988, 45–75.

Hunt, Lynn, *Inventing Human Rights: A History*, New York 2007.

The Paradoxical Origins of Human Rights, in Jeffrey N. Wasserstrom/Greg Grandin/Lynn Hunt/Marilyn B. Young (eds.), *Human Rights and Revolution*, Lanham, MD 2007, 3–20.

Huzzey, Richard, *Freedom Burning: Anti-Slavery and Empire in Victorian Britain*, Ithaca, NY 2012.

Minding Civilisation and Humanity in 1867: A Case Study in British Imperial Culture and Victorian Anti-Slavery, *Journal of Imperial and Commonwealth History* 40/5 (December 2012), 807–825.

Huzzey, Richard/Henry Miller, Petitions, Parliament, and Political Culture: Petitioning the House of Commons, 1780–1918, *Past & Present* 248 (August 2020), 123–164.

Hyam, Ronald, *Britain's Imperial Century, 1815–1914: A Study of Empire and Expansion*, London 1993.

Ignalls, John J. (ed.), *America's War for Humanity Related in Story and Picture, Embracing a Complete History of Cuba's Struggle for Liberty, and the Glorious Heroism of America's Soldiers and Sailors*, New York 1898.

Incognitus, Ricardus, *An Address to the People of the British Dominions, on Behalf of Humanity, and of the Suffering Greeks*, London 1825.

Ingersoll, Edward (ed.), *A Digest of the Laws of the United States of America from March 4th, 1789, to May 15th, 1820*, Philadelphia, PA 1821.

Inikori, Joseph E., Market Structure and the Profits of the British African Trade in the Late Eighteenth Century, *Journal of Economic History* 41/4 (December 1981), 745–776.

Slavery and Atlantic Commerce, 1650–1800, *American Economic Review* 82/2 (May 1992), 151–157.

International Commission on Intervention and State Sovereignty (ICISS) (ed.), *The Responsibility to Protect*, Ottawa 2001.

The Responsibility to Protect: Research, Bibliography, Background. Supplementary Volume to the Report of the ICISS, Ottawa 2001.

International Law Association (ed.), *Report of the Fifty-Second Conference Held at Helsinki, August 14th to August 20th, 1966*, London 1967.

Iriye, Akira, *Global Community: The Role of International Organizations in the Making of the Contemporary World*, Berkeley, CA 2002.

Jack, Malcolm, Destruction and Regeneration: Lisbon, 1755, in Theodore E. D. Braun/John B. Radner (eds.), *The Lisbon Earthquake of 1755: Representation and Reactions*, Oxford 2005, 7–20.

Jackson, Maurice, *Let This Voice Be Heard: Anthony Benezet, Father of Atlantic Abolitionism*, Philadelphia, PA 2009.

Jacob, Cecilia/Martin Mennecke (eds.), *Implementing the Responsibility to Protect: A Future Agenda*, Abingdon 2020.

Jameson, Robert, *Letters from the Havana during the Year 1820: Containing an Account of the Present State of the Island of Cuba and Observations on the Slave Trade*, London 1821.

Janzekovic, John, *The Use of Force in Humanitarian Intervention: Morality and Practicalities*, Aldershot 2006.

Jarrett, Mark, *The Congress of Vienna and Its Legacy: War and Great Power Diplomacy after Napoleon*, London 2014.

Jelavich, Barbara, *History of the Balkans: Eighteenth and Nineteenth Centuries*, vol. 1, Cambridge 1983.

Russia's Balkan Entanglements 1806–1914, Cambridge 1991.

Jennings, Judith, *The Business of Abolishing the British Slave Trade 1783–1807*, London 1997.

Jennings, Lawrence C., France, Great Britain, and the Repression of the Slave Trade, 1841–1845, *French Historical Studies* 10/1 (Spring 1977), 101–125.

The French Press and Great Britain's Campaign against the Slave Trade, 1830–1848, *Revue française d'histoire d'outre-mer* LXVII/246–247 (1980), 5–24.

Slave Trade Repression and the Abolition of French Slavery, in Serge Daget (ed.), *De la traite à l'esclavage: Actes du Colloque international sur la traite des Noirs*, Nantes 1988, 359–372.

French Anti-Slavery under the Restoration: The Société de la morale chrétienne, *Revue française d'histoire d'outre-mer* 81/304 (1994), 321–331.

French Anti-Slavery: The Movement for the Abolition of Slavery in France 1802–1848, Cambridge 2000.

Jessup, Philip C., The Defense of Oppressed Peoples, *American Journal of International Law* 32/1 (January 1938), 116–119.

Joannides, Paul Colin, Delacroix, Byron and the Greek War of Independence, *Burlington Magazine* 125/965 (August 1983), 495–500.

Johnson, John J., *A Hemisphere Apart: The Foundations of United States Policy toward Latin America*, Baltimore, MD 1990.

Johnson, Samuel, *A Dictionary of the English Language*, vol. 1, London 1755.

Jones, Wilbur Devereux, The Origins and Passage of Lord Aberdeen's Act, *Hispanic American Historical Review* 42/4 (November 1962), 502–520.

Joseph, Gilbert M., From Caste to Class War: The Historiography of Modern Yucatán (c. 1750–1940), *Hispanic American Historical Review* 65/1 (February 1985), 111–134.

The United States, Feuding Elites, and Rural Revolt in Yucatán, 1836–1915, in Daniel Nugent (ed.), *Rural Revolt in Mexico: US Intervention and the Domain of Subaltern Politics*, Durham, NC 1998, 173–206.

Journal Printing Company (ed.), *Cartoons of the Spanish–American War by Bart with Dates of Important Events from the Minneapolis Journal*, Minneapolis, MN 1899.

Kampmann, Christoph, Das 'Westfälische System', die Glorreiche Revolution und die Interventionsproblematik, *Historisches Jahrbuch* 131 (2011), 65–92.

The English Crisis, Emperor Leopold, and the Origins of the Dutch Intervention in 1688, *Historical Journal* 55/2 (June 2012), 521–532.

Kampmann, Christoph/Ulrich Niggemann (eds.), *Sicherheit in der Frühen Neuzeit: Norm, Praxis, Repräsentation*, Cologne 2013 (Frühneuzeit Impulse 2).

Kaplan, Lawrence S., The Monroe Doctrine and the Truman Doctrine: The Case of Greece, *Journal of the Early Republic* 13/1 (Spring 1993), 1–21.

Karns, Margaret P./Karen A. Mingst, *International Organizations: The Politics and Process of Global Governance*, Boulder, CO 2010.

Kaufmann, Chaim D./Robert A. Pape, Explaining Costly International Moral Action: Britain's Sixty-Year Campaign against the Slave Trade, *International Organization* 53/4 (Autumn 1999), 631–668.

Kayaoğlu, Turan, *Legal Imperialism: Sovereignty and Extraterritoriality in Japan, the Ottoman Empire, and China*, Cambridge 2010.

Keck, Margaret E./Kathryn Sikkink, *Activists beyond Borders: Advocacy Networks in International Politics*, Ithaca, NY 1998.

Keene, Edward, A Case Study of the Construction of International Hierarchy: British Treaty-Making against the Slave Trade in the Early Nineteenth Century, *International Organization* 61/2 (Spring 2007), 311–339.

International Hierarchy and the Origins of the Modern Practice of International Intervention, *Review of International Studies* 39/5 (December 2013), 1077–1090.

Kendrick, Thomas D., *The Lisbon Earthquake*, London 1956.

Kern, Holger Lutz, Strategies of Legal Change: Great Britain, International Law, and the Abolition of the Transatlantic Slave Trade, *Journal of the History of International Law* 6/2 (2004), 233–258.

Kerschbaumer, Florian, Sir Sidney Smith und die Barbaresken-Frage am Wiener Kongress, in Florian Kerschbaumer/Reinhard Stauber/Marion Koschier (eds.), *Mächtepolitik und Friedenssicherung: Zur politischen Kultur Europas im Zeichen des Wiener Kongresses*, Berlin 2014, 89–105.

Kerschbaumer, Florian/Korinna Schönhärl, Der Wiener Kongress als 'Kinderstube' des Philhellenismus: Das Beispiel des Bankiers Jean-Gabriel Eynard, in Anne-Rose Meyer (ed.), *Vormärz und Philhellenismus, Forum Vormärz Forschung* 18 (2012), 99–127.

Keys, Barbara, *Reclaiming American Virtue: The Human Rights Revolutuion of the 1970s*, Cambridge, MA 2014.

Kielstra, Paul Michael, *The Politics of Slave Trade Suppression in Britain and France, 1814–48: Diplomacy, Morality and Economics*, London 2000.

King, James Ferguson, The Latin-American Republics and the Suppression of the Slave Trade, *Hispanic American Historical Review* 24/3 (August 1944), 387–411.

Kiple, Kenneth F., *The Caribbean Slave: A Biological History*, Cambridge, MA 1984.

Kiple, Kenneth F./Brian T. Higgins, Mortality Caused by Dehydration during the Middle Passage, *Social Science History* 13/4 (Winter 1989), 421–437.

Kipling, Rudyard, *Rudyard Kipling's Verse: Definitive Edition*, London 1929.

Kisirwani, Maroun, Foreign Interference and Religious Animosity in Lebanon, *Journal of Contemporary History* 15/4 (October 1980), 685–700.

Klein, Herbert S.,*The Atlantic Slave Trade*, Cambridge 2010.

Klein, Herbert S./Stanley L. Engerman, Long-Term Trends in African Mortality in the Transatlantic Slave Trade, *Slavery & Abolition* 18/1 (1997), 36–48.

Klein, Herbert S./Stanley L. Engerman/Robin Haines/Ralph Shlomowitz, Transoceanic Mortality: The Slave Trade in Comparative Perspective, *William and Mary Quarterly* 58/1 (January 2001), 93–118.

Klein, Natalie, *'L'humanité, le christianisme, et la liberté': Die internationale Philhellenische Vereinsbewegung der 1820er Jahre*, Mainz 2000.

Klingberg, Frank J., *The Anti-Slavery Movement in England: A Study in English Humanitarianism*, New Haven, CT 1926.

The Evolution of the Humanitarian Spirit in Eighteenth-Century England, *Pennsylvania Magazine of History and Biography* 66/3 (July 1942), 260–278.

Kloepfer, Stephen, The Syrian Crisis, 1860–61: A Case Study in Classic Humanitarian Intervention, *Canadian Yearbook of International Law* XXIII (1985), 246–260.

Klose, Fabian, *Menschenrechte im Schatten kolonialer Gewalt: Die Dekolonisierungskriege in Kenia und Algerien 1945–1962*, Munich 2009.

Human Rights in the Shadow of Colonial Violence: The Wars of Independence in Kenya and Algeria, Philadelphia, PA 2013.

Humanitäre Intervention und internationale Gerichtsbarkeit – Verflechtung militärischer und juristischer Implementierungsmaßnahmen zu Beginn des 19. Jahrhunderts, *Militärgeschichtliche Zeitschrift* 72/1 (2013), 1–21.

'To Maintain the Law of Nature and of Nations' – Der Wiener Kongress und die Ursprünge der humanitären Intervention, *Geschichte in Wissenschaft und Unterricht* 3/4 (March–April 2014), 217–237.

Frieden durch Krieg? Zur Janusköpfigkeit militärischer Interventionspraxis im langen 19. Jahrhundert, in Sandrine Mayoraz/Frithjof Benjamin Schenk/ Ueli Mäder (eds.), *Hundert Jahre Basler Friedenskongress (1912–2012): Die erhoffte 'Verbrüderung der Völker'*, Basel 2015, 201–212.

Humanitäre Intervention und Prävention in der internationalen Politik vom 19. bis ins 21. Jahrhundert, in Nicolai Hannig/Malte Thiessen (eds.), *Vorsorge in der Moderne: Akteure, Räume und Praktiken, Schriftenreihe der Vierteljahrshefte für Zeitgeschichte, vol. 115*, Berlin 2017, 27–44.

Protecting Universal Rights through Intervention: International Law Debates from the 1930s to the 1980s, in Norbert Frei/Daniel Stahl/Annette Weinke (eds.), *Human Rights and Humanitarian Intervention: Legitimizing the Use of Force since the 1970s*, Göttingen 2017, 169–184.

'A War of Justice and Humanity': Abolition and Establishing Humanity as an International Norm, in Fabian Klose/Mirjam Thulin (eds.), *Humanity: A History of European Concepts in Practice from the Sixteenth Century to the Present*, Göttingen 2017, 169–186.

Humanitarian Intervention as an Entangled History of Humanitarianism and Human Rights, in Michael Barnett (ed.), *Humanitarianism and Human Rights: A World of Differences?*, Cambridge 2020, 127–139.

Legal Practitioners – Nineteenth Century International Jurisdiction and the Ambiguous Roles of the Members of the Mixed Commissions, in Marcus M. Payk/Kim Christian Priemel (eds.), *Crafting the International Order: Practitioners and Practices of International Law since c. 1800*, Oxford 2021, 48–65.

Klose, Fabian (ed.), *The Emergence of Humanitarian Intervention: Ideas and Practice from the Nineteenth Century to the Present*, Cambridge 2016.

Klose, Fabian/Mirjam Thulin (eds.), *Humanity: A History of European Concepts in Practice from the Sixteenth Century to the Present*, Göttingen 2017.

Klose, Fabian/Mirjam Thulin, Introduction: European Concepts and Practices of Humanity in Historical Perspective, in Fabian Klose/Mirjam Thulin (eds.), *Humanity: A History of European Concepts in Practice from the Sixteenth Century to the Present*, Göttingen 2017, 9–25.

Knight, Franklin W., The Haitian Revolution, *American Historical Review* 105/1 (February 2000), 103–115.

Knudsen, Tonny Brems, The History of Humanitarian Intervention: The Rule or the Exception?, Paper for the 50th ISA Annual Convention, 15–18 February 2009.

Köchler, Hans, *The Concept of Humanitarian Intervention in the Context of Modern Power Politics: Is the Revival of the Doctrine of 'Just War' Compatible with the International Rule of Law?*, Vienna 2001.

Kontorovich, Eugene, The Constitutionality of International Courts: The Forgotten Precedent of Slave Trade Tribunals, *University of Pennsylvania Law Review* 158/1 (December 2009), 39–115.

Koskenniemi, Martti, Lauterpacht: The Victorian Tradition in International Law, *European Journal of International Law* 8/2 (1997), 215–263.

The Gentle Civilizer of Nations: The Rise and Fall of International Law 1870–1960, Cambridge 2001.

Ković, Miloš, *Disraeli and the Eastern Question*, Oxford 2011.

Kramer, Paul A., Race-Making and Colonial Violence in the U.S. Empire: The Philippine–American War as Race War, *Diplomatic History* 30/2 (April 2006), 169–210.

Krasner, Stephen D., Westphalia and All That, in Judith Goldstein/Robert O. Keohane (eds.), *Ideas and Foreign Policy: Beliefs, Institutions, and Political Change*, Ithaca, NY 1993, 235–264.

Sovereignty and Intervention, in Gene M. Lyons/Michael Mastanduno (eds.), *Beyond Westphalia? State Sovereignty and International Intervention*, Baltimore, MD 1995, 228–249.

Kraus, Michael, Slavery Reform in the Eighteenth Century: An Aspect of Transatlantic Intellectual Cooperation, *Pennsylvania Magazine of History and Biography* 60/1 (January 1936), 53–66.

Eighteenth Century Humanitarianism: Collaboration between Europe and America, *Pennsylvania Magazine of History and Biography* 60/3 (July 1936), 270–286.

The Atlantic Civilization: Eighteenth-Century Origins, Ithaca, NY 1966.

Krause, Dan/Daniel Peters (eds.), *Southern Democracies and the Responsibility to Protect: Perspectives from India, Brazil and South Africa*, Baden-Baden 2017.

Kreß, Claus, Major Post-Westphalian Shifts and Some Important Neo-Westphalian Hesitations in the State Practice on the International Law on the Use of Force, *Journal on the Use of Force and International Law* 1/1 (2014), 11–54.

Kroll, Stefan, The Legal Justification of International Intervention: Theories of Community and Admissibility, in Fabian Klose (ed.), *The Emergence of Humanitarian Intervention: Ideas and Practice from the Nineteenth Century to the Present*, Cambridge 2016, 73–88.

Krüger, Peter/Paul W. Schroeder (eds.), *The Transformation of European Politics, 1763–1848: Episode or Model in Modern History?*, Münster 2002.

Kukovansky, Mlada, American Identity and Neutral Rights from Independence to the War of 1812, *International Organization* 51/2 (Spring 1997), 209–243.

Kurzweg, Rudolf, Die Heilige Allianz und das Interventionssystem des Vertrages von Troppau, *Jahrbücher für Geschichte Osteuropas, Neue Folge* 3 (1955), 141–160.

Laderman, Charles, The Invasion of the United States by an Englishman: E. D. Morel and the Anglo-American Intervention in the Congo, in William Mulligan/Maurice Bric (eds.), *A Global History of Anti-Slavery in the Nineteenth Century*, Basingstoke 2013, 171–197.

Sharing the Burden: The Armenian Question, Humanitarian Intervention and Anglo-American Visions of Global Order, New York 2019.

LaFeber, Walter, *The New Empire: An Interpretation of American Expansion 1860–1898*, Ithaca, NY 1998.

Laidlaw, Zoe, Investigating Empire: Humanitarians, Reform and the Commission of Eastern Inquiry, *Journal of Imperial and Commonwealth History* 40/5 (December 2012), 749–768.

Lambert, Andrew, Slavery, Free Trade and Naval Strategy, 1840–1860, in Keith Hamilton/Patrick Salmon (eds.), *Slavery, Diplomacy and Empire: Britain and the Suppression of the Slave Trade, 1807–1975*, Eastbourne 2009, 65–80.

Lambert, Frank, *The Barbary Wars: American Independence in the Atlantic World*, New York 2005.

Landry, Harral E., Slavery and the Slave Trade in Atlantic Diplomacy, 1850–1861, *Journal of Southern History* 27/2 (May 1961), 184–207.

Lane, Calvin, The African Squadron: The U.S. Navy and the Slave Trade, 1820–1862, *Log of Mystic Seaport* 50/4 (Spring 1999), 86–98.

Langley, Lester D., *The Cuban Policy of the United States: A Brief History*, New York 1968.

Slavery, Reform, and American Policy in Cuba, 1823–1878, *Revista de Historia de América* 65/66 (January–December 1968), 71–84.

The Banana Wars: United States Intervention in the Caribbean 1898–1934, Lexington, MA 1985.

Lappenküper, Ulrich/Reiner Marcowitz (eds.), *Macht und Recht: Völkerrecht in den internationalen Beziehungen*, Paderborn 2010.

Lapsansky, Philip, Graphic Discord: Abolitionist and Antiabolitionist Images, in Jean Fagan Yellin/John C. Van Horne (eds.), *The Abolitionist Sisterhood: Women's Political Culture in Antebellum America*, Ithaca, NY 1994, 201–230.

Laqua, Daniel, The Tensions of Internationalism: Transnational Anti-Slavery in the 1880s and 1890s, *International History Review* 33/4 (December 2011), 705–726.

The Age of Internationalism and Belgium, 1880–1930: Peace, Progress and Prestige, Manchester 2013.

Inside the Humanitarian Cloud: Causes and Motivations to Help Friends and Strangers, *Journal of Modern European History* 12/2 (2014), 175–185.

Laqueur, Thomas W., Bodies, Details, and the Humanitarian Narrative, in Lynn Hunt (ed.), *The New Cultural History*, Berkeley, CA 1989, 176–204.

Mourning, Pity, and the Work of Narrative in the Making of 'Humanity', in Richard Ashby Wilson/Richard D. Brown (eds.), *Humanitarianism and Suffering: The Mobilization of Empathy*, Cambridge 2009, 31–57.

Laukötter, Sebastian, *Zwischen Einmischung und Nothilfe: Das Problem der 'humanitären Intervention' aus ideengeschichtlicher Perspektive*, Berlin 2014.

Lauren, Paul Gordon, *Power and Prejudice: The Politics and Diplomacy of Racial Discrimination*, Boulder, CO 1996.

The Evolution of International Human Rights: Vision Seen, Philadelphia, PA 2011.

Lauterpacht, Hersch, The Law of Nations, the Law of Nature and the Rights of Man, in: Transactions of the Grotius Society 29: Problems of Peace and War, *Papers Read before the Society in the Year 1943*, 1–33.

An International Bill of the Rights of Man, New York 1945.

Lassa Oppenheim, International Law. A Treatise, vol. I: Peace, London 1948.

International Law and Human Rights, London 1950.

Law, Robin, An African Response to Abolition: Anglo-Dahomian Negotiations on Ending the Slave Trade, 1838–1877, *Slavery & Abolition* 16/3 (December 1995), 281–310.

Abolition and Imperialism: International Law and the British Suppression of the Atlantic Slave Trade, in Derek R. Peterson (ed.), *Abolitionism and Imperialism in Britain, Africa, and the Atlantic*, Athens, OH 2010, 150–174.

Law, Robin,(ed.), *From Slavery to 'Legitmate' Commerce: The Commercial Transition in Nineteenth-Century West Africa*, Cambridge 2002.

Le Ghait, Alfred, The Anti-Slavery Conference, *North American Review* 154/424 (March 1892), 287–296.

Leiner, Frederick C., *The End of Barbary Terror: America's 1815 War against the Pirates of North Africa*, Oxford 2006.

Lesaffer, Randall/Georges Macours (eds.), *Sovereignty and the Law of Nations (16th–18th Centuries)*, Brussels 2006.

Lester, Alan, Thomas Fowell Buxton and the Networks of British Humanitarianism, in Helen Gilbert/Chris Tiffin (eds.), *Burden or Benefit? Imperial Benevolence and Its Legacies*, Bloomington, IN 2008, 31–48.

Humanitarians and White Settlers in the Nineteenth Century, in Norman Etherington (ed.), *Missions and Empire*, Oxford 2009, 64–85.

Lester, Alan/Fae Dussart, *Colonization and the Origins of Humanitarian Governance: Protecting Aborigines across the Nineteenth-Century British Empire*, Cambridge 2014.

Lewis, Bernard, *Race and Slavery in the Middle East: An Historical Enquiry*, Oxford 1990.

What Went Wrong? The Clash between Islam and Modernity in the Middle East, London 2002.

Lewis, James E., *The American Union and the Problem of Neighborhood: The United States and the Collapse of the Spanish Empire, 1783–1829*, Chapel Hill, NC 1998.

Lewis, Leonard Axel, *The Relation of British Policy to the Declaration of the Monroe Doctrine*, New York 1922.

Lewis, Mark, *The Birth of the New Justice: The Internationalization of Crime and Punishment, 1919–1950*, Oxford 2014.

Lillich, Richard B., Forcible Self-Help by States to Protect Human Rights, *Iowa Law Review* 53 (1967), 325–351.

Intervention to Protect Human Rights, *McGill Law Journal* 15/2 (June 1969), 205–219.

Humanitarian Intervention and the United Nations, Charlottesville, VA 1973.

Humanitarian Intervention: A Reply to Ian Brownlie and a Plea for Constructive Alternatives, in J. N. Moore (ed.), *Law and Civil War in the Modern World*, Baltimore, MD 1974, 229–251.

Linderman, G. F., *The Mirror of War: American Society and the Spanish–American War*, Ann Arbor, MI 1974.

Lingelbach, William E., The Doctrine and Practice of Intervention in Europe, *Annals of the American Academy of Political and Social Science* 16 (July 1900), 1–32.

Linn, McAllister Brian, *The Philippine War, 1899–1902*, Lawrence, TX 2000.

Livingstone, David/Charles Livingstone, *Narrative of an Expedition to the Zambesi and Its Tributaries; and of the Discovery of the Lakes Shirwa and Nyassa, 1858–1864*, London 1865.

Lloyd, Christopher, *The Navy and the Slave Trade: The Suppression of the African Slave Trade in the Nineteenth Century*, London 1968.

Lobban, Michael, Slavery, Insurance and the Law, *Journal of Legal History* 28/3 (2007), 319–328.

LoGerfo, James W., Sir William Dolben and 'The Cause of Humanity': The Passage of the Slave Trade Regulation Act of 1788, *Eighteenth-Century Studies* 6/4 (Summer 1973), 431–451.

Long, Helen, *Greek Fire: Massacres of Chios*, London 1992.

López-Briones, Carmen González, The Indiana Press and the Coming of the Spanish-American War, 1895–1896, *Atlantis* 12/1 (June 1990), 165–176.

Lorimer, James, *The Institutes of International Law: A Treatise of the Jural Relations of Separate Political Communities*, vol. 1, Edinburgh 1883.

Louet, Ernest, *Expédition de Syrie: Beyrouth, Le Liban – Jérusalem, 1860–1864*, Paris 1862.

Expédition de Syrie; Camille de Rochemonteix, Le Liban et l'expédition française en Syrie (1860–1861), Paris 1921.

Louis, William Roger, The Berlin Congo Conference, in William Roger Louis/ Prosser Gifford (eds.), *France and Britain in Africa: Imperial Rivalry and Colonial Rule*, New Haven, CT 1971, 167–220.

Lovejoy, Paul E., *Transformation in Slavery: A History of Slavery in Africa*, Cambridge, 2000.

Autobiography and Memory: Gustavus Vassa, alias Olaudah Equiano, the African, Slavery & Abolition 27/3 (December 2006), 317–347.

Lovrić-Pernak, Kristina, *Morale internationale und humanité im Völkerrecht des Späten 19. Jahrhunderts, Bedeutung und Funktion in Staatenpraxis und Wissenschaft*, Baden-Baden 2013.

Löwenheim, Oded, 'Do Ourselves Credit and Render a Lasting Service to Mankind': British Moral Prestige, Humanitarian Intervention, and the Barbary Pirates, *International Studies Quarterly* 47/1 (March 2003), 23–48.

Lynn, Martin, Consul and Kings: British Policy, the 'Man on the Spot', and the Seizure of Lagos, 1851, *Journal of Imperial and Commonwealth History* 10/2 (1982), 150–167.

Lyons, Francis S. L., *Internationalism in Europe 1815–1914*, Leiden 1963.

Lyons, Martyn, *Post-Revolutionary Europe, 1815–1856*, Basingstoke 2006.

Lypka, Dennis A., The Slave Trade Department of the British Foreign Office and the Suppression of the Transatlantic Slave Trade, MA dissertation, University of Calgary 1977.

MacColl, Malcolm, *The Eastern Question: Its Facts and Fallacies*, London 1877.

MacDonald, Mairi S., Lord Vivian's Tears: The Moral Hazards of Humanitarian Intervention, in Fabian Klose (ed.), *The Emergence of Humanitarian Intervention: Ideas and Practice from the Nineteenth Century to the Present*, Cambridge 2016, 121–141.

MacFarlane, S. Neil, *Intervention in Contemporary World Politics*, New York 2002.

MacGahan, J. A., *The Turkish Atrocities in Bulgaria: Letters of the Special Commissioner of the 'Daily News'*, London 1876.

MacMaster, Richard K., The United States, Great Britain and the Suppression of the Cuban Slave Trade, 1835–1860, PhD dissertation, Georgetown University, Washington, DC 1968.

MacQueen, Norrie, *Humanitarian Intervention and the United Nations*, Edinburgh 2011.

Cold War Peacekeeping versus Humanitarian Intervention. Beyond the Hammarskjöldian Model, in Fabian Klose (ed.), *The Emergence of*

Humanitarian Intervention: Ideas and Practice from the Nineteenth Century to the Present, Cambridge 2016, 231–252.

Madden, Richard Robert, *Address on Slavery in Cuba Presented to the General Anti-Slavery Convention*, London 1840.

Madej, Marek (ed.), *Western Military Interventions after the Cold War: Evaluating the Wars of the West*, Abingdon 2019.

Makdisi, Ussama, *The Culture of Sectarianism: Community, History, and Violence in Nineteenth- Century Ottoman Lebanon*, Berkeley, CA 2000.

After 1860: Debating Religion, Reform, and Nationalism in the Ottoman Empire, *International Journal of Middle East Studies* 34/4 (November 2002), 601–617.

Mandelstam, André N., La généralisation de la protection internationale des droits de l'homme, *Revue de droit international et de législation comparée* 3/XI (1930), 297–325.

Der internationale Schutz der Menschenrechte und die New-Yorker Erklärung des Instituts für Völkerrecht, *Zeitschrift für ausländisches öffentliches Recht und Völkerrecht* 2 (1931), 335–377.

Manning, Patrick, *Slavery and African Life: Occidental, Oriental, and African Slave Trade*, Cambridge 1990.

Slave Trades, 1500–1800: Globalization of Forced Labour, Aldershot 1996.

Mannix, Daniel P./Malcolm Cowley, *Black Cargoes: A History of the Atlantic Slave Trade, 1518–1865*, New York 1962.

Mansfield, J. S., *Remarks on the African Squadron*, London 1851.

Ma'oz, Moshe, *Ottoman Reform in Syria and Palestine, 1840–1861: The Impact of the Tanzimat on Politics and Society*, Oxford 1968.

Marques, Joao Pedro, *The Sounds of Silence: Nineteenth-Century Portugal and the Abolition of the Slave Trade*, New York 2006.

Slave Revolts and the Abolition of Slavery: An Overinterpretation, in Seymour Drescher/Pieter C. Emmer (eds.), *Who Abolished Slavery? Slave Revolts and Abolitionism: A Debate with Joao Pedro Marques*, New York 2010, 3–40.

Marrus, Michael R., International Bystanders to the Holocaust and Humanitarian Intervention, in Richard Ashby Wilson/Richard D. Brown (eds.), *Humanitarianism and Suffering: The Mobilization of Empathy*, Cambridge 2009, 156–174.

Martens, Friedrich, Étude historique sur la politique russe dans la question d'Orient, *Revue de droit international et de législation comparée* 9/1 (1877), 49–77.

Martínez-Fernández, Luis, *Torn between Empires: Economy, Society, and Patters of Political Thought in Hispanic Caribbean, 1840–1878*, Athens, OH 1994.

The Havana Anglo-Spanish Mixed Commission for the Suppression of the Slave Trade and Cuba's Emancipados, *Slavery and Abolition* 16/2 (August 1995), 205–225.

Fighting Slavery in the Caribbean: The Life and Times of a British Family in Nineteenth Century Havana, Armonk, NY 1998.

Martinez, Jenny S., Antislavery Courts and the Dawn of International Human Rights Law, *Yale Law Journal* 117/4 (January 2008), 550–641.

The Slave Trade and the Origins of International Human Rights Law, Oxford 2012.

Mason, Matthew E., The Battle of the Slaveholding Liberators: Great Britain, the United States, and Slavery in the Early Nineteenth Century, *William and Mary Quarterly* 59/3 (July 2002), 665–696.

Keeping Up Appearances: The International Politics of Slave Trade Abolition in the Nineteenth-Century Atlantic World, *William and Mary Quarterly* 66/4 (October 2009), 809–832.

Mathieson, William L., *Great Britain and the Slave Trade 1839–1865*, London 1929.

Matson, Henry James, *Remarks on the Slave Trade and African Squadron*, London 1848.

May, Ernest R., *Imperial Democracy: The Emergence of America as a Great Power*, New York 1961.

The Making of the Monroe Doctrine, Cambridge, MA 1975.

May, Robert E., *Manifest Destiny's Underworld: Filibustering in Antebellum America*, Chapel Hill, NC 2002.

Manifest Destiny's Filibusters, in Sam W. Haynes/Christopher Morris (eds.), *Manifest Destiny and Empire: American Antebellum Expansionism*, College Station, TX 2008, 146–179.

Mayall, James (ed.), *The New Interventionism, 1991–1994: The United Nations Experience in Cambodia, former Yugoslavia, and Somalia*, Cambridge 1996.

Maynard, Douglas H., The World's Anti-Slavery Convention of 1840, *Mississippi Valley Historical Review* 47/3 (December 1960), 452–471.

Mazlish, Bruce, *The Idea of Humanity in a Global Era*, New York 2009.

Mazower, Mark, An International Civilization? Empire, Internationalism and the Crisis of the Mid-Twentieth Century, *International Affairs* 82/3 (May 2006), 553–566.

Ende der Zivilisation und Aufstieg der Menschrechte: Die konzeptionelle Trennung Mitte des 20. Jahrhunderts, in Stefan-Ludwig Hoffmann (ed.), *Moralpolitik: Die Geschichte der Menschenrechte im 20. Jahrhundert*, Göttingen 2010, 41–62.

Governing the World: The History of an Idea, London 2012.

Mazro, Sophia, Translated by Mr. Kelch, *Turkish Barbarity: An Affecting Narrative of the Unparalleled Suffering of Mrs. Sophia Mazro, A Greek Lady of Missolonghi*, Providence, RI 1828.

Mazzini, Giuseppe, On Nonintervention (1851), in Stefano Recchia/Nadia Urbinati (eds.), *A Cosmopolitanism of Nations: Guiseppe Mazzini's Writings on Democracy, Nation Building, and International Relations*, Princeton, NJ 2009.

McCallum, Jack, *Leonard Wood: Rough Rider, Surgeon, Architect of American Imperialism*, New York 2006.

McCarthy, Justin, *Death and Exile: The Ethnic Cleansing of Ottoman Muslims 1821–1922*, Princeton, NJ 1995.

McCartney, Paul T., *Power and Progress: American National Identity, the War of 1898, and the Rise of American Imperialism*, Baton Rouge, LA 2006.

McCloy, Shelby T., *The Humanitarian Movement in Eighteenth-Century France*, New York 1972.

McDougal, Myers S., Humanitarian Intervention to Protect the Ibos, in Richard B. Lillich (ed.), *Humanitarian Intervention and the United Nations*, Charlottesville, VA 1973.

McDougall, Walter A., *Promised Land, Crusader State: The American Encounter with the World*, New York 1997.

McGee, Gale W., The Monroe Doctrine – A Stopgap Measure, *Mississippi Valley Historical Review* 38/2 (September 1951), 238–239.

McGowan, Winston, African Resistance to the Atlantic Slave Trade in West Africa, *Slavery & Abolition* 11/1 (May 1990), 5–29.

McGowen, Randall, A Powerful Sympathy: Terror, the Prison, and Humanitarian Reform in Early Nineteenth-Century Britain, *Journal of British Studies* 25/3 (July 1986), 312–334.

Medlicott, W. N., *The Congress of Berlin and After: A Diplomatic History of the Near Eastern Settlement 1878–1880*, London 1938.

Meissner, Jochen/Ulrich Mücke/Klaus Weber, *Schwarzes Amerika: Eine Geschichte der Sklaverei*, Bonn 2008.

Melton, James van Horn, *The Rise of the Public in Enlightenment Europe*, Cambridge 2001.

Melville, Ralph/Hans-Jürgen Schröder (eds.), *Der Berliner Kongress von 1878: Die Politik der Grossmächte und die Probleme der Modernisierung in Südosteuropa in der Zweiten Hälfte des 19. Jahrhunderts*, Wiesbaden 1982.

Menon, Rajan, *The Conceit of Humanitarian Intervention*, New York 2016.

Meriage, Lawrence P., The First Serbian Uprising (1804–1813) and the Nineteenth-Century Origins of the Eastern Question, *Slavic Review* 37/3 (September 1978), 421–439.

Merk, Frederick, *The Monroe Doctrine and American Expansionism, 1843–1849*, New York 1966.

Meron, Theodor, Common Rights of Mankind in Gentili, Grotius and Suarez, *American Journal of International Law* 85/1 (January 1991), 110–116.

Meyer-Heiselberg, Richard, *Notes from Liberated African Department*, Uppsala 1967.

Midgley, Clare, *Women against Slavery: The British Campaigns, 1780–1870*, London 1992.

Miers, Suzanne, *Britain and Germany in Africa: Imperial Rivalry and Colonial Rule*, New Haven, CT 1967, 83–118.

Britain and the Ending of the Slave Trade, New York 1975.

The Brussels Conference of 1889–1890: The Slave Trade in the Policies of Great Britain and Germany, in Prosser Gifford/William Roger Louis (eds.), *Humanitarianism at Berlin: Myth or Reality?*, in Stig Förster/Wolfgang J. Mommsen/Ronald Robinson (eds.), *Bismarck, Europe, and Africa: The Berlin Africa Conference 1884–1885*, Oxford 1988, 333–345.

Mill, John S., A Few Words on Non-Intervention, December 1859, in John S. Mill, *Dissertations and Discussions Political, Philosophical, and Historical Reprinted Chiefly from the Edinburgh and Westminster Reviews*, vol. 3, London 1867, 153–178.

Vindication of the French Revolution of February 1848, in John S. Mill, *Dissertations and Discussions Political, Philosophical, and Historical Reprinted*

Chiefly from the Edinburgh and Westminster Reviews, vol. 2, London 1867, 379–381.

Miller, Bonnie M., *From Liberation to Conquest: The Visual and Popular Cultures of the Spanish-American War of 1898*, Amherst, MA 2011.

Millis, Walter, *The Martial Spirit: A Study of Our War with Spain*, Boston, MA 1931.

Millman, Richard, *Britain and the Eastern Question 1875–1878*, Oxford 1979.

The Bulgarian Massacres Reconsidered, *Slavonic and East European Review* 58/2 (April 1980), 218–231.

Milton, Patrick, Intervening against Tyrannical Rule in the Holy Roman Empire during the Seventeenth and Eighteenth Centuries, *German History* 33/1 (2015), 1–29.

Minear, Larry, *The Humanitarian Enterprise: Dilemmas and Discoveries*, Bloomfield 2002.

Mintz, Sidney W., *Sweetness and Power: The Place of Sugar in Modern History*, New York 1985.

Mitzen, Jennifer, *Power in Concert: The Nineteenth-Century Origins of Global Governance*, Chicago, IL 2013.

Morgan, Philip D., Ending the Slave Trade: A Caribbean and Atlantic Context, in Derek R. Peterson (ed.), *Abolitionism and Imperialism in Britain, Africa, and the Atlantic*, Athens, OH 2010, 101–128.

Morrow, Glenn R., The Significance of the Doctrine of Sympathy in Hume and Adam Smith, *Philosophical Review* 32/1 (January 1923), 60–78.

Moses, Dirk/Lasse Heerten (eds.), *Postcolonial Conflict and the Question of Genocide: The Nigeria–Biafra War, 1967–1970*, New York 2018.

Moyn, Samuel, Empathy in History, *Empathizing with Humanity, History and Theory* 45/3 (October 2006), 397–415.

On the Genealogy of Morals, *The Nation* 284/15 (April 2007), 25–31.

The Last Utopia: Human Rights in History, Cambridge, MA 2010.

Die neue Historiographie der Menschenrechte, *Geschichte und Gesellschaft* 38/4 (October– December 2012), 545–572.

Human Rights and the Uses of History, London 2014.

Moynier, Gustave (ed.), *L'Afrique explorée et civilisée*, vol. 1–15, Geneva 1879–1894.

Moynier, Gustave, *La question du Congo devant l'Institute de droit international*, Genf 1883.

La fondation de l'État indépendant du Congo au point de vue juridique, Paris 1887.

Muldoon, James, Francisco de Vitoria and Humanitarian Intervention, *Journal of Military Ethics* 5/2 (2006), 128–143.

Mullan, John, *Sentiment and Sociability: The Language of Feeling in the Eighteenth Century*, Oxford 1990.

Mulligan, Michael, Nigeria, the British Presence in West Africa and International Law in the 19th Century, *Journal of the History of International Law* 11 (2009), 273–301.

Mulligan, William, British Anti-Slave Trade and Anti-Slavery Policy in East Africa, Arabia, and Turkey in the Late Nineteenth Century, in Brendan Simms/David J. B. Trim (eds.), *Humanitarian Intervention: A History*, Cambridge 2011, 257–280.

The Anti-Slave Trade Campaign in Europe, 1888–90, in William Mulligan/ Maurice Bric (eds.), *A Global History of Anti-Slavery in the Nineteenth Century*, Basingstoke 2013, 149–170.

Mulligan, William/Maurice Bric (eds.), *A Global History of Anti-Slavery in the Nineteenth Century*, Basingstoke 2013, 149–170.

Murphy, Craig N., *International Organization and Industrial Change: Global Governance since 1850*, Cambridge, MA 1994.

Murphy, Gretchen, *Hemispheric Imaginings: The Monroe Doctrine and Narratives of U.S. Empire*, Durham, NC 2005.

Murphy, Sean D., *Humanitarian Intervention: The United Nations in an Evolving World Order*, Philadelphia, PA 1996.

The Intervention in Kosovo: A Law-Shaping Incident?, *Proceedings of the Annual Meeting (American Society of International Law)* 94/5–8 (April 2000), 302–304.

Murray, David R., Richard Robert Madden: His Career as a Slavery Abolitionist, *Studies: An Irish Quarterly Review* 61/241 (1972), 41–53.

Odious Commerce: Britain, Spain and the Abolition of the Cuban Slave Trade, Cambridge 1980.

Murray, John (ed.), *Report of the Committee of the African Civilization Society to the Public Meeting of the Society Held at Exeter Hall, on Tuesday, the 21st of June 1842*, London 1842.

Nadelmann, Ethan A., Global Prohibition Regimes: The Evolution of Norms in International Society, *International Organization* 44/4 (Autumn 1990), 479–526.

Nagel, Johann Friedrich Gottlieb, *Werden die türkischen Schlachtbänke noch länger von griechischem Blute rauchen? Oder soll der Erbfeind des Kreuzes die Christenheit noch länger höhnen? Ein Wort zu seiner Zeit*, Braunschweig 1821.

Nahlawi, Yasmine, *The Responsibility to Protect in Libya and Syria: Mass Atrocities, Human Protection, and International Law*, Abingdon 2020.

Needell, Jeffrey D., The Abolition of the Brazilian Slave Trade in 1850: Historiography, Slave Agency and Statesmanship, *Journal of Latin American Studies* 33/4 (November 2001), 681–711.

Neely, Tennyson F./Gilson Willets/Margherita Arlina Hamm (eds.), *Greater America: Heroes. Battles. Camps: Dewey Islands, Cuba, Porto Rico*, New York 1898.

Neff, Stephen C., *War and the Law of Nations: A General History*, Cambridge 2007.

Justice among Nations: A History of International Law, Cambridge MA 2014.

Nelson, Bernard H., The Slave Trade as a Factor in British Foreign Policy 1815–1862, *Journal of Negro History* 27/2 (April 1942), 192–209.

Nerval, Gaston, A Latin American View: Egoistic from Its Pronouncement, in Armin Rappaport (ed.), *The Monroe Doctrine*, New York 1964, 92–98.

Neumann, Christopher K., Political and Diplomatic Developments, in Suraiya N. Faroqhi (ed.), *The Cambridge History of Turkey*, vol. 3: *The Later Ottoman Empire, 1603–1839*, Cambridge 2006, 44–62.

Newbury, C. W. (ed.), *British Policy towards West Africa: Select Documents 1786–1874*, Oxford 1965.

Newbury, C. W. *The Western Slave Coast and Its Rulers: European Trade and Administration among the Yoruba and Adja-speaking Peoples of South-Western Nigeria, Southern Dahomey and Togo*, Oxford 1973.

Newton, John, *Thoughts upon the African Slave Trade*, London 1788.

Nichols, Irby C., Jr, The Eastern Question and the Vienna Conference, September 1822, *Journal of Central European Affairs* 21/1 (1961), 53–66.

The European Pentarchy and the Congress of Verona, 1822, The Hague 1971.

Nicholson, Andrea, Transformations in the Law Concerning Slavery: Legacies of the Nineteenth Century Anti-Slavery Movement, in William Mulligan/Maurice Bric (eds.), *A Global History of Anti-Slavery in the Nineteenth Century*, Basingstoke 2013, 214–236.

Nicolson, Harold, *The Congress of Vienna: A Study in Allied Unity 1812–1822*, London 1947.

Nijman, Janne E., Minorities and Majorities, in Bardo Fassbender/Anne Peters (eds.), *The Oxford Handbook of the History of International Law*, Oxford 2012, 95–119.

Ninkovich, Frank, *The United States and Imperialism*, Malden, MA 2001.

Norris, Stephen N., *A War of Images: Russian Popular Prints, Wartime Culture, and National Identity, 1812–1945*, DeKalb, IL 2006.

Nwulia, Moses D. E., *Britain and Slavery in East Africa*, Washington, DC 1975.

Offner, John L., *An Unwanted War: The Diplomacy of the United States and Spain over Cuba, 1895–1898*, Chapel Hill, NC 1992.

Oldfield, J. R., The London Committee and Mobilization of Public Opinion against the Slave Trade, *Historical Journal* 35/2 (June 1992), 331–343.

Popular Politics and British Anti-Slavery. The Mobilization of Public Opinion against the Slave Trade 1787–1807, Manchester 1995.

Transatlantic Abolitionism in the Age of Revolution: An International History of Anti-slavery, c. 1787–1820, Cambridge 2013.

Oldham, James, Insurance Litigation Involving the Zong and Other British Slave Ships, 1780–1807, *Journal of Legal History* 28/3 (2007), 299–318.

Onuf, Nicolas, Humanitarian Intervention: The Early Years, *Florida Journal of International Law* 16/4 (2004), 753–787.

Orford, Anne, *Reading Humanitarian Intervention: Human Rights and the Use of Force in International Law*, Cambridge 2003.

International Authority and the Responsibility to Protect, Cambridge 2011.

O'Sullivan, John, Annexation, *United States Magazine and Democratic Review* 17/1 (July–August 1845), 5–10.

Osiander, Andreas, Sovereignty, International Relations, and the Westphalian Myth, *International Organization* 55/2 (Spring 2001), 251–287.

Osterhammel, Jürgen, Krieg im Frieden: Zu Formen und Typologie von Interventionen, in Jürgen Osterhammel (ed.), *Geschichtswissenschaft jenseits des Nationalstaats: Studien zu Beziehungsgeschichte und Zivilisationsvergleich*, Göttingen 2001, 288–294.

Auf der Suche nach einem 19. Jahrhundert, in Sebastian Conrad/Andreas Eckert/Ulrike Freitag (eds.), *Globalgeschichte, Theorie, Ansätze, Themen*, Frankfurt a. M. 2007, 109–130.

Sklaverei und die Zivilisation des Westens, Munich 2009.

The Transformation of the World: A Global History of the Nineteenth Century, Princeton, NJ 2014.

Schutz, Macht und Verantwortung: Protektion im Zeitalter der Imperien und danach, in Jürgen Osterhammel (ed.), *Die Flughöhe der Adler: Historische Essays zur globalen Gegenwart*, Munich 2017, 160–182.

Ostrander, Gilman M., The Making of the Triangular Trade Myth, *William and Mary Quarterly* 30/4 (October 1973), 635–644.

Otte, Thomas G., Of Congresses and Gunboats: Military Intervention in the Nineteenth Century, in Thomas G. Otte/Andrew M. Dorman (eds.), *Military Intervention: From Gunboat to Humanitarian Intervention*, Aldershot 1995, 19–52.

Owen, David, *English Philantrophy 1660–1960*, Cambridge, MA 1964.

Packard, Peter, *Am I Not a Man and a Brother? With All Humility Addressed to the British Legislature*, Cambridge 1788.

Panzac, Daniel, *Barbary Corsaires: The End of a Legend 1800–1820*, Leiden 2005.

Pappas, Paul C., *The United States and the Greek War for Independence, 1821–1828*, New York 1985.

Paris, Jean Joseph, *Considérations sur la crise actuelle de l'empire ottoman, les causes qui l'ont amenée, et les effets qui doivent la suivre*, Paris 1821.

Parkinson, C. Northcote, *Edward Pellew, Viscount Exmouth, Admiral of the Red*, London 1934.

Pattison, James, *Humanitarian Intervention and the Responsibility to Protect: Who Should Intervene?*, Oxford 2010.

Pauer, Alexander, *Die humanitäre Intervention: Militärische und wirtschaftliche Zwangsmaßnahmen zur Gewährleistung der Menschenrechte*, Basel 1985.

Paulmann, Johannes, Europäische Monarchien in der Revolution von 1848/49: 'Die erste wahrhafte Internationale'?, in Dieter Langewiesche (ed.), *Demokratiebewegung und Revolution 1847 bis 1849: Internationale Aspekte und europäische Verbindungen*, Karlsruhe 1998, 109–139.

Searching for a 'Royal International': The Mechanics of Monarchical Relations in Nineteenth-Century Europe, in Johannes Paulmann/Martin H. Geyer (eds.), *The Mechanics of Internationalism: Culture, Society, and Politics from the 1840s to the First World War*, Oxford 2001, 146–158.

Reformer, Experten und Diplomaten: Grundlagen des Internationalismus, in Hillard von Thiessen/Christian Windler (eds.), *Akteure der Außenbeziehungen: Netzwerke und Interkulturalität im historischen Wandel*, Cologne 2010, 173–197.

Conjunctures in the History of International Humanitarian Aid during the Twentieth Century, *Humanity* 4/2 (Summer 2013), 215–238.

The Dilemmas of Humanitarian Aid: Historical Perspectives, in Johannes Paulmann (ed.), *Dilemmas of Humanitarian Aid in the Twentieth Century*, Oxford 2016, 1–31.

Paulmann, Johannes, (ed.), *Dilemmas of Humanitarian Aid in the Twentieth Century*, Oxford 2016.

Humanitarianism and Empire, in John M. MacKenzie, *The Encyclopedia of Empire*, vol. II: D–J, Malden, MA 2016, 1112–1123.

Humanity – Humanitarian Reason – Imperial Humanitarianism. European Concepts in Practice, in Fabian Klose/Mirjam Thulin (eds.), *Humanity: A History of European Concepts in Practice from the Sixteenth Century to the Present*, Göttingen 2017, 287–311.

Paulmann, Johannes/Martin H. Geyer (eds.), *The Mechanics of Internationalism: Culture, Society, and Politics from the 1840s to the First World War*, Oxford 2001.

Paxman, John M./George T. Boggs (eds.), *The United Nations: A Reassessment. Sanctions, Peacekeeping, and Humanitarian Assistance*, Charlottesville, VA 1973.

Pearson, Andrew, *Distant Freedom: St Helena and the Abolition of the Slave Trade, 1840–1872*, Liverpool 2016.

Pedersen, Susan, *The Guardians: The League of Nations and Crisis of Empire*, Oxford 2014.

Pekesen, Berna, Vertreibung und Abwanderung der Muslime vom Balkan, *Europäische Geschichte Online* (EGO), Institut für Europäische Geschichte (IEG), Mainz 2011, http://www.ieg-ego.eu/pekesenb-2011-de.

Pellion, Général de division, *La Grèce et les Capodistrias pendant l'occupation française de 1828 à 1834*, Paris 1855.

Pemberton, Jo-Anne Claire, The So-Called Right of Civilisation in European Colonial Ideology, 16th to 20th Centuries, *Journal of the History of International Law* 15/1 (2013), 25–52.

Penn, Virginia, Philhellenism in Europe, 1821–1828, *Slavonic and East European Review* 16/48 (April 1938), 638–653.

Pérez, Louis A. Jr, *Cuba between Empires, 1878–1902*, Pittsburgh, PA 1983.

The Meaning of the Maine: Causation and the Historiography of the Spanish–American War, *Pacific Historical Review* 58/3 (August 1989), 292–322.

Cuba and the United States: Ties of Singular Intimacy, Athens, OH 1997.

The War of 1898: The United States and Cuba in History and Historiography, Chapel Hill, NC 1998.

Incurring a Debt of Gratitude: 1898 and the Moral Sources of United States Hegemony in Cuba, *American Historical Review* 104/2 (April 1999), 356–398.

Cuba between Reform and Revolution, New York 2015.

Perkins, Bradford, *Castlereagh and Adams: England and the United States 1812–1823*, Berkeley, CA 1964.

The Causes of the War of 1812: National Honor or National Interest?, New York 1976.

The Cambridge History of American Foreign Relations, vol. 1: *The Creation of a Republican Empire, 1776–1865*, Cambridge 1993.

Perkins, Dexter, *A History of the Monroe Doctrine*, London 1963.

Perkins, Roger/K. J. Douglas-Morris, *Gunfire in Barbary: Admiral Exmouth's Battle with the Corsairs of Algiers in 1816 – the Story of the Suppression of White Slavery*, Homewell 1982.

Peterson, Derek R. (ed.), *Abolitionism and Imperialism in Britain, Africa, and the Atlantic*, Athens, OH 2010.

Petrie, Charles, *Lord Liverpool and His Times*, London 1954.

Philips, James (ed.), *Substance of the Debates on a Resolution for Abolishing the Slave Trade, which was moved in the House of Commons on the 10th June, 1806, and in the House of Lords on the 24th June, 1806*, London 1806.

Phillips, Jonathan, *Heiliger Krieg: Eine neue Geschichte der Kreuzzüge*, Bonn 2012.

Pierson, William D., White Cannibals, Black Martyrs: Fear, Depression, and Religious Faith as Causes of Suicide among New Slaves, *Journal of Negro History* 62/2 (April 1977), 147–159.

Pinker, Steven, *The Better Angels of Our Nature: Why Violence Has Declined*, New York 2011.

Pitts, Jennifer, *A Turn to Empire: The Rise of Liberal Imperialism in Britain and France*, Princeton, NJ 2005.

Boundaries of Victorian International Law, in Duncan S. Bell (ed.), *Victorian Visions of Global Order: Empire and International Relations in Nineteenth-Century Political Thought*, Cambridge 2007, 67–88.

Intervention and Sovereign Equality: Legacies of Vattel, in Stefano Recchia/ Jennifer M. Welsh (eds.), *Just and Unjust Military Intervention: European Thinkers from Vitoria to Mill*, Cambridge 2013, 132–153.

Plymouth Committee (ed.), *Plan of an African Ship's Lower Deck with Negroes in the Proportion of Only One to a Ton*, Plymouth 1788.

Pocock, Tom, *Breaking the Chains: The Royal Navy's War against White Slavery*, London 2006.

Pogany, Istvan, Humanitarian Intervention in International Law: The French Intervention in Syria Re-Examined, *International and Comparative Law Quarterly* 35/1 (January 1986), 182–190.

Poole, Fred/Max Vanzi, *Revolution in the Philippines: The United States in a Hall of Cracked Mirrors*, New York 1984.

Porter, Andrew, Trusteeship, Anti-Slavery, and Humanitarianism, in Andrew Porter (ed.), *The Oxford History of the British Empire, vol. III: The Nineteenth Century*, Oxford 1999, 198–221.

Sir Roger Casement and the International Humanitarian Movement, *Journal of Imperial and Commonwealth History* 29/2 (May 2001), 59–74.

Poyo, Gerald E., Evolution of Cuban Separatist Thought in the Emigré Communities of the United States, 1848–1895, *Hispanic American Historical Review* 66/3 (August 1986), 485–507.

Pratt, Julius W., The Origin of 'Manifest Destiny', *American Historical Review* 32/ 4 (July 1927), 795–798.

Prévost, Stéphanie, The Eastern Question and Britain's Foreign Policy (1876– 1896), in Trevor Harris (ed.), *Art, Politics and Society in Britain 1880–1914: Aspects of Modernity and Modernism*, Newcastle 2009, 121–137.

W. T. Stead and the Eastern Question (1875–1911); or, How to Rouse England and Why?, *19. Interdisciplinary Studies in the Long Nineteenth Century* 16 (2013), www.19.bbk.ac.uk/articles/10.16995/ntn.654/.

New Perspectives on the Eastern Question(s) in Late-Victorian Britain, Or How 'the Eastern Question' Affected British Politics (1881–1901), in Catherine Delmas/Isabelle Gadoin (eds.), *Représentations: 'Naming, Labelling and Addressing'*, Grenoble June 2015, https://hal.archives-ouvertes .fr/hal-02558661/document.

Priesching, Nicole, Die Verurteilung der Sklaverei unter Gregor XVI. im Jahr 1839. Ein Traditionsburch?, *Saeculum. Jahrbuch für Universalgeschichte* 59 (2008), 143–162.

Priestley, Joseph, *A Sermon on the Subject of the Slave Trade; Delivered to a Society of Protestant Dissenters, at the New Meeting, in Birmingham; and Published at Their Request*, Birmingham 1788.

Prokesch-Osten, Comte Anton (ed.), *Dépêches inédites du Chevalier de Gentz aux hospodars de Valachie: Pour servir à l'histoire de la politique européene (1813 à 1828)*, vol. I, Paris 1876.

Prousis, Theophilus C., Russian Philorthodox Relief during the Greek War of Independence, *Modern Greek Studies Yearbook* 1 (1985), 31–62.

Russian Society and the Greek Revolution, DeKalb, GA 1994.

Puryear, Vernon John, *France and the Levant: From the Bourbon Restoration to the Peace of Kutiah*, Berkeley, CA 1968.

Putney, Martha, The Slave Trade in French Diplomacy from 1814 to 1815, *Journal of Negro History* 60/3 (July 1975), 411–427.

Pybus, Cassandra, 'A Less Favourable Specimen': The Abolitionist Response to Self-Emancipated Slaves in Sierra Leone, 1793–1808, *Parliamentary History* 26/Supplement (2007), 97–112.

Pyta, Wolfram, *Konzert der Mächte und kollektives Sicherheitssystem: Neue Wege zwischenstaatlicher Friedenswahrung in Europa nach dem Wiener Kongress 1815*, in: *Jahrbuch des Historischen Kollegs* 2, Munich 1997, 133–173.

Das europäische Mächtekonzert: Friedens- und Sicherheitspolitik vom Wiener Kongress 1815 bis zum Krimkrieg 1853, Cologne 2009.

Kulturgeschichtliche Annäherung an das europäische Mächtekonzert, in Wolfram Pyta (ed.), *Das europäische Mächtekonzert: Friedens- und Sicherheitspolitik vom Wiener Kongress 1815 bis zum Krimkrieg 1853*, Cologne 2009, 1–24.

Hegemonie und Gleichgewicht, in Jost Dülffer/Wilfried Loth (eds.), *Dimensionen internationaler Geschichte*, Munich 2012, 373–388.

Quataert, Donald, *The Ottoman Empire 1700–1922*, Cambridge 2005.

Quinns, John F., 'Three Cheers for the Abolitionist Pope!': American Reactions to Gregory XVI's Condemnation of the Slave Trade, 1840–1860, *Catholic Historical Review* 90/1 (January 2004), 67–93.

Quirk, Joel, *The Anti-Slavery Project: From the Slave Trade to Human Trafficking*, Philadelphia, PA 2011.

Quirk, Joel/David Richardson, Anti-Slavery, European Identity and International Society: A Macro-historical Perspective, *Journal of Modern European History* 7/1 (2009), 68–92.

Quiroz, Alfonso W., Loyalist Overkill: The Socioeconomic Costs of »Repressing« the Separatist Insurrection in Cuba, 1868–1878, *Hispanic American Historical Review* 78/2 (May 1998), 261–305.

Radner, John B., The Art of Sympathy in Eighteenth-Century British Moral Thought, *Studies in Eighteenth-Century Culture* 9 (1979), 189–210.

Raimondo, Justin, Defenders of the Republic: The Anti-Interventionist Tradition in American Politics, in John V. Denson (ed.), *The Costs of War: America's Pyrrhic Victories*, New Brunswick, NJ 1997, 67–74.

Ralfe, James, *The Battle of Navarin, Compared with Other Important Naval Events; Justifying, by Analogy, the Conduct of Sir Edward Codrington Shewing His Right to the Thanks of Parliament, and the Propriety of Granting Pecuniary Compensation to the Men*, London 1829.

Rankin, F. Harrison, *The White Man's Grave: A Visit to Sierra Leone in 1834*, London 1836.

Rathbone, Richard, Resistance to Enslavement in West Africa, in Patrick Manning (ed.), *Slave Trades, 1500–1800: Globalization of Forced Labour*, Aldershot 1996, 183–194.

Recchia, Stefano/Jennifer M. Welsh (eds.), *Just and Unjust Military Intervention: European Thinkers from Vitoria to Mill*, Cambridge 2013.

Reddy, William M., Sentimentalism and Its Erasure: The Role of Emotions in the Era of the French Revolution, *Journal of Modern History* 72/1 (March 2000), 109–152.

Redfield, Peter/Erica Bornstein, An Introduction to the Anthropology of Humanitarianism, in Peter Redfield/Erica Bornstein (eds.), *Forces of Compassion: Humanitarianism Between Ethics and Politics*, Santa Fe, NM 2010, 3–30.

Rediker, Marcus, *The Slave Ship: A Human History*, New York 2007.

Reed, Nelson A., *The Caste War of Yucatán*, Stanford, CA 2001.

Rees, Siân, *Sweet Water and Bitter: The Ships that Stopped the Slave Trade*, London 2009.

Reich, Jerome, The Slave Trade at the Congress of Vienna: A Study in English Public Opinion, *Journal of Negro History* 53/2 (April 1968), 129–143.

Reinalda, Bob, *Routledge History of International Organizations: From 1815 to the Present Day*, London 2009.

Reinerman, Alan, Metternich, Italy, and the Congress of Verona, *Historical Journal* 14/2 (June 1971), 263–287.

Reis, Joao José, Slave Resistance in Brazil: Bahia, 1807–1835, *Luso-Brazilian Review* 25/1 (Summer 1988), 111–144.

Reisman, Michael with the collaboration of Myers S. McDougal, Humanitarian Intervention to Protect the Ibos, in Richard B. Lillich (ed.), *Humanitarian Intervention and the United Nations*, Charlottesville, VA 1973, 167–195.

Renault, François, *Lavigerie, l'esclavage africain et l'Europe, 1868–1892*, vol. II: *Campagne antiesclavagiste*, Paris 1971.

Cardinal Lavigerie: Churchman, Prophet, and Missionary, London 1994.

Repousis, Angelo, 'The Cause of the Greeks': Philadelphia and the Greek War for Independence, 1821–1828, *Pennsylvania Magazine of History and Biography* 123/4 (October 1999), 333–363.

Resnick, Daniel P., The Société des Amis des Noirs and the Abolition of Slavery, *French Historical Studies* 7/4 (Autumn 1972), 558–569.

Richmond, Steven, *The Voice of England in the East: Stratford Canning and Diplomacy with the Ottoman Empire*, London 2014.

Ribi Forclaz, Amalia, *Humanitarian Imperialism: The Politics of Anti-Slavery Activism, 1880–1940*, Oxford 2015.

Richardson, David, Shipboard Revolts: African Authority, and the Atlantic Slave Trade, *William and Mary Quarterly* 58/1 (January 2001), 69–92.

Richardson, David/Suzanne Schwarz/Anthony Tibbles (eds.), *Liverpool and Transatlantic Slavery*, Liverpool 2007.

Richardson, Samuel, *Pamela: Or, Virtue Rewarded*, London 1741.

Clarissa: Or, the History of a Young Lady, London 1748.

Roberts, Adam, *Humanitarian Action in War: Aid, Protection and Impartiality in a Policy Vacuum*, Oxford 1996.

The United Nations and Humanitarian Intervention, in Jennifer M. Welsh (ed.), *Humanitarian Intervention and International Relations*, Oxford 2006, 71–97.

Roberts, Adam/Richard Guelff (eds.), *Documents on the Laws of War*, Oxford 2000.

Roberts, M. J. D., *Making English Morals: Voluntary Associations and Moral Reform in England, 1787–1886*, Cambridge 2004.

Robertson, William Spence, South America and the Monroe Doctrine, 1824–1828, *Political Science Quarterly* 30/1 (March 1915), 82–105.

Robinson, Ronald, The Excentric Idea of Imperialism, with or without Empire, in Wolfgang J. Mommsen/Jürgen Osterhammel (eds.), *Imperialism and After: Continuities and Discontinuities*, London 1986, 267–289.

Robinson, Ronald/John Gallagher, *Africa and the Victorians: The Official Mind of Imperialism*, London 1981.

Rodogno, Davide, Réflexions liminaires à propos des intervention humanitaires des Puissances européenes aux XIXe siècle, *Relations Internationales* 131 (July–September 2007), 9–25.

The 'Principles of Humanity' and the European Powers' Intervention in Ottoman Lebanon and Syria in 1860–1861, in Brendan Simms/David J. B. Trim (eds.), *Humanitarian Intervention: A History*, Cambridge 2011, 159–183.

Against Massacre: Humanitarian Interventions in the Ottoman Empire, 1815–1914, Princeton, NJ 2012.

European Legal Doctrines on Intervention and the Status of the Ottoman Empire within the 'Family of Nations' throughout the Nineteenth Century, *Journal of the History of International Law* 18 (2016), 1–37.

Non-State Actors' Humanitarian Operations in the Aftermath of the First World War: The Case of the Near East Relief, in Fabian Klose (ed.), *The Emergence of Humanitarian Intervention: Ideas and Practice from the Nineteenth Century to the Present*, Cambridge 2016, 185–207.

Roelofsen, Cornelisen G., International Arbitration and Courts, in Bardo Fassbender/Anne Peters (eds.), *The Oxford Handbook of the History of International Law*, Oxford 2012, 144–169.

Rogers, Helen, Kindness and Reciprocity: Liberated Prisoners and Christian Charity in Early Nineteenth-Century England, *Journal of Social History* 47/3 (Spring 2014), 721–745.

Rogers, Henry Wade, International Law in the Late War, *Forum* 27 (July 1899), 578–591.

Rolin-Jaequemyns, Gustave, Le droit international et la phase actuelle de la question d'Orient, *Revue de droit international et de législation comparée VIII* (1876), 293–385.

Note sur la théorie du droit d'intervention, a propos d'une lettre de M. le Professeur Arntz, *Revue de droit International et de legislation comparée* VIII (1876), 673–682.

La Question d'Orient – L'Armistice – La conférence de Constantinople et ses suites (Octobre 1876–Janvier 1877), *Revue de droit international et de législation comparée* VIII (1876), 511–544.

Chronique du droit international: L'année 1877 et les débuts de 1878 au point de vue du droit international, *Revue de droit international et de législation comparée* X (1878), 5–59.

Rosenau, James N./Ernst-Otto Czempiel (eds.), *Governance without Government: Order and Change in World Politics*, Cambridge 1992.

Rosenbaum, Alan S. (ed.), *Is the Holocaust Unique? Perspectives on Comparative Genocide*, Boulder, CO 1996.

Rougier, Antoine, La théorie de l'intervention d'humanité, *Revue générale de droit internationale public* XVII (1910), 468–526.

Russell, Talcott H., The National Idea, *Yale Law Journal* 7/8 (May 1898), 346–351.

Ryan, Maeve, The Price of Legitimacy in Humanitarian Intervention: Britain, the Right of Search, and the Abolition of the West African Slave Trade 1807–1867, in Brendan Simms/David J. B. Trim (eds.), *Humanitarian Intervention: A History*, Cambridge 2011, 231–256.

'A Most Promising Field for Future Usefulness': The Church Missionary Society and the Liberated Africans of Sierra Leone, in William Mulligan/ Maurice Bric (eds.), *A Global History of Anti-Slavery in the Nineteenth Century*, Basingstoke 2013, 37–58.

Ryden, David Beck, *West Indian Slavery and British Abolition, 1783–1807*, Cambridge 2009.

Saab, Ann Pottinger, The Doctor's Dilemma: Britain and the Cretan Crisis 1866–69, *Journal of Modern History* 49/4 (December 1977), 1383–1407.

Reluctant Icon: Gladstone, Bulgaria, and the Working Classes, 1856–1878, Cambridge 1991.

Salih, Shakeed, The British–Druze Connection and the Druze Rising of 1896 in the Hawran, *Middle Eastern Studies* 13/2 (May 1977), 251–257.

Salt, Henry S., *Humanitarianism: Its General Principles and Progress*, London 1891.
What Is Humanitarianism?, *Humane Review* 8 (October 1907), 178–188.

Salter, Mark B., *Barbarians and Civilization in International Relations*, London 2002.

Salvatici, Silvia, *A History of Humanitarianism, 1755–1989: In the Name of Others*, Manchester 2019.

Saunders, Christopher, A Nineteenth Century Farce: The Anglo-Portuguese Mixed Commission at the Cape of Good Hope, *Quarterly Bulletin of the South African Library* 37 (1983), 298–302.

Liberated Africans in Cape Colony in the First Half of the Nineteenth Century, *International Journal of African Historical Studies* 18/2 (1985), 223–239.

Scanlan, Padraic Xavier, The Rewards of their Exertions: Prize Money and British Abolitionism in Sierra Leone, 1808–1823, *Past & Present* 225/1 (November 2014), 113–142.

Scheffler, Thomas, Ethnizität, symbolische Gewalt und internationaler Terrorismus im Vorderen Orient, in Thomas Scheffler (ed.), *Ethnizität und Gewalt*, Hamburg 1991, 221–250.

'Wenn hinten, weit, in der Türkei die Völker aufeinander schlagen…': Zum Funktionswandel 'orientalischer' Gewalt in europäischen Öffentlichkeiten des 19. und 20. Jahrhunderts, in Jörg Requate/Martin Schulze Wessel (eds.), *Europäische Öffentlickeit: Transnationale Kommunikation seit dem 18. Jahrhundert*, Frankfurt a. M. 2002, 205–230.

Schellings, William J., Florida and the Cuban Revolution, 1895–1898, *Florida Historical Quarterly* 39/2 (October 1960), 175–186.

Schlesier, Gustav (ed.), *Schriften von Friedrich von Gentz: Ein Denkmal*, vol. 5, Mannheim 1840.

Schlichte, Klaus, Das formierende Säkulum: Macht und Recht in der internationalen Politik des 19. Jahrhunderts, in Ulrich Lappenküper/Reiner Marcowitz (eds.), *Macht und Recht: Völkerrecht in den internationalen Beziehungen*, Paderborn 2010, 161–177.

Schmidt-Nowara, Christopher, Wilberforce Spanished: Joseph Blanco White and Spanish Antislavery, in Christopher Schmidt-Nowara/Josep M. Fradera (eds.), *Slavery and Antislavery in Spain's Atlantic Empire*, New York 2013, 158–175.

Schnabel, Albrecht/Ramesh Thakur (eds.), *Kosovo and the Challenge of Humanitarian Intervention: Selective Indignation, Collective Action, and International Citizenship*, Tokyo 2000.

Schroeder, Paul W., *Metternich's Diplomacy at Its Zenith 1820–1823*, Austin, TX 1962.

Austria, Great Britain, and the Crimean War: The Destruction of the European Concert, Ithaca, NY 1972.

Did the Vienna Settlement Rest on a Balance of Power?, *American Historical Review* 97/3 (June 1992), 683–706.

The Transformation of European Politics 1763–1848, Oxford 1994.

International Politics, Peace, and War, 1815–1914, in T. C. W. Blanning (ed.), *The Nineteenth Century: The Short Oxford History of Europe*, Oxford 2000, 158–209.

Alliances, 1815–1945: Weapons of Power and Tools of Management, in Paul W. Schroeder (ed.), *Systems, Stability, and Statecraft: Essays on the International History of Modern Europe*, New York 2004, 199–200.

Schroeder, Paul W., (ed.), *Systems, Stability, and Statecraft: Essays on the International History of Modern Europe*, New York 2004

The Transformation of European Politics 1763–1848, Oxford 1994.

Schulte, Jan Erik, From the Protection of Sovereignty to Humanitarian Intervention? Traditions and Developments of United Nations Peacekeeping in the Twentieth Century, in Fabian Klose (ed.), *The Emergence of Humanitarian Intervention: Ideas and Practice from the Nineteenth Century to the Present*, Cambridge 2016, 253–277.

Schulz, Matthias, *Normen und Praxis: Das Europäische Konzert der Großmächte als Sicherheitsrat 1815–1860*, Munich 2009.

Internationale Politik und Friedenskultur: Das Europäische Konzert in politikwissenschaftlicher Theorie und historischer Empirie, in Wolfram Pyta (ed.), *Das europäische Mächtekonzert: Friedens- und Sicherheitspolitik vom Wiener Kongress 1815 bis zum Krimkrieg 1853*, Cologne 2009, 41–57.

Macht, internationale Politik und Normenwandel im Staatensystem des 19. Jahrhunderts, in Ulrich Lappenküper/Reiner Marcowitz (eds.), *Macht und Recht: Völkerrecht in den internationalen Beziehungen*, Paderborn 2010, 113–134.

The Guarantees of Humanity: The Concert of Europe and the Origins of the Russo-Ottoman War of 1877, in Brendan Simms/David J. B. Trim (eds.), *Humanitarian Intervention: A History*, Cambridge 2011, 184–204.

Internationale Institutionen, in Jost Dülffer/Wilfried Loth (eds.), *Dimensionen internationaler Geschichte*, Munich 2012, 213–232.

Schulz, Oliver, *Ein Sieg der zivilisierten Welt? Die Intervention der europäischen Großmächte im griechischen Unabhängigkeitskrieg (1826–1832)*, Berlin 2011.

Schutter, Bart de, Humanitarian Intervention: A United Nations Task, *California Western International Law Journal* 21/3 (1972), 21–36.

Schwarz, Suzanne, Commerce, Civilization and Christianity: The Development of the Sierra Leone Company, in Suzanne Schwarz/David Richardson/Anthony Tibbles (eds.), *Liverpool and Transatlantic Slavery*, Liverpool 2007, 252–276.

Segesser, Daniel Marc, Humanitarian Intervention and the Issue of State Sovereignty in the Discourse of Legal Experts between 1830s and the First World War, in Fabian Klose (ed.), *The Emergence of Humanitarian Intervention: Ideas and Practice from the Nineteenth Century to the Present*, Cambridge 2016, 56–72.

Semmel, Bernard, *Liberalism and Naval Strategy: Ideology, Interest, and Sea Power during the Pax Britannica*, Boston, MA 1986.

Seton-Watson, R. W., *Disraeli, Gladstone and the Eastern Question: A Study in Diplomacy and Party Politics*, London 1971.

Sewell, Mike, Humanitarian Intervention, Democracy, and Imperialism: The American War with Spain, 1898, and After, in Brendan Simms/David J. B. Trim (eds.), *Humanitarian Intervention: A History*, Cambridge 2011, 303–322.

Sexton, Jay, *The Monroe Doctrine: Empire and Nation in Nineteenth-Century America*, New York 2011.

Seybolt, Taylor B., *Humanitarian Military Intervention: The Conditions for Success and Failure*, Oxford 2007.

Shaikh, Farida, Judicial Diplomacy: British Officials and the Mixed Commission Courts, in Keith Hamilton/Patrick Salmon (eds.), *Slavery, Diplomacy and Empire: Britain and the Suppression of the Slave Trade, 1807–1975*, Portland, OR 2009, 42–64.

Shannon, Richard T., *Gladstone and the Bulgarian Agitation 1876*, Hassocks 1975.

Gladstone and British Balkan Policy, in Ralph Melville/ Hans-Jürgen Schröder (eds.), *Der Berliner Kongress von 1878: Die Politik der Grossmächte und die Probleme der Modernisierung in Südosteuropa in der Zweiten Hälfte des 19. Jahrhunderts*, Wiesbaden 1982, 163–178.

Shaw, Caroline, *Britannia's Embrace: Modern Humanitarianism and the Imperial Origins of Refugee Relief*, Oxford 2015.

Shaw, Ibrahim Seaga, The Politics of Humanitarian Intervention: A Critical Analogy of the British Response to End the Slave Trade and the Civil War in Sierra Leone, *Journal of Global Ethics* 6/3, 2010, 273–285.

Sheehan, James J., The Problem of Sovereignty in European History, *American Historical Review* 111/1 (February 2006), 1–15.

Sheridan, Charles Brinsley, *Thoughts on the Greek Revolution*, London 1822.

Shute, Stephen/Susan Hurley (eds.), *On Human Rights: The Oxford Amnesty Lectures*, New York 1993.

Simms, Brendan/David J. B. Trim, Towards a History of Humanitarian Intervention, in Brendan Simms/David J. B. Trim (eds.), *Humanitarian Intervention: A History*, Cambridge 2011, 1–24.

'A False Principle in the Law of Nations': Burke, State Sovereignty, [German] Liberty, and Intervention in the Age of Westphalia, in Brendan Simms/David J. B. Trim (eds.), *Humanitarian Intervention: A History*, Cambridge 2011, 89–110.

Simms, Brendan/David J. B. Trim (eds.), *Humanitarian Intervention: A History*, Cambridge 2011.

Simonen, Katariina, *The State versus the Individual: The Unresolved Dilemma of Humanitarian Intervention*, Leiden 2011.

Sked, Alan, Metternich's Enemies or the Threat from Below, in Alan Sked (ed.), *Europe's Balance of Power 1815–1848*, London 1979, 164–189.

Skinner, Rob/Alan Lester, Humanitarianism and Empire: New Research Agendas, *Journal of Imperial and Commonwealth History* 40/5 (December 2012), 729–747.

Sluga, Glenda, *Internationalism in the Age of Nationalism*, Philadelphia, PA 2013.

'Who Hold the Balance of the World?' Bankers at the Congress of Vienna, and in International History, *American Historical Review* 122/5 (December 2017), 1403–1430.

Smallwood, Stephanie, *Saltwater Slavery: A Middle Passage from Africa to American Diaspora*, Cambridge, MA 2007.

Smiley, Will, War without War: The Battle of Navarino, the Ottoman Empire, and the Pacific Blockade, *Journal of the History of International Law* 18/1 (2016), 42–69.

Smith, Adam, *The Theory of Moral Sentiments*, London 1853.

Smith, George, *The Case of Our West-African Cruisers and West-African Settlements Fairly Considered*, London 1848.

Smith, Johanna M., Slavery, Abolition, and the Nation in Priscilla Wakefield's Tour Books for Children, in Brycchan Carey/Markman Ellis/Sara Salih (eds.), *Discourses of Slavery and Abolition: Britain and its Colonies, 1760–1838*, London 2004, 175–193.

Smith, Joseph, *The Spanish–American War: Conflict in the Caribbean and the Pacific 1895–1902*, London 1994.

Smith, Robert S., *The Lagos Consulate 1851–1861*, London 1978.

Solow, Barbara L./Stanley L. Engerman (eds.), *British Capitalism and Caribbean Slavery: The Legacy of Eric Williams*, Cambridge 1987.

Soulsby, Hugh G., *The Right of Search and the Slave Trade in Anglo-American Relations 1814–1862*, Baltimore, MD 1933.

Spagnolo, John P., Constitutional Change in Mount Lebanon: 1861–1864, *Middle Eastern Studies* 7/1 (January 1971), 25–48.

France and Ottoman Lebanon 1861–1914, London 1977.

Spiers, Edward M., The Use of the Dum Dum Bullet in Colonial Warfare, *Journal of Imperial and Commonwealth History* 4/1 (1975), 3–14.

St Clair, William, *That Greece Might Still Be Free: The Philhellenes in the War of Independence*, London 1972.

Stagg, J. C. A., *The War of 1812: Conflict for a Continent*, Cambridge 2012.

Stanfield, James Field, *The Guinea Voyage: A Poem in Three Books*, London 1789. *Observations on a Guinea Voyage in a Series of Letters Addressed to the Rev. Thomas Clarkson*, London 1788.

Stapleton, Augustus Granville, *George Canning and His Time*, London 1859. *Intervention and Non-Intervention or the Foreign Policy of Great Britain from 1790 to 1865*, London 1866.

Stauber, Reinhard/Florian Kerschbaumer, Revolution, Restauration und Intervention: Beobachtungen zum Politikraum Europa in der Zeit des Wiener Kongresses, in Christoph Kampmann/Ulrich Niggemann (eds.), *Sicherheit in der Frühen Neuzeit: Norm, Praxis, Repräsentation*, Cologne 2013, 156–174.

Stauber, Reinhard/Florian Kerschbaumer/Marion Koschier (eds.), *Mächtepolitik und Friedenssicherung: Zur politischen Kultur Europas im Zeichen des Wiener Kongresses*, Berlin 2014.

Steckel, Richard H./Richard A. Jensen, New Evidence and Crew Mortality in the Atlantic Slave Trade, *Journal of Economic History* 46/1 (March 1986), 57–77.

Stein, Mark, Who's Afraid of Cannibals? Some Uses of the Cannibalism Trope in Olaudah Equiano's Interesting Narrative, in Brycchan Carey/Markman Ellis/Sara Salih (eds.), *Discourses of Slavery and Abolition: Britain and Its Colonies, 1760–1838*, Basingstoke 2004, 96–107.

Stephen, James, *The Crisis of the Sugar Colonies or an Equiry into the Objects and Probable Effects of the French Expedition to the West Indies, and Their Connection with Colonial Interest of the British Empire*, London 1802. *War in Disguise or the Frauds of the Neutral Flags*, London 1805. *An Inquiry into the Right and Duty of Compelling Spain to Relinquish Her Slave Trade in Northern Africa*, London 1816.

Stevenson, Ana, The 'Great Doctrine of Human Rights': Articulation and Authentication in the Nineteenth-Century U.S. Antislavery and Women's Rights Movements, *Humanity* 8/3 (Winter 2017), 413–439.

Stites, Richard, *The Four Horsemen: Riding to Liberty in Post-Napoleonic Europe*, Oxford 2014.

Stowell, Ellery C., *Intervention in International Law*, Washington, DC 1921. La théorie et la pratique de l'intervention, Académie de droit international (ed.), *Recueil des cours* II/40 (1932), 91–148. Humanitarian Intervention, *American Journal of International Law* 33/4 (October 1939), 733–736.

Stuart, Reginald C., *War and American Thought: From the Revolution to the Monroe Doctrine*, Kent, OH 1982.

Stucki, Andreas, Bevölkerungskontrolle in asymmetrischen Konflikten: Zwangsumsiedlung und spanische Antiguerilla auf Kuba, 1868–1898, in Tanja Bührer/Christian Stachelbeck/Dierk Walter (eds.), *Imperialkriege von 1500 bis heute: Strukturen, Akteure, Lernprozesse*, Paderborn 2011, 241–259.

Aufstand und Zwangsumsiedlung: Die kubanischen Unabhängigkeitskriege 1868–1898, Hamburg 2012.

Sulivan, Captain G. L., *Dhow Chasing in Zanzibar Waters and on the Eastern Coast of Africa: Narrative of Five Years' Experiences in the Suppression of the Slave Trade*, London 1873.

Swaminathan, Srividhya, *Debating the Slave Trade: Rhetoric of British National Identity, 1759–1815*, Farnham 2009.

Swatek-Evenstein, Mark, *A History of Humanitarian Intervention*, Cambridge 2020.

Sylvester, Harold J., The Kansas Press and the Coming of the Spanish–American War, *The Historian* 31/2 (February 1969), 251–267.

Taithe, Bertrand, Evil, Liberalism and the Imperial Designs of the Catholic Church, 1867–1905, in Bertrand Taithe/Tom Crook/Rebecca Gill (eds.), *Evil, Barbarism and Empire: Britain and Abroad, c. 1830–2000*, Basingstoke 2011, 147–171.

Missionary Militarism? The Armed Brothers of the Sahara and Léopold Joubert in the Congo, in Owen White/J. P. Daughton (eds.), *In God's Empire: French Missionaries and the Modern World*, Oxford 2012, 129–150.

Task, David F., *The War with Spain in 1898*, Lincoln, NB 1996.

Tatum, Edward H., To Forestall Britain's Desings on Cuba and New World Markets, in Armin Rappaport (ed.), *The Monroe Doctrine*, New York 1964, 22–33.

Taylor, Eric Robert, *If We Must Die: Shipboard Insurrections in the Era of the Atlantic Slave Trade*, Baton Rouge, LA 2006.

Teitel, Ruti G., For Humanity, *Journal of Human Rights* 3/2 (June 2004), 225–237.

Temperley, Harold, *The Foreign Policy of Canning 1822–1827: England, the Neo-Holy Alliance, and the New World*, London 1966.

Temperley, Harold/Lillian M. Penson (eds.), *Foundations of British Foreign Policy: From Pitt (1792) to Salisbury (1902)*, Cambridge 1966.

Temperley, Howard, *White Dreams, Black Africa: The Antislavery Expedition to the Niger 1841–1842*, New Haven, CT 1991.

Tesón, Fernando R., *Humanitarian Intervention: An Inquiry into Law and Morality*, Ardsley, NY 2005.

Tesón, Fernando R./Bas van der Vossen, *Debating Humanitarian Intervention: Should We Try to Save Strangers?*, New York 2017.

Thakur, Ramesh, Global Norms and International Humanitarian Law: An Asian Perspective, *International Review of the Red Cross* 841 (31 March 2001), https://www.icrc.org/eng/resources/documents/article/other/57jqzd.htm.

The Responsibility to Protect: Norms, Laws, and the Use of Force in International Politics, London 2011.

R2P after Libya and Syria: Engaging Emerging Powers, *Washington Quarterly* 36/2 (Spring 2013), 61–76.

The United Nations, Peace and Security: From Collective Security to the Responsibility to Protect, Cambridge 2017.

Thomas, Hugh, *The Slave Trade: The History of the Atlantic Slave Trade, 1440–1870*, London 2006.

Thompson, Andrew, Informal Empire: Past, Present and Future, in Matthew Brown (ed.), *Informal Empire in Latin America: Culture, Commerce and Capital*, Malden, MA 2008, 229–241.

Humanitarian Interventions, Past and Present, in Fabian Klose (ed.), *The Emergence of Humanitarian Intervention: Ideas and Practice from the Nineteenth Century to the Present*, Cambridge 2016, 331–356.

Thompson, Andrew C., The Protestant Interest and the History of Humanitarian Intervention, c. 1685–c. 1756, in Brendan Simms/David J. B. Trim (eds.), *Humanitarian Intervention: A History*, Cambridge 2011, 67–88.

Thornberry, Patrick, *International Law and the Rights of Minorities*, Oxford 1991.

Thornton, John, *Africa and Africans in the Making of the Atlantic World, 1400–1800*, Cambridge 1998.

Todd, Janet. *Sensibility: An Introduction*, London 1986.

Toledano, Ehud R., *The Ottoman Slave Trade and Its Suppression: 1840–1890*, Princeton, NJ 1982.

Tomkins, Stephen, *The Clapham Sect: How Wilberforce's Circle Transformed Britain*, Oxford 2010.

Tone, John Lawrence, *War and Genocide in Cuba, 1895–1898*, Chapel Hill, NC 2006.

Toufayan, Mark, Empathy, Humanity and the 'Armenian Question' in the Internationalist Legal Imagination, *Revue québécoise de droit international* 24 (2011), 171–192.

Trim, David J. B., 'If a prince use tyrannie towards his people': Interventions on Behalf of Foreign Populations in Early Modern Europe, in David J. B. Trim/ Brendan Simms (eds.), *Humanitarian Intervention: A History*, Cambridge 2011, 29–66.

Conclusion: Humanitarian Intervention in Historical Perspective, in David J. B. Trim/Brendan Simms (eds.), *Humanitarian Intervention: A History*, Cambridge 2011, 381–401.

Intervention in European History c. 1520–1850, in Stefano Recchia/Jennifer M. Welsh (eds.), *Just and Unjust Military Intervention: European Thinkers from Vitoria to Mill*, Cambridge 2013, 21–47.

Tuck, Richard, Grotius, Hobbes, and Pufendorf on Humanitarian Intervention, in Stefano Recchia/Jennifer M. Welsh (eds.), *Just and Unjust Military Intervention: European Thinkers from Vitoria to Mill*, Cambridge 2013, 96–112.

Tupper, H. Allen, Jr, *Columbia's War for Cuba: A Story of the Early Struggles of the Cuban Patriots, and of all the Important Events Leading Up to the Present War between the United States and Spain for Cuba Libre*, New York 1898.

Turley, David, *The Culture of English Antislavery, 1780–1860*, London 1991.

Anti-Slavery Activists and Officials: 'Influence', Lobbying and the Slave Trade, 1807–1850, in Keith Hamilton/Patrick Salmon (eds.), *Slavery, Diplomacy and Empire: Britain and the Suppression of the Slave Trade, 1807–1975*, Eastbourne 2009, 81–92.

Turnbull, David, *Travels in the West: Cuba with Notices of Puerto Rico and the Slave Trade*, London 1840.

Tusan, Michelle, Britain and the Middle East: New Historical Perspectives on the Eastern Question, *History Compass* 8/3 (March 2010), 212–222.

Smyrna's Ashes: Humanitarianism, Genocide, and the Birth of the Middle East, Berkeley, CA 2012.

'Crimes against Humanity': Human Rights, the British Empire, and the Origins of the Response to the Armenian Genocide, *American Historical Review* 119/1 (February 2014), 47–77.

Tyrrell, Ian, *Reforming the World: The Creation of America's Moral Empire*, Princeton, NJ 2010.

Urban, C. Stanley, The Africanization of Cuba Scare, 1853–1855, *Hispanic American Historical Review* 37/1 (February 1957), 29–45.

Uya, Okon E., Slave Revolts in the Middle Passage: A Neglected Theme, *Calabar Historical Journal* 1/1 (June 1976), 65–88.

Vacalopoulos, Apostolos E., Piracy during the Last Years of the Greek War of Independence, in Apostolos E. Vacalopoulos/Constantinos D. Svolopoulos/ Béla K. Király (eds.), *Southeast European Maritime Commerce and Naval Policies from the Mid-Eighteenth Century to 1914*, Boulder, CO 1988, 363–377.

Van Alstyne, Richard W., The British Right of Search and the African Slave Trade, *Journal of Modern History* 2/1 (March 1930), 37–47.

Van Cleve, George, 'Somerset's Case' and Its Antecedents in Imperial Perspective, *Law and History Review* 24/3 (Spring 2006), 601–645.

Van der Linden, Marcel, Unanticipated Consequences of 'Humanitarian Intervention': The British Campaign to Abolish the Slave Trade, 1807–1900, *Theory and Society* 39/3–4 (2010), 281–298.

Van Niekerk, J. P., British, Portuguese, and American Judges in Adderley Street: the International Legal Background to and Some Judicial Aspects of the Cape Town Mixed Commissions for the Suppression of the Transatlantic Slave Trade in the Nineteenth Century (pt. 1), *Comparative and International Law Journal of Southern Africa* 37/1 (March 2004), 1–39.

British, Portuguese, and American Judges in Adderley Street: the International Legal Background to and Some Judicial Aspects of the Cape Town Mixed Commissions for the Suppression of the Transatlantic Slave Trade in the Nineteenth Century (pt. 2), *Comparative and International Law Journal of Southern Africa* 37/2 (July 2004), 196–225.

The Role of the Vice-Admiralty Court at St Helena in the Abolition of the Transatlantic Slave Trade: A Preliminary Investigation, pt. 1, *Fundamina: A Journal of Legal History* 15/1 (2009), 69–111.

The Role of the Vice-Admiralty Court at St Helena in the Abolition of the Transatlantic Slave Trade: A Preliminary Investigation, pt. 2, *Fundamina: A Journal of Legal History* 15/2 (2009), 1–56.

Van Nifterik, Gustaaf P., Religious and Humanitarian Intervention in Sixteenth and Early Seventeenth-Century Legal Thought, in Randall Lesaffer/Georges Macours (eds.), *Sovereignty and the Law of Nations (16th–18th Centuries)*, Brussels 2006, 35–60.

Van Wagenen, Michael Scott, *Remembering the Forgotten War: The Enduring Legacies of the U.S.–Mexican War*, Amherst, MA 2012.

Vec, Miloš, *Recht und Normierung in der Industriellen Revolution: Neue Strukturen der Normsetzung in Völkerrecht, staatlicher Gesetzgebung und gesellschaftlicher Selbstnormierung*, Frankfurt a. M. 2006.

Das Prinzip der Verkehrsfreiheit im Völkerrecht: Die Rheinschifffahrt zwischen dem Frieden von Lunéville (1801) und der Mannheimer Akte (1868), *Zeitschrift für Neuere Rechtsgeschichte* 3/4 (2008), 221–241.

Intervention/Nichtintervention: Verrechtlichung der Politik und Politisierung des Völkerrechts im 19. Jahrhundert, in Ulrich Lappenküper/Reiner Marcowitz (eds.), *Macht und Recht: Völkerrecht in den internationalen Beziehungen*, Paderborn 2010, 135–160.

Vick, Brian E., *The Congress of Vienna: Power and Politics after Napoleon*, Cambridge, MA 2014.

Power, Humanitarianism and the Global Liberal Order: Abolition and the Barbary Corsairs in the Vienna Congress System, *International History Review* 40/4 (2018), 939–960.

The London Ambassadors' Conferences and Beyond: Abolition, Barbary Corsairs and Multilateral Security in the Congress of Vienna System, in Brian E. Vick/Beatrice de Graaf/Ido de Haan (eds), *Securing Europe after Napoleon: 1815 and the New European Security Culture*, Cambridge 2019, 114-129.

Vincent, R. J., *Nonintervention and International Order*, Princeton, NJ 1974.

Grotius, Human Rights, and Intervention, in Hedley Bull/Benedict Kingsbury/Adam Roberts (eds.), *Hugo Grotius and International Relations*, Oxford 2003, 241–256.

Von Bippen, Wilhelm, *Johann Smidt ein hanseatischer Staatsmann*, Stuttgart 1921.

Von Gentz, Friedrich, Bemerkungen über das Interventions-Recht, March 1831, in Gustav Schlesier (ed.), *Schriften von Friedrich von Gentz. Ein Denkmal, Fünfter Teil*, Mannheim 1840, 181–185.

Von Kamptz, Karl Christoph Albert Heinrich, *Völkerrechtliche Erörterungen des Rechts der Europäischen Mächte in die Verfassungen eines einzelnen Staats sich zu mischen*, Berlin 1821.

Von Lingen, Kerstin, Fullfilling the Martens Clause: Debating 'Crimes against Humanity', 1899–1945, in Fabian Klose/Miriam Thulin (eds.), *Humanity: A History of European Concepts in Practice from the Sixteenth Century to the Present*, Göttingen 2017, 187–208.

Von Pufendorf, Samuel, *Of the Law of Nature and Nations: Eight Books*, Oxford 1710.

Von Ungern-Sternberg, Antje, Religion and Religious Intervention, in Bardo Fassbender/Anne Peters (eds.), *The Oxford Handbook of the History of International Law*, Oxford 2012, 294–316.

Wadström, Carl Bernhard, *Observations on the Slave Trade, and a Description of Some Part of the Coast of 1788, in: Company with Doctor A. Sparrman and Captain Arrehenius*, London 1789.

Plan for a Free Community at Sierra Leona, upon the Coast of Africa, under the Protection of Great Britain; with an Invitation to all Persons Desirous of Partaking the Benefits Thereof, London 1792.

An Essay on Colonization, Particularly Applied to the Western Coast of Africa, with Some Free Thoughts on Cultivation and Commerce, London 1794.

Adresse au corps législatif et au directoire exécutif de la République Française, Paris 1795.

Walker, Peter/Daniel Maxwell, *Shaping the Humanitarian World*, New York 2009.

Walvin, James, The Public Campaign in England against Slavery, 1787–1834, in James Walvin/David Eltis (eds.), *The Abolition of the Atlantic Slave Trade: Origins and Effects in Europe, Africa, and the Americas*, Madison, WI 1981, 67–68.

The Propaganda of Anti-Slavery, in James Walvin (ed.), *Slavery and British Society 1776–1846*, London 1982.

England, Slaves and Freedom, 1776–1838, Jackson, MS 1986.

The Trader, the Owner, the Slave: Parallel Lives in the Age of Slavery, London 2007.

Walzer, Michael, *Just and Unjust Wars: A Moral Argument with Historical Illustrations*, New York 2000.

Ward, William E. F., *The Royal Navy and the Slavers: The Suppression of the Atlantic Slave Trade*, London 1969.

Warren, Aiden/Damian Grenfell (eds.), *Rethinking Humanitarian Intervention in the 21st Century*, Edinburgh 2017.

Wasserstrom, Jeffrey N./Greg Grandin/Lynn Hunt/Marilyn B. Young (eds.), *Human Rights and Revolution*, Lanham, MD 2007.

Watenpaugh, Keith David, *Bread from Stones: The Middle East and the Making of Modern Humanitarianism*, Oakland, CA 2015.

Wax, Darold D., Negro Resistance to the Early American Slave Trade, *Journal of Negro History* 51/1 (January 1966), 1–15.

Webster, Charles K. (ed.), *British Diplomacy 1813–1815: Select Documents Dealing with the Reconstruction of Europe*, London 1921.

Webster, Charles K., *The Foreign Policy of Castlereagh 1812–1815: Britain and the Reconstruction of Europe*, London 1931.

The Foreign Policy of Castlereagh 1815–1822: Britain and the European Alliance, London [1925] 1963.

Britain and the Independence of Latin America 1812–1830, 2 vols., New York 1970.

Webster, Charles K. (ed.), *British Diplomacy 1813–1815: Select Documents Dealing with the Reconstruction of Europe*, London 1921.

Webster, Jane, The Zong in the Context of the Eighteen-Century Slave Trade, *Journal of Legal History* 28/3 (2007), 285–298.

Weinbren, Dan, Against All Cruelty: The Humanitarian League, 1891–1919, *History Workshop* 38 (1994), 86–105.

Weisberg, Howard L., The Congo Crisis 1964: A Case Study in Humanitarian Intervention, *Virginia Journal of International Law* 12/2 (1972), 261–276.

Weiss, Thomas G., *Humanitarian Intervention: Ideas in Action*, Cambridge 2012.

Weiss, Thomas G./David P. Forsythe/Roger A. Coate, *The United Nations and Changing World Politics*, Boulder, CO 2004.

Weissman, Fabrice (ed.), *In the Shadow of 'Just Wars': Violence, Politics, and Humanitarian Action*, London 2004.

Wester, Karin, *Intervention in Libya: The Responsibility to Protect in North Africa*, Cambridge 2020.

Weitz, Eric D., From the Vienna to the Paris System: International Politics and the Entangled Histories of Human Rights, Forced Deportations, and Civilizing Missions, *American Historical Review* 113/5 (December 2008), 1313–1343.

A World Divided: The Global Struggle for Human Rights in the Age of Nation-States, Princeton, NJ 2019.

Welch, Richard E., Jr, American Atrocities in the Philippines: The Indictment and the Response, *Pacific Historical Review* 43/2 (May 1974), 233–253.

Response to Imperialism, The United States and the Philippine–American War, 1899–1902, Chapel Hill, NC 1979.

Welsh, Jennifer M., *Humanitarian Intervention and International Relations*, Oxford 2006.

Edmund Burke and Intervention: Empire and Neighborhood, in Jennifer M. Welsh/Stefano Recchia (eds.), *Just and Unjust Military Intervention: European Thinkers from Vitoria to Mill*, Cambridge 2013, 219–236.

Wenzlhuemer, Roland, *Connecting the Nineteenth-Century World: The Telegraph and Globalization*, Cambridge 2013.

Wertheim, Stephen, A Solution from Hell: The United States and the Rise of Humanitarian Intervention, 1991–2003, *Journal of Genocide Research* 12/3–4 (September–December 2010), 149–172.

Western, Jon, Prudence or Outrage? Public Opinion and Humanitarian Intervention in Historical and Comparative Perspective, in Fabian Klose (ed.), *The Emergence of Humanitarian Intervention: Ideas and Practice from the Nineteenth Century to the Present*, Cambridge 2016, 165–184.

Wheaton, Henry, *A Digest of the Law of Maritime Captures and Prizes*, New York 1815.

Elements of International Law with a Sketch of the History of the Science, vol. I, London 1836.

Enquiry into the Validity of the British Claim to a Right of Visitation and Search of American Vessel Suspected to be Engaged in the African Slave Trade, Philadelphia, PA 1842.

History of the Law of Nations in Europe and America from the Earliest Times to the Treaty of Washington, 1842, New York 1845.

Wheeler, Nicolas J., *Saving Strangers: Humanitarian Intervention in International Society*, Oxford 2003.

Wheeler, Nicolas J./Justin Morris, Justifying the Iraq War as a Humanitarian Intervention: The Cure Is Worse than the Disease, in Ramesh Thakur/W. P. S. Sidhu (eds.), *The Iraq Crisis and World Order: Structural, Institutional and Normative Challenges*, Tokyo 2006, 444–463.

Whitaker, Arthur, *The Western Hemisphere Idea: Its Rise and Decline*, Ithaca, NY 1954.

The United States and the Independence of Latin America, 1800–1830, New York 1964.

White, Mark J., The Case of the Yucatecan Request: American Foreign Policy at the Close of the Mexican War, *Mid-America. An Historical Review* 72/3 (October 1990), 169–190.

Wilberforce, Robert I./Samuel Wilberforce (eds.), *The Life of William Wilberforce*, vol. 1, London 1838.

The Life of William Wilberforce, vol. 2, London 1838.

The Life of William Wilberforce, vol. 4, London 1839.

Wilkerson, Marcus M., *Public Opinion and the Spanish–American War: A Study in War Propaganda*, New York 1967.

Williams, Eric E., *Capitalism and Slavery*, Chapel Hill, NC 1944.

Williams, Raymond, *Keywords: A Vocabulary of Culture and Society*, New York 1976.

Williams, William Appleman, *The Tragedy of American Diplomacy*, New York 2009.

Wills, Mary, *Envoys of Abolition: British Naval Officers and the Campaign against the Slave Trade in West Africa*, Liverpool 2020.

Wilson, Ellen Gibson, *Thomas Clarkson: A Biography*, New York 1990.

Wilson, Howard Hazen, Some Principal Aspects of British Efforts to Crush the African Slave Trade, 1807–1929, *American Journal of International Law* 44/3 (July 1950), 505–526.

Wilson, J. Leighton, *The British Squadron on the Coast of Africa*, London 1850.

The British Squadron on the Coast of Africa, by the Rev. J. Leighton Wilson, An American Missionary in the Gaboon River, West Coast of Africa, with Notes by Captain H. D. Trotter, Royal Navy, London 1851.

Wilson, Peter, *The International Theory of Leonard Woolf: A Study in Twentieth-Century Idealism*, New York 2003.

Wilson, Richard Ashby/Richard D. Brown, Introduction, in Richard Ashby Wilson/Richard D. Brown (eds.), *Humanitarianism and Suffering: The Mobilization of Empathy*, Cambridge 2009, 1–30.

Winfield, Percy H., The History of Intervention in International Law, *British Yearbook of International Law* 130 (1922/23), 130–149.

Wirz, Albert, Die humanitäre Schweiz im Spannungsfeld zwischen Philantrophie und Kolonialismus: Gustave Moynier, Afrika und das IKRK, *Traverse: Zeitschrift für Geschichte/Revue d'histoire* 5/2 (1998), 95–111.

Wirz, Albert/Andreas Eckert, The Scramble for Africa: Icon and Idiom of Modernity, in Olivier Pétré Grenouilleau (ed.), *From Slave Trade to Empire: Europe and the Colonisation of Black Africa 1780s–1880s*, London 2004, 133–153.

Wisan, Joseph E., *The Cuban Crisis as Reflected in the New York Press (1896–1898)*, New York 1965.

Wise, Steven M., *Though the Heavens May Fall: The Landmark Trial That Led to the End of Human Slavery*, Cambridge, MA 2006.

Wiseberg, Laurie S., Humanitarian Intervention: Lessons from the Nigerian Civil War, *Revue des droits de l'homme* 70/1 (1974), 61–98.

Wolff, Christian, *Jus gentium methodo scientifica pertractatum, 1749*, vol. II, trans. Joseph H. Drake, Oxford 1934.

Wolfe, John B., *The Barbary Coast: Algiers under the Turks 1500 to 1830*, New York 1979.

Wolff, Richard D., British Imperialism and the East African Slave Trade, *Science & Society* 36/4 (Winter 1972), 443–462.

Wood, Marcus, *Blind Memory: Visual Representation of Slavery in England and America 1780–1865*, Manchester 2000.

Woodhouse, Christopher M., *The Battle of Navarino*, London 1965.

The Philhellenes, London 1969.

The Greek War of Independence: Its Historical Setting, New York 1975.

Woods, Joseph, *Thoughts on the Slavery of the Negroes*, London 1784.

Woolf, Leonard S., *International Government: Two Reports Prepared for the Fabian Research Department*, New York 1916.

Yellin, Jean Fagan, *Women and Sisters: The Antislavery Feminists in American Culture*, New Haven, CT 1989.

Yellin, Jean Fagan/John C. Van Horne (eds.), *The Abolitionist Sisterhood: Women's Political Culture in Antebellum America*, Ithaca, NY 1994.

Young, George, *Corps de droit ottoman: Recueil des Codes, Lois, Règlements, Ordonnances et Actes les plus importants du Droit Intérieur, et d'Ètudes sur le Droit Coutumier de l'Empire Ottoman*, vol. 2, Oxford 1905.

Yule, Henry, *The African Squadron Vindicated*, London 1850.

Zamoyski, Adam, *Rites of Peace: The Fall of Napoleon and the Congress of Vienna*, New York 2007.

Zimmermann, Carl R., Philhellenism in the American Press during the Greek Revolution, *Neo-Hellenika* 2 (1975), 181–211.

Index